gua Handbook

Richard Arghiris
Richard Leonardi

Nicaragua is a land born out of poetry, fire and brazen revolutionary spirit. Few countries can boast such an authentic character. The 1979 Sandinista Revolution, more than any other historical episode, is indelibly etched on the Nicaraguan psyche. As a moment of profound self-realization, it continues to inspire great national pride and endless passionate discourse.

Sadly, years of counter-revolutionary violence have left their mark too. Broken infrastructure, poverty, high unemployment and a lingering negative image are the legacies of over a decade of civil war. Fortunately, Nicaragua is today at lasting peace and very much on its way up. But in spite of burgeoning foreign investment, development remains patchy: power shortages are common, many towns lack paved roads, horse and cart are widely used and wood remains the principal source of fuel. Travelling in Nicaragua is a challenging, intense adventure.

Despite the country's continuing hardships, Nicaraguan culture – heavily revitalized by Sandinista arts programmes in the 1980s – is among the most celebrated in Central America. It revels in unique forms of dance, music and festivals, many of them with pre-Hispanic roots. But most of all, Nicaragua breathes poetry, the unrivalled national passion, which has produced some of the most important poets in the history of the Spanish language.

Nicaragua's expressive and tempestuous national temperament runs in striking parallel to its rich and volatile geological scenery. A rugged spine of more than 50 volcanoes punctuates the landscape from the northwest coast to the vast watery expanse of Lake Nicaragua. Elsewhere, nearly 20% of the country's land mass is an officially protected area with a diverse portfolio of ecosystems – rainforests, cloud forests and wetlands among them – guarding more than 10% of the planet's biodiversity.

For those willing to take the plunge, Nicaragua's ethereal natural beauty and endless anarchic charms tend to leave deep and lasting impressions. Through it all, the people, eternally warm and good humoured, are the country's finest asset.

917.285
F

HONDURAS

Bosawás
Biosphere
Reserve

♦ 12

• Raiti

Río Waskup

ATLANTICO
NORTE

Los Manos
○

NUEVA
SEGOVIA

○ Ocotal

JINOTEGA

Somoto
○ MADRIZ

Reserva
Natural
Miraflor ● 9

ESTELÍ

○ Jinotega

Río Grande
de Matagal

Guasaule ○

○ Estelí

7 ○ Matagalpa

CHINANDEGA

El Congo ○

Cordillera Los Maribios

8 MATAGALPA

LEON

○ Sébaco

○ Muy Muy

ATLANTICO
SUR

Chinandega ○

○ Malpaisillo

León ○ 6

Lago de
Managua
(Xolotlán)

BOACO

○ Boaco

La Paz
Centro ○ Mateare

MANAGUA ●

El Rama

MANAGUA
Masaya ○ ● 1

CHONTALES

La Palma ○

Pacific
Ocean

Jinotepe ○

2
○ Granada

GRANADA

CARAZO

Isla de
Ometepe

Lago de
Nicaragua
(Cocibolca)

RÍO
SAN JUAN

RIVAS
Rivas ○ 3

▲
Volcán
Maderas

Solentiname
Archipelago

San Juan
del Sur ○

San Carlos ○

5

4

El Castil

WITHDRAWN

COSTA RICA

N

40 km
40 miles

Laguna de Bismuna

Río Coco

Río Ulang

Laguna Li-Dakura

Dakura

Río Wawo

Laguna Pahara

Bilwe

Laguna Wounta

Caribbean Sea

Kara

Pearl Lagoon/ Laguna de Perlas

Corn Islands

dido

Bluefields

Laguna de Bluefields

Río njuan

piqui

Finca Esperanza Verde, Nicaragua's best-known ecolodge

Don't miss...

See colour maps at end of book

Granada's impressive cathedral makes a beautiful backdrop to the city

Itineraries for Nicaragua

For such a tiny country, there's a lot to see and do in Nicaragua. Fortunately, road communication in the Pacific Basin is good and most areas of interest are less than 200 km from the capital. A great deal of ground can be covered in a matter of days using express intercity buses, local tour operators or hired taxis.

The rest of Nicaragua is off the beaten track with large nature reserves and small villages devoid of travellers and commercialization. Travel on the east side of the country can be particularly time-consuming and comparatively expensive. If time is very limited, plan carefully and weigh the benefits of your chosen destinations against the hours that might be spent in getting there.

ITINERARY ONE: 2 – 3 weeks
The best of southern Nicaragua

After arriving at the international airport, most travellers skip Managua and make a bee-line for the laid-back colonial city of Granada, just one hour away. The city's touristic infrastructure is well developed and it makes a safe base for exploring the region.

In Granada, few visitors can resist a jaunt on Lake Nicaragua, Central America's largest freshwater lake, or a trip to Volcán Mombacho, where you can hike or zip-line through cloud-drenched forests. Alternatively, many head to the mysterious island of Zapatera, or to the rural communities perched on Mombacho's slopes.

A shopping trip to the city of Masaya, just 30 minutes from Granada, is an obligatory venture. Few fail to be refreshed by the tranquil waters of Laguna de Apoyo, whilst side-trips to smoking Volcán Masaya, the pottery town of San Juan de Oriente and the flower-filled village of Catarina are also rewarding.

From Granada, it's just a two-hour bus journey to the city of Rivas. From there, you can hop straight on a bus to the sunny town of San Juan del Sur, 45 minutes away, to enjoy the crashing surf of the Pacific and,

TRAVEL TIP

If you're looking for a guide, the local offices of MARENA, the town hall or the village church are good places to get recommendations.

if in season, the unforgettable spectacle of thousands of hatching sea turtles at the Refugio de Vida Silvestre La Flor.

If you can tear yourself away, backtrack to Rivas and beat a path to the port of San Jorge, 15 minutes down the road. From there, boats regularly depart to the glorious island of Ometepe with its rustic villages and twin volcano complex. You'll need a few days to soak up the ambience and explore everything it has to offer.

If time is not an issue, Ometepe is the departure point for an overnight ferry to the remote Río San Juan province. Once you've arrived in the jungle gateway of San Carlos, you'll have the option to explore the teeming

TRAVEL TIP
In the wet season, rubber boots are essential footwear for the rainforest.

wetlands of Guatuzo or the bucolic artists' colony of the Solentiname archipelago.

A trip down the Río San Juan to the old Spanish fortress of El Castillo, however, is the real highlight of the region. From there, you'll be able to organize expeditions into the virgin rainforests of the Indio-Maíz reserve. Getting back to Managua from this remote area is not as hard as it seems – single propeller airplanes depart from San Carlos to the capital daily – an adventure in themselves.

Volcán Concepción on Ometepe Island is one of the most symmetrical cones in the world

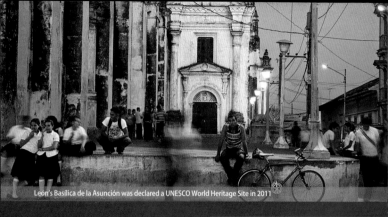
León's Basílica de la Asunción was declared a UNESCO World Heritage Site in 2011

ITINERARY TWO: 2 weeks
Coffee, communities and revolution

The areas north and northwest of Managua are rich in coffee plantations, remote farming communities, verdant nature reserves, smoking volcanoes, rolling mountains and gripping tales of the revolution. Their appeal is often unconventional, but the region is no less rewarding than the more-visited sites in the south.

The vibrant colonial city of León lies under two hours from the capital and is a great place to begin. Be sure to summit a volcano or two, perhaps sand-boarding down the slopes of Cerro Negro, before hitting the Pacific beaches of Las Peñitas and Poneloya. More intrepid travellers can continue to the remote Cosigüina Peninsula before backtracking and cutting east to the coffee capital of Matagalpa, two or three hours away.

Scores of intriguing coffee fincas pepper the hills around Matagalpa, including the German-built Selva Negra and the award-winning Esperanza Verde, both impressive proponents of sustainable organic technologies. An hour north of Matagalpa up a winding mountain road is the refreshing highland city of Jinotega with its access to fine nature reserves and Apanás lake.

From Jinotega, you can descend the mountains as far as the crossroads at Sébaco, where a northbound branch leads to the agricultural city of Estelí, where the finest cigars in Central America are rolled. The massive Reserva Natural Miraflor, just outside the city, is the best community tourism project in the country and offers visitors the rewarding chance to experience rural life up close.

From Estelí it's possible to continue north to the sleepy village of Somoto and, in the dry season, take a lazy trip through its nearby canyon. Beyond, the village of Totogalpa offers glimpses of lost-in-time rural life, as does Ciudad Antigua, which is best accessed from the border town of Ocotal. Now a stone's throw from Honduras, getting back to the capital is simply a matter of jumping on a southbound express bus.

ITINERARY THREE: 2 – 3 weeks
Caribbean dreams

Nicaragua's Caribbean coast is a world unto itself, with few roads and almost zero touristic infrastructure. It offers some seriously challenging adventure travel for those bold enough to tackle it, and, beyond the well-visited Corn Islands, careful planning is required to safely navigate this wily frontier land.

Bluefields, the heart and soul of the Southern Atlantic Autonomous Region, is a sensible place to start. A lightly dilapidated but reasonably populated coastal port, it offers a manageable introduction to the multicultural world of the Caribbean. Just one hour away along jungle-shrouded rivers, the diverse communities of the Pearl Lagoon basin offer the chance to really relax into the local way of life.

If it's beaches you're seeking, the fabled paradise atolls of the Corn Islands lie five to eight hours from Bluefields by ferry. Some serious hammock-time is mandatory, but don't forget to check out the scintillating coral reefs just off shore.

Back on the mainland, the adventure really begins as you head north to Bilwi, the Miskito capital of the North Atlantic Autonomous Region. There are no roads from Bluefields so, unless you're prepared to slog up the coast on random fishing boats, a plane is the best way in. From Bilwi, you have the option to visit all kinds of interesting end-of-the-world communities, including the village of Waspam on the Río Coco. This is deep in Miskito territory and the ride only gets wilder the further you go.

South of Waspam, a rugged seasonal road connects with the interior of Nicaragua. Several bumpy hours away the mining triangle towns of Rosita, Bonanza and Siuna promise fascinating encounters with indigenous communities and provide access to the majestic Bosawás Biosphere Reserve. From the mining triangle the road continues its long, arduous route back to Managua, concluding one of the most awesome journeys this side of space travel.

Golden sands and irie times on Little Corn Island

Masked dancers perform the legendary Güegüence at the Festival de San Sebastián

Red-eyed tree frog (*Agalychnis callidryas*) in a bromeliad flower

Contents

NORTHERN HIGHLANDS

CARIBBEAN COAST

LEON & THE OCCIDENTE

MANAGUA

MASAYA & LOS PUEBLOS

GRANADA

RIVAS ISTHMUS & OMETEPE ISLAND

RIO SAN JUAN

Contents

Footprint features

Essentials

Planning your trip

Best time to visit Nicaragua

Most people prefer to visit western and northern Nicaragua during the rainy season or shortly after the rains have ended. During the dry season the Pacific Basin receives practically no rain at all and from mid-February until the rains arrive in late May the region is very hot and dry. During the rainy season the Pacific Basin is bright green and freshened daily by the rains, which normally last for less than two hours in the afternoon before clearing and then falling again during the night. December is an extraordinarily beautiful time to visit the Nicaraguan Pacific, with all the landscape in bloom, the air still fresh and visibility excellent across the volcanic ranges.

The dry season becomes shorter the further east you travel, and in the Caribbean Basin it can rain at any time of year. For diving and snorkelling, March to mid-May and late September to October offer the best chances of finding calm waters with great visibility. For birdwatching in the rainforest areas of the Río San Juan, the dry season is best as you'll have the chance to see the many migratory species and nesting birds. **Note**: Nicaraguans consider the dry season (December-May) summer and the rainy season winter, which can lead to confusion considering the country lies well north (11-16°) of the equator.

During Easter week and between Christmas and New Year all of Nicaragua rushes to the beach, lake and riverfront areas to swim, drink and dance; avoid these dates if you don't want to encounter massive crowds and fully booked hotels.

What to do in Nicaragua

Nicaragua has a number of options for independent and organized special-interest travel. Many activities, like whitewater rafting, free climbing or windsurfing, provide good opportunities for the experienced adventure traveller who wants to explore without tourist infrastructure or a safety net. Those listed below are ones which have been developed by local tour operators and are accessible to independent travellers. Further details are available in the relevant chapters.

Archaeology

Although the archaeology is not as inspiring as the Mayan temples further north, Nicaragua's pre-Columbian history is fascinating. Around the country, museums display artefacts that have been discovered in each region; the best are at the **Palacio Nacional de la Cultura** in Managua (page 48), the **Museo Antiguo Convento de San Francisco** in Granada (page 118), **Museo El Ceibo** on Isla Ometepe (page 142), and the **Museo Arqueológico** in Juigalpa (page 78). In Lake Nicaragua, there are some remains on the islands of **Zapatera** (page 129) and **Ometepe** (page 139), where you can see some large basalt statues. Petroglyphs are also present on many islands in Lake Nicaragua as well as numerous sites around the mainland. Colonial archaeology can be examined in the UNESCO World Heritage Site of **León Viejo** (page 218). A guide is recommended since English-language books on Nicaragua's archaeological heritage are virtually non-existent.

Packing for Nicaragua

Travelling light is recommended. Your specific list will depend largely on what kind of travelling you plan to do. Cotton clothes are versatile and suitable for most situations. A hat, sun lotion and sunglasses will protect you from the instant grilling that the Nicaragua sun could cause. A light sweater or very light jacket is useful for those heading into the highlands or rainforest. English-language books are very rare in Nicaragua, so bring reading material with you. Contact-lens wearers and people with special medical needs must bring all prescription medicines and lens-cleaning products. If you intend to hike in the volcanoes you will need very sturdy, hard-soled trekking shoes, which should also ideally be lightweight and very breathable. A lightweight pack filled with energy bars and a flask is useful. Take mosquito netting if travelling on the cheap or to the jungle or Caribbean coastal regions. Wellington boots, worn by the locals in the countryside, will allow you to tackle any rainforest trail. Insect repellent is a must in these areas. Rain poncho, zip-lock bags and heavy-duty bin liners/ trash bags (for backpacks) are highly recommended for rainforest travel. A fairly powerful torch is useful all over Nicaragua's countryside as electric power is either irregular or non-existent. A penknife and a roll of duct tape are the traveller's indispensable, all-purpose items. For maps, see page 27.

Birdwatching

According to the latest count Nicaragua is home to over 700 species of bird, including boat-billed flycatcher, collared aracari, black-headed trogon, wood stork, roseate spoonbill, long-tailed manikin and osprey. The national bird is the turquoise-browed mot mot, beautiful and common in the highlands of Managua. The sheer number of birds in Nicaragua is amazing. **Reserva Biológica Indio-Maíz** (page 186) in Río San Juan area has primary rainforest with the scarlet macaw still filling the sky with red plumage. The **Refugio de Vida Silvestre Los Guatuzos** (page 178) has gallery forest and ample wetlands teeming with birds. The **Archipiélago Solentiname** (page 175) has 2 islands that are massive nesting sites. In the northern mountains of **Jinotega** (page 247) and **Matagalpa** (page 238) the cloud forests are home to many prize bird species like the quetzal. The **Montibelli Private Nature Reserve** (page 72), **Laguna de Apoyo** (page 94) and the **Reserva Natural El Chocoyero** (page 72), located just outside the capital, also offer a chance to see many interesting species including 1000 or so nesting parakeets. For those with time, patience and rugged constitutions, the hard-to-reach **Bosawás Biosphere Reserve** (pages 250 and 299) promises some of the best birding in Central America with over 400 resident species.

Climbing

Guided climbs are non-technical in nature. There is potential for technical climbing, but routes are undeveloped and you need to have to your own gear as there are no climbing outfitters or stores. The most popular location is the **Maribios** volcanic range (page 215), set on a broad plain just 20-30 miles inland from the Pacific Ocean and made up of more than 20 volcanoes, 5 of which are active. Another key spot is the island of **Ometepe** (page 139) which has 2 cones affording sparkling lake views. While the Pacific volcanoes are no higher than 1700 m, the climbs are not as easy as they might seem. Most routes start just above sea level and are steep with difficult conditions

How big is your footprint?

Even small groups of travellers can have a big impact on the environment and local communities, especially where local people may be unused to their conventions or lifestyles and natural environments may be sensitive. Here are a few tips:

→ Where possible choose a destination, tour operator or hotel with a proven ethical and environmental commitment.

→ Spend money on locally produced (rather than imported) goods and services. Use common sense when bargaining – your few dollars saved may be a week's salary.

→ Use water and electricity carefully – travellers may receive preferential supply while the needs of local communities are overlooked.

→ Rather than giving money or sweets to children some visitors prefer to donate to a project, charity or school.

→ Learn about local etiquette and culture, consider local norms and behaviour, dress appropriately for local cultures and situations.

→ Protect wildlife and other natural resources – don't buy souvenirs or goods made from wildlife unless they are clearly sustainably produced and are not protected under CITES legislation.

→ Always ask before taking photographs or videos of people.

→ Stay in local rather than foreign-owned accommodation. The economic benefits for host communities are far greater and there are more opportunities to learn about local culture.

→ Community tourism is growing in Nicaragua, offering the chance to participate in, and directly contribute to, rural communities. For more information, see individual chapters.

including sharp rocks, sand and loose terrain, combined with serious heat.

Cycling

The options for cycling in Nicaragua are good, with a network of relatively flat, paved roads connecting the traditional villages of the **Pueblos Blancos**. For those who like their biking rugged, the hills around **Matagalpa** have lots of potential. In the dry season, confident cyclists should consider a foray into the **North Atlantic Autonomous Region**. The villages from Bilwi to Waspam are joined by an extensive web of flat, easy-to-traverse and relatively empty dirt roads and expansive pine forests, but you will need a good map, equally good Spanish and even some wilderness experience to safely navigate the region. (For more information on cycling, see Transport in Nicaragua, page 26).

Diving and snorkelling

There are professional dive operators on both of the **Corn Islands** (page 281). To find any depth a boat trip is needed, but the reefs lining both islands are beautiful and the marine life is rich. Snorkelling in the waters that wash the Corn Islands is world class and a real joy. Though scuba gear can be rented for diving, snorkellers would be wise to bring their own gear as most equipment available outside the dive operations is of poor quality. Snorkelling is also good around the **Pearl Cays** (page 286), but access is by expensive charter boat. The Pacific Coast, beaten by waves, is usually too rough for diving or snorkelling. **Laguna de Apoyo** (page 94) offers diving opportunities for those interested in taking part in scientific research.

Fishing

Nicaragua is a fisherman's paradise, with its wide selection of rivers, lakes and seas. Deep-sea fishing can be arranged in **San Juan del Sur** (page 166) or **Marina Puesta del Sol** (page 227) in the Pacific and bonefishing is possible on the **Corn Islands** (page 274). Lake Nicaragua is great for bass fishing. The island of **Zapatera** (page 129) and its archipelago are home to Central America's biggest annual freshwater tournament. In **Pearl Lagoon** (page 286) and **Alamikamba** (pages 20 and 298) on the Caribbean side and on the **Río San Juan** (pages 169 and 182) tarpon and snook fishing is very good.

Spectator sports

Baseball

Baseball is the national sport in Nicaragua. The first league games were organized over 100 years ago and there is a very hard-fought national championship for the first division and many minor divisions. Nicaraguans follow the major leagues in the United States with more fervour than many Americans. The regular season begins in Nov and runs until the championships in Feb. Games are played all over the country during the dry season on Sun in stadiums that are in themselves a cultural experience.

Boxing

Another big passion for Nicaraguans is boxing, with 5 world champions in the lighter categories to be proud of. Though most fights of importance take place outside Nicaragua, it may be possible to watch low-level Nicaraguan fights as well as quality boxers in training at the **Alexis Argüello gymnasium**, Barrio San José Oriental, de la Clínica Santa María, 2 c sur, 1 c arriba, Managua.

Bullfighting

Bullfighting in Nicaragua is a strange hybrid of bullfighting and bull rodeo. The bull is not killed or injured, just intensely annoyed. The beast is brought inside the ring roped by a few mounted cowboys and tied to a bare tree in the centre. Someone mounts its back using a leather strap to hold on and the angry bull is released from the tree. The rider tries to stay on top and a few others show the animal some red capes for as long as they dare, before running off just before (in most cases) being impaled. When the bull gets too tired, a fresh one is brought in, mounted and shown more capes. Every patron saint festival has a bullfight. One of the most famous takes place at the Santa Ana festival in La Orilla, see page 85.

Cockfighting

Cock fights are legal and take place every Sun all over the country. Like bullfighting, cockfighting in Nicaragua is non-lethal, but it is bloody and birds do occasionally die. Most of them will live to fight another day, though. The biggest time for the fights (*pelea de gallo*) is during the patron saint festival of each town. To find the fight rings you will need to ask around (they do not have signs). The fight ring in Estelí is one of the most serious, with bets of over US$3000 being waged.

Surfing

Nicaragua's Pacific Coast is home to countless beautiful breaks, many of which are only just starting to become popular. Most surfing is done along the coast of Rivas, using **San Juan del Sur** (page 154) as a jumping-off point to reach breaks to the north and south. The country's biggest and most famous break is at **Popoyo** (page 158) in northern Rivas. It is possible to rent boards in San Juan del Sur, but in most cases you will need to bring everything with you, as even wax can be hard to find at times. Many used to rave at the tube rides and point breaks that lie empty all year round, but recent complaints include surf operators converging on breaks with a boat full of clients.

Six of the best: volcano adventures

Volcán Masaya

The Parque Nacional Volcán Masaya is home to one of the world's most accessible volcano complexes – and one of the most active. Perpetually smoking and threatening cataclysm, the yawning chasm of its Santiago crater was long thought to be a gateway to hell. Surrounded by stark black lava fields and swathed in sulphurous vapours, it's not hard to see why. Page 91.

Volcán Mombacho

As the ever-present backdrop to the city of Granada, Volcán Mombacho, 1345 m high, is the one of the easiest volcanoes to experience in the country. Its lower slopes are dotted with tranquil villages that can be visited with the UCA Tierra y Agua community tourism project. Its upper slopes are home to cloud forests, hiking trails and heart-pounding zip-lines. Page 130.

Volcán Maderas

On Isla Ometepe, the slopes of Volcán Maderas are littered with ancient petroglyphs depicting everything from pre-Columbian deities to lizards, crocodiles and frogs. Now extinct and swathed in vegetation, Maderas is home to numerous distinct life zones, including misty cloud forests at its higher altitudes. You'll enjoy views of its tranquil crater lake from the 1394 m summit. Pages 141 and 142.

Volcán Cerro Negro

Reminiscent of a stark lunar landscape, Cerro Negro, 675 m, is one of Latin America's youngest volcanoes, emerging from the earth in just 1850. Vegetation has yet to colonize its slopes, which are instead covered in rolling dunes of black sand and gravel – the perfect environment for the popular new sport of volcano boarding. Don't miss this high-speed thrill. Page 216.

Volcán San Cristóbal

At 1745 m, Volcán San Cristóbal is Nicaragua's highest volcano and, following a decade of frequent eruptions, it remains in a volatile state. It is a challenging ascent through tropical dry forests which finally rewards persistent climbers with awesome views of its 500-m-wide crater. Be sure to use a guide and check on the current safety status before setting out. Page 217.

Volcán Cosigüina

Volcán Cosigüina is renowned for the diverse wildlife inhabiting its tropical dry forests, including a precious population of scarlet macaws – the last remaining in Pacific Nicaragua. The volcano once stood at a height of 3000 m, but following the most violent eruption in Latin American recorded history, it now stands at an altitude of 859 m. Nonetheless, the views from its summit are inspirational, encompassing El Salvador to the north and Honduras to the east. Page 228.

Trekking

Most of Nicaragua's Pacific Basin is great walking country. You will need to speak some Spanish to get by, but once outside the city a whole world of beautiful landscapes and friendly people awaits you. Fences outside cities in Nicaragua are for animals, not people, and if you respect the privacy and rights of the local residents you need not worry about trespassing. Local guides are helpful and you should ask around each village to see who can accompany you and how far. Accommodation will be in hammocks (see Camping, page 29). Due to wild

Six of the best: final frontiers

San Juan del Norte

Located at the yawning mouth of the Río San Juan, the Caribbean port of San Juan del Norte marks the end of a long, meandering trip on jungle-shrouded river. No roads connect it with the outside world and the surrounding rainforests – the ancestral home of the indigenous Rama people – are among the most pristine in Central America. Page 188.

Bosawás Biosphere Reserve

Few places are as wild and untamed as the Bosawás Biosphere Reserve, the largest protected area in Nicaragua. The reserve can be accessed from the remote highlands of Jinotega or the equally remote environs of the mining triangle, but neither journey is easy. However, few destinations are so rewarding – the wildlife, forests and scenes of rugged natural beauty are nothing short of spectacular. Pages 250 and 299.

Pearl Lagoon Basin

The diverse and hospitable communities of the Pearl Lagoon Basin, an hour outside of Bluefields by high-speed *panga*, are home to an intriguing blend of Afro-descendant and indigenous cultures. Creole, Garífuna and Miskito villages sit side by side and maintain a traditional lifestyle very much grounded in fishing and subsistence agriculture. Page 286.

Waspam

Perched on the banks of the mighty Río Coco, Waspam is the spiritual heart of the ancient Miskito Kingdom. As a trading centre for scores of remote communities up and down the river, it is just the starting point for a rare cultural odyssey that leads deep into a mysterious and extraordinary lost-in-time indigenous world. Page 297.

Las Minas

A trio of old mining outposts – Bonanza, Rosita and Siuna – offer glimpses into a lawless frontier-land that's more than a little reminiscent of the Wild West. Thanks to the rising price of gold, these towns are booming again after years of neglect, but still remain isolated with only rough airstrips and a long, painful dirt road (often washed out in the wet season) to connect them with the capital. Page 297.

Alamikamba

Alamikamba lies at the end of the road on the banks of the winding Prinzapolka river. It has experienced numerous episodes of boom and bust serving as an indigenous trading post, river port, ranching centre and hub for banana production. Today it is the seat of government for the local municipality and offers some of the best sport fishing anywhere. Page 298.

driving habits, avoid walking along the road wherever possible and use the volcanoes as landmarks. It is possible to trek the **Maribios** volcano range (page 215) in northwestern Nicaragua, starting at the extinct lake-filled crater of **Volcán Cosigüina**, which is the most westerly point of Nicaragua, and taking in all 21 cones, 5 of which are active. The route passes through many ranches and farms, where you can ask for directions if you need to. Another great place for trekking is the island of **Ometepe** (page 139) with its breathtaking beauty, friendly people and many dirt trails; it is essential to use local guides here.

Getting to Nicaragua

Air

Managua is home to the country's only working international airport, Aeropuerto Internacional Agusto C Sandino. It handles direct flights from a limited range of carriers in the USA, Central and South America. Travellers outside those areas will usually have to transit in the US, although it is sometimes cheaper to fly into Costa Rica and catch a connecting flight/bus from there.

Buying a ticket

Good Nicaragua deals are often hard to come by. Generally speaking local carriers **TACA** and **COPA** are less expensive from the USA, Central and South America than US and European carriers, although code sharing means you can often combine the two from Europe. For a list of airlines serving Managua's international airport, see Arriving in Managua, page 44.

Flights from UK There are no direct flights from the UK to Managua. **British Airways**, www.british-airways.com, uses Miami as a hub to connect with Central American carriers. **Delta Airlines**, www.delta.com, and **American Airlines**, www.aa.com, also fly from London to Managua via the US, but the most direct flights are from Gatwick on **Continental Airlines**, www.continental.com, with a stop in Houston. Prices range from US$900-1400. UK residents can look for deals on www.traveljungle.co.uk.

Flights from the rest of Europe Nicaragua does not receive any directs flights from Europe and travellers are required to transit through the US. Another option is to fly **Iberia**, www.iberia.com, directly from Madrid to Costa Rica or Guatemala, then use a local carrier to reach Managua (around US$700-1000 in addition to the cost of getting to Madrid from your home city).

Flights from North America Several US carriers now fly directly to Managua including **American Airlines**, **Continental Airlines**, **Spirit Airlines** and **Delta Airlines**. TACA, www.taca.com, the Central American group airline, also flies daily from Miami direct to Managua and has a direct flight twice a week from Los Angeles. **COPA**, www.copaair.com, the national carrier of Panama has twice-weekly flights from Houston. Flights from Miami cost US$400-550; from Houston or Los Angeles US$550-850; and upwards of US$800 from Canada. From Montreal, cheap charter flights are available from November to March. **Spirit Air** flies direct to Managua from Fort Lauderdale often at bargain rates of under US$200.

Flights from Australia and New Zealand The most efficient route to Nicaragua from Australia, at a cost of around US$1800, is direct from Sydney with **Qantas**, www.qantas.com.au, to Los Angeles, then to Houston with **Continental Airlines** for a direct flight from Houston to Managua or a **TACA** flight to Managua via El Salvador. From Auckland with the same connections and routes the fare comes to about US$1600.

Flights from Central America TACA flies to Managua from all countries in Central America several times daily, as does the Panamanian carrier **COPA**, with superior in-flight service to Managua from Guatemala, Costa Rica and Panama, although connections are less frequent. **Nature Air**, www.natureair.com, operates flights from a range of provincial airports in Costa Rica and Panama. Return flights to Managua normally cost around US\$260 from Guatemala or Panama and US\$220 from Costa Rica.

Airport information

Managua's Aeropuerto Internacional Agusto C Sandino, www.eaai.com.ni, is a small but modern international airport with a range of amenities including parking, restaurants, souvenirs shops, car rental agencies, a tourist information booth and ATMs. Claro operates a sales stand on the main concourse where you can pick up a Nicaraguan mobile phone for as little as US\$15. The airport is situated on the Carretera Norte about 20 minutes from the city centre and you are strongly advised to use officially licensed taxis working the grounds. The domestic terminal is located next to the main terminal in a separate building.

Ticket agents

UK
STA Travel, 52 Grosvenor Gardens, Victoria, London SW1W 0AG, T0800-819-9339, www.statravel.co.uk.
Trailfinders, 63 Conduit St (just off Regent St), London W15 2GB, T020-7408-9000, www.trailfinders.com.

Rest of Europe
Die Reisegalerie, Grüneburgweg 84, 60323 Frankfurt, Germany, T069-9720-6000, www.reisegalerie.com.
Images du Monde, 14 rue Lahire, 75013 Paris, France, T1-4424-8788, www.imagenes-tropicales.com. Also with an office in Costa Rica.
Thika Travel, Kerkplein 6, 3628 AE, Kockengen (gem. Breukelen), Netherlands, T0346-242526, www.thika.nl.

North America
Discount Airfares Worldwide On-Line, www.etn.nl/discount.htm. A hub of consolidator and discount agent links.

STA Travel, T1-800-781-4040, www.statravel.com. Branches throughout the US and Canada.
Travel CUTS, 187 College St, Toronto, ON, M5T 1P7, T1-800-667 2887, www.travelcuts.com. Specialist in student discount fares, IDs and other travel services.

Australia and New Zealand
Exito Latin American Travel Specialists, 6740 E Hampden Av, Denver, Colorado 80224, T1-800-655-4053, www.exitotravel.com.
Flight Centres, 82 Elizabeth St, Sydney 2000, T133-133, www.flightcentre.com.au; Unit 3, 239 Queen St, Auckland, T0800-243544, www.flightcentre.co.nz. With branches in other towns and cities.
STA Travel, 841 George St, Sydney, T134-782 (general enquires), www.statravel.com.au; 267 Queen St, Auckland, www.statravel.co.nz, T0800-474-400. Also in major towns and university campuses.
Travel.com.au, 76-80 Clarence St, Sydney, T1300-130483, www.travel.com.au.
Trailfinders, 8 Spring St, Sydney, NSW 2000, www.trailfinders.com.au, T1300-780-212.

Road

Bus
International buses are a cheap and efficient way to travel between Nicaragua and other Central American countries. Buses are available to and from Honduras, El Salvador,

International bus routes

Costa Rica
Ticabus leaves Managua at 0600, 0700, 1200 and San José at 0600, 0730 and 1230, US$29, executive US$38, 8½ hours. **King Quality** leaves Managua at 1330 and San José at 0300 US$44, 8½ hours. **Transnica** leaves Managua at 0500, 0700, 1000, 1300 (executive) and San José at 0400, 0500, 0900, 1200 (executive), US$28, Executive Service US$40, 8½ hours.

El Salvador
Ticabus leaves Managua at 0500 and San Salvador at 0500, US$35, executive US$48, 12 hours. **King Quality** leaves Managua at 0330 ('Quality class'), 0530 ('Cruceros Class'), 1100 ('King Class'), and San Salvador at 0530 ('Cruceros Class') and 1130 ('Quality Class'), 'Cruceros class', US$31, 'Quality Class' US$53, 'King Class' US$77, 11 hours.

Guatemala
Ticabus leaves Managua at 0500 and Guatemala City at 1300, US$55, executive US$66, 30 hours including an overnight stay in El Salvador. **King Quality** leaves Managua at 0230 ('Cruceros Class'), 1530 ('Quality Class') and Guatmela City at 0400 ('Cruceros Class') and 0630 ('Quality Class'), 'Cruceros class' US$67, 'Quality Class' US$75, 'King Class' US$99, 15 hours.

Honduras
Ticabus leaves Managua at 0500 (continues to San Pedro Sula, US$37, 14 hours) and Tegucigalpa at 0915, US$23, eight hours (departs San Pedro Sula at 0500). **King Quality** leaves Managua at 0330 ('King Class'), 1130 ('Quality Class'), and Tegucigalpa at 0600 ('King Class') and 1400 ('Quality Class'), 'Quality Class' US$44, 'King Class' US$71, 8½ hours. **Transnica** leaves Managua at 1400 and Tegucigalpa at 0500, US$29, eight hours.

Mexico
Ticabus leaves Managua at 0500 and Tapachula at 0700, US$77, 36 hours including overnight stay in El Salvador. **King Quality** also has daily services between Managua and Tapachula, 'Quality Class' US$78, 'King Class' US$100.

Panama
Ticabus leaves Managua at 0600, 0700, 1200 and Panama City at 1100, US$69, executive 90, 28-32 hours, including a two- to six-hour stopover in Costa Rica.

Guatemala, Costa Rica and Panama. When leaving Managua you will need to check in one hour in advance with your passport and ticket. Three good companies operate the international routes to and from Managua. **Ticabus** ① *de Antiguo Cine Dorado, 2 c arriba, T2222-6094, www.ticabus.com*; **King Quality** ① *at the end of 27 de Mayo St, opposite Plaza Inter, T2228-1454, www.king-qualityca.com* (both arrive at Barrio Martha Quezada); and **Transnica** ① *Managua Rotonda, Metrocentro, 300 m norte, 25 m este T2277-2104, www.transnica.com*. The buses all have air conditioning, toilet and reclining seats; most have TV screens and offer snacks. See box, page 23, for major routes into Nicaragua and one-way costs.

Car and motorcycle
There are three land crossings into Nicaragua from Honduras. Via Tegucigalpa, the most direct is the **Las Manos** crossing, entering just north of Ocotal. See page 267 for more details on Las Manos and El Espino crossings. The most travelled route into Nicaragua

is via the lowlands adjacent to the Golfo de Fonseca using the crossing at **El Guasaule**, north of Chinandega (see page 225), south from Choluteca, Honduras. This entrance is also the nearest crossing for those coming from El Salvador via Honduras. An alternative is **El Espino**, which enters via the northern mountains and passes Estelí en route to Managua. The only road crossing that connects Nicaragua to Costa Rica and unites Central America via road is at **Peñas Blancas** (see box, page 161), 144 km south of Managua. Motorists and motorcyclists must pay US$20 in cash on arrival at the border (cyclists pay US$2, and up to US$9 at weekends, although this tends to vary from one customs post to the next). For motorcyclists crash helmets are compulsory. Several cyclists have said that you should take a 'proof of purchase' of your cycle or suggest typing out your own 'cycle ownership' document to help at border crossings. Motorists also pay the same entry tax per person as other overland arrivals. Make sure you get all the correct stamps on arrival, or you will encounter all sorts of problems once inside the country. Do not lose the receipts, they have to be produced when you leave; without them you will have to pay again. Up to four hours of formalities are possible when entering Nicaragua with a vehicle. On leaving, motorists pay five córdobas, as well as the usual exit tax.

Sea and river

The water crossing into Nicaragua from Costa Rica is via **Los Chiles** using the Río Frío. There is road access to Los Chiles from La Fortuna, Costa Rica. Exit stamps and taxes must be paid in Los Chiles before boarding public boats for the journey down the Río Frío to San Carlos for immigration and customs for Nicaragua (see box, page 174). It is possible to enter Nicaragua at Potosí by boat from El Salvador, but the crossing can be tricky and schedules are unreliable.

Transport in Nicaragua

A decent road system covers the west of Nicaragua and the country's small size makes car or bus travel practical and fairly simple. Buses run between all Pacific and central cities and villages on a daily basis and fares are very cheap. A 4WD is needed to get off the beaten path in all parts of the country. Boat and plane are the only options for long-distance travel on the Caribbean Coast and in the rainforest areas of the north and south where roads are generally horrible to non-existent.

Air

La Costeña ① *T2263-2142, www.lacostena.com.ni*, operates services to Bluefields, Corn Island, Las Minas (Bonanza/Siuna/Rosita), Bilwi (previously known as Puerto Cabezas), San Carlos and Waspam (see relevant chapters for details). No seat assignments are given and flights are often fully booked or overbooked – always allow for possible delays of up to 48 hours. Early arrival at the airport is essential and La Costeña now requires you to check in two hours prior to departure. The airline no longer accepts unpaid advance reservations, but you can buy tickets in advance over the telephone with a credit card. Changing dates on tickets is possible up to 72 hours in advance of departure (a US$10 fee applies thereafter) and open-ended returns are valid for up to three months. Note domestic return flights should always be reconfirmed immediately on arrival at a destination. There is a 9-kg hand luggage limit; stowed luggage maximum is 20 kg on most flights. Domestic departure tax is US$2.

Road

The road network has been greatly extended and improved in recent years. The Pan-American Highway from Honduras to Costa Rica is paved the whole way (384 km), as is the shorter international road to the Honduran frontier via Chinandega. The road between Managua and Rama (for boat access to Bluefields) is paved, but not in good condition. A high proportion of Nicaragua's roads are unpaved with lots of mud bogs in the wet season and dusty washboard and stone-filled paths in the dry season. Be flexible with your schedules.

Bus

This is how most Nicaraguans get around and schedules are pretty reliable except on Sundays. It is best to arrive early for all long-distance buses, especially if it is an express or an infrequent service. On routes that leave every hour or half-hour you only need to check the destination above the front window of the bus and grab a seat. You can flag down most buses that are not marked 'Express'. Fares are collected as you board city buses and en route on intercity buses. For express buses, you often need to purchase your ticket in advance at the terminal or from the driver; some buses have reserved seating. Most Nicaraguan buses are 'retired' US school buses and have very limited legroom. Sitting behind the driver may alleviate this problem for tall passengers and is a good idea if you plan to get off before the final destination. Buses often fill up to the roof and can be very hot and bumpy, but they are a great way to meet and get to know the Nicaraguan people. Most major destinations have an express service, which makes fewer stops and travels faster; for longer journeys an express bus could mean cutting travel times in half.

Car

Petrol stations are very rare in the countryside; it's best to fill up the tank (unleaded, premium grade fuel and diesel are available everywhere) if going into the interior. There are 24-hour petrol stations in the major cities, elsewhere they close at 1800. 4WD drive for travel within the Pacific Basin is not necessary, although it does give you dramatically more flexibility across the country and is standard equipment in mountain and jungle territory. It is obligatory to wear a seatbelt. You may be stopped on a routine check and the law states that all cars must carry an emergency triangle reflector and fire extinguisher. Note that in Nicaragua you must hold your lane for 30 m before and after a signal. If you are involved in a car accident where someone is injured, you may be held for up to two days, guilty or not, while blame is assessed. Hiring a driver covers this potentially disastrous liability. Be careful when driving at night, few roads are lit and there are many people, animals and holes in the road. See also Police and the law, page 36.

Car hire Renting a vehicle costs around US$25-40 a day for a basic car, rising to US$60-100 for a 4WD. Weekly discount rates are significant and if you want to cover a lot of sites quickly it can be worthwhile. A minimum deposit of US$500 is required in addition to an international driver's licence or a licence from your country of origin. Insurance is US$10-25 depending on cover. Before signing up check the insurance and what it covers and also ask about mileage allowance. Most agents have an office at the international airport and offices in other parts of Managua.

Road warrior – driving and surviving in Nicaragua

Anyone familiar with driving in Latin America will be aware to some extent of the challenge that lies ahead, although there are some specific Nicaraguan variations on the theme. Three delectable kinds of driving experiences await you in this tropical state of motoring madness.

City In the Managua battle-zone the visiting gladiator must steer clear of axle-breaking holes and city buses – smoking beasts, filled to the ceiling with sweating commuters and professional thieves and manned by some of the most aggressive men on earth. The crazed and ruthless bus driver mounts his challenge, horn wailing, sharpened metal spikes spinning from chromed wheels. The bus driver will never slow down, yield or even acknowledge anyone, except a boarding or disembarking passenger. Taxi drivers too must be respected for what they are: rogue messengers from planet anarchy, routinely breaking every rule of legal driving in ways previously unimaginable. Don't be surprised by the crash-the-red-light-by-driving-into-oncoming-traffic-to-overtake-waiting-cars-at-the-intersection manoeuvre or their maniacally obsessive horn usage.

The open road Out of the confines of Managua you can breathe deep, relax and run free, but you still need grand prix reaction time to avoid ox and horse carts, people sitting on the road shoulder, potholes as deep as the 12th circle of hell and your fellow road warriors blissfully passing on blind corners and hills. There is no speed limit, just a limit on common sense, patience and judgement. The open-road Nicaraguan driver does, however, give ample room to the oncoming car, the overtaker and the undertaker. No matter how conservative you set out to be, you will be forced into aggressive overtaking. Be sure to use your horn to warn the vehicle you are passing in the daytime and your headlights at night. Be decisive and give space to the other gladiators, they will return the favour.

Off road The real fun of driving in Nicaragua lies beyond the limits of its paved universe. Rock-filled and river-sliced passages lead to places forgotten by earth and roadside services. Driving here is more akin to an off-road endurance test with mud bogs and raging rivers to be forged in the rainy season and relentless banging over rocky dust roads in the dry. The pace is slower and when you are not busy coating well-dressed women and children with thick layers of billowing dirt or sheepishly asking for an ox cart to pull you out of a bog, friends can be made and rides offered – even if a horse really would have been a better choice.

Cycle

A mountain bike is strongly recommended. If you hire one, look for a good-quality, rugged bike with low gear ratios for difficult terrain, wide tyres with plenty of tread for good road-holding, cantilever brakes and a low centre of gravity for improved stability. Imported bike parts are impossible to find in Nicaragua so buy everything you need before you leave home. Most towns have a bicycle shop of some description, but it is best to do your own repairs and adjustments whenever possible. Take care to avoid dehydration by drinking regularly. In hot, dry areas with limited water supplies, be sure to carry an ample supply on the bike. Because of traffic it is usually more rewarding to keep to the smaller roads or to paths. Watch for oncoming, overtaking vehicles, protruding or unstable loads on trucks. Make yourself conspicuous by wearing bright clothing and a helmet.

Hitchhiking

Hitchhiking is a common way to travel in the countryside, less so in the cities. Men will find it significantly more difficult to get a ride if they do not have a female companion. Pick-up trucks are the best bet, you should offer to help pay for fuel. Picking up hitchhikers is a great way to make friends, but not advisable if there is more than one man, unaccompanied by at least one woman. In the deep countryside it is considered quite rude not to offer a ride if you have room, particularly for women with babies.

Truck

In many rural areas and some cities, flat-bed trucks – usually covered with a tarpaulin and often with bench seating – are used for getting to places inaccessible by bus or to fill in routes where no buses are available. The trucks charge a fixed fare and, apart from eating a bowlful of dust in the dry season or getting soaked in the wet, they can be a great way to see the country. Communication with the driver can be difficult, so make sure you know more or less where you are going; other passengers will be able to tell you where to jump off. Banging the roof of the driver's cabin is often necessary to tell the driver he has arrived at your destination.

Sea and river

In a country with two oceans, two great lakes and numerous lagoons, estuaries and rivers, a boat is never far away and is often the only means of travel. The main Pacific ports are Corinto, San Juan del Sur and Puerto Sandino. The two main Atlantic ports are Bilwi and Bluefields. Public river boats are often slow but private boats can be hired at some expense if you are short on time, travelling in a large group, wish to view wildlife or want to make stops along the way. There are regular services between the two Corn Islands and a big boat runs from Bluefields to Big Corn three or four times a week. Apart from the Bluefields route and regular high-speed *panga* services to Pearl Lagoon, boat travel along the Pacific and Caribbean coasts is usually difficult. In Lake Nicaragua you can choose between big ferries and old wooden *African Queen* models. There is a weekly service connecting Granada, Ometepe Island and San Carlos.

Maps

Since road signage is weak, it is important to have a map and some basic Spanish to get even a little way off the main highway. Unfortunately, detailed road maps are yet to be adopted in Nicaragua and internationally produced maps are often poor quality, but they are improving. **National Geographic Adventure**, **Reise Know-How** and **International Travel Maps** have all produced worthy efforts – look for them in book stores before leaving home. Detailed maps (1:50,000) can also be bought at the government geological survey office, **INETER** ① *across from the Nicaraguan Immigration main office in Managua, T2249-3590*, useful if you are planning to escape the beaten track and/or go trekking.

Sleeping price codes

$$$$ over US$150 $$ US$30-65
$$$ US$66-150 $ under US$30

Unless otherwise stated, prices are for two people sharing a room in the high season, including taxes and service charges.

Where to stay in Nicaragua

Nicaragua has a rapidly expanding portfolio of lodging options, from million-dollar private ecolodges to backpacker hostels. Most quality lodging is limited to the Pacific Basin and other select areas. Note beach hotels raise their rates for Holy Week and almost all hotels charge higher prices for the Christmas holiday season with sell-outs common months in advance. **Note**: It is wise to pull the bed away from the wall in the tropics so whatever is crawling on the wall does not see your head as a logical progression.

Hotels and Hospedajes
Outside Managua, hotels at the top end of the **$** range are pleasant and some good deals can be found. Budget travellers have the option to stay in basic *hospedajes* (guesthouses) and they should bring a padlock, toilet paper, soap, insecticide, mosquito net, a sheet sleeper and a decent towel. Do not put toilet paper or any non-organic material in any toilet; you will find a little wastebasket for that purpose. Electric showers are common in highland areas and getting them to work is a matter of finding the right water pressure. Never touch the shower head once the water is running or you'll get a nasty shock. In remote areas, meals are often included in the price and electricity is produced by a diesel generator that runs for only a few hours after sunset.

Hostels
New hostels are opening all the time, especially in the cities of León and Granada, where you'll find no shortage of choice. Most of them offer economical dorm beds for US$5-10 along with a range of amenities including free coffee, breakfast, Wi-Fi, lockers, tours and information. Private rooms in hostels are not necessarily good value and couples and groups may get more bang for their buck in small hotels. As ever, hostels are a sociable option and the best place to meet other travellers or get together groups for tours.

Fincas and ecolodges
Private coffee *fincas* are an increasingly popular option in rural areas, especially in the Northern Highlands and along the volcanic slopes of Isla Ometepe. Most of them are peaceful retreats steeped in bucolic surroundings. To qualify as an ecolodge, a hotel needs to address the issues of renewable energy, water recycling, fair wages and social responsibility. There are comparatively few places that actually manage this and their facilities are sometimes more rustic than luxury. Wilderness lodges are a different category of accommodation. They vary wildly in cost and philosophy but are generally united by their pristine natural setting and access to protected areas. The decent ones will be able to recommend excursions and hook you up with professional guides.

Camping

In the heat of Nicaragua the thought of putting yourself inside a tent – or worse, inside a sleeping bag inside a tent – can be unpleasant. However, relief from the heat can be found in the northern mountains or on the slopes of the volcanoes. In more remote areas you can usually find a roof to hang your hammock under (ask for permission first). A mosquito net, which you should bring from home, will keep off the vampire bats as well as the insects.

Food and drink in Nicaragua

Nicaragua has a great selection of traditional dishes that are usually prepared with fresh ingredients and in generous portions. The midday heat dictates that you get out and tour early with a light breakfast, head for shelter and enjoy a long lunch and rest, then finish with an early dinner.

Food

Gallo pinto, the dish that keeps most of Nicaragua alive, is a mixture of fried white rice and kidney beans, which are boiled apart and then fried together. Equally popular *nacatamales* consist of cornmeal, pork or chicken, rice, *achote* (similar to paprika), peppers, peppermint leaves, potatoes, onions and cooking oil, all wrapped in a big green banana leaf and boiled. Lunch is the biggest meal of the day and normally includes a cabbage and tomato salad, white rice, beans, tortilla, fried or boiled plantain and a meat or fish serving. *Asado* or *a la plancha* are key words for most foreigners. *Asado* is grilled meat or fish, which often comes with a chilli sauce. *Carne asada*, grilled beef, is popular street food. *A la plancha* means the food is cooked on a sizzling plate or flat grill. In the countryside *cuajada* is a must. It is a soft feta-type cheese made daily in people's homes, lightly salted and excellent in a hot tortilla. There are other white cheeses: *queso seco* is a slightly bitter dry cheese and *queso crema* a moist bland cheese that is excellent fried. Regional dishes are described in the relevant chapters.

Drink

Since Nicaragua is the land of a thousand fruits, the best drink is the *refresco* or *fresco*, fruit juices or grains and spices mixed with water and sugar. Options include pineapple, carrot, passion fruit, beetroot, orange, mandarin, lemonade, grenadine, tamarind, mango, star-fruit, papaya and more. Two favourites are *cacao* and *pithaya*. *Cacao*, the raw cocoa bean, is ground and mixed with milk, rice, cinnamon, vanilla, ice and sugar. *Pithaya* is a cactus fruit, which is blended with lime and sugar and has a lovely deep purple colour. The usual fizzy **soft drinks** are also available and called *gaseosas*. For **beer** lovers there are four national brands (all lagers), the strongest being *Cerveza Victoria*, with *Toña* a softer choice. *Flor de Caña* has been called the finest rum in the world and its factory – more than 100 years old – is a national institution. Nicaraguans often spend a night round the table with a bottle of *Flor de Caña*, served up with a bucket of ice, a plate of limes and a steady flow of mixers. Although Nicaraguan **coffee** is recognized as one of the world's finest, most Nicaraguans are unable to pay for the expensive roasts and prefer to drink instant coffee. In the cities ask for *café percolado*, which is often quite good if it's available.

   Note: Water is safe to drink in Managua, Granada, León and other major towns. Bottled water is available throughout the country and is recommended as a precaution, but in the cities it is fine to drink frescos and drinks with ice cubes made from the local tap water.

Eating price codes

$$$ over US$12 $$ US$6-12 $ under US$6

Prices refer to the cost of a meal for one person with a drink, not including service charge.

Restaurants in Nicaragua

Anyone looking for international cuisine will be disappointed as choices and quality tend to be poor. The most expensive dish is not always the best, but a crowded mid-range restaurant is a good indication of a successful kitchen. Many restaurants offer *comida corriente* (also called *comida casera*), a set menu that works out far cheaper than ordering à la carte. Generally speaking, *fritanga* (street food), costs about US$1.50 and is best for the cast-iron stomach crowd, while the US$2-3 *comida corriente* is often tastier, though a bit salty and/or oily. The good eating starts at US$4 and runs up to US$12 a dish in most places. Some travellers complain that Nicaraguan cuisine is excessively bland and the more jaded among them carry bottles of hot sauce wherever they go.

Entertainment in Nicaragua

The favoured entertainment when not eating out is to drink and dance. All cities and most big villages have a *discoteca* and if you can bear music played at deafening volumes the dancing is very unpretentious and surprisingly varied. Bars range from upmarket business chat rooms in Managua to rough cowboy bars in the countryside and are an excellent place to take the pulse of the local population. Political discussion is a common thread, though in the countryside and villages leaving early might be in order at the weekends to avoid fist fights and the town drunk wrapping his arms around you and explaining his life story. Note that pool halls are designed for men only and a woman visitor will draw a great deal of attention.

Shopping in Nicaragua

Nicaragua is one of the richest countries in the region for handmade crafts, though many of them, like the wicker furniture, are difficult to take back home. Variety, quality and prices are favourable. Every city and town has its market. Usually the meats, fruits and vegetables are inside the market, while the non-perishable goods are sold around the outside. Some kind of handmade crafts or products of local workmanship can be found in most markets around the country. It may take some digging to find some markets as Nicaragua is not a mainstream tourist destination and the markets are not adapted to the visitor. The major exceptions are the craft market in Masaya, which is dedicated to the talents of the local and national craftsmen, and the central market in Managua, Roberto Huembes, which has a big section dedicated to crafts from all over the country. Crafts sold at hotels tend to be significantly more expensive.

Items to look out for include: cotton hammocks and embroidered handmade clothing from Masaya; earthenware ceramics from San Juan de Oriente, Condega, Somoto, Mozonte, Matagalpa and Jinotega; wooden tableware from Masaya; wooden rocking chairs from

Masatepe; wicker furniture from Granada; *jícaro* cups from Rivas; *agave* Panama hats from Camoapa; leather goods from León and Masaya; home-made sweets from Diriomo; *agave* rope decor from Somoto; coconut and seashell jewellery from the Caribbean Coast and islands; paintings and sculptures from Managua; balsa wood carvings and primitivist paintings from the Solentiname archipelago.

Shoppers will find visits to artisan workshops interesting and buying direct from the artisan is often rewarding. Prices in the Nicaraguan markets are not marked up in anticipation of bargaining or negotiation. A discount of 5-10% can be obtained if requested, but the prices quoted are what the merchant or artisan hopes to get.

Festivals in Nicaragua

Local celebrations of each town's patron saint are listed throughout the book.

1 Jan New Year's Day.
Mar/Apr The week leading up to Easter Sun is **Semana Santa** (Holy Week), with massive celebrations countrywide, religious processions starting on Palm Sun and ending on Easter Sun. All rivers, lakes and beachfronts are full of holiday-makers, most businesses close at 1200 on Wed and don't reopen until the Mon following Easter.
1 May Labour Day.
30 May Mother's Day, many businesses close after 1200.
19 Jul Anniversary of the 1979 Revolution, most offices close.
14 Sep Battle of San Jacinto, the first victory against William Walker.
15 Sep Nicaragua's Independence from Spain, nationwide celebrations, all businesses close and there are school parades.

2 Nov Día de los Difuntos (Day of the Dead), when families visit grave sites and decorate their tombs with flowers and fresh paint; most businesses close after 1200.
7-8 Dec La Purísima, a celebration of the Immaculate Conception of Virgin Mary and the most Nicaraguan of all celebrations. It's celebrated countrywide with home altars being visited by singers after 1800 on the 7th and massive fireworks. Most businesses close at 1200 on 7 Dec and don't reopen until 9 Dec.
24-25 Dec Christmas is celebrated with the family on the evening of the 24th, most businesses close at 1200 on 24 Dec and reopen on 26 Dec, although some stay closed from 23 Dec to 2 Jan.
31 Dec New Year's Eve is normally spent with family members, or at parties for Managuans, most businesses close at 1200.

Essentials A-Z

Accident and emergency

Police: 118. **Fire**: 115. **Ambulance**: 128.
In case of emergency, contact the relevant emergency service and your embassy (see page 33) and make sure that you obtain police/medical reports in order to file insurance claims. See also listings in the directories throughout the guide for local services.

Children

Nicaragua is not a difficult country to travel in with children and the Nicaraguan people, renowned for their kindness and openness, are even friendlier if you have kids in tow. However, the lack of sophisticated medical services in rural Nicaragua can make travelling with babies less attractive. Travel outside Managua, León and Granada is not recommended for people with children under 2. Children over the age of 5 will find much of interest, not least Nicaraguan children of their own age. Many of the luxuries taken for granted at home (eg snacks) will be unavailable, so warn your children in advance. Hotels do not charge for children under 2 and offer a discount rate for 2-11 year olds; those aged 12 and above are charged as adults. Very small children sitting on their parent's lap should travel free on public buses and boats. On internal flights children under the age of 2 pay 10% the normal fare; 2-11 year olds pay 50% and anyone aged 12 or older pays the adult fares. The website www.babygoes2.com has useful advice about travelling with children.

Customs and duty free

Duty free import of 200 cigarettes or 500 g of tobacco, 3 litres of alcoholic drinks and 1 large bottle (or 3 small bottles) of perfume is permitted. Avoid buying products made from snakeskin, crocodile skin, black coral or other protected species on sale in some Nicaraguan markets; apart from the fact that they may be derived from endangered species, there may be laws in your home country outlawing their import. Note that taking pre-Columbian or early colonial pieces out of Nicaragua is illegal and could result in 2 years in prison.

Disabled travellers

Nicaragua is not an ideal place for disabled travellers. The country has very little in the way of conveniences for disabled people, despite the fact that many Nicaraguans were left permanently disabled by the war years of the late 1970s and 1980s. Outside of Managua Nicaraguans are warm, helpful people and sympathetic to disabilities. Emotional solidarity may not compensate, however, for lack of wheelchair ramps, user-friendly bathrooms and hotel rooms designed for the disabled. There are elevators in the international airport and hotels such as the **Holiday Inn** and **Crowne Plaza**; the **Hotel Seminole Plaza** has special rooms for the disabled on its 1st floor at a slightly higher cost. Nicaraguan public buses are not designed for disabled people, but most long-haul bus attendants will be helpful to travellers who need extra help – if you arrive early. The local airline **La Costeña** has small Cessna aircraft that use a drop-down door ladder, but they are also very helpful with passengers in need of assistance. If using a tour operator it would be wise to book a private tour to assure proper flexibility. For wildlife viewing the Solentiname and Río San Juan areas are ideal as there is a great deal of nature to be seen by boat throughout the region, though private transportation on the river and lake is essential. If you fancy a challenge, **Ometepe Expeditions**, ometepexpeditions@ hotmail.com, T8363-5783, recently made history by guiding a disabled group to the summit of Volcán Concepción; an impressive feat televised by the BBC.

Dress

Most Nicaraguans make an effort to dress well whatever their economic means. In particularly rural or conservative areas, a very scruffy or dirty appearance may raise an eyebrow or two. Women should be aware that topless bathing is unacceptable and that short skirts tend to elicit a great deal of attention from men. Male travellers shouldn't expose their chests anywhere but on the beach. Everyone must dress respectfully when entering rural churches.

Drugs

Recreational drugs of any kind are illegal in Nicaragua and society puts marijuana in the same category as heroin – and prosecutes accordingly. Men with long hair and earrings may arouse more suspicion in local police and run a greater risk of being considered drug users; not a problem as long as they are not. If you find yourself in any trouble with the law, drug-related or otherwise, contact your embassy or consulate in Managua right away (see page 69). They may or may not be sympathetic to your plight, but they should at least be able to put you in touch with a lawyer.

Electricity

Voltage is 110 volts AC, 60 cycles, and US-style plugs are used throughout the country.

Embassies and consulates

For the Nicaraguan embassy or consulate in your own country, consult the Ministry of Exterior Relations, www.cancilleria.gob.ni/

embajadas, who maintain an up-to-date list on their website. For your own embassy or consulate in Managua, see page 69.

Gay and lesbian

Nicaragua is moving forward with its acceptance of gay and lesbian lifestyles with the abolition of sodomy laws in 2008. There are very small gay scenes in Managua, Granada, San Juan del Sur and León, but it is important to bear in mind that many rural areas remain decidedly macho and quite conservative in outlook. Whilst you do not need to conceal your sexuality, be aware that public displays of gay affection may not always be received warmly. By the same token, some gay travellers have reported almost constant amorous attentions from heterosexual men. The best advice is to relax, proceed carefully and play it by ear. For more general information, try the **International Gay and Lesbian Travel Association**, www.iglta.com.

Health

Health risks

No vaccinations are specifically required to enter Nicaragua, however, most doctors will recommend immunization against tetanus, diptheria, hepatitis A, hepatitis B, typhoid and, in some cases, rabies.

The major health risks posed are those caused by insect disease carriers such as mosquitoes and sandflies, especially during the wet season and along Nicaragua's Caribbean Coast. The key parasitic and viral diseases are malaria, South American tyrpanosomiasis (Chagas disease) and dengue fever. You are always at risk from these and dengue fever is particularly hard to protect against as the mosquitoes can bite throughout the day as well as at night (unlike those that carry malaria and Chagas disease); try to wear clothes that cover arms and legs and also use effective mosquito repellent. Mosquito nets dipped in permethrin provide a good physical and chemical barrier at night.

Some form of diarrhoea or intestinal upset is almost inevitable, the standard advice is to be careful with drinking water and ice; if you have any doubts about the water then boil it or filter and treat it. In a restaurant buy bottled water or ask where the water has come from. Food can also pose a problem, be wary of salads if you don't know whether they have been washed or not. Intestinal parasites are relatively common in rural areas with symptoms including profuse diarrhoea and/or vomiting. For a proper diagnosis, submit stool samples to a local laboratory for up to 5 consecutive days – if the results are positive, consult a doctor for immediate antibiotic treatment.

There is a constant threat of tuberculosis (TB) and although the BCG vaccine is available, it is still not guaranteed protection. It is best to avoid unpasteurized dairy products and try not to let people cough and splutter all over you.

Further information
www.btha.org British Travel Health Association.
www.cdc.gov US government site that gives excellent advice on travel health and details of disease outbreaks.
www.fco.gov.uk British Foreign and Commonwealth Office travel site has useful information on each country, people, climate and a list of UK embassies/consulates.
www.fitfortravel.scot.nhs.uk A-Z of vaccine/health advice for each country.
www.numberonehealth.co.uk Travel screening services, vaccine and travel health advice, email/SMS text vaccine reminders and screening of returned travellers for tropical diseases.

Insurance

Always take out travel insurance before you set off and read the small print carefully. Check that the policy covers the activities

you intend or may end up doing. Also check exactly what your medical cover includes (eg ambulance, helicopter rescue or emergency flights back home). Also check the payment protocol. You may have to cough up first before the insurance company reimburses you. To be safe, it is always best to dig out all the receipts for expensive personal effects like jewellery or cameras. Take photos of these items and note down all serial numbers. You are advised to shop around.

Internet

Since most Nicaraguans can't afford computers there is no shortage of internet cafés offering full computer services. Many internet cafés also offer low-rate international telephone services and internet calls (Skype) through their hook-ups. Many lodgings now offer Wi-Fi, including most hostels and nearly all hotels in the **$$$$-$$** ranges.

Language

Spanish is the official language although understanding Nicaraguan Spanish can be difficult for many non-fluent speakers. However, people are usually helpful and happy to repeat themselves. English will generally only be spoken in the more upmarket hotels in Managua, Granada and León, as well as at tour operators and car rental agencies. On the Caribbean Coast Spanish, Creole English, Mayagna, Rama and Miskito are all spoken. See page 332.

Media

Newspapers and magazines
The country's oldest and most influential daily is **La Prensa**, www.laprensa.com.ni, centre-right in leaning; though normally anti-Sandinista they are willing to criticize all politicians. The other major daily is centre-left **El Nuevo Diario**, www.elnuevo diario.com.ni, which, despite a tendency

to be sensationalist and focus on crime news, does have some very good provincial coverage. 2 left-leaning daily news sources include **La Jornada**, www.lajornada.net, and **El 19**, www.el19digital.com; both have ceased printing and are only available in digital format. There are numerous weekly papers which are generally hard to find outside Managua or are only available on-line. They include **7 Días**, www.7dias.com, a populist magazine with light news and filler; **La Brújula**, www.labrujula.com.ni, with short reports and a small distribution mainly around university campuses; and **Confidencial**, www.confidencial.com.ni, an investigative news magazine edited by Carlos Fernando Chamorro, son of the assassinated **La Prensa** director.

Radio
Since the volatile days leading up to the success of the Revolution, when the mobile station Radio Sandino kept the rebels and population up to date on the fighting and where to attack next, radio has been an essential means of transmitting the latest in events to Nicaraguans. **Radio Sandino** (AM 740) has long since been above-ground and can be found just north of the Mirador Tiscapa restaurant in Managua, though the populist voice of the FSLN, **Radio Ya** (AM 600), is the number-one rated. The polar opposite to the Sandinista radio stations has always been **Radio Corporation** (AM 540), Nicaragua's oldest station, which holds the Liberal Party line.

Television
Visitors are quite often amazed at the penetration of television in Nicaragua. The most out-of-the-way, humble of homes are wired-up and tuned in nightly to the collective passion of after-dark viewing, the **telenovela** (or soap). The most influential station is **Canal 2** which has good nightly news broadcasts (1830 and 2200 weekdays). The Sandinista **Canal 4** has news broadcasts weekdays at 1830 and **Canal 8** has the most bloody of the sensationalist newscasts that are sweeping Nicaragua television at 1800 nightly.

Money

Currency ➔ *US\$1=C\$22.88; £1=C\$35.9; €1=C\$30.7 (Dec 2011)*
The unit of currency is the **córdoba** (C\$), divided into 100 centavos. Notes are used for 10, 20, 50, 100 and 500 córdobas and coins for 1 and 5 córdobas and 5, 10, 25 and 50 centavos. 100 córdoba notes can be a problem to change for small purchases, buses and taxis, so use them at supermarkets as well as in restaurants and hotels and hang on to the smaller notes for other purchases. Nicaraguans often use the generic term 'pesos' to describe the córdoba. 'Cinco reales' means 50 centavos. On the Caribbean Coast 'bucks' means córdobas.

Exchange
For money exchange, US dollars are the currency of choice and identification is required. It's usually quicker and easier to change money with 'coyotes' on the street, but calculate what you expect to receive before handing over any cash and carefully count what they give you before walking away. You can pay for almost anything in US dollars as well, but the exchange rate will be unfavourable, change will be given in córdobas and anything larger than a US\$5 note may trigger a change crisis. Also, only notes in mint condition will be accepted. Avoid 500 córdoba notes as no-one will have change for one.

Credit cards, debit card and ATMs
Traveller's cheques (TCs) are a nuisance in Nicaragua, with only 2 banks and 1 *casa de cambio* willing to cash them. **VISA**, **MasterCard** and **American Express** are widely accepted with VISA being the most prevalent. ATM machines are increasingly common, easily found in Managua and other major cities. Debit cards using the

Cirrus and MasterCard credit systems work with the 'Red Total' or 'Credomatic' which can be found in shopping malls, **Banco de América Central (BAC)** and Texaco, Shell and Esso station stores. However, it would be unwise to rely too heavily on debit/ credit cards; if there are communication problems with the outside world, which is not uncommon, Nicaraguan ATMs will not approve the transaction and you will have to try again later. For this reason, never allow your cash to run out, especially when travelling between places. Take all the cash you need (and some more) when visiting the Atlantic departments and Río San Juan region, which have limited or no ATM facilities. Details of banks are provided in the Directory section of each chapter.

Cost of living and travelling

Most visitors to Nicaragua are surprised to find prices higher than expected. The cost of public transport, however, ranges from reasonable to very cheap. A normal taxi fare is US$1-2 with buses costing less than US$1 in almost all domestic cases. The cost of local flights is rising with oil prices, starting at around US$120 for a round-trip from Managua. Car rental is comparable with other countries around the world. Food can be cheap depending on the quality: dishes from street vendors cost from US$1-2; moderate restaurants have marginally more healthy fare that ranges from US$3-5; and quality restaurants charge US$5-10 per dish. As a rule, hotels in Nicaragua are not good value and those in Managua tend to be overpriced; anything under US$30 in the capital usually means very poor quality. Outside Managua, hotels are more reasonable and you can find some very good deals in all price brackets.

Opening hours

Generally 0800-1700. **Banks** open Mon-Fri 0830-1600; Sat 0830-1200 (or 1300). **Churches** are usually open daily during the daytime but be respectful when entering during services if you only want to look around. **Government offices** officially open Mon-Fri 0800-1700, but at the time of research Ortega was closing all government departments at lunch time.

Police and the law

You may well be asked for identification at any time, and if you cannot produce it you will be jailed. In the event of a vehicle accident in which anyone is injured, all drivers involved are automatically detained until blame has been established (see page 25). It's best to carry an international driver's license to avoid losing your normal one. Never offer a bribe unless you are fully conversant with the customs of the country. Do not assume that an official who accepts a bribe is prepared to do anything else that is illegal. If an official suggests that a bribe must be paid before you can proceed on your way, be patient (assuming you have the time) and they may relent. Note that Nicaraguan police pride themselves on being the least corrupt in Latin America, and as such, they generally do not ask for bribes.

Post

Correos de Nicaragua, www.correos.gob.ni, is very slow but reliable. The average time for a letter to the USA is 18 days while European letters normally take 7-10 days. The cost of mailing normal-sized letters is: US$0.80 to Europe, US$0.55 to North America and just over US$1 to Australia and Asia. Parcels should be left open to be inspected and sealed at the post office. Courier services from Nicaragua, available from companies like DHL and UPS, are expensive. For details on Correos de Nicaragua offices see regional chapters.

Safety

Crime is not a major issue for visitors to Nicaragua as long as sensible precautions are taken. Money belts and leg pouches are useful, but keep small amounts of cash in your pocket. Spreading money and credit cards around different parts of your body and bags is a good idea.

Don't try to mount Managua's overflowing buses with luggage or rucksacks. Once settled in a hotel, the best way to get around town is by bus or taxi during the daytime and by taxi at night. **Note**: Managua taxis are now a risk in themselves and you should take extreme care when using them (see box, page 68). Avoid dark areas and places that are not full of people. Bus stops are notorious hotspots for pickpockets. Outside Managua Nicaragua is very safe, but there are thieves in Granada and Estelí and pickpockets throughout the country. Public buses in the north central and northeastern extremes of Nicaragua are subject to hold-ups by thieves. Most country bars should be avoided on Sun when fights often break out. See specific chapters for relevant warnings. Rape is not a common threat for travellers in Nicaragua, although normal precautions should be taken. See also, Women travellers, page 40.

In hotels hide valuables away in cases or in safe deposit boxes. Budget travellers should bring locks for doors and luggage. If something goes missing ask the hotel manager to investigate and then ask them to call the police if nothing can be resolved.

Student travellers

If you are in full-time education you will be entitled to an **International Student Identity Card** (ISIC), www.isic.org, which is distributed by student travel offices and travel agencies in 77 countries. The ISIC gives you discounted prices on all forms of public transport and access to a variety of other concessions and services.

Tax

There is an arrival tax of US$10 payable at immigration when you enter Nicaragua by air and an exit tax of US$35 payable at the airline check-in counter when you leave (although it's sometimes included in the price of your ticket). All hotels, restaurants and shops charge 15% IVA (VAT).

Telephone

The Nicaraguan telephone company, **ENITEL**, is now owned by the behemoth international phone network, Claro. They have offices in all cities and most towns and theirs is often the only telephone in a small village. Calls can be placed to local or international destinations with pre-payment for an allotted amount of time. To make a reverse-charge (collect) call to any country in the world you will need to name the country in Spanish and say '*una llamada por cobrar*'. The average rate for direct calls to Europe or the USA is about US$3 for the 1st min and then US$1 per min thereafter; collect calls cost more. **US operators**: dial 171 for Sprint, 174 for AT&T and 166 for MCI. **European operators**: for Belgium dial 172; Canada 168; Germany 169; The Netherlands 177; Spain 162; and the UK 175. Public phones accept phonecards, which are available for purchase in petrol station convenience stores. Phone numbers in Nicaragua have 8 digits; landlines are preceded by the digit 2, mobiles by 8. To make international calls from Nicaragua, dial 00 and then the country code. To call into Nicaragua, dial your international access then 505 and the number, minus the 1st · zero. **Claro** sells pre-pay mobile phones at affordable prices, as does their competitor, **Movistar**, although their network is not as comprehensive. When you need to top up credit, you can buy a *recarga* from *pulperías* or wherever you see a sign.

Time

The official time is 6 hrs behind GMT (7 hrs during daylight saving). Note that a European or North American sense of punctuality does not exist in Nicaragua.

Tipping

The 10% service charge often included in restaurant bills is not mandatory, although most people choose to pay it. This charge usually goes to the owners, so if you want to tip a waiter or waitress it's best to give it to them directly. For porters at the airport or in an upmarket hotel the normal tip is US$0.50 per bag. Taxi drivers do not expect tips unless hired out on an hourly or daily basis. About US$0.20 is usual for people who offer to look after your car (usually unnecessary, but a way to make a living). The going rate for local guides at national parks is US$5 or more, while kids in the market who help you with translations expect about US$3-5. A tip of anything lower than 5 córdobas will likely be considered an insult.

Tourist information

Useful websites
www.babelfish.altavista.com
Very useful translating engine for English-only speakers who want to understand the Spanish language sites.
www.cdc.gov/travel/destination Nicaragua.aspx Useful for health information and other travel recommendations.
www.groups.yahoo.com/group/ NicaraguaLiving Internet forum, a way to chat to people in the country and travellers.
www.lanic.utexas.edu/la/ca/Nicaragua/ A good general portal from the Latin American Network Information Center.
www.laprensa.com.ni The country's best newspaper, a good source for information on what is happening in Nicaragua.

www.manfut.org A comprehensive compilation of newspaper stories about Nicaragua, in Spanish.
www.marena.gob.ni Nicaragua's official ministry for the environment with information on national parks and reserves.
www.nicaliving.com Community based website with lots of news articles and discussion forums.
www.nicanet.org The latest activist issues.
www.nicaragua.com General English language website that gives a good overview of the country.
www.timeanddate.com/worldclock Useful site for sunset and sunrise data and other information.
www.vianica.com A very handy website that has good travel information including bus schedules and descriptions of popular attractions.
www.visitanicaragua.com The government tourist board is a good place to start.

Online maps
www.eaai.com.ni/english/turismo/nic. shtml The Nicaraguan airport authority has a good map for free download.
www.maps.com The best internationally produced map of the country, enter Nicaragua in their search engine.
See also Maps, page 27.

Tour operators

Many tour operators specializing in Latin American travel will arrange trips to Nicaragua if requested, although sadly few of them know the country well. Recommended tour operators are listed below. For tour operators in Managua, see page 65.

UK
Exodus Travels, T020-8675-5550, www.exodus.co.uk.
Geodyssey, T020-7281 7788, www.geodyssey.co.uk.

Journey Latin America, T020-8747-3108, www.journeylatinamerica.co.uk.
Pura Aventura, T01273-676712, www.pura-aventura.com.
South American Experience, T020-7666-1260, www.southamericanexperience.co.uk.
Steppes Travel, T01285-880980, www.steppeslatinamerica.co.uk.

Rest of Europe
Sawadee Reizen, Netherlands, T020-4202220, www.sawadee.nl.
Rese Konsulterna, Sweden, T031-758-3199, www.resek.se.
Tropical Tours, Greece, T210-324 9504, tropical@ath.forthnet.gr.
Nuove Esperienze, Italy, T06-39725999, www.nuove-esperienze.it.

North America
Destination by Design, Inc, T186-63927865, www.destinationbydesign.com.
Unique Travel Concepts, T800-8798635, www.uniquetravelconcepts.com.
Latin American Escapes, T530-879-9292, www.latinamericanescapes.com.
Big Five Tours & Expeditions, T800-2443483, www.bigfive.com.

Australia and New Zealand
World Expeditions, Australia, T1300-720 000, www.worldexpeditions.com.au.
World Expeditions, New Zealand, T09-2684161, www.worldexpeditions.co.nz.

Visas and immigration

Visitors to Nicaragua must have a passport with a minimum validity of 6 months. In rare cases you may be asked to show proof of an onward ticket or some cash. Most visitors, including those from the UK, USA and EU countries, do not require visas and will simply pay the tourist card fee – US$10 at the airport and US$12 plus US$1 Alcaldía fee at land and river immigration checkpoints; see individual chapters for details. Tourist cards are usually valid for 90 days and under

the 2006 Central America Border Control Agreement (CA-4) permit the carrier to travel between Nicaragua, Guatemala, Honduras and El Salvador without additional paperwork. You are still required to pass border formalities and obtain appropriate entrance and exit stamps, however. For a list of countries whose citizens require a visa, see www.nicaragua.com/visas. Visa application at the border is not recommended as approval can be very slow. If you need an extension of your tourist card beyond the standard 90 days you receive upon entering the country, you will have to visit the **Dirección de Migración y Extranjería**, costado oeste de la DGI Sajonia, Edif Silvio Mayorga, Managua, T2222-7538 ext 3, www.migracion.gob.ni, Mon-Fri 0800-1300. However, it is highly recommended that you use the much faster and conveniently located Migración office in the Metrocentro shopping centre. Take your passport, preferably in the early morning, and ask for an extension form; the current rate for a 30-day extension is US$23. The whole procedure should not take more than 1-2 hrs, unless queues are unusually long. Note that citizens of Colombia, Cuba, Ecuador, Bangladesh, China and India may have difficulties acquiring an extension. If you overstay your visa or tourist card you will be charged US$2 per day, payable upon exit. Non-US citizens transiting through the United States must submit their details to the Electronic System for Travel Authorization website, www.esta.cbp.dhs.gov/esta/, in advance of travel.

Weights and measures

The metric system is the official one in Nicaragua but in practice a mixture of metric, imperial and old Spanish measurements (including the *vara*, which is equivalent to about 1 m and the *manzana* which is 1.73 acres) is used. Petrol in gallons, speed in kph, fabric in yards, height in centimetres and metres, weight in pounds and temperature in Celsius.

Women travellers

A lone female walking down the street is a sight to behold for Nicaraguan men: horns will sound, words of romance (and in Managua some less than romantic phrases) will be proffered and in general you may well feel as if you are on stage. Attitudes to foreign women are generally more reserved, although this is changing rapidly. Touching a woman, Nicaraguan or foreign, is not socially acceptable and is normally greeted with a hearty slap or a swift kick. The best advice is to dress for the amount of attention you desire; it is not necessary to travel clothed as a nun, but any suggestive clothing will bring double its weight in suggestions. In Managua it is dangerous to walk alone at night for either gender; there is more risk of robbery than rape, but it should be avoided. 2 women walking together are less likely to be targeted by thieves. For more advice, see www.journeywoman.com.

Working in Nicaragua

Finding paid work in Nicaragua is a monumental challenge for Nicaraguans and even more so for visitors who hope to get by in the country by working for a short period. It is a good idea to research your own country's aid programmes to Nicaragua and to make contact well in advance of arrival. The sister-city programmes that most countries have with Nicaragua are good examples. Finding English teaching work may be possible although rents are high and survival on a teaching salary will be difficult. It is best to go through an organization that will help with any legal documentation and accommodation. There are numerous opportunities for volunteer work. The following list is a selection of organizations, although it is by no means exhaustive:

Centro de Prevención y Rehabilitación de Adolecentes y Jóvenes (COPRAJ), www.nicablue.orgwww.nicablue.org, is a small but highly rewarding project that works to educate and rehabilitate troubled Bluefields' adolescents.

El Porvenir, www.elporvenir.org, is an off-shoot of **Habitat for Humanity** and deals with water, reforestation and sanitation projects.

Global Exchange, www.globalexchange. org, is an interesting, socially aware organization involved with human rights.

Habitat for Humanity, www.habitat.org, is involved with housing projects in the northern highlands.

The Miraflor Foundation, www.miraflor-foundation.org, needs teachers to work in Miraflor nature reserve, Spanish speakers and a 6-month commitment is preferred.

The Nicaragua Solidarity Campaign, www.nicaraguasc.org.uk, can arrange volunteer work within rural communities.

Quetzaltrekkers, www.quetzaltrekkers.com, need volunteers to get involved with their tour agency in León.

Witness for Peace, www.witnessforpeace. org, is dedicated to peace, economic justice and social development.

Contents

Managua & around

At a glance

◉ **Getting around** Taxis are the best way to navigate Managua's sprawling layout.
◔ **Time required** 3-4 days.
☾ **Weather** Daytime highs of 30-32°C year round; nights tend to be cool from Oct to early Jan.
✖ **When not to go** At the end of the dry season (Mar to mid-May), when blowing dust and smoke from surrounding farmlands combine with 36-38°C heat.

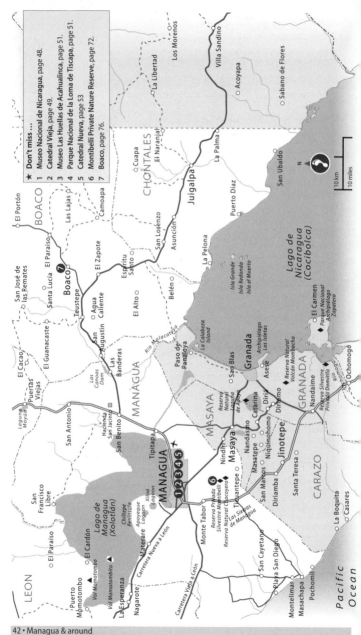

★ Don't miss ...
Museo Nacional de Nicaragua, page 48.
1 Catedral Vieja, page 49.
2 Museo Las Huellas de Acahualinca, page 51.
3 Parque Nacional de la Loma de Tiscapa, page 51.
4 Catedral Nueva, page 53
5 Montibelli Private Nature Reserve, page 72.
6 Boaco, page 76.

If, as the local saying goes, Nicaragua is the country where 'lead floats and cork sinks', Managua is its perfect capital. It's certainly hard to make any sense of a lakefront city which ignores its lake and where you can drive around for hours without ever seeing any water. Managua has 20% of the country's population, yet there is little overcrowding; it has no centre and lots of trees (from the air you can see more trees than buildings); it is a place where parks are concrete, not green, spaces – there are too many of those already; and where, when directions are given, they refer to buildings that haven't existed for over 30 years. Managua is the capital without a city, a massive suburb of over a million people (there was a downtown once but it was swept away in the 1972 earthquake). And yet, despite having no centre, no skyline and no logic, Managua is still a good place to start your visit. It is full of energy and is the heartbeat of the Nicaraguan economy and psyche.

The extinct volcanoes and crater lakes within and surrounding the city provide a dramatic setting, and the rugged central mountains, the warm Pacific waters and Sierra de Managua's mountain forests all lie an hour or less away in opposite directions: to the east are the cowboy departments of Boaco and Chontales, famous for their great cheese, sprawling cattle ranches and pre-Columbian remains; to the west is the wave-swept Pacific Coast, which has everything from rustic fishing villages to expensive vacation homes and five-star resorts; and to the south are the rich tropical vegetation and wildlife of the Sierra de Managua nature reserves of Chocoyero and Montibelli.

Arriving in Managua → *Population: 1.2 million (census 2005). Altitude: 40-200 m. Colour map 3, B3.*

Getting there

Air **Managua International Airport** (see page 21 for details on getting to Managua from abroad), on the eastern outskirts of Managua, is small and manageable. Upon landing you will need to pay US$5 at the immigration counter, before retrieving your bags and passing through customs. If you want to rent a car, there are counters through the sliding glass doors on your left after the customs point. Taxis to Metrocentro, Bolonia or Martha Quezada should cost US$5-10, journey time is 20-30 minutes in good traffic. Be sure to have precise directions in Spanish to your desired destination. When returning to the airport from the capital, a taxi hailed on the street will charge US$5-6 but, due to safety concerns, you are advised to book a radio-taxi through your hotel.

Bus International bus companies provide comfortable transportation from all capitals of Central America. The three main ones are **Transnica**, near Metrocentro; **King Quality** opposite Plaza Inter; and **Ticabus** in Martha Quezada district (see page 23). Taxis wait at the bus stations; transfers to central hotels are normally around US$4-5.

Car From the south, the Carretera a Masaya leads directly to Managua's new centre, Metrocentro, and a range of good restaurants and accommodation; try to avoid arriving from this direction from 0700-0900 when the entrance to the city is heavily congested. The Pan-American Highway (Carretera Panamericana) enters Managua at the international airport, skirting the eastern shores of Lake Managua. Stay on this highway until you reach the old centre before attempting to turn south in search of the new one. Avenida Bolívar runs south from the old centre past the Plaza Inter shopping centre and into the heart of new Managua; turn east onto the Pista de la Resistencia to reach the Metrocentro shopping mall. If arriving from León and the northwest you need to head east from Km 7 of Carretera Sur to find new Managua. ➤➤ *For further transport details, see page 66.*

Getting around

On foot Managua has nothing that even remotely resembles a city grid or urban planning and walking is a challenge and unsafe for those who are not familiar with the city's 600 barrios. The best bet is to get to Metrocentro and not travel more than five blocks on foot.

Bus Local bus routes are confusing as they snake around the city and you must know where you need to get off so you can whistle or holler when the destination grows near. It's best to avoid rush hours and sit near the driver. Major routes include the 119 which passes the Centroamérica roundabout, travels through the heart of Metrocentro and past Plaza España. Route 110 takes you from the northbound bus terminal of Mercado Mayoreo to La UCA where Express buses leave southwards.

Taxi This is the preferred method of transport for newcomers and although some drivers are grumpy or looking to make a week's pay in one journey, most Managua *taxistas* are very helpful and happy to share the city's hidden attractions. Unfortunately, hiring a Managua taxi is not as safe or straightforward as you might hope, but once mastered it is an efficient way to explore Managua (see box, page 68).

Directions in Managua and beyond

How do you find anything in a country without street names or numbers? Sometimes visitors feel as if they are going round in circles, quite literally in the case of Managua with its epidemic of dizzying *rotondas* (roundabouts). The Nicaraguan system is foolproof – as long as you know every landmark that exists, or used to exist, in the city which means that, more often than not, foreigners spend most of their time completely lost.

In Managua, directions are based around the lake, so it is essential to know where the lake is and keep a bird's eye view of the city in your mind. With the location of Lake Managua you have north (*al lago*); away from the lake is south (*al sur*). Then you need to use basic Spanish and the sun. Where the sun comes up (*arriba*) is east and where it goes down (*abajo*) is west. City blocks are *cuadras* (abbreviated in this book as 'c'), and metres are better known here by their old Spanish approximation – *varas* (vrs). The key element once you fix your compass is the landmark from which directions begin, which can be a hotel, park, pharmacy, factory or, in worst-case scenarios, where a factory used to be before the earthquake in 1972! Once you find the landmark, getting to your ultimate destination is simple. For example, take El Caramanchel, Plaza Inter, 2 c sur, 15 varas abajo (see page 61): to sip Nicaraguan rum here first you need to locate Plaza Inter, then go two blocks south and continue 15 m west.

Outside Managua you may also hear the standard orientation points of *norte*, *sur*, *oeste* and *este*. In Granada, *al lago* refers to the east; on the Pacific Coast *al mar* refers to the west, on the Caribbean side it means east. In mountainous areas, *arriba* and *abajo* may also indicate the rise and fall of the land, so it can get confusing. In smaller towns, many directions are given from the Parque Central or Iglesia (central church). It is useful to remember that nearly all the façades of Catholic churches in Nicaragua face west; so when stepping out of the church the north is to your right, south to the left, etc. If the worst comes to worst, hire a taxi, give the driver the coordinates and let him figure it out.

Tourist information

The Nicaraguan Institute of Tourism, **INTUR** ⓘ *T2254-5191, www.visitanicaragua.com, Mon-Fri 0800-1300*, is one block south and one block west of the Crowne Plaza Hotel (the old Intercontinental). They have maps, flyers and free brochures in English, but are generally not geared up for public visits – it helps if you have specific questions in mind. The airport INTUR is just past the immigration check and has similar documents to the main office, though staff are less knowledgeable. The website of Managua's Alcaldía (City Hall), www.managua.gob.ni, contains news and useful links. Information on nature reserves and parks can be found at the Ministerio de Medio Ambiente y Recursos Naturales, **MARENA** ⓘ *Km 12.5, Carretera Norte, T2263-2617, www.marena.gob.ni, Mon-Fri 0800-1300*.

Safety

Like most capitals, Managua suffers from a healthy criminal population, so be sure to take all the usual precautions. With over 600 barrios, a definitive breakdown of Managua safety is a book in itself. As a general rule, at night don't ever walk more than a few blocks anywhere in Managua. There are almost no police during the night time and with no centre there are few places where the streets will be busy. The Metrocentro area is safer, but it's still best not to walk alone after dark. Parts of Martha Quezada are now unsafe at all hours, particularly on the roads between the Ticabus terminal and Plaza Inter – ask locally about the situation before making any excursions on foot.

The only place in the city that lends itself to walking is the *malecón* and central park area of old Managua, but do not walk here at night under any circumstances. Even during the daytime take precautions, don't carry any more than you need and avoid walking alone. Be careful when visiting the Catedral Nueva and the Parque de la Paz, which are next to barrios with many thieves.

Using taxis is one way to avoid risks in Managua, but all visitors should now take extreme care when hiring one. Tourists, especially backpackers and lone travellers, are being targeted by gangs of unlicensed *piratas* who scout the bus stations and later rob their passengers. For more advice on using taxis safely in Managua, see box, page 68. See also page 36 for more safety information.

Background

The southern shore of Lake Managua has been inhabited for at least 6000 years and was once an area of major volcanic activity with four cones, all of which are now extinct. Managua means 'place of the big man' or 'chief' in the Mangue language of the Chorotega indigenous people who inhabited Managua at the arrival of the Spanish. At that time it was a large village that extended for many kilometres along the shores of Lake Managua (whose indigenous name is Ayagualpa or Xolotlán). When the Spanish first arrived Managua was reported to have 40,000 inhabitants, but shortly after the conquest, the population dropped to about 1000, partly due to a brutal battle waged by the Chorotegas against Spanish colony founder Francisco Hernández de Córdoba in 1524. Managua remained a stopping-off point on the road between León and Granada, and so avoided some of the intercity wars that plagued the country after Independence. In 1852 it was declared the capital of Nicaragua as a compromise between the forever-bickering parties of León and Granada, even though its population was still only 24,000. Today it remains the centre of all branches of government and it often seems that life outside Managua is little noticed by the media and political leaders.

The land under Managua is very unstable and the city experiences a big earthquake every 40 years or so, with those of 1931 and 1972 generating widespread damage and erasing a city centre populated by 400,000 residents. Managua's crippled infrastructure was further damaged by the looting of international relief aid in 1972 and aerial bombing in 1979 by the last Somoza and his National Guard troops. Following the troubled years of the 1980s and the resulting waves of migrations from the countryside, the capital now has an inflated population of over one million. Since 1990 the city has been rebuilding and trying to catch up with its rapid population growth. Investment has intensified in the early 21st century, solidifying Managua as the economic heart of the country.

Places in Managua

It is safe to say that Managua is an acquired taste, and one that few tourists will ever acquire. The city overwhelms most first-time visitors with its haphazard semi-urban development, ample evidence of poverty and lack of a focal point. However, there are some interesting sites, sweeping views, great opportunities for eating out and dancing and, most of all, it is the transport hub of the country with all but one internal flight originating here and an extensive network of bus services that cover all the paved, and a great deal of the unpaved, road system of Nicaragua.

Attractions for the visitor in Managua are not as plentiful as you might expect but there are two good museums, two very different and interesting cathedrals, a nice park and an entertaining market. The city also has many private art galleries which provide the only available glimpse of modern Nicaraguan painting and sculpture. Performances in the national theatre are usually good, if you are lucky enough to be in town when there is a show on. ▸▸ *For listings, see pages 55-70.*

Lakefront and the old centre

The only place in the city to see Lake Managua is around the small *malecón* (waterfront) in what used to be the city centre. From the *malecón*, Avenida Bolívar runs south away from the lake past the main tourist attractions of Managua (Teatro Nacional, Casa Presidencial, Catedral Vieja and Palacio Nacional de la Cultura). The boulevard then crosses the Carretera Norte past the revolutionary statue to the workers, to the park-like area that surrounds the parliament building.

Malecón

From Managua's *malecón*, the **Península Chiltepe** can be seen jutting out into the water. It is part of an ancient volcanic complex that includes two beautiful crater lakes, Apoyeque and Xiloá. Much of the *malecón* was destroyed when Hurricane Mitch swept into town in 1998, but it has now been rebuilt and is the site of a new touristic development, **Puerto Salvador Allende** ① *www.epn.com.ni/Puerto-Salvador-Allende.aspx*, built by the FSLN and named after the famous Chilean President. The port boasts rancho-style eateries, shops and a marina, and is a popular place to spend a Sunday afternoon. Boat tours depart from the pier and visit nearby **Isla de Amor** ① *Tue-Sun 1100, 1300, 1500, 1700; 45 mins; adults US$3.50, top floor 'VIP' rate US$5; children US$1.50, top floor 'VIP' rate US$2.50.* The stage with the giant acoustic shell right next to the *malecón* is used for concerts as well as political speeches and rallies. The area in front of the stage, **El Parque Juan Pablo II**, has been turned into a monument and park in honour of Pope John Paul II who preached here in 1996.

Teatro Nacional

① *T2222-7426, www.tnrubendario.gob.ni, US$1.50-US$20, depending on show, most programmes Thu-Sun.*
Past the statue of Simón Bolívar is the 35-year-old Teatro Rubén Darío or Teatro Nacional, a project of the last Somoza's wife, which survived the earthquake of 1972 and provides the only quality stage in Managua for plays, concerts and dance productions. There are occasionally temporary art exhibitions in the theatre so, in the day, ask at the window to view the exhibit and you can probably look inside the auditorium as well.

Parque Rubén Darío

Just south of the theatre is the Parque Rubén Darío, a small park with one of the most famous monuments in Nicaragua. Sculpted from Italian marble in 1933 by Nicaraguan architect Mario Favilli and restored in 1997, it is said to be the aesthetic symbol of modernism, the poetry movement which Darío founded. Passages from some of his most famous poems are reproduced on the monument.

Parque Central and around

In front of the Darío statue is the Parque Central. Now central to almost nothing, it was once surrounded by three- to five-storey buildings and narrow streets that made up the pre-1972 Managua. The **Templo de la Música** erected in 1939 is at the centre of the park and there's a monument above the burial site of the revolutionary Sandinista ideologue, Carlos Fonseca. Next to the park is a dancing, musical fountain complete with its own bleachers. Around the fountain are two of Managua's most historic buildings, the Palacio National and Old Cathedral, as well as the garish **Casa Presidencial**, with its own 'oval office' facing the lake that has been described (generously) as 'post-modernist eclectic'.

Palacio Nacional de la Cultura

Directly across from the presidential office is the attractive neoclassical Palacio Nacional de la Cultura. Finished in 1935 after the original had been destroyed in an earthquake in 1931, the cultural palace was once the seat of the Nicaraguan Congress and the site of Edén Pastora's (Comandante Cero) famous August 1978 revolutionary raid and hostage

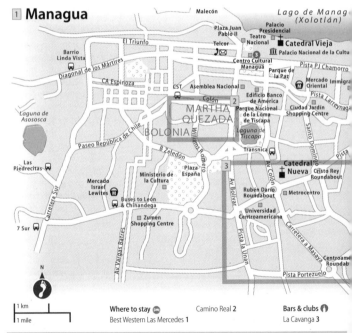

1 **Managua**

| Where to stay | Camino Real 2 | Bars & clubs |
| Best Western Las Mercedes 1 | | La Cavanga 3 |

taking (see page 312). The elegant interior houses two gardens and the **Museo Nacional de Nicaragua** ① *T2222-4820, Tue-Sat 0900-1600, Sun 0900-1500, US$2 (guided tour only, sometimes available in English), US$2.50 extra charge to video, US$1 to photograph*, as well as the national archive and national library. The National Museum has a fine pre-Columbian collection, some of which is on permanent display in the Pacific and Northern archaeology display halls; there's also a statue exhibit from the islands of Ometepe and Zapatera, as well as a natural history hall. The museum has temporary exhibits and several murals, including a very dramatic one depicting the history of Managua and the earthquake (upstairs at the south end of the Salón Azul).

Catedral Vieja

Next to the Palacio de la Cultura is the Old Cathedral. Baptized as La Iglesia Catedral Santiago de Los Caballeros de Managua, it is now known simply as La Catedral Vieja. The church was almost finished when it was shaken by the big earthquake of 1931, and when the earth moved again in 1972 it was partially destroyed. It has been tastefully restored; only the roof of narrow steel girders and side-window support bars were added to keep it standing. There is something romantic about this old and sad cathedral in ruins; a monument to what Managua might have been. Recent tremors have closed the old church indefinitely, though the Mexican government has promised funds to restore it.

Centro Cultural Managua

① *On the south side of the Palacio de la Cultura, T2222-5921.*

The Centro Cultural Managua was built out of the ruins of the Gran Hotel de Managua, the best hotel in town from the 1940s to 1960s. Now, as a cultural centre, it has a selection of before-and-after photos of quake-struck Managua in 1972 and small artists' studios upstairs. The centre is also home to the national art school and the national music school. There are art exhibits downstairs in the galleries and temporary antique and craft shops. The central area is used for performances (check the Thursday newspapers or ask staff to see what is coming up). On the first Saturday of every month an artisans' fair gives craftsmen from outside Managua a chance to show and sell their wares.

Parque de la Paz

Across the Carretera Norte from the Centro Cultural Managua, the Peace Park is a graveyard for a few dozen truckloads of AK-47s and other weapons which are buried here; some can be seen sticking out of the cement. The park was built as a monument

Museo Las Huellas de Acahualinca

Few think of little 'New World' countries like Nicaragua when looking for mankind's ancient footprints. Yet most scholars agree that the Americas were populated somewhere between 9000 and 50,000 years ago by waves of migrants that crossed over the Bering Strait. Virtually nothing is known about these ancient peoples. However, in 1874, during digging for quarry stone near the shores of Lake Managua, one of the oldest known evidences of human presence in Central America was found: footprints of men, women and children left in petrified volcanic mud, 4 m beneath the topsoil. *Las Huellas de Acahualinca* ('footprints in the land of sunflowers') were radiocarbon-dated to 4000 BC. Archaeologists from around the world have come to examine the site and in 1941 another site was found, with prints made by the same prehistoric people as well as tracks made by birds, deer and racoons.

The tracks and footprints were imprinted in fresh volcanic mud, the product of a burning cloud eruption, characterized by a discharge of ashes, gases, water and volcanic fragments. Such clouds destroy vegetation upon descent and form mud capes, which may take days or months to harden.

What were these ancient ancestors doing when they made these perfectly preserved footprints? After numerous theories, some of which involved dramatic images of natives fleeing a volcanic eruption, the Nicaraguan National Police made an anthropometric study of the footprints. They determined that they had been made by 10 different people, with an average height of 140-150 cm, walking upright, some weighed down, perhaps with children or supplies. The volcanic mud was most likely from one of Managua's now-extinct volcanic cones. The footprints were undoubtedly covered in volcanic sand shortly afterwards, preserving an ancient passage and a modern enigma.

to the end of the Contra conflict, with a big lighthouse, a mini-amphitheatre and a tank with a palm tree growing out of it. The plaques on the northern wall include names of most of the big players in the conflict and its resolution. Sadly, according to reports, the park is now unsafe to visit; check with a taxi driver about the current security situation.

Asemblea Nacional

Heading south from the old centre down the Avenida Bolívar is the Asemblea Nacional (parliamentary building), a square red-roofed building. The complex is marked by a white 16-storey building, a true giant in Managua and by far the tallest in Nicaragua. It served as the Bank of America before the Revolution and is now an office building for the *diputados* (parliamentary members). Just south of the government administrative offices that accompany the congress is the **Arboretum Nacional**, which houses 180 species of plant including Nicaragua's national flower, the *sacuanjoche* (*Plumeria rubra*) of which there are five varieties. The most common species has delicate flowers with five white petals and yellow centres at the end of the dry season. The national tree, the *madroño* (*Calycophyllum candidissimumx*), also has tiny white flowers, used in Purísima celebrations, at the end of the rainy season.

West of the old centre

Museo Las Huellas de Acahualinca

ⓘ *Along the lake, 2 km due west of the Museo Nacional, T2266-5774, Tue-Fri 0900-1600, Sat-Sun 0900-1500, US$2 with an additional US$2 charged to take photographs and US$3 to use video cameras. Taxi recommended as it is hard to find.*

This museum has been created around the original site where ancient footprints (see box, opposite) were unearthed at a stone quarry. The 6000-year-old footprints have been left exactly as they were found in excavation and represent some of the oldest evidence of human occupation in Nicaragua. The museum also has a small display of ceramic artefacts found at the site (the oldest ceramics date from 1000 BC, 3000 years later than the footprints) and an illustration of the estimated height of the people who made the footprints. This little museum is a must for lovers of archaeology and indigenous history.

Barrio Martha Quezada to Plaza España

Two blocks south of the government offices is the historic pyramid-shaped Intercontinental building, now home to the Crowne Plaza, and its newer shopping centre (see Metrocentro, below). Directly west from the old Intercontinental is Barrio Martha Quezada, home to budget accommodation and two of the international bus stations. Avenida Bolívar runs up the hill from the Intercontinental and down to a traffic signal which is the road that runs west to Plaza España or east for Carretera a Masaya and Metrocentro. Plaza España, marked by the grass mound and statues of Rotonda El Güegüence, is a series of small shops, banks, airline offices and a big supermarket. Just to the north of Plaza España and west of Martha Quezada is Managua's gallery district, which provides some more comfortable accommodation as well.

Laguna de Tiscapa and Metrocentro

On the south side of the Tiscapa crater lake is the Carretera a Masaya, which runs through the closest thing Managua has to a centre. The bizarre New Cathedral stands on the north side of the big fountains of Rotonda Rubén Darío, which marks Metrocentro. To the south is the Metrocentro shopping complex and a new Intercontinental Hotel. The Carretera a Masaya runs south past single-storey shops and restaurants and the monstrous headquarters of Casa Pellas to the plain grass Rotonda Centroamérica (roundabout), and further south past the Camino de Oriente shopping centre and eventually the city's most upmarket mall, Galerías Santo Domingo.

Parque Nacional de la Loma de Tiscapa

ⓘ *Tue-Sun 0900-1730, US$1 admission for pedestrians, US$2 admission for cars.*

The Parque Nacional de la Loma de Tiscapa has a fabulous panoramic view of Managua and is great for photographing the city and trying to figure out its layout. It is reached by the small road that runs directly behind the Crowne Plaza Hotel, passing a Second World War monument to Franklin D Roosevelt and up the hill to the summit.

At the top, a giant black silhouette of Augusto C Sandino stands looking out over the city and the crater lake, **Laguna de Tiscapa**, on the south side of the hill. The perfectly round lake has been polluted by years of street run-off but is undergoing an intense clean-up and is home to many turtles as well as the occasional caiman. This park is also the site of the former presidential palace (ruined by the earthquake in 1972) and has much historical significance. Sandino signed a peace treaty here in 1933 and, after dining here with the then President Sacasa one year later, was abducted and shot under orders of the first Somoza who would later push Sacasa out of office in 1936 and found a 43-year family dynasty. Both father and son dictators used part of the palace to hold and torture dissidents. The old torture cells can be seen from the eastern part of the park near the drop-off to the crater lake. Next to the statue of Sandino are two tanks, one said to have been a gift to the first Somoza from Mussolini and the other taken from the National Guard during the Sandinista battle for León in 1979. The graffiti on the tank was written by rebels in memory of a fallen female revolutionary named Aracely. The remains of the presidential palace are used for temporary exhibits; the park is popular with families on Sundays.

The **Tiscapa Canopy Tour** ⓘ *T8886-2836, Tue-Sun 0900-1630, US$15*, is a breathtaking zip-line ride that is operated from the park using three long metal cables and four huts with platforms to traverse the lake clipped to a harness and at times more than 70 m in the air. The tour finishes at the bottom of the lake (which is sadly polluted and unfit for swimming) and an old bread truck is used to bring participants back to the summit. Down inside the crater there is a nature walk that is interesting only during the rainy season. Avoid

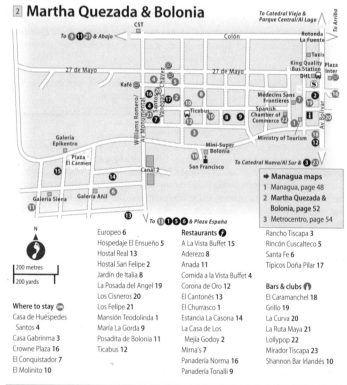

② Martha Quezada & Bolonia

Where to stay 🛌
Casa de Huéspedes
  Santos **4**
Casa Gabrinma **3**
Crowne Plaza **16**
El Conquistador **7**
El Molinito **10**

Europeo **6**
Hospedaje El Ensueño **5**
Hostal Real **13**
Hostal San Felipe **2**
Jardín de Italia **8**
La Posada del Angel **19**
Los Cisneros **20**
Los Felipe **21**
Mansión Teodolinda **1**
María La Gorda **9**
Posadita de Bolonia **11**
Ticabus **12**

Restaurants 🍴
A La Vista Buffet **15**
Aderezo **8**
Anada **11**
Comida a la Vista Buffet **4**
Corona de Oro **12**
El Cantonés **13**
El Churrasco **1**
Estancia La Casona **14**
La Casa de Los
  Mejía Godoy **2**
Mirna's **7**
Panadería Norma **16**
Panadería Tonalli **9**

Rancho Tiscapa **3**
Rincón Cuscatleco **5**
Santa Fe **6**
Típicos Doña Pilar **17**

Bars & clubs 🍸
El Caramanchel **18**
Grillo **19**
La Curva **20**
La Ruta Maya **21**
Lollypop **22**
Mirador Tiscapa **23**
Shannon Bar Irlandés **10**

➡ **Managua maps**
1 Managua, page 48
2 Martha Quezada &
  Bolonia, page 52
3 Metrocentro, page 54

200 metres
200 yards

What lies beneath

In 1972 the Tiscapa fault ruptured, less than 5 km beneath the lakefront, sending forth a 6.6 earthquake that rocked the city and crumbled (and later burned) all that could be considered downtown. The quake came cruelly just after midnight on Saturday 23 December, a day before Christmas. Most of Managua was inside, enjoying big parties; many were never found. Half the population (then 200,000) was left homeless, and at least 5000 Nicaraguans were killed.

There are plenty of reasons not to rebuild the high-rises that once constituted the city's downtown. In fact, 14 good reasons, and that is counting only the principal seismic fault lines that run underneath greater Managua. As a consequence, today's 21st-century Managua is one of the greenest capitals in the world, wide open spaces stretch in every direction, with sprawling barrios and a couple of new low-rise office and hotel buildings looking very much out of place. Much of what was downtown became a sort of monument valley, home to a confused garden of statues, concrete parks and a few new government buildings. With a proper sense of Nicaraguan irony, the new presidential office was built directly over the epicentre of the 1972 quake.

taking photographs until you're at the top of the hill, as the access road to the park passes Nicaragua's national military headquarters which are located next to the Crowne Plaza Hotel.

Catedral Nueva

ⓘ *Access for pedestrians is from the Metrocentro junction and for cars from the east side entrance. Avoid flash photography and entering during Mass via the side doors.*

Some 500 m south of the Laguna de Tiscapa is the Catedral Metropolitana de la Purísima Concepción de María, designed by the Mexican architect Ricardo Legorreta, who has said his inspiration was found in an ancient temple in Cholula, Mexico. Begun in 1991 and finished in September 1993, it is popularly known as La Catedral Nueva (New Cathedral). This mosque-like Catholic church faces south-north, instead of the usual west-east, and is basically a squat, anti-seismic box with a beehive roof. Each of the roof's 63 domes has a small window, which lets heat out and light in. In addition, a row of massive side doors that are opened for Mass allow the east to west trade winds to ventilate the church. The stark concrete interior has a post-nuclear feel with a modern altar reminiscent of a UN Security Council setting. Many visitors are fascinated by the Sangre de Cristo room, which vaguely recalls a Turkish bath and holds a life-size, bleeding Christ icon encased in a glass and steel dome, illuminated by a domed roof with hundreds of holes for the sun to filter through. At night, the dome sparkles with the glow of light bulbs in the holes. The bell tower holds the old bells from the ruins of the Catedral Vieja. The church has capacity for 1500 worshippers at any one time, but is filled well beyond that every Sunday at 1100, for what is the most popular Mass in the capital.

Bolonia

With its quiet tree-lined streets, Bolonia is inner Managua's finest residential neighbourhood, and home to all of Nicaragua's major television networks, most of its embassies, some art galleries well worth visiting and several good eating and sleeping options. The area is bordered by Plaza España to the south, Martha Quezada to the north, Laguna Tiscapa to the east and the sprawling barrios that run to Mercado Israel Lewites to the west.

East of Metrocentro

Mercado Roberto Huembes

The Roberto Huembes market or Mercado Central is the best place for shopping in the capital. It is an interesting visit just for the fruit, vegetable and meat sections, which are found inside the structure proper, along with flowers and other goods. At the northwest corner of the market is a very big craft section with goods from all over the country. While the market in Masaya is more famous and more pleasant to shop at, the artisan section of

③ Metrocentro

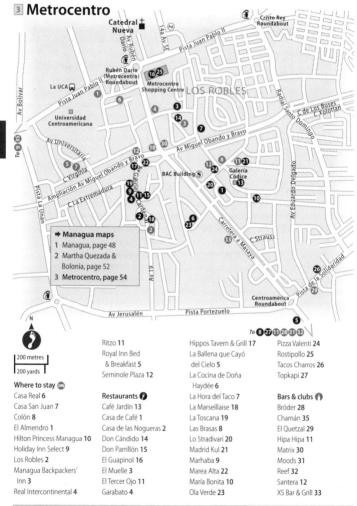

Managua maps
1 Managua, page 48
2 Martha Quezada & Bolonia, page 52
3 Metrocentro, page 54

Where to stay

Casa Real 6
Casa San Juan 7
Colón 8
El Almendro 1
Hilton Princess Managua 10
Holiday Inn Select 9
Los Robles 2
Managua Backpackers' Inn 3
Real Intercontinental 4
Ritzo 11
Royal Inn Bed & Breakfast 5
Seminole Plaza 12

Restaurants

Café Jardín 13
Casa de Café 1
Casa de las Nogueras 2
Don Cándido 14
Don Parrillón 15
El Guapinol 16
El Muelle 3
El Tercer Ojo 11
Garabato 4
Hippos Tavern & Grill 17
La Ballena que Cayó del Cielo 5
La Cocina de Doña Haydée 6
La Hora del Taco 7
La Marseillaise 18
La Toscana 19
Las Brasas 8
Lo Stradivari 20
Madrid Kul 21
Marhaba 9
Marea Alta 22
María Bonita 10
Ola Verde 23
Pizza Valenti 24
Rostipollo 25
Tacos Charros 26
Topkapi 27

Bars & clubs

Bróder 28
Chamán 35
El Quetzal 29
Hipa Hipa 11
Matrix 30
Moods 31
Reef 32
Santera 12
XS Bar & Grill 33

Huembes is in some ways more complete, if more jumbled and difficult to move about. The market is a few kilometres north of the Centroamérica roundabout and the shopping entrance is next to the fire station. The market is also used for buses to Masaya, Granada, Rivas and the border with Costa Rica.

◉ Managua listings

For sleeping and eating price codes and other relevant information, see pages 28-30.

◉ Where to stay

If you are going to splash out on a fancy hotel during your visit to Nicaragua, this is the place to do it, as many of the hotels in the **$** category are in areas that are not very safe or attractive. See box, page 45, for directions and addresses.

Managua Airport *p44, map p48*
$$$ Best Western Las Mercedes, Km 11 Carretera Norte, directly across from international terminal of airport, T2255-9910, www.lasmercedes.com.ni. Conveniently located for flight connections, with large, tree-filled grounds, tennis court, pool and barber shop. Rooms are predictably comfortable, but check before accepting one. There can be noise and fumes from the airport during peak hours. Local phone calls can be made here when airport office is shut; the outdoor café is the best place to kill time while waiting for a plane.
$$$ Camino Real, Km 9.5 Carretera Norte, T2255-5888, www.caminoreal.com.ni. A popular option for delayed passengers or those en route to other destinations. Rooms are comfortable, modern and well equipped, but those close to the pool are often noisy (early-risers take note). Plenty of space, a conventions centre, spa facilities, restaurant, casino and all the amenities you'd expect of a well-established lodging in this price range.

Martha Quezada *p51, map p52*
This area is becoming less safe every year, particularly the area around Ticabus that has most of the **$** lodging. Note that budget

hotels tend to charge per person, meaning many of the rates listed below will halve for single travellers.
$$$$-$$$ Hotel Crowne Plaza, 'el viejo Hotel Inter', in front of the Plaza Inter shopping centre, T2228-3530, www.crowneplaza.com. This is one of the most historic buildings in Managua, home to the foreign press for more than a decade, Howard Hughes when he was already off the deep end, and the new Sandinista government briefly in the early 1980s. Some rooms have lake views, but are generally small for the price. Occasional good deals and discounts through the website, but otherwise poor value.
$$$ Mansión Teodolinda, INTUR, 1 c al sur, 1 c abajo, T2228-1060, www.teodolinda. com.ni. This hotel, popular with business people, has good quality, unpretentious rooms, all with private bath, hot water, safe, Wi-Fi, kitchenette, cable TV, telephone. There's also a pool, bar, restaurant, gym, vehicle rental agency, transport to/from the airport and laundry service.
$$ El Conquistador, Plaza Inter, 100 m sur, 100 m abajo, T2222-4789, www.hotelel conquistador.info. 19 airy rooms with a/c, hot water, cable TV, telephone and Wi-Fi. There's a pleasant courtyard patio and a range of services including tours, restaurant, parking, business centre and laundry. Prices include breakfast.
$$ Los Cisneros, Ticabus, 1 c al norte, 1½ c abajo, T2222-3535, www.hotelloscisneros. com. Comfortable apartments and rooms overlooking a lush garden with hammock space. All have cable TV, a/c and Wi-Fi (at extra cost), but only the apartments have hot water. Serves breakfast, offers legal advice and speaks English. Rooms and apartments

are cheaper with fan. Los Cisneros can organize transit to the airport and tours all over the country, Recommended.

$$ María La Gorda, Iglesia El Carmen, 1 c al sur, ½ c arriba, ½ c al sur, T2268-2455. 8 simple, secure rooms with a/c, private bath, hot water and cable TV. There's internet, laundry services, airport transit, breakfast included and free local calls. Just west of Martha Quezada, good value.

$$-$ Hotel Ticabus, inside Ticabus terminal, T2222-6094. A convenient if generic option for those arriving or leaving at anti-social hours, or for those who do not wish to set foot outside the bus station for whatever reason. Upper tier rooms (**$$**) have bath, a/c and cable TV. The cheaper ones (**$**) have a fan, no TV and a shared bathroom.

$ Casa de Huéspedes Santos, Ticabus, 1 c al lago, 1½ c abajo, T2222-3713, www.casadehuespedessantos.com. Ramshackle cheapie with interesting (and slightly off-kilter) courtyard space and basic rooms. Some have bath, others have washbasins outside. There's a café, breakfast is served and internet is available (Wi-Fi or terminal). Quite shabby but a good place to meet travellers.

$ Casa Gabrinma, Ticabus 1 c al sur, ½ c arriba, opposite radio *La Primerísima*, T2222-6650. This family hotel has 4 basic rooms with fan and cable TV. Cheap food, group discounts, friendly, possibly religious and quiet.

$ El Molinito, Ticabus, ½ c lago, T2222-2013. 14 small, basic rooms with private bath, TV and fan. Some ultra-cheap rooms have shared bath. Good value, simple, clean and hot during the day. There's also a fridge available for clients. Friendly.

$ Hospedaje El Ensueño, Ticabus, 1 c lago, ½ c abajo, T2228-1078. Family-run hotel with 8 clean, dark, windowless rooms with private bath, fan and cable TV. Parking and kitchen available.

$ Hostal San Felipe, Ticabus, ½ c al lago, T2222-3178, hostalsanfelipe1@hotmail.com. Newish budget place near the bus station offering rooms with cable TV and fan. They come with or without private bath; some

have hot water. There's also internet, parking, restaurant and laundry service.

$ Jardín de Italia, Ticabus, 1 c arriba, ½ c lago, T2222-7967, www.jardindeitalia.com. Well-known budget hotel with 8 rooms. Each has private bath, fan, Wi-Fi and cable TV. The ones with a/c cost more (**$$**). There's a garden, and services include tours, airport transfer and parking. Mixed reports – take care of your belongings.

$ Los Felipe, Ticabus, 1½ c abajo, T2222-6501, www.hotellosfelipe.com.ni. This hotel has a lovely garden, pool, restaurant, and many brightly coloured parrots. They're all caged, however, and in desperate need of stimulation. The 28 rooms have private bath, cable TV, Wi-Fi and telephone; cheaper with fan. A good deal for budget travellers, but can't be enthusiastically recommended due to the bird cages.

Metrocentro *p51, map p54*

$$$$ Hilton Princess Managua, Km 4.5, Carretera a Masaya, T2255-5777, www.managua.hilton.com. Classy decor and a wide range of facilities including bar, laundry, secretary and internet. Ask for a room facing the pool. The restaurant is good, if expensive. Check the website for deals.

$$$$-$$$ Holiday Inn Select, Av Juan Pablo II, T22255-6010, www.holidayinn.ni. Comfortable, if inconveniently located, with 155 rooms. All have private bath with hot water, a/c, telephone, Wi-Fi, cable TV. Facilities include pool, gym and business centre. Ask about room packages and special deals with rental cars.

$$$$-$$$ Real Intercontinental Metrocentro, Metrocentro shopping plaza, T2276-8989, www.realhotelsandresorts.com. Nicaragua's finest international hotel, popular with business travellers. It has 157 rooms with hot water, a/c, telephone, Wi-Fi and cable TV. Facilities include pool, restaurant, bar and secretary service. Special weekend and multi-day rates with some tour operators. Certain rooms can be noisy on weekend nights. Recommended.

Hotel Crowne Plaza – revolution and chocolate bars

Built in 1969, Managua's pyramid-shaped Crowne Plaza was originally called the Hotel Intercontinental and has a richer history than your average business hotel. Best known to the world's international press corps, which used the hotel as a base while covering the Revolution and, later, the Contra War, the pyramid has also served as a hostel for an eccentric millionaire and two Nicaraguan governments.

Despite the fact that it was built right on the Tiscapa fault, the hotel was one of the few buildings that withstood the great earthquake that devastated Managua in 1972. At the time of the earthquake, the paranoid North American billionaire Howard Hughes and his many employees occupied the entire seventh and eighth floors of the hotel. Hughes had come to do business with the last Somoza dictator, but spent most of his days sitting naked on his favourite high-backed leather chair engrossed in films. The respected hotel chief was given the heavy responsibility of keeping the sophisticated palate of 'The Aviator' happy, a delicate practice that consisted of heating an endless supply of canned Campbell soups, Hughes' daily diet,

which were then sent upstairs on a silver tray with a Hershey's chocolate bar. When the 1972 earthquake hit, the millionaire dashed downstairs to his car, and was driven directly to the airport where his private plane was already warmed up and ready for take-off, his jet circled once over the horror of the ruined city, alight in flames, never to return to Nicaragua again.

On 17 July 1979, after Somoza Debayle resigned from power and fled to the United States, the Nicaraguan legislature met on the top floor of the hotel and chose Francisco Urcuyo as the new provisional president. He would rule for 43 hours. For several weeks after the Sandinista victory on 19 July, the eight-storey 200-room building became the offices for the Junta del Gobierno de Reconstrucción Nacional, which had taken control of a country in ruins. At the hotel Nicaragua's new authorities carried out government business, received foreign visitors and diplomats, and held emergency cabinet meetings.

Today the building is Nicaragua's Hotel Crowne Plaza, offering rooms with a view of Managua's past and future.

$$$ Casa Real, Rotonda Rubén Darío, 2 c abajo, 2 c al sur, ½ c arriba, T2278-3761, www.hcasareal.com. This business and NGO hotel has a quiet, central location and a leafy courtyard. The spacious and relaxing rooms have private bath, hot water, a/c, telephone, cable TV and Wi-Fi. French, German and English spoken. Breakfast included.
$$$ Hotel Colón, Edif BAC, 2 c arriba, T2278-2490, www.hcolon.net. Bright, comfortable, clean rooms with a/c, cable TV, Wi-Fi and hot water. Close to good restaurants. Pleasant and tidy, if slightly overpriced. Breakfast included.
$$$ Hotel Los Robles, Restaurante La Marseillaise, 30 vrs al sur, T2270-1074,

www.hotellosrobles.com. Managua's best B&B offers 14 comfortable rooms with classy furnishings, cable TV, a/c, hot water, Wi-Fi and luxurious bath tubs. The beautiful colonial interior is complimented by a lush, cool garden, complete with bubbling fountain. It's often full, so book in advance. Recommended.
$$$ Hotel Ritzo, where restaurant Lacmiel used to be, 3 c arriba, 25 vrs al sur, T2277-5616, www.hotelritzo.net. 10 sparse, comfortable rooms decorated with Nicaraguan art. There's 24-hr room service, cable TV, Wi-Fi, hot water and a/c. Good coffee and close to restaurants. Breakfast included.
$$$ Hotel Seminole Plaza, Intercontinental Metrocentro, 1 c abajo, 1 c al sur, T2270-0061,

www.seminoleplaza.com. Somewhat generic, but comfortable rooms with private bath, hot water, cable TV, a/c, Wi-Fi and telephone. There's a small pool, sauna, gym, restaurant and bar, and 1st-floor rooms are wheelchair accessible. Pleasant location within walking distance of numerous bars and restaurants, rooms on the pool side are quieter. Good value. Breakfast included. Recommended.

$$ Casa San Juan, Reparto San Juan, Calle Esperanza 560, T2278-3220, sanjuan@ cablenet.com.ni. Rooms in this friendly, family-run hotel are clean, fresh and comfortable. They have a/c, bath, Wi-Fi and cable TV. Other services include internet, airport transfer, vehicle rental, laundry and ticket reservation.

$$ Hotel El Almendro, Rotonda Rubén Darío, 1 c sur, 3 c abajo (behind big wall, ring bell), T2270-1260, www.hotelelalmendro. com. 2 blocks from La UCA (university), this private and secure hotel has comfortable, good-quality rooms with hot water, a/c, cable TV, telephone and Wi-Fi. They also have a pool, pleasant garden space, private parking and studio apartments (**$$$**) with kitchenette, cooking facilities and utensils. It's a decent choice. Breakfast included.

$$ Royal Inn Bed & Breakfast, Reparto San Juan, Calle Esperanza 553, T2278-1414, www.hroyalinn.com/en/. This intimate hotel has cosy rooms and good attention to detail. Services include hot water, a/c, cable TV, radio, Wi-Fi, garden, breakfast and very good coffee. The Nicaraguan touch.

$ Managua Backpackers' Inn, Monte Los Olivos, 1 c al lago, 1 c abajo, ½ c al lago, Casa 55, T2267-0006, www.managuahostel.com. The only budget hostel in the Metrocentro area is kitted out with thrifty dorms and simple private rooms. There's also a pool, hammocks and shared kitchen. They offer tourist information and are happy to help. Not bad.

Bolonia *p53, map p52*
$$$ Hostal Real, opposite German Embassy, T2266-8133, www.hostalreal. com.ni. A very interesting and unusual hotel laden with exuberant antiques and art. Rooms vary greatly, and some of the interiors are exceptionally beautiful, particularly near the reception area. Very popular so book in advance. Wi-Fi and breakfast included.

$$$ Hotel Europeo, Canal 2, 75 vrs abajo, T2268-2130, www.hoteleuropeo.com. ni. Each room is different, and some have interesting furnishings. The rooms out back are best. Features include a/c, private bath with hot water, cable TV and Wi-Fi. There's a restaurant, bar, business centre, secure parking, laundry service, guard and pool. Price includes continental breakfast. Staff are friendly and helpful. A quiet location.

$$$ La Posada del Angel, opposite Iglesia San Francisco, T2268-7228, www.hotelposada delangel.com.ni. This hotel, filled with interesting art work and antique furniture, has lots of personality. Good, clean rooms have private bath, hot water, cable TV, a/c, minibar, Wi-Fi and telephone. There's a pool, restaurant, office centre and laundry service. Breakfast is included. Book in advance.

$$ Estancia La Casona, Canal 2, 1 c lago, ½ c abajo, T2266-1685. Located on a quiet street close to galleries, this family-run hotel has 9 rooms with private bath, hot water, a/c, cable TV. Breakfast is included, English and French are spoken, and internet services available.

$$ Posadita de Bolonia, Canal 2, 3 c abajo, 75 m al sur, casa 12, T2268-6692, www.posaditadebolonia.com.ni. This intimate hotel has 8 rooms with private bath, a/c, cable TV, telephone, Wi-Fi. It's in a quiet area, close to several galleries, and operates as a Costeña agent, selling plane tickets to the Corn Islands. The friendly owner speaks English and is helpful. Complete breakfast included.

⑦ Restaurants

With the exception of the street vendors and lunch buffets almost all establishments accept Visa cards and many accept MasterCard and American Express.

The Metrocentro shopping centre has several good **$** restaurants in its food court on the bottom level. Along with US standards and Nicaraguan chains like **Rostipollo**, **Tip-Top** and **Quick Burger**, it has cheaper versions of good Nicaraguan restaurants like **Doña Haydée**, **Marea Alta** and **María Bonita** (see below). Most restaurants will make a big salad or a rice and bean dish for vegetarians. Nicaraguan lunch buffets are not all-you-can-eat: rather, you are charged for what you ask to be put on your plate, but this is still the most economical way to eat a big meal in Managua. Most Nicaraguans drink coffee like water so it is hard for them to comprehend a special place set aside just to enjoy a little black brew. Aside from a few Western-style coffee houses, the closest things to cafés in Managua are the many pastry shops.

Martha Quezada *p51, map p52*
$$ Anada, Estatua de Montoya 10 vrs arriba, T2228-4140. Daily 0700-2100. Nicaragua's original non-meat eatery and still one of the best. They serve wholesome vegetarian food, juices, smoothies, breakfasts and soups.
$$ Corona de Oro, INTUR, 1 c arriba, 2 c sur. Chinese cuisine, for the jaded international traveller in search of flavour.
$$ La Casa de Los Mejía Godoy, costado oeste del Hotel Crowne Plaza, T2222-6110, www.losmejiagodoy.com. Mon-Tue 0800-1630, Wed-Sat 0800-1300. This famous terraced restaurant regularly hosts nationally renowned live music acts. They serve Nicaraguan cuisine, wholesome breakfasts and good, cheap lunch buffets (Mon-Fri only). Very popular and recommended.
$$ Rancho Tiscapa, gate at Military Hospital, 300 vrs sur, T2268-4290. Laid-back ranch-style eatery and bar. They serve traditional dishes like *indio viejo*, *gallo pinto* and *cuajada con tortilla*. Good food and a great, breezy view of new Managua and Las Sierras. Recommended.
$ Aderezo, Ticabus 2 c arriba, ½ c sur. Clean, pleasant little place serving home-cooked *comida típica*.

$ Comida a la Vista Buffet, Ticabus, 2 c abajo. Often packed out at lunchtime. Cheap buffet food.
$ Mirna's, near Pensión Norma, 0700-1500. Good-value breakfasts and *comidas*, lunch buffet 1200-1500 popular with travellers and Nicaraguans, friendly service. Recommended.
$ Típicos Doña Pilar, ½ c from Santos on Santos Vargas Chávez. Cheap buffet-style Nicaraguan food, very good, from 1700.

Cafés and bakeries
Café y Té Jordan, 1st floor Crowne Plaza, see Where to stay, T2222-3525. Although the atmosphere and decor is very hotel-like, they do have a salad bar, *café veneciano*, and are unique in that they offer Earl Grey tea.
Panadería Norma, Ticabus, 2 c abajo, ½ c al lago. Unpretentious café-bakery serving rolls, sweet breads and hot black coffee.
Panadería Tonalli, Ticabus, 3 c arriba, ½ c al sur. Pleasant little bakery serving nutritious wholemeal breads, cakes, cookies and coffee. Proceeds go to social projects.

Metrocentro *p51, map p54*
$$$ Casa de las Nogueras, Av Principal Los Robles No R 17, T2278-2506. A popular and often-recommended high-class dining establishment. They serve fine international and Mediterranean cuisine on a pleasant colonial patio. The interior, meanwhile, boasts sumptuous and ornate decoration. A Managua institution.
$$$ Don Cándido, where El Chamán used to be, 75 vrs sur, T2277-2485, www.restaurante doncandido.com. The place to enjoy a good grilled steak. Carnivores will delight at the array of well-presented options, including cuts of churrasco, tenderloin, rib-eye, filet, New York and many others. All meat is certified 100% Aberdeen Angus.
$$$ La Marseillaise, Calle Principal Los Robles, T2277-0224. Closed Sun. Classy (although there have been mixed reviews in the past) French restaurant with a good wine list and a sophisticated array of gastronomic offerings including salmon and lobster.

\$\$\$ Lo Stradivari, costado sur de Edif Pellas, T8927-3739, www.lostradivari.com. Low-key, no-frills ambience at this Italian restaurant. Excellent home-made pastas, good salads, outdoor seating and good wine sauces. Recommended.

\$\$\$ María Bonita, Altamira, la Vicky, 1½ c abajo, T2270-4326. Mexican and Nicaraguan food, including a lunchtime buffet during the week. However, it's most popular on weekend nights, with live music and a noisy, happy crowd. Nice ambience and friendly staff.

\$\$\$-\$\$ Don Parrillón, Zona Hippos, 2 c sur, T2270-0471. Another meat and grill option conveniently located in the heart of Managua's Zona Rosa. Look for the little chimney chugging away on the street.

\$\$\$-\$\$ Marea Alta, Colonial los Robles 75, T2278-6906, www.mareaalta.net. Daily 1200-2200. Has good fresh fish, including sushi. Skip the shellfish but try the grilled dorado fish or tuna. There's outdoor seating and a relaxed ambience.

\$\$\$-\$\$ Marhaba, Hotel Seminole, 2 c sur, T2278-5725. Mediterranean cuisine served in an atmospheric setting. Turkish hookah pipes are available for an after-dinner smoke, should you feel inclined. The kitchen is open late and the bar serves cocktails.

\$\$ El Muelle, Intercontinental Metrocentro, 1½ c arriba, T2278-0056. Managua's best seafood. There's excellent *pargo al vapor* (steamed red snapper), *dorado a la parilla*, *cocktail de pulpo* (octopus), and great ceviche. It's a crowded, informal setting with outdoor seating. Highly recommended.

\$\$ El Tercer Ojo, Hotel Seminole, 2½ c sur, T2277-4787, el.com.ni. Daily 1500-0200. 'The Third Eye' strives for fusion cuisine with mixed success. The interior is imaginative and interesting. Good DJs on some nights, but approach the food cautiously; you may be better off sticking to drinks.

\$\$ Garabato, Hotel Seminole, 2½ c sur, 2278-3156. A clean, popular restaurant serving classic Nicaraguan dishes to a mixed crowd of tourists and locals. Pleasant ambience, friendly service and charming

rustic decor. There's occasional live music, souvenirs for sale and Wi-Fi too.

\$\$ Hippos Tavern and Grill, Colonial los Robles, ½ c al sur, T2267-1346, www.zona hippos.com. Tavern-style place serving grilled American-style food, cold beer and good salads. Nice ambience and music. A popular spot for people-watching and after-work cocktails.

\$\$ La Ballena que Cayó del Cielo, next to Camino de Oriente, T2277-3055. Good hamburgers, good grilled chicken, all in a laid-back open-air seating.

\$\$ La Cocina de Doña Haydée, opposite Pastelería Aurami, Planes de Altamira, T2270-6100, www.lacocina.com.ni. Mon-Sun 0730-2230. Once a popular family kitchen eatery that has gone upscale. They serve traditional Nicaraguan food – try the *surtido* dish for 2, the *nacatamales* and traditional *Pío V* dessert, a sumptuous rum cake. Popular with foreign residents.

\$\$ La Hora del Taco, Monte de los Olivos, 1 c al lago, on Calle Los Robles, T2277-5074. Good Mexican dishes including fajitas and burritos. A warm, relaxed atmosphere.

\$\$ Las Brasas, in front of Cine Alhambra, Camino Oriente, T2277-5568, www. restaurantelasbrasas.com. This restaurant is the best value in town, serving decent, traditional Nicaraguan fare in an outdoor setting. It's a good place to come with friends and order a half bottle of rum; it comes with ice, limes, coke and 2 plates of food. Great atmosphere.

\$\$ La Toscana, La Marsellaise 1½ c al lago, 2277-0153. Clean and well-presented Italian pizzeria with apparently authentic offerings.

\$\$ Madrid Kul, frente al Hotel Colón, T2252-4391. A big, bold restaurant with a vast thatched roof and seating on spacious mezzanine floors. They serve tapas and sangria, among other classic Spanish dishes.

\$\$ Ola Verde, Doña Haydée, 1 c abajo, ½ c lago, T2270-3048, www.olaverde.info. All-organic menu of mostly veggie food, but some organic meat dishes too. Servings can be small and service mediocre, but there's a good store with organic coffee to keep you busy while you wait.

$ El Guapinol, Metrocentro, www.restaurante elguapinol.com. From 1000 daily. The best of the food-court eateries with very good grilled meat dishes, chicken, fish and a hearty veggie dish (US$5). Try *Copinol*, a dish with grilled beef, avocado, fried cheese, salad, tortilla and *gallo pinto* US$4.

$ Pizza Valenti, Colonial Los Robles, T2278-7474. Best cheap pizza in town, packed on Sun nights – national 'eating out with the family' night. They do home delivery.

$ Rostipollo, just west of Centroamérica roundabout, next to McDonald's inside the Metrocentro food court, T2277-1968, www.rostipollos.com.ni. Headquarters for a Nicaraguan chain that is, quite impressively, franchised right across Central America and Mexico. They do great chicken cooked over a wood fire, Caesar salad, lunch specials and combo dishes.

$ Tacos Charros, Plaza el Café, 1 c abajo. The place for cold beer and tasty tacos. Check out the great photos of Pancho Villa, Mexico's enigmatic revolutionary hero.

$ Topkapi, Camino de Oriente, across from Alhambra cinema, T2278-2498. This locals' haunt serves pizza, tacos and Nicaraguan food. Good people-watching from the outdoor seating.

Cafés

Café Jardín, Galería Códice, Colonial Los Robles, Hotel Colón, 1 c sur, 2½ c arriba, No 15, T267-2635. Mon-Sat from 0900. Here you can sip espresso in the confines of an art gallery, and eat sandwiches and salads.

Casa de Café, Lacmiel, 1 c arriba, 1½ c sur, T2278-0605. Mon-Sun 0700-2200. The mother of all cafés in Managua, with an airy upstairs seating area that makes the average coffee taste much better. Good turkey sandwiches, desserts, pies and *empanadas*. There's another branch on the 2nd level of the Metrocentro shopping plaza, but it lacks the charm and fresh air. Popular and recommended.

Bolonia *p53, map p52*

$$$ El Churrasco, Rotonda El Güegüence, T2277-1719. This is where the Nicaraguan president and parliamentary members decide the country's future over a big steak. Try the restaurant's namesake which is an Argentine-style cut with garlic and parsley sauce. Recommended.

$$ Santa Fe, across from Plaza Bolonia, T2268-9344. Tex Mex-style with walls covered in stuffed animal heads. They do a pretty good beef grill and taco salad, but bad burritos. Noisy and festive at lunchtime.

$ A La Vista Buffet, Canal 2, 2 c abajo, ½ c lago (next to Pulpería América). Lunch only 1130-1430. Nicaragua's best lunch buffet. They do a staggering and inexpensive variety of pork, chicken, beef, rice dishes, salads and vegetable mixers, plantains, potato crêpes and fruit drinks. Popular with local television crews and reporters, as well as local office workers, who are often queuing down the street at midday. Highly recommended.

$ El Cantonés, Canal 2, 1 c sur, 20 vrs abajo, T2266-9811. Acceptable Chinese food, quality varies from dish to dish.Try the rice with shrimp and egg rolls (*tacos chinos*). Service is friendly; eat in or take out.

$ Rincón Cuscalteco, behind Plaza Bolonia, T2266-4209. Daily 1200-2200. Good, cheap *pupusas salvadoreñas*, as well as *vigorón* and *quesillos*. Cheap beer and very relaxed.

🎵 Bars and clubs

Bars

Bar Grillo, next to INTUR, near Crowne Plaza Hotel. Live and recorded music in a rustic, colourfully painted gazebo. They serve snacks like *tostones con queso*. Informal young crowd.

El Caramanchel, Plaza Inter, 2 c sur, 15 vrs abajo, T268-6230. Tue-Sat 1900-dawn. Formerly the infamous heavy metal hang-out, **Bar Changó, El Caramanchel** (The Shack) now plays salsa, electrónica and dance music. They also serve Mexican and Colombian snacks, as well as a range of cocktails. Friendly ambience and nice setting under a huge tree.

El Quetzal, Centro América roundabout, 1 c arriba, opposite Shell. Thu-Fri after 1800. Fun crowd who fill the big dance floor and dance non-stop. No entrance fee, loud live music, *ranchera*, salsa, merengue. Few (if any) tourists.

La Casa de los Mejía Godoy, see Restaurants, costado oeste del Hotel Crowne Plaza, T2222-6110, www.los mejiagodoy.com. This is a chance to see two of Nicaragua's favourite sons and most famous folk singers. A very intimate setting, check with online programme to make sure either Carlos or Luis Enrique is playing. Fri is a good bet, entrance US$10.

La Cavanga, trendy bar inside Centro Cultural Managua. Live jazz and folk music weekends, but don't walk at night here.

La Curva, Plaza Inter, 2 c sur, behind Crowne Plaza, T222-6876. This thatched roof bar is low-key most of the week and has live music on weekends with a US$2 entrance. Try the star-fruit (*melocotón* in Nicaragua) and *pitahaya* margaritas, keep track of your bar tab or it may grow.

La Ruta Maya, Montoya, 150 m arriba, www.rutamaya.com.ni. Entrance US$5. Good bands play Thu-Sun, with reggae often on Thu, fine folk concerts and political satirists. Often features nationally and internationally renowned performers; check the website for programmes.

Mirador Tiscapa, Laguna de Tiscapa. Daily 1700-0200. Open-air restaurant and bar with a dance floor and live band on weekends. It's overpriced and service is slow, but the setting above the crater lake is lovely.

The Reef, Zona Viva, Galerías Santo Domingo, T2276-5289. The Reef styles itself as a 'Surf Bar', but with the nearest beach some miles away, this appears to be no more than a clever marketing ploy. Still, on Sat afternoon, 1600-2000, clients are permitted to wear their swimming costumes.

Santera, Costado Este de BAC, T2278-8585. In addition to live poetry, theatre and music performances, Santera features an eclectic mix of musical genres, including jazz, pop, reggae and salsa, The general ambience is low-key, relaxed, bohemian and friendly. Snacks and national beers are served.

Shannon Bar Irlandés, Ticabus, 1 c arriba, 1 c sur. Fabled Irish pub serving fast food, whisky and expensive Guinness. A Managua institution and popular with an international crowd.

Clubs

The biggest rage in Nicaragua dancing is *reggaeton*, a Spanish language rap-reggae. Dancing is an integral part of Nicaraguan life, at any age, and the line between *el bar* and *la discoteca* is not very well defined. Generally, people over 30 dance at bars and the discos are for 18-30 years. Part of this may be due to the music being played at a deafening volume in discos. If your ears can take the pain, the party is always good and, as long as there is music, Nicaraguans will take to the floor. Most discos play a variety of dance music, though hip-hop and *reggaeton* are omnipresent. Most of the establishments in the bar section above offer dancing.

Bar Chamán, Universidad Nacional de Ingeniería (UNI), 1½ c norte, T2272-1873, www.chamanbar.com. US$3 entrance which includes US$1.50 drink coupon. A young, devout dancing crowd sweats it out to salsa, rock and *reggaeton*.

Bróder, Km 7.5 Carretera a Masaya, Plaza Familiar, www.elhipa.com.Wed-Sat, from 2000 until you drop, Thu ladies free. The place for cocktails like *pantera rosa* (Pink Panther). A young crowd, *reggaeton* and rock.

Hipa Hipa, Km 7.5 Carretera a Masaya, Plaza Familiar, www.elhipa.com. Dress smartly for this popular disco, a favourite among Managua's rich kids. The best action is on Wed, Fri and Sat night, cover includes a few beverages.

Lollypop, Hotel Mansión Teodolinda, 50 vrs al lago. A happening new gay disco in the swanky neighbourhood of Bolonia. Good DJs and dance music.

Matrix, Km 4.5 Carretera a Masaya, www.grupostarcity.com. Often packed out with well-to-do revellers, this is a good club to dance in until the early hours. The bar is on the pricey side.

Moods, Zona Viva, Galería Santo Domingo, Modulo 1, www.moodsmanagua.com. Smart, sexy disco with beautiful people, DJs and dry ice. Dress well.

XS Bar & Grill, Km 5, Carretera a Masaya, T2277-3086. Wed-Sat after 2000, entry US$6. One of the most popular discos in Managua, with pumping techno, trance, *reggaeton* and hip-hop.

Entertainment

Cinema

If possible, see a comedy; the unrestrained laughter of the Nicaraguan audience is sure to make the movie much funnier.

Alianza Francesa, Altamira, Mexican Embassy, ½ c norte, T2267-2811, www.alianzafrancesa.org.ni. French films every Wed and Sat at 2000, free admission, art exhibits during the day.

Cinemas Galerías 10, 2nd floor, Galerías Santo Domingo, Carretera a Masaya, T2276-5065, www.galerias.com.ni. Plush, modern and thoroughly a/c cinema in Managua's swankiest mall.

Cinemas Inter, Plaza Inter, T222-3828, www.cinemas.com.ni. 8 screens showing American films, subtitles in Spanish, buy weekend tickets in advance.

Cines Alhambra, 3 screens, Camino de Oriente, T2278-7278, www.cinesalhambra. com. Mostly US films with Spanish subtitles, occasional Spanish and Italian films, US$3, icy a/c. You'll find a 2nd branch at Multicentro Las Américas, Bello Horizonte.

Metrocentro Cinemark, Metrocentro. T2271-9042, www.cinemarkca.com. 6 screens, small theatres with steep seating, very crowded so arrive early, impossible to see well from front rows, US$4. Flyers with film schedules are free at supermarkets and petrol station mini-markets.

Dance and theatre

Managua has no regular dance and theatre performances so it will take a bit of research to time your visit to coincide with a live show. To find out what's on the cultural and musical calendar for the weekend in Managua, Granada and León, check the *La Prensa* supplement *Viernes Chiquito* every Thu.

Ballet Tepenahuatl, one of many folkloric dance companies in Managua, gives regular performances in the **Centro Cultural Managua** as well as the **Teatro Nacional Rubén Darío**. Performances as well as folkloric, salsa and merengue dance classes take place at the **Escuela de Danza**, across from main entrance of La UNI University near La UCA. **Teatro Nacional Rubén Darío** also has plays in the main theatre and a small one downstairs. You could call the country's best-known theatrical group, **Comedia Nacional**, T2244-1268 to see what's on. The **Centro Cultural Managua** also has regular weekend performances.

Festivals

19 Jul 19 de Julio is the anniversary of the fall of the last Somoza in 1979, a Sandinista party in front of the stage with the big acoustic shell at the *malecón*. The party attracts around 100,000 plus from all over the country; don't forget to wear black and red.

1-10 Aug On 1 Aug a statue of **Santo Domingo**, Managua's patron saint and Nicaragua's most diminutive saint is brought from his hilltop church in Santo Domingo in the southern outskirts of Managua, in a crowded and heavily guarded (by riot police) procession, to central Managua. With party animals outnumbering the devotees, this may be the least religious and least interesting of any of the Nicaraguan patron saint festivals. Domingo must be the smallest saint celebrated in Nicaragua, too, about the size of a Barbie doll and reported to be a replica, with the original in a safe box. On the final day, there is the country's biggest *hípica*, a huge parade of very fine horses and very well lubricated (drunk) riders from all over the country, while the saint is marched back up to the Iglesia Santo Domingo.

7 Dec La Purísima, celebrating the purity of the Virgin countrywide and particularly in Managua in the more than 600 barrios of the city. Private altars are erected to the Virgin Mary and food gifts are given to those who arrive to sing to the altars, with some families serving up as many as 5000 *nacatamales* in a night. Considering the truly difficult economic circumstances of the Managuans, this outpouring of faith exhibited in generosity to the general public is all the more moving. The festival runs from 1800-2100 with massive fireworks echoing throughout the city (making walking rather hazardous) at 1800 and 2400.

O Shopping

Handicrafts

The best place for handicrafts in Managua is the **Mercado Central Roberto Huembes**, where there's an ample selection from most of the country artisans. On the 1st Sat of every month there is a craft fair at the **Centro Cultural Managua**, which gives some more unusual crafts a chance to be seen and sold. **Mamá Delfina**, in Reparto San Juan next to IBW Internet in a beautiful colonial-style home, has a very interesting selection of artisan crafts and antiques and is probably the most beautiful store in Managua. For pottery try **Cerámica por la Paz**, Km 9.5, Carretera a León, T2269-1388; even if you don't find the perfect earthenware piece they have great T-shirts. Across from La Casa de Mejía Godoy is the upmarket artisan shop **Tiempo Azul**, which sells some very original designs you won't find elsewhere but at a healthy mark-up. The most complete of the non-market artisan shops is **Galería Códice**, Colonial Los Robles, Hotel Colón, 1 c sur, 2½ c arriba, No 15, T2267-2635, www.galeriacodice.com, Mon-Sat 0900-1830, which has a great selection of crafts from most of Nicaragua including

rarely found items like rosewood carvings from the Caribbean Coast and ceramic dolls from Somoto. **Note** All the markets have some crafts, but avoid the **Mercado Oriental**. Possibly the biggest informal market in Latin America, this is the heart of darkness in Managua, the centre for black market items. Travelling the labyrinth of its bowels is for hard-core adventure travel and survival television programmes, but not worth the risk for simple shopping. If you can't resist, strip off all valuables, bring a photocopy of your passport and a local who knows the market well.

Shopping malls

The 3 big shopping malls are the Plaza Inter, Metrocentro and Galerías Santo Domingo, always full on weekends and a good place to people-watch. The **Plaza Inter** has better deals, with some low-price stores and good cinemas. They often programme events on the patio to the east of the mall. The **Metrocentro** is bigger and broader and attracts a more affluent crowd, reflected in the prices. The **Galerías Santo Domingo** is the newest, shiniest and most upmarket of the 3 and home to a plethora of franchise restaurants, expensive stores and nightclubs. The cinemas are better in Santo Domingo and Plaza Inter, but the food court is much better in Metrocentro, where several good Nicaraguan restaurants offer fair prices and quick service. Metrocentro also has a little area of banks underneath the southern escalator; some of these are open late on Sat. The other main shopping area is **Centro Commercial Managua** in the Centroamérica barrio, good prices and selection, the best place to get a watch fixed or pick up some inexpensive clothing without visiting an outdoor market.

Supermarkets

3 big chains are represented in Managua, **Supermercado La Colonia** being the best. It is located in Plaza España and at the roundabout in the Centroamérica neighbourhood. Both branches have a salad

bar with some cheap cafeteria-style dishes for lunch, and a good selection of Nicaraguan books and magazines. **Supermercado La Unión**, on Carretera a Masaya, is similar to La Colonia, also a few blocks east of the Plaza Inter and several blocks west of Plaza España. **Supermercados Pali**, branches of which can be found scattered around the city, is the cheapest, with goods still in their shipping boxes and no bags supplied at the checkout counter. Supermarkets have good prices for coffee and rum if you are thinking of taking some home, and they are great for finding imported goods such as tea.

☼ What to do

Baseball
The national sport and passion is baseball, which has been established in Nicaragua for more than 100 years. Games in Managua are on Sun mornings at the national stadium, **Estadio Denis Martínez**, just north of the Barrio Martha Quezada. It was in front of this stadium that one of the most symbolic scenes of the 1978-1979 Revolution occurred – the destruction of the statue of Somoza on horseback. The pedestal remains empty in front of the stadium while the remains of the horse can be seen at Loma de Tiscapa. Check the local newspapers for the game schedule. Seats range from US$1-5 per person.

Canopy tour
Tiscapa Canopy Tour, T8886-2836, www.canopytoursnicaragua.com. Tue-Sun 0900-1630, US$15. A breathtaking zip-line ride that is operated from the park using 3 long metal cables and 4 huts with platforms to traverse the lake clipped to a harness at times more than 70 m in the air. The tour finishes near the shore of the lake and an old bread truck is used to bring participants back to the summit. Down inside the crater there is a nature walk that is interesting only during the rainy season. Kayak rentals are planned for the near future.

Tour operators
See also local tour operators in Granada, Ometepe, León, Matagalpa, the Corn Islands and Pearl Lagoon.
Careli Tours, Planes de Altamira, opposite the Colegio Pedagógico La Salle, T2278-6919, www.carelitours.com. One of Nicaragua's oldest tour operators with a professional service, very good English speaking guides and traditional tours to all parts of Nicaragua.
Gray Line Tours, Lotería Nacional, 1 c abajo, 1 c sur, contiguo a Financia Capital, T2277-2097, www.graylinenicaragua.com. Good, professional company with a range of tours including good-value 1-day tours, night tours of Managua and folkloric performances. Manager Marlon speaks French and English.
Solentiname Tours, Apartado Postal 1388, T2270-9981, www.solentiname.com.ni. Eco-friendly tours of the lake, Caribbean Coast, colonial cities and Río San Juan. Spanish, English, German, French and Russian spoken.
Tours Nicaragua, Centro Richardson, contiguo al Banco Central de Nicaragua, T2265-3095, www.toursnicaragua.com. One of the best, offering captivating and personalized tours with a cultural, historical or ecological emphasis. Guides, transfers, accommodation and admission costs are included in the price. English speaking, helpful, professional and highly recommended. All tours are private and pre-booked, no walk-ins please.

Travel agents
Turismo Joven, Km. 5.5 Carretera a Masaya, Frente al Colegio Teresiano, T2278-3788, www.otecviajes.com, travel agency, representative for ISIC, affiliated to YHA. **El Viajero**, Plaza España, 2 c abajo, No 3, T2268-3815, helpful manager, cheap flights to all parts. In the Plaza España area are: **Aeromundo**, T2270-2030, www.aeromundo cwt.com.ni; **Atlántida**, T2266-8720; and **Capital Express**, T2266-5043, capital@ibw.com.ni.

⊖ Transport

Air

Domestic flights Nicaragua's sole domestic airline is **La Costeña**, T2263-2142, www.lacostena.com.ni, which operates a small fleet of single-prop Cessna Caravans and 2-prop Short 360s. In the Cessnas there is no room for overhead lockers, so pack light and check in all you can. For checked luggage on all flights there is a 15-kg (30-lb) weight limit per person for one-way flight, 25 kg (55 lb) for round-trip tickets, any excess is payable on check-in. US$2 exit tax on domestic flights.

Tickets can be bought at the domestic terminal, which is located just west of the exit for arriving international passengers, or from travel agents or tour operators.

Fuel and ticket prices are rising, and schedules are subject to change at any time.

To **Bilwi**, 0630, 1030, 1430, US$97 one-way, US$148 return, 1½ hr. To **Bluefields**, La Costeña, 0630, 1000, 1400, US$83 one-way, US$128 return, 1 hr. To **Corn Islands**, 0630, 1400, US$107 one-way, US$165 return, 1½ hrs.

To **Minas**, 0900, US$92 one-way, US$139 return, 1 hr. To **San Carlos**, 1330, US$82 one-way, US$120 return, 1 hr. To **Waspam**, 1000, US$155 return, 1½ hrs. For return times see individual destinations.

International flights You should reconfirm your flight out of Nicaragua 48 hrs in advance by calling the local airline office during business hours Mon-Sat. Most good hotels will provide this service. There's a US$35 exit tax on all international flights, sometimes included in the price of your ticket. You'll find some souvenir shops, fast-food outlets and cafés inside, with better options before security and immigration. There are also ATMs and money-changing facilities.

Airlines AeroCaribbean, Monte de los Olivos 1 c arriba, 15 vrs. al lago. T2277-5191, aerocar@cablenet.com.ni. **AeroMéxico**, Optica Visión, 75 vrs arriba, 25 vrs al lago, T2266-6997, www.aeromexico.com.

American Airlines, Rotonda El Güegüense 300 vrs al sur, T2255-9090, www.aa.com. **Continental Airlines**, Edif Ofiplaza, piso 2 edif 5, T2278-7033, www.continental.com. **Copa Airlines**, Carretera a Masaya Km 4.5 edif CAR 6, T2267-0045, www.copaair.com. **Delta Airlines**, Hotel Seminole, 350 vrs sur, Casa 58, T2270-0535, www.delta.com. **Spirit Airlines**, International airport, T233-2884, www.spirit air.com. **Taca Airline**, Edif Barcelona, Plaza España, T2266-6698, www.taca.com.

Bus

City bus City buses are usually run-down and very full and try not to come to a full stop if only 1 or 2 people are getting on or off; they slow down and the assistant yanks you on or off. City buses in Managua charge US$0.30 per ride; pay when you get on. They run every 10 mins 0530-1800, and every 15 mins 1800-2200; buses are frequent but their routes are difficult to fathom. Beware of pickpockets on the crowded urban buses. Crime is prevalent at bus stops and on city buses, if there are no seats available (which is often) you are at more risk – avoid peak hours 0700-0930 and 1600-1830.

Intercity buses Bus Expresos are dramatically faster than regular routes. Check with terminal to confirm when the next express will leave. Payment is required in advance and seat reservations are becoming more common. There are also microbuses serving some of the major destinations. These are comparatively speedy and as comfortable as it gets. However, there's little space for luggage, and you may have to pay extra to stash large objects.

All fares and schedules below are subject to sudden and inexplicable change. Stay focused and alert at the bus stations and, once on board, check the going fare with a fellow passenger to avoid extra charges.

La UCA (pronounced La 'OO-ka'), close to the Metrocentro and opposite the University, serves just a few destinations. The microbuses are cheap, fast and highly recommended if travelling to Granada, León or Masaya. To **Granada**, every 15 mins or when full, 0530-2100, US$0.95, 1 hr. To **Diriamba**, every 30 mins or when full, 0530-2000, US$1.10, 45 mins. To **Jinotepe**, 0530-2000, every 20 mins or when full, US$1.10, 1 hr. To **León**, every 30 mins, 0730-2100, US$1.90, 1½ hrs. To **Masaya**, every 15 mins or when full, 0530-2000, US$0.60, 40 mins.

Mercado Roberto Huembes, also called Mercado Central, is used for destinations southwest. To **Granada**, every 15 mins, 0520-2200, Sun 0610-2100, US$0.60, 1½ hrs. To **Masaya**, every 20 mins, 0625-1930, Sun until 1600, US$0.35, 50 mins. To **Peñas Blancas**, every 30 mins or when full, US$2.40, 2½ hrs; or go to Rivas for connections. To **Rivas**, every 30 mins, 0600-1900, US$1.90, 1¾ hrs. To **San Juan del Sur**, every 30 mins, 1000-1600, US$2.60, 2½ hrs; or go to Rivas for connections To **San Jorge** (ferry to Ometepe), every 30 mins, 0600-2100, US$1.90, 2 hrs; or go to Rivas for connections.

Mercado Mayoreo, for destinations east and then north or south. To **Boaco**, every 30 mins, 0500-1800, US$1.50, 2 hrs. To **Camoapa**, every 40 mins, 0630-1700, US$2, 3 hrs. To **El Rama**, 8 daily, 0500-2200, US$8, 8 hrs; express bus 1400, 1800, 2200, US$9.50, 6 hrs. To **Estelí**, every 30 mins, 0400-1800, US$2.20, 3½ hrs; express buses, hourly, 0600-1700, US$3.10, 2½ hrs. To **Jinotega**, hourly, 0400-1730, US$3.50, 3½ hrs; or go to Matagalpa for connections. To **Juigalpa**, every 20 mins, 0500-1730, US$2.50, 2½ hrs. To **Matagalpa** every 30 mins, 0330-1800, US$2, 2½ hrs; express buses, 12 daily, US$2.50, 2 hrs. To **Ocotal**, express buses, 12 daily, 0545-1745, US$4.50, 3½ hrs. To **San Rafael del Norte**, express bus, 1500, US$5, 4 hrs. To **San Carlos**, 0500, 0600, 0700, 1000, 1300, 1800, US$9, 7-10 hrs. To **Somoto**, hourly, 0400-2000, US$3.10, 3½ hrs.

Mercado Israel Lewites, also called Mercado Boer, for destinations west and northwest. Some microbuses leave from here too. To **Chinandega**, express buses, every 30 mins, 0600-1915, US$2.50, 2½ hrs. To **Corinto**, every hr, 0500-1715, US$3.50,

3 hrs. To **Diriamba**, every 20 mins, 0530-1930, US$1.10, 1 hr 15 mins. To **El Sauce**, express buses, 0745, 1445, US$3.25, 3½ hrs. To **Guasaule**, 0430, 0530, 1530, US$3.25, 4 hrs. To **Jinotepe**, every 20 mins, 0530-1930, US$0.50, 1 hr 30 mins. To **León**, every 30 mins, 0545-1645, US$1.25, 2½ hrs; express buses, every 30 mins, 0500-1645, US$1.50, 2 hrs; microbuses, every 30 mins or when full, 0600-1700, US$1.90, 1½ hrs. To **Pochomil**, every 20 mins, 0600-1920, US$0.80, 2 hrs.

International buses If time isn't a critical issue, international buses are a cheap and efficient way to travel between Nicaragua and other Central American countries. Buses are available to and from **Honduras**, **El Salvador** and **Guatemala** in the north, **Costa Rica** and **Panama** to the south. When leaving Managua you will need to check in 1 hr in advance with passport and ticket. 4 companies operate the international routes to and from Managua. The buses all have a/c, toilet, reclining seats; most have television screens and offer some sort of snacks. See Essentials, page 21, for examples of routes in and out of Managua.

Car
Car hire All agencies have rental desks at the international airport arrivals terminal. There are more than 15 car rental agencies in Managua. The rates are all very similar, although vehicles from the more successful agencies tend to be in much better condition. It is not a good idea to rent a car for getting around Managua, as it is a confusing city, fender benders are common and an accident could see you end up in jail (even if you are not at fault) until blame is determined. Outside the capital, however, main roads are better marked and a rental car means you can get around more freely. (Taxis can also be hired by the hour or by the day, see below.)

For good service and 24-hr roadside assistance, the best rental agency is **Budget**, with rental cars at the airport, T2263-1222, and Holiday Inn, T2270-9669.

The art of taxi hire

Despite the Managua taxi driver's liberal interpretation of Nicaraguan driving laws, his knowledge of the city is second to none and taxis are often the best way to get around the city. Since 2009, however, a number of travellers have reported disturbing experiences with unlicensed piratas, who scout the bus stations for unsuspecting victims or use well-dressed women to befriend potential targets on intercity buses. The experience usually involves the victim being robbed at knife or gunpoint and forced to make cash withdrawals at several different ATMs. These types of incident have been reported in Managua, Masaya and Rivas.

If you must hire a taxi on the street, follow this basic procedure and under no circumstances get into a vehicle with someone you've just met, no matter how friendly or harmless they may seem:
1. Check that the number on the side of the vehicle matches the license plate (and make a mental note of it).
2. Lean into the passenger window and state your desired destination (veiling your accent as best possible to try and keep the rates down).
3. If the driver nods in acceptance, ask him how much – *¿por cuánto me lleva?*

4. Haggle if necessary, and insist upon a private fare, not a colectivo (shared taxi) – this will cost double, but it is worth it.
5. Ask to see the driver's identification.
6. Sit next to the driver at all times.

It is normal for most drivers to quote the going rate plus 5 to 20 córdobas extra for foreigners. When you reach your destination pay the driver with the most exact money possible (they never have change, an effective built-in tip technique). Some drivers have been known to feign communication problems for short fares at night, looking for a healthy profit.

The minimum charge is 15 córdobas per person (there will be a slight discount for two people riding together); within the same general area the fare should be about 20 córdobas; halfway across town no more than 30 córdobas; and all the way across town 50 córdobas, to the airport 120 córdobas. Radio taxis do not stop for other passengers and charge double for short prebooked trips and from the airport into the city (US$10, US$15 return). For an early morning or late night journey it is especially wise to call a radio taxi, they are private, safer and in most cases in better condition than the other taxis.

Their main office is just off Carretera Sur at Montoya, 1 c abajo, 1 c sur, T2255-9000. Average cost of a small Toyota is US$50 per day while a 4WD (a good idea if exploring) is around US$100 per day with insurance and 200 km a day included; 4WD weekly rental rates range from US$600-750. Check website for details: www.budget.com.ni. Also at the airport are **Avis**, T2233-3011 (and at Hotel Intercontinental, T2278-2188), www.avis.com.ni and **Hertz**, T2233-1237 (also at Hotel Seminole Plaza, T2270-5896, and at Hotel Crowne Plaza, T2222-2320), www.hertz.com. Another reliable agency

is **Toyota Rent a Car**, www.toyotarentacar. com, which has cars at the airport, T2266-3620, the Hotel Princess, T2270-4937, and the Camino Real, T2263-2358.

Taxis

Taxis without red licence plates are '*piratas*' (unregistered); avoid them. Taxis can be flagged down in the street. They also cruise the bus stations and markets looking for passengers. Find out the fare before you board the vehicle. Fares are always per person, not per car. For tips on the art of taxi hire in Managua see box, opposite. Have the telephone number of your hotel with you. Street names and numbers are not universal in the city and the taxi driver may not recognize the name. Make sure you know the coordinates if you are heading for a private residence. If you are going to Barrio Martha Quezada, ask for the Ticabus terminal if you do not know your exact destination.

Radio taxis pick you up and do not stop for other passengers, they are much more secure for this reason and cost twice as much: **Cooperativa 25 de Febrero**, T2222-4728; **Cooperativa 2 de Agosto**, T2263-1512; **Cooperativa René Chávez**, T2222-3293; **Cooperativa Mario Lizano**, T2268-7669. Get a quote on the phone and reconfirm agreed cost when the taxi arrives.

Taxis can also be hired by the hour or by the day for use inside Managua and for trips anywhere in the country. This should be done with a radio taxi company, negotiating the fare per hour, per day or per journey. Some guidelines are: US$10 per hr inside Managua; US$50 per day inside Managua; a trip to Volcán Masaya, US$50, Granada US$65; León US$75, Estelí US$100, border with Honduras US$150. Some good *taxistas* are **León Germán Hernández**, T2249-9416, T8883-3703 (mob); **Dionisio Ríos Torres**, T2263-1838; and **Freddy Danilo Obando**, T8777-8578.

❶ Directory

Banks
The best bank for foreigners is **Banco de América Central (BAC)** as they accept all credit cards and TCs. BAC offers credit card advances, uses the Cirrus debit system and changes all TCs with a 3% commission. Any other bank can be used for changing dollars to córdobas or vice versa. See page 35 for more details on ATMs. BAC's slick new office headquarters is at Edif Pellas, Km 4 Carretera a Masaya, T2277-3624. There is a BAC in Plaza España, T2266-7062, and at Metrocentro, T2278-5510.

Doctors
Dr Enrique Sánchez Delgado, T2278-1031; Dr Mauricio Barrios, T2255-6900. **Gynaecologist**, Dr Edwin Mendieta, T2266-5855. **Ophthalmologist**, Dr Milton Eugarrios, T2278-6307. **Paediatricians**, Dr Alejandro Ayón, T2276-2142; Dr César Gutiérrez Quant, T2278-3902, T2278-5465 (home).

Dentists
Dr Claudia Bendaña, T2277-1842; and **Dr Mario Sánchez Ramos**, T2278-1409, T2278-5588 (home).

Embassies and consulates
Austria, Rotonda El Güegüense, 1 c al norte, T2266-3316. **Argentina**, Las Colinas C Prado Ecuestre 235B, T2276-2654. **Brasil**, Km 7.5 Carretera Sur, T2265-0035. **Canada**, Bolonia Los Pipitos, 2 c abajo, T2264-2723. Mon-Thu 0900-1200. **Costa Rica**, Las Colinas II Entrada, 1 c al lago, 1 c arriba, T2276-0115. 0900-1500. **China**, Altamira 3ra etapa, Panadería Sampsons 50 m al lago, T2267-4024. **Colombia**, Las Colinas 2nd entrance, 1 c arriba ½ c al lago No 97, T2276-2149. **Denmark**, Bolonia Salud Integral, 2 c al lago, 50 vrs abajo, T2254-5059. **Finland**, Edif El Centro, 2nd floor, rotonda El Güegüense, 600 m al sur, T2278-1216. 0800-1200, 1300-1500. **France**, Iglesia El Carmen, 1½ c abajo, T2222-6210, 0800-1600. **Germany**, Plaza España, 200 m lago, T2266-3917. Mon-Fri 0900-1200. **Guatemala**, just after Km 11 on Carretera a Masaya, T2279-9835. Fast service, 0900-1200 only. **Honduras**, Las Colinas No. 298, T2276-2406. **Italy**, Rotonda El Güegüense, 1 c lago, T2266-6486. 0900-1200. **Japan**, Rotonda El Güegüense 1 c abajo, 1 c al lago, T2266-1773. **Mexico**, Km 4.5, Carretera a Masaya, 1 c arriba, T2278-1859. **Netherlands**, Colegio Teresiano, 1 c sur, 1 c abajo, T2276-8630. **Panama**, Col Mantica, Cuartel General de Bomberos, 1 c abajo, No 93, T2266-8633. 0830-1300, visa on the spot, valid 3 months for a 30-day stay, US$10. **Russia**, Frente Colegio Dorís María 164, T2276-2005. **Spain**, Las Colinas Av, Central No 13, T2276-0966. **Sweden**, Plaza España,

1 c abajo, 2 c lago, ½ c abajo, Apdo Postal 2307, T2255-8400. 0800-1200. **Switzerland**, Banpro Las Palmas, 1 c abajo, T266-3010. **UK**, La Fise, 40 vrs abajo, T2278-0014. 0900-1200. **USA**, Km 4.5, Carretera del Sur, T2266-6010. 0730-0900. **Venezuela**, Km 10.5, Carretera a Masaya, T2276-0267.

Hospitals

The best are **Hospital Alemán-Nicaragüense**, Km 6 Carretera Norte Siemens, 3 blocks south, T2249-0611, operated with German aid, mostly Nicaraguan staff; **Hospital Bautista**, near Mercado Oriental, T2264-9020, www.hospitalbautistanicaragua. com; **Hospital Metropolitano Vivian Pellas**, Km 9.5 Carretera a Masaya, 250 vrs abajo, T2255-6900, www.metropolitano.com.ni; and **Hospital Militar**, T2222-2763 (go south from Hotel Crowne Plaza and take 2nd turn on left). Make an appointment by phone in advance if possible. Private clinics are an alternative. **Policlínica Nicaragüense**, in Bolonia across from AGFA, T2266-1261, consultation US$30. **Med-Lab**, 300 m south of Plaza España, is recommended for tests on stool samples, the director speaks English.

Internet

Internet cafés are spread all over Managua, but they come and go with the seasons. You can try scouting around the main plazas and shopping centres, and near the UCA. Alternatively ask at your hotel for the nearest paid hook-up if you don't see one. Expect to pay US$0.50-US$1 per hr.

Language schools

Academia Europea, Hotel Princess, 1 c abajo, ½ c sur, T2278-0829, is the best school in Managua, with structured classes of varying lengths and qualified instructors. **Universidad Centroamericana**, better known as La UCA, T2278-3923 and T2267-0352, www.uca.edu.ni, runs Spanish courses that are cheaper than some private institutions, but with larger classes.

Laundry

There are very few public launderettes in Nicaragua and nearly all are confined to cities where there are high concentrations of expats and tourists. Ask your hotel or *hospedaje* to arrange laundry or dry cleaning. In Bolonia, **Dryclean USA**, Plaza Bolonia, 1 c arriba, T2266-4070; and **American Dry Cleaners**, Rotonda El Güegüence, 2 c sur, T2268-0710.

Post

Correos de Nicaragua, www.correros.gob.ni, is at 21 locations around Managua. The main office is Palacio de Comunicación, Parque Central, 1 c abajo. The tall building was a survivor of the 1972 earthquake, but is looking the worse for wear.

Note courier and express mail **Correos de Nicaragua** is slow so you may want to use an express courier. **DHL**, west side of Plaza Inter, T2251-2484, delivers letters to the USA and Europe, US$35-50. A little cheaper is **UPS** across from the German Embassy in Bolonia at Rotonda El Güegüence, 2 c norte, T2254-4892.

Telephone

Inside the Edif Enitel, **Claro** has telephone, mobile, fax and internet services, T2222-7272, www.claro.com.ni. **Movistar**, Km 6.5 Carretera a Masaya, Edif Movistar, T2277-0708, www.movistar.com.ni, is the main competitor, and both companies have branches all over the city, including in the main shopping centres. Many cybercafés facilitate national and international calls, as well as Skype (internet calls).

Useful numbers

Fire Dial 115 if an emergency; the central number is T2222-6411. **Police** Dial 118 in an emergency. The local police station number will depend on what *distrito* you are in. Main branch at Roberto Huembes, T2278-3945. **Red Cross** Dial 128 in an emergency; to give blood call, T2265-1517.

Las Sierras and Pacific beaches

West and south of Managua are two dramatically different regions that make attractive one-to three-day trips. To the west is the Pacific Ocean and the wave-swept beaches of Nicaragua's central coast with everything from surfer ecolodges to luxury resorts. South of Managua is the surprisingly biodiverse area of Las Sierras, with broad swathes of tropical dry forest, mild climates and a great diversity of wildlife and vegetation. ▶ *For listings, see pages 74-75.*

Las Sierras de Managua → *For listings, see pages 74-75.*

Behind the suburban sprawl that is Managua, Las Sierras rise 950 m above sea level into a broad area of forest and mountains. Considering it is less than 30 km from a city of more than a million people, the diversity of wildlife and vegetation that can be found here is remarkable. Accommodation is extremely limited but the area can be visited as a day trip from Managua or Granada. There are two entrances to Las Sierras, from the Carretera Sur and the Carretera a Masaya, the former offering brilliant views of crater lakes, the great lake basin and numerous volcanoes, the latter with access to the excellent nature reserves of Montibelli and El Chocoyero.

Getting there and around

Getting there To get to Las Sierras, take a bus heading for Diriamba and Jinotepe from the Mercado Israel Lewites, just west of the Alcaldía in Managua. Alight just after Las Nubes (the towers on the summit of the Carretera Sur) and walk up from the Carretera Sur on the tower road to see the fantastic views. To visit Montibelli or El Chocoyero, take a bus from Mercado Israel Lewites (or La UCA, Managua's University bus terminal) to La Concepción or San Marcos. Tell the driver you want to get off at the entrance; it is then a long dusty or muddy walk depending on the season, though you will meet lots of people along the way. Taxis can be hired for the trip. Agree in advance on the cost and how long you wish to stay. Expect to pay US$40-60 if you want the taxi to wait while you spend time walking. In the rainy season you will need to hire a 4WD. See Managua, page 67, for more information.

Getting around Buses pass regularly on both the Carretera a Ticuantepe and Carretera Sur. Once off the main roads walking or driving are the options. You might get a transfer from the Belli family if you book Montibelli in advance, see page 74.

Along the Carretera Sur

The Carretera Sur is one of the most dramatic roads in Nicaragua, with expansive views and several crater lakes to be seen as it rises up into the mountainous region of Las Sierras de Managua. At Km 6 is the little park **Las Piedrecitas**, which fills up at weekends with children, families and couples and has a cheap café serving bad hamburgers. The park has a great view of **Laguna de Asososca** ('blue waters' in Náhuatl), the principal reservoir of drinking water for Managua. It is a pretty lake and the view extends to Lake Managua and the Chiltepe Peninsula where two more crater lakes are hidden. At Km 9 is another crater lake, **Laguna de Nejapa** ('ash waters'), in the wooded crater of an old volcano that is almost dry during the summer. The highway continues south and turns right at a traffic signal 1 km past the final petrol station. From there the road rises gradually past some of the wealthiest homes in Nicaragua.

The section of road from Km 19 to Km 21 has no development, perhaps a coincidence, but some might tell you otherwise, as there is a **haunted house** at Km 20. Past the haunted house the highway twists and climbs to the summit, with its transmitter towers known as **Las Nubes**. You can turn left at the summit, just beyond the towers, and take a narrow road that runs along the ridge. Close to the end of the paved road, a small turning leads to a spectacular view of the valley of Lake Managua, Peninsula Chiltepe, the Pacific Ocean and the northern volcanic chain, Los Maribios, that runs from the province of León and into Chinandega.

Reserva Privada Silvestre Montibelli

ⓘ *Km 19, Carretera a Ticuantepe, turn right at the sign for the reserve and follow signs for 2.5 km, by reservation 3 days in advance only, T2270-4287, www.montibelli.com, Tue-Sun.*

Montibelli Private Nature Reserve is a family-owned nature park in greater Managua and one of the Pacific Basin's best forest reserves for birdwatching. Montibelli protects 162 ha of forest at an altitude of 360-720 m. The combination of its forest and elevation allow a more comfortable climate than Managua, with temperatures ranging from 18-26°C. The sandy Sierras' soil is super-fertile, but also very susceptible to erosion, making projects like Montibelli all the more valuable for their preservation of the mountain wildlife and vegetation. The property once had three separate shade-coffee haciendas; today only 22 ha are dedicated to coffee production and another 8 ha to fruit cultivation, the rest is set aside as forest reserve. The tropical dry forest has three principal nature walks, 1-3 km in length, which you can combine up to 7 km. The forest is home to 115 species of tree, and there are more than 100 species of bird including toucans, parrots, mot-mots, trogons, manikins and hummingbirds. There are also an impressive 40 species of butterfly as well as wild boar, agouti and howler monkeys. The old coffee hacienda house acts as a small museum and on the back patio meals are served by prior arrangement. Birdwatching or a butterfly tour with a local guide is US$45 per person with breakfast. The reserve also offers guided trekking for US$15 per person (minimum of two). Every Sunday there are group nature walks that finish with a farm style *parillada* of grilled meats and the Belli family's excellent organic coffee.

Reserva Natural El Chocoyero

ⓘ *Km 21.5, Carretera a Ticuantepe, turn right at the sign for the reserve and then follow signs for 7 km, T2276-7810. There is a park ranger station at the entrance, US$4, the rangers act as guides.*

The park's 184 ha houses 154 species of flora and 217 species of fauna and there are 2.5 km of trails, the best one being Sendero El Congo for its howler monkeys. It is also easy to see agouti, hummingbirds, butterflies and coral snakes, but the big attraction here are parakeets (the park's name comes from the ubiquitous *chocoyo*, Nicaraguan for parakeet). Pacific parakeets (*Aratinga strenua*) nest here in staggering numbers – there are around 700-900 couples. The best place to see them is at the El Chocoyero waterfall where the cliffs are dotted with tiny holes that they use for nesting. Arriving in the early afternoon allows time to explore the park and see them coming home to nest – a glorious racket. **Camping** is possible in the park, but bring plenty of insect repellent.

Managua's Pacific Coast → *For listings, see pages 74-75.*

The province of Managua has swathes of empty beaches and some tourist infrastructure exists in a few places, including Pochomil, Masachapa, the resort Montelimar and the ecolodge of Los Cardones. All the beaches in this region are washed by strong waves and currents and there are excellent conditions for surfing near the settlement of San Diego.

The beaches themselves are not terribly attractive with greyish sand and a good deal of litter near population centres but the ocean is warm and the sun shines for more than 300 days of the year and the beaches immediately in front of hotels are cleaned daily. The dry season means bigger crowds and often stronger winds; the rainy season brings with it more mosquitoes. Avoid Montelimar from November to March when charter flights from Montreal fill the resort. For surfing, March to November is best.

Getting there and around

Getting there Buses to Masachapa and Pochomil (60 km from Managua) leave from the Mercado Israel Lewites in Managua. To visit Montelimar or Los Cardones you will need a private car or taxi or ask your hotel to pick you up. A taxi to the coast from Managua should cost no more than US$40 (less if you are sharing a ride), though if you want them to wait expect to pay US$60.

Getting around Walking along the beach is the best way to get around the area and from one beach town to the other, though passing Masachapa at high tide can be tricky as there are many rocks, and access to Montelimar is blocked by a rocky bluff from the south.

Along the Carretera a Masachapa

At Km 32 on the Carretera Nueva a León is the turning to the Carretera a Masachapa – a long stretch of forest-lined highway paved with smooth cement cobblestones that runs through 25 km of pasture, forest and sugar cane. When the road ends, turn right and you will come to Masachapa. The first exit to the right is for the private beaches of the Montelimar Beach Resort; continue straight on for the little fishing village of Masachapa, or turn left and continue 1 km for the entrance to the broad public beaches of Pochomil.

Pochomil and Masachapa beaches

The tourist centre of Pochomil (US$1.50 per car, free if you come by bus) has countless restaurants, mostly poor value, and a main beach that is not very clean. Further south the beach is cleaner, the sand lighter in colour and more attractive. The huge, garishly painted presidential summer house is here. Along a rocky break at high tide are natural saltwater waterfalls, created by waves crashing over a neat shelf of rocks, great for cooling off. Further south is a cove with more very expensive homes and beyond **Pochomil Viejo** is another long beach. At low tide it is possible to drive in a 4WD for almost an hour along this stretch of sand from Masachapa south to just short of **La Boquita** in Carazo.

North of the tourist centre is the rocky shore of **Masachapa**, which has many tidal pools at low tide. The surf here is strong and swimming is a considerable risk. If you are up early, head to the centre of Masachapa beach where the fishermen roll their boats on logs up the beach with the morning's catch. If the fishing has been good it is a very happy and busy time – fishing is the lifeblood of the village, aside from tourism.

Montelimar and Playa San Diego

North of Masachapa, reached by a slightly inland road, is the infamous beach house of the last Somoza dictator which was turned into **Montelimar Beach Resort** by 1980s Minister of Tourism Herty Lewites. Further north of Montelimar, the beaches become increasingly deserted, until you arrive at a small lodge at **Playa San Diego**, called Los Cardones. It was built by an Israeli/French couple around a small coastal estuary and backed by tropical dry forest; it's a great place for surfing and relaxing.

⦿ Las Sierras and Pacific beaches listings

For sleeping and eating price codes and other relevant information, see pages 28-30.

⦿ Where to stay

Montibelli Nature Reserve *p72*
$$ Eco-Albergue Oropendula, inside Montibelli Reserve, T270-4287, www.monti belli.com. Simple cedar and stone cabins each with a deck that looks onto the forest reserve, private baths, with good beds, recommended. Meals are US$4-10 per dish.

Pochomil *p73*
$$$ Vistamar, Petronic, 600 m sur, turn right at sign, then 400 m on sandy road, T2269-0431, www.vistamarhotel.com. This seafront hotel has 17 attractive cabins with ocean views, private bath, a/c and hammocks; some have kitchenettes. The beautiful grounds have 3 swimming pools and many different varieties of hibiscus. The restaurant (**$$$**) does good seafood soup.
$$ Ticomo Mar, just south of the presidential beach house, T2265-0210. Simple rooms at a pleasant location, they come with a/c and bath. Parking available.
$$ Villas del Mar, just north of Pochomil centre, T2269-0426. There's a fun party atmosphere at the crowded, overpriced restaurant, and the rooms have private bath and a/c. Use of pool is US$5 per person.
$ Alta Mar, 50 m south of bus station, T2269-9204. Situated on a bluff with a great view of the ocean, but the rooms are generally poor value and suffocating, with dirty shared baths. The restaurant, however, is very good (**$$**), and serves fish at the tables on the sand. Popular with backpackers largely because of a lack of choice.

Masachapa *p73*
$$$$-$$$ Montelimar Beach Resort, 3 km north of Masachapa, T2269-6769, www.barcelo montelimarbeach.com. Price includes all meals and national drinks.

Most of the rooms are in bungalows surrounded by towering palms. Rooms have a/c, minibar, cable TV, private bathroom, a giant swimming pool, 4 restaurants, several bars, disco, fitness centre, shops, BAC bank to change TCs, laundry, tennis, casino (US$50 per person for use of all facilities for 6-hr day, including buffet lunch). This hotel is part of Nicaraguan history. It was once the sugar plantation of German immigrants. During the Second World War the first General Somoza confiscated the land. His son made the estate into the family's favourite beach house, built an airstrip and turned the sugar plantation into one of the best in the country. The Sandinista government then took over and after the Revolution turned it into an attractive beach resort. After the Sandinistas lost the elections in 1990, new President Violeta Barrios de Chamorro sold the resort to the Spanish hotel chain Barceló, which runs it today. It is set along an impressive beach with 3 km of uninterrupted sand. The beach is good for swimming with a very gradual shelf and (relatively) weak current. The resort is normally full of Canadian tourists between Nov and Mar.
$$ Ecológico, Petronic, 300 m south, T8887-5144. 10 rooms with private bath, a/c, swimming pool, TV. Only comes alive during holidays.
$$ La Bahía, behind Petronic, T2222-4821. Attractive little rooms with private bath a/c, TV, parking, swimming pool, friendly staff, bar and restaurant. Not a great location.

Montelimar and Playa San Diego *p73*
$$$ Finca Río Frío, Km 45, Carretera a Masachapa, T2266-2709, rzq@ibw.com.ni. A lovely farmhouse and ranch inland from the ocean along the highway. The farm has a charming log cabin with 4 rooms with 1 bed in each, shared toilets and showers, swimming pool, sun deck and a big thatched-roof dining area. This is the

farm and rural tourism project of Rodrigo Zapata, son of Nicaragua's legendary musical artist Camilo Zapata, the father of Nicaraguan folk music (see page 320). Rodrigo rents the entire farm to visitors who can relax around the pool, plant trees, milk cows, horse ride and swim in the river that passes through the property and gives the farm its name. Guests can use the kitchen or receive 3 meals a day for US$20 per person, advance reservations only. Transfers round-trip to the farm in van are US$40 total.

$$$ Los Cardones Ecolodge, Km 49, Carretera a Masachapa, then 15 km to the coast, follow signs, T8364-5925, www.los cardones.com. Surf and yoga retreats. This upmarket lodge has simple bungalows with brick walls, tile floors and thatched roofs.

The little complex, not easy to find, lies on a beautiful and wild stretch of beach next to the tiny coastal settlement of San Diego and backed by 7 ha of greenery. The owners are surfers and can direct guests to a variety of waves from little sand-bottom breaks to a harrowing shallow rock reef tube ride called 'Haemorrhoids'. Food is served by the owners and includes pizza and the original *nacatamal de pescado*. Horse rental and other tours offered.

⊖ Transport

Pochomil *p73*

Buses to **Managua**, every 20 mins, 0400-1745, US$1, 2 hrs. This can be a tedious ride with many stops.

East of Managua

East of the great lake basin of Lago de Managua and Lago de Nicaragua, the land rises and breaks into a mountainous region of dramatic peaks bridged by wide, gentle plains to form the departments of Boaco and Chontales. The region was heavily populated before the conquest and it remains rich in pre-Columbian archaeology, which is on display in Juigalpa. When the Spanish arrived they quickly recognized it as prime cattle grazing land and it has now been one of Central America's richest cattle and dairy lands for more than two centuries. Few foreign visitors bother to explore these provinces with their wide open spaces and traditional toughened cowboys, some of whom still ride with holstered guns. Accommodation is sparse due to the lack of tourism, but the region is worth visiting for anyone who wants to see real Nicaraguan cowboy culture, buy an authentic Nicaraguan woven sombrero or learn more about Nicaragua's Chontal indigenous culture. Travellers might also want to check out Cuapa, the site of pilgrimage after repeated appearances of the Virgin Mary to a humble local man during the Contra war of the 1980s. ▸▸ *For listings, see pages 79-80.*

Getting there and around

Buses to all towns and cities in the region leave from the Mercado Mayoreo in Managua. Either provincial capital can be visited in a day trip from Managua or Matagalpa, though an overnight stop allows for better exploration. If short on time, getting around is easiest by taxi or a hired car. Bus connections between attractions are frequent but slow.

The road to Boaco and Chontales → *For listings, see pages 79-80.*

Leaving Managua on the Pan-American Highway, the road leads north to the small town of **San Benito** (Km 35). To the north lie the Northern Highlands and to the east begins the Carretera a Rama highway that leads eventually to the town of **El Rama** (270 km away) and the Río Escondido that drains into Bluefields Bay. A very good paved highway goes past the **Las Canoas** lake, created by damming the Río Malacatoya that drains into Lake Nicaragua. The water is used to irrigate thousands of hectares of sugar cane and rice that is cultivated south of the highway and runs all the way to Lake Nicaragua's shoreline. There are several places to eat a tasty lake bass (*guapote*) fried whole, including **Restaurante El Viajero**, where a plate of fried *guapote* is US$3, with rice and cabbage salad. At Km 74 the road forks: to the left is the highway to Boaco, which is paved as far as Muy Muy and then continues to the Caribbean town of Bilwi – more than 400 km of unpaved adventure and the only road link from the Pacific to the Caribbean. At Km 88 is the pleasant hilltop town of Boaco, capital of the department of the same name.

Boaco

Surrounded by mountains and perched on a two-tiered hill, Boaco's setting is impressive and its high-low division gives it the nickname *Ciudad de Dos Pisos* ('two-storey city'). The relaxed cowboy atmosphere is reminiscent of some northern mountain towns, but the city is actually a commercial meeting place for the workers and owners of the sprawling cattle ranches that make up the department. Boaco has the history of a frontier town, having passed centuries on the edge of western and eastern Nicaragua. It has been moved west twice: in 1749 as a result of attacks from indigenous groups, then again in 1772 due to a harsh outbreak of cholera.

The original location is now called **Boaco Viejo** and is more scenic and laid back than modern Boaco. Inside its 250-year-old church there are pre-Columbian statues from the region. This is also the site of some interesting dances during the festival of Santiago celebrated from 22-31 July – the 25th being its most important day with a ritual dance and mock fights between *'Moros'* and *'Cristianos'* recalling Spanish history of more than 500 years ago. Thirteen dancers represent each warring party, though the 'Moors' invariably end up being baptized year after year. Ask if you can watch cheese being made at the factory by the entrance to Boaco, next to the open-air saddle workshop (they start at 1100 daily). Boaco is also a good place to buy cowboy boots.

The streets of the upper level are pleasant to walk around. Above the church is a lookout point with an improbable lighthouse and a fabulous view of the town and the surrounding hills.

Camoapa

The pleasant town of Camoapa is 20 km past Boaco on a rough rocky road that passes through the outskirts of Boaco Viejo, which lies to the north of the highway. This is one of the prettiest regions in Boaco and the friendly locals are curious to see foreigners. Situated at 520 m above sea level Camoapa has a good climate and is known around Nicaragua for its *agave* hats, similar to the 'Panama' hat of southern Ecuador, though not quite as fine a weave. People of Camoapa also make purses and other items out of the fibre known as *pita*. Just down from the central park is Elsa Guevara Arróliga's very good artisan shop, **Artesanías Palmata** ⓘ *Cooperativa Camoapa 20 vrs abajo, T2549-2338*, with 50 years of family experience. They will explain the delicate process of preparing *pita* to be woven into hats and bags. It's a good place to pick up a local sombrero (the finer ones require three months of work), which are excellent in the heat of Nicaragua for their breathability.

There is a charming church in the centre of town, the **Iglesia San Francisco de Asís**, which dates from 1789 and enjoys protection as a national monument. The interior has been completely remodelled, but the façade is original and the biggest of the three icons representing San Francisco was carved in Spain and dates from the late 1600s. If staying in

Camoapa you can organize an excursion to the **Río Caña Brava**, 25 minutes from the town; the river here is great for swimming and lined with forest. Few locals would hesitate to mention the pride of rural Camoapa, a 128-m *puente colgante* (hanging bridge) that passes 30 m above a particularly dangerous part of the river, 40 minutes by 4WD from the village. The festival for Camoapa in the name of San Francisco de Asís is on 24 June.

San Lorenzo

South past the Empalme de Boaco (the intersection in the highway) the road passes a paved turning to the left at Km 88 which leads to San Lorenzo, one of the most attractive villages in the region. Nestled in a narrow mountain pass, surrounded by lush green hills, this little village of 1400 people has a pleasant air; its cleanliness and beauty make it well worth a stop if you have your own transport. The locals are friendly and welcoming and often quite surprised to see foreigners. The central park is halfway up the cobblestone ridge and there is a small church, remodelled in 1977, with a white-tiled floor that contrasts with its dark wood ceiling. You can get some extremely crunchy but excellent *rosquillas* in the village. The feast day of San Lorenzo is 10 August, when there is a rodeo at the entrance to the village.

Cuapa

Continuing along the highway to Juigalpa and on to El Rama, the striking, extraterrestrial-looking 600-m monolith of **Cerro Cuisaltepe** ('eagle mountain') appears to the east, beyond Km 91, believed to be part of an ancient volcano. This region is geologically one of the oldest in Nicaragua and volcanic activity ceased millions of years ago. The highway passes a prison and, later, a large slaughterhouse before reaching the dirt road turning to the small but famous village of Cuapa, marked by a little monument to the Virgin Mary.

Continuing east, the highway passes through pleasant countryside and at Km 134 another impressive monolith becomes visible to the south. **Piedra de Cuapa** is reminiscent of Cerro Cuisaltepe and is equally mysterious in form and appearance. At Km 149, there is a monument to more than 70 Sandinista government troops who died in an ambush by the Contras in 1985. The words, written by Chilean poet Pablo Neruda, are a reminder that this area was heavily contested during the war years.

At Km 152, another statue of the Virgin marks the entrance to an access road to a monument and open-air church at the spot where the Virgin appeared to a priest helper, Bernardo Martínez (known as Bernardo de Cuapa), on 8 May 1983. At the time Nicaragua was suffering from Contra rebel attacks against the Sandinista military and personal liberties were vanishing rapidly all over the country. The Virgin, known as **La Virgen de Cuapa**, appeared on a cedar tree and told Bernardo that the Nicaraguan people must unite their families and pray for peace. "Nicaragua has suffered much since the earthquake," she said. "It is in danger of suffering even more. You can be sure that you all will suffer more if you don't change." Bernardo told of his experience publicly and there was a media frenzy. In Nicaragua everything becomes political, and Bernardo's vision was no exception. The Sandinista administration, dealing with Contra attacks in an area that was unsympathetic to its cause, saw the Virgin's message as anti-Sandinista and denounced Bernardo as a counter-revolutionary. The experience changed his life and he went on to become a priest until his death in 2000. An elaborate monument stands on the beautiful hillside where the Virgin appeared in 1983; the only noise is the wind rustling the trees and parrots squawking in the distant forest. Even an atheist would find the setting special. On 8 May every year, some 5000 pilgrims celebrate the happening with mass, prayers and confessions, in the hope of seeing her again. During her life Mother Teresa of Calcutta visited the site twice.

The village itself just 1 km down the main road is sleepy and uninteresting, though pleasant enough. The local church holds the official icon representing the Virgen de Cuapa, which is brought to the site of her appearance every 8 May.

Juigalpa

A hot and sprawling rural capital, Juigalpa is not terribly attractive, but its setting is beautiful and it is a great base for exploring the Sierra de Amerrisque mountain range, which lies to the east. Nineteenth-century naturalist Thomas Belt lived in the valley to the east and wrote about this area in his book *The Naturalist in Nicaragua* (see page 329). You'll get a great view of the Río Mayale, the Valle de Pauus and the Amerrisque range if you go to the east end of the street on which the museum (see below) stands. There, up on the left, is the lookout park, Parque Palo Solo, 'one tree park', which has an endless view of the mountains and valley.

On Parque Central, the very modern **Catedral de Nuestra Señora de la Asunción**, constructed in 1966 to replace the crumbling church built in 1648, appears starkly modern for Nicaragua with its two giant grooved bell towers. The cathedral has an interesting stained-glass treatment on the façade that is indecipherable from the outside; from inside the images appear to represent cowboys, women and Christ. Juigalpa has a raucous patron saint **festival** on 14-15 August, when the image of the Virgin is taken from the hospital (where she stays all year long to help with healing) to the cathedral at the head of a procession of cowboys and about 30 bulls. As in the rest of the country the bulls are mounted and brave young men run around in front of them with capes. As with most towns in this region, Juigalpa also has a brightly painted, very well-kept and attractive cemetery, on the main highway.

The town's claim to fame, and rightly so, however, is its superb **Museo Gregorio Aguilar Barea** or **Museo Arqueológico** ① *bus station ½ c sur, ½ c arriba, T2512-0784, Mon-Fri 0800-1130, 1400-1630, Sat 0800-1130, US$2*. Founded in 1952, the museum has more than 100 pre-Columbian statues, of all different sizes, and with varying reliefs, but always in the same cylindrical form. Many are in excellent condition, despite being carved out of relatively soft rock and having been exposed to the rain and sun for more than 600 years. The works date from AD 800-1200 and include one which, at over 4 m in height, is believed to be the tallest statue of its kind in Nicaragua and perhaps in Central America. Their smooth cylindrical form differentiates these statues from pieces found on the other side of Lake Nicaragua and its islands. They are sublime works, depicting men, women, priests, gods and warriors. The warriors hold knives; others hold hatchets or, if idle, their hands are crossed. The effort made to amass this collection and protect it in this private museum is staggering considering its limited funds. The curator, Carlos Villanueva, is a young, enthusiastic and sincere champion of national heritage, who knows the surrounding hills and their pre-Columbian treasures better than anyone in Chontales. It was Carlos who discovered the biggest ceremonial *metate* (used to crush corn for tortillas) encountered anywhere in Nicaragua (87 cm long and 46 cm tall). It is on display at the museum, along with many others. He has also recently discovered a previously unknown ceremonial site with eight statues. The museum also holds some colonial relics, taxidermy of native species and historic photography. One of the most beautiful statues – *La Chinita*, also known as the *Mona Lisa Chontaleña* (Mona Lisa of Chontales) – has now returned after a three-year loan to the Louvre in Paris.

Carlos Villanueva will take visitors on archaeological expeditions (including camping and two to three days on horseback). Contact him at the museum or T2512-0511 at home. The nearest archaeological site is just a few kilometres outside Juigalpa at the entrance to the highway to Cuapa, where numerous burial mounds and the ruins of some ancient homes lie behind a small school.

For sleeping and eating price codes and other relevant information, see pages 28-30.

🛏 Where to stay

Boaco *p76*
$ Hotel Alma, southeast corner of Parque Central, T2542-2620. Basic rooms with fan and shared bath. Friendly and a good location.
$ Hotel Boaco, across from Cooperativa San Carlos, T2542-2434. This clean and friendly hotel has 22 tiny rooms with tired beds; some have private bath. Parking available.
$ Sobalvarro, Parque Central, T2542-2515. This well-located hotel has a nice front patio and 15 very basic rooms with shared bath.

Camoapa *p76*
$ Hotel Las Estrellas, Parmalat, 1 c norte, 1½ c arriba, T2549-2240. The best in town has 17 small, no frills rooms with private bath, hot water, cable TV. The attached restaurant serves beef.
$ Hotel Taisiwa, Puente entrada de Managua, 50 vrs arriba, T2549-2158. Basic rooms with shared or private bath.

Juigalpa *p78*
$ Hospedaje Angelita, Parque Central, ½ c abajo, T2512-2408. Small, airless rooms with mosquito netting, shared bath and outhouse toilets. They are nice people, the grandmother makes some interesting crafts.
$ Hotel Casa Country, across from Parque Palo Solo, T2512-2546. This attractive 2-storey house has 5 good value rooms with a/c, private bath and cable TV; some have good views. The best in town, recommended.
$ Hotel La Quinta, across from the hospital on the highway at Km 141, T2512-2574. 38 rooms with private bath, hot water, a/c, TV. There is also a restaurant (**$$**), which is not very popular with the locals, but serves moderately priced steak dishes and good soups. The **La Quinta** disco charges US$2 entry for dancing, with a pleasant upper-

view deck, complete with stuffed bulls' heads and wagon wheels. It's very noisy here on weekend nights.
$ Hotel Rubio, cemetery on highway, 2½ c sur, T2512-0630. Clean and basic rooms with private bath and fan. Grumpy staff, parking available.

🍴 Restaurants

Boaco *p76*
There are lots of little places to eat, beef is the main dish.
$$-$ La Casona, next to Texaco, T2542-2421. Daily 0800-2200. Serves surf 'n' turf, traditional dishes, grilled chicken, good, moderate prices.
$ Alpino, Iglesia Santiago, 1½ c arriba, T2542-2270. Daily 0800-2100. Hamburgers, good *churrasco*, good value. Recommended.

Camoapa *p76*
$$-$ Restaurante & Disco Atenas, Iglesia, 1 c arriba, T2549-2300. Mon-Thu 1000-2400, Fri-Sat 1000-0200. Good beef and pork dishes, dancing to recorded music on weekend evenings after 2000.

San Lorenzo *p77*
$ El Taurete, across from the church. Serves cheap *carne asada* and tacos.
$ Restaurante El Mirador, down the hill, 50 m from Parque Central. Very cheap chicken and taco dishes, very friendly owners and lukewarm beer. There is a lookout point with little benches across from the eatery.

Juigalpa *p78*
$$ Restaurante Palo Solo, at the park by the same name, up from the museum. Has a great view of the valley and mountains and serves good fruit juices, fruit salad and *plancha palo solo*, a *carne asada* served with onions. For spice lovers, try *pollo a la diabla* (devil's chicken).

$ Comedor Quintanilla, just past the cemetery opposite Hotel Rubio. Serves the best cheap meal in town, wildly popular at lunch with locals, 3 meals a day, all less than US$2, with big servings, fruit juices, *sopa huevos de toro* (bull's balls soup).

⊖ Transport

Boaco *p76*
Buses leave from the central market to **Managua**, every 30 mins, 0330-1715, US$2, 2 hrs.

Camoapa *p76*
Buses to **Managua**, 7 daily, US$2.50, 3 hrs. Express buses once daily to **Managua**, 0610, US$3, 2 hrs.

Juigalpa *p78*
From the terminal, buses to **Managua**, every hour from 0330-1700, US$2.50, 3 hrs. If you are staying on the highway and don't want to go into town to catch the bus you can wait at Esso petrol station on the highway exit to Managua.

ⓘ Directory

Boaco *p76*
Bank Bancentro, next to Asociación de Ganaderos, T2542-1568. **Fire** T2542-1471. **Hospital** José Nieborowski on exit to Managua, T2542-2542. **Police** T2542-2274. **Red Cross** T2542-2200.

Camoapa *p76*
Bank Bancentro, north side of the church, T2549-2687. **Police** T2549-2210. **Red Cross** T2549-2118.

Juigalpa *p78*
Banks Bancentro, T2512-1477; and BDF, T2512-2467, both on Parque Central. **Fire** T2512-2387. **Hospital** Asunción, T2512-2332. **Police** T2512-2727. **Red Cross** T2512-2233.

Contents

Masaya & Los Pueblos

At a glance

◉ **Getting around** Masaya and Los Pueblos Blancos are connected by a good network of roads. Buses, taxis and Asian-style tuc-tucs are the main forms of transport.

◉ **Time required** 4-7 days.

◉ **Weather** Tropical weather systems typical of Pacific Central America. Dry season runs Nov-Apr; wet season May-Oct.

◉ **When not to go** Most of the region is green year round, though Masaya, Nindirí and the national parks are less enjoyable in the dry season. Nov-Jan the upper-rim villages of Laguna de Apoyo, like Catarina and San Juan de Oriente, can be chilly by Nicaraguan standards.

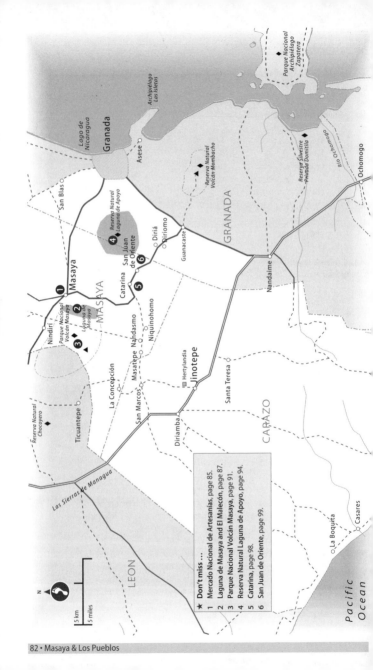

Don't miss...

1. Mercado Nacional de Artesanías, page 85.
2. Laguna de Masaya and El Malecón, page 87.
3. Parque Nacional Volcán Masaya, page 91.
4. Reserva Natural Laguna de Apoyo, page 94.
5. Catarina, page 98.
6. San Juan de Oriente, page 99.

Home to communities deeply rooted in their distant indigenous past, Masaya and the surrounding *pueblos blancos* are distinguished by their archaic folklore and vibrant craftwork. Irresistibly sleepy until fiesta time, these ancient settlements play host to bustling workshops, Nicaragua's best artesanía market, and a famously hospitable population who are directly descended from the ancient Chorotega peoples. Among their attributes is a fierce and indomitable spirit that has been roused time and again during difficult periods. It was here that the legendary chief Dirangén fought against the Spaniards; here that bloody rebellions erupted against Somoza; and here that the nation made a final stand against US invader William Walker. It is perhaps no surprise that the region also spawned Augusto Sandino, Nicaragua's most celebrated revolutionary.

The area's cultural assets are well complimented by dramatic physical landscapes, including an intensely sulphuric and other-worldly volcano complex. Dark and perpetually smoking, the tempestuous Santiago crater has been threatening cataclysm for centuries. Hiking trails snake up and around the angry giant, promising unforgettable olfactory encounters, stirring views and vivid natural spectacles. Nearby, infinitely more sedate Laguna Apoyo is the country's most attractive crater lake, with eternally warm, soothing waters heated by underwater vents. This is a special, peaceful place that is largely unspoiled (although increasingly threatened) by human activities. The surrounding mesa of highland villages, known as Los Pueblos Blancos, with their historic churches and interesting festivals, extends all the way from Laguna de Apoyo to the Pacific Coast. Although sparsely settled with wealthy vacation homes and sleepy fishing villages, it's an appropriately wild stretch, washed by strong surf and violent currents.

Ciudad de Masaya

Masaya has long been a vibrant centre for Nicaraguan culture and is home to several beautiful churches. Shaken by an earthquake in 2000, this attractive town suffered damage to around 80 houses and most of its churches. However, some attractive homes remain and the city is full of bicycles and traditional horse-drawn carriages, the latter used as taxis by the local population. Protected from lava flows of the Santiago Crater by the Laguna de Masaya, the city is renowned across Nicaragua for its folklore and its craft tradition. The indigenous barrio of Monimbó is possibly the richest artisan centre on the isthmus with many of its handmade goods being offered for sale across Central America. ▸▸ *For listings, see pages 89-91.*

Arriving in Masaya → *Population: 140,000. Altitude: 234 m. Colour map 3, B3.*
Getting there and around There are frequent bus services from Managua's Roberto Huembes market and La UCA bus station, as well as Granada's bus terminals. Many buses (including those with final destinations other than Masaya) do not pass through the city centre, but drop you at the ESSO station on the highway, several blocks north of the Parque Central. Taxis are available in Masaya, both the motorized and horse-drawn variety. ▸▸ *For further details, see Transport, page 90.*

Tourist information **INTUR** ⓘ *Banpro, ½ c sur, just south of the artisans' market, T2522-7615, masaya@intur.gob.ni, Mon-Fri 0800-1300,* has a branch office in Masaya. They have maps of the city and information on events.

Safety Masaya is generally a very safe city for visitors, but there have now been a few isolated reports of the same kind of taxi robberies that are afflicting Managua (see box, page 68). Be vigilant and do not ride in colectivos. As with any place subject to frequent fiestas, drunken street brawls can sometimes occur (usually after dark), but these almost never involve outsiders. Don't stroll on the *malecón* late at night.

Background
Masaya has always been home to very hard-working and skilled craftsmen. The first tribute assessments of 1548 for the Spanish crown stipulated that Masaya was to produce hammocks and *alpargatas* (cloth shoes). Around 300 years later, when US diplomat and amateur archaeologist EG Squier visited Masaya, he noted that, along with Sutiava (León), Masaya was a thriving centre of native handicraft production. Composed of at least three pre-Columbian villages – Masaya, Diriega and Monimbó – Masaya was briefly the colonial capital of Nicaragua when Granada rose up in rebellion, and it has always been involved in major political events in Nicaragua. In November 1856, William Walker's occupying troops lost a critical and bloody battle here to combined Central American forces, triggering his eventual retreat from Granada and Nicaragua. In September 1912, Masaya was the scene of battles between Liberal army forces and the US Marines. The insurrection against Somoza was particularly intense here, with the indigenous community of Monimbó showing legendary bravery during popular rebellions in February and September 1978. Finally in June 1979, the Revolution took control of Masaya and it was used by retreating Managuan rebels as a refuge before the final victory a month later. Since the war years, Masaya has returned to making fine crafts, serving as the commercial centre for Los Pueblos Blancos and the heart of Nicaragua's Pacific culture.

Places in Masaya

Mercado Nacional de Artesanías

ⓘ *Southeast corner of Parque Central, 1 c arriba, daily 0900-1800; folkloric performances Thu 1900-2200. There is a DHL office open daily 1000-1700 inside the market in case you end up buying more than you can carry.*

Most people come to Masaya to shop, and the country's best craft market is here in the 19th-century Mercado Nacional de Artesanías. The late Gothic walls of the original market were damaged by shelling and the inside of the market burned during the

Ciudad de Masaya

Where to stay 🛏
Cailagua **4**
Hostal Santa María **1**
Maderas Inn **3**
Monimbó **2**
Regis **5**

Sleeping 🍴
Che Gris **1**
Comedor Criolla **4**

Comidas Criollas **13**
Fruti Fruti **14**
La Cazuela de
  Don Nacho **5**
La Jarochita **2**
Los Corredores **3**
Munchis **7**
Panadería Norma **15**
Plaza Pedro Joaquín
  Chamorro **9**

Telepizza **11**

Bars & clubs 🍸
Coco Jambo **6**
Disco Bar Ritmo
  de Noche **10**
La Ronda **8**

Masaya festivals

The festivals of Masaya and the Pueblos de la Meseta are some of the richest, most evocative and staunchly celebrated in Nicaragua.

2-8 February, Virgen de la Candelaria (Diriomo) Festival for the patron saint, brought from Huehuetenango, Guatemala in 1720. Processions run from 21 January to 9 February with 2 February being her main feast day. On 2 February, a pilgrimage leaves from La Iglesia Guadalupe in Granada and arrives in Diriomo at 1000 to join the festivities. Dancing is performed by both children and adults, wearing masks and traditional costume. The dancers lead the procession up to the icon of La Virgen.

16 March, La Virgen de la Asunción (Masaya) Also known as the festival of the cross, commemorating how the icon miraculously diverted lava flows during the 1772 volcanic eruption.

3 April, Jesús del Rescate (Masaya) A procession of ox carts travel from Masaya to San Jorge.

24 April, Tope de las imágenes de San Marcos (San Marcos) This is the famous meeting of the icons of the four main saints of the region: San Sebastián (from Diriamba), Santiago (from Jinotepe), the black Virgen de Montserrat (from La Concepción) and San Marcos himself. They are paraded around in pairs until they all finally meet at El Mojón (on the highway between Diriamba and Jinotepe). It is a huge party with traditional dancing. The next day there is more dancing in the Parque Central and the four saints come out of the church together to tremendous fireworks, confetti and processions.

Week before Palm Sunday, San Lázaro (Masaya) A fun, if highly surreal, celebration in which dogs are dressed up in costumes.

Mid-May, Santísma Trinidad (Masatepe) This festival for the patron saint lasts over a month from mid-May and includes famous horse parades.

Revolution of 1978-1979. Work to repair the walls began in 1992 and the interior was also restored for its grand opening in May 1997. After two decades of sitting in ruin it was reopened and is now dedicated exclusively to handmade crafts. Masaya and its surrounding villages house an abundance of talent, which is clearly evident here. There are 80 exhibition booths and several restaurants inside the market and it's a great place to shop without the cramped conditions or hard sell of a normal Latin American market. Every Thursday night from 1900 to 2200 there is a live performance on the stage in the market. These usually include one of Masaya's more than 100 folkloric dance groups with beautifully costumed performers and live marimba music accompaniment, mixed with a more modern music ensemble.

The market sells local leather, wood, ceramic, stone and fabric goods, as well as some crafts from around Nicaragua. Although most vendors try to keep a broad variety to guarantee steady income, there are some stalls that specialize. One of them is **Grupo Raíces** ① *Módulo H-6, T2552-6033*, which has a fine selection of ceramics from Condega, San Juan de Oriente and Jinotega, as well as soapstone sculptures from San Juan de Limay. They are located in the south wing of the market. Nearby, on the outside of the southern block of stalls, is a stall that has the finest examples of *primitivista* paintings from Solentiname and Masaya artists, as well as a good selection of books. Just north of the main entrance is a special stall that has a great selection of festival **masks** and **costumes**; these are not made for tourists but festival participants. Boys will greet you at the market

17-29 June, San Pedro (Diría) Festivities include bullfights and violent ritualized fighting with cured wooden palettes.

24 June, San Juan Bautista (San Juan de Oriente) An often wild festival for the patron saint with ritual fighting in the streets between believers and lots of *chichero* music (brass and drum ensembles).

24-26 July, San Santiago (Jinotepe) Festival for the local patron saint.

26 July, Santa Ana (Niquinohomo) Patron saint festival with folkloric dancing and fireworks.

15 August, Día de la Virgen de la Asunción (Masaya) Monimbó festival honouring Mary Magdalene.

17-27 September, San Sebastián (Diriamba) The legendary *Güegüence* is performed by masked dancers in bright costumes accompanied by music played with indigenous and mestizo instruments, which together have come to represent the very identity of Pacific Nicaraguan mestizo culture.

30 September-early December (San Jerónimo, Masaya) 80 days of festivities, making it one of the longest parties in Latin America. Celebrations include processions and dances performed to the driving music of marimbas, such as *El Baile de las Inditas* and *Baile de las Negras* (Sundays throughout October and November), *Baile de los Diablitos* (last Sunday of November) and, most famous for its brutally humorous mocking of Nicaragua's public figures and policies, *El Toro Venado* (last Sunday in October and third Sunday in November).

Last Friday in October, Noche de Agüizotes (Masaya) A festival commemorating bad omens, in which participants dress up like ghouls and monsters.

26 November, Santa Catalina de Alejandría (Catarina) Patron saint festival.

31 December-1 January (San Silvestre, Catarina) The big fiesta in Catarina, with flower-festooned parades.

with a handful of English words; they can help you find what you are looking for and will translate with the merchants for a tip of US$1-2.

Masaya's most famous craft is its cotton **hammocks**, which are perhaps the finest in the world and a tradition that pre-dates the arrival of the Spanish. The density of weave and quality of materials help determine the hammock's quality; stretching the hammock will reveal the density of the weave. You can visit the hammock weavers (normally in very cramped conditions) in their homes; the highest concentration is one block east from the stadium on the *malecón* and one block north of the *viejo hospital*. With a deposit and 48-hours' notice, you can also custom-order a hammock in the workshops. If you have no intention of buying a hammock it is better not to visit the workshops.

Laguna de Masaya and El Malecón

The best view of the deep blue 27-sq-km Laguna de Masaya and the Masaya volcanic complex is from the *malecón*, or waterfront, usually populated with romantic couples. There is also a **baseball stadium**, named after the Puerto Rican baseball star Roberto Clemente, who died in a flying accident in Florida while en route to Nicaragua with earthquake relief aid in 1972. The lake is 300 m below, down a steep wall. Before the pump was installed in the late 19th century, all of the town's water was brought up from the lake in ceramic vases on women's heads – a 24-hour-a-day activity according to British naturalist Thomas Belt who marvelled at the ease with which the Masaya women dropped down into the crater and glided back out with a full load of water. The lake has suffered from city run-off for the last few decades and the city is looking for funding to clean its waters, which are not good for swimming at the moment. There are more than 200 petroglyphs on the walls of the descent to the lake that can also be seen reproduced in the Museo Nacional in Managua (see page 49). There are no official guides to take you to the petroglyph sites, but you can try the INTUR office near the market, or ask around locally.

La Parroquia de Nuestra Señora de la Asunción

Nearly every barrio in Masaya has its own little church, but two dominate the city. In Masaya's leafy Parque Central is La Parroquia de Nuestra Señora de la Asunción, a late-baroque church that dates from 1750. It was modified in 1830 and has undergone a complete restoration with financial help from Spain. The clean lines and simple elegance of its interior make it one of the most attractive churches in Nicaragua and well worth a visit. There is a subtle balance to its design, particularly inside, and its extensive use of precious woods and native tile floor add to its charm.

Iglesia de San Jerónimo

San Jerónimo, though not on Parque Central, is the spiritual heart of Masaya. This attractive domed church, visible from kilometres around, is home to the city's patron Saint Jerome (whose translation of the bible was the standard for more than a millennium) and a focal point for his more than two-month-long festival. The celebration begins on 30 September and continues until early December, making it by far the longest patron saint festival in Nicaragua and perhaps in Latin America (see box, page 86). The church of San Jerónimo was badly damaged by the earthquake in 2000. The walls survive with four sets of temporary exterior supports; however, it is awaiting proper funding to restore it.

Comunidad Indígena de Monimbó

The famous indigenous barrio of Monimbó is the heart and soul of Masaya. During Spanish rule the Spanish and Indian sections of major cities were clearly defined. Today, nearly all the lines have been blurred, yet in Monimbó (and in the León barrio of Sutiava, see page 204) the traditions and indigenous way of life have been maintained to some extent. The Council of Elders, a surviving form of native government, still exists here and the beating of drums of deerskin stretched over an avocado trunk still calls people to festival and meetings and, in times of trouble, to war. In 1978, the people of Monimbó rebelled against Somoza's repressive Guardia Nacional. They achieved this entirely on their own, holding the barrio for one week using home-made contact bombs and other revolutionary handicrafts to hold off what was then a mighty army of modern weapons and tanks. This and other proud moments in Monimbó's revolutionary past are documented in the flag-draped **Museo Comunitario y Etnográfico La Insurreción de Monimbó** ① *Damas Salesianas 1½ c arriba, orlancabrera@hotmail.com, Mon-Fri 0900-1600, US$0.50*, where you'll find a modest collection of historical photos and artefacts.

Today the crafts of Monimbó are largely aesthetic and the people of the southern barrio are masters of all kinds of domestic and decorative crafts. This neighbourhood should be the most famous artisan barrio in Central America, yet curiously commerce dictates otherwise. A visit to some of the workshops around Monimbó will quickly reveal why: here you will see leather goods with 'Honduras' written on them, flowery embroidered dresses that say 'Panama' and ceramics with 'Costa Rica' painted in bright letters are everywhere. Even Guatemala, which has perhaps the finest native textiles in the western hemisphere, imports crafts from Monimbó – of course with their country's name on it. It is possible to do an artisan workshop tour independently, though hiring a local guide will make it much easier. The highest concentration of workshops is located between the unattractive Iglesia Magdalena and the cemetery. You can start from the Iglesia San Sebastián on Avenida Real de Monimbó, go two blocks away from the centre of town and then turn right.

Fortaleza de Coyotepe

ⓘ *Carretera Masaya Km 28. Daily 0900-1600, US$2. Bring a torch/flashlight, or offer the guide US$2 to show you the cells below. The access road is a steep but short climb from the Carretera a Masaya, parking U$1.*

Just outside Masaya city limits is the extinct volcanic cone of Coyotepe (Coyote Hill) and a post-colonial fortress. The fortress was built in 1893 by the Liberal president José Santos Zelaya to defend his control of Masaya and Managua from the Conservatives of Granada. In 1912, it saw action as the Liberals battled the US Marines (allied with the Conservatives) and lost the fortress. During the battle Liberal General Benjamín Zeledón was killed; his death would inspire future rebel leader Augusto C Sandino and give status to Zeledón as a martyred hero. Though donated to the Boy Scouts of Masaya during the 1960s, the fortress was used by the second General Somoza as a political prison. His National Guard used it to shell rebel-held civilian neighbourhoods in Masaya in 1979. When the Sandinistas took power Coyotepe remained a political prison. In 1990 it was finally returned to the Boy Scouts after the Sandinista electoral defeat. There are 43 cells on two floors that can be visited; people have reported hearing the distant echo of screams. The top deck offers a splendid 360° view of Masaya, Laguna de Masaya and the Masaya volcanoes and on to Granada and its Volcán Mombacho.

◉ Ciudad de Masaya listings

For sleeping and eating price codes and other relevant information, see pages 28-30.

◎ Where to stay

Quality lodging in Masaya is very limited, due to its proximity to Managua and Granada.
\$\$ Hostal Santa María, Banpro, 1 c arriba, ½ c sur, info@hostalsantamarianic.com, T2552-2411. This centrally located hotel has a range of clean, comfortable rooms with private bath, cable TV and a/c (cheaper with fan). There's a small pool in the garden.
\$\$ Hotel Monimbó, Plaza Pedro Joaquín Chomorro, 1 c arriba, 1½ c norte, T2522-6867, hotelmonimbo 04@hotmail.com. 7 clean, comfortable rooms with private bath, hot water, a/c and cable TV. There's a pleasant patio and garden space with relaxing hammocks. Other services include Wi-Fi, laundry, restaurant-bar, tours and transportation. Breakfast included.

\$\$ Maderas Inn, Bomberos, 2 c sur, T2522-5825, www.hotelmaderasinn.com. A friendly little place with a pleasant family ambience and a variety of rooms kitted out with private bath, a/c, cable TV. Continental breakfast is included in the price, but there are also cheaper rooms without breakfast or a/c (**\$**). Services include medical consultations, Wi-Fi, tours, parking, laundry and airport transfer. There's also hammock space for chilling out.
\$ Cailagua, Km 30, T2522-4435, cailagua@ hotmail.com. Comfortable hotel with 22 rooms, secured parking, private bath, a/c, cable TV, swimming pool, restaurant. Noisy location, far from centre; for the exhausted driver.
\$ Hotel Regis, La Curacao, 40 vrs norte, T2522-2300, hotelregismasaya@hotmail. com. Very friendly and helpful owner. Rooms are clean and basic, with shared bath and fan. The price is right, but there are at least

3 other economical options on the same block. Ultra-cheap for single travellers.

🍴 Restaurants

$$ La Cazuela de Don Nacho, northeast corner of the Mercado de Artesanía, T2522-7731. Fri-Wed 1000-1800, Thu 1000-0000. There's a jaunty atmosphere at this pleasant market-place eatery, usually buzzing with diners. They serve *comida típica* and à la carte food like shrimps, *filet mignon*, *filete de pollo* and *churrasco* steak.

$$ La Jarochita, east side of the Parque Central, 50 vrs norte, T2522-2186. Daily 1100-2200. The best Mexican in Nicaragua; some drive from Managua just to eat here. Try *sopa de tortilla*, and chicken *enchilada* in *mole* sauce, *chimichangas* and Mexican beer. Recommended.

$$ Munchis, Bomberos, 2 c sur. A rather ad-hoc interior but the dishes here are good and should satisfy most carnivores. Offerings include BBQ *brochetas* and a range of other grilled meat and chicken dishes. Cocktail deals in the evening.

$$ Restaurante Che Gris, southeast corner of the Mercado de Artesanía, T2552-0162. Very good food in huge portions, including excellent *comida típica*, *comida corriente* and à la carte dishes like steaks, chicken and pork.

$$-$ Los Corredores, Iglesia Parroquia La Asunción, 1 c norte, ½ c abajo, T2552-2291. A big, new colonial-style building with a well-finished interior. They serve burgers, club sandwiches, grilled meats and other meaty fare. Economical lunch-time deals (**$**) Mon-Fri 1100-1500, but dinner is served too. Occasionally hosts live music.

$$-$ Telepizza, Iglesia La Asunción 25 vrs norte, T2522-0170. Filling, wholesome pizza, thick or thin based, but nothing amazing. Delivery service.

$ Comedor Criolla, northeast corner of Parque Central, 5 c norte. Popular locals' haunt serving cheap Nica fare, buffet food, breakfasts and lunch.

$ Comidas Criollas, south side of Parque Central. This large, clean, buffet restaurant serves up healthy portions of Nica fare.

$ Plaza Pedro Joaquín Chamorro, also known as **Tiangue de Monimbó**, in front of Iglesia San Sebastián in Monimbó. Good *fritangas* with grilled meats, *gallo pinto* and other traditional Masaya food, very cheap.

Cafés, juice bars and bakeries
Fruti Fruti, northeast corner of Parque Central, 3½ c norte. Tasty, sweet, fresh fruit smoothies, including delicious *piña coladas*.
Panadería Norma, northwest corner of the artisan market, ½ c norte. Good, fresh-brewed coffee, bread, cakes and pastries.

🍸 Bars and clubs

Coco Jambo, next to the *malecón*, T2522-6141. Fri-Sun from 1900. US$2, very popular disco, mixed music, lots of fun.
Disco Bar Ritmo de Noche, next to the *malecón*, T2522-5856. Fri-Sun 1900-0100. Open-air dance bar, also fun.
La Ronda, south side of Parque Central, T2522-3310. Tue-Thu 1100-2400, Fri-Sun 1100-0200. Music and drinks, beautiful building with a young festive crowd.

🛍 Shopping

There is a **Palí** supermarket next to Claro on the west side of Parque Central. The municipal market is located on the east side of town, several blocks from the Parque Central. It is hectic and dirty but a great place to pick up hand-crafted wooden furniture and other artisan crafts; prices are invariably cheaper than the tourist market downtown.

🚍 Transport

Bus
The regular market or Mercado Municipal is where most buses leave from, it is 4 blocks east of the south side of the artisan market. Express bus to **Managua** (Roberto

Huembes), every 20 mins, 0500-1900, US$0.60, 50 mins. To **Jinotepe**, every 20 mins, 0500-1800, US$0.50, 1½ hrs. To **Granada**, every 30 mins, 0600-1800, US$0.50, 45 mins. To **Matagalpa**, 0600, 0700, US$2.75, 4 hrs.

From Parque San Miguelito, between the artisan and regular markets on Calle San Miguel, express buses leave for La UCA in **Managua**, every 30 mins, 0530-1900, US$0.80, 40 mins. You can also board any bus on the Carretera a Masaya to **Managua** or towards **Granada**. Note the sign above front windshield for destination and flag it down. For **Parque Nacional Volcán Masaya** take any Managua bus and ask to step down at park entrance. Buses to **Valle de Apoyo** leave twice daily, 1000, 1530, 45 mins, US$0.70, then walk down the road that drops into the crater.

    International bus North and southbound **Transnica** (reservations T2552-3872), and **King Quality** buses stop at the Texaco station on the highway. **Ticabus**, agency, in front of the old Farmacia Aguilar, Ciber Centro, T2552-0445, stops at the Esso.

Taxi
Fares around town are US$0.40 per person anywhere in the city. Approximate taxi fares to: **Granada** US$15, **Laguna de Apoyo**, US$7, **Managua** US$20, **airport** US$25. Horse-drawn carriages (*coches*) are for local transport inside Masaya, US$0.50.

⊕ Directory

Banks All banks will change dollars. The BAC, opposite the northwest corner of the artisan market, has an ATM; as does **Banpro**, opposite the southwest corner. There's a **Bancentro** on the west side of the plaza with a Visa ATM. You'll also find street changers around the plaza. **Fire** T2522-2313. **Hospital** T2522-4166. **Internet** Several around town including **Cyber Pro**, southeast corner of artisan market, 1 c arriba; and **Cyber Space**, Plaza Miguelito, ½ c arriba. **Police** T2522-4222. **Post** Correos de Nicaragua is 1 block north of police station, T2522-2631. **Red Cross** T2522-2131. **Telephone** Claro is on the west side of Parque Central, T2522-2891.

Around Masaya

The city of Masaya is set among some spectacular geography that includes the Laguna de Apoyo crater lake nature reserve and the Volcán Masaya National Park. Both sites are within half an hour of the city and offer unique nature experiences. Masaya's tiny sister city is Nindirí, a truly ancient settlement with a charming colonial church, rich culture and a relaxed pace of life.
▶▶ *For listings, see pages 96-97.*

Parque Nacional Volcán Masaya

ⓘ *Daily 0900-1700, US$4, including entrance to the museum. The visitor centre (the Centro de Interpretación Ambiental) is 1.5 km up the hill from the entrance, T2522-5415, pvmasaya@ ideay.net.ni.*

The heavily smoking Santiago crater of the Volcán Masaya complex is one of the most unusual volcanoes in the Americas and reported to be one of only four on earth that maintain a constant pool of lava (neither receding nor discharging) in its open crater. Just 30 minutes from the Metrocentro in Managua, with a 5-km paved road that reaches the edge of its active crater, this is undoubtedly one of the most accessible active volcanoes in the world. What the park protects is a massive caldera with more than half a dozen cones that have risen up inside it over the last seven millenniums. It is a place of eerie beauty, the rugged lunar landscape punctuated by delicate plant life, remarkably resilient animal life and a panorama view of the great lake valley. The main attraction, the smoking cone, seems almost peaceful – until one recalls that it is an open vent to the centre of the earth and prone to sudden acts of geological violence.

Getting there and around

Getting there Any bus that runs between Masaya and Managua can drop you at the park entrance, Km 23, Carretera a Masaya, though the long, hot walk without shade make a hired taxi (US$1.50 from the entrance), tour company or private car a valuable asset. Hitching is possible, as are guided hikes, US$0.70-3 per person payable at the museum before you set out. Note that certain trails may be closed for safety reasons or for maintenance. At the summit parking lot (Plaza de Oviedo) there are soft drinks for sale. There is also a picnic area with *asadores* (barbecues) opposite the museum.

Safety

The 1.5-km hike from the gate to the visitor centre is not terribly steep, but it is intense for lack of shade. Be sure to pack sunscreen and water. The crater itself is another 2-3 km uphill through the lava fields. Watch out for any significant change in smoke colour, or any persistent rumbling, which may indicate a pending eruption. Do not spend more than 20 minutes at the crater's edge, especially with children, as the steam and smoke are quite toxic. Asthmatics may want to avoid the area altogether (or should at least pack the appropriate inhalers).

Background

At first glance it's not obvious that the park is actually located inside a massive extinct crater, Ventarrón (10 km by 5 km), which includes all the park's cones and the crater lake. From the summit of the active cone, you can see the ancient walls of the Ventarrón caldera sweeping around the outside of the park. Ventarrón is believed to have erupted in 4550 BC in a massive explosion. Since then, successive lava flows have filled in the cauldron and mountains have risen in its centre, the lake being the last remaining part of the original crater that has not been filled with rock and earth.

The current active complex was called Popogatepe ('burning mountain') by the Chorotega people. In 1529, the Spanish chronicler Gonzalo Fernández de Oviedo y Valdés (known simply as Oviedo) visited the volcano. He wrote that there were many ceremonies at the base of the mountain, with the Chorotegas supposedly sacrificing young women and boys to appease Chacitutique, the goddess of fire. In the adjacent village of Nindirí, Chief Tenderí of the Chorotegas told Oviedo that they would go down into the crater to visit a magical fortune-teller who lived there. She was a very ugly old woman, naked, with black teeth, wrinkled skin and tangled hair (there is a beautiful rendition of her in the park's museum painted by the Nicaraguan master Rodrigo Peñalba). The old fortune-teller predicted eruptions, earthquakes, the quality of the coming harvest, wars and victories; she even told the chief that he should go to war with the Christians (the Spanish). Oviedo became convinced that she was the Devil. After visiting the volcano, he commented that any Christian who believed in Hell would surely fear the crater and be repentant for his sins. Around the same time Friar Francisco de Bobadilla hiked to the summit to perform an exorcism and place a large wooden cross above the lava pool to keep the door to Hell (the lava pool) shut. A cross still stands in its original place above the crater, though it has been replaced several times. Another friar, less religious perhaps, or at least more capitalistic – Friar Blas de Castillo – organized an expedition into the west crater. Armed with a cross and a flask of wine and wearing a conquistador's helmet, Friar Blas descended into the crater to extract what he was sure was pure gold. With the help of his assistants and a metal bowl dangling on a long chain, he managed to extract some molten lava, which, to his profound disappointment, turned into worthless black rock when exposed to cool air.

The final eruption of the Nindirí crater occurred in 1670 and the lava flow can still be seen on the left side of the access road when climbing the hill to the summit. Volcán Masaya burst forth on 16 March 1772 with a major lava flow that lasted eight days. The eruption threatened to destroy the town of Nindirí, but the lava flow was supposedly stopped in its path by the **Cristo del Volcán**, a church icon, and diverted into the Laguna de Masaya, thus saving the city. A colourful mural depicting the event can be seen inside the park museum. Another violent eruption occurred in 1853, creating the Santiago crater as it stands today, some 500 m in circumference and 250 m deep. The crater erupted again in 1858 and fell silent until the 20th century, when it erupted in 1902, 1918, 1921, 1924, 1925, 1947, 1953, and 1965, before collapsing in 1985. The resulting pall of sulphurous smoke made a broad belt of land to the Pacific uncultivatable. From 1996 to 2000 the crater gave increasing signs of life, with sulphur output rising from 150 to over 400 tonnes per day and a noticeable increase in seismic activity. Since 1997, the increasingly unstable land under the lookout from the west side means the lava pool can no longer be seen from there. (The photographs you see on posters and brochures of the magma pool were taken from that side of the crater.) In early 2001 the crater's gaseous output came almost to a complete stop and on 23 April 2001 the resulting pressure created a minor eruption. Debris pelted the parking area at the summit (during visiting hours) with hundreds of flaming rocks at 1427 in the afternoon, and exactly 10 minutes later the crater shot some tubes of lava on to the hillside just east of the parking area, setting it ablaze. Miraculously there were only minor injuries but several vehicles were badly damaged by falling stones.

Trails around Parque Nacional Volcán Masaya

The park boasts 20 km of trails that meander around this intense volcanic complex. This area includes fumaroles at the base of **Comalito**, a small extinct cone; the crater lake of **Laguna de Masaya**; and two extinct craters, **Masaya** and **Nindirí**, whose cones support the active crater of **Santiago**, along with three smaller extinct cones. The park is beautiful, a surreal moonscape punctuated by orchids and flowers such as the *sacuanjoche* (*Plumeria rubra*), Jesus flower (*Laelia rubescens*) and many species of small lizard. Racoon, deer and coyote share the rockscape, and mot-mots, woodpeckers and magpie jays nest in hillsides and trees. The real heroes of the park, however, are the bright green parakeets, that nest in the truly toxic environment of the active Santiago crater. The bird is known as the *chocoyo coludo* in Nicaragua; its popular name in English is the Nicaraguan green conure (*Aratinga strenua*). The *chocoyos* can be spotted late in the afternoon returning to their nests in the interior walls of Santiago, soaring happily through suffocating clouds of hydrochloric acid and sulphur dioxide, chattering away as they enter their cliff dwellings. The holes are tunnels which have a chamber at the end and can be as deep as 3 m inside the mountain. In July they lay two to four eggs. Most scientists attribute protection for the eggs as motivation for the *chocoyos'* adaptation to the lethal environs of the crater.

A short path from the visitor centre leads up to **Cerro El Comalito** and the fumaroles there, with good views of Mombacho, the lakes and the park's extraordinary volcanic landscapes. **Sendero Los Coyotes** is a 5.5-km trail that accesses Laguna de Masaya. **Sendero de las Pencas** is a hike through lava flows that is interesting in the dry season because of the flowers to be found in the area. The **San Fernando crater**, straight up the hill from the summit parking area (Plaza de Oviedo), offers great views of Santiago and the valley below, as well as the interior of the forested crater. For a view of Masaya city and Laguna de Masaya, you need to make a 20-minute hike around the crater to its narrow east rim, where there are dozens of vultures nesting. Beware of **snakes** on this trail in the rainy season when the grass is tall. The hike up the 184 stairs to the **Cruz de Bobadilla** has been closed indefinitely for fear that the hillside beneath it may collapse. The **Cueva Tzinancostoc** is a gaseous cave formed by lava and full of bats.

Los Coyotes, Comalito and La Cueva can only be visited with a park ranger and all tickets must be bought at the museum (before you get to the summit), US$0.70 per person. The rangers there can tell you what is open, which depends on activity in the crater, their current staff size and fire hazards. If you want a good look at the red hot lava simmering beneath the earth's surface, a **night tour** is presently your best chance. They depart daily, 1700, US$10, six-person minimum, book at least one day in advance. You'll observe flocks of parakeets returning to roost, swarms of bats departing to feed, various rock tunnels, and a newly formed crater opening, glowing red and emitting pungent, sulphurous clouds.

Nindirí → For listings, see pages 96-97.

At Km 25 on the east side of the Carretera a Masaya near the volcano park is the historic village of Nindirí. A cemetery marks the first entrance; the third or southernmost entrance leads directly to Parque Central. Inhabited continually for the last 3000 years, this attractive, well-kept village is built in one of Central America's richest areas for pre-Columbian ceramics. A quiet place, Nindirí makes quite a contrast from the hustle and bustle of Masaya just down the road. The leafy and colourful Parque Central is marked by a tall monument to **Tenderí**, the legendary Chorotega chief who was in charge of this area when the Spanish arrived in 1526. In 1528 Diego Machuca laid the plans of the town, which was not officially named a city until over 400 years later. The town church **La Iglesia Parroquial** is a charming primitive baroque structure that was first built in 1529, restored in 1798 and once again in 2004. It is a lovely church with tile floors, adobe walls and a traditional tile roof. It has a slightly indigenous feel to it and is home to the patron saint Santa Ana as well as the famous **Cristo del Volcán**, credited with stopping the lava flow of 1772 from annihilating the village (see page 93). The central park is well tended and the site of a performance celebrating the passion of Christ on the Wednesday evening before Easter during Semana Santa.

The **Museo Tenderí** ① *corner house, Biblioteca Municipal, 1 c abajo, T2552-4026, Mon-Fri 0800-1600, donation requested*, is so overflowing with relics that it is difficult to distinguish one piece from another. It's home to more than 1500 pre-Columbian pieces and a few very interesting colonial period artefacts. The elderly woman who owns the museum will show you around and may be coaxed into playing an ancient indigenous flute that represents three different animals. Her deceased husband accumulated the collection. If she is not around ask the neighbours to help you find her.

Reserva Natural Laguna de Apoyo → For listings, see pages 96-97.

One of Nicaragua's most beautiful sites, this stunning crater lake is drawing increased attention with its tranquil, Mediterranean-blue waters, unique fish species and mysterious healing properties. Heated by thermal vents deep below the surface, the water is clean, clear and comfortably warm. Its light sulphur content makes it a fine skin tonic and an effective mosquito repellent. Swimming here is a rejuvenating experience, but many come just to gaze at the hypnotic waters that turn azure when directly illuminated by the sun.

Ecological mysteries under threat

As yet unspoiled, Laguna de Apoyo is Nicaragua's most beautiful crater lake and a true ecological jewel. Declared a nature reserve in 1991, the lake's surrounding tropical dry forests are home to a rich array of mammals including opposums, anteaters, pacas, jaguarundis, howler monkeys, white-headed capuchins, armadillos and agoutis. Bird life is equally prolific, with oropendolas, falcons and hummingbirds among the 171 species.

The **Proyecto Ecológico**, located on the northern shores of the lake, has spent many years observing and documenting this diverse wildlife. Founded in 1996 and managed by Dr Jeffrey McCrary, the project's most fascinating discovery is three new species of fish unique to the lake. These exciting finds could change the way that scientists think about evolution, as the lake itself is a relatively young phenomena and only 23,000 years old. Dr McCrary also thinks there are other endemic species waiting to be discovered.

But the lake's fragile ecosystem faces serious threats. Pollution from motorboats, leaking septic tanks, forest fires, deliberately introduced foreign species and illegal wood cutting are among them. But the most serious dangers come from a handful of foreign investors. Having acquired large tracts of land very cheaply, these developers are deforesting it, dividing it and selling it on, piece by piece.

Some speculate that this deforestation has contributed to the problem of the lake's rapidly diminishing water supply. The water level has dropped by 10 m in the last several years and continues to drop 30 cm per year. Deforestation of the area around the Pueblos Blancos has been particularly detrimental, where rainfall filters down to the subterranean rivers that feed the lagoon. Water levels are also being effected by human extraction, and some speculate that new cracks were formed by an earthquake in 2000, and these are also draining the lagoon.

Protecting the lagoon for future generations will be a real challenge. Part of the problem is finding a united approach to managing the reserve, which falls under the jurisdiction of several districts. Some foreigners have taken advantage of this lack of co-ordination by building properties illegally, often on unsafe land. Meanwhile, the sheer ruthlessness of some developers, who boast about their ability to 'buy ministers', mean conservationists are in for a tough fight.

If developments continue, Laguna de Apoyo's unique evolutionary arc will be permanently and disastrously interrupted. Like Laguna de Masaya and Tiscapa, it will become little more than a dead crater lake. Whilst environmentalists like Dr McCrary and groups like AMICTLAN (Asociación de Municipios Integrados por la Cuenca y Territorios de la Laguna de Apoyo) are working to raise awareness, it will require real political will to ensure the lake's long-term survival.

The Proyecto Ecológico is managed by FUNDECI-GAIA, one of Nicaragua's oldest NGOs. They are actively engaged in a broad range of conservation work including reforestation and the monitoring of local animal species. They offer several exciting volunteer programmes of both a scientific and hands-on nature, as well training in resource management, conservation and ecology. Research scientists and students are particularly welcome. If you would like to learn more, contact the Proyecto Ecológico directly, north shore of lake, T8882-3992, www.gaianicaragua.org. Their blog contains the latest news, www.lagunadeapoyo.blogspot.com.

Others choose to hike through the thickly forested surroundings, observing birds and other prolific wildlife.

Arriving in Reserva Natural Laguna de Apoyo

Getting there Access to the inside of the crater, its forest and lake shores is from two cobbled roads, one that starts near Monimbó and the other from the Carretera a Granada at Km 37.5. Both end in a tiny settlement called Valle de Apoyo that sits at the edge of the crater's north rim. From there, a steep road slices down the northern wall of the crater to the lake shore. It's easiest to go by car, but infrequent buses do run to the inside of the crater. There are daily buses to Valle de Apoyo from Masaya, or regular buses between Masaya and Granada; get off at Km 37.5 and walk up the 5-km access road. Hitchhiking is possible though traffic is sparse on weekdays. In Granada, several hostels including the **Bearded Monkey**, **La Libertad** and **El Chelero** offer daily transfers to Apoyo; they depart around 1000-1100, US$6 round-trip. The other alternative is a taxi from Granada (US$10-15) or Masaya (US$5-$7) or Managua (US$20-25).

Getting around Once you reach lake level, a left (east) turn takes you to the Spanish school, ecological station and **Monkey Hut**. To the right (west) are **Hotel Norome**, **San Simian**, the best nature walks, and tracks to Mirador de Catarina and Mirador de Diriá. Walking is the best way to enjoy the lake shore and nature.

Background

Created by a massive volcanic explosion some 23,000 years ago, the drop from the extinct crater's highest point to the lake is more than 400 m, and the lake itself is 6 km in diameter. The maximum depth of the water is yet to be discovered, but it is known to be at least 200 m deep (more than 70 m below sea level), making it the lowest point in Central America. When the Spanish arrived, Laguna de Apoyo was a central point for the Chorotega indigenous tribes, whose capital is thought to have been at Diriá, along the south upper rim of the crater above the lake. The basalt used for many of their ceremonial statues came from inside the crater. Today the reserve's only indigenous remains are petroglyphs submerged on the lower walls of the crater lake which can be seen using diving gear. The crater has seen some increased development in recent years, but at least half of it still consists of thick tropical dry forest (see box, page 95).

⊚ Around Masaya listings

For sleeping and eating price codes and other relevant information, see pages 28-30.

⊖ Places to stay

Parque Nacional Volcán Masaya *p91*
$$ Hotel Besa Flor, Km 19.8 Carretera a Masaya, 200 m sur, 500 m oeste, T2279-9845, www.hotel-besa-flor.de. Lovely hotel located close to Volcán Masaya national park. 5 rooms have private bath with hot water, Wi-Fi and free local calls. There's also a lush garden and access to a private nature

reserve. Spanish, English and German are spoken. Recommended.
$$ Hotel Volcán Masaya, Km 23, Carretera a Masaya, T2522-7114, hotelvolcan@hotmail. com. Great location in front of the volcano park, with spectacular views from the shared patio. Rooms have private bath, a/c, fridge and cable TV. The lobby area is good for relaxing.

Reserva Natural Laguna de Apoyo *p94*
$$$$-$$$ The Villas, on the western shores of the lake, T2552-8200, www.the

villasatapoyo.com. Formerly Norome Resort and Villas, this comfortable lodging boasts 66 high-quality villas (**$$$$-$$$**) and apartments (**$$$**) set back from the lake. Apartments have a/c, private bath and all amenities, but you'll pay US$10 more for one with a fully equipped kitchen. On the lakeshore there is a bar, restaurant, swimming pool, jacuzzi, and dock. Note this is a controversial project due to environmental impacts on lake water.

$$ San Simian, south of Norome Resort, T8813-6866, www.sansimian.com. A peaceful spot with 5 great *cabañas* with Balinese-style outdoor shower or bathtubs – perfect for a soak under the starry sky. Facilities include restaurant, bar, dock, hammocks, kayaks and a catamaran (US$15 per hr). Day use US$5. Yoga, massage, Spanish classes and manicure/pedicure can be arranged. Recommended.

$ Estación Ecológica (FUNDECI-GAIA), north shore of lake, follow signs for Apoyo Spanish School, T8882-3992, www.gaia nicaragua.org. Friendly, low-key lodging managed by biologist Dr Jeffry McCrary, an expert on the laguna's ecology. Accommodation is in simple dorms and rooms with tasty home-cooked meals served 3 times daily. Activities include reforestation (volunteers receive discounts), Spanish school, diving, kayaking and birdwatching. The research station also offers biology courses and is a great place to learn about conservation. It's close to the lake and walking trails and is highly recommended.

$ Monkey Hut, foot of the access road, 100 m north, T8887-3546, www.themonkey hut.net. Dorms, single and double rooms, and a lovely *cabaña* in front of the lake. Breakfast and dinner included. Can be booked with transfer from Granada. Canoe, kayak and sailing boat rentals and you can use facilities for US$6 if not a guest. A beautiful property with excellent views and a young backpacking clientele.

🍴 Restaurants

Nindirí *p94*

$$ El Bucanero, Km 26.5, Carretera a Masaya. A Cuban-owned favourite with sweeping views of Laguna Masaya and a loud, party atmosphere. There's a constantly changing menu of international and Nicaraguan dishes, including good beef. Worth it for the views.

$$-$ Restaurante La Llamarada, Iglesia, ½ c norte, T2522-4110. Daily 0900-2000. Attractive setting in the village, try the *lomo relleno*.

$$-$ Restaurante La Quinta, Alcaldía, ½ c norte. Mon-Fri 1000-2400, Sat-Sun 1000-0200. Great *plato típico* that includes pork, fried pork skin, beans and cream, fried cheese, fried plantains, grilled beef and tortilla.

🎯 What to do

Reserva Natural Laguna de Apoyo *p94*
Diving
Estación Ecológica (FUNDECI-GAIA), north shore, T8882-3992, www.gaia nicaragua.org. Visibility is generally good and native species include rainbow bass, freshwater turtles and various species which you will be asked to record for the purposes of scientific research (see box, page 95). A 2-tank dive with the project costs US$60; PADI open water certification US$305.

🚌 Transport

Reserva Natural Laguna de Apoyo *p94*
Buses to **Masaya**, 0630, 1130, 1630, 1 hr, US$0.50. To **Granada**, take a Masaya bus, exit on the highway and catch a Granada-bound bus. **Shuttles** to **Granada** depart daily from the Monkey Hut Hostel, around 1600, 30 mins, US$6 (return). **Taxi** to **Granada** costs US$10-15, to **Masaya** US$5.

Nindirí *p94*
Buses to **Granada**, **Masaya** and **Managua** pass every 15 mins along the Carretera.

❶ Directory

Reserva Natural Laguna de Apoyo
p94
Language schools
Apoyo Intensive Spanish School, inside
Estación Ecológica (FUNDECI-GAIA), T8882-

3992, www.gaianicaragua.org. Nicaragua's
oldest Spanish school and still one of the
best. One-to-one instruction with complete
immersion, 1 week US$220, 2 weeks US$430,
3 weeks US$630, 4 weeks US$810; all rates
include meals and lodging, native instructors
and 3 excursions per week. Excellent tutors.

Los Pueblos Blancos

The Carretera a Los Pueblos runs south from Masaya and upon leaving the city rises to an average 500 m above sea level. Due to its elevation, it is one of the most agreeable areas in Nicaragua. The mesa is cooler than the lake valley where León, Managua and Granada sweat out the afternoon sun and most of it remains green throughout the dry season. Los Pueblos are shared politically by the separate provinces of Masaya, Granada and Carazo, but they are really one continuous settlement. This area, like Monimbó and Nindirí, is the land of the Chorotegas. Although you will not hear local languages nor see a particular style of dress (as in the Guatemalan highlands, for example), most of the people of Los Pueblos are of Chorotega ancestry. The Chorotega Empire stretched from the Gulf of Fonseca in Honduras to what is today the Nicoya Peninsula of Costa Rica. Made up of 28 chiefdoms, the capital for this large, remarkably democratic empire was here in the highlands of La Meseta. It is believed that the chiefs from all 28 local governments came to meet here every seven years to elect a new leader. Today the local people have a very quiet but firm pride in their pre-Conquest history and culture. ▸▸ *For listings, see pages 104-106.*

Arriving in Los Pueblos de la Meseta

Getting there and around Los Pueblos de la Meseta have a very fluid network of buses in between towns and to Masaya and Managua; less so to Granada. A hired taxi from Managua is not too expensive due to relatively short distances involved with most villages less than 50 km from the capital. Outside Masaya there are limited taxis, but bicycle rickshaws can usually be found within a village. At the entrance to Catarina is a highway that cuts across the Meseta from east to west passing through the outskirts of Niquinohomo, Masatepe, Jinotepe and Diriamba and continuing to the Pacific Coast.

Catarina

This attractive hillside colonial-period village has a simple church built in 1778 and an obvious love of potted plants. From the highway, the town climbs up the extinct cone of the Apoyo volcano until its highest point overlooking the majestic deep blue crater lake of Laguna de Apoyo. Between the highway and the lookout point are numerous horticultural nurseries and Nicaraguans come here from around the country to buy their houseplants. There are also a number of artisans who specialize in heavy carved wooden furniture, bamboo furniture and baskets. The lookout point above the crater lake, **Mirador de Catarina**, has an entrance fee of US$0.80 if you come by car. On the rim of the Mirador there is a row of restaurants that share the magnificent view across the lake. From the lookout you can see the dormant Mombacho Volcano and its cloud forest as well as the city of Granada, Lake Nicaragua and part of the Las Isletas archipelago. This area is crowded on Sundays with families and young couples, but quiet during the week. Due to its perch-like position it is breezy all year round but in the dry season the wind can be a bit strong. The walk down into the crater is easy, with spectacular views; the hike back up is quite strenuous – it's only about 500 m, but a very steady climb. Ask at the mirador for the trailhead and then keep asking on the way down as it's easy to get lost (see also Laguna de Apoyo, page 94). For more information on trails and activities around Catarina, stop by the new **Centro de Visitantes de la Reserva Natural de Laguna de Apoyo** ① *entrada principal de San Juan de Oriente, 1 c norte, 1 c arriba, T2558-0456, www.apoyolalaguna.com, Tue-Sat 0800-1700*. Catarina's patron saint, Santa Catalina, is celebrated on 26 November, but the town's big fiesta is for San Silvestre, on 31 December and 1 January (see box, page 86).

San Juan de Oriente

Across the highway from Catarina and just south is the traditional Chorotega village of San Juan de Oriente, which has gained international recognition for its elegant ceramic earthenware. Local clay has been used here to make hand-shaped pottery for at least 1000 years. Until about 25 years ago, all the houses in the village were made of adobe, however these have been replaced by stone-block constructions. Today, the distinguishing feature of the village is the tremendous creativity and dexterity of its population.

After the Spanish conquest, much of the ornamental expertise evident in pre-Columbian ceramics was lost, but the tradition continued until the 20th century. For many years, the village was known as San Juan de los Platos, because of the rustic ceramic plates it produced. In addition to plates, the villagers continue to make clay pots for plants and storing water (*tinajas*), which are still used today throughout rural Nicaragua.

In 1978, the Nicaraguan Ministry of Culture and the country's Central Bank initiated a programme of training scholarships. Eleven people from the village learned how to use a potter's kick-wheel for the first time, how to balance the mixture of the native clay with sand for added strength, and how to polish and paint pieces in the pre-Columbian style that had been lost in the centuries since the conquest. These 11 artists formed the **Artesanos Unidos**, the town's first co-operative. After the success of the Revolution, the Sandinista administration helped to support and promote the co-operative's work and the influx of foreigners provided a more affluent clientele.

In true Nicaraguan fashion, the skills and knowledge have been unselfishly passed on to other members of the community. Today at least 80% of the villagers who are old enough are involved in some aspect of pottery production and sales. The creativity of their designs and the quality of their work is excellent and their products can be found in many markets and shops across Central America. To buy direct from the source or to see the artisans at work, you can visit the artisans' co-operative, **Cooperativa Quetzal-Coatl** ① *25 m inside the 1st entrance to the town, T2558-0337, www.cooperativaquetzalcoatl. wordpress.com, daily 0800-1700*.

The ceramic artists sell direct from their home workshops and may invite you in to see the process, these include: **Francisco Calero** ① *Taller Escuela de Cerámica, ½ c arriba, T2558-0300*; **Róger Calero** ① *Iglesia, 2 c sur, T2558-0007*; **Juan Paulino Martínez** ① *across from Restaurante Quilite, T2558-0025*; and **Duilio Jiménez** ① *opposite los juzgados, next to the women's co-operative*, who is very welcoming. The most acclaimed of the ceramic artists is **Helio Gutiérrez** ① *2nd entrance, 1 c abajo, 300 m sur, T2558-0338*.

San Juan's small and precious early 17th-century church was badly shaken by the Laguna de Apoyo earthquake in 2000, which was followed a week later by the earthquake in Masaya. It has now been restored.

Diriá

Heading south towards the Mombacho Volcano on the highway that separates Catarina and San Juan de Oriente, there is another set of historic twin villages: Diriá and Diriomo. Diriá, in historical terms, is the most important of all Los Pueblos de la Meseta. It was here that the Chorotega elders met to elect new officials and from where the fierce Chorotega chief Diriangén ruled when the Spanish arrived to impose their dominance. Today it is one of the sleepiest of the highland pueblos, only really coming to life during festivals. **La Parroquia de San Pedro** church was first erected in 1650, damaged and rebuilt after an earthquake in 1739 and restored once again in 2003. It is a charming, simple construction in the Spanish colonial style with the bell tower a safe distance from the church in this highly seismic zone.

Diriá occupies part of the shoreline and upper rim of the Laguna de Apoyo. In some ways the lookout point here is more spectacular than the more developed complex at Catarina. There are several simple bars and eateries and a small Virgin Mary that stares out across the lake-filled crater. Access to the Diriá mirador is from the south of the church due east past the baseball diamond and the seminary. The people of Diriá are fond of statues and their central park has three interesting ones. On the north side is Moses with his Ten Commandments and on the south side is King Solomon. In the shaded part of the park is Chief Diriangén ready for battle and surrounded by idols. At the exit of the town is a mother nursing her child, the focal point for many festivals.

Diriomo

This farming centre is a charming town with a friendly populace that seems more open and relaxed than its twin, Diriá. Sorcery and folk healing is widely practised in Diriomo, a likely centre for magical activity prior to the Spanish conquest. Charms, potions, spells, incantations and readings are available from the various *brujos* and *curanderos* that work in town. If you're in the market for such spiritual remedies, or would simply like to know more, ask around for personal recommendations or enquire at the Alcaldía to find a reputable practitioner.

Nicaragua's traditional sweets, known as *cajetas*, are an art form in Diriomo. The most famous of the sweet houses is **La Casa de las Cajetas** ① *Parque Central, opposite the church, T2557-0015, cajeta@datatex.com.ni, tours available, call ahead,* founded in 1908 by the grandmother of the aging Socorro, who oversees operations today with the help of her grandchildren. The sweets are a combination of sugar, rice and various fruits; the most unusual is the *cajeta de zapoyol* which is made from the seed of the *zapote* fruit. Another, slightly less sophisticated, sweet house is that of **Hortensia González** ① *Enitel, 2 c norte,* whose family has 60 years of experience in making excellent *cajetas* (*dulce de leche,* or caramel sweet).

The **Iglesia Santuario de Nuestra Señora de Candelaria**, home of the town's patron saint, is a very attractive church but it suffered some damage in the earthquakes of 2000. The church was built over the course of over 100 years from 1795 using a mixture of stone and brick, each stone being carried from a hill more than 1 km away. The church's cupola is said to have been inspired by the architecture of Tuscany while the façade combines baroque and neoclassical design – a result of its long period of construction. The roof is supported by 12 solid posts of cedar, each 12 m in height. This is one of the most visually pleasing structures in Nicaragua and deserves to receive funding to repair its damage.

Niquinohomo

This quiet colonial-period village founded in 1548 by the Spanish is best known for its famous son, the nationalist rebel General Augusto C Sandino (perhaps the only

Nicaraguan who claims more attention is the León poet Rubén Darío). Tellingly, the name Niquinohomo is Chorotega for 'Valley of the Warriors'.

The town's entrance is marked by a small church and a statue of Sandino, a bronze relief of the nationalist warrior in memory of his legendary determination and integrity. The rebel general's childhood home is today the **public library** ⓘ *Parque Central, opposite the gigantic cross that guards the church, Mon-Fri 0900-1200 and 1400-1800*, and houses a small display on the life of Sandino.

The pride of the village is the town's stately church, finished in 1689. Both the classic exterior and clean simple interior of this long and elegant colonial church are pleasing to the eye, despite an unfortunate cement cross at the front. For the most part, the village is pleasant, if a bit lacking in energy. The Niquinohomo cemetery, on the far west side of the town, is well kept, brightly painted and pretty.

The village is also known for its original bamboo lamps, shaped mostly as pineapples, seen throughout Nicaragua. You can visit the artisan, Juan Norori, at his shop **Artesanías Pueblos Blancos** ⓘ *Empalme de Niquinohomo, 1 km norte, T2607-1278*.

Nandasmo

Nandasmo is several kilometres west of Niquinohomo and borders the south side of the beautiful Laguna de Masaya. The village itself feels neglected; it is a place few outsiders see and foreigners are greeted with wide eyes. However, it has a pleasant climate and a steady breeze from the lake. From the highway it is a 5-km walk to the Laguna de Masaya, where the views of the volcanoes and the city of Masaya are spectacular. It is possible to walk to Masaya from here although you will have to rely on local farmers to keep you on the right path. Past the entrance to Nandasmo, the highway leads to Masatepe and becomes an endless roadside market, with furniture makers displaying their wares in front of their workshop-homes. The village comes to life – in a big way – for its patron saint festival on 26 July.

Masatepe

This colonial-period village and ancient Chorotega settlement is now the furniture capital of Nicaragua; its production dwarfs the rest of the nation's shops combined. Dining room sets, wicker baby cribs, hardwood bed frames and dressers, and the wonderful rocking chairs that are found in almost every house in Nicaragua, are made here in every style and type of wood imaginable. This is when many travellers wish they were going home on a boat rather than a plane. In addition to the countless roadside workshops that sell their products, there is a big store at the entrance to the town, in the old railway station. The town itself is warmer than most of the other pueblos of the region. Rickshaw taxis wait at the town entrance to take visitors on a small tour of the village for US$3 and, although the **Iglesia San Juan Bautista de Masatepe** is not particularly interesting, it has a views of the smoking Masaya Volcano. The pueblo is famous also for its *cajeta* sweets, said to be among the best in Nicaragua, and it is the home of one of Nicaragua's fàvourite dishes, the *sopa de mondongo* (tripe soup).

San Marcos

Eight kilometres west of Masatepe, the pueblos highway enters the scenic coffee-growing department of Carazo and the university town of San Marcos, home to Central America's only US-accredited English-speaking university, with courses given mostly by North American professors. **Ave María College of the Americas** ⓘ *T2535-2314, www.avemaria.*

El Güegüence: comedy and identity

In Nicaragua the name is omnipresent. The play *El Güegüence* is about humour, corruption, the power of language and the clever art of revenge, and it defines the very essence of what it means to be Nicaraguan.

Although the play's author is anonymous, it was almost certainly first written down between 1683 and 1710 in a mixture of Náhuatl and Spanish. The author was a master of languages and colonial law and had a sharp sense of humour. The play is both hilarious and profound in its use of language and comic timing. It is laced with double meanings, many to insult the Spanish colonial ruler who plays the sucker. The humour is often vulgar and all the characters in the play are targets. The great José Martí called it a "master comedy" and León's vanguard poet, Salomón de la Selva, said it was, "as good as or better than what we know of Greek comedy before Aristophanes". The work has been analysed by just about every Nicaraguan intellectual of any note who all have their own conception of the play's deeper meaning. However, they agree it to be a master play of American indigenous theatre and a source of cultural pride for Nicaragua.

The plot is simple: *El Güegüence* is an indigenous trader in goods, some contraband, all of great variety, some of high value. He is called in by the local colonial chief of police for a bribe. He first plays semi-deaf, then stupid to avoid the subject of payment in a very funny 'who's on first?' type of skit. Eventually he is brought in to meet with the governor and he befriends him with his ingenuity, his humour and brilliantly funny lies. *El Güegüence* then manages to marry off one of his boys to the daughter of the governor by changing his reality from that of abject poverty to feigning immense wealth.

El Güegüence is the need of the Nicaraguan sense of humour to maintain pride, combat state corruption, salvage a seemingly hopeless situation with wit and break the chains of class structure. The use of laughter and irony to face difficult situations and the capacity to laugh at oneself are essential to the Nicaraguan character.

edu.ni, is in the south of the town, its large student population (mostly well-off Central Americans) adding a vibrant atmosphere quite different to the rest of the mesa.

In 2005, the oldest evidence of organized settlement was unearthed in San Marcos in an archaeological excavation by the National Museum. The ceramic and human remains date from 2500 BC making San Marcos older than the organized settlements in Managua and Los Angeles, Ometepe, previously believed to be the most ancient. The Spanish did not place much importance in the town, suggesting that it was not densely populated at the time of their arrival, and it remained a big ranch until the mid-19th century. Today, the town is clean and pleasant with a lively Parque Central, especially during the patron saint festival for San Marcos, which culminates on 24 April in the **Tope de las imágenes de San Marcos** (see box, page 86). The rather plain-looking church is colourful inside with a series of murals on the aqua ceiling. Above the altar is a fresco of Saint Mark in the tropics, complete with volcanoes in the distance. San Marcos is also the birthplace of Anastasio Somoza García (the first of the two rulers), whose mother owned a bakery in town and whose father had a coffee farm just outside the village. Somoza's home town is just a few kilometres down the road from Niquinohomo, the birthplace of his nemesis, Augusto C Sandino.

South from San Marcos is the highway to the Carazo department's two principal towns, **Jinotepe** and **Diriamba**. One kilometre before Jinotepe is the Nicaraguan version of Disneyland, a Herty Lewites-inspired theme park called **Hertylandia** ① *T2532-2155, hertyland@hotmail.com, Wed-Sun 0900-1800, US$5 entry to both sections, US$2 entry to amusement section only, additional charges for each ride US$0.50-2*. Herty Lewites, ex-rebel gunrunner, Minister of Tourism and Mayor of Managua from 2000 to 2004, tried to mount a bid for president in 2006 but died of a heart attack four months before the election. Hertylandia is a very simple amusement park in a green and spacious setting. The rides are specifically aimed at children. There are two separate sections, one with a big swimming pool and water slide and the other with mechanical rides.

Jinotepe
① *INTUR office, Palí, 1 c sur, T2532-0298, carazo@intur.gob.ni, Richard Acuña has information on the region and maps.*
Another pleasant highland colonial built on top of a Chorotega village, Jinotepe has a coffee- and agriculture-based economy and some pretty, older homes. The town prides itself on being the cleanest of the pueblos, although conditions at the bus station do little to support that theory. On the whole, though, it is clean and attractive. The city has a fine neoclassical church with some modern stained-glass windows, **La Iglesia Parroquial de Santiago** (1878), that almost appears to be a scale model of the Cathedral of León.

Diriamba
In comparison with many other pueblos on the mesa, Diriamba is a slightly grungy, disorganized place. Here the locals are a bit different from the rest. The bicycle-powered taxis have been modified to use little motors and the population tends to hang out more in the streets. The town's people are famously good looking, open and friendly. Diriamba was one of the most important Chorotega settlements in Nicaragua when the Spanish first arrived in 1523 and it has been heavily populated for over a millennium. A statue of Chorotega Chief Diriangén, Nicaragua's oldest symbol of resistance, stands proudly over Parque Central, although the spear is now missing from his outstretched hand. It was at Diriamba that the late 17th-century anti-establishment comedy and focal point of Nicaraguan culture, *El Güegüence*, is thought to have originated, and it is performed during the town's patron saint festival for San Sebatián (see box, page 86).

One of the grandest of the pueblos churches can be found in front of Diriamba's tired-looking Parque Central. Most of the buildings around the park were destroyed by the National Guard as the populace rebelled against Somoza in the 1978 Revolution, but the church stands proud with an elegant domed interior flooded with ambient light and sporting much fine woodwork. The **Museo Ecológico Trópico Seco** ① *costado sur Policía Nacional, T2534-2129, www.adeca.org.ni/museo_eco, Mon-Fri 0800-1200, 1400-1700, Sat 0800-1200*, provides an interesting ecological and geographical overview of the region and deals with conservation issues such as the effect of agriculture on local ecosystems.

The Pacific Coast of La Meseta → *For listings, see pages 104-106.*

La Boquita
The department of Carazo has 40 km of Pacific Ocean coastline with crashing waves and light grey sand. La Boquita, 25 km on rough paved highway from Diriamba, is a popular beach during the dry season and particularly Semana Santa (Easter week), which can be

a raucous occasion here. For the rest of the year it is a fairly quiet, slightly artificial tourist centre that is popular with Nicaraguan families. It's not a spectacular spot, but pleasant enough and there are many little ranch-style restaurants that serve fresh fish against the background sound of the sea. If you are driving, there is a US$1.50 entrance fee to the parking area. Do not swim in the estuary in the dry season when it becomes polluted.

Casares
South of La Boquita, where the Río Casares drains into the Pacific, is the small, authentic and friendly fishing village of Casares. At the northern part of the beach are the homes of wealthy Managuans. There is little tourist infrastructure here, little shade, and a few very cheap places to eat. Fishing is done in little fibreglass boats with outboards. The ocean has strong currents here and it is not unusual for bathers to get caught out, even when close to the shore. Travel further south is possible by 4WD only and even they are known to get stuck attempting the river crossings. If you're heading south, the best access is from the Santa Teresa exit of the Pan-American Highway.

⊚ Los Pueblos Blancos listings

For sleeping and eating price codes and other relevant information, see pages 28-30.

⊜ Places to stay

San Marcos *p101*
$$ Hotel Casa Blanca, across from the Baptist church, T2535-2717, www.hotel casa blanca.com.ni. A very friendly, pleasant hotel with a family atmosphere and 16 clean rooms; some have a/c. There's Wi-Fi, hammocks, relaxing garden, breakfast included and 2 conference centres. Ask about the monthly rate for 'snow birds'. Recommended.
$$ Hotel and Restaurante Lagos y Volcanes, La Concepción, San Marcos, 4 km sur, Instituto Guillermo Ampie, 1.5 km arriba, lagosyvolcanes@hotmail. com. Surrounded by citrus trees and offering great views of Laguna Masaya, this hotel has 15 attractive rooms with good beds, cable TV, bath and hot water. Facilities include a good restaurant and pool.

Jinotepe *p103*
Jinotepe has the region's best accommodation, making it a good base for exploring the other pueblos.

$$ Casa Mateo, Esso station, 4 c sur, 2½ c arriba, T2532-3284, www.hotelcasa mateo.com. Formerly **Hotel Casa Grande**, this comfortable 3-storey hotel has 40 good rooms, some with a/c. Services include Wi-Fi, tours, massage and laundry. There's also a decent restaurant attached serving breakfasts (included in rates) and *comida típica*. Proceeds go to fund Quinta Esperanza, a centre for abused or neglected children. Excellent central location and the best place in town. Discounts for missionaries.

Diriamba *p103*
$$ Tortuga Verde, Residencial Regina, Km 40.5 carretera sur, about 1 km outside Diramba. T2534-2948, www.ecolodgecarazo. com. This well-presented eco-hotel has a range of comfortable rooms with Wi-Fi, cable TV, fan and hot water. It also has a beautiful lush garden that was once part of a coffee plantation. Recommended.
$ Diriangén, Shell station, 1 c arriba, ½ c sur, T2534-2428. 11 simple rooms with private bath, fan, parking. A friendly, family-run place.

La Boquita *p103*
$ Hospedaje La Boquita, on the beach. Locally owned hotel with a mix of ocean

front rooms with private bath and a/c, and some much cheaper lodgings with fan. A great location. Friendly.

$ Parador Suleyka. Formerly **Palmas del Mar**, this hotel has been recently acquired by new owners and was undergoing renovation at the time of research. When complete it should have 14 rooms with private bath and fan. Located at the heart of the tourist centre.

Casares p104

$$ Hotel Lupita, Cruz Verde, 800 m sur, T2552-8708, lupita41@ibw.com.ni. 16 rooms on Casares Beach with private bath, a/c, cable TV, swimming pool, steps to the beach, clean and pretty with nice views.

🍴 Restaurants

Catarina p98

$$ El Túnel, at the Mirador de Catarina on the far north side of the wooden deck, T2558-0303. 0700-2000. Order *a la plancha*, which comes as a sizzling plate of meat served with fried plantains, fried cheese, rice and salad, US$7.

Diriá p100

$ Cafetería La Plaza, north side of the church, T557-0207. Simple, open-air place offering good *comida corriente*.

Diriomo p100

$ El Aguacate, on the Carretera from the petrol station at town entrance 150 vrs al norte. Wild game dishes like *cuzuco* (armadillo) and *guardatinaja* (paca), traditional dishes are also excellent, good value.

Masatepe p101

$$-$ Mi Terruño Masatepino, Km 54, Carretera a Masatepe, T8887-4949. Daily 0900-2100. Traditional dishes like *indio viejo* and Masatepe's own *sopa de mondongo*. *Cuajada* with tortilla is great here, as is the *sopa de albóndiga*, a popular soup that has

meatballs made of chicken, eggs, garlic and corn meal. *Sopa de iguana* can often be found here. Most meals are US$3-5. A very big dish of assorted traditional foods is US$10, but feeds 2. Also try one of Nicaragua's grainy local drinks like *posol* and *tiste* served in an original *jícaro* gourd cup. Great coffee produced locally and roasted at home. This is the pueblos' most authentic eating experience and well worth a visit. The sign outside says simply *platos típicos*.

San Marcos p101

$ La Casona Coffee Shop, ENITEL, 1 c norte. 'Where cool people hang out', according to their own publicity material. A very fine eatery, popular with students and serving good coffee, cakes, pastas and salads. Recommended.

Jinotepe p103

$$ Bar y Restaurante Sardina, Km 49.5 Carretera Sur, T8889-4261. Outdoor dining and drinking under a ranch-style thatched roof. Good seafood and beef dishes, pleasant atmosphere and service.
$$ Buen Provecho, next to Colisseo, T2532-1145. Sun-Fri 1100-1500. Try the baked chicken or beef in asparagus.
$$-$ Pizzería Colisseo, Parque Central, 1 c norte, T2532-2150, colisseo@ibw.com.ni. Tue-Sun 1200-2200. The most famous pizzas in Nicaragua. Some customers drive from Managua to eat here. They serve pasta too.
$ Casa Blanca, Cruz Lorena, 1 c arriba, T2532-2379. Daily 1000-2200. Something different – Chinese food.

Diriamba p103

$$ Mi Bohio, Museo, 1 c arriba, T2534-2437. Founded in 1972, a good, clean restaurant serving chicken in wine sauce, soups and *ceviche* among other dishes.

La Boquita p103

At least one good restaurant serving excellent seafood.

⊖ Transport

Catarina and San Juan de Oriente
p98
Buses pass through Catarina every 15 mins to **Masaya**, **San Marcos** or **Rivas**. Buses to **Granada** are less frequent; take a bus towards Masaya and get off on the highway to Granada for a connecting bus.

Diriá and Diriomo *p100*
Buses run along the highway nearby. For **Granada** take any bus heading east, get off at Empalme de Guanacaste and take bus heading north. For **Masaya** and **Managua** buses pass every 20 mins.

Niquinohomo and Masatepe
p100 and p101
Buses pass on the highway between **Catarina** and **San Marcos** every 15 mins. Express bus to **Managua**, every 30 mins, 0500-1700, US$1.50, 1 hr 15 mins.

San Marcos *p101*
Buses run to **Managua** via La Concepción highway and to **Jinotepe** and **Rivas** (south) and **Masatepe** (east). Buses west connect with the Carretera Sur (Carretera Panamericana), from where buses can be caught south to **Diriamba** or north to **Managua**. To **Managua** every 20 mins, 0600-2000, US$1, 1 hr.

Jinotepe *p103*
As the capital of the western pueblos region, Jinotepe has good bus connections with many express options to **Managua**, some of which go to the centrally located La UCA (University stop) next to Metrocentro. The rest use Mercado Israel Lewites (also called Mercado Boer). To **Managua**, every 20 mins, 0530-1800, US$1.10, 1 hr 15 mins to Mercado Lewites. Express bus to **Managua**, every 15 mins, 0600-2000, US$1.10, 1 hr 25 mins to la UCA. To **Rivas**, express buses every 30 mins, 0540-1710, US$1.50, 1 hr 45 mins; and 9 regular buses daily. To **Granada**, express buses hourly, 0600-1600, US$1.10, 1 hr 25 mins; and 6 regular buses daily. To **Masaya**, express buses every 15 mins, 0500-1800, US$0.55, 1 hr 15 mins.

Diriamba *p103*
Buses run to central terminal at **Jinotepe** every 15 mins, US$0.25. To **Managua**, every 20 mins, 0530-1800, US$1, 1 hr 15 mins.

⊕ Directory

San Marcos *p101*
Bank BAC, next to Ave María College, T2535-2339, cash from credit cards and TCs. **Police** Parque Central, T2535-2296.

Jinotepe *p103*
Bank Bancentro, north side of the church, T2532-1432, can change Amex TCs. **Fire** T2532-2241. **Hospital** T2532-2611. **Police** T2532-2510. **Red Cross** T2532-2500.

Contents

At a glance

⊖ **Getting around** The city of
Granada is easily navigable on foot.
Outside attractions can be reached
by taxi, boat or local bus.

⊗ **Time required** 5-7 days.

☀ **Weather** Granada is hot year
round but due to its lakefront
location it does not suffer from
as much dust and smoke during
the dry season as other towns.
The prettiest time of year is the
rainy season, Jun-Oct.

⊗ **When not to go** If planning a
trip on the lake, avoid the windy
months, Nov-Mar.

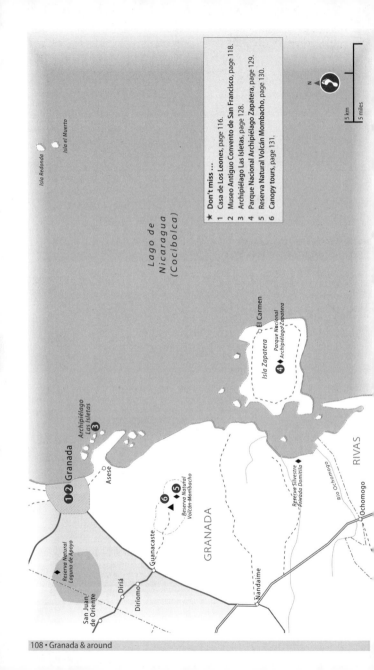

Isla Redonda

Isla el Muerto

Lago de
Nicaragua
(Cocibolca)

Archipiélago
Los Isletas

② Granada

Asese

Isla Zapatera

El Carmen

Parque Nacional
Archipiélago Zapatera ④

Reserva Natural
Volcán-Mombacho

⑥⑤

Guanacaste

Reserva Silvestre
Privada Domitilla

RÍO OCHOMOGO

RIVAS

Ochomogo

GRANADA

Nandaime

Diriá

Diriomo

San Juan
de Oriente

Reserva Natural
Laguna de Apoyo

★ Don't miss ...
1 Casa de Los Leones, page 116.
2 Museo Antiguo Convento de San Francisco, page 118.
3 Archipiélago Las Isletas, page 128.
4 Parque Nacional Archipiélago Zapatera, page 129.
5 Reserva Natural Volcán Mombacho, page 130.
6 Canopy tours, page 131.

N

5 km
5 miles

A bastion of old money and conservatism, Granada is Nicaragua's most handsome and romantic city. Plied by horse-drawn carriages and overlooked by regal volcanoes, it's an endlessly photogenic place that blends wistful colonial grandeur with teeming local street life. Centuries of attacks by marauding pirates and North American filibusters mean that many of the city's elegant Spanish houses, colourful churches and thronging public squares are careful reconstructions of earlier structures. Fortunately, Granada has remained faithful to its original design and despite its numerous reinventions has maintained its good looks. Today, Granada has earned its place as a major tourist hub. Weary travellers will delight in the city's well-developed infrastructure, its reputable hotels and restaurants, and its abundance of helpful tour operators. Others may argue that Granada – Nicaragua's most visited destination – is in danger of losing itself under the growing swell of foreign interest.

For the moment, however, Granada remains very much a Nicaraguan city – one full of history, spirit and indomitable good character. Beyond its fine restaurant scene and disarming aesthetic charms, you'll find scores of outdoor attractions to entice you. The expansive waters of Central America's largest freshwater lake, Lake Nicaragua (or Lago Cocibolca, as it's known locally), are home to hundreds of scattered isles and enclaves, many of them occupied by lost-in-time fishing communities. Some of them, like Isla Zapatera, contain striking evidence of ancient inhabitation. Then there's Volcán Mombacho, looming darkly to the south. This is Nicaragua's best-managed wildlife reserve, boasting well-tended trails, commanding views, diverse flora and fauna and, for those seeking adrenalin-charged encounters with the arboreal canopy, high-speed zip-lines. Finally, the peaceful and bucolic farming villages surrounding the city are worthy destinations in themselves. Granada, it seems, is not just a pretty face.

Granada

Granada's burgeoning tourist trade has forged an inevitable disparity between the locals and foreigners. The Parque Central is the hub of the city's social life and is often thronging with activity: strolling families, hawkers, street kids, scavenging dogs, canoodling lovers and groups of tourists straight off the bus. The city centre is prettified and perfect for strolling, but real estate prices have soared here in recent years with expats and foreign businesses staking a hefty claim in Granada's future. Despite this, the city remains fascinating: between the carefully crafted colonial façades, there is still plenty of local colour, often supplied by the inhabitants of the city's impoverished and ramshackle barrios. Many of the old houses around town remain the property of families who have been here for generations and it's hard not to steal glances through the open doors of those high-ceilinged homes, catching intimate glimpses of everyday Granadino life. The challenge of the future is a balancing act between authenticity and pretence, substance and form, progress and identity. The current King of Spain summed it up during a visit here: "Don't touch anything", he remarked. ▸▸ *For listings, see pages 118-127.*

Arriving in Granada → *Population: 111,500. Altitude: 60 m. Colour map 3, B4.*

Getting there
Boat There is a ferry service from San Carlos, a challenging 12- to 14-hour journey across Lake Nicaragua that connects with river boats from Río San Juan and Los Chiles, Costa Rica. En route it stops at Altagracia, Isla Ometepe.

Bus There are express buses from Managua's UCA terminal and slow buses from Roberto Huembes market, as well as services from Rivas in the south. International bus companies **Transnica**, **King Quality** and **Ticabus** stop in Granada on some of their routes north from Costa Rica.

Car If coming from the north, take the Carretera a Masaya, turn right at the Esso station upon entering the city and then left up Calle Real towards the centre. If coming from the south, use the Carretera a Granada. You will enter at the cemetery; continue north to the Calle Real and turn east towards the lake to reach the centre.

Getting around
Granada's city centre is small and manageable on foot. Parque Central is the best reference point and the cathedral is visible from most of the city. There are three main streets: leading from the Fortaleza de La Pólvora, at the western extreme of the old centre, **Calle Real** runs east (*al lago*) past several churches to the central square. The road continues as Calle El Calmito east of the park and on to the lake. Running perpendicular is **Calle Atravesada**, one block west of Parque Central, behind the Hotel Alhambra. This street runs from the old railway station in the north of the city past Parque Central and south to Granada market. It has most of the cheap eating and night entertainment. The other important route, **Calle Calzada**, starts at the big cross on Parque Central and runs east towards the lake, past many beautiful homes, colourful restaurants and small *hospedajes*, ending at Lake Nicaragua and the city port. Much of the city's beauty can be appreciated within an area of five blocks around the centre. The east side of the Parque Central is generally much quieter with far fewer cars and trucks. ▸▸ *For further details, see Transport, page 126.*

Community tourism around Granada

Granada may well be the country's most conventional tourist destination, but it offers opportunities for some great alternative experiences too. Founded in 1984, **UCA Tierra y Agua** (Union of Agriculture and Fishing Cooperatives 'Earth and Water') is a union of nine co-operatives, one women's association and more than 150 families who supplement their farming-based income with tourism services. This excellent organization arranges tours and homestays in three different communities and your money will directly contribute to their upkeep.

At the base of Mombacho volcano, **La Granadilla** and **Nicaragua Libre** are farming communities offering guided hikes in the cloud forest reserve, horse riding, cycling and tours of the plantations. Your guide will explain the many responsibilities of agricultural life and, if

you wish, introduce you to members of the community. At **Agua Agrias** you can hike within an attractive nature reserve and bathe in freshwater streams and lakes. Economical and often delicious meals are available at all three communities.

The best way to learn about Nicaraguan life is to live it. A homestay with a Nicaraguan family, no matter how brief, will afford you a priceless opportunity to observe the daily rhythms of life. And if you roll up your sleeves and muck in, all the better. Rustic homestays are available at La Granadilla for around US$3 per person per night. There's a comfortable hostel at Nicaragua Libre, US$5 per person per night.

For more information and help planning your visit, contact **UCA Tierra y Agua**, Shell Palmira 75 vrs abajo, Monday, Wednesday, Friday 0830-1400, T2552-0238, www.ucatierrayagua.org.

Tourist information

INTUR ⓘ *Iglesia San Francisco, opposite the southwest corner, on Calle Arsenal, T2552-6858, www.visitanicaragua.com, Mon-Fri 0800-1300*, one of the better INTUR offices. Plenty of flyers, maps and brochures and, if you're lucky, English-speaking staff. Elsewhere, a good source of local information is the tourist directory, **Anda Ya**, www.andayanicaragua.com, available in hotels and restaurants throughout town.

Safety

The centre of Granada is generally safe, but can become very empty after 2100 and some thefts have been reported. Police presence is almost non-existent on week nights so always take precautions. Avoid walking alone at night, avoid the barrios outside the centre. Take care along the waterfront at any time of day and avoid it completely after dark.

Background

Granada was founded by Captain Francisco Hernández de Córdoba around 21 April 1524 (the same year as León, and Nicaraguan historians have been arguing ever since to establish which was the first city of Nicaragua). The original wall, which divided the Spanish and Indian sectors of Granada, can be seen today just southeast of the Xalteva church. In 1585, a French chronicler described a religious procession in the city as rich in gold and emeralds, with Indian dances that lasted for the duration of the procession and a line of very well-dressed Spaniards, although the total Spanish population was estimated at only 200. Granada became a major commercial centre and when the Irish friar Thomas

A time of dreams and roses: Granada's poetry festival

I want to express my anguish in verses
that speak of my vanished youth, a time
of dreams and roses ...
Rubén Darío (1867-1916)

Each February, Granada's elegant colonial courtyards, historic houses, public squares and churches reverberate to the sounds of poetic verse. Since 2005, an annual festival of poetry has been attracting over 100 scribes and thousands of spectators from around the world. Concerts, art exhibits, theatrical performances and impassioned debates accompany the lyrical occasion, but it is recitals from some of the world's finest poets, both Nicaraguan and international, that make it such an important event. Attended with all the vigour of a Catholic mass, these recitals are a rousing testament to Nicaragua's long-standing infatuation with poetic form.

Granada's poetic roots reach back to the Vanguardia movement of the late 1920s, an alliance of formidable wordsmiths like José Coronel Urtecho, Joaquín Pasos and Pablo Antonio Cuadra, who would meet in the city's public spaces to exchange ideas. Radical and confrontational, the Vanguardia's contributions were important and lasting, and marked a significant departure from Rubén Darío's *modernismo*.

Today, escaping the enduring shadow of this great 'Father of Modernism' is once again the challenge of Nicaragua's newest generation of poets, who are striving to define themselves in a political climate that is largely unsympathetic to creative endeavour. The closure of UCA humanities programmes, the rising cost of books, falling literacy rates and the growing popularity of television mean that they have their work cut out for them. Still, Granada's annual poetry festival, organized and funded privately, is a sign of impending cultural revitalization. The attending crowds of mainly working-class Nicaraguans demonstrate that public enthusiasm for literature has not abated, even if government support has. And the themes of Nicaraguan poetry – poverty, war, identity and nature – are as eternal as words themselves. Conceivably, Nicaragua's love of verse will last forever.

For more information, see www.festival poesianicaragua.com (Spanish only).

Gage visited in 1633 he marvelled at the city's wealth, most of which came from trade with Peru, Guatemala and Colombia.

Thanks to the lake and Río San Juan's access to the Atlantic, Granada flourished as an inter-oceanic port and trading centre, soon becoming one of the wealthiest, most opulent cities in the New World. But it was not long before reports of Granadino wealth began to reach the ears of English pirates occupying the recently acquired possession of Jamaica, which they wrested from Spain in 1665. Edward Davis and Henry Morgan sailed up the Río San Juan and took the city by surprise on 29 June 1665 at 0200 in the morning. With a group of 40 men they sacked the churches and houses before escaping to Las Isletas. In 1670 another band of pirates led by Gallardillo visited Granada via the same route. After destroying the fort at San Carlos, they sacked Granada and took with them men and women hostages.

In 1685, a force of 345 British and French pirates, led by the accomplished French pirate William Dampier, came from the Pacific, entering near where the Chacocente wildlife refuge is today (see page 158). The local population were armed and waiting to fight off the pirates but were easily overwhelmed by the size of the pirate army. They had, however, taken the precaution of hiding all their valuables on Isla Zapatera. The pirates burned the Iglesia San Francisco and 18 big houses, then retreated to the Pacific with the loss of only three men.

Granada saw even more burning and destruction in what were the biggest nationalist uprisings for Independence from Spain in 1811-1812 and during persistent post-Independence battles between León and Granada. When León's Liberal Party suffered defeat in 1854 they invited the North American filibuster William Walker (see box, page 117) to fight the Conservatives, thus initiating the darkest days of Granada's post-colonial history. Walker declared himself president of Nicaragua with the *cede* in Granada, but after losing his grip on power (which was regional at best) he absconded to Lake Nicaragua, giving orders to burn Granada, which once again went up in flames.

Places in Granada

Despite the repeated ransackings and burnings, Granada has maintained an unmistakable colonial charm. The architectural style has been described as a mixture of Nicaraguan baroque and neoclassical. Having been rebuilt on a number of occasions, the city has a fascinating visual mix of Spanish adobe tile roof structures and Italian-inspired neoclassical homes with some ornate ceiling work and balconies. It is interesting to compare the architecture of Granada with that of León, which was spared much of the looting and burning that the wealthier city of Granada suffered over the centuries.

Catedral Nuestra Señora de la Asunción
As a result of Granada's troubled history, its churches have all been rebuilt several times. Sadly, most have not retained much in the way of architectural interest or beauty. Last rebuilt and extended after William Walker's flaming departure in November 1856, the Catedral de Granada on Parque Central has become a symbol for Granada. The original church was erected in 1583 and rebuilt in 1633 and 1751. After Walker was shot and buried in Honduras in 1860, reconstruction began again on the cathedral, but was held up by lack of funds in 1891. The work in progress was later demolished and restarted to become today's church, finally opened in 1915. The cathedral has neoclassic and Gothic touches and its impressive size and towers make it a beautiful backdrop to the city, but the interior is plain. An icon of the Virgin, much-loved patron saint of Granada, is housed over the main altar. Mary has been proclaimed several times by the Nicaraguan government as the supreme ruler of Nicaragua's armed forces, responsible for defending the city against numerous attacks.

Parque Central
Parque Central is officially called Parque Colón (Columbus Park), though no one uses that name. Its tall trees and benches make it a good place to while away some time. There are food stalls selling the famous and tremendously popular Granada dish *vigorón*, which consists of a big banana leaf filled with cabbage salad, fried pork skins, yucca, tomato, hot chilli and lemon juice.

Next to the cathedral is a big cross, erected in 1899, with a time capsule buried underneath. It was hoped that by burying common artefacts and personal belongings from the 19th century, it might ensure a peaceful 20th century. Despite the fairly violent period that followed, Granada did enjoy a reasonable amount of peace.

Calle Real
The most attractive of the Granada churches is **Iglesia La Merced**, which can be seen as part of a very nice walk from Parque Central down the Calle Real to the old Spanish

Fortaleza de la Pólvora (see below). La Merced, built between 1751 and 1781 and also damaged by William Walker, has maintained much of its colonial charm and part of the original bell towers and façade. The pretty interior, painted an unusual tropical green colour, has an attractive altar and a painting of the Virgin on its north side. In front of the

Granada

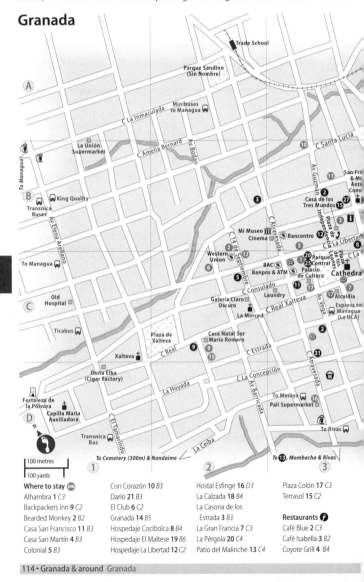

Where to stay 🛏

Alhambra **1** *C3*
Backpackers Inn **9** *C2*
Bearded Monkey **2** *B2*
Casa San Francisco **11** *B3*
Casa San Martín **4** *B3*
Colonial **5** *B3*

Con Corazón **10** *B3*
Darío **21** *B3*
El Club **6** *C2*
Granada **14** *B5*
Hospedaje Cocibolca **8** *B4*
Hospedaje El Maltese **19** *B6*
Hospedaje La Libertad **12** *C2*

Hostal Esfinge **16** *D3*
La Calzada **18** *B4*
La Casona de los
  Estrada **3** *B3*
La Gran Francia **7** *C3*
La Pérgola **20** *C4*
Patio del Malinche **13** *C4*

Plaza Colón **17** *C3*
Terrasol **15** *C2*

Restaurants 🍴

Café Blue **2** *C3*
Café Isabella **3** *B2*
Coyote Grill **4** *B4*

church is a cross constructed in 1999 as a symbol of hope for peace in the 21st century. You can ascend the bell tower of La Merced for great views of the city's tiled rooftops, Cocibolca and Volcán Mombacho, particularly striking at dusk (US$1).

Lago de Nicaragua

Corrales

C El Arsenal

Guadalupe

C San Juan del Sur

Dock

Plaza España

Complejo Turístico

To San Carlos

To Las Isletas

To Puerto Asese

mito

④

D'Fruit 24 B3
Don Luca's 19 B4
Doña Conchi's 5 C2
Don Simón 25 C3
El Garaje 6 B4
El Tercer Ojo 21 B3
El Zaguán 7 C3

⑤

Euro Café 20 C3
Garden Café 1 B3
Imagine 8 B3
Kathy's Waffle House 27 B3
Las Colinas del Sur 13 D3
Los Bocaditos 11 C3
Los Portales 12 B3

Mediterráneo 14 C3
Mona Lisa 30 B4
Panadería Luna 9 C2
Querube's 31 C3
Roadhouse 18 B4
TelePizza 15 B3

⑥

Bars & clubs ●
Centralito 10 B4
Kelly's Bar 16 C3
Nectar 22 C3
Nuestro Mundo 17 C3
O'Sheas 23 C4

One block south and two blocks west of La Merced is the **Casa Natal Sor María Romero** ① *Tue-Sun 0800-1200, 1400-1700, free*, a small chapel and humble collection of artefacts and books from the life of María Romero Meneses (born in Granada 1902, died in Las Peñitas, León 1977). María was a local girl who became a Salesian nun at 28 and spent the rest of her life caring for the poor and ill, founding both a heathcare centre for the poor and a home for street children in Costa Rica. She is said to have assisted in various miracles and may become the first saint in the history of Central America – her beatification was approved in Rome on 14 April 2002 by Pope John Paul II.

Further down the Calle Real is the **Plaza de Xalteva**, which has unusual stone lanterns and walls, said to be a tribute to ancient Indian constructions. Unlike León and Masaya, Granada no longer has an indigenous barrio of any kind, yet you can see the remains of the walls from the colonial period that separated the Spanish and indigenous sectors marked by a small tile plaque. The church on the plaza, **Iglesia Xalteva**, was yet another victim of William Walker. It was rebuilt at the end of the 19th century and is reminiscent of a New England church – a bit lacking in flair. From the plaza, it's possible to take an interesting detour to Granada's old hospital, a once-handsome structure now fallen into heavy dilapidation. Head one block west on Calle Real then go two blocks north. Make your presence known to the security guard before entering the hospital grounds, which are very eerie and photogenic.

Continuing further west along the Calle Real you'll arrive at the charming little **Capilla María Auxiliadora**. This church has some interesting features on its façade and some lovely detail work inside and is worth a visit. At the end of the street is the 18th-century fort and ammunitions hold, **Fortaleza de la Pólvora** ① *open during daylight hours, US$1-2 donation to the caretaker*. The fort was built in 1749 and used primarily as an ammunitions hold, then as a military base and finally a prison. You can climb up inside the southeastern turret on a flimsy ladder to have a good view down the Calle Real.

Calle Atravesada

There are a few sights of interest along the Calle Atravesada. Dating from 1886 and beautifully restored, the **old train station**, is now a trade school. Next to it is the 'Parque Sin Nombre' (park with no name). This little park was called Parque Somoza until the Revolution, when it was changed to **Parque Sandino**. When the Sandinistas lost in the 1990 elections, the park once again needed a new name. Some wise locals have since decided it best to allow the park to remain anonymous, though Parque Sandino remains its official name. Several blocks south and opposite Calle Arsenal is **Mi Museo** ① *Mon-Fri, 0800-1200, 1330-1700*. This museum has an array of well-presented archaeological relics, including many rotund funerary pots that were once 'pregnant' with lovingly prepared human remains. Past Parque Central on the same street towards the volcano is the bustle and hustle of Granada's **market**. A visit here is a must, if only to compare the noisy, pungent chaos with the relative order of the more well-tended tourist drags. Arrive early in the morning to observe the activity as its most frenetic.

Plaza de Independencia and around

Next to Parque Central is Plaza de Independencia, which has a movie-set quality to it. The bishop of Granada lives in the red house, at one time the presidential palace for William Walker. The **Claro** office is next door and just a few doors down is the historic **Casa de Los Leones** (its NGO name is **Casa de Los Tres Mundos**) ① *T2552-4176, www.c3mundos. org, daytime US$0.50; extra admission charged for live concerts on weekend nights*, with its

William Walker – the paradox of a villain

It is a name that is a complete mystery to most first-time visitors to Central America. Yet for Nicaraguans, North American William Walker is the epitome of foreign intervention, the model of the evil invader. Had Walker been successful, the history of the isthmus and the United States would be radically different, for it was his plan that Nicaragua should become a new US state to relieve anti-slavery pressure on mid-19th century US plantation owners. History, however, did not favour slave masters; on 12 September 1860, Walker was put against an adobe wall and shot by firing squad in Honduras and seven months later the US Civil War began.

Walker not only brought the bickering states of Central America together against a common enemy, but he was also a fascinating and paradoxical character. Young Billy Walker, the son of a banker from Scotland, spent much of his early childhood taking care of his ill mother, reading Byron and history books. His friends at school were unimpressed and called him 'missy'. He may not have been overly macho, but neither was he slow. By the age of 16 he had earned a graduate degree in Classics from the University of Tennessee. At the age of 19 he received his doctorate in medicine from the University of Pennsylvania and travelled to Europe to pursue advanced medical studies. For a short time he lived in the Latin quarter of Paris. By the age of 22, Walker had become fluent in Spanish, French and Italian and had a good knowledge of Greek and Latin. He had also found time to study US law and pass the bar exam.

Walker found work as an editor at *The New Orleans Delta* (where an unknown poet named Walt Whitman worked under him) and his editorials demonstrated a pacifist, anti-slavery and anti-interventionist stance. His newspaper even exposed a plot to take over Cuba and make it a slave state, foiling the project. In New Orleans, Walker had met the love of his life, Ellen Martin, an upper-class girl who was witty, beautiful, mute and deaf. Walker learned sign language and got engaged, but both Ellen and Walker's mother died shortly afterwards from cholera.

Now alone, Walker moved to California during the gold rush and became hardened by the turn of events in his life. Massacres of Native Americans in California perpetrated by gold prospectors and land grabbers were commonplace and, as their defence lawyer, Walker became acquainted with selective law – and with murderers getting off scot-free. Love was gone from his life and Walker was now a proponent of slavery and expansionism. Poorly planned and executed military attempts by Walker at setting up colonies in Northern Mexico and Baja California failed. Yet Walker returned to the US more popular than ever. In Nicaragua the Liberals of León were unable to defeat the Conservatives of Granada and the Liberal leader looked to the north for help. The job was given to William Walker, setting the stage for the bloody invasion. What the Liberals did not know was Walker's detailed plan to legalize slavery in Nicaragua and annex it to the US. Every year Nicaraguans celebrate his failure.

17th-century Moorish stone door frame that survived all the burning. The building was once the municipal theatre, then a private house where poet-priest Ernesto Cardenal was born. Now it is a cultural centre particularly renowned for its vibrant art exhibits, music and occasional poetry readings; check their website for details on upcoming events.

One block east from the northeast corner of Plaza de la Independencia is the bright blue **Iglesia San Francisco** (1524), Nicaragua's oldest standing church with original steps. It was burnt down in 1685 by the group of pirates led by William Dampier, rebuilt, then modified in 1836 before being reduced to flames in 1856 on Walker's departure. It was finally rebuilt in 1868 with a fine restoration of the interior and a controversial decoration of the façade – some complain that it now looks like a birthday cake. The legendary human rights priest Fray Bartolomé de las Casas preached here while visiting Granada in the 1530s.

Connected to the church is the mustard yellow **Museo Antiguo Convento de San Francisco** ⓘ *T2552-5535, daily 0830-1730, US$3, US$2.50 extra to photograph.* Originally founded as a convent in 1529, it was also burnt down in 1685 by Dampier. In 1836, after the religious orders of Central America had been forced to leave by the Central American Federation, it became a university, and then, in 1856, it was used as a garrison by William Walker, who burned it down once again before leaving the country. The old convent was rebuilt and became the most important secondary school in town, the Colegio de Granada, which later became the Instituto Nacional de Oriente until it closed in 1975. Restoration began in 1989 with help from the Swedish government. There is a mural in the entrance that leads to a small shop and café. The interior garden is dominated by towering 100-year-old palms, often full of squawking parakeets. In the east wing of the building is one of the country's most interesting pre-Columbian museums, housing large religious sculptures from the island of Zapatera in Lake Nicaragua (see page 129). The sculptures date from AD 800-1200; of particular note are the double standing or seated figures bearing huge animals, or doubles, on their heads and shoulders. The museum also has temporary exhibitions, historic photographs of Granada, some colonial-period religious art and a gallery of Solentiname naïve painting.

Calle Calzada

East from the Parque Central, the brightly coloured and well-manicured Calle Calzada contains the city's highest concentration of restaurants and foreign tourists. This is the place for people-watching and enjoying a good cold beer. The parade of gringo eateries peters out about halfway towards the lake, where you'll find the **Iglesia Guadalupe**. This church has seen plenty of action, thanks to its location near the water. Walker's forces used it as a final stronghold before escaping to the lake where Walker was keeping well away from the fighting, on a steamship. Originally constructed in 1626, its exterior has a melancholy, rustic charm, although the post-Walker interior lacks character. Beyond the church you'll pass the red cross and a baseball field before arriving at the lake and ferry port. Head south along the shore and you'll reach the fortress-like gates of the **complejo turístico**, a large recreation area of restaurants, discos and cafés, popular with the locals, particularly over Christmas and New Year.

◉ Granada listings

For sleeping and eating price codes and other relevant information, see pages 28-30.

● Where to stay

Granada *p110, map p114*
$$$ Casa San Francisco, Corrales 207, T2552-8235, www.casasanfrancisco.com.

This attractive, tranquil hotel is composed of 2 colonial houses with 13 lodgings that vary greatly. There's 1 house with 2 suites and 2 comfortable rooms with private bath, cable TV, a/c, pool and a modern kitchen. The other has 8 rooms and 1 suite, a pool and restaurant. The friendly and helpful staff speak English.

\$\$\$ Hotel Alhambra, Parque Central, T2552-4486, www.hotelalhambra.com.ni. Granada's landmark hotel has a stunning location on the plaza. Rooms vary dramatically in quality and price. The ones overlooking the park are best. There's also a pool and terrace for drinks, and a restaurant – not owned by the hotel – that receives a lot of criticism for poor service. Often full with groups.

\$\$\$ Hotel Colonial, Calle La Libertad, Parque Central, 25 vrs al norte, T2552-7581, www.hotelcolonialgranada.com. This centrally located, colonial-style hotel has a range of pleasant, comfortable lodgings, including 27 heavily decorated rooms with 4-poster beds and 10 luxury suites with jacuzzi. There are 2 pools, a conference centre, a tour agency, and the restaurant serves breakfast only.

\$\$\$ Hotel Darío, Calle La Calzada, de la Catedral, 150 vrs al lago, T2552 3400, www.hoteldario.com. Right in the heart of town and housed by the smart green and white neoclassical building you can't fail to notice. The interior is handsome, with comfortable rooms and beautiful grounds. Breakfast is included in the price.

\$\$\$ La Gran Francia, southeast corner of Parque Central, T2552-6002, www.lagranfrancia.com. This traditional colonial building has elegeant rooms with private bath, hot water, cable TV, a/c, minibar and internet access. Standard rooms are dark and face a wall, junior suites (**\$\$\$\$**) have big wooden doors that lead on to small balcony with a lovely view and lots of light; worth the extra money.

\$\$\$ Patio del Malinche, Calle El Caimito, de Alcaldía, 2½ c al lago, T2552-2235, www.patiodelmalinche.com. This beautiful and tastefully restored colonial building has 15 clean, comfortable rooms overlooking an attractive garden and pool. There's a bar and tranquil patio space in which you can have breakfast or simply relax. Rooms are equipped with a/c, cable TV, fan, hot water, safe and Wi-Fi. Tidy and elegant.

\$\$\$ Plaza Colón, frente al Parque Central, T2552-8489, www.hotelplazacolon.com. Atmospheric colonial grandeur at this long-established hotel on the plaza. Rooms have all the usual luxury amenities, including a/c, minibar, cable TV, hot water and internet, but those with balconies also have fantastic views over the square. There's a pool, restaurant and a small army of staff to care for your needs. Recommended.

\$\$\$-\$\$ Hotel Granada, opposite Iglesia Guadalupe, T2552-2974, www.hotelgranadanicaragua.com. **Hotel Granada** has been renovated and offers 3 classes of room. The hotel grounds are rambling and boast the largest swimming pool in town, as well as conference rooms, restaurant and an art gallery.

\$\$\$-\$\$ La Casona de los Estrada, Iglesia San Francisco, ½ c abajo, T2552-7393, www.casonalosestrada.com.ni. Decorated with fine furnishings, this small, homely hotel has 6 pleasant, well-lit rooms with private bath, hot water, a/c, Wi-Fi and cable TV. There's a pleasant plant-filled courtyard, English and French are spoken, and prices include breakfast.

\$\$ Casa San Martín, Calle La Calzada, catedral, 1 c lago, T2552-6185, www.hcasasanmartin.com. 7 clean, cool, spacious rooms in a beautiful colonial home. All have cable TV, private bath, Wi-Fi and a/c or fan. Nice decor and garden terrace, very authentic Granadino feel. Staff speak English.

\$\$ Hospedaje El Maltese, Plaza España, 50 m sur, opposite *malecón* in Complejo Turístico, T2552-7641, www.nicatour.net. 8 very clean rooms with private bath, nice furnishings, Italian spoken, restaurant **La Corte Del Maltese**, Mon-Fri 1600-2200. Don't walk here at night alone.

\$\$ Hotel Con Corazón, Calle Santa Lucía 141, T2552-8852, www.hotelconcorazon.com. As the name suggests, this 'hotel with heart' strives to be ethical and donates its profits to social causes. Rooms are simple, minimalist and comfortable; all are fitted with a/c, cable TV and fan. There's a pleasant colonial patio, bar, pool, hammocks and a restaurant serving international food (**$$**). Often recommended by former guests.

$$ La Pérgola, Calle el Caimito, de la Alcaldía, 3 c al lago, T2552-4221, www.lapergola.com.ni. Originally a 19th-century colonial home, with 11 comfortable rooms set around a leafy courtyard from where you can see Volcán Mombacho. Each room has a/c, cable TV, orthopaedic bed and minibar. Hotel services include parking, tours, transfers, Wi-Fi and bar. Clean, tidy and professional. Breakfast included.

$$ Terrasol, Av Barricada, T2552-8825, www.hotelterrasol.com. Rooms are comfortable, modern and adorned with good artwork. Each has cable TV, private bath and a/c (cheaper with fan). Some have balconies with views of the street. The restaurant downstairs has had good reports, thanks to the managers who have a background in the food industry.

$$-$ El Club, Parque Central, 3 c abajo, T2552-4245, www.elclub-nicaragua.com. This Dutch-owned hotel has 2 suites with mezzanine floors, as well as several small, windowless, fading rooms with private bath, a/c, cable TV and Wi-Fi. The cheapest are quite cramped. The bar lays on a loud party on Thu, Fri and Sat nights, when you won't get much peace. Prices include breakfast.

$ Backpackers Inn, Esquina Calle Real Xalteva y Av Barricada, 25 m sur, T2552-4609, www.backpackers-inn.com. A very clean and attractive hostel for independent travellers. There's a colonial courtyard, traditional art work, good hammocks, well-tended garden, café, business centre and restaurant. Other services include Wi-Fi, laundry and tours.

$ Bearded Monkey, Calle 14 de Septiembre, near the fire station, T2552-4028, www.the beardedmonkey.com. A sociable, popular hostel with dormitories, private rooms and hammocks for seriously impoverished backpackers. There's a plethora of services to keep you entertained including restaurant, bar, cable TV, internet access, cheap calls, evening films, bike rentals,

and free tea and coffee. Use lockers, as everybody is free to walk in and out.

$ Hospedaje Cocibolca, Calle La Calzada, T2552-7223, www.hospedajecocibolca.net. A friendly, family house with 24 clean, simple rooms. There's Wi-Fi, a kitchen, free coffee in the morning and plenty of chess sets. A few rooms have cable TV and a/c (**$$**) Very nice owners and a brilliant location on the Calzada. Recommended.

$ Hospedaje La Libertad, Av 14 de Septiembre, T2552-4087, www.la-libertad. net. Managed by the friendly Chepe, this relaxed and sociable hostel offers economical dorm beds (single sex and mixed) and simple private rooms. There's a well-stocked bar, leafy courtyard, good hammocks, internet terminals, Wi-Fi, free coffee and large lockers. La Libertad also offers a range of tours with 'Jimmy the Man' and supports local artists. Pleasant atmosphere.

$ Hostal Esfinge, opposite market, T2552-4826, esfingegra@hotmail.com.ni. Lots of character at this friendly old hotel near the market. They offer a variety of simple rooms, including those with bath, shared bath and a/c (**$$**). There's a shared kitchen, washing area, ping-pong table, lockers, fridge and a leafy garden with pleasant hammocks and seating. Nica-owned and recommended for down-to-earth budget travellers.

$ La Calzada, Calle Calzada, near Iglesia Guadalupe, T2552-7684, www.hospeda jelacalzadanica.blogspot.com. This family-run guesthouse has 8 big, simple rooms with fan and private bath; cheaper with shared bath. Authentically Nicaraguan, but has seen better days. Internet available.

Apartments and long-term rentals

If you're in town for a few weeks or more, renting a furnished house or apartment will often work out more cost-effective than staying in a hotel. There are plenty of properties available, many of them advertised in expat-run cafés and restaurants. A few agencies also specialize in vacation rentals:

Granada Property Service, 2nd floor of Café DecArte, Calle Calzada, del Parque Central, 1 c al lago, T2552-7954, www.gps nicaragua.com. A range of houses and apartments, all comfortable, but most are on the expensive side. They also have properties in San Juan del Sur.

Granada Rentals, Calle Corrales, opposite Oro Travel, T2552-0313, www.granada rentals.com. A wide range of houses, all available for short- or long-term let.

🍴 Restaurants

Granada *p110, map p114*

$$$ Imagine, Calle La Libertad, del Parque Central, 1 c al lago, T8842-2587, www.imagine restaurantandbar.com. A very decent and creative restaurant that utilizes fresh and organic ingredients to produce dishes like seared sushi tuna, 100% grain-fed lamb chops, flaming breast of duck and mango bread with chocolate fondue. Recommended.

$$$ Mediterráneo, Calle Caimito, T2552-6764. Daily 0800-2300. Mediterranean cuisine served in a Spanish-owned colonial house with an attractive and tranquil garden setting. Mixed reviews; good seafood but bad paella. Popular with foreigners.

$$$-$$ Doña Conchi's, Calle La Libertad, northwest corner of the Parque Central, 2½ c abajo. Wed-Mon 1100-2300. A very beautiful restaurant, illuminated by candles and adorned with rustic decorations. They serve quality dishes like grilled salmon, sea bass and lobster (**$$$**), as well as slightly cheaper, reasonably good (if very garlicky) pasta (**$$**). Lovely garden seating and pleasant service. Recommended.

$$$-$$ El Zaguán, on road behind cathedral (east side), T2552-2522. Mon-Fri 1200-1500 and 1800-2200, Sat and Sun 1200-2200. Incredible, succulent grilled meats and steaks, cooked on a wood fire and served impeccably. Undoubtedly the best beef cuts in Granada, if not Nicaragua. Meat-lovers should not miss this place. Highly recommended.

$$ Coyote Grill, Parque Central, 3 c al lago, La Calzada, T2252-2457. Same owner as **Pizza Luca** next door. They serve burgers, chicken, steak, salads, fajitas, fries and American-style fare. Some outdoor seating, but indoors is comfortable too.

$$ Don Luca's, Calle La Calzada, catedral, 2 c al lago, T2552-7822. Excellent wood-oven pizza, calzone, and pasta. Wine and coffee too. Indoor seating or tables on the Calzada. Not bad.

$$ El Garaje, Calle Corrales, del Convento de San Francisco, 2½ c al lago, T8651-7412. Mon Fri 1130-1900. A wonderfully understated Canadian-owned restaurant and undoubtedly one of Granada's best options. The menu changes weekly and includes tasty specials like Jamaican curry, roast turkey, Mediterranean salad and Szechuan steak wrap. Fresh, healthy, beautifully presented home-cooking. Good vegetarian options too. Highly recommended.

$$ El Tercer Ojo, Calle El Arsenal, south corner of the Convento San Francisco, T2552-6451. This lounge-restaurant has interesting, exotic decor, reminiscent of some Far Eastern locale. Unfortunately, the food was mediocre at our last visit.

$$ Kathy's Waffle House, opposite Iglesia San Francisco. 0730-1400. The best breakfasts in Granada. It's always busy here in the morning, especially at weekends. You'll find everything from waffles and pancakes to *huevos rancheros*, all with free coffee refills. Highly recommended.

$$ Las Colinas del Sur, Shell Palmira, 1 c sur, T2552-3492. Daily 1200-2200, Tue lunch only 1200-1500. Seafood specialities, excellent lake fish, try the *guapote* fried whole, boneless fillets, avocado salad, far from centre, but worth it, take a taxi. Recommended.

$$ Los Chocoyos, Calle Corrales, north corner of the Convent, inside **Casa San Francisco**, see Where to stay, T2552-8235. Daily 1200-2300. A range of tasty international cuisine including Mexican, Italian and French, served in a colonial setting.

$$ Mona Lisa, Calle La Calzada, 3½ c al lago, T2552-8187. Undoubtedly the best pizzas in Granada; stone-baked, tasty and authentic. Friendly and recommended.
$$ Roadhouse, Calle La Calzada, 2 c al lago. Popular with Nicaraguans, this rocking American-style restaurant serves lots of beer and a range of wholesome burgers. Their fries, flavoured with cajun spices, are the best thing they do. Inside tends to be rowdier than outside.
$$-$ Café Isabella, 108 Calle Corrales, Bancentro, 1 c norte, ½ c abajo. Open for breakfast and lunch, this café has a large terrace overlooking the street and interior garden. They serve some vegetarian dishes.
$$-$ Los Portales, on Plaza de los Leones, T2552-4115. Daily 0700-2200. Simple Mexican food, sometimes overpriced but there are good people-watching opportunities to make up for it.
$ Café Blue, southwest corner of Parque Central, 1½ c sur. Mon-Sat. Cosy little restaurant with a casual café ambience. They serve a range of cheapish breakfasts, including fruit, pancakes, bacon and eggs, as well as economical lunches, which mainly consist of meat and chicken fare.
$ Los Bocaditos, Calle el Comercio. Mon-Sat 0800-2200, Sun 0800-1600. A bustling, but clean, locals' joint with buffet from 1100-1500, breakfast and dinner menu.
$ Restaurant Querube's, Calle el Comercio, opposite Tiangue 1. Clean and popular locals' joint near the market. They serve greasy, high-carb Nicaraugan and Chinese fare from a buffet, and do set lunches and breakfasts.
$ TelePizza, Bancentro, 1½ c al lago, T552-4219. Daily 1000-2200. Good, tasty pizzas, but not outstanding. Popular with Nicaraguan families, if you've had enough of the gringo places. They deliver too.

Cafés, bakeries and juice bars

D'Fruit, Calle Calzada, del Parque Central, 2½ c al lago. The place for your fruit juice fix, whether your vitamins are running low or just need to quench your thirst.

Don Simón, Parque Central, T884-1393. Daily 0700-2100. Great views over the plaza. They serve simple breakfasts, good pastries, coffee, espresso, cappuccino, sandwiches.
Euro Café, Calle La Libertad, on the corner of Parque Central. Coffee and cappuccinos, as well as muffins, cakes and other baked goods. Their hot paninis are a tasty option if you need food on the go.
Garden Café, Entitel, 1 c al lago. A very relaxed, breezy café with a lovely leafy garden and patio space. They do breakfasts, sandwiches, coffees, muffins and cookies. They have a small book collection and Wi-Fi. Friendly and pleasant.
Panadería Luna, Calle Xalteva, Lotería Nacional 100 vrs al lago. The best bakery in town with a good selection of European-style white and brown bread, cookies, cakes and other treats. They serve sandwiches and coffee too, and there's a second branch on the popular Calle La Calzada.

⚓ Bars and clubs

Granada *p110, map p114*
The action tends to gravitate towards Calle La Calzada with a kind of thronging carnivalesque atmosphere Fri-Sun evenings.
Centralito, Calle La Calzada, Parque Central, 2½ c al lago. Popular with Nicas as well as foreigners, **Centralito** often sees spirited (and well-oiled) crowds gathered at its outdoor tables. A good place to meet the locals, get loud and ridiculous, and soak up the local ambience.
El Club, see Hotel El Club, page 120. A modern bar with a European ambience, pumping dance music and a mixture of locals and foreigners. Stylish and a cut above the rest. Most popular Thu-Sat, when parties run late into the night.
Kelly's Bar, Calle el Caimito, Alcaldía, 1 c al lago. Feisty boozer that's popular with a young beer-swilling crowd. Happy hour is every day 1600-1800, They show sports on TV, have a selection of games, and play rock from the 70s, 80s and 90s.

There's also a kitchen and they boast over 30 types of cocktail.

Nectar, Calle La Calzada, Parque Central, 1½ c al lago. Another popular drinking establishment on the Calzada, although this one has lounge-style ambience and comfortable indoor seating, should you wish to avoid the hoi-polloi of the world outside. Avoid the nachos too.

Nuestro Mundo, southeast corner of Parque Central, next to the Alcaldía. A large space with 2 floors of diversions. Featured entertainment include billiards, live music, table football, Nintendo, karaoke and cable TV.

O'Shea's, Calle La Calzada, Parque Central, 2 c al lago. **O'Shea's** is one of Central America's few authentic Irish bars. Sadly, the food is mediocre and the interior grim, but they do have outdoor seating and, most importantly, they serve Guinness.

⊕ Entertainment

Granada *p110, map p114*
Cinema
Cine Karawala, Calle Atravezada, behind Hotel Alhambra, T2552-2442. 2-screen cinema that only seems to open Fri-Sun.

⊛ Festivals

Granada *p110, map p114*
Feb Poetry Festival, a captivating and popular literary festival that draws national and international crowds (see box, page 112), check website for dates, www.festivalpoesianicaragua.com.
Mar Folklore, Artesanía and Food Festival for 3 days in Mar (check locally for dates).
Aug 1st weekend in August is **El Tope de los Toros** with bulls released and then caught one at a time, much tamer than Pamplona, though occasionally the bulls get away sending everyone running for cover. **Assumption of the Virgin** (14-30).
Dec Celebrations for the **Virgin Mary** on 7 Dec and **Christmas**.

○ Shopping

Granada *p110, map p114*
Antiques and artisan crafts
Granada is the best place to hunt for antiques in Nicaragua. Keep in mind that pre-Columbian pieces cannot be taken out of the country and colonial-period relics may also be considered national patrimony and subject to the same laws.

There are not many good places to buy general *artesanías*, most are marked-up, but if you are not planning to visit Masaya and Los Pueblos Blancos, this might be the only chance. There are usually some on sale in the Parque Central and inside the shops surrounding it. *Vendedores* also wander about town with trays of ceramics or other wares. There's primitivist art inside the centro comercial near the BAC.
ArtesaNic, Puente Papa Q, 1 c abajo, Calle La Libertad, T2552-1543, www.artesanic.com. Authentic and durable 18th-century reproductions.
Casa de Antigüedades Felicia, Calle El Beso, Casa 114, T2552-4677. Religious relics, furniture, Nicaraguan art, owner Felicia Sandino also offers to take care of shipping.
Casa Elena, Iglesia Xalteva, 2 c sur, ½ c abajo, Casa 215, T2552-6242. Tue-Sun 1000-1800. Crafts from Mexico and Nicaragua.
El Recodo, Calle La Libertad, from Parque Central, 4 c abajo, ½ c al sur, T2552-0901, www.casaelrecodo.com. Great colonial furniture and artisan crafts for sale in what is apparently Granada's oldest building.
Exapiel, Entitel, 100 vrs al lago, next to Garden Café, T2552-2003. For bags and belts handcrafted from Italian leather.
Mercedes Morales, La Merced, 1½ c sur, for appointment phone T8887-1488.

Books
Hispamer, Convento San Francisco, ½ c abajo, Calle El Arsenal, A good selection of Spanish-language books.
Mockingbird Books, next to Café Euro, northwest corner of Parque Central.

Has a selection of second-hand books including novels and travel guides.

Cigars

There is some rolling done in Granada although most of the wrap and filler are brought from Estelí where the best cigars are made outside Cuba (see Estelí page 253).

Doña Elba Cigars, Calle Real, Iglesia Xalteva, ½ c abajo, T8860-6715, www.elbacigars.com. A long-established factory where you can learn more about cigar-making or just pick up some fresh *puros*.

Mombacho Cigars, 422 Calle La Calzada, www.mombachocigars.com. A swish new Canadian outfit offering rolling demonstrations from their elegant headquarters on the Calzada.

Galleries

Casa de los Tres Mundos, Plaza de Independencia, T2552-4176, www.3mundos.org, has changing exhibits in a gorgeous space.

Casa Sacuanjoche, southeast corner of Parque Central, 1 c al lago, 1½ c sur, T552 6151, www.galeria.casa sacuanjoche.com, has paintings by local artist Alvaro Berroteran.

Galería Calzada, Parque Central, 1½ c al lago, Calle Calzada. A new gallery featuring prints and originals by local and national artists. Pleasant garden.

Markets

El Mercado de Granada, Parque Central, 1 c abajo, then south on Calle Atravesada, is a large green building surrounded by many street stalls. It's dark, dirty and packed and there have been plans to move it for years but for now it remains in its claustrophobic location.

Supermercado Palí, just west of the market. Also dark and dirty, with a selection of low-price goods.

La Colonia, on the highway to Masaya, from the Esso at the end of Av Elena

Arellano, 1½ c al lago. The best (and most modern) supermarket.

☉ What to do

Granada *p110, map p114*
Boating, kayaking and windsurfing
Mombotour, Centro Comercial Granada No 2, next to BAC, T2552-4548, www.mombotour.com. Having acquired the reputable 'Island Kayaks' agency, Mombotour offer kayak lessons and guided tours of the Isletas, which can be combined with longer birding expeditions. A 2½-hr kayak tour costs US$30 including guide, transportation and entrance fees; book in advance.

NicarAgua Dulce, Marina Cocibola, Bahía de Asese, T2552-6351, www.nicaraguadulce. com. An ecologically aware outfit that contributes to local communities. They offer kayak rental by the hour or day to explore the lesser-visited Asese Bay, which can be done with or without a guide, or additional bicycle rental if you wish to explore the peninsula by land. Boat tours of the Isletas are offered, as well as tours to their idyllic private island, Zopango, where you can chill out in a hammock, swim or stroll along the botanical track. Taxi to the marina is supplied when you book a 3-hr tour or more.

Zapatera Tours, Calle Palmira contiguo a la Cancha, T8842-2587, www.zapatera tours.com. This long-established company specializes in lake tours with trips to las Isletas, Zapatera, Ometepe and the Solentiname archipelago. They also offer biking, hiking and windsurfing.

Canopy tours

See also page 131.

Mombacho Canopy Tour, located on the road up to the Mombacho cloud forest reserve, T8997-5846, canopy@cablenet.com. ni. Daily 0900-1700 (book at least 24 hrs in advance). US$30, US$10 student discount. It combines well with a visit to the cloud forest reserve which is on this side of the volcano.

Mombotour, Centro Comercial Granada No 2, next to BAC, T2552-4548, www.mombotour.com. US$38 per person. Cost includes transfers by 4WD up and down the mountain from Granada; transfers normally leave at 0900 and 1300 daily but you must book in advance.

Cycling
Cycling is a great way to explore the area, particularly the Península de Asese. Many agencies rent out bikes, but these are specialists:

Bicimaximo, east side of the Parque Central, next to Va Pues, T8387-6789, info@bicimaximo.com. Cycle rentals at US$4 for a half day, US$6 for an 8- to 12-hr day.

Detour, Alcaldía, 150 vrs al lago, Calle Caimito. Good bicycles with shock absorber, locks, maps, helmets, tips and repair kit at US$2 per hr, US$5 for a half day, US$8 for a full 24 hrs.

Cultural and community tourism
UCA Tierra y Agua, Shell Palmira, 75 vrs abajo, T2552-0238, www.ucatierrayagua.org. Daily 0830-1630. This organization will help you organize a visit to rural communities around Granada including La Granadilla, Nicaragua Libre and Aguas Agrias (see box, page 111). Very interesting and highly recommended for a perspective on local life and the land.

Health and spa
Pure Natural Health and Fitness Center, Calle Corrales, from Convento San Francisco, 1½ c al lago, T8481-3264, www.purenica.com. A range of well-priced packages and therapies including excellent massage, reiki and beauty treatments. Classes include meditation, yoga, kick-boxing and aerobics. Weights and cross-trainers available in the gym. Professional, friendly and highly recommended (especially for yoga). If you visit, be sure to meet Snoopy, the giant African tortoise!

Seeing Hands, inside EuroCafe, off the northwest corner of Parque Central. This excellent organization offers blind people an opportunity to earn a living as masseurs. A range of effective, professional massages are available, from a 15-min back, neck and shoulder massage, US$3, to a 1-hr table massage, US$12.50.

Tour operators
Tour operators come and go with the seasons in Granada. The following list is not exhaustive, but includes some of the more established companies:

De Tour, Alcaldía, 150 vrs allago, T2552-0155, www.detour-ameriquecentrale.com. This relatively new operator offers a range of interesting cultural and historical tours, including trips to the gold mines of Chontales. Other possibilities are coffee tours, horse riding, kayaks, community tourism and bicycle rental. Different and worth a look.

Oro Travel, Convento San Francisco, ½ c norte, T2552-4568, www.orotravel.com. Granada's best tour operator offers quality, specialized tours and trips, many including transfers and hotels. Owner Pascal speaks French, English and German. Friendly and helpful. Recommended.

Tierra Tour, Calle la Calzada, catedral, 2 c lago, T0862-9580, www.tierratour.com. This well-established Dutch-Nicaraguan agency offers a wide range of affordable services including good-value trips to Las Isletas, cloud forest tours, birding expeditions and shuttles. Helpful and friendly.

Va Pues, Parque Central, blue house next to the cathedral, T552-8291, www.vapues.com. This award-winning agency offers canopy tours, turtle expeditions, Zapatera cultural heritage tours, car rental, domestic flights and a 'romantic getaway' tour to a private island. They work closely with a sister company, **Agua Trails**, www.aguatrails.com, which operates out of Costa Rica and specializes in the Río San Juan region on the border.

⊖ Transport

Granada p110, map p114
Boat and ferry
For short expeditions, you can easily find boats by the lakeside *malecón* and in the Complejo Turístico. Otherwise try: **Marina Cocibolca**, www.marinacocibolca. net. Check the Marina's administrative offices for information on costs and schedules for visits to the Isletas, Zapatera, and nearby private reserves.

For long-distance ferry trips, services depart from the *malecón* and schedules are subject to change, www.epn.ni. The ferry to **San Carlos** leaves the main dock on Mon and Thu at 1400, and stops at **Altagracia, Ometepe** after 4 hrs (US$4 1st class, US$2 2nd class), **Morrito** (8 hrs, US$5 1st class, US$3, 2nd class), **San Miguelito** (10 hrs, US$5.50 1st class, US$3 2nd class) and finally **San Carlos** (14 hrs, US$9.50 1st class, US$4 2nd class). This journey is tedious, take your own food and water, and a hammock, a pillow and a sleeping bag if you have them. Although you'll still be sleeping on a hard bench or floor, the 1st-class deck is much more comfortable than the crowded and noisy 2nd-class deck below – worth the extra dollars. The ferry returns from San Carlos on Tue and Fri following the same route. For **Altagracia** you can also take a cargo boat with passenger seats on Wed and Sat (1200, 4½ hrs, US$2). It is faster to go overland to **San Jorge** and catch a 1-hr ferry to **Ometepe**, see San Jorge, page 136 for more details.

Bus
Intercity bus For the border with **Costa Rica** use **Rivas** bus to connect to **Peñas Blancas** service or use international buses.

Express minibuses to La UCA in **Managua** from a small lot just south of Parque Central on Calle Vega, every 20 mins, 0500-2000, 45 mins, US$0.95. Another express service departs from a different terminal, shell station, 1 c abajo, 1 c norte, which goes to the sketchy Mercado Oriental, US$0.95. Either can drop you on the highway exit to **Masaya**, US$0.60, from where it's a 20-min walk or 5-min taxi ride to the centre. Buses to Mercado Roberto Huembes, Managua, US$0.60, also leave from a station near the old hospital in Granada, west of centre, but they're slower and only marginally cheaper.

Leaving from the Shell station, Mercado, 1 c al lago: to **Rivas**, 7 daily, 0540-1510, 1½ hrs, US$1.50, most depart before midday; to Nandaime, every 20 mins, 0500-1800, 20 mins, US0.70; to **Niquinohomo**, every 30 mins, 0550-1800, 45 mins, US$1, use this bus for visits to **Diriá, Diriomo, San Juan de Oriente, Catarina**; to **Jinotepe**, 0550, 0610, 0830, 1110, 1210 and 1710, 1½ hrs, US$0.80, for visits to **Los Pueblos**, including **Masatepe** and **San Marcos**. There's a second terminal nearby, Shell station, 1 c abajo, 1 c norte, serving **Masaya**, every 30 mins, 0500-1800, 40 mins, US$0.50.

International bus To **San José**, Costa Rica, daily. See individual offices for schedules: **King Quality**, Av Arellano, from Shell Guapinol, 1½ c al sur, www.king-qualityca.com; **Ticabus**, Av Arellano, from the old hospital, 1½ c al Sur, T2552-8535, www.ticabus.com; **Transnica**, Calle Xalteva, Frente de Iglesia Auxiliadora, T2552-6619, www.transnica.com.

A shuttle to **Laguna Apoyo** leaves daily from The Bearded Monkey Hostel, stopping at Hospedaje La Libertad and Hostal El Chelero in Granada before dropping passengers at the Monkey Hut by the lake shore, 1000-1100, ½ hr, US$2. They return at 1600-1700.

Paxeos, Parque Central, blue house next to cathedral, T2552-8291, www.paxeos.com. Daily shuttles to **Managua airport**, US$12; **León**, US$20; **San Juan del Sur**, US$23; and **San Jorge**, US$18. Also try Tierra Tour (see Tour operators, above) for competitive rates.

Car hire
Budget Rent a Car, at the Shell station near the north city entrance, T2552-2323,

provides very good service. Also try **Dollar**, in Hotel Plaza Colón, T2552-8515; or **Alamo**, in Hotel Colonial, T2552-2877. If you rent a car in Managua you can leave it here, or you can hire it in Granada and drop it off in Managua or other northern destinations. However, cheaper rates can be found in Managua with other companies.

Horse-drawn carriages

Coches are for hire and are used as taxis here, as in Masaya, Rivas and Chinandega. Normal rate for a trip to the market or bus station should be no more than US$1.50. The drivers are also happy to take foreigners around the city and actually make very good and willing guides if you can decipher their Spanish. Rates are normally US$5 for 30 mins, US$10 for 1 hr.

Taxis

Granada taxi drivers are useful for finding places away from the centre, fares to anywhere within the city are US$0.50 per person during the day, US$1 at night. To **Managua** US$25, but check taxi looks strong enough to make the journey.

Directory

Granada *p110, map p114*
Banks Banco de Centro América (BAC) Parque Central, 1 c abajo, on Calle La Libertad, has an ATM and will change TCs and US dollars. ATM at Esso Station (15-min walk from town centre) accepts Cirrus, Maestro, MasterCard as well. **Banpro**, BAC, 1 c al sur, has a less reliable ATM and money changing facilities. **Bancentro**, BAC, 1 c al norte, has a Visa ATM. **Western Union**, fire station, ½ c sur, Mon-Sat 0800-1300, 1400-1700. **Doctors** Dr Francisco Martínez Blanco, Clínica de Especialidades Piedra Bocona, Cine Karawala, ½ c abajo,

T2552-5989, general practitioner, speaks good English, consultation US$10.
Fire T2552-4440. **Hospital** T2552-2719. **Internet** Internet cafés can be found all over town, while most hostels and hotels also offer internet access as well as international calls. **Language schools** Granada is becoming a hot-bed for Spanish schools, with many rising and falling with the city's increasing popularity. These ones are well-established and proven: **Casa Xalteva**, Iglesia Xalteva, ½ c al norte, T2552-2436, www.casaxalteva. com. Small Spanish classes for beginners and advanced students, 1 week to several months. Homestays arranged, and voluntary work with children. Recommended. **APC Spanish School**, west side of Parque Central, T2552-4203, www.spanishgranada. com. Flexible immersion classes in this centrally located language school. There are volunteer opportunities with local NGOs. **One on One**, Calle La Calzada 450, T2552-6771, www.1on1tutoring.net. One on One uses a unique teaching system where each student has 4 different tutors, thus encouraging greater aural comprehension. Instruction is flexible, by the hour or week, with homestay, volunteering and activities available. **Laundry** Mapache Laundry Service, Calle Calzada and El Cisne, from the Parque Central 2 c al lago, ½ c norte, T2552-6711, 0900-1800, fast service, US$5 for a medium load; and **La Lavandería**, almost opposite, Calle La Libertad, good lads, similar rates. **Police** T2552-2929. **Post** Calle El Arsenal, from Convento San Francisco, ½ c al lago, DHL, next to Casa de los Tres Mundos, T2552-6847. **Red Cross** T2552-2711. **Telephone** Claro (Enitel) on northeast corner of Parque Central. Movistar, from the northeast corner of the Parque Central, ½ c norte.

Around Granada

Despite Granada's five centuries of European settlement, there remains plenty of pristine nature close to the old city. The shores of Lake Nicaragua offer access to the well-populated archipelago of Las Isletas and the mysterious and largely unvisited indigenous ceremonial sites of Parque Nacional Archipiélago Zapatera. On the mainland it is hard to miss the sulking mountain of Mombacho, its cloud forest draped in mist most of the year, but nevertheless great for hiking in and canopy touring. On the south side of the volcano there are expansive tropical dry forests including the private nature reserve of Domitila. Past the trees are vast plains of sugar cane, rice and cattle pasture that lead to the tough cowboy town of Nandaime, a distant echo of Granada's colonial sister city, lost forever in a 16th-century Mombacho landslide. ▸▸ *For listings, see page 132.*

Archipiélago Las Isletas → *For listings, see page 132.*

Just five minutes outside Granada, in the warm waters of Lake Nicaragua, is the chain of 354 islands called Las Isletas. The islands are big piles of basalt rock covered in lush vegetation growing in the fertile soil that fills in the islands' rocky surface. The number of mango trees on the archipelago is staggering (the abundance of fruit in general is an important part of the local diet along with fish) and magnificent giant ceiba and guanacaste trees dominate the landscape. Bird life is rich, with plenty of egrets, cormorants, ospreys, magpie jays, kingfishers, Montezuma oropendulas and various species of swallow, flycatcher, parrot and parakeet, as well as the occasional mot-mot. A great way to appreciate the bird life is to head out for a dawn kayaking expedition with NicarAgua Dulce or **Mombotour**, see page 124 for further details.

The islands were created by a massive eruption of the Mombacho volcano that watches over the lake and islands to the west. You can see from the tranquillity of Las Isletas' waters how much of the mountain was blown into the water during the eruption. The islands' population consists mainly of humble fishermen and boatmen, though many of the islands are now privately owned by wealthy Nicaraguans and a handful of foreigners who build second homes and use them for weekend and holiday escapes. The school, cemetery, restaurants and bars are all on different islands and the locals commute mostly by rowing boat or by hitching rides from the tour boats that circulate in the calm waters. Fishing is the main source of income and you may well see the fishermen in the water laying nets for the lake's delicious *guapote* or *mojarra*. Many also find work building walls or caretaking on the islands owned by the weekenders.

The peninsula that jets out between the islands has small docks and restaurants on both sides. The immediate (north) side of the islands is accessed by the road that runs through the tourist centre of Granada and finishes at the *malecón* and docks. This is the more popular side of the archipelago and boat rides around the islands are cheaper from here (US$15 per hour per boat). In addition to the many luxurious homes on this part of the islands, is the tiny, late 17th-century Spanish fort, **San Pablo**, on the extreme northeast of the chain; it can be visited from the north side of the peninsula. Real estate companies have moved into this side of the archipelago and it is not unusual to see 'For Sale' signs in English.

Some 3 km from downtown on the southern side of the peninsula lies Bahía de Asese, where boats also offer one-hour rides around the islands. You will see large signs for Asese and a turning as you advance through the Complejo Turístico. Once you arrive at the bay, you will find boat schedules for Zapatera (see below) at the **Marina Cocibolca** ⓘ *T228-1223, www.marinacocibolca.net*. Despite the fact that there are fewer canals here you will have a better chance to see normal island life since this southern part of the archipelago is populated by more locals, some of them quite impoverished. An hour on this side is normally US$15 with both sides charging US$1.50 for parking. A taxi or horse-drawn carriage to the docks costs US$4 or less.

Parque Nacional Archipiélago Zapatera → *For listings, see page 132.*

Although most important relics have been taken to museums, this archipelago of 11 islands remains one of the country's most interesting pre-Columbian sites. Isla Zapatera, the centrepiece and Lake Nicaragua's second largest island, is a very old and extinct volcano that has been eroded over the centuries and is covered in forest.

Arriving in Archipiélago Zapatera

Getting there The island system is 40 km south of Granada. The journey to the islands takes one hour from Granada by *panga* (skiff), more if there are lake swells. The passage between the protected waters of Las Isletas and Zapatera can be especially rough. Public boats depart irregularly from Puerto Asese and the average cost of hiring a private boat is US$100-150. Several Granada tour companies offer one-day trips that include lunch, boat and guide, including **Zapatera Tours**, page 124, and **Oro Travel**, page 125. **Tours Nicaragua** in Managua, page 65, offer a visit to Zapatera as part of a sophisticated week-long archaeological trip guided by a National Museum archaeologist. Note there have been some isolated reports of park rangers turning away visitors who do not have permission from MARENA, so it is best to use a tour operator to avoid being disappointed. All hiking on Zapatera is guided. Beyond a single simple restaurant and rustic lodgings, there are no facilities on the island or shops of any size. Bring all the supplies you need, including food and water.

Around Archipiélago Zapatera

Isla Zapatera has both tropical dry and wet forest ecosystems depending on elevation, which reaches a maximum height of 625 m. It is a beautiful island for hiking, with varied wildlife and an accessible crater lake, close to the northwest shore of the island. The main island is best known for what must have been an enormous religious infrastructure when the Spanish arrived, though many of the artefacts were not 'discovered' until the mid-19th century. There are conflicting reports on the island's indigenous name, ranging from *Xomotename* (duck village) to *Mazagalpan* (the houses with nets). Archaeological evidence dating from 500 BC to AD 1515 has been documented from more than 20 sites on the island. Massive basalt images attributed to the Chorotega people were found at three of these sites and some can be seen in the Museo Convento San Francisco in Granada and the Museo Nacional in Managua. US diplomat and amateur archaeologist Ephraim George Squier, on his visit to the island in 1849, uncovered 15 statues, some of which he had shipped to the US where they are in a collection at the Smithsonian Museum in Washington, DC. Another 25 statues were found by the Swedish naturalist Carl Bovallius in 1883, in what is the most interesting site, Zonzapote, which appears to have been part of an ancient ritual amphitheatre. In 1926, the US archaeologist Samuel Kirkland Lothrop theorized that Bovallius had uncovered a Chorotega temple consisting of several sacred buildings each with a separate entrance, idols and sacrificial mounds. But the evidence is not conclusive and further studies are needed.

Reserva Natural Volcán Mombacho → *For listings, see page 132.*

Just 10 km outside Granada is one of only two cloud forests found in Nicaragua's Pacific lowlands. As well as the forest reserve, the volcano is home to coffee plantations and some ranches. The summit has five craters: four small – three covered in vegetation and one along the trails of the nature park – and one large that lost one of its walls in a tragic mudslide in 1570 (see Nandaime, page 131).

Arriving in Reserva Natural Volcán Mombacho

Getting there Take a bus between Nandaime or Rivas and Granada or Masaya. Get off at the Empalme Guanacaste and walk (or take a taxi) 1 km to the car park. From here you can take a truck to the top of the volcano (great view), 25 minutes; they leave every couple of hours from the parking area. The last trip is at 1500, although if there are enough people they will make another trip. It is also possible to walk the 5.5 km to the top using the steep cobblestone road (see below). Bring water, hiking shoes and a light sweater or better still a rain jacket or poncho.

Admission and information Park administration is in Granada, T2552-5858, www. mombacho.org. Thursday-Sunday, 0830-1700, US$12 adult, US$6 children, which includes transfer to the reserve from the parking area and the aid of a park guide. Tickets are sold at the parking area at the base, along with purified water and snacks. There's a small but pretty butterfly sanctuary and orchid house near the park entrance at the foot of the volcano.

Around the Reserva Natural Volcán Mombacho

The nature reserve is administered by the non-profit **Cocibolca Foundation** and is one of the best organized in Nicaragua. It's home to many species of butterfly and the famous Mombacho salamander (*Bolitoglossa mombachoensis*) which is found nowhere else in the world. Among other resident fauna, the biologists have counted some 60 species of mammal, 28 species of reptile, 10 species of amphibian, 119 species of bird and a further 49 species that are migratory visitors. More than 30,000 insect species are thought to exist, though only 300 have been identified to date. The volcano has terrific views of extinct craters and, if cloud cover permits, of Granada, Lake Nicaragua and Las Isletas. The cloud often clears for a few hours in the afternoon, 1400-1530 being your best bet for a good view.

Paths are excellently maintained and labelled. For those who want to see a pristine, protected cloud forest the easy way, this is the perfect place. Most visitors opt for a one- or two-hour stroll along the **Sendero Cráter**, an easy trail that leads through magnificent cloud forest full of ferns, bromeliads and orchids (752 species of flora have been documented so far). It has various lookout points and a micro-desert on the cone where you'll encounter steaming fumaroles and a stunning view of Cocibolca, Granada, Laguna de Apoyo and Volcán Masaya. An optional guide costs US$5 per group. Hardcore hikers may be disappointed by this relatively tame and well-tended trail, but there is an opportunity for a more challenging excursion too. The **Sendero El Puma** is only 4 km in length but takes around four hours to cover because of the elevation changes. This is the best walk for seeing wildlife, which can be very elusive during the daytime. A guide is obligatory, some speak English and they charge US$15 per group.

The main beauty of the park is its vegetation; if you wish to examine the amphibian, reptile and birdlife of the reserve, you will have to sleep in the research station itself and go hiking at night and in the early morning. They have one big room with several beds, shared baths, kitchen and an outhouse. Cost per person with meals and a night tour is US$30. The research station offers simple, cheap sandwiches and drinks to visitors and has a good model of the volcano and historical explanations.

Canopy tours
Canopy tours are not designed for nature watching, but to give you a bit of a rush and a sense of what it's like to live like the birds and monkeys up in the trees. Most people find it takes a long time for their smile to wear off. Mombacho has three canopy tours. On the forest reserve (west face) is the **Mombacho Canopy Tour** (see page 124), which includes lessons on a practice cable at ground level, assistance of one of the company guides, and all gear, and has 15 platforms from which you can buzz along a cable from platform to platform, high up in the trees and a suspended 1500-m-long bridge. The Mombacho tour is over coffee plants and has some very big trees; the service includes refreshments in a little viewpoint overlooking the valley after your adventure. The second canopy tour is on the east face of the mountain and is run by **Mombotour** (see page 125). This is a world-class canopy tour designed by the inventor of the sport, with 17 platforms 3-20 m above the ground on the lake side of Volcán Mombacho. The tour concludes with a stomach-churning vertical descent on a rappel line. The third canopy tour is new and operated by a Mombacho Canopy breakaway group, **Miravalle Canopy Tour**, located close to the entrance of the volcano reserve. It consists of 17 platforms and 2 km of 11 different zip-lines.

South from Granada → For listings, see page 132.

Nandaime
Nandaime (which translates roughly as 'well-irrigated lands') has an interesting history. Little is known about the original settlement, which was near the shores of the lake opposite the Zapatera Archipelago and was visited by the Spanish explorer Gil González Dávila. It was the most important town for the Chorotega southern federation and could have been responsible for administering the religious sites on Isla Zapatera. The city was then moved for unknown reasons to a second location further west along the base of the Mombacho volcano and could have grown to be a sister city to Granada – had it survived. It was reported to have been a town with the same classic colonial design as Granada, home to a "formal and solid Catholic church". However, in 1570 an earthquake caused the rim of the Volcán Mombacho crater lake to collapse and the village was annihilated in a massive landslide. A third settlement was established at Nandaime's current position.

Nandaime has two pretty churches, **El Calvario** and **La Parroquia** (1859-1872). It is a peaceful cowboy town for most of the year, but becomes a raucous party town for the patron saint festival of Santa Ana in the last week of July (the most important day is 26 July). The festival includes the dance of the *Diablos de al Orilla*, which is a colourful, spectacular display of more than 40 men, who accompany the saint on an annual pilgrimage to the tiny settlement of **La Orilla**, closer to the southern face of Volcán Mombacho. There is a bullfight in La Orilla and much dancing and drinking, and the following days in Nandaime include more dancing in colonial period costume, cross-dressing, more drinking and some parading around on horseback.

Reserva Silvestre Privada Domitila
① *María José Mejía (the owner), Calle Amelia Benard, Casa Dr Francisco Barbarena, Granada, T8881-1786, www.domitila.org, or Amigo Tours, Hotel Colonial, Granada, T2552-7299 (who*

act as agent), arrange reservations. To get to Domitila you will need to hire a taxi or car, though a 4WD is needed in the rainy season. Entrance to the park is US$5 and guides cost from US$10-40. Reservations to stay or visit the reserve must be made at least three days in advance. The forest is quite bare at the end of the dry season; ideal months to visit would be Nov-Jan.

Five kilometres south of Nandaime is the turning to an 8-km unpaved road that heads towards the lake and private nature reserve of Domitila. Just south of this turning, the Pan-American Highway passes over the region's most important river, Río Ochomogo, the ancient border between the worlds of the Chorotega and that of the indigenous Nicaraguans to the south. Today it marks the end of Granada and the beginning of the isthmus department of Rivas (see page 136). Most of the pristine low-altitude tropical dry forest that has not been cut for grazing is located at the back of the Mombacho volcano. However, further south there is a small swatch of it at this private wildlife reserve. Entry to the reserve is expensive, but it is home to more than 100 howler monkeys and 165 bird, 65 mammal and 62 butterfly species have been documented on their land. Due the small size of the reserve, nature watching is a more rewarding experience.

Lodging is available in eco-friendly rustic and attractive thatched huts at US$65 per person with three meals included, although food is average at best. The reserve management also offers horse riding and sailing excursions.

◉ Around Granada listings

For sleeping and eating price codes and other relevant information, see pages 28-30.

● Sleeping

Archipiélago las Isletas *p128*
$$$$ Jicaro Island Eco-lodge, on Jicaro island, T2552-6353, www.jicarolodge.com. Nicaragua's most upscale nature resort has 9 beautifully presented casitas and a secluded setting that makes it a fine spot for honeymoons or romantic getaways. Massage and yoga treatments are available, as well as a range of soft adventure tours.

Reserva Natural Volcán Mombacho
p130
$ Treehouse Poste Rojo, Pozo de Oro, 10 km outside Granada on the road to Nandaime, T8903-4563, www.posterojo. com. A happening new backpacker joint known affectionately as the **Tree House Hostel**. It has attractive and rustic wooden lodgings connected by Robinson Crusoe walkways. Activities include volunteering and full-moon parties. Buzzing and sociable.

● Restaurants

Archipiélago las Isletas *p128*
$$ Restaurante Puerto Asese, at the dock of Asese in Las Isletas, T2552-2269. Tue-Sun, 1100-1800. Good-value fish specialities, relaxed service, great views.

Contents

At a glance

⊖ **Getting around** Isla Ometepe can be explored by bus, car, mountain bike, motorcycle or horse. 4WD vehicles or high-speed *pangas* are needed to reach many beaches around San Juan del Sur.
✪ **Time required** 5-7 days.
☽ **Weather** During the dry season (Nov-Apr) everything is brown; the area is much prettier during the rainy season (May-Oct), although gnats and mosquitoes can be a problem then. Surfing is best Apr-Dec.
✖ **When not to go** Strong winds Nov-Mar can make exposed beaches quite uncomfortable (and the crossing from San Jorge to Ometepe Island quite rough). To avoid the crowds, don't come at Christmas or Holy Week.

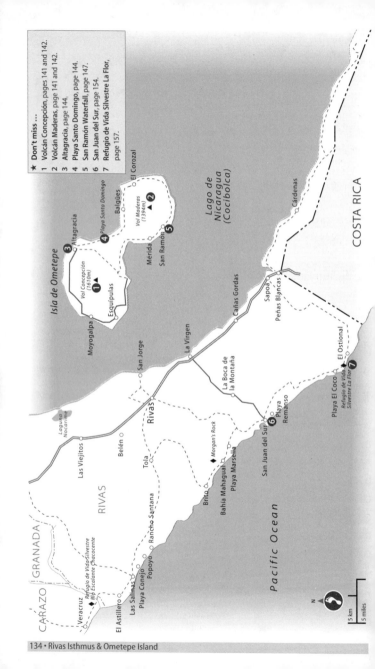

★ Don't miss ...
1 Volcán Concepción, pages 141 and 142.
2 Volcán Maderas, page 141 and 142.
3 Altagracia, page 144.
4 Playa Santo Domingo, page 144.
5 San Ramón Waterfall, page 147.
6 San Juan del Sur, page 154.
7 Refugio de Vida Silvestre La Flor,
   page 157.

Isla de Ometepe

Altagracia 3

*Vol Concepción
(1610m)* 1 ▲

Moyogalpa

Esquipulas

Balgües

El Corozal

4 Playa Santo Domingo

*Vol Maderas
(1394m)* 2 ▲

Mérida

San Ramón 5

*Lago de
Nicaragua
(Cocibolca)*

Cárdenas

San Jorge

La Virgen

*Laguna
Nocarime*

GRANADA

CARAZO

RIVAS

Las Viejitos

Belén

Tola

*Refugio de VidaSilvestre
Río Escalante Chococente*

Veracruz

El Astillero

Las Salinas

Playa Conejo

Popoyo

Rancho Santana

La Boca de
la Montaña

Cañas Gordas

Sapoa

Peñas Blancas

El Ostional

7 *Refugio de Vida
Silvestre La Flor*

Playa El Coco

COSTA RICA

Rivas

Brito

Bahía Mahagual

Playa Marsella

Morgan's Rock

San Juan del Sur

6 Playa
Remanso

Pacific Ocean

N

5 km
5 miles

The slender, well-travelled isthmus of Rivas separates the Pacific Ocean from Lake Nicaragua. Geographically speaking, this is the youngest part of the country, having emerged from the ocean four or five million years ago to fuse North and South America into a single continent. Swathes of ultra-fertile lowlands dominate the landscape as the isthmus tapers towards the Costa Rican border – a mere half hour from the provincial capital. Thanks to its rich terrain, sublime shorelines and prime position on the Pan-American Highway, the isthmus of Rivas is now enjoying a special prosperity and growing international interest.

Beyond the black-sand shores and sprawling ranches of its east coast, Isla Ometepe rises from the waters of Lake Nicaragua with perfectly symmetrical twin cones – an archetype of volcanic beauty. There is an enchanted and other-worldly feel to the island, where ancient stone relics hint at a lost civilization as bloodthirsty as it was mystically inclined. Today, Ometepe is home to a growing community of organic farmers who are transforming the island into a bastion of ecological soundness. Although you can hike, swim, cycle, kayak and volunteer here, much of the island's pleasure comes from simply lazing in a hammock.

By contrast, the west coast of the Rivas Isthmus is rocky and wave-swept, with low mountains and more than 130 km of Pacific beaches, including two of the world's most important turtle nesting sites. For better or worse, the region's rugged splendour has not been overlooked by international developers, who are constructing a slew of beachfront retirement homes and gated communities around the town of San Juan del Sur. Once little more than a quiet fishing village, it's now swollen with foreign prospectors, surfers and party-goers. Still, the sunsets are immense, development is in its early stages, and a poor infrastructure means much of the coast has been spared, for now.

Rivas

The capital of the department that carries its name, Rivas is a pleasant city with two beautiful churches, a happy, friendly population and lots of horse-drawn carriages with car tyres, particular to this area. It carries the nickname 'city of mangoes' for the trees that grow seemingly everywhere around the city. Sadly, few travellers bother to visit this town, preferring to head straight for San Jorge along the route that leads to Isla de Ometepe.
▸▸ *For listings, see pages 137-138.*

Arriving in Rivas → *Population: 41,764. Altitude: 139 m. Colour map 3, B4.*

Getting there and around Rivas is a transport hub and there are frequent bus services from Managua, Granada, San Juan del Sur and the border with Costa Rica at Peñas Blancas. Colectivo taxis can be hired from San Juan del Sur or the border. Bicycle rickshaws are popular for short trips around town, whilst connections between Rivas and the dock at San Jorge are best by taxi. ▸▸ *For further details, see Transport, page 138.*

Tourist information **INTUR** ⓘ *Texaco, 1 c abajo, T2563-4914, elcantor2000@yahoo.com.* Good maps of Nicaragua and general information. **Note**: The waterfront area of town is not safe at night.

Places in Rivas
Founded in 1720 and named after a high-level Spanish diplomat in Guatemala, Rivas was, and still is, a ranching centre. For the filibuster William Walker (see page 117), who fought and lost three battles here, it was never a very happy place. The **Templo Parroquial de San Pedro** on Parque Central dates from 1863 and is the city's principal church, with a design reminiscent of the cathedral in León. Inside there is a famous fresco depicting the heroic forces of Catholicism defeating a withered Communism in a seemingly one-sided sea battle. There is also the gaily painted **Iglesia San Francisco** to the west of the park, which is the older of the two churches.

The **Museo de Antropología e Historia** ⓘ *Escuela International de Agricultura, 1 c arriba, 1½ c norte, Mon-Fri 0900-1200, 1400-1700, Sat 0900-1200, US$2,* is the region's best museum. It has a dwindling, poorly labelled but precious, collection of archaeological pieces as well as taxidermic displays and some ecological information. The main attraction is the beautiful old **Hacienda Santa Ursula** in which the museum is housed. The hacienda is said to have been built in the late 18th century and its charming corridors and views make it well worth a visit.

San Jorge
It may seem like an extension of Rivas, but San Jorge is actually a separate town, one that most visitors see only on their way to the ferry for Ometepe. To catch the **ferry**, head east from the roundabout on the highway towards the lake, as far as the Parque Central. Here you will pass the **Iglesia de San Jorge**, a little Gothic-Mudéjar (a mixture of Christian and Muslim architecture from Spain) church, with the ruins of an ancient convent behind. From the church it is two blocks north, then east again all the way to *el muelle* (the dock). The cross over the road between the highway and the church is known as **La Cruz de España** and, together with a small mural painting and a few plaques, commemorates the fateful arrival of the Spanish.

⊛ Rivas listings

For sleeping and eating price codes and other relevant information, see pages 28-30.

⊕ Where to stay

Rivas *p136*

$$ Nicarao Inn Hotel, northwest corner of Parque Central, 2 c abajo, T2563-3836, www.hotelnicaroinn.com.ni. The finest hotel in Rivas has 18 tastefully decorated, comfortable rooms, all with a/c, cable TV, hot water and Wi-Fi. Services include laundry, car rental, conference centre, restaurant and bar. Polite and professional. Breakfast included.

$ El Coco, on highway near where bus from the border stops. Noisy, basic, small rooms, some with private bath. Interesting bar, *comedor* with vegetarian food and a nice garden.

$ Español, across from the southeast corner of Iglesia San Pedro, T2563-0006. Dusty old cheapie with 5 basic rooms, each has bath and fan. Clean but faded. Restaurant attached.

$ Hospedaje Hilmor, across from the northeast corner of Iglesia San Pedro, T2563-5030. A range of economical rooms. Some have private bath and TV, others are ultra-basic with shared bath. Shared kitchen is available and breakfasts are cooked on request and at extra cost. The owner is friendly, chatty and helpful – ask about her good-value lodgings in San Juan del Sur. Recommended.

$ Hospedaje Lidia, Texaco, ½ c abajo, near bus stop, T2563-3477. 12 rooms, clean, family atmosphere, some with private bath, noisy, helpful. Recommended.

San Jorge *p136*

There are a few ultra-cheap *hospedajes* scattered around the port, otherwise most lodgings in San Jorge start at around US$20.

$$ Hotel California, el puerto, 200 vrs abajo, T8804-6699, www.myhotelcalifornia.com. North American-owned, motel-style place

with lush gardens and Wi-Fi. It has clean, comfortable rooms with cable TV, a/c and private bath (a few have hot water). Airport pickup available and prices include breakfast.

$$ Hotel Dalinky, el puerto, 200 vrs abajo, T2563-4990, www.hoteldalinky.com. Large, clean, fairly pleasant double rooms with a/c, cable TV and bath. Services include pool, parking, restaurant, Wi-Fi and transportation. There's a handful of cheaper rooms with fans and no a/c. Full breakfast included.

$$ Hotel Hamacas, el puerto, 100 vrs abajo, 25 vrs sur, T2563-0048, www.hotelhamacas. com. As the name suggests, lots of hammocks, mostly slung across porches. The rooms are large and clean with a/c and cable TV (cheaper with fan). Services include Wi-Fi, a paddling pool for kids and billiards. A pleasant spot with lots of quiet green spaces. Breakfast included.

⊘ Restaurants

Rivas *p136*

For economical street food, you'll find several cheap *comedores* on the north side of Parque Central.

$$ El Mesón, Iglesia San Francisco, ½ c abajo, T2563-4535. Mon-Sat 1100-1500. Very good, try *pollo a la plancha* or *bistec encebollado*.

$$ La Lucha, Km 118.5, south of Rivas on lake side of highway, wild game menu and traditional dishes, *guardatinaja asada* (grilled paca), *cuzuco en salsa* (armadillo in tomato sauce), *huevo de toro asado* (grilled bulls' balls), *garrobo en caldillo* (black iguana soup) or *boa en salsa* (boa constrictor in tomato sauce), good service, big seating area, friendly.

$$ Rancho Coctelera Mariscazo, Estadio de Rivas, 800 vrs sur, on the Carretera Panamericana. One of the best seafood restaurants in Nicaragua, with great fish dishes *a la plancha*, excellent *sopa de mariscos* (seafood soup). Simple decor, friendly service, very good value. Highly recommended.

$$-$ Vila's Rosti-Pizza, south side of
Parque Central, T2563-0712. A grand old
building that looks almost too elegant to
house the fast-food joint that it does. Vila's
offers roast chicken, tacos, pizza and other
wholesome grub. Locals seem to rate it.
$ Guajiros, northwest corner of Parque
Central, 1 c norte, 1½ c abajo. Good, clean,
unpretentious dining at this intimate little
Cuban restaurant. They serve national dishes,
buffet fare and *comida* à la carte.
$ Pizza Hot, north side of the plaza, T563-
4662. Fast food including burgers, fried
chicken and reasonable enough pizza.
$ Rayuela, across from police station,
T563-3221. Prices here are a steal with very
cheap tacos, *repochetas* and sandwiches.
A clean and pleasant *comedor* that's often
recommended by the locals.

Bakeries

Ballesteros, northwest corner of Parque
Central, 2 c abajo. A large, popular bakery
that's good for a cheap breakfast of bread
and cake.

San Jorge *p136*
Plenty of cheap places around the dock area.
$$-$ El Gran Diamante, San Jorge Plaza,
300 vrs sur, 800 vrs arriba. Seafood restaurant
perched on the lake, with panoramic views
of Ometepe's volcanoes.
$$-$ El Refugio, Portuaria, 200 vrs sur,
T2563-4631. Daily 0900-2200. Overlooking
the water and specializing in seafood.
The beef is reportedly good.
$ Restaurante Ivania, Alcaldía Municipal,
1 c abajo, 2½ c sur, T2563-4764. Daily 0600-
2300. Good fish soup or shrimp *ceviche*.

⊕ What to do

San Jorge *p136*
Boat trips
Ometepe Tours, at the dock, T2563-4779.
For boats to the island, hotel reservations,
car rental, tours on the island, student
groups and information.

⊖ Transport

Rivas *p136*
Bus
Managua, every 30 mins, 0630-1700,
US$2, 2½ hrs; express buses, US$2.50,
2 hrs; microbuses, US$3, 1½ hrs. To **Granada**
every 45 mins, 0530-1625, US$1.50, 1¾ hrs.
To **Jinotepe**, every 30 mins, 0540-1710,
US$1.50, 1¾ hrs. To **San Juan del Sur**,
every 30 mins, 0600-1830, US$1, 45 mins.
To **Peñas Blancas**, every 30 mins, 0500-
1600, US$0.75, 1 hr.

International buses Ticabus, Pulpería
El Diamante, de la Estación Texaco, 150 vrs
norte, T8847-1407, www.ticabus.com, and
Transnica, Shell, 4 c al lago, T8898-5195,
www.transnica.com, have buses bound for
Costa Rica and **Honduras** stopping at the
Texaco station on the highway.

Taxi
From the centre of Rivas to the dock at
San Jorge, US$1 colectivo (US$4 private).
To **San Juan del Sur**, US$1.75 colectivo
(US$7.50 private). To **Peñas Blancas**, US$2
colectivo (US$8 private). In all cases beware
of overcharging and exercise caution (see
box, page 68).

San Jorge *p136*
Boat and ferry
Services are always subject to change. To
Moyogalpa, hourly, 0700-1730, ferry US$3,
boat US$2, 1 hr. To **San José del Sur**, 0930,
1000, 1640, 1700, ferry US$3, boat US$2, 1 hr

Bus
There are 7 daily buses to **Managua**, 0830-
1630, US$2.50, 2½ hrs. A **taxi** direct from/
to **San Juan del Sur** costs US$8; colectivo
US$2. Taxi to **Rivas** terminal US$1.

⊕ Directory

Rivas *p136*
Banks The plaza has 2 banks: a Banpro
on the west side, and a Banco Procredit

with a Visa ATM on the northwest corner. There's also a BAC ATM, plaza, 2 c oeste. **Fire** T2563-3511. **Hospital** T2563-3301. **Police** T2563-3732. **Post** Correos de **Nicaragua**, Gimnasio Humberto Méndez, ½ c abajo, T2563-3600. **Red Cross** T2563-3415. **Telephone** Enitel, Parque Central, west side, T2563-0003.

Isla de Ometepe

The ancient Nahuas of Mexico were delivered to Ometepe by a dream, so the legend goes, after many years of fruitless wandering. Two ethereal volcanoes comprise this mysterious realm: Concepción is larger, active and periodically spews ash; Maderas is smaller, extinct and swathed in cloud forest. Each evening at dusk, their green slopes erupt with the chattering of exotic birds. Ometepe's pre-Columbian heritage survives in the form of bizarre petroglyphs and a statuary that is testament to a shamanic reverence for animal spirits. The island's inhabitants, descended from these cultures, are mostly fishing and farming communities, and some of Nicaragua's kindest people. This is a fine place for volunteering or learning about organic farming. The rich volcanic soil means agriculture here has always been organic, but a wave of foreigners are introducing more sophisticated, ecologically aware permaculture techniques. Thus far, tourist development has kept within the style and scale of the island, although there are now murmurings of larger, less sympathetic construction projects. ▶▶ *For listings, see pages 147-153.*

Arriving on Isla de Ometepe → *Population: 37,000. Colour map 3, B4.*

Getting there **Boat** connections from Granada and San Carlos are possible, but the most user-friendly are the one-hour boats and ferries from San Jorge to Moyogalpa, running almost hourly throughout the day, with reduced services on Sunday (see Transport, page 138). The best choice is the ferry, which has three levels, a toilet, snack bar, television (with *telenovelas* blasted through concert speakers over the noise of the motors) and room for six cars.

Car If you have a high-clearance 4WD you may want to take it across on the ferry (US$20 each way). Arrive at least one hour before the ferry departure to reserve a spot (if possible call the day before, T2278-8190, to make an initial reservation). You will need to fill out some paperwork and buy a boarding ticket for each person travelling. Make sure you reserve your spot as close to the ferry ramp as possible, but leave room for trucks and cars coming off the ferry.

Getting around Taxis (vans and pick-ups) wait for the boat arrivals, as do buses. Most of the island is linked by a bus service, otherwise trucks are used. Walking, cycling, motorbiking or horse riding are the best ways to see the island; however, it can be dusty in the dry season.

Tourist information **Ometepe Expeditions** ⓘ *75 m from the port in Moyogalpa, behind the white fence and in front of Hotel Ometepetl, T8363-5783, ometepexpeditions@hotmail.com,* are the island's best tour operator and a good source of information. There's usually someone there who speaks English.

Safety

Several hikers have fallen to their deaths trying to summit Ometepe's volcanoes unguided. Always use professional and qualified guides, and beware local scammers. In recent years, motorbikes have taken over the island and some tourists have been in nasty and expensive accidents. Clarify all insurance details before hiring a vehicle, and if you've never ridden before, understand that a quick jaunt up and down a football pitch does not qualify you to ride on the roads.

Background

Ceramic evidence shows that the island has been inhabited for at least 3500 years, although some believe this figure could be 12,000 years or more. Little is known about the pre-Conquest cultures of the island. From ceramic analysis carried out by US archaeologist Frederick W Lange (published in 1992), it appears the people of 1500 BC came from South America as part of a northern immigration that continued to Mexico. They lived in a settlement in what is today the town of Los Angeles and were followed by waves of settlement to both the western and eastern sides of the island.

Mystery also surrounds the people who inhabited the island at the time of the Conquest. A visiting priest reported in 1586 that the natives of the island spoke a language different from any of those spoken on the mainland. Yet the large basalt statues found on Ometepe appear to be of the same school as the ones found on Zapatera and attributed to the

Ometepe

To Granada ▶

To San Carlos

San Marcos   San Mateo   Puerto de Gracia
              San José del Norte
La Flor   Altagracia

9 Moyogalpa   El Chipote

                Volcán   La Primavera
                Concepción   Playa Santo Domingo
                (1610m)   Urbaite
Punta   Balgües   Bona Fide
Jesús   Socorro
María   Esquipulas   San José   El   La Palmera
          Los Angeles   del Sur   La Unión   Porvenir
                                   Isthmus   Santa Cruz
                         Sinacapa of Istián
              Charco Verde   Quiste

Lago de Nicaragua
                        San Antonio
                                   San Ramón
                        Mérida   Waterfall
                                   Volcán   San
                                   Maderas   Pedro
                                   (1394m)
                              San Ramón
                                            Tichuna

N

5 km
5 miles

Where to stay 🛏
Albergue Ecológico
  Porvenir **22**
American & Café **14**
Buena Vista **16**
Caballito Mar **4**

Central **5**
Charco Verde Inn **6**
Chico Largo Hostel **19**
Costa Azul **18**
El Encanto **20**
El Indio Viejo **17**
Finca del Sol **8**
Finca Ecológica El
  Zopilote **23**
Finca Magdalena **13**
Finca Playa Venecia **15**
Finca Santo Domingo **2**

Hacienda Mérida **7**
Hospedaje Castillo **21**
Hospedaje Ortiz **9**
Hospedaje Soma **24**
Hotelito Aly **25**
Island Landing **10**
Istiam **1**
Little Morgan's **11**
Ometepetl **26**
Totoco Eco-Lodge **12**
Villa Paraíso **3**

Restaurants 🍴
American Café **9**
Café Campestre **1**
Comedor Santa Cruz **2**
Corner House **3**
Julia's **4**
Las Manos Mágicas **5**
Los Ranchitos **6**
Natural **7**
Yogi's Café & Bar **8**

Petroglyphs ••

Chorotegas. Dr J F Bransford, a medical officer for a US Navy, came to Nicaragua in 1872 as part of an inter-oceanic exploratory team. His observations (published in 1881 by the Smithsonian Institute) remain one of the few sources of information about this mysterious place. During his digs in 1876 and 1877, near Moyogalpa, he noted that the Concepción volcano was forested to the top and 'extinct' (it would become very much alive five years later) and that the isthmus between the two volcanoes was passable by canoe during the rainy season. The island's population was estimated at 3000, with most living in Altagracia and some 500 others scattered around the island. Most people he described fitted the description of an Ometepino today – basically Chorotega in appearance; however, on the very sparsely populated Maderas side of the island lived a tall people – many of the men were over 6 ft – with decidedly unusual facial features. These people were more suspicious by nature and reluctant to talk or share the location of the big basalt idols of the islands. From this, Bransford concluded that they still worshipped the gods represented in the statues (by contrast, the other inhabitants of the island had happily revealed the location of their statues). There is little evidence of these people today, but their religious statues can be found next to the church in Altagracia and in the Museo Nacional in Managua (see page 53).

Around Isla de Ometepe

Geology, vegetation and wildlife

ⓘ *Climbing is good on both volcanoes. The vegetation and wildlife of Maderas is superior in both quantity and diversity, but there are more hikers to scare off animals.*

Ometepe's two volcanoes rising up out of Lake Nicaragua appear prehistoric and almost other-worldly. The two cones are part of a recently ordained UN Biosphere Reserve and they are connected by a 5-km-wide lava-flow isthmus. The island is always in the shadow of one of its two Olympian volcanic cones. The dominant mountain, one of the most symmetrical cones in the world and covered by 2200 ha of protected forest, is **Volcán Concepción** (1610 m high, 36.5 km wide). It is an active volcano that last blew ash in March 2010 and had its most recent major lava flow in 1957. The volcano was inactive for many years before it burst into life in 1883 with a series of eruptions continuing until 1887. Concepción also erupted from 1908 until 1910, with further significant activity in 1921 and 1948 to 1972. Thanks to its hot lava outbursts, one of the cone's indigenous names was *Mestlitepe* (mountain that menstruates). The other well-known name is *Choncotecihuatepe* (brother of the moon); an evening moonrise above the volcano is an unforgettable sight.

Volcán Maderas (1394 m high, 24.5 km maximal diameter) last erupted about 800 years ago and is now believed to be extinct. The mountain is wrapped in thick forest and is home to the only cloud forest in Nicaragua's Pacific Basin other than Volcán Mombacho. The Nicaraguans called the mountain *Coatlán* (land of the sun). The 400 m by 150 m cold, misty crater lake, **Laguna de Maderas**, was only discovered by the non-indigenous population in 1930 and has a lovely waterfall on the western face of the cone. Maderas has 4100 ha of forest set aside and protected in a reserve.

Both cones have monkey populations, with the Maderas residents being almost impossible to miss on a full-day hike on the cone. The forest of Maderas also has a great diversity of butterfly and flower species, as well as a dwarf forest and the island is home to numerous parrots and magpie jays; the latter are almost as common as the pigeons in the squares of European cities. The **Isthmus of Istiam**, the centre of the island's figure-of-eight shape and a fertile lowland finger that connects the two volcanoes' round bases, has several lagoons and creeks that are good for kayaking and birdwatching. Off the northeast

Climbing the volcanoes

Volcán Concepción There are two main trails leading up to the summit. One of the paths is best accessed from Moyogalpa, where there is lots of accommodation. The other is from Altagracia. Climbing the volcano without a local guide is not advised under any circumstances and can be very dangerous; a climber died here in 2004 after falling into a ravine. Ask your hotel about recommended tour guides; many of the locals know the trail well but that does not make them reliable guides; use extreme caution if contacting a guide not recommened by a tour operator or well-known hotel. See page 152 for recommended guides. The view from Concepción is breathtaking. The cone is very steep near the summit and loose footing and high winds are common. Follow the guide's advice if winds are deemed too strong for the summit. From **Moyogalpa** the trail begins near the village of La Flor and the north side of the active cone. You should allow eight hours for the climb. Bring plenty of water and breathable, strong and flexible hiking shoes. From **Altagracia** the hike starts 2 km away and travels through a cinder gully, between forested slopes and a lava flow. The ascent takes five hours, 3½ hours if you are very fit. Take water and sunscreen. Tropical dry and wet forest, heat from the crater and howler monkeys are added attractions.

Volcán Maderas Three trails ascend Maderas. One departs from Hotel La Omaja near **Mérida**, another from Finca El Porvenir near **Santa Cruz**, and the last from Finca Magdalena near **Balgües**. Presently, the trail from Finca Magdalena is the only one fit enough to follow, but check locally. You should allow five hours up and three hours down, although relatively dry trail conditions could cut down hiking time considerably. Expect to get very muddy in any case. Ropes are necessary if you want to climb down into the Laguna de Maderas after reaching the summit. Swimming in the laguna is not recommended, as one tourist got stuck in the mud after jumping in. Rather farcically, she had to be pulled out with a rope made of the tour group's trousers. Hiking Maderas can no longer be done without a guide, following the deaths of British and American hikers who apparently either got lost or tried to descend the west face of the volcano and fell. While some hikers still seem reluctant to pay a local guide, it is a cheap life insurance policy and helps the very humble local economy. Guides are also useful in pointing out animals and petroglyphs that outsiders may miss. There is an entrance fee of US$2 to climb Maderas. The trail leads through farms, fences and gets steeper and rockier with elevation. The forest changes with altitude from tropical dry, to tropical wet and finally cloud forest, with howler monkeys accompanying your journey. Guides can be found for this climb in Moyogalpa, Altagracia and Santo Domingo or at Finca Magdalena where the hike begins.

side of the isthmus are a couple of islands that also shelter rich birdlife, in addition to the legendary **Charco Verde** on the southern coast of Concepción (see page 144).

Petroglyph sites

Ometepe has much to offer the culturally curious as well, with numerous pre-Columbian sites. A six-year survey in the mid-1990s revealed 73 sites with 1700 petroglyph panels and that is just the tip of the iceberg. A guided visit is recommended to one of the petroglyph sites, which are known according to the name of the farm they are found on. To list but a few: **San Marcos** has an eagle with outstretched wings; **Hacienda San Antonio** has geometric figures; **Altagracia**, in the house of Domingo Gutiérrez, shows a rock with an 'x' and a cross used to make sacrifices to the cult of the sun; **Hacienda La Primavera** has various images; **La Cigüeña** shows the southern cross and various animals; and **El Porvenir** has a sundial and what some believe to be an alien being and a representation of the god of death. **La Palmera**, **Magdalena**, **San Ramón** and **Mérida** all have interesting petroglyph sites and **Socorro** has some sun calendars.

Moyogalpa

Moyogalpa is the port of entry for arrivals from San Jorge. It is a bustling, commercial town with a decidedly less indigenous population than the rest of the island. There is little of cultural or natural interest here but, thanks to its growing traveller and expat scene, it is becoming an increasingly popular stopover, particularly those leaving on an early boat or climbing Concepción from the western route. The name Moyogalpa translates as the 'place of mosquitoes', but there aren't really any more here than elsewhere in the region.

One interesting excursion from Moyogalpa (dry season only) is to walk or rent a bicycle to visit **Punta Jesús María**, 4-5 km away. It is well signposted from the road: just before Esquipulas head straight towards the lake. Jesús María has a good beach and a panoramic view of the island. In the mornings you can watch the fishermen on the long sandbar that extends into the lake. During the end of the dry season there are temporary places to eat and drink.

There is a small museum, cybercafé and artisan store called **Museo Ometepe** ① *up the street that runs from the dock to the church, ½ block from the Pro Credit office, T2569-4225, daily 0800-2000, US$2.* The crafts available here are hard to find anywhere else in Nicaragua. There are plantain rope hats from Pul, *jícaras* from La Concepción, oil paintings by local artists from Esquipulas and Moyogalpa, seed necklaces from Moyogalpa, wood sculptures from Altagracia and pottery from San Marcos. You can also buy beautiful all-natural canteens known as a *calabazos* – a big round *jícaro* fruit, hollowed and smartly decorated, with a rope strap attached and drinking hole plugged with a corn cob.

Moyogalpa to Altagracia

Most transport uses the southern route to Altagracia as it is faster and completely paved. The northern route is very rough but is more natural and scenic; it runs east from Moyogalpa along the north shores through the tiny villages of **La Concepción**, **La Flor** and **San Mateo**. There are commanding views of the volcano with its forests and 1957 lava flow visible beyond rock-strewn pasture and highland banana plantations. To the north lies the deep blue of Lake Nicaragua. A fork to the left leads to the coast and the small, indigenous settlement of **San Marcos**; to the right it leads to **Altagracia**, past a baseball field (matches on Sundays) and a school. A tiny chapel marks your arrival in Altagracia. The town entrance is just southeast of the cemetery, and is perhaps the most scenic in all Nicaragua with its backdrop of Volcán Concepción.

The southern route, which is more heavily populated, is the quickest route to Altagracia, Playa Santo Domingo and the Maderas side of Ometepe. The road passes the town of **Esquipulas**, where it is rumoured that the great Chief Niqueragua may have been buried, and the village of **Los Angeles**, which has some of the oldest known evidence of ancient settlers on the island, dated at 1500 BC. Between Los Angeles and the next settlement, San

José del Sur, a turning leads to the **Museo El Ceibo** ① *0800-1730, El Sacremento, T-15, www. elceibomuseos.com, daily 0800-1700, US$6*, which has the best collection of pre-Columbian artefacts on the island, including numerous clay funerary urns and statues, as well as a fine collection of antique bills and coins, many dating to the beginning of the Republic. At the fairly developed **San José del Sur**, evacuated in 1998 under threat of massive mudslides from Concepción, the road rises to spectacular views of Volcán Maderas across the lake.

Just past San José del Sur is the rough, narrow access road to **Charco Verde**, a big pond with a popular legend of a wicked sorcerer, Chico Largo, who was said to have shape-shifting powers. Today his discarnate spirit guards the pond, ruling all those who have sold their soul to him. In the rainy season this is one of the most scenic parts of the island. At the end of the road are a petrol storage tank and a twig-covered beach. Just east is the **Bahía de Sinacapa**, which hides an ancient volcanic cone under its waters, along with an island called **Quiste**. There is a good lookout nearby, **Mirador del Diablo**, where you can breathe in the best sunset on the island.

Altagracia

This calm, unpretentious town is the most important on the island and it hides its population of around 20,000 well – except at weekends (there is usually dancing on Saturday nights, not to mention the odd fight among the local cowboys) and during festivals and holidays (see page 151). Altagracia predates the arrival of the Spanish and was once home to two tribes who named their villages **Aztagalpa** (egrets' nest) and **Cosonigalpa**. The tribes were divided by what is now the road from Parque Central to the cemetery. Their less than amicable relationship forced the people of Cosonigalpa to flee to what is now San José del Sur and to the bay of Sinacapa. The Spanish renamed the village, but the population remains largely indigenous. In the shade of the trees next to Altagracia's crumbling old church, built in 1924 to replace a much older colonial temple, is a **sculpture park** ① *daily 0900-1700, US$1.50*, which contains some of the most famous pre-Columbian statues in Nicaragua. They are estimated to date from AD 800 and represent human forms and their alter egos or animal protectors. The most famous are the eagle and the jaguar, which is believed to have been the symbol of power. On the plaza, the **Museo de Ometepe** ① *Tue-Sun 0900-1200, 1400-1600, US$2*, has displays of archaeology and covers local ethnographic and environmental themes (in Spanish only).

Playa Santo Domingo

The sweeping sandy beach at Santo Domingo is reached via a newly paved road which begins near Altagracia's southern exit. The road winds through plantain plantations, past a miniature church, down a steep section and across a tiny bridge where women do laundry in a large creek. Further upstream, the water is very clean and great for swimming. Its source is **El Ojo de Agua** ① *0700-1800, US$1*, where you'll find refreshing man-made swimming pools, a small ranch and some gentle walking trails. Beyond here, the road continues over an elevated pass that allows a view of both cones before dipping into beautiful (and cooler) tropical dry forest and Santo Domingo.

This long sandy coastline is one of the prettiest freshwater beaches in Nicaragua and with the forest-covered Volcán Maderas looming at the beach's end, it is truly exotic. The warm water, gentle waves and gradual shelf make it a great swimming beach. If you wade out you'll be able to see the cone of Concepción over the forest; a dual volcano swimming experience. The lake here is reminiscent of a sea (visitors are often surprised to see horses going down to drink from its shores, forgetting that it is fresh water). On

Romeo and Ometepetl – a lake story

Centuries ago, there was no Lake Nicaragua or any islands. Instead, there was a lush valley with fruit-bearing trees, full of deer and the songs of beautiful birds. This was a valley of the gods. Tipotani, the supreme god, sent Coapol to watch over the valley and for that it was called the Valle de Coapolca. Coapol was not alone in his duties; other gods such as Hecaltl, Xochipilli, Oxomogo and Cachilweneye helped tend the garden. But despite all the lush trees, green fields and healthy animal life, there was no source of water in the valley. Its lushness was created and maintained by the gods. Several tribes lived around the edge of the Valle de Coapolca and entered the valley often, to use its forests for hunting, to pick its wild fruits and for romance.

One summer afternoon the beautiful Ometepetl from the Nicaraguas tribe met the brave and handsome warrior Nagrando, from the neighbouring Chorotega tribe, and it was love at first sight. The god Xochipilli sent harmonious breezes across the pastures, while other gods offered gentle rain and singing birds. The gods married them for this life and the afterlife. But Ometepetl and Nagrando had to keep their love secret, as their tribes were rivals and war was possible at any moment. (The tribal chiefs had long since passed laws that their sons and daughters could not mix.) One day when they came to the valley to make love, they were seen by some soldiers and Nagrando was sentenced to death for his insolence. The supreme god Tipotani warned the couple of impending danger and the couple was led to a safe hiding place. Still, they knew that the chief's pronouncement was inexorable and they decided they would rather die together than live apart.

After reciting a prayer to the gods, they held each other tightly, kissed an eternal kiss and slit their wrists. Their blood began to fill the valley; the skies went dark and opened in torrential rains. Thunder clapped across the sky and rain filled with meteorites, as shooting stars ran across the heavens. Nagrando, delirious and writhing in pain, rose to his feet, stumbled and fell away from Ometepetl. The valley filled with water. The gods looked on and Nagrando's body came to rest as the island of Zapatera, while Ometepetl became the island of Ometepe, her breasts rising above the waters of the torrential floods. The instigators of the tragedy, those who put politics above love, were drowned in the floodwaters and the punished bodies from each tribe formed the archipelagos of Las Isletas and Solentiname.

this side of the island the trade winds blow nearly all year round and keep the heat and insects at bay. At times the wind is too strong for some visitors. During the early rainy season there can be many gnats if the wind dies. The width of the beach depends on the time of year: at the end of the dry season there's a broad swathe of sand and at the end of the rainy season bathers are pushed up to the edge of the small drop-off that backs the beach. It is not unusual to see a school of freshwater sardines (silversides) bubbling out of the water being chased by a predator. Around the beach there are many magpie jays, parrots, vultures, ospreys and hawks.

Santa Cruz

The diminutive settlement of Santa Cruz lies at the foot of Volcán Maderas, just south of Playa Santo Domingo. There are several good hotels here, including El Porvenir, which has

Mark Twain – "The Nicaragua route forever!"

Samuel Clemens, better known as Mark Twain, first saw the Pacific Coast of Nicaragua on 29 December 1866, after a long boat journey from San Francisco. He described the approach to the bay of San Juan del Sur thus: "…bright green hills never looked so welcome, so enchanting, so altogether lovely, as do these that lie here within a pistol-shot of us." Travelling on the inter-oceanic steamship line of Cornelius Vanderbilt between the Pacific and the Caribbean, Twain was writing a series of letters to a San Francisco newspaper *Alta California*, letters that were published in book form over 60 years later, in 1940, in a collection called *Travels with Mr Brown*.

He crossed Nicaragua in three days. The first was spent overland in a horse-drawn carriage from San Juan del Sur to the port of La Virgen on Lake Nicaragua. During the only land part of his journey from San Francisco to New York he was amazed at the beauty of the Nicaraguan people and their land. He and his fellow passengers gleefully exclaimed: "the Nicaragua route forever!" It was at the end of that 3½-hour carriage ride that he first saw the great lake and Island of Ometepe. "They look so isolated from the world and its turmoil – so tranquil, so dreamy, so

steeped in slumber and eternal repose." He crossed the lake in a steamship to San Carlos and boarded another that would take him down the Río San Juan to El Castillo, where passengers had to walk past the old fort to change boats beyond the rapids there. "About noon we swept gaily around a bend in the beautiful river, and a stately old adobe castle came into view – a relic of the olden time – of the old buccaneering days of Morgan and his merry men."

Back on the river, Twain enjoyed the beauty that today is the Indio-Maíz Biological Reserve: "All gazed in rapt silent admiration for a long time as the exquisite panorama unfolded itself. The character of the vegetation on the banks had changed from a rank jungle to dense, lofty, majestic forests. There were hills, but the thick drapery of the vines spread upwards, terrace upon terrace, and concealed them like a veil. Now and then a rollicking monkey scampered into view or a bird of splendid plumage floated through the sultry air, or the music of some invisible songster welled up out of the forest depths. The changing vistas of the river ever renewed the intoxicating picture; corners and points folding backward revealed new wonders beyond."

some of the best petroglyphs on the island. Importantly, the road forks at Santa Cruz – one route goes north towards Balgües, the other heads south to Mérida and San Ramón – making it a good, strategic base for exploring both sides of Maderas.

Balgües and around

The road to Balgües is rocky and scenic, although there are currently plans to pave it. The village itself is a little sad in appearance, but the people are warm and friendly, especially if you are travelling with a local. The feeling that everyone knows everybody on Ometepe is magnified here as most Ometepinos have a relative around every corner. This village is the entrance to the trailhead for the climb to the summit of Maderas (see box, page 142). There are several interesting **organic farms** in the area, including the famous Finca Magdalena, Finca Campestre and Bona Fide farm, where you can study permaculture techniques.

Mérida

From the fork at Santa Cruz the road goes south past small homes and ranches and through the towering palms of the attractive village of Mérida, in an area that was once an expansive farm belonging to the Somoza family. The road drops down to lake level and curves east past an old pier where Somoza's coffee production used to be shipped out to the mainland. It's possible to hire kayaks from Caballitos Mar (see Where to stay, page 150) if you wish to explore the nearby Río Istiam, an attractive waterway replete with birds, mammals and caiman.

San Ramón

Further along the eastern shores of Maderas is the affluent town San Ramón. The 'biological station' is the starting point for a hike up the west face of Maderas Volcano to a beautiful 40-m cascade, also called San Ramón. This is a much less athletic climb than the hike to the summit, but sadly it has lost much of its charm due to the bad management of the biological station, which has cleared much of the forest for grazing and cash crops. They have also installed an armed guard who you will need to pay to pass, US$5. At the time of research, locals were forging an alternative trail to the waterfall, enquire at the tourist information centre next to the dock in Moyogalpa. Note that it is sunny and hotter on this side of the mountain with less breeze from the trade winds from the east. Furthermore, transport is not as frequent on this side of the island and you may have a long walk if you are not on a tour. Hotels and Moyogalpa tour companies offer packages that are reasonable if you can get together at least two other hikers.

◉ Isla de Ometepe listings

For sleeping and eating price codes and other relevant information, see pages 28-30.

◖ Where to stay

Moyogalpa *p143, map p140*
$$-$ Hospedaje Soma, opposite Instituto Smith, up the hill from the port, left at the church and straight on for 250 m, a 10-min walk, T2569-4310, www.hospedajesoma. com. A tranquil spot offering a mix of dorms, private rooms, and cabins (**$$** with a/c). There's a large leafy garden, hammock space, BBQ, fire pit and communal kitchen. Better to book in advance.
$$-$ Island Landing, Muelle Municipal, 20 vrs arriba, almost next to the port. A comfortable and attractive hotel with a range of options. For the impoverished there are hammocks and dorms; for the better off there are private rooms, well-equipped apartments (**$$**) and comfortable *casitas* with open-air kitchen and dining space.

Island Landing has breezy views of the lake, volcano and the bustling port. Friendly and hospitable. Recommended.
$ American Café and Hotel, Muelle Municipal, 100 vrs arriba, a white building on the right, T8645-7193, simonesantelli14@ gmail.com. Excellent value, handsome, comfortable, spacious, well-furnished and immaculately clean rooms. All have good mattresses, attractive fixtures and hot water. Hosts Bob and Simone are very friendly and hospitable. Italian, German, Spanish and English spoken. A good source of information and the best rooms in town. Recommended.
$ El Indio Viejo, Muelle Municipal, 1 c sur, 3 c arriba, T2569-4262. This brightly coloured Moyogalpa cheapie (formerly **Hospedaje Central**) has ultra-basic dorms and private rooms. It seems to be steadily improving, but tread carefully and keep a close eye on your stuff. Bar and restaurant attached.
$ Hotelito Aly, Muelle Municipal, 200 vrs arriba, T2456-3270, hotelitoaly@yahoo.com.

This long-standing Nica-run cheapie has small, reasonably comfortable rooms with private bath and TV (cheaper without either). The newly renovated rooms upstairs are better but the attached restaurant is so-so.
$ Ometepetl, Muelle Municipal, 10 vrs arriba, T2569-4276, ometepetlng@hotmail.com (also reservations for Istián, Santo Domingo, below). This long-standing favourite has reasonably comfortable, clean, colourful (and now faded) rooms with or without a/c and bath. There's a restaurant attached, vehicle rental and tours on request. OK.

Moyogalpa to Altagracia *p143, map p140*

$$ Hotel Charco Verde Inn, almost next to the lagoon, San José del Sur, T8887-9302, www.charcoverde.com.ni. Pleasant *cabañas* with private bath, a/c, terrace and doubles with private bath and fan. Services include restaurant, bar, Wi-Fi, tours, kayaks, bicycles, horses and transportation. An Ometepe favourite with good reports.
$$-$ Finca Playa Venecia, 250 m from the main road, San José del Sur, T8887-0191, www.fincavenecia.com. Very chilled out, comfortable lodgings and a lovely lakeside garden. They have 4 rooms (**$**) and 15 *cabañas* (**$$**), some with lake view and some cheaper ones with fan. There's a good restaurant in the grounds, Wi-Fi, horses, tours, motorcycles, transportation and English-speaking guides. Recommended.
$ Chico Largo Hostel, next to Finca Playa Venecia, T8886-4069, www.chicolargo.net. 2 economical dorms, one with lake views, one without. They also have a few private rooms with bath and fan. Services include ATV rental, a camping area and a grill for cooking. Various tours offered including a boat tour to Isla Quiste, Río Istiam and the cascada at San Ramón. Friendly and relaxed.

Altagracia *p144, map p140*

$ Hospedaje Castillo, Parque Central, 1 c sur, ½ c oeste, T2552-8744, www.el castillo.com. Pleasant, friendly hotel with

19 rooms, most have bath outside, a few have private bath and a/c. There's a restaurant, bar and internet facilities, credit cards are accepted and TCs changed. They also rent out bikes and motorbikes and run tours to the volcanoes. The most upmarket option in town.
$ Hospedaje y Restaurante Ortiz, del Hotel Central, 1 c arriba, ½ c al sur, follow signs near the entrance to town, T8923-1628, www.hospedajeortiz.com. A very friendly, relaxed hotel managed by the hospitable Don Mario. They offer a range of pleasant budget rooms with shared bath. English is spoken and services offered include tours to the volcanoes, bicycles, fishing, book exchange, laundry, bar and restaurant. An amiable family atmosphere. Highly recommended for budget travellers.
$ Hotel Central, Iglesia, 2 c sur, T2552-8770, doscarflores@yahoo.es. 19 rooms and 6 cabañas, most with private bath and fan. There's a restaurant and bar, bicycle rental, tours, laundry service, parking, and hammocks to rest your weary bones. Dominoes and chess to keep you entertained in the evening. Credit cards accepted. Friendly and recommended.

Playa Santo Domingo *p144, map p140*

$$ Hotel Costa Azul, Villa Paraíso, 50 vrs sur, T2569-4867, www.hotelcostaazul. com.ni. The Costa Azul has 12 big, clean, well-lit rooms with good solid furniture, a/c, private bath and TV with DVD. There's also a restaurant serving *comida típica* and breakfasts. Bike and motorbike rental, tours and guides available.
$$-$ Finca Santo Domingo, Playa Santo Domingo, north side of Villa Paraíso, T2569-4862, www.hotelfincasantodomingo.com. Friendly lakeside hotel with a range of rooms (**$$-$**) and a handful of bungalows across the road (**$**), all with private bath. The rooms are generally clean and brightly coloured, but reports are mixed. You'll pay more for a space with a/c and lake views. There's also an *artesanía* store, bicycle

rental, internet terminal, laundry service and various tours. The restaurant serves *comida típica* and has good views.

$$-$ Villa Paraíso, beachfront, T2569-4859, www.villaparaiso.com.ni. One of Ometepe's longest-established and most pleasant lodgings. It has a beautiful, peaceful setting with 25 stone *cabañas* (**$$**) and 5 rooms (**$**). Most have a/c, private bath, hot water, cable TV, minibar and internet. Some of the cabins have a patio and lake view. Often fully booked, best to reserve in advance.

$ Hotel Buena Vista, Playa Santo Domingo, Villa Paraíso, 150 m norte, T8690-0984. Great views, you really feel the lake from here. This hotel has 2 cell-like rooms with private bath and fan; there's a restaurant, a pleasant terrace and hammocks. Seems to attract a young backpacker crowd. Sadly, there have been reports of thefts, so keep a very close eye on your belongings.

Santa Cruz *p145, map p140*
$$ Finca del Sol, from the fork in the road, 200 m towards Balgües, T8364-6394, www.fincadelsol.blinkweb.com. A lovely natural place with comfortable and ecologically designed *cabañas*. All are equipped with solar power, orthopaedic mattresses, TV, DVD player, shower and compost toilet. They grow their own organic fruit and vegetables and also farm sheep. A maximum of 8 guests are permitted at any one time and you will definitely need to book in advance. Recommended.

$ Albergue Ecológico Porvenir, Santa Cruz, T2552-8782, doscarflores@yahoo.es. Stunning views at this tranquil, secluded lodge at the foot of Maderas. Rooms are clean, comfortable and tidy, with private bath and fan. Scores of petroglyphs are scattered throughout the grounds, making it one of the island's most important archaeological sites. Excellent value. Recommended.

$ El Encanto, 100 m north of Santa Cruz, on the beach road, T8867-7128, www.goelencanto.com. A very tranquil and well-

tended *finca* with beautiful views and lots of sleepy, breezy porches. The rooms are good, clean and comfortable, and there's a pleasant restaurant with fine volcanic vistas. Various tours and dorm beds are also available. An excellent, secluded location close to the beach and trails. Friendly and highly recommended.

$ Finca Ecológica El Zopilote, from the fork in the road, 300 m towards Balgües, T8369-0644, www.ometepezopilote.com. El Zopilote is a funky organic *finca* that's popular with backpackers, hippies and eco-warrior types. They offer dorm beds, hammocks and *cabañas*, but are often full so it's best to book in advance. Offerings include full-moon parties, voluntary work placements, use of kitchen, tours and horse riding. Tranquil and alternative.

$ Hotel Istiam, Villa Paraíso, opposite the beach, 1 km north of Santa Cruz, T8844-2200, ometeptlng@hotmail.com, reservations through Ometepetl in Moyogalpa. Basic and often seemingly abandoned, this friendly, family-run place has a wonderfully isolated location on the beach road. Rooms are simple but clean, with fan and bath. Restaurant, tours, kayaks, horses, wind-surfing and bike rental available. Recommended.

$ Little Morgan's, from the fork in the road, 200 m towards Balgües, T8949-7074, www.littlemorgans.com. **Little Morgan's** is a fun, popular place with hospitable Irish management, a pool table and a well-stocked bar. They offer rustic dormitories, hammocks and 2 *casitas*, as well as guided tours, kayaks (there's access to a good sheltered bay), fishing, bicycles, horses and massages. Some of the hotel's structures are artfully reminiscent of Lord of the Rings.

Balgües and around *p146, map p140*
$$$ Totoco Eco-Lodge, Balgües, sign from the road, 1.5-km steep climb uphill, T8425-2027, www.totoco.com.ni Totoco is an ethically oriented and ecologically aware project that includes a permaculture farm,

eco-lodge and development centre. They have 4 very comfortable custom-designed *cabañas* (more in the works) with solar power, hot showers and compost toilets. There's a great restaurant with superb views and they offer a range of excellent tours. Totoco is also a good source of general information and a 'one-stop shop' for all your travel needs. A very honest and professional business that has earned its eco credentials. Highly recommended.

$$-$ Finca Magdalena, Balgües, signs from the road, 1.5-km steep climb uphill, T8498-1683, www.fincamagdalena. com. Famous co-operative farm run by 26 families, with accommodation in a small cottages, *cabañas* (**$$**), doubles (**$**), singles, dorms and hammocks. Camping possible. Stunning views across lake and to Concepción. Friendly, basic, and often jammed to the rafters with backpackers. Good meals served for around US$2. You can work in exchange for lodging, 1 month minimum. Locally produced coffee and honey available for sale.

Mérida *p147, map p140*
$$-$ Hacienda Mérida, el Puerto Viejo de Somoza, T8868-8973, www.hmerida.com. Popular hostel with a beautiful setting by the lake. Lodgings have wheelchair access and include a mixture of dorms and rooms, some with views (**$$**). There's a children's school on-site where you can volunteer, also kayak rental, good quality mountain bikes, internet and a range of tours available, including sailing. The restaurant serves fresh, hygienically prepared food – good for vegetarians. Recommended.
$ Caballitos Mar, Mérida, follow signs from the road, T8842-6120, www.caballitosmar. com. Great new Mérida alternative that has the best access to the Río Istiam and good kayaks for day or night tours. Fernando, the Spanish owner, is friendly and helpful and cooks up a very decent paella. Rooms are basic there are only a few of them at present; however, the neighbour also has

cheap beds if they're full with guests and there are hammocks, too. Recommended.

🍴 Restaurants

Moyogalpa *p143, map p140*
Almost all lodges serve meals, see Where to stay, above.

$$ Los Ranchitos, Muelle Municipal, 2 c arriba, ½ c sur, T2569-4112. One of the best in town, with a dirt floor, thatched roof, and excellent food, including fish, vegetarian pasta, vegetable soup, chicken in garlic butter, steak, pork and other hearty meat dishes, all served in the usual Nica way, with rice, beans, plantain and salad. Recommended.
$$-$ The American Café, the pier, 100 vrs arriba. Had enough of *gallo pinto*? This is the place for home-made food with flavour, including chilli con carne, pancakes and waffles. Very tasty and good value. They also have a small second-hand book collection. Recommended.
$$-$ The Corner House, Muelle Municipal, 200 vrs arriba, opposite the petrol station. Great new café-restaurant offering decent coffee and espresso, sandwiches, creative salads and tasty breakfasts, like eggs Benedict. All ingredients are sourced locally. Friendly owners. Recommended.
$$-$ Yogi's Café and Bar, Hospedaje Central, ½ c sur. A great place for good American food, beer and big-screen movies. Yogi is an enormous, but gentle, black labrador and not to be confused with the owner, Jerry, who is a very decent fellow and always open to philosophical conversation. Yogi's Café now features a single guest room (**$**), which can be earned in exchange for volunteer work such as painting, cooking, cleaning or dog-walking. Recommended.

Altagracia *p144, map p140*
All hotels serve food and you'll find a few economical *comedores* dotted around town – try the main plaza. Otherwise, head for one of the island's best:

$$ Las Manos Mágicas, Alcaldía, 2 norte, ½ c abajo. Daily 1700-2200. Don't miss this fantastic (if somewhat random) little Italian restaurant. The aptly named 'magic hands' serves authentic pizzas and home-made pasta in a pleasant garden setting. Friendly management and delicious food. Highly recommended.

Playa Santo Domingo *p144, map p140*
$$ Natural, Playa Santo Domingo, on the edge of the strip. Charming little hippy shack on the beach. They serve vegetarian food that's reasonably tasty but not good value. OK.
$ Julia's, Playa Santo Domingo, next to Natural. Tiny ramshackle comedor with a thatched roof. Possibly the cheapest and most unpretentious dining on the beach. **Comedor Gloriana** next door offers similar fare. Reasonable but not spectacular.

Santa Cruz *p145, map p140*
$ Comedor Santa Cruz, from the fork in the road, 50 m towards Balgües. Home cooking from the irrepressible Doña Pilar, who serves up the usual hearty Nica meat, fish and chicken fare. Service is achingly slow, so bring a book or a deck of cards. Friendly and entertaining. Recommended.

Balgües *p146, map p140*
$$ Café Campestre. Road-side café-restaurant that serves one of the best curries in Nicaragua (hot, spicy and highly recommended). There's tamer fare too, including burritos, burgers, sandwiches and other tasty, well-prepared creations that are sure to please the gringo palate. Juices, coffee and breakfast offered too. Recommended.

⊕ Festivals

Moyogalpa *p143*
Jul The town's patron saint festival (**Santa Ana**) is a very lively affair. Processions begin on 23 Jul in the barrio La Paloma

and continue for several days. On 25 Jul there is a lovely dance with girls dressed in indigenous costume and on 26 Jul there's a huge party with bullfights at a ring north of the church. Dates for some of the festivities vary according to the solar cycle. 2nd week of Dec, an impressive new marathon takes endurance runners up Concepción (25 km), Maderas (50 km) or both (100 km).

Altagracia *p144*
Oct-Nov The town's patron saint, **San Diego de Alcalá**, is celebrated from 28 Oct to 18 Nov with many dances and traditions, particularly the **Baile del Zompopo** (the dance of the leaf-cutter ant), which is famous throughout the country. The indigenous population celebrate their harvest god, Xolotl, every Nov. The story goes that one year when the harvest was being annihilated by red ants, the tribe shamans practised some ritual sacrifices and instructed the people to do a special dance to drums with branches of various trees. The disaster and starvation were averted and a tradition was born. When the Franciscans arrived in 1613 they brought with them an image of San Diego whose patron saint day coincided with that of the annual celebration for Xolotl and the red-ant dance. Over time, the friars convinced the indigenous locals to substitute one god for another, and the dance is still performed on 17 Nov.
Dec The **Purísima** celebrations to the Virgin Mary on 7 Dec are a marathon affair here of singing to a large, heavily decorated image of Santa María on the back of a pick-up truck in what is truly a Fellini-esque setting.

ⓞ What to do

Moyogalpa *p143*
ATVs, biking and motorbiking
Bikes and motorbikes are now ubiquitous on Isla Ometepe (see Safety, page 139) and are a great way to get around. Most hotels have units for rent and charge US$5-7 per

day for bicycles, US$20-30 for motorbikes or mopeds. In Moyogalpa, enquire at the bars near the dock, or try Robinson, who has many new cycles, motorbikes and a few ATVs (US$50 per day); find him 4 blocks uphill from the port, then 1 block south, T8691-5044, robinson170884@gmail.com. Ensure your unit is robust if aiming to cross the rough dirt roads on the north side of Concepción or on the east side of Maderas.

Kayaking
At the time of press, **Island Landing**, close to the dock, was planning to offer kayak rental in addition to bikes and motorbikes.

Tour operators
Ometepe Expeditions, 75 m from the port, behind the white fence and in front of Hotel Ometepetl, T8363-5783, ometepexpeditions@hotmail.com. A highly reputable agency that worked with the BBC to guide a group of disabled people to the summit of Concepción. They offer a range of tours including half- and full-day hikes to the volcanoes and cloud forests. Experienced, knowledgeable, English speaking and helpful. One of the best and highly recommended.
Unión Guías de Ometepe, 150 m from the port, close to Ometepe Expeditions, T8827-7714, www.ugometepe.com. Formed in 2006, this union of 30 guides offers an interesting range of half- and full-day tours, including hikes up Maderas and Concepción. A good organization that's worth supporting. Recommended.

Altagracia p144
Archaeology
Professor Hamilton Silva, north side of the Catholic church, or enquire in the town's museum, T8905-3744, is a resident expert and writer on Ometepe's history and archaeology. He speaks a little English and leads very interesting and good-value tours to the island's petroglyph sites. At weekends he can be found at his home in

Mérida, from Margarita's bar 70 m south, an archaeological site in itself. Recommended.

Santa Cruz p145
Windsurfing
Hotel Istiam, Villa Paraíso, opposite the beach, 1 km north of Santa Cruz, T8844-2200, ome teptlng@hotmail.com. Ideally positioned to catch the strong the winds hitting Playa Santo Domingo, **Hotel Istiam** has a small wind-surfing operation. Kayaks are available too, but conditions on this exposed part of the island can be rough and at times quite challenging.

Balgües p146
Organic farming
Bona Fide, www.projectbonafide.com. Also known as Michael's farm, **Bona Fide** offers innovative courses in permaculture as well as volunteer opportunities for those wishing to learn more about the science and work of organic farming. An interesting project.

Mérida p147
Kayaking
Caballitos Mar, follow signs from the road, T8842-6120, www.caballitosmar.com. The best starting point for kayak excursions down the Río Istiam, where you might spot caiman and turtles if you're lucky. Rentals are available for US$5 per hr, negotiable. Dawn is the best time for wildlife viewing, pack sunscreen and check lake conditions before setting out. For the brave, there are also night tours.

☉ Transport

All times are Mon-Sat; on Sun there are very few buses. All schedules subject to change; always confirm times if planning a long journey involving connections. Hitching is possible.

Moyogalpa p143
Boat and ferry
Schedules are always subject to change. To **San Jorge**, hourly, 0500-1730, ferry US$3, boat US$2, 1 hr. Reduced service on Sun.

Bus

Buses wait for the boats in Moyogalpa and run to **Altagracia** Mon-Sat, every 1-2 hrs, 0530-1830, US$1, 1 hr; Sun, several from 0530-1830. To **San Ramón** Mon-Sat, 0830, 0930, US$1.25, 3 hrs. To **Mérida**, Mon-Sat, 1445, 1630, US$2, 2 hrs; Sun 1245. To **Balgües**, Mon-Sat, 1030, 1530, US$2, 2 hrs; Sun 1020. For **Charco Verde**, and San José del Sur, take any bus to Altagracia and ask the driver where to get out. For Playa Santo Domingo or Santa Cruz, take any bus bound for Balgües, San Ramón or Mérida; or go to the Santo Domingo turn-off before Altagracia and get a connection there.

Car hire

Ometepe Rent a Car, Hotel Ometepetl, T2459-4276. A good strong 4WD is a must, US$35-50 for 12 hrs, US$60 for 24 hrs. They can also provide a driver, though advance notice is needed.

Taxi

Pick-up and van taxis wait for the ferry, price is per journey not per person, some have room for 4 passengers, others 2, the rest go in the back, which has a far better view, but is dusty in dry season. To **Altagracia** US$12-15, to **Santo Domingo** US$20-25, to **Mérida** US$30. Try Transporte Ometepe, T8695-9905, robertometeour@yahoo.es.

Moyogalpa to Altagracia *p143*
Boat and ferry

Boats depart from San José del Sur to **San Jorge**, 0540, 0730, 1330, 1520, ferry US$3, boat US$2, 1 hr. Reduced service on Sun.

Altagracia *p144*
Bus

For **Playa Santo Domingo** use any bus to San Ramón, Mérida or Balgües. To **Moyogalpa**, Mon-Sat every 1-2 hrs, 0430-0530, US$1, 1hr; Sun several daily, 0430-1700. To **Balgües**, Mon-Sat, 8 daily, 0430-1700, US$1, 1 hr; Sun 1040. To **Mérida**, Mon-Sat, 6 daily, 0730-1600, US$1, 2 hrs.

To **San Ramón**, Mon-Sat, 1030, 1400, US$1.30, 3 hrs.

Ferry

The port of Altagracia is called **San Antonio** and is 2 km north of the town; pick-up trucks meet the boat that passes between Granada and San Carlos. To **San Carlos**, Mon and Thu 1800-1900, upper deck (1st class) US$7, lower deck US$2.50, 11 hrs. To **Granada**, Tue and Fri, 2300-0000, upper deck (1st class) US$4.50, lower deck US$2, 3½ hrs. You strongly advised to travel on the upper deck and wear warm clothes. A sleeping bag, pillow and anti-sickness tablets are useful too.

❶ Directory

Moyogalpa *p143*

Banks Banco Procredit, Muelle Municipal, 3 c arriba, with Visa ATM and dollar-changing facility, but best to bring all the cash you need. There's a Western Union attached and another ATM in the grocery store across the street. You can also change money (but not TCs) in the 2 biggest grocery stores or in hotels. **Comercial Hugo Navas** also gives cash advances on credit cards (MasterCard and Visa). **Hospital** T2569-4247. **Internet** Cyber Ometepe, also known as Museo Ometepe, on main road up from dock, T2569-4225. Comercial Arcia has many computers and telephone service. **Police** T2569-4231. **Port Authority** T2569-4109. **Post and telephone** Entitel, T2569-4100, from the dock, 2 c arriba, 1½ sur, for both postal and telephone services.

Altagracia *p144*

Internet Hospedaje Castillo, US$1 per hr. They will also change TCs (at a poor rate).

San Juan del Sur and around

Although it has become one of Nicaragua's central tourist destinations, San Juan del Sur has not lost its small town, fishing village feel, with an abundance of little boats anchored just off its golden sands. But the many kilometres of Pacific shoreline north and south of the town's sweeping half-moon bay are even prettier, drawing increasing numbers of visitors to their luxury ecolodges, isolated surfing spots and empty, wave-swept beaches (the town is said to have more real estate agents than school children). The real attraction is the olive ridley turtles that have been coming to this stretch of coast for thousands of years – sometimes as many as 20,000 over a four-night period. The dry season along Nicaragua's Pacific Coast is very parched and brown, but most of the year the landscape is fluorescent green, shaded by rows of mango trees and dotted with small, attractive ranches and flower-festooned front gardens. Roadside stalls offer many fruits, such as watermelon, mango, níspero and some of the biggest papaya you'll see anywhere. ▶▶ *For listings, see pages 162-168.*

San Juan del Sur → *For listings, see pages 162-168. Population: 14,621. Altitude: 4 m.*
Colour map 3, C4.

Not long ago this was a secret place, a tiny coastal paradise on Nicaragua's Pacific Coast. In recent years, however, this little town on a big bay has become very popular, first as an escape from the built-up beaches across the international border in Costa Rica, then as a magnet for real estate developers, US retirees and the international surf crowd. In addition, cruise ships now anchor in its deeper waters and tourists have begun to arrive in quantity. San Juan del Sur has become a major destination, buzzing with activity and increasingly starting to resemble Costa Rica. Whilst the town is no longer the place to experience a country off the beaten path, there are still plenty of empty beaches nearby and the local coastline remains among the most beautiful in Central America.

Arriving in San Juan del Sur

Getting there Most of the buses come from Rivas, though a few leave direct from Managua. If coming from the border with Costa Rica take any bus towards Rivas and step down at the entrance to the Carretera a San Juan del Sur in La Virgen. A taxi is also a possibility from the border with Costa Rica and some hotels will pick you up at the border if you warn them well in advance. If driving, it is very straightforward: look for the turning in La Virgen from the Pan-American Highway (Carretera Panamericana) and head west until the road ends in San Juan del Sur.

Getting around You can get anywhere in San Juan by walking; if you are visiting outlying beaches you can arrange transport with local hotels or the ones at your destination. Additionally, there are many shuttle services making frequent trips north and south of the town. For the wilder and truly untamed stretches further away from town you will need a decent 4WD or even a boat.

Safety Under no circumstances walk to Playa Yankee or Playa Remanso, the beaches north of San Juan del Sur, as this road is a haunt of thieves. There have also been reports of unpleasant robberies on the beaches themselves, so check the security situation before heading over. Don't linger on the sand after dark in San Juan del Sur.

Background

Andrés Niño, the first European to navigate the Pacific Coast of Nicaragua, entered the bay of San Juan del Sur in 1523 while looking in vain for a possible passage to Lake Nicaragua or the Caribbean. So San Juan del Sur remained a sleepy fishing village until after Nicaragua's Independence from Spain. It began working as a commercial port in 1827 and in 1830 took the name Puerto Independencia. Its claim to fame came during

San Juan del Sur

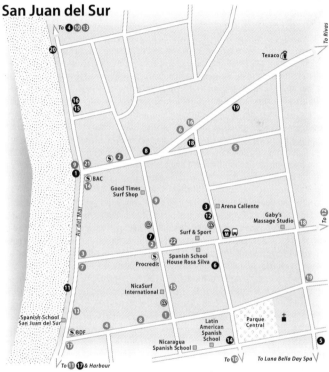

Where to stay
Azul Pitahaya **2**
Casa Oro Youth Hostel **1**
Casa Marina **13**
Casablanca **14**
Colonial **15**
El Puerto **16**
Encanto del Sur **10**
Esperanza **17**
Estrella **7**
Gran Océano **8**
Hostal Beach Fun
  Casa 28 **9**
La Estación **3**
La Posada Azul **4**
Pelican Eyes **12**
Royal Chateau **18**
Secret Cove Inn **5**
South Seas Hostel **6**
Victoriano **11**
Villa Isabella **19**

Restaurants 🍴
Bambú Beach Club **4**
Bar Timón **1**
Barrio Café **7**
Black Whale Bar & Grill **15**
Comedor Margarita **3**
El Colibrí **5**
El Pozo **6**
Eskimo **16**
Gato Negro **8**
Josseline's **11**
Jugaso **12**
La Cascada **17**
O Sole Mio **18**
Pan de Vida **19**
Pau Hana **20**
Pizzería San Juan **14**

Bars & clubs 🍸
Big Wave Dave's **2**
Crazy Crab Beach Club **10**
Dorado's Bar & Grill **21**
Iguana Bar **9**
The Pier **13**
Republika **22**

the California gold rush when thousands of North Americans, anxious to reach California (in the days before the North American railroad was finished), found the shortest route to be by boat from the Caribbean, up the Río San Juan, across Lake Nicaragua, overland for only 18 km from La Virgen (see page 160) and then by boat again from San Juan to California. It is estimated that some 84,880 passengers passed through the town en route to California, and some 75,000 on their way to New York. In 1854 the local lodge, El United States Hotel, charged a whopping US$14 per day for one night's lodging and food of bread, rice, oranges and coffee made from purified water. But as soon as the railway in the USA was completed, the trip through Central America was no longer necessary. The final crossing was made on 8 May 1868 with 541 passengers en route to San Francisco. The steamship was taken over for a while by William Walker to re-supply his invasion forces in the mid-1850s. In 1857, Walker escaped to Panama and later to New Orleans via San Juan. Walker was believed to be attempting another attack on Nicaragua via San Juan del Sur in 1858, but was blocked by the British Navy ship *Vixen*. There was some very tough fighting here during 1979 Revolution in the hills behind San Juan, as Somoza sent his best troops to take on Commandante Zero, Edén Pastora, and his rebel southern front. As victory approached, a ragged group of Somoza's National Guard managed to escape out of San Juan (threatening to burn it down), just as southern Rivas was being taken by Pastora-led rebels. In recent years, San Juan has seen an influx of wealth both from Managua's upper class and foreign capital and there are many expensive homes being built along the low ridge that backs the beach and in the northern part of the bay and beyond.

Places in San Juan del Sur

Mark Twain described San Juan del Sur as "a few tumble-down frame shanties" in 1866, and said the town was "crowded with horses, mules and ambulances (horse carriages) and half-clad yellow natives". Today there are plenty of half-clad people, though less and less are natives and most are enjoying the sun and sea. Most of the horses and all of the mules have been replaced by bicycles, which is the preferred form of transport.

What makes San Juan del Sur different from other Nicaraguan beach towns is the growing ex-patriot crowd that has migrated here from across Europe and North America. San Juan is a natural bay of light-brown sand, clear waters and 200-m cliffs that mark its borders. The sunsets are placed perfectly out over the Pacific, framed by the boats bobbing in the bay. The beach is lined by numerous small restaurants that offer the fresh catch of the day, along with lobster and shrimp. Surfers can climb in a boat and find access to very good breaks along the same coastline, one that has a year-round offshore breeze. Deep-sea fishing is also possible. Swimming is best at the northern end of the beach. See What to do, page 166.

Pacific Coast south of San Juan del Sur → *For listings, see pages 162-168.*

① *If staying in San Juan del Sur most of these beaches are easier reached by boat for a day trip.* A well-kept earth and rock road runs south from the bridge at the entrance to San Juan del Sur. Signs mark the way to a housing and apartment development called **Parque Marítimo El Coco** and also serve as directions to the superb beach and turtle nesting site of **La Flor** (see below). There are also signs for **Playa Remanso**, the first beach with lodging south of San Juan. There are big houses being built here above a pretty beach good for swimming. However, there have been some questions raised about the treatment of locals by this establishment and others along the coast that are trying to block public access to the coast. Nicaraguan law stipulates that all Nicaraguan beaches must be open to the public (the term 'private beach' is either a hollow promise or they are breaking the law), but the law does not clarify how access must be granted. The beaches are rapidly being shut down to people of lower economic status (90% of the population), creating hard feeling among the Nicaraguans whose families have been visiting these beaches for hundreds of years and now find they are off limits because foreigners have suddenly grown fond of them. Both **Remanso** and the beautiful **Playa El Yankee**, to the south, are good surfing beaches but El Yankee has a hotel project planned on disputed land in front of a gorgeous beach. The road is rough here and you will have to cross streams that are small during the dry season, but will require high-clearance and 4WD vehicles from June to November. The drive is over a beautifully scenic country road with many elevation changes and vistas of the ocean and the northern coast of Costa Rica.

Playa El Coco is a long copper-coloured beach with strong surf most of the year. Much of it is backed by forest and there are several families of howler monkeys that live between here and **La Flor**, two beaches to the south. There is a growing development at the north end of the beach with a mixture of condos, bungalows and homes for rent. This is the closest lodging to La Flor without camping. The housing complex at Playa El Coco is involved in community projects which includes free schooling for local children and the beach is open to the public. Prices for rental range from one night in a one-room apartment for US$85 to US$1900 for one week in a big house.

Refugio de Vida Silvestre La Flor
① US$10, US$2.50 student discount, access by 4WD or on foot.
Just past Playa El Coco and 18 km from the highway at San Juan del Sur, the La Flor wildlife refuge protects tropical dry forest, mangroves, estuary and 800 m of beachfront. This beautiful, sweeping cove with light tan sand and many trees is an important site for nesting sea turtles (see box, page 159). The best time to come is between August and November. Rangers protect the multitudinous arrivals during high season and are very happy to explain, in Spanish, about the animals' reproductive habits. Sometimes turtles arrive in their thousands, usually over a period of four days. Even if you don't manage to see the turtles, there is plenty of other wildlife. Many birds live in small, protected mangroves at the south end of the beach and you may witness a sunset migration of hundreds of hermit crabs at the north end, all hobbling back to the beach in their infinitely diverse shells. Camping can be provided (limited number of tents) during the turtle season, US$25 per night. Bring a hammock and mosquito netting, as insects are vicious at dusk. The ranger station sells soft drinks and will let you use their outhouse; improved facilities are planned.

Pacific Coast north of San Juan del Sur → *For listings, see pages 162-168.*

There is an unpaved access road to beaches north of San Juan del Sur at the entrance to the town. It is possible to travel the entire length of the Rivas coast to Chacocente from here, though it is quite a trip as the road does not follow the coast but moves inland to **Tola** (west of Rivas) and then back to the ocean, and the surface is changeable from hard pack dirt to sand, stone and mud. In the rainy season a 4WD or sturdy horse is needed for these trails. Some of the beaches in this part of Rivas are spectacular with white sand and rugged forested hillsides and, like the coastline south of San Juan del Sur, they are being quickly cordoned off. This area is seeing big development and building projects, including gated communities and retirement resorts, and Tola itself has become a service town for the growing numbers of construction workers.

Playa Marsella has plenty of signs that mark the exit to the beach. It is a slowly growing resort set on a pleasant beach, but not one of the most impressive in the region. North of here, **Los Playones** is playing host to ever-increasing crowds of surfers with a scruffy beer shack and hordes of daily shuttle trucks. The waves are good for beginners, but are often heavily oversubscribed. **Maderas** is the next beach along, where many shuttles claim to take you (they don't, they drop you at the car park at Los Playones). This is a pleasant, tranquil spot, good for swimming and host to some affordable lodgings, best booked in advance. **Bahía Majagual** is the next bay north, a lovely white-sand beach tucked into a cove.

On the road to Majagual before reaching the beach is the private entrance to **Morgan's Rock** a multimillion dollar private nature reserve and reforestation project with tree farming, incorporating more than 800 ha of rare tropical dry coastal forest and the stunningly beautiful Playa Ocotal. Don't even think about dropping by to check it out without first digging deep in your wallet as this is the most expensive place to sleep in Nicaragua and, most reports say, worth every *peso*. While the hotel may not win awards for social consciousness, it is on the progressive edge of conservation and sustainable tourism in ecological terms. If you can afford a few nights here, it is one of the prettiest places on the Central American coast and the cabins are set up high on a bluff wrapped in forest overlooking the ocean and beach (see Where to stay, page 164).

To the north of Morgan's are more pristine beaches, like **Manzanillo** and **El Gigante** and all have development projects. One that has really got off the ground is **Rancho Santana** ⓘ *www.ranchosantana.com*. This is a massive housing and resort project located on the west side of the earthen highway between Tola and Las Salinas, behind a large ostentatious gate and a grimacing armed guard. Rancho Santana is a very organized and well-developed project for luxury homes built by foreign investors and retirees. The popular surf spot Playa Rosada is included in the complex's claim of four 'private' beaches. California-style hilltop luxury homes are being built here with stunning Pacific views and the 'state within a state' ambience includes a slick clubhouse called **Oxford** and a private helipad.

Further north from Rancho Santana is the legendary surf spot **Popoyo**. This place is getting crowded with surfers from around the world and with good reason. The surf here is very big with a good swell and still has waves when the rest of the ocean looks like a swimming pool. There is also lodging at a surf camp here. See www.surf nicaragua.com for information.

One of the prettiest beaches on the northern Rivas coast is **Playa Conejo**, now taken over by **Hotel Punta Teonoste**. It is located near Las Salinas with very funky and creative bungalows along the beach and a memorable circular bar right above the sand. Sadly the land behind the bungalows is completely treeless and the sun and wind are ferocious here in the dry season. Having said that, this is the nearest decent accommodation to Chacocente Wildlife Refuge, 7 km north of the hotel (see below) and access via the highway from Ochomogo is year round.

Refugio de Vida Silvestre Río Escalante Chacocente

ⓘ *There is a US$4 entrance fee to the park. There is no public transport to the park and a 4WD is necessary during the turtle-laying season from Aug to Nov. There are 2 entrances to the area, 1 from Santa Teresa south of Jinotepe. Follow that road until the pavement ends and then turn left to the coast and El Astillero. Before you reach the bay of Astillero you will see a turning to the right with a sign for Chacocente. At Km 80 from the Pan-American Highway is the bridge over the Río Ochomogo that separates the province of Granada from Rivas; the Pan-American*

Sea turtles – the miracle of life

Every year between July and February thousands of beautiful olive ridley turtles (*Lepidochelys olivacea*) arrive at La Flor and Chacocente, two wildlife refuges set aside to aid in their age-old battle against predators with wings, pincers, four legs and two.

The sea turtles, measuring up to 80 cm and weighing more than 90 kg, come in waves. Between August and November as many as 20,000 arrive to nest in a four-night period, just one of many arrivals during the nesting season. Each turtle digs a hole with her rear flippers, patiently lays up to 100 eggs, covers them and returns to the water – mission complete. For 45 days the eggs incubate under the tropical Nicaraguan sand. The temperature in the sand will determine the gender of the turtle: temperatures below 29°C will result in males and 30°C and above will be females, though very high temperatures will kill the hatchlings. After incubation in the sand, they hatch all at once and the little turtles run down to the sea. If they survive they will travel as far as the Galapagos Islands.

The huge leatherback turtle (*Dermochelys coriacea*), which can grow up to 2 m and weigh over 300 kg, is less common than the olive ridley and arrives alone to lay her eggs.

Turtle eggs are a traditional food for the Nicaraguans, and although they are not eaten in large quantities, poaching is always a threat. Park rangers and, during peak times, armed soldiers protect the turtles from animal and human threats in both Chacocente and La Flor wildlife refuges. If you have the chance to witness it, don't miss out and get talking to the rangers who have a great passion for their work. Extreme caution must be exercised during nesting season as, even if you see no turtles on the beach, you are most likely to be walking over nests. Limit flash photography to a minimum and never aim a flash camera at turtles coming out of the water.

Camping is the best way to see the turtles in Chacocente or La Flor, but a pre-dawn trip from either San Juan del Sur or Playa El Coco to La Flor, or from Las Salinas to Chacocente is also possible.

Highway is in excellent condition here as it continues south to Rivas. On the south side of the bridge a rough dirt road runs west to the Pacific Ocean. This is a 40-km journey through small friendly settlements to the same turning for the reserve.

Tropical dry forest and beach make up Chacocente Wildlife Refuge. The beach is most famous for the **sea turtles** that come to nest every year. This is one of the four most important sea turtle nesting sites on the entire Pacific seaboard of the American continent (another of the four, **La Flor Wildlife Refuge**, is further south, see above). The park is also a critical tropical dry forest reserve for the Nicaraguan Pacific and a good place to see giant iguanas and varied bird life during the dry season, when visibility in the forest is at its best. The beach itself is lovely too, with a long open stretch of sand that runs back into the forest, perfect for stringing up a hammock. Camping is permitted – this may be the most beautiful camping spot along the coast – but no facilities are provided and you will need to come well stocked with water and supplies. The Nicaraguan environmental protection agency **MARENA** has built attractive cabins for park rangers and scientists and it is possible that they will rent them to visitors in the future. At the moment the rangers seem surprised to see visitors but they are very sincere in their efforts to protect the wildlife and diversity of the reserve.

La Virgen to the border

La Virgen

At the turning from the Pan-American Highway for the highway to San Juan del Sur, this little windswept village has some less-than-clean beaches and a stunning view of the big lake and Ometepe. If you come early in the morning you may see men fishing in the lake while floating in the inner tube of a truck. This curious sight is peculiar to this small village. The fishermen arrive at the beach in the early morning and blow up the big tyre tubes, tie bait to a thick nylon cord and wade out, seated in the tubes, as far as 3 km from the coast. When they get out of the water, often fully clothed, the cord can have 15 or more fish hanging from it.

In the 19th century the lake steamships of Cornelius Vanderbilt stopped here (after a journey from New York via the Río San Juan) to let passengers off for an overland journey by horse-drawn carriage to the bay of San Juan del Sur. The North American novelist Mark Twain came here in 1866, doing the trip from west to east (San Francisco–San Juan del Sur–La Virgen–Lake Nicaragua–San Carlos–Río San Juan–San Juan del Norte–New York). He gazed out at the lake and waxed lyrical about the splendour of Lake Nicaragua and Ometepe from his viewpoint in La Virgen (see box, page 146). The dock used by the steamships is no longer visible and there is some debate among the villagers as to where it actually was.

It is here that the distance between the waters of Lake Nicaragua and the Pacific Ocean is shortest, only 18 km blocking a natural passageway between the Atlantic and Pacific oceans. Incredibly the continental divide lies yet further west, just 3 km from the Pacific; the east face of this low coastal mountain ridge drains all the way to the Caribbean Sea via the lake and Río San Juan. The road is paved to San Juan de Sur and follows to a great extent the path used in the 1800s by carriages and ox carts for the inter-oceanic gold rush route of Vanderbilt. What had previously been a full-day's journey through rough terrain became a trip of just under four hours by the construction of this road in earthen form in 1852 by Vanderbilt's company.

La Virgen to Peñas Blancas

The Pan-American Highway continues south from La Virgen to the coastal town of **Sapoá** on the southernmost shores of Lake Nicaragua and **Peñas Blancas**, the one land crossing between Nicaragua and Costa Rica. The landscape changes dramatically as the rainforest ecosystem of the southern shores of Lake Nicaragua meets the tropical dry forest ecosystem of the Pacific Basin, and the stretch of land is rich pasture crossed by numerous streams. It is possible to follow a 4WD track from Sapoá all the way to the town of **Cárdenas**, 17 km away on the shores of Lake Nicaragua and close to the western border of **Los Guatuzos Wildlife Refuge** (see page 178). From here you could try to hire a private boat to Solentiname, Río Papaturro or San Carlos. For information on crossing the border into **Costa Rica**, see box, opposite.

Border crossing: Nicaragua–Costa Rica

Peñas Blancas

Entering Nicaragua

By bus or on foot When entering Nicaragua (immigration open 0600-2000), show your passport at the border, completing Costa Rican exit formalities, and then walk the 500 m to the Nicaraguan border controls. International bus passengers have to disembark and queue for immigration to stamp their passport. Then you must unload your baggage and wait in line for the customs official to arrive. You will be asked to open your bags, the official will give them a cursory glance and then you reload. Passports and tickets will be checked again back on the bus. For travellers not on a bus, there are plenty of small helpers on hand. Allow 45 minutes to complete the formalities. You will have to pay US$12 to enter Nicaragua plus a US$1 Alcaldía charge.

By private vehicle There is no fuel going into Nicaragua until Rivas (37 km). When entering Nicaragua, go through Migración then find an inspector who will fill out the preliminary form to be taken to Aduana. At the Vehículo Entrando window, the vehicle permit is typed up and the vehicle stamp is put in your passport. Next, go to Tránsito to pay for the car permit. Finally, ask the inspector again to give the final check. Fumigation is mandatory, US$1. Note: INTUR requires that all visitors to Nicaragua purchase car insurance, US$5.

Money exchange The border is your last chance to sell córdobas if leaving or sell colones if arriving.

Transport from Peñas Blancas Rivas, every half hour, 0600-1800, US$0.75, one hour. From here buses connect to **Managua**, every half hour, 0330-1800, US$2.50, 2¾ hours or to **Granada**, every 45 minutes, 0530-1625, US$1.50, 1¾ hours, try to board an express bus from Rivas to your destination. Express buses from Peñas Blancas to **Managua**, every half hour, 0700-1800, US$3.50, 3½ hours.

Leaving Nicaragua

By bus or on foot When leaving Nicaragua, pay US$1 mayor's fee to enter the customs area at the border and then complete formalities in the new customs building where you pay US$2 to have your passport checked. Then walk the 500 m to the Costa Rican border and simply have your passport stamped. Buses and taxis are available from the border – hitching is difficult.

By private vehicle When leaving the country, first pay your exit tax at an office at the end of the control station, receipt given. Then come back for your exit stamp, and complete the *Tarjeta de Control Migratorio*. Motorists must then go to Aduana to cancel vehicle papers; exit details are typed on to the vehicle permit and the stamp in your passport is cancelled. Find the inspector in Aduana who has to check the details and stamp your permit. If you fail to do this you will not be allowed to leave the country – you will be sent back to Sapoá by the officials at the final Nicaraguan checkpoint. Fumigation is US$0.50 and mandatory. Foreign drivers entering Costa Rica from Nicaragua must also pay US$15 for an insurance policy from the National Insurance Institute (INS).

San Juan del Sur and around listings

For sleeping and eating price codes and other relevant information, see pages 28-30.

Where to stay

Many hotels in the region of San Juan del Sur double and triple their rates for Semana Santa and around Christmas and New Year.

San Juan del Sur *p154, map p155*

$$$$ Pelican Eyes Resort, Parroquia, 1½ c arriba, T2563-7000, www.pelicaneyesresort.com. Beautiful, peaceful, luxurious houses and hotel suites with private bath, a/c, cable TV, sitting area, great furnishings and views of the bay. Sailing trips on the *Pelican Eyes* boat can be arranged. The best in town with a plethora of comforts and amenities.

$$$$-$$$ Casa Marina, Av del Mar, opposite Josselin's, T2568-2677, www.casamarinasjds.com. For better or worse, these high-rise timeshare condos are a sign of the times in San Juan del Sur. Large apartments (8-person capacity) have 2 bedrooms, 2 bathrooms, kitchen, living room and unobstructed views of the bay (**$$$$**). Also smaller, cheaper, 1-bedroom apartments (4-person capacity, **$$$**). Modern and comfortable.

$$$ Casablanca, Av del Mar, opposite Bar Timón, T2568-2135, www.elhotelcasablanca.com. Clean, comfortable rooms with a/c, cable TV, private bath, safe, refrigerator and hot water. There's a small pool, parking, free Wi-Fi and continental breakfast included in the price. Friendly and relaxed.

$$$ La Estación, mercado, 2 c al mar, T2568-2304, www.laestacion.com.ni. Built on the ruins of the old railway station, although you would never have guessed from looking at this modern building. La Estación has 18 rooms in total, including suites with sea views, various doubles and singles, all clean, comfortable and well tended. Services include restaurant-bar, Wi-Fi, a/c and hot water.

$$$ La Posada Azul, BDF, ½ c arriba, T2568-2698, www.laposadaazul.com. La Posada Azul is a tranquil and intimate lodging with just a handful of comfortable, well-furnished rooms. A beautiful wooden building with lots of history and character. There's a lush garden, self-service bar and a modest pool. Services include a/c, private bath, hot water and Wi-Fi. Full breakfast included.

$$$ Victoriano, Paseo Marítimo, costado norte Enitel, T2568-2005, www.hotelvictoriano.com.ni. This gorgeous clapboard mansion is actually a restored English Victorian-era family house. Rooms are simple, stylish and elegant with a/c, cable TV, DVD, Wi-Fi and all the usual amenities. Great restaurant-bar, pool and garden. One of the best in town and a place to be seen.

$$$ Villa Isabella, across from the northeast corner of the church, T2568-2568, www.villaisabellasjds.com. This lovely, well decorated wooden house has 17 clean rooms with private bath, a/c, disabled access, ample windows and light. There's a pool, garage parking, Wi-Fi, free calls to USA, video library and breakfast included in the price. English spoken, very helpful. Discounts for groups.

$$ Colonial, mercado, 1 c al mar, ½ c sur, T2568-2539, www.hotel-nicaragua.com. This well-managed hotel has a pleasant, relaxing garden, and 12 comfortable rooms with a/c, cable TV, Wi-Fi, hot water. Full breakfast included, bikes, tours and transportation to/from the airport or beaches can be arranged. 40% of profits support social and ecological projects.

$$ El Puerto, Texaco, 1 c al mar, T2568-2661, hotel-el-puerto@gmx.net. Simple, comfortable, economical rooms with private bath and a/c (cheaper with fan). Good value, friendly and clean. There's also Wi-Fi and free coffee in the morning.

$$ Gran Océano, northwest corner of Parque Central, 1½ c al mar, T2568-2219, www.hotel granoceano.com.ni. A popular hotel that also specializes in sports fishing expeditions. They have 22 rooms with private bath, a/c, hot water and cable TV. The top-floor rooms are much more spacious and comfortable, but also more expensive. There's a swimming pool, bar, Wi-Fi and parking. Breakfast included.

$$ Hotel Azul Pitahaya, mercado, 1 c al mar, T2568-2294, www.hotelazulsanjuan.com. Comfortable rooms with good mattresses, hot water, cable TV and a/c. There's Wi-Fi in the café downstairs, which serves familiar gringo food. Tours, surf board rental and transportation available. Breakfast included.

$$ Hotel Encanto del Sur, iglesia, 100 m sur, T2568-2222, www.hotelencantodelsur.com. One of the best deals in town. This hotel has 18 clean, modern, comfortable rooms with private bath, cable TV, Wi-Fi and a/c, cheaper with fan (**$**). Quiet and away from the action. Recommended.

$$ Royal Chateau, Texaco, 300 m sur, T568-2551, www.hotelroyalchateau.com. Motel-style place with a green lawn and 20 clean, pleasant unremarkable rooms, all with a/c, cable TV and bath. (cheaper with fan). Other services include Wi-Fi, parking and 24-hr guard. Breakfast included.

$ Casa Oro Youth Hostel, Hotel Colonial, 20 vrs sur, T2568-2415, www.casaeloro.com. A very popular hostel with clean, economical dorms (the ones upstairs are better), simple but pleasant private rooms and a plethora of services including Wi-Fi, computer terminals, shuttles, tours and surf lessons (see Tour operators, page 167). They also have a self-service kitchen, daily surf reports, and a breezy bar-terrace that's great for evening drinks. Breakfast served 3 times a week. Youthful, fun and buzzing.

$ Estrella, mercado, 2 c sur, T2568-2210. Weathered and fading old cheapie with simple rooms, partitioned walls, good breezes, sea views and shared bath. Overlooks the beach and is equipped with Wi-Fi, computer terminals. Famously discourteous staff and management, but an old favourite and now a SJDS institution.

$ Hostal Beach Fun Casa 28, mercado, 1 c al mar, 1 c norte, T2568-2441, javieralara@hotmail.com. Long-standing budget favourite with a range of simple economical private rooms, with or without bath and TV. A few have a/c (**$$**). Services include free Wi-Fi, use of computer terminal and shared kitchen. Tours, transport to/from the beaches and ATV rental offered. English spoken.

$ Hotel Esperanza, BDF, 30 vrs sur, T8325-5279, www.hotelesperanza.com. Slightly grungy, but friendly. They have both dorms and private rooms. Services include internet, Wi-Fi, purified water, free coffee, BBQ pit, kitchen, games, hammocks and lockers for valuables. Very relaxed and the only hostel on the beach.

$ Secret Cove Inn, mercado, 2 c sur, ½ c abajo, T8672-3013, info@thesecret covenicaragua.com. Intimate and friendly B&B lodging with a handful of clean, comfortable, well appointed rooms. They offer tours and information, use of kitchen, hammocks, Wi-Fi and a chilled-out communal area. Very relaxed, welcoming and helpful. Nice owners. Recommended.

$ South Seas Hostel, Texaco, 1½ c al mar, T2568-2084, www.southseasnicaragua.com. A pleasant Nica-owned budget lodging with a relaxed family atmosphere. They have clean, comfortable, simple rooms with fan and shared bath (**$$** with a/c), and there's also a great kitchen for your own cooking, a pool and a sun terrace. Discounts for longer stays. Recommended.

Apartments and short-term rentals

There's no shortage of foreign properties in and around San Juan del Sur, many of which are represented by local real estate agents – drop in and enquire. Alternatively, David Golichowski at **Good Times Surf Shop** (see Surfing, page 167) is a well-connected source of information. He can give advice and help arrange rentals at beachfront properties out of town.

South of San Juan del Sur *p156*

$$$$-$$$ Parque Marítimo El Coco, 18 km south of San Juan del Sur, T8999-8069, www.playael coco.com.ni. Apartments and houses right on the sand and close to La Flor Wildlife Refuge. Suits 4-10 people, most have a/c, all have baths, TV and cleaning service included. There's a general store and restaurant in the complex. The beach, backed by forest, can have strong waves. Rates vary according to season, weekday nights are less expensive. Interesting rural excursions are offered.

$$ Latin Latitudes, Playa Yankee, T8671-9698, www.latinlatitudes.com. Bed and breakfast that's received good reports from former guests. This great-looking house, 10 mins from the beach, has just a few rooms and suites (book in advance), all comfortable, clean and well appointed. Plenty of hammocks to chill out in and Wi-Fi access too. Full breakfast included.

North of San Juan del Sur *p157*

$$$$ Morgan's Rock Hacienda & Ecolodge, Playa Ocotal, sales office in Costa Rica, T506-8670-7676, www.morgans rock.com. Famous 'ecolodge' with precious wood bungalows and unrivalled views of the ocean and forest. The cabins are built on a high bluff above the beach and are connected to the restaurant and pool by a suspension bridge. The food, included in the price, has received mixed reviews; the hotel has rave reviews. Also included is a night-time wake-up call to observe the turtles on the beach. Tours are extra. The beach is lovely but the forest much prettier from Jun-Nov. Highly recommended if you've got the dosh.

$$$ Buena Vista Surf Club, Playa Maderas, www.buenavistasurfclub.com, T8863-4180. The **Buena Vista** boasts several attractive (but rustic) tree houses up on the cliffs, each with private bath, fan and mosquito nets. The communal 'rancho', where guests gather to eat and drink, has superb views of the ocean. Breakfast and dinner included;

minimum 2-night stay. Board rental and tours available.

$$$ El Empalme a Las Playas, at the fork in the road between Playa Marsella and Playa Maderas, T8803-7280, www.playa marsella.com. A friendly, personable lodging just minutes from the beach and surf. Accommodation is in rustic cane and thatch *cabañas*; each is equipped with a private bath and fan. Lots of pleasant greenery and wildlife around. Breakfast included. Often recommended.

$$$ Hotel Punta Teonoste, Playa Conejo, Las Salinas, reservations in Managua at Hotel Los Robles, T2267-3008, www.punta teonoste.com. Charming cabins overlooking a lovely beach. The bathroom and shower outside units are in a private open-air area, there's weak water pressure, unusual decor, private decks with hammock and circular bar at beach. All meals included. Avoid windy months from Dec-Mar.

$$-$ Hostal Hamacas, Bahía de El Astillero, de la escuela 50 vrs norte, T-4144, www.hostalhamacas.com. A tranquil spot located on the Bay of El Astillero near Tola. They offer a range of apartments (**$$**) and private rooms (**$**), all with private bath and TV, some with a/c (**$$**). A good jumping-off point for beaches and surf, as well as turtle tours. Lots of colourful hammocks, as the name might suggest.

$ Camping Matilda, Playa Maderas, T2456-3461. The best lodgings in Playa Madera. They have 8 rooms with private bath, 2 small dormitories and some funny little houses that look just like dog kennels. Very friendly, relaxed and pleasant. Often full.

$ Los Tres Hermanos, Los Playones, T8879-5272. Scruffy little shack popular with surfers and budget travellers, conveniently located next to the shuttle drop-off. There are just 10 dorm beds, usually full, and you can pitch a tent for US$2. Beer, water and *comida típica* available. Security may be an issue.

⑦ Restaurants

San Juan del Sur *p154, map p155*
There are many popular, but overpriced, restaurants lining the beach, where your tourist dollars buy excellent sea views and mediocre food. Only the better ones are included below. For budget dining you can't beat the market.

$$$ Bambú Beach Club, Malecón Norte, 200 m from the bridge, www.thebambu beachclub.com. Conceived and executed by a German-Austrian-Italian trio, the **Bambú Beach Club** is one of San Juan's finest dining options and often recommended. Mediterranean-inspired seafood with a hint of Nica.

$$$-$$ Bar Timón, across from Hotel Casablanca. Probably the best of the beachfront eateries, serving lobster, prawns and a host of other seafood dishes. No plastic furniture here. Popular and Nicaraguan.

$$$-$$ El Colibrí, mercado, 1 c este, 2½ sur. The best restaurant in town, with an excellent and eclectic Mediterranean menu, great decor and ambience, fine wines and really good food, much of it organic. Pleasant, hospitable and highly recommended.

$$$-$$ El Pozo, mercado, ½ c sur. Smart and stylish, with a robust international menu and an attractive, young clientele. Food and atmosphere is decidedly Californian. Lots of good reports.

$$$-$$ La Cascada, Pelican Eyes, Parque Central, 1½ c arriba. One of the best restaurants in town with fine seafood and excellent views overlooking the harbour. Recommended.

$$ Black Whale Bar and Grill, Malecón, opposite Eskimo Ice Cream. Laid-back surfers' hangout with a pool table, table football and a well-stocked fridge of beer. They serve American-style grub, but some say their 'famous' Monster Burger is more bread than burger. Live music on Fri, discounts on Sat. Open late.

$$ Josseline's, on the beach. One of the better beachside eateries, offering the usual seafood fare like shrimps, fillets and lobster. Some limited meat and chicken dishes too.

$$ Jugaso, mercado, 5 vrs norte, opposite Arena Caliente. Breezy little café that serves flavourful daily specials like Mediterranean salad and mango chicken. Also does tasty sandwiches, omelettes, coffee and juices. Friendly and recommended.

$$ O Sole Mio, Texaco, 1 c al mar. Friendly pizzeria-trattoria with an authentic Italian ambience.

$$ Pau Hana, Malecón Norte. Hawaiian-themed beach-front restaurant serving breakfasts, lunches, dinners, beers and fruity tropical cocktails. Open-mic on Tue night, if you fancy sharing your talents with the world.

$$ Pizzería San Juan, southwest corner of Parque Central, ½ c al mar. Tue-Sun 1700-2130. Often buzzing with expats and visitors, this restaurant serves excellent and authentic Italian pizzas – large enough to satisfy 2 people. Recommended, but perhaps not for a romantic evening meal.

$ Comedor Margarita, mercado, ½ c norte. *Comida típica* and other cheap fare. Unpretentious, wholesome and good-value daily specials. A nice change. Recommended.

Cafés, bakeries and ice cream parlours

Barrio Café, mercado, 1 c al mar, www.barriocafesanjuan.com. Familiar café food for homesick Westerners, including pancakes, bagels, coffee, burgers, sandwiches, wraps and cakes. A good place for breakfast and checking emails on the Wi-Fi.

Eskimo, seafront, Hotel Estrella, 2½ c norte. Sweet cold cones, sundaes and banana splits.

Gato Negro, mercado, 1 c al mar, 1 c norte. Popular gringo café with good, if slightly pricey, coffee, a reading space, breakfasts and snacks. This is also one of the best bookshops in the country, with the largest collection of English-language books on

Nicaragua, in Nicaragua, and plenty of fiction too. Chocolate chip and banana pancakes are great for sweet teeth. Recommended. **Pan de Vida**, Texaco, ½ c al mar. Brick-oven bakery that's good for cookies and freshly baked loaves of bread.

♪ Bars and clubs

San Juan del Sur *p154, map p155*
Big Wave Dave's, Texaco, 200 m al mar, T2568-2203, www.bigwavedaves.net. Tue-Sun 0830-0000. Popular with foreigners out to party and hook up with others. Wholesome pub food and a busy, boozy atmosphere.
Crazy Crab Beach Club, Malecón Norte, at the end of the road. The only thing in San Juan del Sur that passes for a disco, Crazy Crab sees a good mix of locals and foreigners, most of them under 30 years old. A great place to let loose on the dance floor.
Dorado's Bar and Grill, formerly María's, Malecón, opposite Timón and Iguana Bar. This popular local's haunt was under renovation at the time of research. Once completed, it's bound to take centre stage in San Juan's buzzing bar scene with an all-new disco on the 2nd floor and a roof-top bar on the 3rd.
Iguana Bar, Malecón, next door to Timón, www.iguanabeachbar.com. Also known as **Henry's Iguana**, a very popular hang-out with tourists, often buzzing and a good place to knock back rum and beer. They also do food, including sandwiches, burgers, beer and cheese-drenched nachos. Various happy hours and events, check the website for the latest.
The Pier, Malecón norte. Popular beachfront hang-out with an eclectic international crowd, live music and DJs. A relaxed, friendly ambience inside and bonfires on the sand outside. Happy hour 1900-2100 every night. Everything from rock to world music. Recommended.
Republika, mercado, ½ c al mar. Intimate café-style bar, low-key, with a friendly crowd and occasional live music and BBQ.

⚙ What to do

San Juan del Sur *p154, map p155*
ATV rental
Hostal Beach Fun Casa 28, mercado, 1 c al mar, 1 c norte, T2568-2441, javieralara@hotmail.com. A wide range of ATVs available for an hour, half day or full day.

Canopy tour
Da' Flying Frog, just off road to Marsella, T8613-4460. US$30. 17 platforms, 2.5 km of zip-line and great views from the canopy. One of Nicaragua's longest, promising adrenalin-charged thrills.

Diving
The waters around San Juan del Sur are home to a wrecked Russian trawler and a plethora of sea creatures including rays, turtles and eels.
Neptune Watersports, www.neptune nicadiving.com. This PADI centre offers 2-tank dives. Open water certification and training to Dive Master level. They also do fishing and snorkelling tours.

Fishing
Depending on the season, the waters around San Juan harbour all kinds of game fish, including marlin, jack and dorado. Many hotels and surf shops offer fishing packages, including **Gran Océano**. Otherwise try:
Super Fly Sport Fishing, advance reservation only, T8884-8444, www.nica fishing.com. Fly fishing and light tackle, deep-sea fishing, Captain Gabriel Fernández, fluent in English with lots of experience, also fishes north Pacific Coast and Lake Nicaragua.

Health and spa
Buena Vida, Mercado, 1 c al mar, ½ c norte, www.buenavidafitness.com. This centre offers interesting 'fitness vacations' which include daily high-intensity workouts, jungle hikes, ocean swims and instruction in nutrition and health. Regular options for day

visitors include yoga classes in the garden, juice bar and gym.

Gaby's Massage Studio, mercado, ½ c este, T568-2654, estrelladeluna@hotmail.com. Professionally trained in Managua, Gaby has nearly 10 years' experience and combines techniques from shiatsu, reflexology and aromatherapy.

Spa del Sur, El Colibrí, 2 c sur, behind the church, Azul, T8381-7671, www.spadelsur. com. A wide range of health and beauty treatments, including massage, haircuts, nail treatments, facials, waxing, Thai foot massage, body scrubs and body wraps.

Paintballing

El Gran Nelson, Km 127.5 Carretera San Juan del Sur, T2560-0122, karenr1828@ yahoo.com. If you fancy some SAS-style action head to this recreation centre on the highway. Then shoot your friends and family, with paint-balls, of course. Fun and different.

Sailing

Pelican Eyes Sailing Adventures, Parroquia 1½ c arriba, T2563-7000, www.pelicaneyes resort.com. Sails to the beach at Brasilito, US$90 per person full day, US$60 per person half day, discount for hotel guests, minimum 10 people, leaves San Juan at 0900.

Surfing

The coast north and south of San Juan del Sur is among the best in Central America for surfing, access to the best areas are by boat or long treks in 4WD. Board rental costs US$10 per day; lessons US$30 per hr. Although the town is quite inundated with surf shops, only the most established and reputable are given below:

Arena Caliente, mercado, ½ c norte, T815-3247, www.arenacaliente.com. Friendly Nica-run surf shop with board rental, surfing lessons and transport to beaches. Affordable accommodation (**$**) is available in town along with various 'surf camp' packages. Other options include snorkelling, spearfishing, canopy tours and horse riding.

Good Times Surf Shop, mercado, 1 c al mar, ½ c norte, T8675-1621, www.goodtimessurf shop.com. Also known as 'Outer Reef S.A.', This well-established and professional surf shop specializes in quality and customized surfboard rentals, lessons, and tours. Tours include day trips as well as multi-day and boat trips to surf hard-to-reach waves. Friendly, helpful and highly recommended. Dave claims he "will never piss on your leg and tell you it's raining".

NicaSurf International, mercado, 1 c al mar, ½ c sur, T2568-2626, www.nicasurf int. com. Board rental, classes, trips and tons of merchandise.

Surf and Sport, mercado, ½ c al mar, T8984-2464, www.sanjuandelsurf.com. Board rental, night fishing, surf tours, lessons, whale watching, booze cruises and transportation to the beaches.

Tour operators

Casa Oro, Hotel Colonial, 20 vrs sur, T2568-2415, www.casaeloro.com. Casa Oro runs a popular surf school with economically priced instruction, new boards and experienced teachers. Additionally, they offer sea-turtle tours, horse-riding trips on the beach, sailing, fishing and canopy tours. Works with local communities. Professional and well established.

⊖ Transport

San Juan del Sur *p154, map p155*
Bus

To **Managua** express bus 0500, 0530, 0600, 1730, US$3.50, 2½ hrs, ordinary bus every hr 0500-1530, US$2.50, 3½ hrs. Or take a bus/taxi to Rivas and change here. To **Rivas**, every ½ hr, 0500-1700, US$1, 40 mins. For **La Flor** or **Playa El Coco** use bus to **El Ostional**, 1600, 1700, US$ 0.70, 1½ hrs. Return from El Coco at 0600, 0730 and 1630.

Shuttles Several companies run shuttles to the beaches north and south of San Juan del Sur, including **Casa Oro Youth Hostel**

and **Arena Caliente**. Both have at least 3 daily departures to **Los Playones**, next to Maderas, and 1 daily departure to **Remanso**, US$5. Note schedules are affected by tides and may not operate in inclement weather.

Boat

Rana Tours, kiosk opposite Hotel Estrella on the seafront, T8877-9255. Runs transport to the northern beaches like **Michal**, **Marsella** and **Maderas**. They depart at 1100 and return at 1630, US$10 per person.

4WD

You can usually find a 4WD pick-up to make trips to outlying beaches or to go surfing. You should plan a day in advance and ask for some help from your hotel. Prices range from US$20-75 depending on the trip and time. You can also hire 4WDs, contact **Alamo Rent a Car**, inside hotel Casa Blanca, T2277-1117, www.alamonicaragua.com.

Taxi

Taxi Colectivo is a very feasible way to get to Rivas and slightly quicker than the bus. They depart from the market, US$1.75 per person, or US$7.50 for the whole taxi.

⊕ Directory

San Juan del Sur *p154, map p155*
Banks Banco Procredit, mercado, 1 c al mar, has a Visa ATM and will change dollars; BDF, mercado, 2 c al mar, 1 c sur, has a Visa ATM; BAC (ATM only, all networks), Malecón, next to Hotel Casablanca. Some hotels might change dollars too. **Fire** T8993-4797. **Internet** Several places in town,

Leo's (US$1 per hr, daily 0800-2100) and at **Super-Cyber Internet Service** (US$1 per hr, 0800-2200, internet calls as well). **Language schools** APC, BDF, 20vrs sur, T8678-7839. One-to-one classes, homestays, activities. Nicaragua Language School, southwest corner of Parque Central, ½ c al mar, T2568-2142, www.nicaspanish.com. One-to-one immersion classes, volunteer opportunities and customized classes. Free internet. **Playas del Sur**, Enitel, 50 vrs norte, opposite the beach, T8668-9334, www.playasdelsurspanishschool.com. Operated by a women's collective and one of the oldest schools in Nicaragua. They offer flexible programmes of one-to-one tuition, homestays, activities and voluntary work. All teachers have 8-12 years' experience. Spanish School House Rosa Silva, mercado, 50 m al mar, T8682-2938, www.spanishsilva.com. 20 hrs of 'dynamic' classes cost US$120, student accommodation or homestay are extra. Activities include swimming, hiking and cooking. All teachers are English-speaking. Teaching by the hour, US$7. Spanish School San Juan del Sur, T2568-2432, www.sjdsspanish.com. Regular morning classes, tutoring with flexible hours. **Spanish Ya**, Texaco, 100 vrs norte T8898-5036, www.learnspanishya.com. One-to-one classes, accommodation, activities and volunteer opportunities. DELE courses and diplomas. **Laundry** Various around town. Try: Lavandería Gaby, mercado, ½ c arriba, around US$3 for a medium-sized load. **Police** T2568-2382. **Post** 150 m left (south) along the seafront from the main junction.

Contents

Río San Juan

At a glance

⊕ **Getting around** There are few roads in the sparsely inhabited Río San Juan province. Most travel takes place on the rivers using *pangas* or other motor-powered boats.

◔ **Time required** 6-9 days. Travel in the region is time-consuming and/or comparatively expensive.

☼ **Weather** Water levels on the river are significantly lower during the dry season, but it can rain heavily at any time of year – pack accordingly and protect your luggage from downpours.

✕ **When not to go** High water levels during the wet season, May-Nov, speed transit along the waterways but can also make hiking in the forests unpleasant and challenging – expect hordes of insects and knee-high mud.

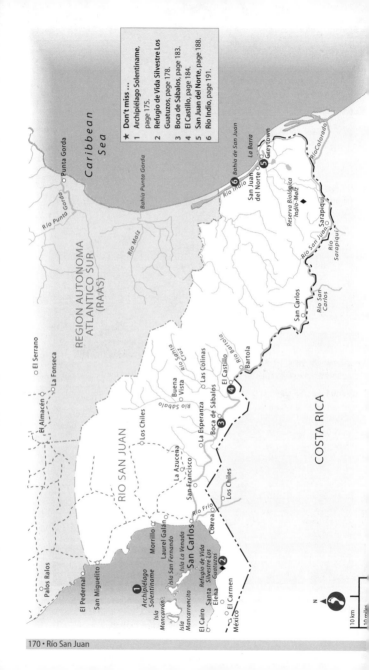

Caribbean Sea

Punta Gorda

Bahía Punta Gorda

Río Punta Gorda

Río Maíz

Bahía de San Juan

La Barra

Greytown

Río Indio

San Juan del Norte

6

5

Reserva Biológica Indio-Maíz

Río San Juan

Río Sarapiquí

Sarapiquí

REGION AUTONOMA ATLANTICO SUR (RAAS)

El Serrano

La Fonseca

El Almacén

RIO SAN JUAN

Los Chiles

Buena Vista

Río Santa Cruz

Las Colinas

Río Sábalo

La Esperanza

La Azucena

Boca de Sábalos

3

El Castillo

4

Río Bartola

Bartola

San Carlos

Río San Carlos

San Francisco

Río Frío

Cobrea

Los Chiles

Los Chiles

COSTA RICA

Palos Ralos

El Pedernal

San Miguelito

Archipiélago Solentiname

1

Isla Mancarrón

Isla Mancaroncito

Morrillo

Laurel Galán

Isla San Fernando

Isla La Venada

San Carlos

Refugio de Vida Silvestre Los Guatuzos

2

El Cairo

Santa Elena

El Carmen

México

N

10 km

10 miles

The evening symphony of tropical birds, high-pitched cicadas, ardent tree frogs and vociferous howler monkeys hints at the multitude of strange creatures inhabiting the darkened rainforests of the San Juan river. A natural canal between the Pacific and Atlantic oceans, this waterway has long drawn enterprising nations keen to exploit its commercial and military potential: the British navy, Napoleon III and the US government among them. Fortunately they all failed, and the river remains one of the great natural attractions of Central America – a mini Amazonas, visited by frequent bouts of life-giving rain and replete with surreal, uniquely adapted biological forms and vigorous plant life. Connected to the outside world by just two roads, boat is the main form of transport here. From the scattering of upstream ecolodges, downstream to the very heart of the Indio-Maíz rainforest reserve, and beyond, to the steamy Bay of San Juan, travelling this river is an entrancing and unforgettable experience.

Part of this remote region embraces the southeastern sector of Lake Nicaragua, which includes the precious wetlands and rainforest reserve of Los Guatuzos Wildlife Refuge; one of the finest birdwatching locations in the country. On the lake itself lies the Solentiname archipelago, a chain of pretty, drowsy islands that were once the site of an interesting social experiment. In 1965, the poet-priest Ernesto Cardenal came here to preach liberation theology and instruct the locals in artistic methods. His dream was a kind of radical Christian-Communist utopia that combined religion and revolution, spiritual love and community conscience. The result was a school of primitivist art whose output is internationally renowned. Vivid and colourful, this art captures the spiritual essence of rustic life, as well as Nicaragua's scintillating natural world.

San Carlos and Archipiélago Solentiname

Steamy, seedy San Carlos is a major cross-road, regional gateway, border crossing point (with Costa Rica, south along the Río Frío) and unavoidable transport hub. It's also the provincial capital of the isolated Río San Juan department. Most people arrive by plane from Managua but a single north-bound highway also connects it with the capital – after years of disrepair it is finally paved, cutting overland journey times to just five hours. For those who don't want to fly, bus or drive, there's always the ferry. West of San Carlos, the waters of Lake Nicaragua stretch away into obscurity, offering connections to tranquil Isla Ometepe, and eventually the colonial city of Granada. Among the lake's other sublime treasures is the Los Guatuzos Wildlife Reserve, buzzing with nature on its southern shores; and the soporific Solentiname archipelago, a chain of idyllic islands where time unravels and life finds itself in the colours and brush strokes of painted canvases. ▶ *For listings, see pages 179-182.*

San Carlos and the border → *For listings, see pages 179-182. Colour map 3, C6.*

San Carlos stands in contrast to the immense natural beauty that surrounds it. Scruffy, ramshackle and incurably chaotic, the place has a sultry 'last outpost' feel. Few would imagine that the city hides a historic fortress and that elegant colonial homes once lined its cobblestone streets. History has been unkind to the city, though progress is slowly coming to the town where the only banks and hospital in the entire region are to be found. The nearby Costa Rican border means dubious characters are often passing through, but the locals are very friendly and philosophical about the future of this jungle gateway. This is where the last buses arrive from the outside world after a protracted journey through forests and wetlands. The big boat from Granada docks here after 15 or so hours on the lake. Once a day, the single-propeller Cessna buzzes the rusting tin roofs of the village as it arrives from Managua onto San Carlos' landing strip. And the long narrow river and lake boats arrive from the surrounding settlements and wilderness. Whatever may be said about the city's looks, it remains a vital centre of gravity in an otherwise remote and disconnected universe.

Arriving in San Carlos

Getting there and around There is one daily flight to San Carlos from Managua, three boats per day from Los Chiles in Costa Rica (Monday-Saturday), and boats twice weekly from Granada which stop at Ometepe (see pages 110 and 139). The city is small and easily navigated on foot, although there is a confusing feel to the streets, which cling to the slopes of a hill. A taxi from the airport should cost around US$1, otherwise it's a 30-minute walk to the centre of town. ▶ *For further details, see Transport, page 181.*

Tourist information The **tourist office** ⓘ *on the waterfront malecón T2583-0301, Mon-Fri 0800-1200, 1400-1700,* has a selection of maps and flyers. They're helpful, but speak Spanish only. **Note:** You may see a number of white plastic jugs and cola bottles floating in the river; these are not garbage, but rather markers for shrimp nets. The river is very rich in *camarones del río* (freshwater prawns).

Places in San Carlos

Since the so-called 'discovery' of the Río San Juan by the Spanish Captain Ruy Díaz in 1525, San Carlos has had strategic importance for the successive governments of Nicaragua. Its location at the entrance to the Río San Juan from Lake Nicaragua and at the end of the Río Frío, which originates in Costa Rica, has meant that controlling San Carlos means controlling the water passages from north to south and east to west. The town was first founded in 1526, with the name Nueva Jaén, under the orders of King Carlos V of Spain but it did not officially become a port until 1542. The town (and a fortress that has not survived) were abandoned for an unknown length of time and were re-founded as San Carlos during the 17th century.

A new fortress was built but was sacked by pirates in 1670; part of it survives today as a small **museum** ① *0900-1200, 1400-1700, admission free*, and the town's principal tourist attraction. The fort was used for supply backup and troop fallbacks during attacks on the frontline fortress of El Castillo by Dutch and British pirates in the 17th century and British Naval forces in the 18th century. San Carlos was embroiled in the post-Independence struggles between León and Granada. It was a changeover stop for passengers of the Vanderbilt inter-oceanic steamship service and William Walker's forces also occupied the fort during Walker's attempt at a hostile takeover of both the steamship line and Nicaragua.

San Carlos

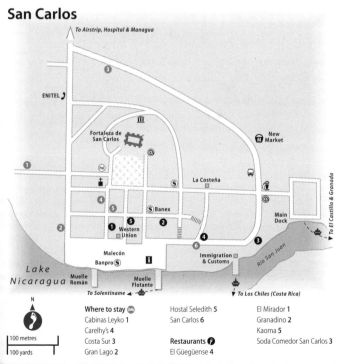

Where to stay	Hostal Seledith 5	El Mirador 1
Cabinas Leyko 1	San Carlos 6	Granadino 2
Carelhy's 4		Kaoma 5
Costa Sur 3	**Restaurants**	Soda Comedor San Carlos 3
Gran Lago 2	El Güegüense 4	

Border crossings: Nicaragua–Costa Rica

The Nicaragua-Costa Rica border runs along the southern bank of the Río San Juan but has been the subject of much government tension and debate. The Costa Rican border reaches the south banks of the Río San Juan 2 km downriver from El Castillo but the river in its length is Nicaraguan territory. Officially Costa Rican boats are only allowed to navigate the river for commercial purposes. It is best to travel in Nicaraguan boats on the river, as Costa Rican ones could be detained or turned back depending on the political climate (see box, page 189).

San Carlos to Los Chiles

This is a frequently used crossing point between Nicaragua and Costa Rica. Crossing from the Río San Juan to other parts of Costa Rica is not legal, though there are plans to establish several new border posts; ask in San Carlos if any other official points of entry or departure have opened up.

Nicaraguan immigration The border is open seven days a week 0800-1600 (closed for lunch). Exit stamps, costing US$2, must be obtained in San Carlos Monday-Friday only. Entrance stamps into Costa Rica are only available via Los Chiles. Check with the police in advance for the latest situation.

Transport There are three boats per day from San Carlos to Los Chiles, 1030, 1300, 1500, US$8, two hours, schedules are subject to change.

San Juan del Norte (see page 188)

Crossing to Costa Rica here is not legally permitted at time of printing, nor is entering Nicaragua without passing through San Carlos; the exception are package customers of the Río Indio Lodge, which has special permission for its clients.

Nicaraguan immigration There is no official immigration in San Juan del Norte. Projections suggest that the new San Juan del Norte airport will include immigrations and customs for international arrivals and departures. Whether this will open up the legality of boat arrivals and departures remains to be seen.

When Mark Twain visited San Carlos in 1866 on the Vanderbilt line (see box, page 146) he described it simply as Fort San Carlos, making no mention of any town. In 1870 the English naturalist Thomas Belt arrived after the long journey up the Río San Juan where rubber tappers were working in the nearby forests. He spent the night on one of the docked steamships and wrote of skirmishes between the Guatuzo and the rubber-extracting residents of San Carlos.

On 13 October 1977 Sandinista rebels from Solentiname attacked and took the military base after a four-day trek through jungle in Costa Rica, but they were forced back into Costa Rica after other attacks around Nicaragua failed. It was the first military victory of the Revolution and after the final triumph in 1979, the Sandinista administration set up a base in San Carlos that was used to fight Contra insurgents in the 1980s. The city's waterfront was burnt down in 1984 and was rebuilt in the ramshackle manner that can be seen today.

The town continues to act as a trading centre for local goods and as a jumping-off point for Nicaraguan migrant workers en route to Costa Rica, and for a small but growing number of tourists. In 2009, a series of city improvements were initiated by INTUR, the national tourism office, as part of their ambitious Río San Juan 'Ruta del Agua' campaign

These included a complete renovation of the *malecón*, improvement of the bus station, a new immigration centre, a new tourist information office, the training of hospitality staff, general infrastructure improvements and the establishment of a new Carnaval Aquático, celebrated each year in November. Thanks to their hard work, San Carlos is looking smarter than ever.

Río Frío to the border

This is the river that connects northern Costa Rica with Lake Nicaragua and the Río San Juan. Passengers from Costa Rica pass through customs at San Carlos and then continue to Managua (by bus or plane), or down the Río San Juan towards the Caribbean. Once you pass into Nicaraguan territory, the river enters a reserve, marked by a little green guard house. The reserve is the superb **Refugio de Vida Silvestre Los Guatuzos** (see page 178). The east bank is also home to a small project within the reserve called **Esperanza Verde** (see page 180), a nature reserve with an investigative centre and some basic accommodation. Although the river is used mainly as a commuter route, there is some beautiful wildlife and vegetation and it is rare not to see at least one clan of howler monkeys along the banks or even swimming across the river; while they tend to avoid swimming at all costs, the monkeys can manage a very methodical doggy paddle if necessary.

As late as the 1870s the indigenous **Guatuzo** people (Maleku) inhabited the river banks of this area (the indigenous name for the river was Ucubriú). The naturalist Thomas Belt recounted battles between the rubber tappers and the Guatuzo people who were fighting to stop the invasion of their land. The Spanish were never able to subjugate the Guatuzo and they gained a reputation for hostility and were left alone for years; the original explorers of the Río Frío are thought to have been attacked and killed by Guatuzo arrows. However, when the India-rubber trade grew and the supply of trees along the Río San Juan was exhausted, the rubbermen were forced to explore the Río Frío. This time they came heavily armed, killing anyone in their path. By 1870, just the sight of a white man's boat along the river sent the indigenous population fleeing into the forest in desperate fear. After that, the end of the culture was quickly accomplished by illegal kidnapping and slave trading with the mines and farms of Chontales. (Today the Guatuzo are known as the Rama and they populate the Rama Cay in Bluefields Bay, see page 284.)

Archipiélago Solentiname → *For listings, see pages 179-182.*

The Solentiname archipelago is a protected area, designated a Monumento Nacional, and one of the most scenic parts of Lake Nicaragua. It is made up of 36 islands in the lake's southeastern corner which, despite being just one hour in a fast boat from San Carlos, remain remote. The islands are sparsely populated and without roads, telephones, electricity or running water: this is Nicaragua as it was two centuries ago, with only the outboard motorboat as a reminder of the modern world. The islands are home to some of the most industrious and talented artists in the country. The ecosystem is transitional from tropical dry to rainforest and much of the islands' interiors are pasture and agricultural land. About 46 species of fish inhabit the waters around the islands and birdwatching opportunities are good, with many parrots, oropendolas and ospreys around. At night you can see the fishing bat, a spectacular and eerie hunter, as it drags its claws through the lake water at night picking off unwary fish near the surface.

Arriving in Archipiélago Solentiname

The archipelago has four main islands, from east to west they are: La Venada, San Fernando, Mancarrón and Mancarroncito, which are detailed below. There are many other beautiful islands that can be visited for the day or for a camping trip, but ask permission from the locals. There is plenty to keep you occupied on the islands, including visits to local artists, boating, swimming and nature walks. The main problem is the lack of public boats – services from San Carlos depart just twice a week. This means you will have to hire a boat or use a tour operator to organize your trip or allow plenty of time to find transport when you're out there. You could probably kayak between some of the islands, if you're strong and experienced enough. ▸▸ *See also Transport, page 182, for further details.*

Background

The islands are the result of ancient volcanic activity, now heavily eroded and partially submerged. Solentiname has been populated since at least AD 500 and is thought to have been populated up until AD 1000, when historians believe it became a ceremonial site. Today the inhabitants are mostly third and fourth generation migrants from Chontales and Isla de Ometepe.

The islanders make a living from subsistence farming and artistic production. In the early 1960s, 12 local farmers were given painting classes at the initiative of the idealistic and much-revered Catholic priest/poet/sculptor Ernesto Cardenal. In addition, the local inhabitants were trained in balsa woodcarving. This small amount of training was passed from family to family; mother to son and father to daughter and soon the entire archipelago was involved in sculpting or painting. The style is *primitivista* and many of the painters have become internationally known and have been invited to study and exhibit as far away as Finland and Japan. The balsa woodcarvings can be found around Central America and the artisans have expanded their themes in recent years. Both the woodwork and oil paintings represent local ecology and legends, with the paintings normally depicting dense tropical landscape and the balsa works recreating individual species of the region.

Ernesto Cardenal ran his church innovatively with participative masses and a call to arms against the oppression of the Somoza government in the 1970s. The islanders, organized by Cardenal and led by local boy Alejandro Guevara, made the first successful rebel attack on a military base at San Carlos in October 1977; one month later Somoza sent helicopters to raze Mancarrón Island. Cardenal, who was defrocked by Pope John Paul II, went on to be the Sandinista Minister of Culture and an international celebrity. The 80-something icon still writes poetry, sculpts and visits Solentiname occasionally to stay in his small house on Isla Mancarrón near to his old church, which sadly is no longer in use. Cardenal's glowing memoir of all that was great about the Revolution and his role at the Ministerio de Cultura was published recently. The 666-page work, called *Revolución Perdida*, reveals some amazing scenes about his life as the international fundraiser for arms for the Sandinista rebel underground. It also documents in detail his administration of Nicaragua's blossoming culture in the 1980s, the biggest success of the Sandinista years. The book is in Spanish only and available at hotels on the islands and in Managua.

Isla La Venada

Named for its once-plentiful population of deer, La Venada (also known as Isla Donald Guevara) is a long narrow island that is home to many artists, including Rodolfo Arellano who lives on the southwestern side of the island. He and his wife are among the island's original painters and his daughters and grandchildren all paint tropical scenes and welcome visitors to see and purchase their work. You can also rent a bed in his house. On the north side of the island is a series of semi-submerged caves with some of the best examples of petroglyphs which are attributed to the Guatuzo people. One of the caves links up with the opposite side of the island and was probably used during low water levels. The cave can be visited by boat, though the entrance is dangerous if the lake is rough.

Isla San Fernando

This island, also known as Elvis Chavarría, is also famous for its artisan work and painting. It has some of the prettiest houses in the archipelago and is home to the famous Pineda artist family. Rosa Pineda is very friendly and will show you her work. Nearby, on a beautiful hill, is a new museum, the **Museo Archipiélago Solentiname** ① *T2583-0095 (in San Carlos), US$2*. The museum has a small pre-Columbian collection, with some interesting explanations of local culture and ecology. There is also mural painted by the Arellano family from La Venada. The museum has a fabulous view of the islands and is not to be missed at sunset. If it is closed, ask around to find out who has the key.

Isla Mancarrón

This is the biggest island in the chain and has the highest elevation at 250 m. The famous revolutionary/poet/sculptor/Catholic priest/Minister of Culture, Ernesto Cardenal, made his name here by founding a *primitivista* school of painting, poetry and sculpture, and even decorating the local parish church in naïve art. The church is open and there is a museum just behind the altar (ask permission to visit). It contains the first oil painting ever made on Solentiname, a bird's eye view of the island, and many other curiosities. Next to the church there is a monument to the Sandinistas and the tomb of the deceased rebel commander Alejandro Guevara who was from this island.

Mancarrón is good for walking and it is home to many parrots and Montezuma propendolas. Ask in the village for a guide to show you the way to the mirador, which has super views of the archipelago. Also at the mirador you can see a coyol palm tree which is used to make a sweet palm wine. The indigenous name for the palm is *mancarrón*, giving the island its name. The village has two small stores and cold drinks, bottled water, crackers and snacks. You can visit the homes of the island's talented artisans.

Isla Mancarroncito

Mancarroncito is a big, wild, mountainous island with primary forest. There is some good hiking in the forest, although the terrain is steep. Ask at your guesthouse for a recommended guide.

Other islands

On the north side of Mancarrón there is a tiny island with an inlet that holds the wreck of a sunken steamship from the inter-oceanic route. Only the chimney, now covered in tropical vegetation, is still visible above the water. On the far west end of the archipelago, just off the west coast of Mancarroncito, is another bird-nesting site on a little rock pile island, with hundreds of egret and cormorant nests.

Isla de Zapote, which is in front of the Los Guatuzos river of the same name, is home to over 10,000 bird nests, making it perhaps the richest bird-nesting site in Nicaragua. Most of the nests belong to cormorants or white egrets, although there are other egrets, herons, roseate spoonbills, wood storks and two species of ibis among the others.

Between San Fernando and Mancarrón is the small forest-covered island of **El Padre**, named after a priest who once lived there. It is the only island with monkeys (howlers) which were introduced only 25 years ago and are now thriving. With a few circles of the island by boat you should be able to find some of them.

Refugio de Vida Silvestre Los Guatuzos → For listings, see pages 179-182.

Los Guatuzos Wildlife Refuge occupies the southern shores of Lake Nicaragua and the southern banks of the first few kilometres of the Río San Juan. Nicaraguan biologists consider it the cradle of life for the lake, because of its importance as a bird-nesting site and its infinite links in the area's complex ecological chain. More than a dozen rivers run through the reserve, the most popular for wildlife viewing being the **Río Papaturro**. The ecosystems are diverse with tropical dry forest, tropical wet forest, rainforest and extensive wetlands. Best of all are the many narrow rivers lined with gallery forest – the ideal setting for viewing wildlife.

Flora and fauna
The vegetation here is stunning with over 315 species of plant, including some primary forest trees over 35 m in height and 130 species of orchid. The quality and sheer quantity of wildlife is the reason most visitors come here; it is astonishing. This little park is brimming with life, especially at sunrise, and while there are places in Nicaragua and Central America with a longer species list, you can often see as much wildlife in a few hours in Los Guatuzos as you will in several days elsewhere.

Eighty-one amphibious species have been documented so far, along with 136 species of reptile, 42 species of mammal and 389 species of bird. The most noticeable residents of the gallery forest are the **howler monkeys** (*mono congo*), named after the loud growl of the male monkey, which can be heard up to 3 km away. The reserve is loaded with howlers particularly along the Río Papaturro, where you can see 30-50 monkeys in an average four-hour period. More difficult to spot, but also present, are white-faced and spider monkeys. Of the reptiles, the easiest to spot are the caimans, iguanas and turtles, especially if it is sunny. A long way upriver are a number of Jesus Christ lizards, famed for their hind-leg dashes across the surface of the water. There are also sloths, anteaters and jaguars. However, the most impressive aspect of the reserve is the density of its birdlife. As well as the many elegant egrets and herons, there are five species of kingfisher, countless jacanas, the pretty purple gallinule, wood storks, the roseate spoonbill, jabiru, osprey, laughing falcon, scarlet-rumped tanagers, trogons, bellbirds and six species of parrot.

Background
The original inhabitants of the area that included the Solentiname archipelago were fishermen, hunters and skilled planters with crops of corn, squash, cacao and plantains. They called themselves the **Maleku**. The Maleku language had sprinklings of Náhuatl as spoken by the Nicaraguas (a root of Aztec Náhuatl), but was basically Chibcha (the language root of the Miskito, Rama and Mayangna). Their name for Lake Nicaragua was Ucurriquitúkara, which means 'where the rivers converge'. The Spanish name for these people was the **Guatuzo** because they painted their faces red, in a colour reminiscent of the large tropical rodent, the *guatuza* (agouti), which is very common to the region. It was the extraction of rubber, which began in 1860, that spelled the beginning of the end for Guatuzo culture. In the 1930s and 1940s the current residents began to move in

but you can still see traces of the original Maleku or Guatuzo people in a few residents of Solentiname and the reserve administrators allow them to practise small-scale agriculture and ranching.

Centro Ecológico de Los Guatuzos

ⓘ *Managua office T2270-5434, www.losguatuzos.com, US$6 including tour of the grounds and projects; canopy bridge US$10 extra.*

Some local residents have become involved in the research and protection of the reserve at the Centro Ecológico de Los Guatuzos run by the Nicaraguan non-profit environmental NGO **Fundación de Amigos del Río San Juan (Fundar)**. The ecological centre has over 130 species of orchid on display, a sad butterfly farm (broken into and robbed constantly by local forest animals), a turtle hatchery and a caiman breeding centre. In addition to some short trails with vicious mosquitoes, there is a system of wobbly canopy bridges to allow visitors to observe wildlife from high up in the trees. If you don't suffer from vertigo, this is a wonderful experience allowing you to get right up close to the wildlife. A recommended guide is Armando (Spanish-speaking only), who is a native of the river and an expert on orchids.

⦿ San Carlos and Archipiélago Solentiname listings

For sleeping and eating price codes and other relevant information, see pages 28-30.

⦿ Where to stay

San Carlos *p172, map 173*
$$ Gran Lago Hotel, Caruna, 25 vrs al lago, T8823-3488. This hotel has views of the lake and serves fruit breakfast in the mornings. The rooms are comfortable enough, with private bath, a/c, cable TV and 24-hr water. Purified water and coffee available throughout the day.
$ Cabinas Leyko, Policía Nacional, 2 c abajo, T2583-0354. One of the better places in town, with clean, comfortable rooms, good mattresses, private bath and a/c. Cheaper with fan and shared bath.
$ Carelhy's Hotel, iglesia católica, ½ c sur, T2583-0389. 15 clean and simple rooms; 5 have a/c. Each room has 2 beds and can sleep 3. Can help arrange tours or transport. Internet in the works. Discount for longer stays or groups.
$ Costa Sur, Consejo Supremo Electoral, 50 m sur, T5283-0224. A little way out of town and reportedly an hourly rental. Nice and cheap, with 10 very simple, shabby rooms with or without private bath and fan.

$ Hostal Seledith, Enacal, 1 c abajo, T2583-0376, www.hostalcyberseledithrsj.blogspot.com. 11 simple, wooden rooms, each with a small table, chair, fan and bath. Family-run and economical for single travellers.
$ Hotelito San Carlos, next to Clínica San Lucas, T2583-0265. Pleasant family-owned place with small, basic, cleanish rooms with shared bath.

Isla San Fernando *p177*
$$ Cabañas Paraíso, T8824-1860 (mob), gsolentiname@ifxnw.com.ni, Managua office in Galería Solentiname, T2278-3998. The lack of trees means that the views are spectacular and the sun hot. Rooms are very clean, bright and crowded, with private bath. Feels a bit Miami, but friendly. Excursions in very fine boats are offered.
$$ Hotel Celentiname or **Doña María**, T2276-1910. This laid-back place is the most traditional of the hotels here. It has a lovely location facing another island and a lush garden filled with big trees, hummingbirds, iguanas and, at night, fishing bats. The rustic cabins have private bath and nice decks. Sad dorm rooms are not much cheaper with shared baths. Generated power, all meals included. Friendly owners. Recommended.

Isla Mancarrón *p177*

$$ Hotel Mancarrón, up the hill from the cement dock and church, T2277-3495, hotelmancarrun@gmail.com. Great birdwatching around this hotel that has access to the artisan village. Rooms are airy, screened, equipped with mosquito netting and private bath. The managers are personal and friendly. Prices include 3 great home-cooked meals per day. Recommended.
$ Hospedaje Reynaldo Ucarte, main village. 4 decent but basic rooms with shared baths. Meals available on request. Friendly, nice area with lots of children and trees.

Refugio de Vida Silvestre Los Guatuzos *p178*

$$$ Esperanza Verde, Río Frío, 4 km from San Carlos, T2583-0127, fundeverde@yahoo.es. In a beautiful area rich in wildlife, these 280 ha of private reserve inside the Los Guatuzos Wildlife Refuge have good nature trails for birdwatching. There are 20 rooms with single beds, fan, shared bath. Prices include 3 meals per day.
$$ La Esquina del Lago, at the mouth of the Río Frío, T2849-0600, www.riosanjuan.info. Surrounded by vegetation and visited by 61 species of bird, this tranquil and hospitable lodge on the water is owned by former newspaper-man Philippe Tisseaux. A range of tours are available, including birdwatching and world-class sports fishing. Excellent food, which uses fresh fish and home-grown herbs. Free use of kayak and free transport from San Carlos, a 5-min ride away (speak to **El Güegüense**, below, to arrange transit to the hotel). Highly recommended.
$ Centro Ecológico de Los Guatuzos, Río Papaturro, T2270-3561, www.losguatuzos.com. An attractive wooden research station on the riverfront. 2 rooms have 8 bunk beds in each, shared bath. Meals for guests US$2-3, served in a local house. Guided visits to forest trails, excursions to others rivers in the reserve.

Night caiman tours by boat. Private boat to and from San Carlos can be arranged. All tours in Spanish only, some Managua tour operators arrange programmes with an English-speaking guide (see page 65).

❼ Restaurants

San Carlos *p172, map 173*

$$$-$$ Granadino, opposite Alejandro Granja playing field, T2583-0386. Daily 0900-0200. Considered the best in town, with a relaxed ambience and pleasant river views. *Camarones en salsa*, steak and hamburgers. Not cheap.
$$-$ El Güegüense, southeast corner of the plaza, 2 c arriba, 1 c sur, just east of the *malecón*. Attractive Solentiname art on the walls of this eatery. They serve Nica fare, including breakfasts, lunches and dinners. Can call through transport to La Esquina del Lago, see Where to stay, above.
$$-$ Kaoma, across from Western Union, T2583-0293. Daily from 0900 until the last customer collapses in a pool of rum. Nautically themed and also decorated with dozens of oropendola nests. There's fresh fish caught by the owner, good *camarones de río* (freshwater prawns), and dancing when the locals are inspired. Views of the river from the wooden deck and occasionally refreshing breezes. Recommended.
$ El Mirador, iglesia católica, 1½ c sur, T2583-0367. Daily 0700-2000. Superb view from patio of Lake Nicaragua, Solentiname, Río Frío and Río San Juan and the jumbled roofs of the city. Decent chicken, fish and beef dishes starting at US$3 with friendly service. Recommended, though it closes if the *chayules* (mosquitoes) are in town.
$ Soda Comedor San Carlos, Muelle Principal, 100 m sur. One of many cheap and popular places in the area serving economical Nica food.

O Shopping

San Carlos *p172, map 173*
Stock up on purified water and food for
a long journey. The market is a cramped
nightmare, but in front of immigration
there are stalls to buy goods. High-top
rubber boots or wellingtons are standard
equipment in these parts, perfect for jungle
treks and cost US$6-9, though large sizes
are rarely found.

O What to do

San Carlos *p172, map 173*
Tour operators
Ryo Big Tours, Malecón, T2583-0266.
A broad range of tours, including visits to
Solentiname, Los Guatuzos and El Castillo,
which last a day or more. Also runs caiman
and kayak tours, and historical tours of San
Carlos. If you're in search of something
different. You could try their traditional
bow and arrow fishing trip.
San Carlos Sport Fishing, La Esquina del
Lago hotel, at the mouth of the Río Frío,
T2849-0600, www.riosanjuan.info. Operated
by Phillipe Tisseaux, who has many years of
experience fishing the Río San Juan, where
plenty of tarpon, snook and rainbow bass
can be caught. He also offers birdwatching,
kayaking and cultural tours. Recommended.

O Transport

San Carlos *p172, map 173*
Air
The flight to Managua is breathtaking.
On a clear day you can see Solentiname,
Ometepe, Las Isletas, Granada, Volcán
Mombacho, Laguna de Apoyo, Volcán
Masaya and Lake Managua. La Costeña has
1 daily flight from San Carlos to **Managua**,
1425, US$82 one-way, US$120 return, 1 hr
(see page 66 for outgoing schedules).
Taxi from airstrip to dock US$1. Arrive 1 hr
before departure because the single-prop
Cessna Caravan 208B touches down,

unloads and takes off again all within 5 mins
and you must be ready to jump on – also
because overbooking is common. There are
no reserved seats and only 5 seats with a
decent view, all on the left.
  Airline office La Costeña, Fortaleza
San Carlos, 1 c sur, 2 c arriba, T583-0271.

Bus
From San Carlos to **Managua**, daily,
0600, 0800, 1145, 1430, 1800, 2000,
2200, US$9, 5-6 hrs.

Motorboat
Small motor boats are called *pangas*; long,
narrow ones are *botes* and big broad ones
are known as *planos*.
  Public Arrive at least 30 mins in advance
to ensure a seat on a short ride; allow 1 hr or
more for long trips. All schedules are subject
to random changes; check locally before
setting out. To **Solentiname**, Tue, Fri, 1400,
US$4, 2½ hrs, stopping at islands **La Venada**,
San Fernando, **Mancarrón**. To **Los
Guatuzos**, stopping at **Papaturro**, Tue, Wed,
Fri, 0700, US$5, 3½ hrs. To **Los Chiles**, Costa
Rica, daily 1030, 1300, 1500, US$8, 2 hrs. To
El Castillo (and Sábalos), Mon-Sat (express)
0430, 0530, 0600, 0700, 1030, 1130; (slow)
0500, 0830, 1200, 1430, 1530; Sun (express)
0630, 0800,1030; (slow) 1330. Avoid the
slow boat if you can, it's a gruelling 6-hr ride.
To **San Juan del Norte**, Tue, Thu, Fri, 0600,
12-14 hrs, US$14; express services run Tue
and Fri in the wet season, 7-9 hrs, US$30.
The ferry to **Granada** leaves from main dock
in San Carlos, Tue and Fri 1400, US$9.50 1st
class, US$4 2nd class, 14 hrs. 1st class has a
TV, nicer seats and is usually less crowded;
it's worth the extra money. Bring a hammock
if you can and expect a challenging journey.
  Private Motorboats are available for
hire; they are expensive but afford freedom
to stop and view wildlife. They are also
faster, leave when you want and allow you
to check different hotels for space and
conditions. Beyond El Castillo downriver
there are only 2 boats per week, so private

transport is the only other option. Ask at tourism office for recommendations. Average round-trip rates: **El Castillo** US$190-250, **Solentiname** US$100-150, **San Juan del Norte** US$800-950. Some *pangueros* (boatmen) who have been recommended include: Armando Ortiz, Norman Guadamuz, Martín López, Ricardo Henríquez. Packages are available from **Tours Nicaragua** (see page 65) who specialize in this region, providing complete trips with private boat transfers, bilingual naturalist guide and boat tours of wildlife reserves; expensive unless you have a group of at least 4 travellers.

Taxi
Taxis wait for arriving flights at the landing strip; if you miss them you will have to walk to town (30 mins). To get to the landing strip, taxis can be found in town between the market and *muelle flotante*. All fares are US$1, exact change is essential. Drivers are helpful.

Archipiélago Solentiname *p175*
Boat
Solentiname to **San Carlos**, Tue, Fri 0430, US$4, 2½ hrs. **Los Guatuzos** and **Río**

Papaturro to **San Carlos**, Mon, Tue, Thu 0600, US$5, 3½ hrs.

⊙ Directory

San Carlos *p172, map 173*
Bank BDF, Fortaleza San Carlos, 1 c sur, 1 c arriba, T583-0144. There is a **Banpro** with a Visa ATM on the *malecón*, as well as a **Banex**, 1 block south of the plaza, and a **BDF**, Fortaleza San Carlos, 1 c sur, 1 c arriba, T2583-0144. You are advised to bring as much cash as you'll need to the region due to the possible failure of the ATM or unforeseen issues with your card network. No TC changes, but you can change dollars, córdobas or colones with the coyotes at the entrance to immigration and customs. Expect long bank queues on, or near, the 15th or 31st of each month. **Fire** T2583-0149. **Hospital** T2583-0238. **Police** T2583-0350. **Post** Correos de Nicaragua, across from Los Juzgados de Distritos, T2583-0000. **Telephone** Enitel office is on road from landing strip to town, T2583-0001.

Along the Río San Juan

The vast and extraordinarily beautiful Río San Juan is Lake Nicaragua's sole outlet to the sea. Three major rivers that originate in Costa Rica and more than 17 smaller tributaries also feed this mighty river, which is up to 350 m wide at points. A staggering amount of water flows out of this river to the sea every day. At San Carlos enough water enters the river in a 24-hour period in the dry season to supply water to all of Central America for one year – a gigantic resource that Nicaragua has yet to exploit. For the visitor it is an opportunity to experience the rainforest and to journey from Central America's biggest lake all the way to the thundering surf of Nicaragua's eastern seaboard. From San Carlos, the river passes the easternmost sector of Los Guatuzos Wildlife Refuge before entering a long stretch of cattle ranches that lead to the historic town and fort of El Castillo. Past El Castillo, the Indio-Maíz Biological Reserve runs the remaining length of the river's north bank to the scenic coastal estuaries of the Caribbean Sea.
▶▶ *For listings, see pages 191-194.*

Arriving in San Juan → *Colour map 4, C1-3.*
Getting around The river drops an average of 18 cm per kilometre on its 190-km journey from Lake Nicaragua to the Caribbean. Travel is only possible by boat, with a regular daily service to El Castillo and sparse public boat operations downriver. To really explore the river,

private boat hire is necessary, though expensive. All travel times between tributaries in this section are estimates based on a private boat with capacity for six to eight passengers and a 45 horse power motor or better, travelling downstream. If you are travelling upstream add 20-35%; for heavy boats, smaller motors and travel at the end of the dry season, add much more time. If travelling in a light boat with a big motor during the rainy season when the rivers are full, travel times can be cut almost in half depending on the bravado of the navigator. ▸▸ *For further details, see Transport, page 194.*

Background

In 1502 Christopher Columbus explored the Caribbean Coast of Nicaragua in search of an inter-oceanic passage. He sailed right past the Río San Juan. The river was populated by the Rama people, the same that can be found today on a small island in the Bay of Bluefields. In the 17th century the biggest Rama settlement was estimated at more than 30,000 in the Boca de Sábalo; at the same time, the capital of Nicaragua had some 40,000 residents. Today the Rama are making a return to the southern forests of Nicaragua, though only in the Río Indio area along the Caribbean Coast.

When Francisco Hernández de Córdoba established the cities of Granada and León, he sent Spanish Captain Ruy Díaz in search of the lake's drainage. Díaz explored the entire lake, reaching the mouth of the river in 1525. He was able to navigate the river as far as the first principal northern tributary, Río Sábalo, but was forced to turn back. Córdoba was unfazed and sent a second expedition led by Captain Hernando de Soto (later the first European to navigate the Mississippi river). Soto managed to sail as far as Díaz and was also forced to turn back due to the rapids.

Explorers were busy looking for gold in Nicaragua's northern mountains and the river was ignored until 1539, when a very serious expedition was put together by the Spanish governor of Nicaragua, Rodrigo de Contreras. This brutally difficult journey was undertaken by foot troops, expert sailors and two brave captains, Alonso Calero and Diego Machuca. Having passed the first set of rapids, they encountered more rapids at El Castillo; Machuca divided the expedition and marched deep into the forest looking for the outlet of the river. Calero continued the length of the river and reached its end at the Caribbean Sea on 24 June 1539. This happened to be Saint John the Baptist's saint's day, so they named the river after him. He then sailed north in search of Machuca as far as the outlet of the Río Coco. However, Machuca had left on foot with his troops and returned all the way to Granada without knowledge of what had happened to the Calero party. The newly discovered passage was exactly what the Spanish had been hoping for. It was quickly put into service for the transport of gold, indigo and other goods from their Pacific holdings to Hispañola (Dominican Republic and Haiti today) and then to Spain. The river was part of the inter-oceanic steam ship service of Cornelius Vanderbilt in the mid-1800s and was used by William Walker for his brief rule in Granada. During the Contra conflict, parts of the river were contested by Edén Pastora's southern front troops in attacks against the Sandinista government army.

San Carlos–Río Sábalo–El Castillo → *Travel time about 2 hrs.*

Outside the limits of San Carlos, the river is lined with wetlands, providing good opportunities for birdwatching. Deforestation in this section of the river (until El Castillo) is getting increasingly worse and, despite numerous reforestation projects, barges can be seen transporting giant trunks of cedar. The Río Sábalo is an important tributary named after the large fish found in this region, the *sábalo* (tarpon). The town at its mouth, **Boca de Sábalos**, is melancholy, muddy and friendly. There is an earth path that leads to a spooky-looking African palm plantation and factory, where palm oil is made. From the road it is possible to connect with the **Río Santa Cruz** and navigate that small and beautiful river to El Castillo. The road in the dry season goes deep into the backcountry and wildlife viewing at the forest edge is very good; you may well see spider, howler and white-faced monkeys, flocks of parrots and many birds of prey. There are decent lodges around the mouth of the Río Sábalo (see Where to stay, page 191) and the people of Sábalo seem happy to see outsiders. There are some small rapids just past the river's drainage into the Río San Juan. The fishing for *sábalo real* (giant tarpon) is quite good here. They can reach up to 2.5 m and weigh in at 150 kg. *Robalo* (snook) is also a popular sport fish and much better to eat than tarpon. Just downriver from Sábalo is the charming, clean and friendly town of El Castillo, 60 km from San Carlos and home to a famous 17th-century fortress.

El Castillo → *For listings, see pages 191-194.*

The peaceful little village of El Castillo could well be the most attractive riverfront settlement in Nicaragua. Located in front of the **El Diablo rapids**, El Castillo is a sight to behold: tiny riverfront homes with red tin roofs sit on stilts above the fast-moving river. Behind, on a round grassy green hill, a big, 330-year-old Spanish fort dominates the view of the town. Most people come to see the fort, but the village makes a longer stay worthwhile.

Tourist information Right in front of the town dock is a little office for **INTUR**, often unmanned, but good for advice on hiring boats if it's open.

Fortaleza de la Inmaculada Concepción

When British pirate Henry Morgan made off down the Río San Juan with £500,000 sterling after sacking Granada, the Spanish said ¡Basta! (enough!). Construction of the fort at El Castillo began in 1673 on the top of a hill that affords long views to the east (the route of attacks) and in front of one of the river's most dangerous rapids. In 1674 French pirates encountered a half-finished fortress, but were warded off. Work was completed in 1675 and today the fort is Nicaragua's oldest standing colonial building (in its original state). Tipped to become a UNESCO World Heritage Site, this was the biggest fortress on the Central American isthmus and the second biggest in all the Spanish American colonial empire when it was finished.

In the 18th century the fort came under siege from the British several times. In 1762 the British Navy came up the Río San Juan to take the fort and control the river. A new

El Castillo

To ③ ④ ⑤

Sportsground

El Diablo Rapids

Health Centre

Fortaleza de la Inmaculada Concepción

Centro de la Interpretación de la Naturaleza

Río San Juan

To San Carlos

Dock

Lomas de Nelson

N

Not to scale

Where to stay
Albergue El Castillo 1
Nena Lodge 6
Posada del Río 3
Richarson 4
Universal 2
Victoria 5

Restaurants
Bar Cofalito 1
Borders Coffee 2
Cafetín Cristina 4
El Chinandegano 5
Vanessa's 3

Canal dreams

The dream of making the Río San Juan into part of an inter-oceanic canal was born as early as 1567, when King Phillip II of Spain ordered a feasibility study. By the mid-17th century the English had moved in on Spanish holdings in the Caribbean and had created a base for attacks on Central America. Their goal was to conquer the Río San Juan and "divide the Spanish Empire in half". From then on, renowned scientists, engineers, business people and public figures would advocate the canal idea and become more directly or indirectly involved in its promotion. In the 19th century, the US president Ulysses ordered a study to find the best option for a Central American inter-oceanic canal. It concluded that the Nicaraguan route was more feasible than Panama or Tehuantepec, Mexico.

In 1901 the US House of Representatives passed a bill in favour of the US government building the canal in Nicaragua. However, just as the Senate hearings on the proposal were about to begin, a Caribbean volcano erupted, killing thousands. A sharp lobbyist for the Panama Canal project distributed a Nicaraguan postage stamp depicting Volcán Momotombo in eruption to all the senators, with the footnote that a Nicaraguan canal would have to pass by this active volcano. This was not actually true (it was the active Concepción volcano on the Island of Ometepe that would be passed), but it was convincing enough and the canal project was awarded to Panama.

national hero was born in El Castillo – a teenage girl called Rafaela Herrera, the daughter of a decorated captain of the Spanish forces who had recently died. The soldiers of the fort were ready to concede defeat, but Rafaela, who had received training in armament, took command of the fortress and troops and fired the first rounds of cannon herself against the British. She is said to have killed a British commander with her third shot. The battle lasted five days. One night, under heavy attack from the boats under cover of darkness, Rafaela ordered sheets to be soaked in alcohol, placed on big branches and set alight upriver. The flaming torches illuminated the enemy for counter fire and the river carried the burning debris downstream toward the enemy's wooden boats. The British were forced to retreat.

In 1779 English chancellor Lord George Germain devised a serious attack on the Río San Juan that was aimed at securing British domination of Lake Nicaragua and control of the province. Seven warships were brought to the mouth of the Río San Juan with a force of 600 British soldiers and 400 Miskito warriors. Also on the mission was a young Captain Horatio Nelson, later to become the British Navy's greatest hero. The fortress at El Castillo had two weaknesses and Nelson's attack exposed both. Firstly, the fort had no water supply, so the Spanish were unable to take water from the river while under siege. Secondly, there is high ground just behind the fort, which allowed the fort attackers to shoot down into the fortress. Nelson brought the troops ashore well before the fort and travelled overland through the forest (legend has it he killed a jaguar on the way and narrowly avoided dying from a snake bite) to attack the fortress from the high hill behind. Today, the hill is a cemetery known as Lomas de Nelson. The British won the battle and took control of the fort, but Matías de Galvez, the captain general of Central America, was every bit as capable as the British generals who masterminded the invasion. Galvez decided to let the jungle do his work for him and, using massive troop reinforcements in San Carlos, kept the British forces bottled up in the fort. Soon the Miskito got tired of waiting and left. Jungle diseases, especially dysentery and malaria, set in and in less than a year the great majority of the invasion forces had died. The British decided to abandon the fort. Many Nicaraguan history books claim Nelson lost his eye in battles at the fort, others say he lost the use of an arm. In fact neither occurred here, but his health was so affected by dysentery that he had to be carried off the boat on a cot when he returned to Jamaica.

A museum and library were built inside the fortress in the 1990s. The **museum** ① *0900-1200, 1400-1700, US$2*, is one of the country's finest with a very complete history of the region (in Spanish) and the views alone are worth the price of admission. There is also an educational museum behind the fortress, **Centro de Interpretación de la Naturaleza** with displays and explanations of local wildlife and vegetation as well as a butterfly farm.

El Castillo–Río Bartola → *Travel time about 25 mins.*

Travelling downstream from the fortress means riding the small but tricky rapids in front of the town. Locals fish here and Nicaraguan boat drivers have no problems zigzagging through the rapids, though the occasional reckless boatman has flipped over here. Just 2 km downriver, there's a narrow cut through the forest up a hill and a Nicaraguan flag marks the border with Costa Rica, which reaches the southern banks of the river here and follows most of the river to the Caribbean Sea. The confluence of the Río San Juan and Río Bartola marks the beginning of the splendid Indio-Maíz Biological Reserve.

Reserva Biológica Indio-Maíz → *For listings, see pages 191-194.*

This is Central America and Nicaragua's second largest nature reserve and perhaps its most pristine. A few square kilometres here house more species of bird, tree or insect than the entire European continent. The reserve protects what North American biologists have called "the largest extent of primary rainforest in Central America", its trees reaching up to 50 m in height. Indio-Maíz also has numerous wetland areas and rivers. Its westernmost border is marked by the Río Bartola; at the east is the Caribbean Sea; and the northern and southern limits are marked by the Río Punta Gorda and Río San Juan respectively. There is no accommodation inside the reserve at the time of printing, but the banks of the river have been changed (downgraded in terms of level of protection) from biological reserve to wildlife refuge, in theory allowing for construction of ecolodges along the Nicaraguan bank of the river and opening up the reserve to more tourism.

Background

Inside the reserve's pristine forest are several ancient extinct volcanoes, the highest being **Cerro La Guinea** at 648 m. The reserve is home to over 600 species of bird, 300 species of reptile and amphibian, and 200 species of mammal, including many big cats and howler, white-face and spider monkeys. Rainfall in the park ranges from just under 3000 mm a year in Bartola to 5000 mm in San Juan del Norte. Sadly little research has been done in the reserve and most of its wildlife and vegetation remains a mystery but over the past decade UCLA biologists have been enlisting the help of student volunteers. They report that the density and diversity of the wildlife at the field site (the forest behind Bartola and the MARENA station) is "impressive, even by neotropical standards". As well as the three primate species, the students discovered two bird species previously undocumented in Nicaragua and made a list of birds that include 11 different species of heron, two of ibis and stork, 12 species of hawk, kite and falcon, and eight species of parrot and macaw. They also documented 11 species of hummingbird, six kingfisher, three toucan, seven woodpecker, 19 antbirds and no less than 27 species of flycatcher. The biologists also encountered 28 species of reptile and 16 species of mammal including three-toed sloth, jaguarundi, river otter, tapir, deer, agouti, paca, white-faced, spider and howler monkey. The sheer beauty of the reserve means that non-enthusiasts will also enjoy the enchantment of a virgin rainforest.

Río Bartola–Río San Carlos → Travel time about 1 hr.

This is one of the most scenic sections of the river, in particular the area around the rapids of **Machuca** and just upriver from the mouth of Río San Carlos, which originates in Costa Rica. The forest is in good condition on both sides of the river and the trees are teeming with parrots. As the vegetation rises out of succulent rainforest, it's easy to see why Mark Twain (see box, page 146) and other observers have been so enchanted over time.

At the mouth of the pristine **Río Sarnoso** is a shipwreck from the 19th-century inter-oceanic steam ship service, though the locals like to claim it is a Spanish galleon wreck. Jaguar can be seen here, one of the most difficult jungle animals to spot thanks to their preference for night hunting and large territories (up to 11 sq km). To enter the Río Sarnoso you will need to receive advance permission from MARENA in Managua (see page 45) and show the letter to the guards east or west of the river.

At the confluence of the **Río San Carlos** there is a checkpoint for the Nicaraguan military and MARENA, where passports must be presented. Across the banks in Costa Rica there is a general store and a basic eatery. Permission can be obtained from the Costa Rican military to make a quick supply or food stop (córdobas are difficult to use on the Costa Rican side, so keep a supply of small note dollars).

There once was a Spanish fortress on the island that lies at the confluence of the San Carlos and San Juan rivers, which predated the structure at El Castillo. The **Fortaleza San Carlos** (not to be confused with the old fort at San Carlos on the lake) was built in 1667 with room for 70 musketeers and a few artillerymen to operate four cannon. Three years later, pirate Lawrence Prince attacked the little wooden fortress with 200 men. Only 37 Spanish soldiers had survived the climate and insects, but nonetheless put up stout resistance, killing six and wounding eight of the pirates and managing to send a boat up to Granada to ask for reinforcements. They never came and the Spaniards had to surrender. Prince sent his fastest canoe double-manned with Miskito oarsmen to overtake the Spanish messenger. He then went on to sack Granada, prompting the construction of the great structure at El Castillo (see page 184).

Río San Carlos–Río Sarapiquí → Travel time about 1 hr.

Past the Río San Carlos the stunning beauty of the Indio-Maíz reserve on the north bank continues, while the south bank is a mixture of forest and ranch settlements, with some clear cutting. There are sandbars and beaches most of the year and slow navigation will allow opportunities to spot crocodiles and turtles, as well as monkeys and toucans in the canopy. The muddy, debris-filled **Río Sarapiquí** drains into the Río San Juan at the second river checkpoint for the military and MARENA. The Sarapiquí is in Costa Rica and there is a small village where basic boat and motor repairs can be made. This was the scene of several significant battles between the Edén Pastora-led southern front Contra forces and the Nicaraguan Sandinista military in the 1980s. At the confluence of the two rivers on the Costa Rican side is **Doña Adilia's** (see page 192), a small friendly lodge and the last chance for a bed before the end of the river.

Río Sarapiquí–Río Colorado → *Travel time about 1 hr.*

Past the drainage of the Sarapiquí, the Río San Juan travels northeast passing some of the river's 300 islands, including the **Isla Nelson**. Petrol is available on the Costa Rican side, which is dotted with sprawling ranches. The Nicaraguan territory (which includes the river and its islands) is pristine rainforest mixed with some secondary growth where land was reclaimed for the biological reserve. At one of the widest parts of the river it branches southeast and northeast. To the southeast is the mighty **Río Colorado** in Costa Rica. To the northeast is the **Río San Juan**. Thanks to sediment build-up in the bay of San Juan since the mid- to late-1800s, the majority of the water now drains out of the Río Colorado to the sea. There is another checkpoint here. Past the intersection of the two rivers, the Río San Juan becomes narrow and runs almost due north.

Río Colorado–Caribbean Sea → *Travel time about 2 hrs.*

This section of the Río San Juan is normally quite good for sighting monkeys, toucans, scarlet macaws and king vultures. As it approaches the sea, the Río San Juan begins to snake wildly. It twists and turns past wetlands and the broad, handsome swamp palms that are common in this area, until it meets the sea at a dark sandbar called simply **La Barra** (the bar). The emerging and submerging sandbar (according to the tides and the force of the San Juan river) has fooled navigators for hundreds of years and has been responsible for many a sailor's death. After hours of dense jungle, the sight of the windswept beach is exhilarating. Here the Caribbean is muddy, filled with sediment from the river and literally teeming with bull sharks that are feeding on the many fish in this rich combination of fresh and salt water. Swimming is only for the suicidal (you could not pay a local to swim here) – strong surf and currents aid the sharks in ripping apart any flesh within its reach.

Bahía de San Juan → *For listings, see pages 191-194.*

North of the sandbank is a series of connected coastal estuaries known collectively as the Bay of San Juan. If sunny, the bay is glorious, with deep-blue water reflecting dense green rainforest and shores lined with flowering waterlilies and grass. This is the end of the earth: a tropical paradise. It is also one of the wettest places in the Americas, with an average annual rainfall of 5000 mm. Sitting forlornly in the bay is the more than 100-year-old dredger that started the canal project to connect the two seas. Today its rusted body is covered with vegetation. There is superb fishing and an ecolodge in front of the dredger.

San Juan del Norte

The end-of-the-world feeling is not lost in this little village of winding paths, homes on stilts and flooded yards. Fishing for brown and white lobster are the main sources of income. White lobster (*langosta blanca*), however, is in fact cocaine. The locals comb the beach or coastal waters for big bails of the drug that have been thrown overboard by Colombian speed boats being chased by the coastguard. The ocean currents dictate that a great deal ends up on the coast here. What was once a peaceful little lobster fishing village has become severely corrupted in the last few years thanks to the instant riches available from *langosta blanca*. Nonetheless, the residents of San Juan del Norte are very friendly, a mix of Afro-Caribbeans from Bluefields and El Limón in Costa Rica, Hispanics from the Pacific, and some of the indigenous Rama from Bluefields Bay. The village lines the west bank of the Río Indio, one of Nicaragua's most beautiful rivers, and 200 m wide at this point. There is a new paved road resembling a central avenue with little palms and brightly

Costa Rica and Nicaragua: a bridge too far?

They appear on the world map as perfect opposites. The nature- and peace-loving Costa Ricans living happily in their tourist mecca, the self-proclaimed Switzerland of Central America and darling of international ecotourism. Across the Río San Juan, lies bad-boy Nicaragua, a country synonymous with war and natural disasters, whose inhabitants are always fighting among themselves and daring to defy the United States, driving their own economy into the ground.

It was not always this way, but the tables have been turned over the years, creating bitterness on both sides. During the war against William Walker in 1856, Costa Rica rushed to help Nicaragua fight Walker and occupied southern Lake Nicaragua and the then lucrative inter-oceanic route of the Río San Juan. After Walker was defeated, Costa Rica hoped to annex Granada, Chontales and Rivas, leaving Nicaragua with Río San Juan and Lake Nicaragua. However, they had to settle for Guanacaste, the Nicoya Peninsula and the southern banks of the Río San Juan, sowing the seeds of an animosity that lives on today.

Following the Contra War, several human rights watch groups documented abuses by the Costa Rican military against Nicaraguan immigrant farm workers and Nicaraguan migrants found little humour in the claim that Costa Rica had no military, a feat achieved by calling their large (larger than the entire Nicaraguan military and police force combined), well-trained troops the 'Civil Guard'. It was the same non-existent Costa Rican military that was caught dressed in battle fatigues patrolling the Río San Juan in a camouflage boat in 1998, with automatic rifles and mounted machine-guns at the ready. The news sent Nicaraguans into outrage. Nicaraguans called for a total ban of Costa Rican boat travel inside its borders. Costa Rica threatened to expel all Nicaraguan immigrant workers and both countries lapsed into uncomfortable diplomatic attempts at repair.

Since then, feelings have calmed and Costa Ricans are once again allowed to navigate the river for commercial purposes, but allowing military patrols inside Nicaragua is a sticking point that remains un-resolved. Though the actual ownership of the river has never been in doubt, Nicaragua has long been suspicious of Costa Rica's desires to incorporate it.

In October 2010, tensions between the two countries flared once again when Nicaragua commenced dredging a 33-km section of the river close to a Costa Rican-owned nature reserve, Isla Calero. According to Costa Rica, Nicaragua had made illegal incursions into Costa Rican territory and was causing significant environmental damage in the process. Nicaragua argued it had every right to dredge its own river and a protracted stand-off ensued whilst both sides sent reinforcements to the region. Costa Rica eventually took its complaints to the World Court in the Hague, and in March 2011, the court ruled that both parties should withdraw their forces from the disputed area.

A tentative peace has returned to Río San Juan, but with Nicaragua assessing the viability of several new hydroelectric projects, it is only a matter of time before this vital resource becomes a point of contention once again. Meanwhile, most people who live on both sides of the river find all this bickering to be counterproductive. In most instances, they are commercially interdependent, and otherwise share almost all aspects of daily life and culture.

painted benches and two footpaths. This runs parallel to the river about 50 m inside the village. Across the river is a 400-m-wide strip of land full of coconut palms, dense forest and beach that separates the copper-coloured Río Indio from the crashing Caribbean Sea. It is a delightfully surreal experience to watch the jungle river flow south as the sun sets over the bright green rainforest that separates the two bodies of water, while being serenaded by the muffled roar of the sea.

Greytown

At the edge of one of the lagoons are a decaying wooden dock and a tattered Nicaraguan flag which marks the entrance to the historic and long-deserted frontier town of Greytown. This is all that remains of the original San Juan del Norte, known to most as Greytown after the British governor of Jamaica in 1847 when the town was re-baptized by the British. In 1850 the US was flexing its naval muscles in the region and the two powers signed a pact to unify and build a canal in Nicaragua with both British and US navies controlling its waters. In 1854 the town was bombed from a US battleship. It seems the attack was provoked by a boating accident in which the boat of US representative Mr Boland sunk the vessel of a Nicaraguan *indígena*. The locals demanded that the captain of the US boat be captured and tried. Mr Boland refused, a fight broke out and the honourable Boland was unceremoniously smashed over the head with a beer bottle. The US government fined the Nicaraguan government 24,000 pesos for the bump on Boland's head and gave Nicaragua 24 hours to pay up. Nicaragua refused and a hail of 210 cannon balls fell on Greytown, destroying the town but failing to set it alight. That afternoon US troops torched the town house by house.

Twelve years later Mark Twain slept here on his journey from San Francisco to New York and described the town as a "peopled paradise ... composed of 200 old frame houses and some nice vacant lots, and its comeliness is greatly enhanced, I may say is rendered gorgeous, by the cluster of stern-wheel steamboats at the water front. The population is 800 and is mixed – made up of natives (Nicaraguans), Americans, Spaniards, Germans, English and Jamaicans." He added that "the transit business has made every other house a lodging camp and you can get a good bed anywhere for a dollar." Today the only beds are in the town's cemeteries, which are preserved as a national monument. Greytown was taken over in 1982 by Edén Pastora and his Contra army unit, which provoked further bombardment by the Nicaragua Sandinista government. When Pastora's forces retreated, it was burned down by the Sandinista military and left as it is today. However, Greytown's economic demise had actually come much earlier when the inter-oceanic service was finally discontinued. It was briefly brought back to life by late 19th-century canal projects, but then relegated to obscurity in the 20th century and reduced to 300 inhabitants.

After the 1982 burning, there was nothing left of the town until it was re-founded upriver in 1990 as San Juan del Norte. The jungle that had taken over Greytown was cut down, ironically, by Edén Pastora in early 2004 so he could land his aeroplane here and get to his new shark-fishing business in today's San Juan del Norte. The old town lies just to the north side of the clearing. There is a quiet, often water-filled trail that leads through Catholic, American, Masonic and Anglican cemeteries; the faded tombstones entwined in rainforest. The only other sign of Greytown is the bell from the town church, an old creaking windmill and the front steps of the Pellas family house. In 2011, Edén Pastora's landing strip was upgraded to receive commercial flights from San Carlos, Costa Rica and Panama. Once fully operational, the new and somewhat insensitively located airport will usher big changes to the region. The economic benefits will surely be welcome, but the once quiet and haunting atmosphere of ruined old Greytown will be lost for good.

Río Indio

If you have chartered a boat, a trip further down the Río Indio is recommended to see wildlife, virgin forest and occasional encounters with the indigenous Rama (please respect their culture and right to privacy), who are returning to the region after centuries of exile. Upriver is truly spectacular, like a miniature Amazon, with kilometre after kilometre of virgin forest. It is important to leave early to see wildlife, and to bring plenty of petrol and water. You will need permission from the military and MARENA checkpoint at the north end of town on the riverfront. The river provides opportunities for serious adventure, but your budget must be healthy as there is no public transport. The Rama people navigate the river in canoes to buy weekly supplies in San Juan, but will only be able to offer a one-way ride to the jungle. The river goes into the heart of the Indio-Maíz reserve. Ask around locally to see what the current security situation is.

◉ Along the Río San Juan listings

For sleeping and eating price codes and other relevant information, see pages 28-30.

◉ Where to stay

Río Sábalo *p183*
$$$ Monte Cristo River Resort,
2 km downriver from Boca de Sábalos, T2583-0197, www.montecristoriver.com. Comfortable rooms with private bath. There are also apartments, a swimming pool, dance floor and **Mark Twain Bar**. Sometimes loud weekend parties arrive from El Castillo to use the dance hall. Rate covers 3 meals and all activities, including kayaking, fishing and horses. There's a special backpacker rate (**$$** per person) with much the same on offer.
$$ Hotel Sábalos, on confluence of San Juan and Sábalo rivers, T2271-7424, www.hotelsabalos.com.ni. This simple and friendly wooden hotel has a good location, with views up and down the river, great for watching locals pass in canoes. 9 wooden rooms have private bath and fan. The best resting spot on upper San Juan. Recommended.
$$ Sábalos Lodge, in front of El Toro rapids, just downriver from Río Sábalo, T2278-1405 (Managua), www.sabaloslodge.com. Funky and attractive mix of huts, cabins, shacks, some with bath inside, and hammocks. One nice unit on the river has a sitting room and

deck, all open to the outside with mosquito netting. Mixed reports, beautiful grounds but not much forest around.

El Castillo *p184, map p184*
$$ Hotel Victoria, el muelle, 400 vrs arriba, at the end of the end road, T2583-0188, www.hotelvictoriaelcastillo.com. This friendly and hospitable hotel has 9 wood-panelled rooms with cable TV, a/c and private bath (**$** with shared bath). Downstairs there's a pleasant restaurant overlooking the water and a nearby stream filled with turtles and caimans. Tours with accredited guides include horse-riding and night tours. The best place in town. Recommended.
$$ Posada del Río, el muelle, 400 vrs arriba, next to Hotel Victoria, T8925-9988. This intimate little hotel has 6 wooden rooms with private bath, a/c and hot water. In addition to the restaurant, there's a shared balcony and porch with deck-chairs and hammocks.
$ Albergue El Castillo, next to fortress above city dock, T8924-5608. Comfortable, if simple, wooden rooms and great views from a shared balcony overlooking the river. Only 1 room has a private bath; for extra side ventilation, the best rooms are Nos 1 and 10, but you have noisy bats for company in No 10. Noisy early morning as the public boats warm up (0500) motors. 25 mins of internet and breakfast included.

$ Hotel Richarson, el muelle, 300 vrs arriba, then follow the sign, T8644-0782. Sometimes seems to be abandoned; if the owner isn't there, ask around. The rooms are small and cleanish, and they have private baths with shower curtain doors. Friendly and quiet, but has seen better days. Richarson now offers restaurant service, including fish, chicken and pasta.

$ Nena Lodge, el muelle, 350 vrs arriba, T8821-2135, www.nenalodge.com. This new hotel has a range of simple budget rooms equipped with mosquito nets, soap and towels. Many of them open onto a communal balcony slung with hammocks. There is a tour agency on site, running trips to Finca Los Cocos, Sendero Bartola and Sendero Aguas Frescas, among others.

$ Universal, el muelle, 50 vrs arriba, T8666-3264. Friendly owners, good views and 8 small, clean, wooden rooms. A nice budget choice, but you'll find other cheapies in the adjacent buildings.

Río Bartola *p186*

$$$ Refugio Bartola, confluence of Río San Juan and Río Bartola, T8376-6979, refugiobartola@yahoo.com. Simple wooden rooms with private bath, high ceilings and solid beds. Prices include 3 meals, juice and coffee, bats in roof and frogs in toilet at no extra charge. There's a research station on site, with lots of creepy creatures in jars, including what could be the world's largest cockroach. There's also a private reserve with a labyrinth of trails. You need a guide (US$5, plus tip) as it's easy to get lost, and be sure to ask questions. Snakes, some deadly, are a real danger on a night hike. Recommended.

Río Sarapiquí *p188*

$ Cabinas La Trinidad or **Doña Adilia's**, at confluence of Río San Juan and Río Sarapiquí on Costa Rican bank, mobile T506-2391-7120, hurbinacom@yahoo.com. Little rooms (not terribly clean and bring your own mosquito net) with private bath and fan, run by a friendly, kind family. Nice

garden with good birdwatching, billiards table, restaurant with decent set meals, US$3. Doña Adilia also has a small store selling supplies and will accept córdobas. You need to check in with the Costa Rican guard station across from the lodge on the Río Sarapiquí if you just want to pick up something at the store and if you want to spend the night here. It's the only resting spot on the lower Río San Juan.

Bahía de San Juan *p188*

$$$$ Río Indio Lodge, between Indio and San Juan rivers, near San Juan del Norte, T506-2231-4299, www.rioindiolodge.com. Multi-million dollar lodge, designed for upscale fishing packages but excellent for wildlife safaris, birdwatching and rainforest walks. 20 big wooden cabins have screened windows, 2 queen-sized beds, ceiling fans, good ventilation, hot water and a private nature-viewing porch. Food is the only weakness: very Americanized buffet-style menu. But this is still Nicaragua's finest rainforest jungle lodge, and recently named one of the top 10 jungle lodges in the world.

San Juan del Norte *p188*

$ Cabinas El Escondite, behind the military base north of the pier, ask for Rasta, T8414-9761. Spacious wooden cabinas with bunk beds, private bath and a pleasant garden. The owner, Rasta, speaks English and cooks the best Caribbean food in town (**$$-$**). Great host and relaxed vibe. Recommended.

$ Cabinas Monkey, el muelle, 150 vrs norte on the Calle Principal, T8407-6757. Nice little budget cabins with fan, mosquito net, hard beds, sporadic plumbing, private bath, lots of hummingbirds in the garden and complimentary condoms in the rooms. Good value.

$ Hospedaje Anderson, from the Calle Principal, 1 c abajo, T8414-1368. Small, simple, wooden rooms with shared bath. Quite basic.

$ Hotelito Evo, Proyecto habitacional, Grupo 'Bed and Breakfast', Casa 18, west of the pier, ask around for Enrique's place, T2583-901. This cosy B&B has a relaxed family atmosphere and 7 simple rooms, most with private bath. The owner, Enrique, is friendly and knows the history of the town. Breakfast included and other meals available.

🍽 Restaurants

El Castillo p184, map p184
Eating is good here – the freshwater prawns (camarones de río) and snook (robalo) are both excellent.
$$$-$$ Bar Cofalito, on the jetty. Has a great view upstairs overlooking the river and serves excellent camarones de río, considered by many the best in town, with fresh fish most evenings.
$$$-$$ Borders Coffee, next to the dock. Good but pricey pasta in organic tomato sauce, vegetarian fare, curries, shrimps, and fresh organic cappuccinos at this friendly little café. Nice views of the river and a good place to wait for your boat. They can also arrange stays at a nearby finca.
$$-$ El Chinandegano, el muelle, 300 vrs arriba. Fish, chicken and other Nica fare. Reasonable and well presented, but the flavours aren't stunning. Overlooks the water and has economical rooms for rent.
$ Cafetín Cristina, el muelle, 50 m abajo. A bit dingy, but budget travellers will be pleased with filling tacos for US$1 and other cheap grub.
$ Vanessa's, el muelle, 1 c arriba. Great spot by the rapids, with fish and river shrimp. Can be hit and miss; check the catch is fresh before ordering.

San Juan del Norte p188
Drinks in town consist of Costa Rican beer, Nicaraguan rum and Coca-Cola.
$$-$ Doña Marta's, el muelle, 350 m sur along the waterfront, the building with the blue tin roof. Doña Marta's serves very tasty, reasonably priced fish and shrimp. It has a great waterfront setting and is the best restaurant in town.

$$-$ El Chele, follow Calle Principal south to the end and then bear left for 100 m. A slightly insalubrious bar-restaurant (avoid the toilet) but the service is friendly enough. So-so chicken, fish and other typical fare.
$$-$ Soda Tucán, el muelle, 150 m sur on Calle Principal. Small, clean comedor serving economical Nica fare. Various tours offered by the owners.

🛍 Shopping

El Castillo p184, map p184
Just east of the dock is a general store that sells purified water and other basic supplies. If travelling far on the river it may be wise to buy some of the heavy-duty yellow (or orange) plastic bags sold here. Protect all luggage against the rain with a double layer of plastic.

🎯 What to do

El Castillo p184, map p184
Tour operators
Guías Turísticas Río San Juan, tourist office by the pier. This group of 9 guides offers a range of tours on and off the water; horse rides, kayak excursions and night tours to observe the caimans among them.
'The First Step' Adventure and Eco-Tours, inside Bar Cofalito's, next to the dock, T8432-8441, www.firststepecotours.com. Kayaking, fishing, hiking and custom-made adventures. Popular tours include a 3-day adventure to Boca San Carlos to explore waterfalls and jungle, and a 5-day trip to San Juan del Norte (for the experienced) to see wildlife in the Indio Maíz reserve. Miguel is an English-speaking native who has spent some 18 years exploring the Río San Juan area. Fun and recommended.

San Juan del Norte p188
Tour guides
There are several guides in town, but very few speak English. Prices are standard, but guides of particular note are:

Edgar 'Rasta' Coulsen, Cabinas el Escondite, behind the military base north of the pier, T8414-9761. Born in old Greytown, Rasta is one of Nicaragua's best guides and an important community figure. He offers trips to Greytown, US$65; caimain watching, US$100; night walks, US$100; mangrove tours, US$120; and 3-day trips into the Indio-Maíz reserve to visit Rama communities and see basalt rock formations. Highly recommended.
Quicksilver Tours, T8909-7635. Adonis Coulsen is an experienced native guide. He offers similar tours to his cousin, Rasta, and speaks some English.

⊖ Transport

El Castillo *p184, map p184*
All schedules are subject to change; check times locally.
San Carlos; Mon-Sat (express) 0600, 1030; (slow) 1030, 1200, 1430, 1530; Sun (express) 0500, 1400; (slow) 0530, 1530, US$3.75 express, US$2 slow boat, 1½-2½ hrs. To **San Juan del Norte**, Tue, Thu, Fri 0900, US$12.50, 8-9 hrs. In the west season, express services run Tue and Fri 0800, 5-6 hrs, US$25.

San Juan del Norte *p188*
All schedules are subject to change; check times locally.
To **San Carlos**, stopping at **El Castillo**, Thu and Sun 0430, US$12.50 (US$25 express).

A new service between San Juan del Norte and **Bluefields** opened in 2010, only to close in 2011. There is a good chance it will reopen again in the future; check with local hotels for the latest news. The ride is 3-4 hrs and extremely bumpy.

⊙ Directory

El Castillo *p184, map p184*
Banks There are no banks here. Bring all the cash you need before setting out. **Internet** You'll find public terminals at Soda Vanessa's, Border's Cafe and Albergue El Castillo. **Telephone** Enitel, T552-6124.

San Juan del Norte *p188*
Banks There are no banks and the most common currency is Costa Rican colones thanks to the (relatively) easy access to El Limón, Costa Rica. You can pay in córdobas or dollars, but expect change in colones. Village locals may be willing to change money at wilderness rates, options are few, ask around. **Internet** No internet cafés, but there is crushingly slow Wi-Fi at the public library. **Nicaraguan immigration** There is Nicaraguan customs and immigration at San Juan del Norte, but officially entrance and exit stamps for international travel cannot be obtained here. **Telephone** There are 2 shops that offer the use of a mobile telephone, when it is working. The service is via Costa Rica to Nicaragua.

Contents

León & El Occidente

At a glance

⊖ **Getting around** The city of León is reasonably compact and can be covered on foot or by taxi. Elsewhere, public buses and microbuses travel to the major sights; more remote destinations may require 4WD.

⏱ **Time required** 7-10 days.

☀ **Weather** León and its surroundings are hotter and drier than Managua and the rest of the Pacific Basin. Daytime temperatures are normally 31-33°C with nights dipping to 24-26°C. The exception is Nov-Jan when the streets are not cooked for quite so long.

✖ **When not to go** Mar-May are brutally hot months when the smoke from farmers burning their fields mixes with wind-blown dirt to make air conditions – and hiking especially – miserable. That said, you will not want to miss Semana Santa in León.

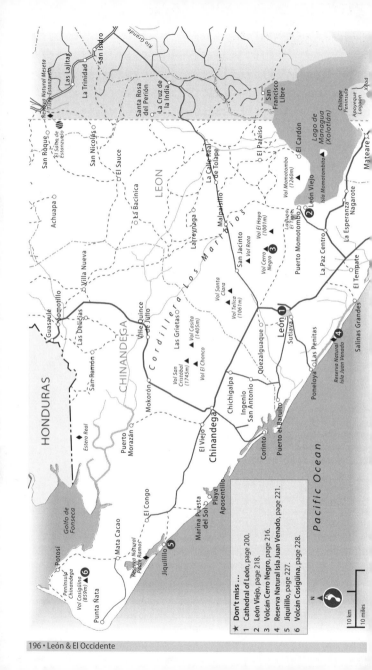

HONDURAS

Golfo de
Fonseca

Pacific Ocean

Río Grande

Reserva Natural Meseta
Tisey-Estanzuela

San Isidro

Las Lajitas

La Trinidad

San Roque

El Salto de
Estanzuela

San Nicolás

El Sauce

Santa Rosa
del Perión

La Cruz de
la India

San Francisco
Libre

San Nicolás

La Calle Real
de Tolape

El Paraíso

El Cardón

León
Viejo

Vol Momotombo
(1260m)

Isla Momotombito

Lago de
Managua
(Xolotlán)

Chiltepe
Peninsula

Apoyeque
Lagoon

Xiloá

Mateare

Achuapa

La Bácinica

Latreynaga

Malpaisillo

San Jacinto

Vol El Hoyo
(1001m)

Laguna
El Tigre

Puerto Momotombo

La Esperanza

Nagarote

LEÓN

Villa Nueva

Guasaule

Somotillo

Las Delicias

San Ramón

CHINANDEGA

Mokorón

Vile Quince
de Julio

Las Grietas

Vol Santa
Clara

Vol Telica
(1061m)

Vol Casita
(1405m)

Vol Cerro
Negro

Vol Rota

León

Sutiava

La Paz Centro

El Tempate

Vol San
Cristóbal
(1745m)

Vol El Chonco

Quezalguaque

Salinas Grandes

Chichigalpa

Ingenio
San Antonio

Poneloya

Las Peñitas

Reserva Natural
Isla Juan Venado

El Viejo

Puerto
Morazán

Estero Real

Chinandega

Corinto

Puerto el Barrito

Mata Cacao

El Congo

Marina Puesta
del Sol

Playa
Aposentillo

Potosí

Península
Chinandega

Vol Cosigüina ▲ (859m)

Punta Ñata

Reserva Natural
Padre Ramos

Jiquilillo

★ Don't miss ...
1 Cathedral of León, page 200.
2 León Viejo, page 218.
3 Volcán Cerro Negro, page 216.
4 Reserva Natural Isla Juan Venado, page 221.
5 Jiquilillo, page 227.
6 Volcán Cosigüina, page 228.

N

10 km
10 miles

Nicaragua's sweltering northwestern provinces are the setting for immense and extraordinary panoramas, scorched skies and violently shifting geological tempers. This a land born of fire, home to one of the most densely active volcanic chains in the world: the Cordillera Los Maribios. No fewer than 21 volcanoes occupy the range, each with its own character and distinct set of challenges. Smoking craters, steaming pools, teeming forests, tranquil lakes and stark, rolling, black-sand slopes perfect for high-speed boarding – all await exploration.

Within this tempestuous terrain lie the ruins of León Viejo, Nicaragua's accursed first capital, destroyed by forces of nature and haunted by its notorious past. Fortunately, León was rebuilt and today survives as one of Central America's finest colonial cities. The spiritual home of Nicaragua's greatest poets, León is the artistic and intellectual heart of the country – and since 1979, a hotbed of Sandinista activity. A wealth of satirical murals, commemorative sites, bombed-out ruins and bullet-marked buildings are evidence of León's turbulent revolutionary past. Today, the city's student population lends it a youthful edge and a vibrant nightlife. After a day pounding the streets, you can relax in one of the city's many bars, drink a beer, chat about politics with the locals and take in a rousing live music performance.

Beyond the city, the departments of León and Chinandega enjoy miles of Pacific coastline accented by beaches, barrier islands and coastal lagoons. If you need a break from the heat and frenetic chaos of downtown León, an excursion to the sleepy beaches of Poneloya and Las Peñitas, 20 minutes west, is always refreshing and welcome. The bucolic retreat of Jiquilillo, perched on the remote and less-visited shores of the Cosegüina Peninsula, is the place for serious hammock time.

León

The crumbling old Spanish city of León is full of intellectual vitality and artistic tradition; a place to unravel Nicaragua's past and glimpse its future. The colonial capital has fine examples of old Spanish architecture and it is full to the brim with students from all over the country who come to study in its fine secondary schools and universities. With a dozen colonial churches and Central America's largest cathedral, this fervently Catholic city is home to some of Nicaragua's most beautiful religious celebrations and traditions. Despite the sweltering year-round heat of the León valley, the city enjoys an advantageous position set between the ruggedly majestic Maribios volcanoes to the east and the crashing surf of the warm Pacific Ocean to the west.
▶▶ *For listings, see pages 207-211.*

Arriving in León → *Population: 155,000. Altitude: 109 m. Colour map 3, A2.*

Getting there
León can be reached by regular bus and microbus services from Managua and Chinandega, and by less frequent services from Estelí and Matagalpa. International buses also stop in León if arriving from Guatemala, Honduras or El Salvador.

Getting around
The city is laid out in the classic Spanish colonial grid system, based around a central plaza. The plaza, named Parque Jérez, is commonly referred to as Parque Central. The majestic León Cathedral faces west and sits on the park's east side. Roads running east–west are *Calles* and those running north–south *Avenidas*. Calle Rubén Darío runs directly west from Parque Central, through Sutiava and all the way to the Pacific Ocean. Avenida Central runs from the cemetery in the extreme south, past the Guadalupe church right into the central plaza and continues north of the plaza past banks, restaurants and the Iglesia La Recolección. Though taxis are cheap, US$0.75 during the day, León is a terrific city for walking, with each barrio supporting its own unique church and beautiful colonial homes.
▶▶ *For further details, see Transport, page 213.*

Tourist information
The Nicaraguan Institute of Tourism, **INTUR** ① *Parque Rubén Darío, 1½ c norte, T311-3682*, has limited information and flyers; staff speak Spanish only. **UNAN** ① *next to Restaurante El Sesteo, on Parque Central*, is a small office run by the tourism students of the university. They sell a good map of the city and other miscellaneous items. Most youth hostels are well stocked with flyers and can often supply helpful information on local attractions.

Background

The present city was founded in 1610 after the abandonment of its cursed original location, known today as León Viejo (see page 218). The site was chosen to be close to the large indigenous settlement of Sutiava and to the Pacific, but with a 21-km buffer between it and the sea to protect against pirate attacks. The indigenous people of Sutiava are Maribios, a group distinct from the Nicaraguas and Chorotegas that populated the rest of the Pacific Basin at the time of the arrival of the Spanish. The Maribios are most famous in Nicaraguan history books for scaring the living daylights out of the Spanish and their horses by dressing in the human skin of a ceremonial victim – worn inside out. The Maribios are thought to be related to the native inhabitants of southern and Baja California, with whom they share strong linguistic similarities.

Despite its tumultuous beginnings, León was the capital of Nicaragua for 242 years. (In 1852, the Nicaraguan Congress moved the country's capital to Managua as a compromise with Granada, which spent much of the mid-19th century contesting León's capital status.) As the administrative centre of Nicaragua, León was home to the Bishop of Nicaragua, as well as the country's first secondary school and university. Unlike Granada, León was not rich in commerce and therefore not a big target for pirates. The exception to this happened 75 years after the city's relocation, when an unholy alliance of British and French pirates descended upon it. Using the volcano San Cristóbal as a navigational tool, a makeshift army of 520 men entered what is today the port of Corinto and marched overland to León on 9 April 1685. The Spanish agreed to pay the demanded ransom of 300,000 gold pieces and food to sustain 1000 men for four months. The pirates waited, but after realizing the Spanish were stalling while waiting for troop reinforcements, the pirates set fire to the city on 14 April 1685 and retreated to the Pacific.

León produced one of the heroes of the fight for liberation from Spain, Miguel Larreynaga, who helped draft the original Central America constitution and can be seen on the 10 córdoba note today. After Independence was declared on 15 September 1821, the Liberal Party of León (which would go on to figure heavily in Nicaragua's future) was pitted against the Conservative Party of Granada in what was to be a violent struggle for power. In 1844, León was invaded and conquered by the Salvadoran General Malespin, with the help of the conservative army of Granada, in a war that damaged the town centre and left the Veracruz Church in Sutiava in ruins.

At the turn of the 20th century, Liberal president José Santos Zelaya (who graces the 20 córdoba note) made radical changes to the country that brought a long occupation by the US Marines. Later, nationalist hero Augusto Sandino, a Liberal Party member, was abducted and assassinated under General Somoza García's orders. Somoza himself had become the country's de facto leader by deposing the weak Liberal Party president, Juan Bautista Sacasa, that the US Marines had propped up before they pulled out. When Somoza García was assassinated in León by Rigoberto López in 1956, León's history with the Liberal Party had come full turn.

León became a hotbed for the Frente Sandinista de Liberación Nacional (FSLN) Marxist underground in the 1960s and 1970s and fighting against Somoza Debayle (the son of Somoza García) was fierce in León, with much damage suffered by the old city, some of which can still be seen today. After a final brutal battle which lasted from 3 June to 9 July 1979 and was won by the rebels, the FSLN, led by female Commandante Dora María Tellez, succeeded. The city is still strongly Sandinista, with every mayor since 1979 coming from the FSLN party. The private sector and Spanish government's foreign aid project have invested heavily in restoring the city; although not as thoroughly painted and restored as Granada, León is slowly regaining its visual glory.

Places in León

The simplest and richest pleasure in the city is walking its historic streets, noting the infinite variety of colonial doors, ceiling work and window irons as well as sneaking peeks inside the grand houses to see their lush interior gardens. Though damaged in 1685, 1844 and 1979, León has retained much more of its colonial Spanish structural and design flavour than the oft-burned Granada. Reason enough to visit León are its many curious and beautiful churches: the city has more than a dozen of them, including the cathedral, Central America's grandest church.

Cathedral of León

ⓘ *It's possible to climb the cathedral for commanding views of the city and countryside, US$1.*
The Cathedral of León, officially the **Basílica de la Asunción**, is the pride of both city and country. This impressive structure – a UNESCO World Heritage Site since 2011 – is the work of 113 years of labour, but it is not the first cathedral to stand in front of León's central park. Five years after the founding of León in its current location, a simple cathedral made of clay bricks and tiles was consecrated by the first Bishop of new León in 1615. The church was improved by the next Bishop of Nicaragua, with funds from Spain, but it was burned by the pirate invasion of 1685. Another construction was built, bigger still than the first, with three altars and five chapels. This church would survive about 60 years before the construction of the current cathedral began in 1747. Due to the size of the task and constant shortage of funds, it was not open for worship until 1780 and not finished in its current from until 1860. The Atlas figures in the central bell tower were added as a stylistic and structural enhancement in 1905. The Cathedral of León did not receive its pews until 1877 and all masses before that date were celebrated on foot or sitting and kneeling on the floor.

Legend has it that the plans for the cathedrals of Lima in Peru and León were switched by mistake, but there is no evidence to support that charming excuse for such a big church in such a little country. The plans were drawn by Guatemalan architect Diego de Porres and two Franciscan Friars from Guatemala also worked on the design and layout of the temple, which has been described as 'Central American baroque' with its squat towers and super-thick walls. This design stems from the experience gained from building churches in the seismically active valley of Ciudad Antigua. But there are both Gothic and neoclassical elements in this great structure. The fact that the cathedral was built from back to front over more than a century is clearly evident, with the back of the cathedral (the side of the market) exhibiting different design influences from the front (on the plaza). The exterior was painted in the mid-1990s and is in need of a fresh coat, but the interior's white-washed walls and ceiling give the church a peaceful, elegant look. Inside are large oils for the Stations of the Cross; recently restored for the first time since the 19th century.

The cathedral also houses a very fine **ivory Christ**, the consecrated **Altar of Sacrifices** and the **Choir of Córdoba**. The most famous image is called the *Cristo de Pedrarias*. This Gothic work of Christ on the cross comes from the old cathedral of León Viejo; the damage on his right foot happened during the pirate attack of 1685. He is celebrated with fireworks every 2 July in León. Most controversial and least admired about the church are the column statues of the **12 Apostles**. At the foot of the Apostle Paul column, guarded by a sorrowing lion, is the **tomb of Rubén Darío**, Nicaragua's greatest poet and one of the greats of the Spanish language. Two of Nicaragua's other great poets are also buried nearby, **Salomón de la Selva** and **Alfonso Cortés** (whose starkly beautiful verses appear above his tomb).

West of the cathedral

There are several interesting and historic buildings on **Parque Central**. These include the **archbishop's house**, next to the south side of the cathedral, and the historic **Seminario de San Ramón**, founded in 1680, which today houses a primary school. You can ask permission to enter the school; in the eastern hall are the portraits of all the Bishops of Nicaragua and, from post-colonial times, the Bishops of León. The Gothic **Colegio de Asunción** (primary and secondary school), just to the west, is often mistaken for a church.

On the southwest corner of the Parque Central stands the grand old Palacio Municipal, a 1930s structure that has been gently decaying since its Somoza-era heyday. Today it houses the unashamedly pro-Sandinista **Museo de la Revolución** ① *daily 0800-1800, US$1.50*, where visitors can learn about the 1979 revolution and hear gripping war stories from former FSLN fighters. The tour is entirely in Spanish and is supplemented by displays of historic newspaper clippings and intriguing old photos of the city. Your visit concludes with a trip to the roof for great views over the plaza and surrounding streets.

One block west and south of Parque Central is the beautifully restored **Teatro Municipal José de la Cruz Mena** ① *Mon-Fri 0800-1230 and 1400-1700, plays and concerts from US$1-15*. The theatre was built in the 19th century and was home to many important concerts of touring groups from Europe during the early 20th century. Later the theatre fell into disrepair and was badly burned in 1956. It has now been reopened after more than 40 years of neglect and was declared National Cultural Patrimony in 2007. The theatre is named after León's greatest classical composer (you can see a portrait of him in **El Sesteo** restaurant, see page 210). Maestro Mena suffered from leprosy and for that reason, at the premier of his award-winning composition titled *Ruinas*, he was not allow to enter the theatre to hear its debut performance. Witnesses say that he sat outside on the front steps of the theatre, crying with joy as he listened to the orchestra play his composition inside the elegant theatre. Soon after, he died of leprosy.

Two blocks west of Parque Central is the **Convento y Iglesia San Francisco**. The church was damaged in 1979 during fighting in the Revolution but maintains much of its ancient charm. It was the city's first convent when founded in 1639. The pillars of the temple and two of its altars remain from the original construction, that of the Sangre de Cristo and of San Antonio de Padua. The façade has been modified greatly over the years, but on the south face of the church the original structure can still be seen. The rest has been converted into a hotel called **El Convento** (see Where to stay, page 210).

Museo de Arte Fundación Ortiz-Guardián ① *opposite Iglesia San Francisco, T2277-2627, www.fundacionortizgurdian.org, Tue-Sun 1030-1800 entrance US$2*, is a lovely colonial home that doubles as one of the finest art museums in Central America with works from Europe, Latin America and Nicaragua. It is worth a visit to see a classic example of a colonial period home. Across the street, is an annexe holding more modern art.

Founded in 1964, the **Museo-Archivo Rubén Darío** ① *Calle Central, Iglesia San Francisco, 1 c abajo, T2311-2388, Tue-Sat 0800-1200, 1400-1700, Sun 0800-1200, entry and guided tour free but donations appreciated*, has an interesting collection of the national hero's personal possessions, photographs, portraits and a library with a wide range of books of poetry in Spanish, English and French. See also box, page 205. The great metaphysical poet Alfonso Cortés (see box, page 206) lost his mind in this house and was said to have been chained to the bars that are next to Darío's bed. Cortés died here in 1969 and was buried near to Darío in the cathedral.

East of the cathedral

On Calle Central, east of the cathedral, is the **Iglesia El Calvario**. Built in the mid-1700s, it was restored in 2000, the towering Momotombo Volcano in the background making for a dramatic setting. Inside are representations of Jesus and the two men he was crucified with. The life-size sculptures are unusual for their stark realism, a rare quality in colonial religious art. Both the interior and the gaily painted exterior of the neoclassical church are attractive and the façade is said to show the stylistic influence of the French in 18th-century Spanish architecture.

León

San Felipe

Av Central

5 C NE

4 C NE

Lavandería **22**

Honorary
Spanish Consul

12

3 C NE

La
Recolecció

Tierra
Tours

19 **4**

2

8 **3**

11

14

13 Zaragoza

Centro Popular
de la Cultura

INTUR

UNAN
(University)

BAC
ATM

La Merced

S **S**

Pool Tables **21**

UNAN **10** **18**

6

San Francisco

2

6

Mausoleo Héroes
y Mártires

7 **15**

C Central/Rubén Darío

Museo-Archivo
Rubén Darío

Museo
Ortiz-Gurdián

Parque
Rubén
Darío

Parque
Central

Cathedral

5

C Jorge de Marcoleta

San Juan
de Dios

1 **16** **23**

Museo de la
Revolución

Teatro Municipal
José de la Cruz Mena

Lavamático

10

18

Museo de Leyendas
y Tradiciones

5 & Va Pues Tours

San Nicólas
de Laborío

20

To Guadalupe

To Comunidad Indígena
de Sutiava & Poneloya

6 AV NO   5 AV NO   4 AV NO   3 AV NO   2 AV NO   1 AV NO

N

200 metres

200 yards

Where to stay
Austria **10** *D4*
Bigfoot Hostel **17** *C5*
Calle de los Poetas **7** *D1*
Casa de Huéspedes
El Nancite **15** *C5*

Casa Vieja **13** *B5*
El Albergue de León **1** *B5*
El Convento **6** *D2*
Europa **8** *B6*
Hostal Clínica **18** *D3*
Hostal La Casa
Leonesa **12** *B4*
Hostel Iguana **2** *B3*
La Casona Colonial **14** *B4*

La Perla **11** *C3*
La Posada del Doctor **19** *B5*
Lazybones Hostel **3** *C3*
Los Balcones **16** *C5*
San Juan de León **4** *B5*
Sonati Hostel **9** *B5*
Siesta Perdida **21** *D3*
Tortuga Booluda **5** *D1*
Via Via **20** *C5*

Restaurants 🍴
Barbaro **1** *D3*
Café La Rosita **2** *D3*
Cafetín San Benito **3** *C3*
Cocinarte **5** *E2*
Comedor Lucía **11** *C5*
Comedor Poneloya **18** *C4*
El Desayunazo **19** *B3*
El Mississipi **12** *D6*

To Chinandega & San Jacinto

NE

TSA Tours Travel

To Bus Terminal (3 blocks) & Market

San Juan Bautista

Parque San Juan

Mercado San Juan

Quetzaltrekkers

C NE

Western Union

Museo Entomológico

Union Supermarket Cinemas

1 C NE

El Calvario

SE

2 C SE

3 C SE

Cimac

4 C SE

⑤

El Sesteo 6 D4
La Buena Cuchara 20 E3
La Casa Vieja 13 C2
La Mexicana 4 B3
Marrakech 22 B4
Terraza Mediterráneo 8 C3
Pan y Paz 7 C5
Pure Earth Café 9 C5

⑥

Bars & clubs 🎵
Café Taquezal 23 D3
Camaleón 14 C4
Don Señor 21 C3
Jack's 10 C3
Olla Quemada 15 D1
Oxygen 2 16 D3

North of the cathedral

Two blocks north of Parque Central is the lovely **Iglesia La Merced**. This is León's second most important church and home of the patron saint of León, the Virgen de las Mercedes. The first La Merced church was founded in León Viejo in 1528 (see page 218). The present church was founded in 1615, before being burnt down during the pirate raid of 1685. It was rebuilt by a team of architects from Guatemala who came to work on the cathedral. It was demolished and rebuilt once again in the late 1700s. In the early 19th century there was a fire in the main altar that holds the Virgen de las Mercedes. Legend has it that a local black slave rushed into the flames to rescue the Virgen and broke the glass case holding the image with his bare hands. In gratitude for his heroism he was granted his freedom. The current main altar was made out of marble to replace the burnt one. The interior is arguably the most ornately decorated in Nicaragua with fine woodwork and delicately sculpted altars. It is said to be the most representative of León's 18th-century churches. The exterior was restored in 1999, but funds ran short of a paint job.

Two blocks north of the cathedral's lions on Avenida Central is the **Iglesia La Recolección**, with a beautiful baroque Mexican façade that tells the entire story of the Passion of Christ. It was built in 1786 and has a neoclassical interior with lovely mahogany woodwork. Two blocks north and one block east of La Recolección is the simple yet handsome **Iglesia San Juan Bautista**, which sits on the east side of the Parque San Juan, otherwise known as the *parquecito*. The church dates from 1739 but was remodelled in the following century. Three blocks west and two blocks north, the **Iglesia San Felipe** was built at the end of the 16th century for the religious services of the black and mulatto population of the city. It was rebuilt in the 18th century in a manner true to its original form, a mixture of baroque and neoclassical.

One and half blocks from the Parque San Juan, next to La Merced, is the **Centro Popular de la Cultura**, which has frequent exhibitions and events (see schedule on bulletin board in front lobby). Three blocks west, the **Iglesia de Zaragoza** was built from 1884 to 1934 and has two octagonal turrets and an arched doorway with tower above. It resembles a fortress more than a church and is unattractive inside.

The **Museo Entomológico** ① *ENEL, 30 vrs arriba, opposite Western Union, T2311-6586, www.bio-nica.info, daily 0900-1200, 1400-1600, US$0.50,* is the amazing collection of Nicaragua's foremost expert on its insect life, Dr Jean-Michel Maes; it includes butterflies from around the world.

South of the cathedral

Three blocks south and half a block west of the cathedral is the **Museo de Leyendas y Tradiciones** ① *T2311-2886, www.museoleyendasytradiciones.com, Mon-Sat 0800-1200, 1400-1700, Sun 0800-1200, US$1.* This project of Doña Carmen Toruño is a physical demonstration of some of the many legends that populate the bedtime stories of Nicaraguan children. León is particularly rich in legends and Doña Carmen has handcrafted life-size models of the characters of these popular beliefs to help bring them to life. Most impressive of the displays is the *carreta nahua* (haunted ox cart) a story symbolic of the harsh labour Spanish masters required of their Indian subjects, so much so that the ox cart became a symbol of literally being worked to death.

Three blocks west of the museum, the **Iglesia de San Nicolás de Laborío**, founded in 1618 for the local indigenous population, is the most modest of the León churches. It is constructed of wood and tiles over adobe walls with a simple façade and altar. The interior is dark, cool and charming, with the feel of a village parish more than a city church. The local padre is friendly and willing to chat. If the church is closed you can knock on the little door at the back. The celebration for San Nicolás is 10 September.

If the heat and noise of the city is getting too much, consider an excursion to **Centro Iniciativa Medio Ambiental (CIMAC)** ① *Iglesia de San Sebastián, 4 c arriba, Mon-Fri 0800-1200, 1400-1730, US$1,* an ecological garden some four blocks east of the Museo de Leyendas y Tradiciones. There is a broad range of local flora on show, including plenty of shady fruit trees, and a gentle interpretive trail that takes no more than half an hour to traverse.

Comunidad Indígena de Sutiava → *For listings, see pages 207-211.*

Like Monimbó in Masaya, Sutiava is the one of the last remaining examples of indigenous urban living. The Sutiavans have a fiercely independent culture and a language that survived despite being surrounded by the numerically superior Chorotega culture in pre-Columbian times and later by the Spanish. Until the 20th century they managed to maintain a significant level of independence, including the indigenous community's land holdings of more than 72,000 acres, west of León proper. The community finally succumbed to pressure from León elites who had been eyeing the communal lands for centuries and Sutiava was annexed to the city in 1902, making it nothing more than a barrio of the colonial city, and opening up communal lands to non-indigenous ownership. It is no surprise that Sutiava was a major player during the planning and recruitment stages of the Sandinista-led Revolution, as the community has been involved in numerous anti-government rebellions since Nicaragua achieved Independence from Spain.

The entrance to the community is marked by the change of Calle Rubén Darío into a two-lane road with a central divider full of plants, including *sacuanjoche* in some unusual

Rubén Darío: the prince of Spanish letters

The great Chilean poet Pablo Neruda called him "one of the most creative poets in the Spanish language" when, together with the immortal Spanish poet Federico García Lorca, he paid tribute to Rubén Darío in Buenos Aires in 1933. In front of more than 100 Argentine writers, Lorca and Neruda delivered the tribute to the poet they called "then and forever unequalled".

Darío is without a doubt the most famous Nicaraguan. He is one of the greatest poets in the history of the Spanish language and the country's supreme hero. Born Felix Rubén García Sarmiento in Metapa, Nicaragua in 1867, Rubén Darío was raised in León and had learnt to read by the age of four. By the time he was 10, little Rubén had read *Don Quixote*, *The Bible*, *1001 Arabian Nights* and the works of Cicero. When he was 11, he studied the Latin classics in depth with Jesuits at the school of La Iglesia de La Recolección. In 1879, at the age of 12, his first verses were published in the León daily newspaper *El Termómetro*. Two years later he was preparing his first book. Later, he became the founder of the Modernist movement in poetry, which crossed the Atlantic and became popular in Spain. His most noted work, *Azul*, revolutionized Spanish literature, establishing a new mode of poetic expression.

As well as being a poet, Darío was a diplomat and a journalist. He wrote for numerous publications in Argentina, the United States, Spain and France. In 1916 he returned to the city of León, and, despite several attempts at surgery, died of cirrhosis on the night of 6 February. After seven days of tributes he was buried in the Cathedral of León.

Ox that I saw in my childhood, as you steamed
in the burning gold of the Nicaraguan sun,
there on the rich plantation filled with tropical
harmonies; woodland dove, of the woods that sang
with the sound of the wind, of axes, of birds and wild bulls:
I salute you both, because you are both my life.

You, heavy ox, evoke the gentle dawn
that signaled it was time to milk the cow,
when my existence was all white and rose;
and you, sweet mountain dove, cooing and calling,
you signify all that my own springtime, now
so far away, possessed of the Divine Springtime.

'Far Away', Rubén Darío. From *Selected Poems* by Rubén Darío, translated by Lysander Kemp, University of Texas, Austin, 1988.

colours. Also of note are the neatly presented fruit stands on the street corners and the lack of colonial structures – Sutiava retained its native buildings until long after Spanish rule had ended. The best way to witness the true pride and culture of the barrio is during fiesta time. However, there are also several sites of interest and Sutiava cuisine is superior to León's, so a visit to eat is also worthwhile.

Unlike the secular buildings, the churches of Sutiava date from colonial times and are simple, elegant structures. The **Iglesia Parroquial de San Juan Bautista de Sutiava** was first constructed in 1530 by missionaries, and reconstructed from 1698-1710. The human rights priest Bartolomé de las Casas, known as the 'Apostle of the Indians', preached here on several occasions. The featureless dirt plaza in front of the church was baptized in his name in 1923. The church is one of the most authentic representations of Nicaraguan

Alfonso Cortés: the insanity of genius

None of Nicaragua's poets can match the striking simplicity of the metaphysical poet Alfonso Cortés, who spent most of his life in chains, but who, in an impossibly microscopic script, wrote some of the most beautiful poems the Spanish language has ever seen.

Alfonso Cortés was born in León in 1893. He lived in the very same house that had belonged to Rubén Darío and which today is the Museo-Archivo Rubén Darío. It was in this house that Cortés went mad one February night in 1927. He spent the next 42 years in captivity, tormented most of the time but, for the good fortune of Nicaragua, with lucid moments of incredible productivity. Cortés was kept chained to one of the house's colonial window grilles and it was from that vantage point that he composed what poet-priest Ernesto Cardenal called the most beautiful poem in the Spanish language, *La Ventana* (The Window):

A speck of blue has more intensity than all the sky; I feel that there lives, a flower of happy ecstasy, my longing.
A wind of spirits, passes so far, from my window sending a breeze that shatters the flesh of an angelic awakening.

Later, at the age of 34, Alfonso Cortés was committed to a mental institution in Managua, where he was to live out the rest of his life. In these incredibly adverse conditions, Cortés produced a number of great poetic works, most of which were published with the help of his father. When he was not writing he was tied to his bed, with only his guitar, hanging on the wall, for company.

According to Cardenal, the poet spoke slowly while shaking and stuttering, his face changing from thrilled to horrified, then falling totally expressionless. He used to say, "I am less important than Rubén Darío, but I am more profound". Alfonso Cortés died in February 1969, 53 years later than Darío. Today, just a couple of metres separate these two great Nicaraguan poets, both buried in the Cathedral of León.

baroque and thankfully has survived years of invasion and civil war. The indigenous influences, such as the ceiling, saints and other subtle styling clues, are what make the church famous today. The colonial altar was donated by the King of Spain and brought to Sutiava in pieces. There is an interesting representation of the Maribio Sun God, carved in wood in the mid-nave on the ceiling; it has become the definitive icon for indigenous pride along with a certain tamarind tree near by (see below).

Inside the handsome **Casa Cural de Sutiava** (1752), on the south side of the plaza in front of the church, is the **Museo de Arte Sacro** ① *Mon-Fri 0800-1200 and 1400-1600, Sat 0800-1000, US$0.70*. The museum contains a display of colonial religious relics, some of which were rescued from León Viejo, with many gold and silver pieces; there is, however, a lack of explanations or qualified guides. Two blocks north of the San Juan church is the **Museo de la Comunidad Indígena de Sutiava** or **Museo Adiact** ① *T2311-5371, Mon-Fri 0800-1200 and 1400-1700, Sat 0800-1200, donations greatly appreciated*, marked by a fading mural. This is the indigenous community's museum and the only example in Nicaragua of an indigenous people protecting their cultural patrimony in their own museum. The tiny rooms are crammed full of statues and ceramics from the Maribios culture. The museum is named after the last great leader Adiac who was executed after challenging the local Spanish authority. The old tamarind tree where Adiac was hanged by the Spanish remains a vivid symbol of Sutiava's proud but tragic history. The tree, known to all as **El Tamarindón**, is located three blocks south and two blocks west of the San Juan church. There is a small *tiangue* or indigenous market with native foods and crafts on the third Sunday in April to celebrate the tree and its importance.

The **Ruinas de la Iglesia de Veracruz** is a sad, crumbling stone relic from the 16th century that was destroyed by an attack from Salvadorian General Malespin in 1844. It is two blocks west from the central plaza of Sutiava and often shut off to visitors by a chain-link fence, though the *comunidad indígena* is doing much to try and make the ruins a cultural focal point. On 7 December, when the Catholic **Purísima** celebration to the Virgin Mary is celebrated, the community mounts an unusual semi-pagan altar to the Virgin in the ruins of the old church complete with torch lighting and a replica of the Sun God. Other interesting celebrations include the festival for the second annual planting of corn between 25 July and 15 August. You'll find another ruined 17th-century church one block north of Sutiava's central plaza, **Iglesia Santiago**, which has a small surviving bell tower.

Holy week, or **Semana Santa**, celebrations in Sutiava are the most interesting in Nicaragua. The most spectacular of all events are the sawdust street paintings made on *Viernes Santo* (Good Friday). At the eastern end of Sutiava, marked by a statue of Adiac and a tiny park, two blocks south of the main avenue, the streets leading towards the San Juan church are closed off for the day. Around 1100 you can see the artists framing their sawdust canvas and soaking it in water. Later in the afternoon moist, dyed sawdust is used to make religious paintings, which serve as carpets for the **Santo Entierro** (the funeral procession of the crucified Christ) at around 2100. These short-lived masterpieces are honoured by being trampled by the procession, totally destroying them. Unlike the more famous street paintings of Antigua in Guatemala, no moulds are used for the street in Sutiava, they are created completely freehand. After 1600, when many paintings are complete and others are being finished, a walk up and down the neighbourhood streets is an unforgettable experience. While some of the paintings are amateurish, others are astounding in their detail and scope, especially considering the difficulty of the medium. The leader of the street artist association, Federico Quezada, has invented a new art medium by gluing the coloured sawdust to a wooden 'canvas' to preserve the art of the festival beyond the procession. During Holy Week, Quezada's home is opened as a **gallery** ① *Texaco Guido, 2 c sur, ½ c arriba, T2315-3942, fquesadamoran@yahoo.com, Spanish-speaking only*, and he is happy to show his work by appointment.

Three blocks east of the south side of the San Juan Church is the charming **Iglesia Ermita de San Pedro**. Built in 1706 on top of an even older construct, this church is a fine example of primitive baroque design popular in the 17th century. The adobe and red tile roof temple was refurbished in 1986. Santa Lucía is celebrated in Sutiava throughout most of December, with the focal point being the plaza in front of the parish church; Santa Lucía's day is 13 December.

ⓔ León listings

For sleeping and eating price codes and other relevant information, see pages 28-30.

ⓒ Where to stay

León *p198, map p202*
There's no shortage of cheap beds in León with new hostels and backpacker hotels

are springing up all the time – dorms cost US\$5-10 per night. If you plan on staying in the city a month or more, many houses rent student rooms at competitive rates.
\$\$\$ Hotel El Convento, connected to Iglesia San Francisco, T2311-7053, www.elconvento nicaragua.com. This beautiful, intriguing hotel is decorated with antique art, including

an impressive gold-leaf altar and sombre religious icons. Comfortable rooms have a/c, bath, Wi-Fi, electronic safe, minibar and cable TV. There's a good restaurant (**$$**) with excellent coffee. Recommended.

$$$ La Perla, Iglesia La Merced, 1½ c norte, T2311 2279, www.laperlaleon.com. This handsome old 19th-century building has been carefully remodelled and now boasts elegant a/c rooms, some with bath tubs, several suites, a bar, restaurant, casino and pool. Spacious and grand.

$$ Hostal La Casa Leonesa, catedral, 3 c norte, 15 vrs arriba, T2311-0551, www.lacasaleonesa.com. This typical León house has a lovely elegant interior, Wi-Fi, a swimming pool and 10 rooms of varying size, all with private bath, hot water, cable TV, telephone. Breakfast included. Rooms upstairs are cheaper.

$$ Hotel Austria, catedral, 1 c sur, T2311-1206, www.hotelaustria.com.ni. Very clean, comfortable, straightforward rooms surrounding a lush central courtyard. They have hot water, a/c, telephone and cable TV. Internet and laundry service available. Continental breakfast is included in the price. Friendly and often fully booked.

$$ Hotel Europa, 3 c NE, 4 Av, T2311-6040, www.hoteleuropaleon.com. A reasonable business hotel, although some rooms are much better than others. Expect Wi-Fi, safe, telephone, a/c and hot water as a minimum. Elsewhere there are pleasant patios and quiet enclaves. Other services include restaurant, bar and parking. Cheaper with fan.

$$ La Casona Colonial, Parque San Juan, ½ c abajo, T2311-3178. This pleasant colonial house has 7 good-value, homely rooms with attractive antique furniture, private bath and a/c. Management is friendly and hospitable, and there's a lovely green garden too. Cheaper with fan. Recommended.

$$ La Posada del Doctor, Parque San Juan, 25 vrs abajo, T2311-4343, www.laposadadeldoctor.com. 11 clean and nicely furnished rooms with private bath, hot water, high ceilings, cable TV and a/c, although they're mostly on the small side. Services include

laundry, parking and Wi-Fi. Pleasant little patio and relaxed atmosphere. Continental breakfast included. Cheaper with fan.

$$ Los Balcones, Esquina de los Bancos, 1 c arriba, T2311-0250, www.hotelbalcones.com. A handsome colonial building with an attractive courtyard, bar and restaurant. The 20 rooms have private bath, hot water, a/c and cable TV; some have a good view. Wi-Fi and laundry service available; breakfast included. Rooms on the street side are noisy.

$$-$ Hostel Iguana, Iglesia La Merced, 1½ c norte, T2311-4643, www.hosteliguana.com. A lot of love has gone into **Hostel Iguana**, a colourful place with pleasant chill-out spaces and a fine restaurant attached (try the pasta). The good-value rooms (**$$** with a/c, **$** with fan) are clean and comfortable. The dorm (**$**) has only a few beds so won't get overcrowded. A quiet, attractive and friendly lodging. Recommended.

$$-$ San Juan de León, costado norte de Parque San Juan, T2311-0547, www.hsanjuandeleon.com. This hotel has 20 clean, comfortable rooms on 2 floors, all with private bath, cable TV and a/c (**$** with fan). Wi-Fi, laundry service, lawn, pleasant rooftop patio and kitchen are available. Continental breakfast is included.

$ Bigfoot Hostel, Banco ProCredit, ½ c sur, T8917-8832, www.bigfootnicaragua.com. Sociable, buzzing and popular with the whipper-snappers. This hip backpackers' joint has lots of economical dorm space, a handful of private rooms, TV, pool table, bar, lockers, and a popular restaurant (see **Pure Earth Café**). Their *mojitos* are famous and well worth a taste – happy hour runs 1800-2000.

$ Calle de los Poetas, Calle Rubén Darío, Museo Darío, 1½ c abajo, T2311-3306, rsampson@ibw.com.ni. This comfortable, good-value guesthouse has a relaxed home ambience, spacious rooms with private and shared bath, a beautiful garden and friendly hosts. It's also the base for **Sampson Expeditions** (see page 213). Often full, so arrive early. Discounts for longer stays. Recommended.

$ Casa de Huéspedes El Nancite, Iglesia El Calvario, 1½ c norte, T2311-4117, www.guesthousenancite.com. Tranquil, tasteful and comfortable. This orange-themed guesthouse has a handful of good-value rooms set around a lush courtyard, all with hot water. Wi-Fi, TV and coffee available. Good for couples. Recommended.

$ Casa Vieja, Parque San Juan, 1½ c sur, T2311-4235. Sociable Nica hotel with some long-term residents and a family feel. It has 9 large rooms with fan, communal bath and kitchen, cooking on request, laundry service and telephone. Friendly.

$ El Albergue de León, Gasolinera Petronic, ½ c abajo, T8894-1787, www.hostal albergedeleon.com. A colourful, if slightly grungy, bare-bones hostel with plant-filled courtyards, ultra-cheap dorms and private rooms. Amenities include kitchen, Wi-Fi, DVD, book exchange, coffee, bikes and lockers. Reportedly a good place to pick up volunteer work.

$ Hostal Clínica, 1 Av NO, Parque Central, 1½ c sur, T2311-2031, roxyprincesscutie@hotmail.es. Family-run and very Nicaraguan. Simple single and double rooms have fan and private or shared bathroom. There's an ultra-cheap dorm too. Washing facilities, terrace with hammock space, breakfast and drinks are available. Very friendly.

$ Lazybones Hostel, Parque de los Poetas, 2½ c norte, T2311-3472, www.lazybones.com. Managed by a friendly English-Colombian couple, this excellent hostel has a refreshing pool and lots of extras including free coffee and tea, pool table, Wi-Fi, internet, DVD rental and a daily 10-min long-distance phone call. Clean dorms and private rooms; some have private bath, cheaper without. Check out the mural by one of Managua's best graffiti artists.

$ Siesta Perdida, southwest corner of the Parque Central, ½ c abajo, T8826-2672, www.siestaperdida.com. Ultra-cheap party hostel with basic rooms at the right price. Good, lively crowd at the bar and a range of community tours available at the adjoining

Nicasí office (see What to do, below). Great central location close to the bar and clubs.

$ Sonati Hostel, Iglesia la Recolección, 1 c norte, ½ c arriba, T2311-4251, www.sonati.org. Owned by a biologist and tied to an environmental education organization, **Sonati** is a tranquil new hostel with hammock space and a 'hummingbird garden'. Clean dorms and private rooms are available with the usual hostel amenities like laundry, free organic coffee, book exchange, kitchen, Wi-Fi and water refill. Reforestation and other volunteer opportunities are offered, as well as interesting tours (see **Sonati Trekking**, page 213).

$ Tortuga Booluda, southwest corner of Parque Central, 3½ c abajo, T2311-4653, www.tortugabooluda.com. A very pleasant, friendly hostel with clean dorms (**$**), private rooms (**$**), and an a/c 'suite' with views (**$$**). Internet, Wi-Fi, pancake breakfast, organic coffee, kitchen, pool table, book exchange and Spanish classes available. Discounts for peace corps volunteers and long-term rentals in low season. Relaxed and recommended.

$ Via Via, Banco ProCredit, ½ c sur, T2311-6142, www.viaviacafe.com. Part of a worldwide network of Belgian cafés, this excellent and professionally managed hostel offers clean dorm beds and a range of private rooms, some with TV. There's a tranquil garden and popular restaurant-bar. In the manager's words, 'a meeting place for cultures'. Recommended.

❼ Restaurants

León p198, map p202
$$ Barbaro, Parque de los Poetas, 1 c sur. Efficient and often buzzing bar-restaurant where moneyed Nicas like to be seen. A range of meat, fish and chicken dishes are available, all reasonably tasty and filling, but the quality is inconsistent – the steaks are good, the pasta is bad. An army of staff is on hand.
$$ Cocinarte, costado norte Iglesia de Laborío. Quality vegetarian restaurant and intriguing international menu of Eastern,

Middle Eastern and Nicaraguan cuisine. They use a lot of fresh and organic produce and host a monthly organic market.

$$ El Sesteo, next to cathedral, on Parque Central. The place for watching the world go by, particularly in the late afternoon. Good pork dishes, *nacatamales*, fruit drinks and *cacao con leche*, but everything on the menu is overpriced. Portraits of Nicaraguan cultural greats on the wall.

$$ Marrakech, Iglesia La Merced, 1 c arriba, 2½ c norte. Dinner only, closed Tue. Intimate Moroccan restaurant with soft lighting and authentic art work. They serve tagines, kebabs and baclavas. A romantic option.

$$-$ La Casa Vieja, Iglesia San Francisco, 1½ c norte. Mon-Sat 1600-2300. Lovely, intimate restaurant-bar with a rustic feel. Serves reasonably tasty meat and chicken dishes, beer and delicious home-made lemonade. Popular with Nicas.

$$-$ Pure Earth Café, Banco Procredit, ½ c sur. Open for breakfast, lunch and dinner, closed Tue. Intimate non-profit café that's best on Wed and Sun evenings when you can get a pizza and 2 *mojitos* for US$7 (feeds 2). Otherwise they offer a simple vegetarian menu with good juices, natural teas and organic ingredients grown on site. Some of the café's proceeds go to reforestation and conservation projects.

$$-$ Terraza Meditterráneo, Parque Rubén Darío, 2½ c norte. This popular restaurant serves French and Mediterranean cuisine, fresh fruit juices and Italian wines. Relaxed ambience and an attractive colonial building. There's also a bakery attached where they sell fresh bread, croissants, *pan de chocolate* and cakes. The garden looks great at night when it's lit up with candles and fairy lights. Generally good, but a bit inconsistent. Try the steak.

$$-$ Via Via, see Where to stay, above. A popular place with a recently reworked menu that includes giant plates of pasta, Mexican, Nicaraguan and US dishes. The hand-cut *papas fritas* are quite good, including Belgian and Dutch variations.

$ Cafetín San Benito, northwest corner of the Parque Central, 1 c abajo, ½ c norte. Open Mon-Sat for lunch and dinner. Serves up cheap, wholesome, high-carb Nica grub with a Chinese twist. Get there 1130 and 1730 for fresh servings (later is not so good). Popular with students and budget travellers.

$ Comedor Lucía, Banco Procredit, ½ c sur. Mon-Sat. Reputable *comedor* serving good and reliable *comida típica* and buffet food, popular with locals. Dinner is much simpler and cheaper than lunch.

$ Comedor Poneloya, Catedral, 25 vrs norte, inside Vivero de Empresas. Lunch only. Fresh seafood brought daily from the beach at Poneloya, including fish and crab. Very affordable, friendly and tasty. Often recommended by budget travellers.

$ El Desayunazo, Parque de las Poetas, 3 c norte. Open 0600-1200. A great breakfast spot where you can enjoy blueberry pancakes, fruit salad, waffles and *huevos rancheros*, among others. The burritos are particularly recommended. Friendly, speedy service.

$ El Mississippi, southeast corner of the cathedral, 1 c sur, 2½ c arriba. Also known as La Cucaracha, everyone raves about the bean soup here. Simple, unpretentious dining at this locals' haunt. Tasty, energizing and highly recommended.

$ La Buena Cuchara, Parque Rubén Darío, 3½ c sur. Friendly, homely little *comedor* with tasty and cheap buffet food. Lunch only.

$ La Mexicana, La Iglesia Merced, 2 c norte, ½ c abajo. Economical, no-frills Mexican grub, but tasty and completely authentic. The *chilaquiles* and *burritos de res* are the best offerings, particularly after a cold beer or 2. Popular with the locals, greasy and recommended, in spite of the sullen service.

Cafés and bakeries

Café La Rosita, northwest corner of Parque Central, ½ c abajo. A pleasant colonial building with chequered floors and a tranquil courtyard. They serve good, if pricey, coffee, cappuccino, cakes, sandwiches, salads and

all-day breakfasts. The chocolate brownies are very tasty. Wi-Fi enabled and recommended.
Pan and Paz, northeast corner of the cathedral, 1 c norte, 1½ c arriba. This excellent French bakery serves what is probably the best bread in Nicaragua. They also offer great-value sandwiches, delicious quiches and scintillating fresh fruit juices. Highly recommended.

Sutiava *p204*
$$ Los Pescaditos, Iglesia de San Juan, 1 c sur, 1 c abajo. Daily 1200-2230. Excellent seafood at reasonable prices, go with the waiter to choose your fish from the ice box. Recommended.

🍷 Bars and clubs

León *p198, map p202*
León has a vibrant nightlife, thanks to its large student population. The action moves between different places through-out the week.
Barbaro, see Restaurants, above. Popular with visiting foreigners and Nicas. **Barbaro** serves wine and cocktails in addition to the usual beer and rum tipple. Some people, however, may find the lights a little too bright.
Café Taquezal, southwest corner of Parque Central, ½ c abajo, T311-7282. Mon-Sat 1800-0200. Pleasant atmosphere with good live folk music on Thu nights. Classic León decor. Food served.
Camaleón, Iglesia La Recolección, 35 vrs abajo. **Camaleón** is a hot and sweaty after-party place and something of a León institution. It's best enjoyed in a state of absolute inebriation. So wrong it's almost right.
Don Señor, opposite Parque La Merced. Tue-Sun. Popular with students and young Nicas on Fri nights, with liberal doses of karaoke, dancing and beer. A good place to see the locals cut loose.
Jack's, opposite Parque La Merced, behind Don Señor. Rooftop bar that's popular with Nicas and travellers. Cool and breezy. The

bar downstairs, **El Alamo**, promises some interesting cultural experiences too.
Olla Quemada, Museo Rubén Darío, ½ c abajo. Popular on Wed nights with live music acts and lots of beer; Salsa on Thu. Great place, friendly atmosphere.
Oxygen 2, Teatro Gonzales, 75 vrs abajo. Tue-Sun; ladies' night Fri. Darkened disco that plays everything from R&B to salsa, reggae to techno, rock to pop. Popular with gringos and Nicas, so don your dancing shoes and dress to impress.
Via Via, Banco ProCredit, ½ c sur. Good on most nights, but best on Fri when there's live music. Good, warm atmosphere. Popular with foreigners and Nicas and often praised.

🎭 Entertainment

León *p198, map p202*
Cinema
There is a cinema with 3 screens in the Plaza Nuevo Siglo, next to the La Unión supermarket. It shows mostly US movies with Spanish subtitles, US$2.50.

🎉 Festivals

León *p198, map p202*
Feb Rubén Darío's birthday celebrations.
Mar/Apr León is famed throughout Nicaragua for the beauty of its religious festivals, particularly **Semana Santa** (Holy Week). Starting on **Domingo de Ramos** (Palm Sun) the cathedral has a procession every day of the week and the Parish church of Sutiava has many events (see page 204), as do all of the other churches of León. (A program of processions and events can be obtained from the Nicaraguan Institute of Tourism, INTUR.)
14 Aug Gritería Chiquita (see Gritería, below) was instituted in 1947 to protect León during a violent eruption of the nearby Cerro Negro volcano.
24 Sep Patron saint of León, **La Virgin de las Mercedes**.
7-8 Dec La Purísima or Gritería (the Virgin Mary's conception of Jesus), like Semana

Santa, is celebrated throughout the country, but is best in León, as this is where the tradition began. Altars are built in front of private residences and outside churches during the day. At 1800, a massive outburst of pyrotechnics opens the proceedings in front of the Cathedral of León, complete with dances, then a roaming Mass visits every makeshift altar yelling: "Who causes so much happiness?" which must be answered by: "The conception of Mary!" Visitors receive small gifts in return, like sugarcane and oranges or more modern snacks. The fireworks end at midnight and the next day is a public holiday when everything is closed.

O Shopping

León p198, map p202
Bookshops
Libro Centro Don Quixote, next to Hotelito, Calle Real. New and second-hand books, a few bad ones in English, the owner is very helpful and knowledgeable about León.

Crafts and markets
If you're looking for crafts, try the street markets on the north side of the cathedral. Additionally, **Flor de Luna**, Iglesia San Fransisco, 75 vrs abajo, Mon-Sat 0900-1900, stocks Nicaraguan artesanías, whilst **Kamañ**, southwest corner of the Parque Central, 20 vrs abajo, sells an assortment of handicrafts, bags and simple jewellery.

The best **market** is in the pale green building behind the cathedral which sells meat, fruit and veg inside, and shoes, fans and stereos in the street stalls outside. The inside market is a good place to find out what tropical fruits are in season. There is another market near the Iglesia San Juan, which stocks mostly stationery, bags and school supplies; and one at the bus terminal, which sells everything from vegetables to furniture. Both are dirty and hot.

Supermarkets
La Unión, catedral, 1 c norte, 2 c arriba, is modern and well stocked; there is another good supermarket, **Salman**, behind Hotel El Convento. There's also an inexpensive but dimly lit **Palí** northeast of the centre, near the bus station and market. A convenient **minimart** can be found just south of Via Via and Bigfoot.

O What to do

León p198, map p202
Cultural and community tourism
Casa de Cultura, Iglesia La Merced, 1½ c abajo. Offers a range of courses including traditional and contemporary dance, music and painting. Ask inside for a schedule.
Nicasí Tours, southwest corner of Parque Central, ½ c abajo, T8414-1192, www.nicasi tours.com. The best cultural and community tours in town. **Nicasí** offers a diverse range of activities including rooster fights, cooking, cowboy, city and historical tours. Promises unique insights into the Nica way of life. Recommended.

Horse riding
Rancho Los Alpes, Km 100.5 Carretera León–Poneloya, T8803-7085, rancholosalpes@gmail.com. A working cattle ranch where you can fulfil all your cowboy fantasies. Various trails and tours are available, including forest, beach and volcano excursions. Aside from horse riding, you can participate in farming and communal activities, like making charcoal or milking cows.

Tour operators
Green Pathways, Banco Procredit, ½ c sur, T2315-0964, www.greenpathways.com. Green pathways aspires to carbon-neutral sustainability and donates proceeds to environmental projects. They offer the usual range of local tours, but also specialize in alternative 'adventure in nature' trips further afield. These include whale-watching expeditions, tours of the

Atlantic Coast, birdwatching and tours of the Northern Highlands.

Tierra Tour, La Merced, 1½ c norte, T2315-4278, www.tierratour.com. This Nicaragua travel specialist is Dutch-Nicaraguan owned. They offer good information and affordable tours of León, the Maribios volcanoes and Isla Juan Venado reserve. English, Dutch, Spanish, German and French spoken. Also domestic flights and trips all over the country, as well as shuttles direct to Granada and other places. Well established and reliable.

Va Pues, north side of El Laborio Church, inside Cocinarte restaurant, T2315-4099, www.vapues.com. Popular tours include sandboarding on Cerro Negro, cultural trips to León Viejo, night turtle tours, kayaking, mangrove tours, tours of Sutiava's workshops, horse riding, visits to San Jacinto's mud fields or Pacific coast salt factories, and city tours. English, French, Dutch and Spanish spoken. They have an office in Granada and can organize trips all over the country. Well established and professional.

Trekking

Quetzaltrekkers, Iglesia la Recolección, 1½ c arriba, T2311-6695, www.quetzal trekkers.com. An ethical non-profit organization with proceeds going to street kids. Multi-day hikes to Los Maribios US$20-US$70 including transport, food, water, camping equipment. **Quetzaltrekkers** is volunteer-led and the team is always looking for new additions. They prefer a 3-month commitment and will train you as a guide. Nice guys and recommended.
Sampson Expeditions, Calle Rubén Darío, 1½ c abajo, inside Hostal Calle de Los Poetas, T2311-3306, rsampson@ibw.com.ni. Kayaking in Juan Venado and Laguna El Tigre, volcano expeditions, poetry tours. Rigo Sampson comes from a family of devout hikers and climbers and is Nicaragua's foremost expert on climbing the Los Maribios volcanoes. He also works closely with educational organizations. Professional and highly recommended.

Sonati Trekking, Iglesia la Recolección, 1 c norte, ½ c arriba, T2311-4251, www.sonati.org. Affiliated to an environmental education NGO, Sonati offers ecology-focused tours of the volcanoes, forests, mangroves and nature reserves. There is particular emphasis on flora and fauna. Birdwatching in dry forest and mangrove swamps is also offered.

Volcano boarding

Many tour operators offer boarding on Cerro Negro, but of particular note are:
Bigfoot Adventure, Banco ProCredit, ½ c sur, www.bigfootnicaragua.com. The original and most professional outfit in town will kit you out with a board and safety gear, and transport you to the top of Cerro Negro. The fastest boards have been clocked at 70 kph. Tours depart daily, US$23, plus park entrance fee, around US$5.
Tierra Tour, La Merced, 1½ c norte, T2315-4278, www.tierratour.com. This boarding specialist usually has 2 daily tours to Cerro Negro. Full protective gear, funky suits, boards, transport, guide and park entrance for US$28.

⊖ Transport

León p198, map p202
Bus
The bus terminal is in the far eastern part of town, a long walk (20-30 mins) or short taxi ride from the centre. Small trucks also ferry people between the bus terminal and town for US$0.25. Note express buses to Estelí and Matagalpa leave only if there are enough passengers; travel on Fri if possible, or simply go to San Isidro for connections. To **Managua**, express bus to La UCA, every 30 mins, 0400-1900, US$1.90, 1 hr 45 mins. To **Chinandega**, express bus, every 15 mins, 0500-1800, US$1, 1 hr 45 mins. To **Corinto**, every 30 mins, 0500-1800, US$1, 2 hrs. To **Chichigalpa**, every 15 mins, 0400-1800, US$0.75, 1 hr. To **Estelí**, express bus, 0520, 1245, 1415, 1530, US$2.50, 3 hrs. To **Matagalpa**, express bus, 0420, 0730, 1445,

US$2.50, 3 hrs. To **San Isidro**, every 30 mins, 0420-1730, US$1.50, 2½ hrs. To **El Sauce**, every hr, 0800-1600, US$1.50, 2½ hrs. To **El Guasaule**, 0500, US$2, 2½ hrs. To **Salinas Grandes**, 0600,1200, US$0.40, 1½ hrs.

Buses and trucks for **Poneloya** and **Las Peñitas** leave from Sutiava market, every hr, 0530-1735, US$0.60, 25 mins. Service can be irregular so check to see when last bus will return. There are more buses on weekends.

International buses Contact individual agencies for schedules and costs; Ticabus, San Juan church, 2 c norte, in the Viajes Cumbia travel agency, T2315-2027, www.ticabus.com. **Transnica**, Colegio Mercantil ½ c abajo, T2311-0821, www.transnica.com. Nica Expresso, Agencia Benitours, north side of Iglesia San Juan, 25 vrs norte, T2315-2349. **King Quality**, corner of 2a Calle NE and 3a Ave NE, T2311-2426, www.king-qualityca.com.

Taxi
There are many taxis in the centre, at the bus terminal and on the bypass road. Day-time fares are US$0.75 per person to any destination in the city; US$1 at night. Taxis can also be hired to visit **Poneloya** beach and the fumaroles at **San Jacinto** (see page 217). Rates for longer trips vary greatly, with a trip to **San Jacinto** normally costing US$15-20 plus US$1 for every 15 mins of waiting or a higher flat rate for the taxi to wait as long as you wish. Trips outside must be negotiated in advance. If staying in a **$$** level or above hotel ask the front desk to help with the price negotiation and it should be less than looking for one on the street.

⊙ Directory

León p198, map p202
Banks Banks are clustered on the streets immediately north of the cathedral. A block west of La Unión Supermarket is BAC (Banco de América Central), the best bank for TCs and cash withdrawals from credit/debit

cards, including Maestro and Cirrus networks Other banks offer withdrawals on Visa cards only. If you need to change currency, it's often quicker and easier to use the cash-waving 'coyotes' who hang around outside. **Consulates** Spain, María Mercedes de Escudero, Av Central 405, T2311-4376. **Fire** T2311-2323. **Hospital** Catedral, 1 c sur, T2311-6990. **Internet** At nearly every hotel and almost every street in León; head for Via Via or Bigfoot, where you'll find at least 3 cybers in the same street. **Language schools** León Spanish School, Casa de Cultura, Iglesia La Merced, 1½ c abajo, T2311-2116, www.leonspanishschool. org. Flexible weekly or hourly one-on-one tuition with activities, volunteering and homestay options. Pleasant location inside the casa de cultura. Metropolis Academy, northwest corner of the cathedral, ½ c norte, T8932-6686, www.metropolisspanish. com. A range of programmes from simple hourly tuition to full-time courses with daily activities and family homestay. UP Spanish School, Parque Central, 3½ c norte, www.upspanishschoolleon.com, T8878-3345. Flexible one-on-one classes with experienced and dedicated teachers. Options include homestay, volunteering and activities. Good reports and highly recommended. **Laundry** Lavamático, northeast corner of Parque Central, 4 c norte. Wash and dry, quick service but not economical. Also try Lavamático Express, teatro, ½ c abajo, self-service wash and dry. **Medical services** Plenty of clinics, thanks to the university. For blood tests and others, including parasites, Clínica Metropolitana, Colegio Mercantil, 25 vrs norte, T2311-2750. They also have general doctors and specialists for consultation, US$15-25. There are many other labs and clinics in the area, including some low-cost ones. **Police** T2311-3137. **Post** Correos de Nicaragua,Iglesia La Merced, 2 c abajo, 3½ c norte. **Red Cross** T2311-2627. **Telephone** Claro, on Parque Central at the west side, T2311-7377. Also at bus terminal.

Around León

León's rugged volcanoes, windy beaches and hot, sleepy little villages make interesting excursions from the city. Los Maribios volcanoes are great for climbing and hiking, offering stunning views of the León valley stretching as far as the Pacific Coast. León Viejo is a glimpse of Nicaragua's brutal beginnings as a Spanish colony and a UNESCO World Heritage Site. The little villages that run north and south of León offer glimpses into the lives of local cowboys and farmers, authentic towns cooking under the tropical sun that come to life in the early mornings and late afternoons. ▸▸ *For listings, see pages 223-224.*

Los Volcanes Maribios → *For listings, see pages 223-224. Colour map 3, A1-2.*

A scintillating landscape of sulphurous craters, steaming black sand slopes, simmering pools and imminent eruptions, Los Maribios are reason enough to visit the hot provinces of León and Chinandega. A rocky 60-km spine made up of 21 volcanoes, five of which are active, the cones rise from just above sea level to an average height of 1000 m, filling every vista with marvellous earthen pyramids. These mountains are bathed in sunlight most of the year and are home to rustic farms and tropical dry forest. The principal volcanoes of Los Maribios are described below from south to north.

Getting there and around
The entire range is an easy day trip from León. Most of the volcanoes have unpaved road access, though some can only be reached on foot or horseback. A 4WD is essential for getting close to the trail heads if a summit climb is planned on the same day. Camping is possible on many of the cones. It is strongly recommended that you bring a guide from León or use someone from the local communities at the base of each volcano. The best option is to use one of the mountaineering outfits in León, like **Sampson Expeditions** (see page 213), that can provide 4WD transfers, camping gear and guide.

Volcán Momotombo → *Altitude: 1260 m.*
In the province of León at the southern tip of the Maribios volcano range, this symmetrical cone towering over the shores of Lake Managua has been an inspiration to both national and international poets over the centuries. The climb is a long one, normally taking two days, with an overnight camp just below the end of the tree line. Access to the base of the volcano is via the village of **Puerto Momotombo**, the site of León Viejo. *Momotombo* in Náhuatl means 'great boiling summit', though this cone was called *Mamea* 'the fireplace', by the Chorotega who lived at its base. In many ways, Momotombo is Nicaragua's national symbol and can be seen from as far south as Volcán Masaya. Although only 500 ha of the cone is a forest reserve, there is much nature to see on its lower slopes and its seldom-explored lagoon, known as **Laguna Monte Escalante**. The volcano is still active, although it has only produced fumarolic steam and some ash (which can be seen on its eastern face) since its last big magma flow in 1905. At the western base of the cone is a geothermal plant, operated by an Israeli company which promises to increase its power output.

There are two principal routes to climb the mountain; the easier one requires permission from the power company. Check with the police in Puerto Momotombo for procedures, or better still use a León tour operator that supplies a guide and camping gear and will take you up via the safest route. The northern ascent is longer and more difficult, but affords a visit to the lagoons. Above the tree line there is a two-hour climb through loose rock that must be done carefully to reach the crater. The view from the smoking summit is breathtaking and one of the most spectacular in Nicaragua.

Volcán El Hoyo and Laguna El Tigre → *Altitude: 1089 m.*

There are some magnificent 1000-m cones northwest of Volcán Momotombo, such as Volcán El Hoyo, an active cone (last major eruption 1954) and part of the **Volcán Las Pilas** complex, which is protected by a 7422-ha nature reserve of tropical dry forest. El Hoyo is a very physical climb and offers a frightening view of a perfectly round 80-m hole in its western face that is a bit of a mystery. Below El Hoyo and the extinct **Volcán Asososca** (818 m) is a pristine crater lake of the same name, but known popularly as Laguna El Tigre, or Jaguar Lagoon. (The Spanish misnamed the animals, previously unseen by Europeans: a jaguar is called a 'tiger' – *tigre* – and a puma a 'lion' – *león*.) From the 4WD path up to the western rim of the crater, it is an easy 10-minute walk down to the lake shores. This is one of Nicaragua's cleanest crater lakes and is great for swimming. Kayaking can be arranged with **Sampson Expeditions** (see page 213), which brings kayaks from León. The crater lake has an oval shape 1000 m x 1500 m wide. Its waters are 35 m deep and the temperature averages at 29°C. Camping is also possible on the lakeshore. Hikes and camping in this zone should be done with a guide, as much of the land is privately owned.

Volcán Cerro Negro → *Altitude: 675 m.*

ⓘ *French cyclist Eric Barone set a speed record on the steep gravel slope of Cerro Negro's west face in May 2002, reaching 172 kph before his front forks disintegrated and sent him rolling for 50 m. Very luckily, he survived the crash.*

This fierce little volcano is the newest in the western hemisphere and the most violent of the marvellous Maribios range. In 1850, what was a flat cornfield came to life with 10 days of violent eruption, leaving a hill 70 m high. In the short period since, it has grown to a height of 450 m above its base, with persistently violent eruptions shooting magma and ashes up to 8000 m in the air. Cerro Negro's most recent eruptions in 1992, 1995 and 1999 have coated León in black ash and put on a spectacular night-time display of fire. The eruption in August 1999 created three new baby craters (named by locals '*Las Tres Marías*') at its southern base. The three Marías are simmering quietly, and the main crater is smoking silently as the short, squat mountain keeps everyone nervously waiting for its next hail of rocks, lava and ash. Fortunately, most of the eruptions have come with ample seismic warning. Have a look at www.ineter.gob.ni before climbing Cerro Negro and you can examine the volcano's daily activity recorded at INETER's seismic station next to the cone.

As its name suggests, Cerro Negro is jet-black, made up of black gravel, solidified black lava flows and massive black sand dunes. Hiking on the cone is a surreal experience and quite tiring, for the base is nothing but a giant black sandpit. On the northern fringes of the cone, growing in the volcano's seemingly sterile black sand, is a strange forest full of lizards, birds and flowering trees. This is the only volcano of its kind in Nicaragua and, depending on the route taken, you can choose between a very accessible 4WD drive and hike or a hot day-long excursion.

The most accessible ascent is the partially marked trail that starts at the baby craters near the seismic station and loops around to the east face. The climb is over loose volcanic rock and pebbles, very unstable on the surface, but solid underneath. At the summit, most people traverse the southern lip to reach the west face; the wind can be very strong up here so be careful. The west face descent is great fun but running down can be dangerous. Many people enjoy descending the volcano on wooden boards – a high-speed thrill offered by **Bigfoot Adventures** and **Tierra Tour** in León (see page 213). The experience is not really comparable to snowboarding and most people have more fun sitting rather than standing. The sunsets from the cone are beautiful – however, with such a perilous mountain, descending in the dark may not be advisable. Wait for a full moon.

San Jacinto fumarolic pools

Further north in the Maribios range is **Volcán Rota**, which overlooks the highway that connects the northern mountains and the Pacific Basin. Known as the Carretera Telica–San Isidro, the highway slices through the heart of the range, at a low point between Volcán Rota and **Volcán Santa Clara**. At the base of Santa Clara is San Jacinto, an extraordinary little village that lives with amazing volcanic activity in its own backyard. Fifteen kilometres from the highway between León and Chinandega is the semi-paved entrance to the town with a big sign that says 'Los Hervideros de San Jacinto'. Follow the road to a stone arch where a US$2 admission is charged. The land drops off behind the village to a field of smoking, bubbling and hissing micro-craters, the Maribios range in miniature. They are the result of the water table leaking onto a magma vein of the nearby Volcán Telica (see below). In an ever-changing landscape, the water is heated and rushes to the surface with a heavy dose of sulphuric gases. Local children act as guides; choose one and heed instructions as to where it is safe to walk. As a rule it is best to avoid walking on the crystallized white sulphur and to listen for hissing. Increased caution is required after rains, when the ground is particularly soft and prone to collapse.

Volcán Telica → Altitude: 1061 m

This smoking volcano last erupted in May 2011 and is part of a 9088-ha tropical dry forest reserve. Telica's activity creates the spectacle at San Jacinto and the volcano is one of Nicaragua's most active, with recorded eruptions in 1527 and steady activity ever since. This was one of three cones that erupted in the final weeks before the millennium celebrations, which certainly had the prophets of doom wringing their hands in eager anticipation. There is a long but rewarding hike that starts from just off the highway to Chinandega before the entrance to the village of **Quezalguaque**. The walk follows an ox-cart trail up the north shoulder of the cone, around to its east face and then up to the summit. The lip of the active crater affords a breathtaking view of the vertical interior walls of its crater and down to a smaller crater inside that limits the smoke. The hike can take three to five hours for a round trip, or you can continue to San Jacinto next to Volcán Santa Clara. This hike takes six to eight hours and involves three ascents. The climb should be undertaken with a guide; local guides are available if you start the climb from San Jacinto or, for the northeast route, use a León tour operator (see page 212) to allow 4WD access to the trail plus a guide to make the complete hike. Camping is also possible near the summit at a local ranch.

Volcán San Cristóbal → Altitude: 1745 m.

This is another of Los Maribios' very active volcanoes and the highest in Nicaragua. San Cristóbal has shown almost constant activity since 1999, with the last recorded eruption in December 2010. San Cristóbal shares 17,950 ha of tropical dry forest reserve with **Volcán Casita**. One of the most symmetrical and handsome of the Maribios volcano range, San Cristóbal is a difficult climb that should only be attempted with a guide and by hikers who are physically fit, though 4WD access to the adjacent Volcán Casita means that lesser athletes can still reach the summit to marvel at its 500 x 600-m-wide crater. Some of the ranchers' caretakers are blocking access to the cone so it is critical to have a local with you to ease access and find the best route. Winds are very strong near the summit; avoid the windiest months from November to March if possible.

South of León → *For listings, see pages 223-224.*

León Viejo

ⓘ *The site is open daily from 0800-1700 and costs US$2, which includes parking and a Spanish-speaking guide, usually a native of Puerto Momotombo. A guide will show the ruins and make comments, but ask questions first to gauge the depth of the guide's knowledge. The sun is brutally strong most of the year at the site – avoid 1100-1430, and it is better to visit in the rainy season for the climate, visibility and the lushness of the countryside. Light is better in the late afternoon to photograph the ruins and surrounding volcanoes.*

Inside the quiet lakeside village of Puerto Momotombo, León Viejo or Sitio Histórico Colonial Ruinas de León Viejo, as it is officially known, is a must for anyone interested in colonial history and archaeology. Confirming its historical significance, not just for Nicaragua but for the world, León Viejo was declared a UNESCO World Heritage Site in December 2000 – the first site to receive such status in Nicaragua. It is a very hot and humid place with only the occasional lake breeze. At first sight León Viejo is nothing more than a few old foundations, surrounded by pleasant greenery in the shadow of the imposing Volcán Momotombo, but this unfinished excavation site is all that remains of one of the most tragic of Spanish settlements – one which witnessed some of the most brutal acts of the Conquest and was ultimately destroyed by a series of earthquakes and volcanic eruptions between 1580 and 1610. Nicaraguans will tell you with absolute conviction that León Viejo's destruction was a punishment from God for the crimes committed here.

León Viejo was Nicaragua's first capital, founded in the same year as Granada (1524) by **Francisco Hernández de Córdoba**. The site was selected because of its lakefront location and the existence of an important Chorotega settlement known as **Imabite**. The town was laid out in classic colonial fashion with the cathedral facing west to a central plaza and principal avenues running from the park east–west and north–south. The earliest reports of the town speak of huts made of wood and thatch, and of persistent Indian attacks. León Viejo was the kind of town where if you had money or power you slept with your horse saddled, and this first capital set the stage for a long history of unjust rulers, a tradition that would continue almost unbroken for the next 450 years.

The country's original ruler, **Pedrarias Dávila**, was a brutal old man who, before coming to Nicaragua, had run Panama's first settlement like a Mafia boss. When he was declared governor of Nicaragua on 1 July 1527, he was already in his mid-80s. He married a teenage Spanish girl and ordered the country's founder, Captain Hernández de Córdoba, to be beheaded (as he had done with Balboa in Panama). One of Pedrarias Dávila's most famous acts was the theatrically cruel murder of a dozen indigenous hostages in 1528 in revenge for the murder of a half-dozen Spanish in the nearby mountains. Dávila devised a little game: he sent the *indígenas* one by one into the Parque Central of León Viejo, in front of the village population, with a stick to protect themselves. First a tiny dog was released, which could be fought off easily. Then real killer dogs (which Pedrarias bred as a hobby) were released, and they tore their victims to bits. Old Pedrarias then insisted on leaving the bodies to rot for four days in the tropical sun until the population finally convinced him to let them clean them up. Pedrarias died in March of 1531 and was buried in the La Merced Church.

In 1535, Pedrarias' son-in-law, **Rodrigo de Contreras**, was appointed governor. Along with the Crown Treasurer, Pedro de los Ríos, and Crown Sheriff, Luis de Guevara, he sacked the country and stole everything he could find for almost 10 years. Even after the Spanish Crown ended his political reign and took away some of his slave ranches, Contreras still had control of the country, much in the manner of a tropical Al Capone. In 1550, while Contreras was in Spain to request the return of his land, his wife María de Peñalosa and their two sons, Hernando and Pedro, decided to rebel against the Spanish Crown. They murdered the respected and honest defender of indigenous rights, the Bishop of Nicaragua, Fray Antonio de Valdivieso, at his home. They also killed all loyal government officials, stole the Crown's treasury, pirated ships, travelled to Panama and sacked its capital until they were finally defeated. One son, Hernán, may have drowned, but Pedro got away. María de Peñalosa paid her way out of a trial for treason, and went with her husband to enjoy the high life in Lima, Peru.

After the Contreras rebellion, León Viejo never really recovered, and was left to decay before being destroyed in a series of earthquakes and volcanic eruptions from 1580 until 1609. It was finally abandoned for León's current site in 1610.

Nicaragua's first capital was mostly forgotten, though it lived on in legends, including some that said it was located underneath Lake Managua. But after 357 years lying buried under volcanic ash, excavations began in 1967. In 2000, Nicaraguan archaeologist Ramiro García discovered the remains of Nicaragua's founder, Francisco Hernández de Córdoba, in the tomb of the ruins of La Merced church; his bones resting peacefully next to those of his nemesis Pedrarias Dávila. Córdoba's remains were put in a small glass box and paraded around the country, accompanied by a small guard of honour in the back of a big flat-bed truck. To add to the discovery of the tombs of Córdoba and Dávila, archaeologists from the Museo Nacional in Managua excavated and confirmed the remains of the assassinated Fray Antonio de Valdivieso, Bishop of Nicaragua, in the altar tomb of the old cathedral. He lies in a very large and fairly morbid-looking casket in a special roofed exhibit near the park entrance.

La Paz Centro
At Km 54 of the Carretera Nueva a León is the exit for the paved road that leads 12 km to the lakefront village of Puerto Momotombo and León Viejo. Just north of the exit is the friendly, dusty and sad-looking town of La Paz Centro. The survivors of earthquakes, volcanic eruptions and cruel rulers of León Viejo settled here in the early 17th century. The area has a long history of ceramic production as well as many artisan brick and tile factories. The beautiful clay tiles used on the roofs and floors of the colonial homes of León and surrounding villages are made here in big wood-burning ovens utilizing the local soil. To see this centuries-old way of making bricks and tiles it is best to visit before 0900 or after 1700 when the small factories take advantage of relatively cool temperatures to put their ovens to work.

Few Nicaraguans and increasingly few foreigners pass up the opportunity to eat traditional Nicaraguan food while passing through La Paz and its sister city, Nagarote, to the south (see below). Nagarote is the birthplace of the *quesillo*, the most fattening snack in Nicaragua, but very good if fresh. The *quesillo* consists of a hot corn tortilla stuffed with mild white cheese (similar to mozzarella) and onions, drenched with fresh cream and seasoned, see page 224.

Nagarote
At Km 41 on the Carretera Nueva a León, rising out of the intense heat that bakes the lakeshore plains, Nagarote is a rustic and scenic ranching town and birthplace of a famous dish, *quesillo*, one of Nicaragua's best-loved traditional meals (see La Paz Centro, above). Nagarote is a good place to savour a cold *tiste* – a traditional indigenous drink of corn and *cacao* (raw chocolate bean dried and crushed) served, as it has been for over 1000 years, in the dried and gutted shell of the oval *jícaro* fruit. The most famous place in Nagarote for

a good *quesillo con tiste* is the **Quesillos Acacia**, located at the southern highway entrance to Nagarote.

The centre of Nagarote lies well west of the highway, but is worth a visit if you have private transport. During the morning, ox carts arrive from surrounding farms full of metal milk cans and boys ride into town on bicycles with live chickens dangling from their handlebars. There are many rustic and charming colonial homes and the people of Nagarote are helpful and laid back. Parque Central is sleepy and there's a pretty adobe church with red-tile roof; inside, the dining room chandeliers and green curtains give it a homely feel. One block north is the original home of **Silvio Mayorga**, one of the Sandinista party founders who was killed by the National Guard in Pancasán in 1967. One block north and four blocks east of Parque Central an unassuming little park is home to what is believed to be Nicaragua's oldest living tree. This wide, ancient trunk with several surviving branches is the 950-year-old *genízaro* tree (*Pithecellobium saman*). In pre-Columbian times, this same tree gave shade to a *tiangue*, an indigenous market. At the corner of the park is a curious carved wood sculpture depicting a Chorotega chief on the front side and an indigenous woman at the back. The monument was carved in 1999 out of a single branch of the ancient tree that watches over it.

Mateare

At Km 25, the highway reaches the sleepy fishing and agricultural town of Mateare, where you'll find the finest fish from Lake Managua. Although not as clean as Lake Nicaragua, this part of the lake is much cleaner than along the shores of Managua and the fish here is safe to eat. The locals say once you eat their *guapote* (large-mouth bass) you will never leave Mateare. Most of the locals who do not fish have small farms in the hills across the highway.

The village offers rustic access to the seldom-visited **Isla Momotombito**. It is not easy to arrange but, with some asking around (try at the Araica residence on the east side of Parque Central), the fishermen can take you to the small volcanic island. The best time of year to visit is during the rainy season, when the island is green and the swell on the lake is small. Dry (windy) season trips mean a white-knuckle ride and a lot of water in your face. Boats have turned over on occasion during a big swell. It costs around US$60-80 for the day and you may need to drive out of town to fill up the fisherman's petrol tank in Los Brasiles. The ride is up to an hour depending on the lake swell. **Note**: Beware of snakes; there are literally hundreds on the island and the guards claim to kill more than five a day just to keep their hut snake-free.

The island is situated in the northwest of Lake Managua in the shadow of Volcán Momotombo. Momotombito (little Momotombo) has much bird and reptile life and a legendary family of albino crocodiles. There is a small military outpost on the calm side of the island. Stop there to check in if you wish to hike on the islands. Bring drinks or food as gifts for the (non-uniformed) guards, who are very friendly, usually quite bored and thrilled to see visitors. They might take you hiking for a small fee to see what is left of the island's many pre-Columbian statues.

West of León → *For listings, see pages 223-224.*

Poneloya and Las Peñitas beaches

The crashing surf of the Nicaraguan Pacific lies only 21 km from León, down a newly paved highway. Past the Estela de los Mares the road forks: to the left is the road to the beaches of Las Peñitas and Poneloya. There is a US$1 entrance fee if you come by car on the weekend or during holidays. A visit during the week means you have most of the beach to yourself with just a few fishermen to chat to, the exception being during Semana Santa when the entire coast turns into the biggest party of the year.

Poneloya, the more popular of the two beaches, lies to the north of Las Peñitas – if coming by bus, you will pass through Poneloya first. However, Las Peñitas, further on, tends to be a little cleaner and less crowded, and also has the best hotel and restaurant on the coast, as well as access to the nature reserve of Isla Juan Venado (see below). Both beach towns are passed by a single road lined with a mixture of local houses and luxury holiday homes for the wealthy of León. The locals are very friendly and helpful. The beaches themselves are attractive, with wide swathes of sand, warm water and pelicans. Swimming at either beach must be done with extreme caution; the currents are deceptively strong and foreigners die here every year assuming that strong swimming skills will keep them out of trouble. A good rule is to stay within your depth. You can ask the locals where the best place to swim is, but the truth is you won't see many of them swimming, just wading.

Reserva Natural Isla Juan Venado
This nature reserve is a turtle-nesting site with mangroves, crocodiles, crabs, iguanas and a healthy aquatic birdlife. The island is very close to the mainland and is 22 km long and varies from 25 m to 600 m wide. On the ocean side of the island there are sea turtles nesting from August to December. From the beach it is possible to swim across to Salinas Grandes (see below). It is also possible to camp on the island but the mosquitoes are vicious. To explore the entire canal that runs behind the island you should allow about four hours in a motorboat, costing US\$50-60, or about US\$20 for a short trip. Early morning, late afternoon or at night are the most favourable times to see the reserve, but touring needs to be timed with high tide. Try the fisherman who goes by the name of Toño Ñanga (Antonio González) who lives just 20 m east of the **Bar Comedor El Calamar** in front of an old washed-away pier. Kayaking is also offered here at the hostel **Barca de Oro** and other local tour operators in León, one of which, **Sampson Expeditions** (see page 213), has a house in Salinas Grandes and offers a rewarding circuit with kayaking from Las Peñitas to the beach at Salinas Grandes, traversing the entire wildlife refuge. This journey takes from three to six hours depending on conditions and your level of fitness and includes sea kayaks, a bilingual guide, motorboat for support (and cold drinks), land transfers to Las Peñitas and from Salinas Grandes and time relaxing in their beach house. Prices range from US\$25-75 per person depending on group size. Night tours are also very interesting and useful for spotting crocodiles and sea turtles laying eggs, but take plenty of insect repellent.

Salinas Grandes
At Km 74 on the Carretera Vieja a León is a scenic dirt track that leads through pleasant pastures to the Nicaraguan Pacific and the long wave-swept Pacific Ocean beach of Salinas Grandes. Past a small settlement, the path drops down through lobster and shrimp farms before arriving at the simple beach with fishermen's homes. South of here, where the main road finishes, is where the fisherman roll their boats out of the sea and on to the beach over logs pushed by half the village. Their catch is normally *pargo rojo* or *negro* (red or black snapper) and you can ask for someone to cook you a fresh *pargo* for US\$3. The beach is fairly littered here but is much cleaner to the north and south. About 1 km north is the mouth of a river where the locals like to swim. North of the river outlet is the clean sand of the long barrier **Isla Juan Venado**, a protected nature reserve that runs all the way to Las Peñitas (see above).

From León, the Carretera a Chinandega runs north along the western slope of the Maribios range. The exit for the only paved highway that connects the Pacific Basin with the northern mountains is at Km 101. This scenic road slices in between the volcano range and connects to the Pan-American Highway at San Isidro.

El Sauce

The Carretera a San Isidro passes the rocky savannah of **Malpaisillo** until the exit at Km 150; from here it is 28 km along a paved road in poor condition to the rustic town of El Sauce, a classic colonial ranching village set in a small highland valley. Most of the year not one outsider passes through El Sauce, but every January it comes alive to celebrate *El Señor de Esquipulas*, the black Christ image that was responsible for numerous miracles. One of many stories is about the 18-year-old bride who was being wed in the church of El Sauce around 100 years ago. As she was about to finish her vows she looked above the altar to the Señor de Esquipulas and asked him for the truth. Should she marry, give up her virginity and live a carnal life or should she serve God in heaven? She prayed to the black Christ, asking him for a sign. As the church sat silent waiting for her to say 'I do', she fell to the ground, dying on the steps of the altar. Her virgin death was a sure sign to the people that she was a saint and she is still remembered today in a series of special ceremonies. The celebrations last over a week, but the principal day is 18 January, when people congregate in El Sauce on the culmination of a pilgrimage from as far away as Guatemala.

Lost Canyon Nature Reserve

ⓘ *www.lost-canyon.org. All visits to Lost Canyon are via appointment only and limited to groups of no more than 12 people. Visits are 1 Jun-31 Dec, 0530-1400. A donation of US$25 per visitor includes guided hiking in the reserve (Spanish-speaking park ranger) and lunch at the biological station.*

Founded in 2005 by author and photographer Richard Leonardi, the Lost Canyon Nature Reserve is dedicated to the conservation and restoration of tropical dry forest biodiversity. Between 2006 and 2011, a massive reforestation effort saw 7200 new trees planted across the reserve's 40 ha, which are located inside Lago Xolotlan's northern watershed. Today, Lost Canyon is flourishing and providing much-needed shelter to a variety of endangered species, the Nicaraguan iguana (*Ctenosaura quinquecarinata*) chief among them. Thanks to the reserve's **Nicaragua Iguana Project**, which is working to relocate iguanas from nearby farmland, visitors can usually enjoy first-hand encounters with a specimen or two. Several low-impact trails provide further opportunities for wildlife viewing, but the majority of the park's terrain has no public access in order to minimize disturbance of native fauna. Lost Canyon Reserve is located roughly 1½ hours from León off the Malpaisillo–San Isidro highway; contact in advance for specific directions.

For sleeping and eating price codes and other relevant information, see pages 28-30.

⊙ Where to stay

San Jacinto *p217*

$ Cinema, 1 block south of the entrance to Los Hervideros. Lodging is available in the town's old cinema, which has been refurbished and made into a hostel. Shared bath.

León Viejo *p218*

$ La Posada de León Viejo, Centro de Salud, 2 c norte. 3 rooms with shared bath; hotel does not have kitchen, but can arrange meals for customers. This archaeologists' hostel is located just 4 blocks from the excavation site.

Poneloya and Las Peñitas *p220*

Most of the best eating is at the hotels and hostels.

$$ Posada de Poneloya, Playa Poneloya, from the intersection of Las Peñitas and Poneloya, 150 m abajo, T2311-4612, posadaponeloya@yahoo.com. 19 rooms with private bath, hot water, a/c, with room service, parking. Not very near the beach, but lively on weekends.

$$ Suyapa Beach Hotel, Las Peñitas, T2317-0217, www.suyapabeach.com. A well-kept and professional hotel with a small pool and 24 clean rooms, all with a/c and private bath; a few cheaper ones have fan. Rooms on 2nd and 3rd floor have ocean views and a breeze. Often full with groups. The hotel restaurant (**$$$-$$**) is good quality and located right on the beach.

$$-$ Surfing Turtle Lodge, Isla Los Brasiles, transport from Poneloya, T8640-0644, www.surfingturtlelodge.com. This solar-powered surfers' lodge is located right on the beach. It has comfortable wooden cabins, double rooms and an economical dorm. Options include surf lessons, board rental, massage,

yoga, Spanish lessons, fishing and salsa. Protects the turtles who visit the island. Good reports.

$ Barca de Oro, Las Peñitas, at the end of the beach facing Isla Juan Venado Wildlife Refuge, www.barcadeoro.com.ni, T2317-0275. Friendly, funky hotel and day-trip hang-out with dorm beds and private rooms. Bamboo 'eco-cabañas' sleeping 4 are also available, all kitted with solar lighting and water recycling. Services include kayaking, horse riding, body boarding, turtle watching, book exchange, *artesanías*, pool table, hammocks, tours of Juan Venado and Cerro Negro, and beauty treatments. The restaurant serves seafood, meat and vegetarian dishes. The hotel is the departure point for many trips to Isla Juan Venado.

$ El Oasis, Terminal de Buses, 200 vrs norte, Las Peñitas, T8839-5344, www.oasislas penitas.com. Right on the beach, **El Oasis** has 7 large rooms with poor mattresses; some have phenomenal views. There are also several chill-out spaces with hammocks and gringo day-trippers like to hang out here. The restaurant has great views but the toilets aren't always clean. Tours to Isla Juan Venado available, US$15 per person. Surfboard rental available.

$ Samaki, overlooking the bay, Las Peñitas, T8640-2058, www.LaSamaki.net. 4 tasteful rooms with good mattresses, mosquito nets, running water, Wi-Fi and private bath. Canadian-owned, very relaxed, friendly and hospitable, and home to Nicaragua's only kite-surfing operation. There's an internet terminal, a good selection of wines and fresh food made to order, including delicious, real Asian curries and BBQs. Rates include breakfast. Currently for sale at a reasonable price and highly recommended.

Salinas Grandes *p221*

$$ Rise Up Surf Camp, T8917-8832, www.riseupsurftoursnicaragua.com. | A comfortable and professionally maintained surf camp some 30 mins from León. Good access to the world-class waves of Puerto Sandino. Meals, tours, yoga and massage available. Book beds and transport through **Bigfoot Hostel** or **Green Pathways** in León.

El Sauce *p222*

$ Hotel Blanco, Alcaldía, 1 c sur, 1 c abajo, T2319-2403. 20 rooms around a big tamarind tree with private bath and fan, cooler rooms are on 1st floor, basic, clean and friendly, the best in this region, also good *comida corriente* (**$**).

❷ Restaurants

San Jacinto *p217*

$ At the entrance to the fumaroles there is a small ranch that has cheap set meals and offers soft drinks.

$ Restaurante El Rancho, at the entrance to the village. Greasy food, but very cheap and with cold fruit juices and beer.

La Paz Centro *p219*

$ Quesillos Guiliguiste, near town entrance. The most popular place in Nicaragua to eat *quesillos*. They sell so many here that the ingredients are always fresh and the servings are generous, with fast cafeteria-style service.

Mateare *p220*

$ Bar El Ranchito, Parque Central. Serves fried chicken, fish and cold beer and offers

an up-close glimpse of village personalities (and drinking capacities) along the rural northern lakefront.

$ Mirador Momotombo, Km 31.5, Carretera Nueva a León. Daily 1000-2000. Charming outdoor restaurant with priceless view of Momotombo, Lake Managua and Isla Momotombito, typical beef, pork and chicken dishes at cheap to mid-range prices. The grounds of the restaurant are great for photography.

❸ Transport

Buses pass through **Mateare**, **Nagarote** and **La Paz Centro** on the Carretera every 15 mins between **León** and **Managua**.

León Viejo *p218*

Buses between Puerto Momotombo (León Viejo) and **La Paz Centro** every 1½ hrs, from 0400-1600, US$0.40. Taxi or hired car can be used as roads are good.

Poneloya and Las Peñitas *p220*

Buses to León pass hourly, 0530-1730, 20 mins, US$0.60.

Salinas Grandes *p221*

Buses to **León** daily at 0900 and 1500.

El Sauce *p222*

Buses to **León**, every 2 hrs, 0800-1600, US$1.40, 2½ hrs. To **Estelí**, 1300, US$1.25, 3 hrs. Express bus to **Managua**, 1200, US$2, 3½ hrs.

Chinandega and the Cosigüina Peninsula

The hot plains of Chinandega province were once bursting with thousands of orange trees and caressed by cool breezes. The cotton boom of the mid-20th century brought the local ecosystem to its knees, however, and now the dust and oppressive heat make it a less appealing prospect. That said, the province still boasts forested volcanoes, quiet Pacific beaches and estuary wildlife reserves and is worth a visit in the rainy season when daily showers moderate the sun's fury. The department's modest administrative capital, Chinandega, is a friendly, sleepy place, but no less searing than its surroundings. You'll want to limit your explorations of its colonial churches to the early morning or late afternoon; between 1000 and 1700 temperatures are scorching. ▸▸ For listings, see pages 229-232.

The city of Chinandega sits in the middle of the most extensive plain of volcanic soil in Nicaragua, which some believe to be the most fertile valley in all of Central America. Chinandega is the centre for thousands of hectares of farms that utilize the rich soil to grow sugarcane, bananas and peanuts among many other crops. It is also one of the hottest places in Central America, feeling like an irrigated desert for much of the year.

Arriving in Chinandega

Getting there Chinandega is accessed from a good paved highway north of León or another highway that crosses over from Choluteca, Honduras via El Guasaule. Bus services are frequent from Managua, León and the border.

Getting around Inside Chinandega taxis are cheap and friendly, as are the horse-drawn carriages that ply the hot streets. Walking is also a good way to get around if you can stand the infernal sun. Once outside the city, it is best to travel by 4WD, with the exception of El Viejo and Corinto, both of which have easy taxi access and regular bus service. ▶▶ *For further details, see Transport, page 232.*

Tourist information **INTUR** ① *opposite BAC, T2341-1935*, has a selection of flyers and helpful Spanish-speaking staff.

Background

When the Spanish first arrived in Chinandega, it was a large Nicaraguas (as in Rivas) indigenous settlement with a rather haughty chief (see El Viejo, below). The brutal first governor of Nicaragua, Pedrarias Dávila, found it to be so fertile that he commandeered all of it as one of his own plantations. It was the site of various meetings of Central American states in the 19th century as attempts were made to remake a federation, all of which failed. It used to be known as the 'city of oranges' for its principal crop at the turn of the 20th century, but cotton replaced the orange trees in the 1940s and the heat of the valley began to increase. For decades, cotton was the main export of Nicaragua, until a downturn in the international market prices, combined with exhausted soil, a war of insecticides with local insects and greedy middlemen, ruined the business. Now sugarcane and peanut millionaires utilize the still-fertile soil of the area and there are profitable shrimp farms in the outlying estuaries. Chinandega's patron saint is Santa Ana; her celebrations begin on 17 July and end on 26 July.

Places in Chinandega

Grungy and super-hot Chinandega will not win any beauty contests but the people who live here are very nice and welcoming and the city has two pretty churches that act as bookends for the city centre. At the east end of the centre is the **Iglesia El Calvario**, with its central bell tower and white-painted wood ceilings with chandeliers that are common in this region. The town's central avenue runs west from the church past one of three markets. Six blocks west of the church is the **Parque Central**, unusual for its north orientation to the church. The **Iglesia Santa Ana** is attractive with its typical Nicaraguan baroque design and slightly incongruous Wall Street pillars. Inside there are some gold leaf altars and faded frescos.

Around Chinandega → For listings, see pages 229-232.

Chichigalpa

Chichigalpa is a bustling agricultural centre that is best known for the country's oldest sugar mill, the **Ingenio San Antonio**. The French pirate William Dampier noted the factory's existence on his way to sack León in 1685. It is here that the sugar is processed for Nicaragua's superb rum, **Flor de Caña** (flower of the cane). West of the town, the road runs along palm-shaded railroad tracks that connect the village to the sugar mill. This rail line, with the Maribios volcanoes as a backdrop, is the now famous trademark of *Flor de Caña* and *Toña* beer. There are five trains a day each way from May to November, passengers are taken for US$0.25, or there is a bus for US$0.30. On the edge of Chichigalpa itself is the *Flor de Caña* distillery (www.flordecana.com), the maker of what many believe to be the finest rum in the world, aged up to 21 years and bottled in over 15 flavours. While the installations are not open to the public, the town's *alcaldía* (town hall) may be able to help arrange a special tour; alternatively, contact the distillery well in advance of your visit.

Corinto

From the roundabout at the entrance to Chinandega, it is 25 km southwest to the only deep-water port in Nicaragua. About 60% of the country's commerce passes through here and Asian cars seem to flow out of the town all year round. (Note that entry to the port is barred to all except those with a permit. There is immigration and customs at the port, but the only way in or out of here is on a container ship.) Corinto is the western terminus in a proposed transoceanic 'dry canal' railway system that would link ports on the Pacific and Caribbean coasts, although it seems doubtful the railway will ever materialize. The town itself is on a sandy island, **Punto Icaco**, connected to the mainland by bridges. Near the port are some tired but graceful old wooden buildings with verandas. The old train station is now a beautiful library. The most popular pastime in Corinto (besides drinking) seems to be riding around the central park at night on bicycles. There is also an unspoken contest to see how many passengers one can fit on a bicycle and still do laps of the park; six appears to be the record.

El Viejo to the Cosigüina Peninsula → For listings, see pages 229-232.

ⓘ *All routes on the Cosigüina Peninsula should be done in public bus or 4WD only. It is essential to buy purified water and, if driving, fill up with fuel before leaving El Viejo; there are no petrol stations on the peninsula.*

From El Viejo there is a scenic drive or bumpy bus ride to the Pacific Coast or on to the last of the Maribios volcanoes, **Volcán Cosigüina** (800 m) and the steamy and beautiful **Golfo de Fonseca** at Potosí. Another interesting trip northeast from El Viejo is to **Puerto Morazán**, which has some simple lodging and some of the friendliest people in Chinandega. The town is on the **Estero Real**, the biggest Pacific Basin nature reserve in Nicaragua at 55,000 ha, an endless labyrinth of estuaries and the biggest mangrove forest in Central America. You can hire a fisherman's boat in Puerto Morazán to explore.

El Viejo

Although it is officially a separate city, 5 km from Chinandega, the growth of El Viejo means that it is merging into a single sprawl with Chinandega. This slightly run-down but peaceful place is home to the patron saint of Nicaragua, an ancient church and a large indigenous community. This is one of the most important Catholic sites in a very Catholic country. The 70-cm-tall image in the church of the Immaculate Conception of the Virgin Mary, called **La Virgen del Trono**, is one of the most venerated images in all of Central America. La Virgen del Trono is said to have arrived in Nicaragua on the back of Alonso Zepeda, the brother of Saint Teresa of Spain, who gave the image to her brother before he left for the New World in the late 16th century. Legend has it that when Alonso Zepeda arrived at the indigenous settlement of Tezoatega, later named El Viejo, he grew tired and rested in the shade of a tree. When he left the comfort of the shade he noticed that the load on his back was much lighter. He wrestled the luggage off his back and found that the Virgen del Trono had somehow escaped his pack and, returning to the resting spot, he found her under the tree where he had taken shade. Alonso packed her once again and headed off, only to find down the road that his load was, once again, strangely lighter. He checked for the image of the Virgin and found that she was missing again. He returned to the same tree and found the Virgin once again in its shade. He decided it was here that she wished to stay and the **Basílica de la Inmaculada Concepción de la Virgen María** was built upon that very spot. She remains there today and La Virgen del Trono was officially named Patron Saint of Nicaragua in May of 2000. The church that houses her received the title of Basilica during Pope John Paul II's visit to El Viejo in February of 1996. The original structure dates from 1562 and it was refurbished in 1884.

One of the most famous religious events in Nicaragua is the **Lavada de la Plata** (cleaning the silver). This seemingly innocuous activity is an honour for the devout of the Virgen del Trono, who clean all the silver items associated with the ancient icon every 6 December, before her big day – the huge *Purísima* celebrations that start on 7 December all over Nicaragua in her name. Pilgrims arrive from all over the country and as far away as Guatemala to participate in the cleaning of the icons' silver, stowing away the cotton used to clean her relics for good luck.

Jiquilillo

West of El Viejo, there are some long empty beaches on the coast of the peninsula that are backed by towering cliffs further north. Despite the proximity to population centres like Chinandega and León, this region has a forgotten end-of-the-earth feel and is seen by relatively few foreigners. For those looking to escape the beaten path, this is one of the most accessible areas to get away from it all – if you can take the heat, which is year-round but more bearable from September to December.

The first section of the highway is paved and passes gigantic ranches, so big and wealthy that this part of the road is nicknamed '*Carretera Millonaria*'. Before the pavement ends there are two turnings that lead to the desolate beaches of the extreme northwest of Nicaragua's Pacific Coast. The first exit leads to **Aposentillo** and the second to **Jiquilillo**. Jiquilillo is a quiet, friendly, laid-back community that is now receiving a steady stream of backpackers. Facilities are still very basic, but travellers are reporting great things about the area, which also makes a convenient base for exploring the nature reserve of Padre Ramos.

Marina Puesta del Sol

Reached by another long, winding dirt and rock path off the highway is the resort of Marina Puesta del Sol, located between the sweeping coastline of Aposentillo and the tiny fishing village of **Los Aserradores** on a crystal bay. This very ambitious project has a world-class marina for the international yachting crowd sailing the Pacific, a heliport and pretty hotel rooms and suites with a view of the bay and northern Maribios range.

For those who don't arrive in their yacht, the resort offers one of the prettiest, cleanest beaches in Central America. Fifteen minutes from the hotel and marina structure on foot or five minutes by car or boat, the stretch of **Playa Aposentillo** opens out on the north side of the barrier islands. The resort has an unusual beach hut, a giant palm frond 'hat', as they call it, that shades a stone floor dining and bar area, next to an infinity swimming pool dug right out of the beach, particularly attractive in the bright morning light.

Reserva Natural Padre Ramos

North of the beautiful Playa Aposentillo is the coastal estuary reserve of Padre Ramos, named after a priest from El Viejo who drowned here. This is the most remote and pristine Pacific Coast estuary in Nicaragua, very wild and unknown to all but a handful of the local population. More than 150 species of birds have been recorded in Padre Ramos, as well as ocelots, iguanas, three species of sea turtle and crocodiles. The average temperature here is 29°C with an annual rainfall of 1.5 m. Access is best from the highway to Jiquilillo, as the ranger station is located at the southern part of the Pacific mouth that opens up to the estuary. It is possible to camp here and hire a boat and local guide through the park staff's contacts. If you wish to arrange something in advance contact **SELVA** ① *Comanejante del Area Protegida, Mercado Central, 6 c abajo, 1 c sur, ½ c abajo, El Viejo, T8884-9156, selvanic@ hotmail.com,* the NGO in charge of the reserve.

Volcán Cosigüina → *Altitude: 859 m.*

At the northwesternmost point of Nicaragua, this volcano has some unique wildlife and 13,168 ha of protected tropical dry forest. The forest at the base of the volcano is under threat from farming and burning, and the majority of this part of the peninsula is totally deforested with ground water found below 100 m at some points. The success of the reserve is that it is the last remaining Nicaragua Pacific Coast habitat for the **scarlet macaw**, the star billing in a reserve which has more than 77 bird species as well as 15 species of mammal including the spider monkey, not found anywhere else on the Pacific Coast of Nicaragua.

There are two climbs to the summit, **Sendero El Jovo**, which starts just west of Potosí, where there is very simple accommodation, and **Sendero La Guacamaya**, accessed via El Rosario on the north end of the cone and at the Ranger Station located south of El Rosario. It is possible to sleep in the station by prior arrangement with park managers who have an office in El Viejo, **Fundación LIDER** ① *Mercado Central, 3 c norte, lider@ibw. com.ni, Thu-Sun.* On the south side of the crater there is a charming lodge, **Hostal Hacienda Cosigüina**, that offers both hiking and 4WD trips to the summit and is by far the most comfortable option (see page 230). Other recommended operators include the **Ecodetur** tourism cooperative and NGO based in El Viejo, which offers a range of interesting Cosigüina packages (see page 232).

The view from the summit is why most hikers come to Cosigüina, a sweeping panorama that includes the islands in the Gulf of Fonseca and El Salvador to the north and Honduras to the east, not to mention the emerald lagoon 700 m below the summit of the crater, 1.5 km in diameter and occupying 90% of the bottom of the crater. The conditions for the crater lake were created by the biggest eruption recorded in Latin American history. During a series of eruptions from 20-26 January 1835, the volcano, which was close to 3000 m at the time, blew its top, sending ash as far away as Jamaica, 1300 km to the east, and Mexico, 1400 km to the north.

Border crossings: Nicaragua–Honduras

Guasaule

The distance between the border posts is 500 m.

Immigration Open 24 hours. To enter Nicaragua costs are US$12 plus a US$1 Alcaldía charge; to exit it is US$2 plus the US$1 immigration charge.

Transport Buses run every 30 minutes from the border to Chinandega, US$1. Express Guasaule–Managua, 1130, 1230, 1700, US$3.25, four hours.

Money exchange Money changers offer the same rates for córdobas to lempiras as on the Honduran side. Bancentro, next door to the immigration office, is recommended: good rates, no commission, and will accept a photocopy of passport if yours is being checked by immigration.

Nicaragua–El Salvador

Potosí

Nicaraguan immigration and customs Open 0800-1700, but closed for lunch. Exit is US$2 and Nicaraguan immigration entrance is US$12.

Transport Buses from Potosí–Chinandega, 0230, 0345, 0500, 0620, 0710, 1000, 1500, US$2, three hours. If trying to leave Nicaragua, there is a public boat every Friday 0800. Otherwise you will have to hire private transport, US$60-100.

Potosí

Arriving in Potosí is much like arriving at any other end-of-the-world place. Although it is only 60 km from Chinandega, the rocky road, searing heat and chocolate-brown waters of the prehistoric bay of **Golfo de Fonseca** are other-worldly. For those seeking to relax, there are thermal springs inland from the rusty hull of the shipwreck on the east side of the beach. From the solitary dock in Potosí, it is only 15 minutes by boat to a commercial shipping port in Honduras and two hours to La Unión in El Salvador. Public services to La Unión depart every Friday 0800, around US$15; otherwise you will have to negotiate a private fare with a boatman, US$60-100 – talk to **Hospedaje Brisas del Golfo** (see page 231) about your options. Entrance tax to El Salvador is around US$10. The **immigration office** ① *corner of Av General Cabañas and 7a Calle Pte, La Unión, T2604-4375, 0600-2200*, is next to the post office. You will need to stop here whether coming from or going to Nicaragua.

◉ Chinandega and the Cosigüina Peninsula listings

For sleeping and eating price codes and other relevant information, see pages 28-30.

◉ Where to stay

Chinandega *p225*

$$$ Los Volcanes, Km 129.5, Carretera a Chinandega, at southern entrance to city, T2341-1000. Very pleasant, comfortable rooms with private bath, hot water, a/c, cable TV. There's a smart restaurant and bar, service is professional.

$$ Campestre Terraza, Rotunda entranda a Chinandega, T2340-3058, hotelcampes terraza@yahoo.com. This smart new hotel at the entrance to town has comfortable rooms with a/c, cable TV, hot water and internet. There's a pool and private parking.

$$ Hotel Chinandegano, Esso El Calvario 1½ c arriba, T2341-4800, hotelchdgano@

turbonett.com.ni. Some rooms are windowless, but all are have cable TV, a/c, bath and hot water. Tidy, comfortable, polite and well looked after. Not bad.

$$ Hotel Cosigüina, Esquina de los Bancos, 50 m sur, T2341-3636, www.hotelcosiguina. com. 25 clean, presentable rooms with private bath, warm water, a/c, fridge, telephone, cable TV. Facilities include bar, restaurant and Wi-Fi. There's a restaurant-bar attached and prices include breakfast.

$$ Hotel Pacífico, Iglesia San Antonio, 1½ c sur, T2341-3841, www.hdelpacifico. com. Comfortable, friendly hotel with decent, modern rooms, all have a/c, cable TV, private bath, Wi-Fi and hot water. Breakfast included and laundry service available. Recommended.

$$ Hotel San José, Esquina de los Bancos, 2½ c norte, T2341-2723. Clean, comfortable and friendly. 10 small, plain rooms have private bath, a/c, cable TV and Wi-Fi. Breakfast included. Laundry service and internet available. Friendly and homely.

$$ Los Balcones, Esquina de los bancos, 75 vrs norte, T2341-8994, www.hotel balcones.com. Same owners as the reputable Los Balcones in León. 18 clean, comfortable rooms with cable TV, hot water and a/c. Wi-Fi and breakfast included. Good.

$ Casa Grande, Frente de Gallo mas Gallo, T2341-4283. Management is friendly, English speaking and talkative, but some of the beds are poor. Be sure to get a room with a/c, those without can be uncomfortably warm. Tours to the volcanoes, birdwatching, camping and accommodation at a nearby *finca* are offered. Laundry service available. Long-term stays a possibility.

$ Don Mario's, Enitel, 170 vrs norte, T2341-4054. Great-value rooms and friendly hosts at this homely lodging. Rooms have a/c, private bath and cable TV; cheaper with fan. Chill-out space and tables overlook the plant-filled courtyard and the kitchen is available if you wish. The owners speak excellent English, 'anything you want, just ask'. Relaxed family atmosphere and highly recommended.

$ Hotel California, Esso Calvario, 1 c arriba, ½ c sur, T2341-0936. Clean, simple, reasonably priced rooms that are a good economical deal for a single traveller. Services include private bath, cable TV and fan. Quiet and family-run.

Chichigalpa *p226*
$ Hotel La Vista, Alcaldía, 1 c arriba, 75 vrs norte, T2343-2035. 10 rooms with private bath, a/c, cable TV, includes breakfast, simple rooms with low ceiling, spacious, the best in town.

Corinto *p226*
$ Central, in front of Port buildings. Clean rooms with a/c.

$ Puerto Plata, Corinto, Parque Central, 175 m sur, T2342-2667. A/c available or cheaper with fan, private bath, good.

El Viejo *p226*
$ Casa de Huespedes, near central square. Basic rooms with shared bath.

Jiquilillo *p227*
$$ Monty's Surf Camp, where Bar Los Gemelos used to be, 150 m sur, T2341-8721, www.montysbeachlodge.com. This rustic surf lodge on the beach has a variety of private rooms, some with private bath, some without. Various 'stay and play' packages available, as well as surf school, kayaks, volcano tours and horse riding.

$ Rancho Esperanza, Jiquilillo, 200 m behind Disco ONVI, www.rancho-esperanza. com, T8879-1795. This friendly and relaxed 'low-impact' rancho has a good location on the beach. Various bamboo *cabañas* are available, as well as dorms for the thrifty. 3 meals a day cost US$10. Activities include surfing, kayaking, hiking and community tours. Volunteer opportunities are also available. Good reports.

$ Rancho Tranquilo, near Pulpería Tina Mata, Los Zorros, 10 mins from Jiquilillo, T8968-2290, www. rancho-tranquilo-nica. com. For people looking to escape the gringo trail, Rancho Tranquilo is a relaxed backpacker place with cabins and ultra-cheap dorms. There are also hammocks, vegetarian food and volunteer opportunities. Managed by Tina, a friendly lady from California and the only Gringa in the village.

Marina Puesta del Sol *p227*
$$$$ Marina Puesta del Sol, Los Aserradores, T8883-0781, www.marina puestadelsol.com. 19 suites overlooking the bay and marina, all spacious and modern with generic decor and patios. Some have jacuzzi, and the higher level suites have a great view of bay and volcanoes.

Volcán Consigüina *p228*
$$-$ Hostal Hacienda Cosigüina, Km 60, from Chinandega on highway to Potosí, T2341-2872, www.haciendacosiguina.com. One of Nicaragua's most charming rural lodges set on a 3500-acre hacienda where peanuts, corn, sesame seeds and cashews are grown, and cattle are raised. The farm was founded by a Basque migrant in 1775 and still remains under the same family's care, though the original ranch was destroyed in 1835 by the eruption of Volcán Cosigüina.
$ Ramsar Lodge, Cosigüina, T2315-4099, www.ramsarlodge.com, contact Va Pues agency to book in advance. Rustic cabins, owned and maintained by a group of Nicaraguan families who founded the tourism cooperative COSETUR after they lost their properties in Hurricane Mitch. Activities include swimming in hot springs, guided wetland hikes and ascents of Volcán Cosigüina. True community tourism and recommended.

Potosí *p229*
Contact Héctor for permission to stay in the fishing cooperative (**$**). The fishermen are friendly. You can sling your hammock at the *comedor* 150 m past immigration for US$1.
$ Hospedaje Brisas del Golfo, next to the dock. A row of clean, if stark, concrete block rooms with fan inside, toilet and bath outside.

🍴 Restaurants

Chinandega *p225*
$$ Buenos Aires, Plaza Colonial, 2½ c sur. A good place for an evening meal. This jaunty, brightly coloured restaurant serves meat, chicken and fish dishes under a thatched palapa roof. Specialities include a range of enchiladas, beef steaks and breaded shrimp dishes. Not bad.
$$ Corona de Oro, Iglesia San Antonio, 1½ c arriba, T341-2539. Chinese food with flavour. The chicken curry and shrimp skewers are especially tasty. Often recommended by locals.
$$ El Paraíso, Plaza Colonial, 3 c arriba, on the Guasule highway. A large outdoor restaurant with a vast palapa roof. New and professional, serving the usual meat, chicken and fish fare. A favourite of lunchtime businessmen and moneyed Nicaraguans.
$$-$ El Antiguo, Esso Calvario 1½ c arriba. A well-established and reasonably economical haunt that has good wooden furniture and lunchtime specials.
$ El Mondongazo, south side of Colegio San Luis, T341-4255. Traditional Nicaraguan foods like *sopa mondongo* (tripe soup), beef, chicken and meatball soup.
$ El Refugio, Esso, El Calvario, ½ c sur, T341-0834. Great beef specialities, try the breaded tongue.
$ La Parrillada, Palí, 1½ sur. Economical buffet fare including roast chicken, breaded shrimp, *carne a la plancha*, *gallo pinto* and other national staples.
$ Las Tejitas, Parque Central, 7 c arriba. Cheap and cheerful. They serve buffet food, grilled meats and *comida típica*. Very popular and always packed out. A Chinandega institution.
$ Mi Casita, esquina de los bancos, 1 c arriba. Orange-themed dining hall that serves economical buffet fare. Clean, cheap, cheerful and friendly.

Bakeries and juice bars
Aloha Smoothies, Iglesia Calvario, costado sur. Cheery, Hawaiian-themed juice bar where you can get a fruity dose of vitamins.

Panadería Marella, Shell, 1 c arriba. Sweet rolls, bread and coffee.

Chichigalpa *p226*
$$-$ Rancho Típico, Alcaldía, 3½ c sur, T343-1030. Good beef dishes, seafood, traditional Nicaraguan food.

Corinto *p226*
$ El Español, in Corinto, puente Paso Caballos, 100 vrs abajo, T8851-0677, patipaso@yahoo.com. Good seafood restaurant, also beef, and other meats, pleasant outdoor seating with view of an estuary canal. They are also building hotel rooms planned to open soon. Recommended.

El Viejo *p226*
$$-$ Tezoatega, El Viejo, Basílica 1½ c norte, T2344-2436. Daily 1100-2200. Chicken and beef, good value, outdoor seating, friendly.

Potosí *p229*
$ Bar y Restaurante Gilmari. Fried chicken, steak, fish soup. If you order fish the owner will walk down to the dock, buy one and cook it, usually *pargo* (snapper). Most dishes US$2-3. Pitcher of beer is US$1.75.

⚙ Activities and tours

El Viejo *p226*
Tour operators
Ecodetur, IRO INATEC, 1 c norte, 1 c abajo, T2344-2381, cosiguinatour@gmail.com. Ecotouristic NGO and co-op with knowledgeable local guides offering interesting packages that include hikes to the summit of Cosigüina, community visits, tours of mangrove forests and hot springs.

⊖ Transport

Chinandega *p225*
Bus
Most buses leave from the new market at southeast edge of town. To **Corinto**, every 20 mins, 0430-1800, US$0.40, 30 mins. To

Somotillo, every 3 hrs, 0900-1500, US$2, 2 hrs. To **Guasaule**, every 2 hrs, 0400-1700, US$2, 2 hrs. To **Managua**, every 30 mins, 0430-1700, US$2.50, 3 hrs. To **León**, every 1 mins, 0430-1800, US$1, 1 hr. Buses for **Potosí**, **El Viejo**, Jiquilillo and **Puerto Morazán** leave from the Santa Ana Mercadito northwest of town every 15-40 mins, 0730-1600. A bus links Terminal, Mercado and Mercadito.

   International buses Contact individual agencies for schedules and costs; Ticabus, Policía Nacional 170 vrs al sur, T2341-8596, www.ticabus.com. Transnica, opposite Colegio Bethelemitas on the Carretera Panamericana, next to Hotel Maribios, T8918-3096, www.transnica.com. Nica Expresso, opposite Colegio Bethelemitas, next to the Costa Rican consulate, T2340-1463, www.nicaexpresso.com.ni.

Car hire
There are several companies, including: Toyota Rent a Car, T2341-2303, www.toyota rentacar.com; and Budget, Hotel Cosigüina, T2341-1663, www.budget.com.ni.

Taxi
Taxis are very cheap around Chinandega, with fares of US$0.50 for short trips. Longer trips or night-time service can run to US$1.25. Drivers are very friendly and helpful.

Chichigalpa *p226*
Buses to **León** from 0500-1700, every 11 mins, US$0.70, US$1.

❶ Directory

Chinandega *p225*
Banks For cash on Visa cards and all TCs use BAC, Texaco Guadalupe, 2 c norte, T2341-0078. **Fire** T2341-3221. **Hospital** T2341-4902. **Internet** Across the street from Hotel Casa Grande at IBW or at Hotel Cosigüina. **Police** T2341-3456. **Post** Correos de Nicaragua BANIC, 125 m norte, T2341-0407. **Red Cross** T2341-3132. **Telephone** Enitel, Central Plaza, 1 c arriba, 25 vrs norte, T2341-0002.

Contents

Footprint features

Border crossings

Northern Highlands

At a glance

◉ **Getting around** Most destinations are served by local buses but the rugged terrain can make travel slow going, especially in the wet season. For very remote locations, a 4WD vehicle may be necessary.
◷ **Time required** 7-10 days.
☼ **Weather** Mar-May is dry, hot and dusty in many parts of the Northern Highlands. The rainy season is cooler and dramatically greener. Evenings can be chilly in Jinotega at all times.
✖ **When not to go** Although the rainy season is generally a better time to visit, many areas are prone to flooding Sep-Nov, so it's worth checking conditions before setting out. The Somoto Canyon cannot be visited during the rains.

N

10 km
10 miles

HONDURAS

JINOTEG

Tolecacinte

Jalapa

NUEVA SEGOVIA

Wamblán

Wambuca   El Plantel   Valle
Congjas

Las Manos

Santa Clara

Murra

Plan de Grama

Macuelizo   Moxonte

Susucayan

6 Ciudad
Antigua

Apají   Ocotal

Wiwilí

San José
de Bocay

Grand
Canyon of   Totogalpa
Somoto

Yalagüina   MADRIZ

5   Somoto

El Espino   Palacagüina

Río Coco

El Cuá

Pueblo
Nuevo   Valle Ducali

Condega

Piedra Larga

San Francisco
del Norte   San Juan
de Limay   San Rafael
del Norte   El Jaguar Cloud
Forest Reserve

La Sirena   Lago de
Apandá

4
Reserva
Natural
Miraflor   La Dalia

MATAGALPA

3   Estelí   Jinotega   2   Reserva
Natural Arenál

San Roque   Río Tuma

Achuapa   Reserva Natural Meseta
El Salto de   Tisey-Estanzuela
Estanzuela   Selva Negra
Cloud Forest
Reserve   El Tuma

Las Lajitas

San Nicolás   La Trinidad   1   Esperanza Verde/Yucul

Disparate
de Potter

CHINANDEGA   La Garita   Pancasár

Villa   San Isidro   Matagalpa   La Rosa
Nueva   El Sauce   Chagüitillo   San Ramón

La Bacinica   Sébaco   San Pablo   Matiguás

Santa Rosa   El Caracal
del Peñon

LEON   La Cruz de   Muy Muy
la India   Ciudad Darío   Terrabona   Pineda   Tierra Azul

Río Grande de Matagalpa   Esquipulas   Río de
Larreynaga   La Calle Real   Valle El   Janeiro   Santa
de Tolape   Orégano   El Portó
Vol   San   Laguna   San José de   BOAC
Santa   Jacinto   Francisco   Moyud   El Cacao   las Remates   El Paraíso
Clara   Libre   Puertas   Santa Lucía
Vol El Hoyo   Viejas   El Guanacaste   Boaco   Las Lajas
Vol   (1001m)   San
Cerro Negro   El Paraíso   Antonio   San   Teustepe   Camoap
Vol Momotombo   Agustín   Agua   El Zapote
Puerto   (1260m)   Hacienda   Caliente
Momotombo   El Cardón   San Jacinto   Espíritu Sant
León Viejo   Lago de   Las
Vol Momotombito   Managua   Banderas   El Alto
La Esperanza   (Xolotlán)   San Benito   MANAGUA
El Tempate   Nagarote   Chiltepe   San Lorenzo
Salinas   Peninsula   Belén   Asunció
Grandes   Mateare   Xiloá Lagoon   Tipitapa
MANAGUA

Nicaragua's ruggedly beautiful northern mountains and valleys have staged much of the history that has given the country its dubious international reputation. It was here that indigenous cultures attacked Spanish mining operations in the 16th century and, in the 19th century, fought confiscation of communal lands that were to go to German immigrants for coffee growing. This is where nationalist Sandino fought the US Marines' occupation of Nicaragua from 1927 to 1933 and where the rebel Sandinistas launched their first attacks against the Somoza administration in the 1960s. Then, in the 1980s, the Contras waged war against the Sandinista Government in these mountains.

Today, most visitors would be hard pressed to see where all this aggression came from, or that it existed at all. Most of the northern ranges and plains are full of sleepy villages with ancient churches, rustic cowboys and smiling children. This is where the soil and the homes blend into a single palette: the red-brown clay earth reflected in the brown adobe walls and red-tile roofs. Nothing is rushed here and many of the region's villages are evidence that time travel is indeed possible, with the 21st century in no danger of showing itself around here anytime soon, at least not until the 20th century arrives.

In addition to the area's intense history, rustic beauty and kind population, there are precious cloud forest reserves, pine forests and interesting crafts being made using techniques dating back many centuries. The climate is cooler than the rest of the country with elevations rising to 2000 m. As the searing heat of the Pacific Basin gives way to the misty northern villages, you will see people actually wearing sweaters.

Managua to Matagalpa

The Pan-American Highway leaves Managua just north of the international airport, runs north into Nicaragua's most beautiful non-volcanic mountains and continues all the way to Honduras. There are two interesting routes, one that leads to border crossings through historic villages and another that heads off east near Sébaco to Matagalpa, the heart of coffee-growing country. ▶▶ *For listings, see pages 243-247.*

North of Managua → *For listings, see pages 243-247.*

Hacienda San Jacinto

After Tipitapa, at Km 35 of the Pan-American Highway, is the turning for the cattle ranching departments of Boaco and Chontales (see page 75). Soon after, at Km 39.5 is the short road that leads to the historic ranch of San Jacinto, where William Walker lost a critical battle against rebel Nicaraguan forces from Matagalpa in 1856. The battle is remembered every year on 14 September as a national holiday. The ranch is in a pleasant valley and open as a **museum** ① *T2222-4820, Tue-Sun 0800-1500, though it may be hard to find the caretaker on Sun, US$2*, with objects from the celebrated battle on display.

Laguna Moyuá

At Km 57 the remains of a 1000-year-old lake can be seen, in the form of three lagoons: **Las Playitas**, **Moyuá** and **Tecomapa**, though from the highway they appear to be one calm body of water. During the dry season they recede and disappear from view of the highway, but in the rainy season they form a beautiful contrast to the surrounding dry hills and are full of sandpipers, egrets and ducks. Laguna Moyuá has two islands that show signs of the pre-Columbian populations that inhabited this area and the ruins of what could have been a temple. The lagoons are most famous for their lovely *guapote* and *mojarra* fish, which are offered for sale by children along the roadside. Just north of the fruit stands on the waterfront are several cheap restaurants with fresh *guapote* fish fried daily; worth a stop if you're in a private vehicle.

Ciudad Darío

Near Km 90, on the left-hand side, is the exit for the long three-bridge entrance to Ciudad Darío, a sleepy cowboy settlement set on a hill over the Río Grande de Matagalpa. This is the first of many forgotten villages that dot the northern landscape but one that has found some fame due to a small adobe corner house where the country's national hero, **Rubén Darío** (see page 318), was born in January 1867. Living in Honduras, Rubén's mother was fed up with her husband's abusive ways and decided to return to León to have her child. She only made it as far as her sister's house in the village (then called Metapa), gave birth to Rubén, rested for 40 days and then continued on to León where Darío would receive the education that would help him change Spanish poetry and Nicaragua forever. Today the house is the museum **Casa Natal de Rubén Darío** ① *1 block east, 2 blocks north of bus station, T2776-3846, Tue-Sun 0900-1630, US$2*, where you can see the bed he was born on, the china set that was used to wash his mother and a 19th-century kitchen of the kind that is still in use in much of the countryside today.

A local taxi can take you to the trailhead for an hour's hike to the summit of **Cerro de la Cruz** which has a panoramic view of the city, surrounded by hills and rivers. Legend

Community tourism around Matagalpa

The coffee-rich land around Matagalpa is home to several fascinating agricultural co-operatives. The **Unión de Cooperativas Agropecuarias (UCA) San Ramón** is one of the largest and best organized, providing tours, activities and stays in four different communities. **La Pita**, 17 km from Matagalpa, offers rousing guided hikes in the mountains, including a visit to an old gold mine. You can meet a co-operative of women who create paper from organic waste, ride horses, and participate in the coffee production process. The community of **La Corona** has two refreshing waterfalls: Yasika and Posa Bruja. They offer courses in natural medicine for US$40 per group, tours of the area, and captivating recitals of their indigenous legends. **La Reina**, 18.5 km from Matagalpa, is rich in wildlife and offers guided ecological hikes and horse riding. Two co-operatives comprise the community **El Roblar**: El Privilegio and Daniel Téllez Paz. They're very proud of their organic coffee and provide explanations of the process, great guided hikes with panoramic views, horse riding and lessons in natural medicine. All four communities offer stays with families for US$12 per person per night including breakfast; additionally, La Corona and La Pita have hostels. Meals cost around US$4.50 in all communities, guided hikes are generally US$15 per group.

UCA San Ramón is located opposite the Parque Municipal in San Ramón, T2772-5247, www.agroecoturismorural.com.

as it that this mountain was growing out of control, skywards, at an alarming rate, so a local Franciscan monk hiked to the top and planted a cross on the summit and put an end to the mountain's insolence. No-one can agree how many years it has been there, but every 3 May there is a pilgrimage to the cross with a Mass held at the summit. The patron saint, **San Pedro**, is celebrated on 29 July and from 8 to 14 January there are festivities commemorating the birth of Rubén Darío.

Sébaco

Further north along the Pan-American Highway is the dry lakebed valley and agricultural centre of Sébaco. It is a hot and unattractive town but it has Nicaragua's most colourful vegetables in its **market**. The Pan-American Highway forks here and the market is inside the fork in the highway. The town is the agricultural crossroads of the Northern Highlands and has been called the capital of onions, as this is where Nicaragua's finest are grown, along with huge quantities of rice and sorghum. Also in the market are deep purple beets and bright orange carrots begging to be photographed. Sébaco also has a historic church with a tiny pre-Columbian and colonial-period museum inside. To reach the historic **Vieja Iglesia de Sébaco** turn right at the first entrance to the highway after crossing the bridge, go to the back of the new church and head all the way to the top of the hill and turn right.

Chagüitillo

From the fork at Sébaco, the highway to the right is the Carretera a Matagalpa which rises gradually past the charming village of Chagüitillo at Km 107, home to some important pre-Columbian sites with petroglyphs and the **Museo Precolombino de Chagüitillo** ① T8659-7567, www.mpch.bravehost.com, Mon-Sat 0800-1700, US$0.60. The museum is a simple collection of petroglyphs set against a mural painting depicting pre-Conquest life. There is a mountain stream area called **Salto El Mico**, 1.5 km from the town centre, which has an impressive array of petroglyphs, many depicting monkeys, but also one that locals claim to be an Aztec calendar. Look for a guide in the museum or with local children.

Matagalpa → *For listings, see pages 243-247.*

ⓘ *Population 98,000. Altitude 682 m.*

Set in a broad valley circled by green mountains, including the handsome Cerro de Apante at 1442 m, Matagalpa appears quite attractive at a distance, though less so up close. This important and bustling café-capital of Nicaragua has a vaguely claustrophobic feel to it. The city streets are narrow, filled with cars and trucks, and a circular sprawl of new homes climb the surrounding hills, threaten to enclose the city in concrete. When it rains, the deforested hills that wrap Matagalpa drain into the quickly overflowing Río Grande de Matagalpa and flood through its barrios. However, Matagalpa sells some interesting crafts in local stores and is an excellent jumping-off point for visiting beautiful scenery and some of the world's best coffee farms.

Arriving in Matagalpa

Getting there and around There are frequent buses from Managua's Mercado Mayoreo with regular express services, and lots of buses from Jinotega. Infrequent but direct services exist from Masaya, León and Chinandega and more regular routes from Estelí. Alternatively, get off at Sébaco on any bus passing on the Pan-American Highway and change to a bus heading north to Matagalpa. There are plenty of inexpensive taxis around town. They can also offer transfers to Selva Negra and San Ramón. The centre of town is easy to walk around and safe, but the barrios should not be visited on foot. There are two main streets that run to and from the attractive cathedral south to the little Parque Darío where it is a bit more peaceful. Along these streets are most of the city's sleeping, dining and entertainment options. The rest of this hilly city is a maze of mixed streets of pavement and mud. ➽ *For further details, see Transport, page 246.*

Tourist information INTUR ⓘ *Banco Citi, 1 c sur, T2772-7060*, has limited, patchy details on local attractions. **Matagalpa tours** ⓘ *Banpro, ½ c arriba, T2772-0108, www.matagalpa tours.com*, are an excellent source of information, with a thorough knowledge of the city and the surrounding mountains; they speak Dutch and English. You could also try **CIPTURMAT** in the coffee museum.

Background

Matagalpa is the most famous mountain town in Nicaragua. It is in the heart of coffee country, an industry that was started in the 1870s by German and other European immigrants. In 1881, Matagalpa was the scene of the last significant indigenous rebellion which was sparked by a combination of factors: forced labour laying telegraph lines between Managua and Matagalpa; attempts to ban *chicha* (fermented corn liquor); and the expulsion by the government of the Jesuits, much loved by the locals, who willingly provided free labour for the construction of Matagalpa's cathedral. The rebellion failed and the government troops' revenge was brutal, moving Matagalpa's indigenous community (which is still quite large) forever to the background in the region's affairs. The German influence in Matagalpa continued until the beginning of the First World War, when the government confiscated German-owned coffee farms but the Germans returned after the war and re-established themselves. The farms were confiscated again in 1941 when

Nicaragua declared war on Germany. Many Germans did not return after the end of that war. During the Contra War, Matagalpa was often just behind the front line of battle and many of the residents of the city fought on both sides of the conflict.

The city has prospered in recent years, thanks not only to increased coffee production, but also the fact that it boasts a high percentage of high-quality shade-grown coffee

Matagalpa

N

100 metres
100 yards

Where to stay 🛏
Apante **10**
Bermúdez **9**
Campestre Barcelona **12**
Don Guillermo **3**
El Sueño de la Campana **13**
Finca Esperanza Verde **6**
Fountain Blue **14**
Hospedaje Mirador **4**
Ideal **15**
La Buena Onda **1**
La Profe **11**
La Siesta **2**
Lomas de San Thomás **7**
San José **5**
Selva Negra **8**

Restaurants 🍴
Artesanos Café-Bar **15**
Barrista **1**
Buffet Maná del Cielo **10**
Cafetería Don Chaco **5**
Centro Girasol **7**
El Cafeto **3**
El Mexicano **8**
El Pullazo **2**
Hamburlooca **9**
La Pradera **11**
La Vita é Bella **6**
Pesca Mar **12**
Pique's **13**
Simo's **4**

Bars & clubs 🍸
Madre Tierra **16**
Tequila's **14**

and has developed organic growing practices which bring the highest prices. In many respects, Matagalpa is enjoying a phase of much-needed gentrification with smart new coffee houses, youth hostels and hotels springing up all over town. Still, the economic rollercoaster of international coffee prices always carries a threat.

Places in Matagalpa

Although the main attraction of Matagalpa is the sublime beauty that lies just outside it, the **Catedral de San Pedro de Matagalpa** (1897) is worth a visit and there are two other city churches that are pleasant: the late 19th-century **Templo de San José de Laborio** in front of the Parque Darío and the primitive Nicaraguan baroque **Iglesia de Molagüina**, which is the oldest church in Matagalpa, believed to date from 1751. Adjacent to the Parque Central is the impressive statue for the **Centro Cultural de los Héroes y Mártires**, which occasionally hosts events. East of Parque Darío is the **Museo Casa Cuna Carlos Fonseca** ① *Parque Darío, 1 c arriba, T2772-2932, Mon-Fri 0830-1200 and 1400-1730*, a memorial to the principal intellectual and founder of the FSLN, who was shot by the National Guard less than three years before the success of the Revolution. He lived here as a young boy and the museum houses pictures, writings, stories and objects, like the famous glasses, of this national hero. Contributions are welcome for the maintenance of this old house. If closed, ask next door at the tyre repair workshop.

The city and region is famous for its beautiful *cerámica negra* (black pottery), and it is possible to visit one of the city's ceramic co-operatives. In addition, there are indigenous fabric co-operatives, which make attractive purses, backpacks and much more. The **Coffee Museum** ① *on the main avenue, Parque Morazán, 1½ c sur, T2772-0587, Mon-Fri 0800-1730, Sat 0800-1200*, houses the town's **cultural centre**, offering music and painting classes and displays on the history of local coffee production. Exhibits include photographs and antique objects used in the early days of coffee production in Matagalpa.

Around Matagalpa → *For listings, see pages 243-247.*

Apante Hill

Located within the **Reserva Apante** a few kilometres southeast of Matagalpa, this hill offers commanding views of Matagalpa and the surrounding countryside. It takes two hours to reach the summit on the main trail. There is another trail that takes five hours and another that takes seven hours, concluding in the village of San Ramón. The trails are hard to find and it is recommended that you hire a guide. A guide will be able to lead you to other attractions within the reserve, like streams and waterfalls.

Esperanza Verde

① *Office in San Ramón, Iglesia Católica, 1½ c arriba, T2772-5003, www.fincaesperanzaverde. org. Buses run to Yucul from Matagalpa's north terminal and there are signs for the reserve from San Ramón.*

East of Matagalpa is the largely indigenous town of **San Ramón** founded by a friar from León, José Ramón de Jesús María, in 1800. Legend has it that the village's small church is built on a thick vein of gold, which almost resulted in the demolition of the church until the villagers campaigned to prevent its destruction.

Beyond San Ramón is **Yucul**, home to a nature reserve designated a *Reserva de Recursos Genéticos*. The pine forest shelters a rare species (*Pino spatula sp tecunmanii*) that reportedly has the finest seeds of its kind on the American continent. What has made

Yucul famous in recent years, however, is the well managed ecolodge and private nature reserve of **Esperanza Verde**. There are few finer places in Nicaragua for birdwatching and enjoying the nature of the northern mountains. The award-winning reserve has a butterfly breeding project, organic shade-grown coffee cultivation, hiking trails and great views to the mountains of the region. The forest has howler monkeys, sloths and more than 150 species of bird, plus numerous orchids and medicinal plants. The reserve came to international attention in 2004, winning a *Smithsonian Magazine* award as the best sustainable new ecolodge project in the world. The lodge offers handsome cabins and double rooms for sleeping in, yoga classes, meals and Spanish-speaking guides. A book detailing the reserve's hiking trails is available for US$7.

Reserva Silvestre Selva Negra

① At Km 139.5 on the Carretera a Jinotega, T2772-3883, www.selvanegra.com, an old Somoza-era tank that was destroyed by the rebels serves as an entrance sign to the coffee hacienda and reserve. Any bus heading towards Jinotega will drop you off at the entrance, from where it is a 1.5-km walk to the hotel; or take a taxi from Matagalpa. A range of tours are offered, US$12-20; discount for guests.

The highway rises steeply out of Matagalpa giving panoramic views of the city and the surrounding deforestation. About 7 km beyond Matagalpa, the scenery changes dramatically, with pine trees and oaks draped in bromeliads, in a forest that is green year-round. Eddy and Mausy Kuhl bought this 1470-acre coffee hacienda in 1974 and promptly turned half of it into forest reserve, making them Nicaraguan pioneers in the burgeoning practice of setting aside private nature reserves. The 30 creeks within the reserve have benefited greatly from the reforestation of its higher slopes, which were once used for coffee production. Birdwatching is excellent around the property (but best around the shaded coffee plantation), with more than 200 species documented so far, including trogons, parrots, flycatchers and the elusive but resplendent quetzal. The property has 14 well-marked paths and the hotel cabins are surrounded by forest and flowers; many even have flowers growing out of their roofs.

What makes Selva Negra really special, however, is the way the hacienda's coffee, vegetable, flower and animal farming is organized and operated. The hacienda is a model for sustainability: everything from coffee husks to chicken blood is recycled. Coffee-processing wastewater (a serious pollutant in coffee-growing regions) is run into two-step pressurizing tanks that create methane or 'bio-gas', which is then used on the farm for cooking and other chores. As many as 250 full-time employees work in flower production, with 10 species grown in greenhouses, all vegetables served at the hotel restaurant are grown organically on the farm and meat served at the hotel is also locally raised.

El Disparate de Potter

Past Selva Negra the forest becomes even thicker as the road leads past lush forest and highland ranches, coffee plantations and flower farms. At Km 143 there is a school and then the **Restaurante El Disparate de Potter** (see page 245). Mr Charles Potter, an eccentric English gentleman used to own the land here and had the idea of blowing a hole in the mountain to let the road pass through to Jinotega – you can now climb up the part of the mountain that is left for a good view of the Momotombo and San Cristóbal volcanoes. The border between the provinces of Matagalpa and Jinotega is located here, as well as access to the small but precious Reserva Natural Cerro Arenal (see below). The road then passes appetizing fruit and vegetable stands, a great place to stop and enjoy the fresh mountain air, before looping downwards into the broad valley of Jinotega.

Café Nicaragüense: from German to gourmet

Large-scale coffee growing in Nicaragua is directly tied to German immigration, promoted by 19th-century Nicaraguan governments that offered 500 *manzanas* (350 ha) of land to any investor who would plant 25,000 coffee trees, bringing migrant planters from Germany, US, England, France and Italy.

The pioneer of Nicaragua coffee planting was Ludwing Elster, originally from Hanover, and his wife Katharine Braun, from Baden Baden who settled in Matagalpa in 1852. In 1875, Wilhelm Jericho arrived and founded the Hacienda Las Lajas, promising to lure 20 more German families to Nicaragua. When the Nicaraguan government started

offering the 500 *manzanas* free to inspire production, more than 200 foreign families settled and began growing coffee in Matagalpa and neighbouring Jinotega.

Today Nicaraguan coffee is planted on more than 160,000 *manzanas* by 30,000 different farms with country-leader Jinotega producing around 680,673 100-pound bags of coffee a year, followed by Matagalpa at 624,818 bags. The country's best coffee export customers are the USA, Spain, Belgium and France.

The push for high-quality organic shade coffee has lifted Nicaragua to sixth place in the world in gourmet coffee production, with an annual output of organic coffee three times greater than that of Costa Rica.

Reserva Natural Cerro Arenal

ⓘ *At Km 145.5 on the Carretera a Jinotega. Reputable local guides include Pablo Ubeda and his brother Nico, who are very familiar with the forest. They live near the entrance to the reserve from the highway. You could also telephone the Matagalpa office of MARENA, T2772-3926, for their recommendations.*

This is one of the finest cloud forest reserves in Nicaragua that can be accessed by a paved road. The reserve protects **Cerro Picacho** (1650 m) and its surrounding forest which is over 1400 m. There are numerous giant balsa trees, known as *mojagua* (*Heliocarpus appendiculatus*), the favoured nesting sites for the resplendent quetzal, and the forest is also home to giant oak trees, up to 12 m in circumference and 40 m tall, as well as many strangler figs, tree ferns, bromeliads, orchids, mosses, bamboo and even arboreal cacti. The cloud forest has an abundance of the endangered resplendent quetzal (*Pharomachrus mocinno*), considered sacred by the Maya and agreed by all to be one of the most beautiful birds in the world, and the **Sendero Los Quetzales** is one of the best places in Nicaragua to spot it. The path passes plenty of native avocado (*Aguacate canelo*), one of the bird's favourite snacks (the fruit is ripe between March and May). The quetzal shares the forest with 190 documented species, including Amazon parrot, toucans, emerald toucanets, other trogons and numerous colourful hummingbirds, such as the violet sawbrewing hummingbird (*Campylopterus hemileucurus*). The three-wattled bellbird's distinctive song can often be heard, too. There are also 140 documented species of butterfly here, such as the spectacular purple-blue morpho and the almost-invisible, transparent-winged gossamer. Howler monkeys, agoutis and sloths are reasonably common.

For sleeping and eating price codes and other relevant information, see pages 28-30.

⊖ Where to stay

Ciudad Darío *p236*
$ Casa Agricultor, bus station, 1½ c norte, T2776-2379. Simple, dark rooms; 3 with bath, 5 without, all have a fan and there's secure parking. The owner, Emma López, is hospitable and friendly.

Sébaco *p237*
$ El Valle, on the highway 1.5 km south of town, T2775-2209. Small, simple rooms with fans and TV at this quiet, motel-style place on the highway. Some have a/c.

Matagalpa *p238, map p239*
$$ Don Guillermo, Enitel, 25 vrs oeste, T2772-3182. A new, tastefully attired hotel with 7 big, clean, comfortable, good-value rooms. Each has cable TV, hot water and Wi-Fi. Breakfast is included and there's a night guard on the door. Recommended.
$$ Hotel Campestre Barcelona, Prolacsa 800 m norte, T2772-2439, hotelbarcelonacampestre.com. 22 rooms with private bath, a/c, cable TV, secure parking. North of Matagalpa, quiet with nice views and swimming pool.
$$ Lomas de San Thomás, Escuela Guanuca 400 m este, T2772-4189, snthomas2006@ yahoo.com. The most luxurious hotel in the region. 26 spacious rooms have private bath and hot water, cable TV, telephone, Wi-Fi and minibar. Attractive grounds and great views, but not very central. Good reports.
$ Bermúdez, Parque Darío, 2 c abajo, T2772-6744. Most rooms at this friendly and lightly dilapidated hotel are run-down, some aren't too bad. Dirt cheap for a single traveller too.
$ El Sueño de la Campana, contiguo al Instituto de San Ramón, outside Matagalpa in the community of San Ramón. This rural farm has a range of single and double rooms and

enjoys expansive views of the countryside. Guests can hike or participate in voluntary activities that help the local community.
$ Hospedaje Mirador, Parque Darío, 1½ c abajo, T2772-4084. 27 simple, bare-bones rooms around a courtyard, all have shared bath and no fan. Ramshackle and ultra basic, but the price can't be beaten.
$ Hotel Apante, west side of Parque Darío, T2772-6890. 14 simple rooms with private bath, hot water and cable TV. The management's friendly, there's Wi-Fi and free water and coffee 24 hrs. OK.
$ Hotel Fountain Blue, catedral, 3 c al norte, 2 c oeste, T2772-2733. Try the side door if no one answers the bell. Comfortable rooms with private bath, cable TV, hot water and fan; cheaper with shared bath. A simple breakfast of coffee and bread is included. There's also parking, Wi-Fi and laundry service.
$ Hotel Ideal, catedral, 2 c al norte, 1 c oeste, T2772-2483, hotelidealmat@yahoo.es. A range of cheap rooms, the very cheapest with fan and shared bath, the most expensive with a/c, cable TV and private bath. There's also a bar and conference centre. OK.
$ Hotel La Profe, Shell el Progreso, 20 vrs norte, T2772-2506. A pleasant, family-run place. Simple, tidy rooms have cable TV, fan, private bath and hot water (cheaper with shared bath). Not bad.
$ Hotel La Siesta, Texaco, 1½ c oeste, T2772-2476. A clean, tidy, friendly hotel. Rooms have hot water, cable TV and fan. Cheaper with shared bath. There an international call centre next door with internet facilities.
$ Hotel San José, behind Iglesia San José, T2772-2544, hotelsnjose2009@yahoo.es. 12 comfortable, clean rooms with able TV, fan and hot water (**$$** with a/c). On the small side but not bad. There's a pleasant garden and services include Wi-Fi, laundry and parking.
$ La Buena Onda, Brigadista, 2½ c este, T2772-2135, www.hostelmatagalpa.com. This great new hostel has a range of clean, comfortable dorms, each with private bath.

There are also some spacious private rooms, a library, TV room, DVDs, free coffee, laundry service and a good restaurant attached (see below). For longer-term stays there's an apartment available at US$400 per month. Friendly and helpful with good connections to Matagalpa Tours (page 246). Recommended.

Esperanza Verde p240
$$ Finca Esperanza Verde, office in San Ramón, Iglesia Católica, 1½ c este, T2772-5003, www.fincaesperanzaverde.org. This famous ecolodge has a range of handsome wood and brick cabins with covered patios, solar power, private bath and bunk beds. Various packages are available; consult the website for more. There's also camping at US$6 per person. See also page 240.

Selva Negra Cloud Forest Reserve p241
$$$-$$ Selva Negra, T2772-3883, www.selvanegra.com. A range of rooms (**$$**), and Germanic cottages (**$$$**) on the edge of the rainforest. Large 4-person units for families too (**$$$$**). See also page 241.

🍴 Restaurants

Ciudad Darío p236
$ El Buen Gusto, bus station, 3½ c norte. This clean *comedor* serves home-cooked Nicaraguan fare and some good-looking fairy cakes.
$ El Clementino, Museo, 1 c norte, 10 vrs este. Small, simple *comedor* serving meat, chicken or whatever the señora has prepared. Look out for the chattering parrots.

Sébaco p237
$$ El Sesteo, del BDF, 1½ c abajo. Clean, wonderful a/c and well-staffed. Their menu offers a healthy selection of steaks, chicken, soup and shrimp dishes.
$$ Los Gemelos, Monumento de la Virgen, 1½ c abajo. Regular buffets and a variety of meat and chicken dishes served. There's a

disco on Sat and Sun evenings, playing hip-hop, salsa and dance.
$$ Restaurante Rosario, west side of highway at south entrance to town. Fried chicken or beef dishes, loud music, greasy and friendly.

Matagalpa p238, map p239
$$ Artesanos Café-Bar, Banpro, ½ c arriba. This pleasant café-bar has a wooden, rancho-style interior. They do breakfasts, light lunches and hot and cold drinks including *licuados*, iced coffee and really excellent cappucinos. Popular with locals and tourists.
$$ Buffet Maná del Cielo, Iglesia Molaguina, ½ c norte, T2772-5686. Daily 0700-2100. Variety of typical Nicaraguan buffet food. Cheap and filling. Not bad.
$$ La Buena Onda, see Where to stay, above, T2772-2135, www.hostelmatagalpa.com. Open Wed-Mon for lunch and dinner. Bohemian café ambience and flavourful fare like coconut curry, chicken with mango and filete mignon. Also light snacks, including sweet salads and sandwiches. Recommended.
$$ La Vita é Bella, Col Lainez 10, from Buena Onda, ½ c north, then right down an alleyway to an unmarked house, T2772-5476. An Italian-run restaurant, which has received strong praise from several readers.
$$ Restaurante El Pullazo, on the highway just south of town, T2772-3935. Has a famous and tasty dish with the same name as the establishment: a very lean cut of beef cooked in a special oven and smothered with tomatoes and onions, served with fresh corn tortillas, *gallo pinto* and a fruit juice.
$$ Restaurant La Pradera, Shell la Virgen, 2 c norte, T2772-2543. One of the best in town, ideal for 'meat lovers', also good seafood.
$$ Restaurante Pesca Mar, Cancha del Brigadista, 3 c arriba, T2772-3548. Daily until 2200. Seafood specialities, shrimp in garlic butter, red snapper in onions.
$$ Restaurante Pique's, Casa Pellas, 1 c arriba, T2772-2723. Atmospheric Mexican restaurant serving tacos, tequila, *tostadas* and *chilaquiles*. Popular and friendly.

$$-$ El Cafeto, southeast corner of Parque Morazán, 1 c sur, ½ c oeste. A clean, modern café that's good for salads, sandwiches and other snacks. On the pricey side but OK. Light and airy.

$ Cafetería Don Chaco, next to coffee museum. Closed Sat. They do breakfasts and set menus, but are most famous for their fruit and vegetable shakes. Busy with locals in the morning.

$ El Mexicano, Brigadista, 2½ c este. Mon-Sat 1100-2100. Brightly painted and fully authentic Mexican eatery offering a range of affordable dishes including fajitas, nachos and burritos. Friendly and casual. Recommended for budget travellers.

$ Hamburlooca, La Cancha del Brigadista, 3 c arriba, T2772-7402. Rough 'n' ready burger joint. They do home deliveries too.

Cafés

Barrista, northwest corner of Parque Darío, 2½ c norte. Excellent Americanos, cappuccinos, espressos and other locally sourced caffeinated fare. There's also, Wi-Fi, cakes and snacks to go with your cup of the black stuff. A proper coffee house and recommended.

Centro Girasol, Parque Rubén Darío, 3 c sur, 3 c abajo. This bright, friendly café stocks baked goods and fine coffee. It is a great source of information about sustainable local enterprises and belongs to an organization that supports disabled children – ask inside about volunteer opportunities.

Simos, southwest corner of Parque Darío, ½ c oeste. Good, strong coffee as well as light meals, **Simos** can get quite busy with diners in the evenings. Try the cheesecake if it's in stock. Also has Wi-Fi.

El Disparate de Potter *p241*
$$ Restaurante El Disparate de Potter, T2772-2553. With a bar and food à la carte, good soups and *nacatamales*.

🎵 Bars and clubs

Matagalpa *p238, map p239*
Most discos do not start up until after 2100, and all Matagalpa discos serve dinner. You should get a taxi back from any night spot.
Artesanos Café-Bar, see Restaurants, above. A popular place that draws a diverse crowd of locals and expats. Cocktails, rum and beer, in addition to coffee. Recommended.
Madre Tierra, southwest corner of Parque Darío, ½ c sur. Adorned with political photos, peace flags and iconic, revolutionary portraits, this café-bar has an alternative feel. They serve light meals and cold beer. The action hots up at night, with regular live music and occasional documentary films.
Tequila's, Valle Las Tejas, take a taxi. Raucous disco-bar that's been known to soak its revellers in gallons of soap bubbles. Young and feisty.

🛍 Shopping

Ciudad Darío *p236*
Ciudad Darío was a big shoe-producing town during the Sandinista years and one can still have a customized pair of cowboy boots made in 3 days, for US$30. If you wear smaller than a size 41, you can pick up boots for US$25 right out of the workshop.

Matagalpa *p238, map p239*
Crafts
Cerámica Negra, Parque Darío. This kiosk, open irregularly, sells black pottery in the northern tradition – a style found only in parts of Chile, Nicaragua and Mexico. There is evidence that this school of ceramics dates back to 1500 BC in this region of Nicaragua. For more information contact Estela Rodríguez, T2772-4812.
Colectivos de Mujeres de Matagalpa, Banco Uno, 2½ c arriba, T2772-4462. Mon-Fri 0800-1200, 1400-1730, Sat 0800-1200. Native fabrics, leather goods, ceramics and an orange and coffee liqueur made by

women's co-operatives in El Chile, Molino Norte and Malinche.

La Vita é Bella, see Restaurants, above. A good artisan craft store that also sells locally made chocolates *El Castillo de Cacao*.

Around Matagalpa *p240*
Colectivo de Tejedoras Entre Hilos, Molino Norte, Km 15, Carretera a Jinotega (take bus towards Jinotega or hire taxi, US$3). Mon-Fri 0800-1600, Sat 0800-1200. This women's co-operative produces hand-spun fabrics elaborated into bags and other small items.
Colectivo de Tejidos El Chile, 20 km from Matagalpa off the Carretera a San Dionisio. Founded in 1984 as part of a cultural rescue program, the indigenous community of El Chile makes fabrics, backpacks, camera cases, purses and wallets out of hand-spun fabrics. Visits to the village can be arranged through **Matagalpa Tours** (see below) or take bus towards San Dionisio and get off at the entrance to El Chile.

☉ What to do

Matagalpa *p238, map p239*
Coffee tours
The coffee museum, INTUR, or Matagalpa Tours will help you arrange trips to the many coffee *fincas* in the area including **Finca El Socorro** and **Finca de Pita**. Other interesting, easily arranged options are:
Finca Esperanza Verde, office in San Ramón, Iglesia Católica, 1½ c arriba, T2772-5003, www.fincaesperanzaverde.org. This award-winning 220-acre certified organic farm has 28 acres of ethically managed, sustainably cultivated arabica coffee. Truly ecotouristic and interesting.
Selva Negra, Km 139.5 Carretera Matagalpa-Jinotega, T2772-3883, www.selvanegra.com. At the edge of beautiful rainforest reserve, this famous *finca* offers daily tours of its fascinating, ecologically sound facilities. Call in advance to check times.
UCA San Ramón, opposite the Parque Municipal, San Ramón, T2772-5247,

www.agroecoturismorural.com. This organization can arrange a 'hands-on' experience of coffee production, where you meet farming communities and participate in the process. They also offer more conventional tours of the **SolCafé** processing plant outside Matagalpa.

Tour operators
Matagalpa Tours, Banpro, ½ c arriba, T2772-0108, www.matagalpatours.com. This reputable agency runs tours to the north and further afield. Trekking, hiking, birdwatching and rural community tours are among their well-established repertoire. One of their most interesting options involves visiting Mayagna communities and working mines in the remote northeast of the country. Also offers excellent mountain-bike tours, from 2 hrs to several days. Dutch and English-speaking, helpful and friendly. The best agency in town – for all your adventuring needs. Highly recommended.
Northward Nicaragua Tours, Parque Rubén Darío, 2½ c abajo, T2772-0605, www.adventure-nicaragua.com. A new operation founded by Nicaraguan tour guide and outdoors enthusiast Alvaro Rodríguez. He offers a range of custom-made tours throughout the Nicaraguan countryside.
UCA San Ramón, see above and box, page 237.

☉ Transport

Ciudad Darío *p236*
The bus station in Ciudad Darío is at the small park just north of the iron bridge on south side of town. Buses leave 0415-1900 every 15 mins, US$1.20 north to **Matagalpa**, or US$1.10 south to **Managua**.

Sébaco *p237*
Sébaco is a major transportation hub with northbound traffic to **Matagalpa** and **Jinotega** and northwest to **Estelí**, **Ocotal** and **Somoto**.

Buses pass every 15 mins to/from **Estelí** US$1.20, **Matagalpa** US$1.10 and **Managua** US$1.50. Buses between Matagalpa and Sébaco pass the highway just outside **Chagüitillo** every 15 mins.

Matagalpa *p238, map p239*
Bus
Terminal Sur (Cotransur), is near Mercado del Sur and used for all destinations outside the department of Matagalpa.

To **Jinotega**, every 30 mins, 0500-1900, US$1.40, 1½ hrs. To **Managua**, every 30 mins, 0335-1805, US$2.20, 3-4 hrs; express buses, every hour, 0520-1720, US$2.75, 2½ hrs. To **Estelí**, every 30 mins, 0515-1745, US$1.40, 2-3 hrs; express buses, 1000, 1630, US$1.50, 1½ hrs. Express bus to **León**, 0930, 1200 (Fri only), 1500, US$2.75, 2½ hrs, departs only if there is sufficient demand, otherwise travel to the junction south of San Isidro and change. Express bus to **Masaya**, 0700, 1400, 1530, US$2.75, 4 hrs.

Terminal Norte, by Mercado del Norte (Guanuca), is for all destinations within the province of Matagalpa including **San Ramón** and **El Tuma**. Taxi between terminals US$0.50.

International buses For information on fares and schedules, see individual agencies: Ticabus, northeast corner of Parque Darío, ½ c abajo, opposite La Posada Rotisserie, T2772-4502, www.ticabus.com; Transnica, opposite the Shell Central, T2772-2389, www.transnica.com.

Car hire
Budget Rent a Car, Km 131 at Shell station on entrance to city, T2772-3041.

Taxi
Matagalpa taxis are helpful and cheap. Average fare inside the city is US$0.50. Fare to **Selva Negra** US$4-5 per person.

❶ Directory

Matagalpa *p238, map p239*
Banks Banco de América Central (BAC and Credomatic), Parque Morazán, 1 c sur, on Av Central. Change all TCs and cash on Visa and MasterCard and has ATM for most credit and debit cards with Cirrus logo. Banpro, opposite BAC, offers similar services. **Fire** T2772-3167. **Hospital** T2772-2081. **Internet** There are many places around town, particularly along Av José Benito Escobar, most charge US$0.50 per hr. **Language schools** Matagalpa Spanish School, Banpro ½ c arriba, inside Matagalpa Tours, T2772-0108, www.matagalpa.info. They offer a range of packages, from hourly tuition to intensive courses of 30 hrs per week. There are options for family homestay, voluntary work and cultural tours. Classes are one-to-one, grammar and exercise books provided. **Police** Parque Central, 1 c sur, T2772-2382. **Red Cross** T2772-2059. **Telephone** Enitel, catedral, 1 c arriba, daily 0700-1900, T2772-4600.

Jinotega

Nestled in a valley of green mountains and shaded from the tropical sun, Jinotega has a pleasant climate. Like Matagalpa, it is an important area for the nation's coffee industry, though it is considerably more relaxed and friendly; the helpful and charming people of the city are its greatest assets. Jinotega is the capital of a sprawling province that has almost no infrastructure to date and remains one of the poorest and least developed parts of the country. Like Matagalpa, the province is subject to the whims of international coffee prices.
▶▶ *For listings, see pages 251-253.*

Arriving in Jinotega → *Population 33,000. Altitude 1004 m.*

Getting there and around Jinotega is served by regular bus services from Matagalpa and a few Express buses from Managua's Mercado Mayoreo. A paved highway between Sébaco and Jinotega was completed in 2009 and it bypasses Matagalpa completely. Look for it on the left about 20 minutes out of Sébaco. Taxis are available and inexpensive inside the city. Jinotega is easy to walk around, but avoid walking after 2200 at the weekend.
▶ *For further details, see Transport, page 253.*

Tourist information INTUR ① *Texaco, 1 c norte, Mon-Fri, 0800-1200, 1400-1600, T782-2166,* has information on the town and surrounding areas. See also www.jinotegalife.com.

Background

Jinotega enjoys the highest elevation of any major city in Nicaragua. A small indigenous community in the 17th century, it was sacked by a combination of British and Miskito forces attacking from the east. The US Marines were stationed here during their fight against Sandino who directed his National Sovereignty Army out of nearby San Rafael del Norte much of the time. The city was attacked several times by FSLN rebel groups; one of these attacks cost FSLN rebel hero 'El Danto' Germán Pomares his life. El Danto, who was the most athletic (and seemingly invincible) of the anti-Somoza *guerrilleros*, was hit in Jinotega by 'friendly fire'. Jinotega's interior was the site of constant battles and attacks by the Contras on both military and civilian targets.

Places in Jinotega

Jinotega is not visited by many foreigners, except for those working on international projects. However, it won't be long until its refreshing climes start attracting wealthy North American retirees. The city has grown rapidly to the east of the centre in recent years, which means that the central park is actually now in the west of town. The area around the main plaza and the very attractive cathedral, **El Templo Parroquial** (1805), is full of broad streets and has a tranquil, small-town feel. The Gothic cathedral has an interior that reflects the local climate, with a lovely, clean, cool, whitewashed simplicity and a very complete collection of imagery imported from Italy and Spain. The pulpit is dramatic, with a life-sized suffering Christ encased in

Jinotega

To ⑦ ⑧ & San Rafael del Norte

To ⑪

To ⑦

To Hospital Victoria, Bus Station & ②

Parque Central

Cathedral

Alcaldía

Enitel

INTUR ①

To ⑤

To ⑥ & Matagalpa

N

300 metres
300 yards

Where to stay 🛏
Borbon **5**
Central **1**
Hotelito **4**
Kiuras **2**
La Quinta **7**
Primavera **8**
Solentuna Hem **3**

Restaurants 🍴
Chaba's Pizza **1**
El Tico **2**
La Perrera **6**
La Ronda **5**
Las Marías **8**
McGarry **7**
Roca Rancho **4**
Soda Buffet El Tico **9**
Soppexcca **3**

Bars & clubs 🍸
Discoteca Jaspe **10**

glass below. The city's symbol is the cross-topped mountain, **Cerro La Peña Cruz**, to the west of central park. The cross was put on the mountain by Fray Margil de la Cruz to stop flooding in the city. The population was suffering from weeks of endless rain and floods and believed the mountain, full of water, was responsible for the inundation. The cross saved the city and every 3 May more than 5000 pilgrims hike to the top to take part in a Mass at the summit at 0900. (The hike to the summit takes just over an hour.)

Around Jinotega → For listings, see pages 251-253.

Lago de Apanás

ⓘ *To visit the lake take a bus from Jinotega bound for Austurias-Pantasma (hourly 0700-1500, 1 hr, US$2).*

The beautiful Lago de Apanás, 8 km east of Jinotega, was created by the damming of the Río Tuma in 1964 to form a 54-sq-km shiny blue body of water. The lake is full of *guapote* and *tilapia* and is good for fishing. Small *ranchos* that line the lake will fry fish for you. There are indigenous communities on the north shore, which is the access to the deeply rural towns northeast of here, **El Cuá** and **San José de Bocay**. You can go out on the lake with one of the 87 members of the fishing co-operative **La Unión del Norte** who have three motorboats and many more rowing boats to take people fishing or touring on the glassy waters. They charge US$6 per hour for the motorboat and US$3 per hour in the rowing boats. Ask at El Portillo de Apanás.

Reserva Natural Dantali-El Diablo

ⓘ *The area is managed by the Lina Herrera Cooperative, who can arrange guides and lodging in their wood cabins. For more information, contact Marco García at Aldea Global, T2782-2237, www.aglobal.org.ni, a farmers' association of more than 1000 families, mostly indigenous Choretegas. To get to the reserve, take a bus to El Cuá-Bocay, get off at the turning for Venecia and walk 3.5 km to the community of Gobiado.*

Protected since 2002, this easy-to-reach reserve comprises 400 *manzanas* of attractive highlands; roughly a third is cultivated for coffee production. It has rich biodiversity with 79 species of tree, a variety of medicinal plants and many orchids. There's good birdwatching, and the reserve is home to the challenging peak of **El Diablo** (1640 m), offering ample opportunities for hiking, horse riding and breathing in inspiring views.

Reserva Silvestre El Jaguar

ⓘ *T2279-9219, www.jaguarreserve.org, during the rainy season access to the area is only possible with a 4WD; make sure you get detailed directions and book accommodation well in advance. The entrance fee is US$10, and this includes a guide. Food and drinks are available.*

The paved highway from Jinotega to San Rafael del Norte passes through rolling terrain with cabbage and lettuce fields and 'bearded' oak trees (the 'beards' – Spanish moss – are used by the locals for scrubbing during bathing). At the Empalme San Gabriel is an earthen road that leads to towards **Mancotal**. Thirteen kilometres from the paved highway, after several switchbacks and a steady climb, is the organic coffee farm and private cloud forest reserve of El Jaguar. This is one of the most temperate accommodation options in Nicaragua; the reserve is often in the clouds with cool breezes passing over the mountain top, making it an excellent place to visit from February to April when places at sea level are burning hot.

Owners Georges and Liliana Duriaux are lovers of nature, especially birds, and teams of ornithologists can often be spotted here studying the high-altitude and (for Nicaragua) upper-latitude resident and migratory birdlife. The current list for this 200-acre property, is around 180 species. The shade coffee farm produces some of Nicaragua's finest coffee (recently rated 90 out of 100 by *Coffee Review*), which Georges cooks up at all hours of the day over an open flame. The property has five walking trails, which range from 45 minutes to three hours at a relaxed pace and which pass giant oaks, cedars, prehistoric fern trees, orchids and bromeliads.

San Rafael del Norte

Just 25 km northwest from Jinotega, reached by a paved highway, is the tiny village of San Rafael, a pleasant, authentic mountain town with a gigantic church and a rich history. The dusty streets are a corridor of contrasts, where Franciscan nuns walk smiling past uniformed school children and grizzled cowboys. The population is relaxed and unassuming, with a faith reported to be as big as their magnificent church which, aside from the Sandino museum, is the town's main attraction. **La Iglesia Parroquial** was first built in 1887 with the help of local Franciscan monks from Italy. It was enlarged in 1961 and has grown to be a majestic and beautiful structure. The church sits next to a Franciscan convent and behind a weedy central park where horses graze. Inside are brightly coloured, stained glass and many beautiful icons imported from Italy, including the patron saint of the city. To the left of the main altar is a gigantic altar to the Virgin Mary that reaches from floor to roof, with a built-in waterfall. It is made solely from volcanic rocks taken from a solidified lava flow on Volcán Masaya, more than 200 km to the south. The most famous aspect of the church is a mural next to the entrance on the left depicting the temptation of Christ; the devil's face is said to resemble the Sandinista leader Daniel Ortega. Although it was painted in 1977 before most people even knew who Ortega was, the resemblance is uncanny.

The reason this little village, backed by a clear stream and pine forests, has such a big church is down to Padre Odorico D'Andrea, a Franciscan monk from Abruzzo in Italy, who lived here until his death on 22 March 1990. His memory lives on very much in the hearts of the people of San Rafael and surrounding settlements for the social work he did during his life. Locals are pushing for his sainthood and have constructed a curious chapel on a hill behind San Rafael, with a shrine for his tomb called *Ermita del Tepeyac*. It is a peaceful and pretty place that comes alive on 22 March each year for what the locals already call the celebrations of 'Santo Odorico'.

The **Museo Sandino** ① *Casa Museo Ejército Defensor de La Soberanía Nacional, northeast corner of the Parque Central, ½ c norte, T2265-3359, Mon-Fri 0800-1200 and 1400-1730*, is where General Augusto C Sandino used to send telegrams to his troops in different parts of the northern hills. The 19-year-old girl to whom he dictated his messages, Blanca Aráuz, married Sandino at the church here on 18 May 1927 and died giving birth to a baby girl in 1933. Blanca Aráuz is buried in the cemetery at the town entrance. The museum has recently been restored and although it is often locked, the caretaker (formerly Padre Odorico's driver) lives behind the church and convent.

The festival for San Rafael usually lasts eight days and takes place around 29 September; there are also celebrations for Sandino's wedding on 18 May.

Into the Reserva de Biósfera Bosawás

The Bosawás Biosphere is one of Central America's largest protected areas. Most often accessed from the Atlantic side of the country, details on the reserve's prolific flora and fauna can be found on page 299. The two routes that enter the reserve from Jinotega are neither in particularly good condition, nor easily traversed. On the first route, the **El Cuá–Bocay** road passes the rather stunning **Reserva Natural Peñas Blancas**, on the border of the departments of Jinotega and Matagalpa. Protected as part of the Bosawás Biosphere, this area is home to one of the highest mountains in the country, countless gorgeous waterfalls, misty cloud forests, and some impressive wildlife, including jaguars and resplendent quetzals. Take a bus to **El Cuá** (0400, 1200, three hours, US$2.50, also departures from Matagalpa) and contact the **Cooperativa Guardianes del Bosque**, T2829-6544, who offer nature and community tours and rustic lodging within the reserve. Beyond El Cuá, you'll find a ranger's station at **San Juan de Bocay**, as well as access to the **Reserva Natural Cerro Kilambé**, named after the 1750-m mountain within its borders. Beyond San Juan de Bocay the last place of any size is **Tablazo Yulawas**, where the road ends, the Río Bocay begins and the Bosawás Biosphere stretches away into obscurity. The Río Bocay also connects with the Río Coco further downstream. The second route into the biosphere leads from Jinotega to **Wiwilí**, directly to the Río Coco and the potential starting point for a great odyssey. If you have the time, resources and a seriously adventurous inclination), you could theoretically follow this mighty river all the way to the Caribbean Coast, but most settle for **Waspam**, where flights connect to Managua. Buses depart from Jinotega to Wiwilí at 0430 and 1300, five hours, US$3.

The best time for this trip would be at the end of the rainy season, from January to February. The Río Coco skirts the northern border of Bosawás so you will have to leave the river to go into the reserve. A jungle hammock with built-in netting (where you zip yourself inside) for insect protection is a great asset. Also bring a first-aid kit, water purification tablets and some kind of portable food. You will need locally hired guides. Allow at least a week for this trip and bring more money than you think you will need, in small bills. For further advice on this and to check the security situation of any area you will visit in the Bosawás area get in touch with **MARENA** in Managua (see page 45).

◉ Jinotega listings

For sleeping and eating price codes and other relevant information, see pages 28-30.

◉ Where to stay

Jinotega *p247, map p248*
Most hotels and restaurants lock their doors at 2200, Fri-Sun 2300. Only hardy youths are out in the streets after this time.
$$ Hotel, Café and Restaurant Borbon, Texaco, 1 c abajo, ½ c norte, T2782-2710. The best hotel in the province has 25 very comfortable rooms with private bath, hot water, a/c, Wi-Fi, cable TV. Elegant, quiet and friendly with a good restaurant attached (**$$**) serving traditional dishes.
$ Hotel Central, catedral, ½ c norte, T2782-2063, abrahaniarivera@yahoo.com. 20 simple, newly renovated rooms of varying quality. Rooms upstairs have private bath, cable TV and a great mountain views. Convenient central location.

$ Hotelito, Esso, 2 c al sur, ½ c arriba, T2782-2079. Small, basic, economical rooms, most divided by plasterboard partitions. Sound travels easily and all rooms have a shared outside bath. A few have cable TV. Helpful owners.
$ Hotel Kiuras, Catedral, 1½ c sur, T2782-3938, sarcoson@yahoo.com. Pleasant, comfortable rooms equipped with cable TV, fan, private bath, hot water. There's also Wi-Fi and parking.
$ Hotel Sollentuna Hem, Esso, 1 c arriba, 2½ c norte, T2782-2334, sollentuna.hem@ gmail.com. This clean, safe, family hotel has 16 rooms, all with private bath, cable TV, fan and hot water. The owner lived in Sweden for many years, and offers a range of beauty treatments including massage and pedicure. Breakfast and dinner are served, and coffee tours are available. Other services include Wi-Fi, laundry and parking. Pleasant and professional.

$ La Quinta, Parque Central, 7 c norte, over the bridge, T2782-2522, becquerfernandez@yahoo.ca. This Nicaraguan mini-resort has a pleasant setting among the pine trees. There's a range of rooms and cabins (**$$**), all comfortable and well equipped with cable TV, private bath and hot water. Amenities include Wi-Fi, parking, a swimming pool, restaurant, karaoke bar and disco. Helpful English-speaking management. Recommended.
$ Primavera, Esso station, 4 c norte, T2782-2400. This cheap hotel has 26 clean, plain rooms with shared bath. A handful have cable TV and their own bath. Breakfast is served but not included in the price. Friendly and authentic. A good local atmosphere.

Reserva Natural Dantali-El Diablo *p249*
$$-$ La Bastilla Ecolodoge, Comarca Las Colinas, Jigüina, call ahead for directions, T2782-4355, www.bastillaecolodge.com. Certified by the Rainforest Alliance, this ecologically sound lodge is situated in La Bastilla coffee estate. You can tour the facilities, hike in the surrounding reserve and spend the night in comfortable cabins or on a luxury camping platform.

Reserva Silvestre El Jaguar *p249*
$$$-$ El Jaguar Cloud Forest Reserve, T2279-9219 (Managua), www.jaguarreserve.org. 2 wood cabins (**$$$**) at the edge of the forest with spectacular views if clear, private baths, small kitchens and living space and a biological station with dorm rooms (**$**).

San Rafael del Norte *p250*
$ Hotel Rocío, petrol station, 20 vrs sur, T2784-2313. Small, intimate and very clean *hospedaje*, with private or shared bath. Serve 3 set meals a day, each US$1.50, good value.

Into the Reserva de Biósfera Bosawás *p250*
$$ La Sombra Ecolodge, Municipio El Tuma-La Dalia, Macizo de Peñas Blancas, access from Matagalpa in a 4WD, contact lodge for directions, T845-3732, www.

lasombraecolodge.com. This wooden eco-lodge is surrounded by lush forests and hiking trails. Rooms are clean and comfortable and open onto a great balcony overlooking the garden. Activities include horse riding and hikes to numerous beautiful waterfalls.

🍽 Restaurants

Jinotega *p247, map p248*
$$ La Perrera, Km 186 Carretera Matagalpa–Jinotega. Oft-praised restaurant just out of town, serving international fare and seafood.
$$ Roca Rancho, Esso, 1 c sur, 2½ c arriba. Tue-Sun 1200-0000. This fun, friendly restaurant looks like a beach bar. They serve *comida típica*, shrimps, burgers and *bocas*. There's live music on Thu.
$$-$ La Ronda, Texaco, 3 c oeste, T2782-3516. Fun, popular restaurant specializing in local and Chinese-flavoured fare.
$$-$ McGarry, Tienda Rosy, 1½ c este, T2782-4020. This long-standing locals' favourite, 30 years in service, has a simple, unpretentious interior to match its menu of meat, chicken and fish.
$$-$ Restaurante El Tico, across from La Salle athletic field, T782-2530. Daily 0800-2200. 44-year-old establishment in new, very modern location, popular with couples, moderately priced dishes, try surf and turf (*mar y tierra*) or *pollo a la plancha*, also cheap dishes and sandwiches. Recommended.
$$-$ Soda Buffet El Tico, Esso, 2½ c sur. Reputable buffet restaurant serving good Nicaraguan food. Clean, professional and popular with tourists.
$ Chaba's Pizza, Esso, 2 c sur, 2½ c arriba, T2782-2692. When you've had enough of *pollo frito* and *gallo pinto*, try these pizzas.
$ Las Marías, Esso, 2½ c sur. Good locals' lunch buffet with pork, chicken and beef-based Nica dishes. Family-run and friendly.

Cafés
Soppexcca, Ferretería Blandón Moreno, 1 c abajo, www.soppexcca.org/en.
The best coffee in town, produced by an

environmentally aware and progressive co-operative. Highly recommended.

San Rafael del Norte *p250*
$ Bar y Restaurante Los Encuentros, at the exit from town on the highway to Yalí. Outdoor seating overlooking the confluence of hot and cold rivers, backed by pine forests, very pretty and a popular bathing spot. Whole chicken for US$5, beers are US$0.80.
$ Comedor Chepita, south of the museum. Offers lunch and dinner, speciality of the day.

🍷 Bars and clubs

Jinotega *p247, map p248*
As usual, the action takes place Fri-Sun. Karaoke seems to be a particularly popular form of entertainment in Jinotega.
Discoteca Jaspe, Esso, 1 c abajo, ½ c al norte. Popular place attracting a youthful crowd.

⊙ What to do

Jinotega *p247, map p248*
Tour operators
Cooperativa Lina Herrera, contact Marco García at Aldea Global, T2782-4027. Aside from guided birdwatching, hiking and horse riding within the Reserva Natural Dantali-El Diablo, this co-operative lets you experience rustic communities with cooking, music and story-telling.
UCA Soppexcca, Ferretería Blandón Moreno, 1 c abajo, www.soppexcca.org/en. This great

organization comprises 15 organic coffee co-operatives who operate sustainably and offer tours to see how their award-winning beans are cultivated and prepared for international export.

⊖ Transport

Jinotega *p247, map p248*
Most destinations will require a change of bus in Matagalpa. To **Matagalpa**, every ½ hr, 0500-1800, US$1.50, 1½ hrs. Express bus to **Managua**, 10 daily, 0400-1600, US$4, 3½ hrs. To **San Rafael del Norte**, 10 daily, 0600-1730 US$1, 1 hr. Taxis in Jinotega are available for local transport, average fare US$.50.

San Rafael del Norte *p250*
Buses to **Jinotega**, 0550, 0615, 0630, 0930, 1000, 1145, 1200, 1345, 1400, 1530, 1730, 1900, US$1, 1 hr. Express bus to **Managua**, Mon-Sat, 0400, US$5, 4 hrs.

⊙ Directory

Jinotega *p247, map p248*
Banks For cash from cards or TCs there is a BAC, catedral, 2 c norte, T2782-4413. Banpro and Bancentro, catedral, 10 vrs al norte, have ATMs and currency change. **Fire** T2782-2468. **Hospital** Victoria, T2782-2626. **Police** T2782-2215. **Post** Correos de Nicaragua, behind Bancentro, T2782-2292. **Red Cross** T2782-2222. **Telephone** Enitel, Alcaldía, 1 c arriba, 2½ c sur, T2782-2022.

Estelí

Beyond Sébaco, the Pan-American Highway climbs through the villages of San Isidro and La Trinidad before reaching the cigar capital of Central America, Estelí, at Km 148. Estelí appears to be a jumbled, unattractive place, yet this unpretentious town is one of the most lively and industrious in Nicaragua. It is the biggest commercial centre in the north, with an endless array of small family shops and restaurants along its two main boulevards and many side streets. There are also good schools and universities here, which draw students from all over the northern region and, as a result, the population is young and optimistic. The climate, too, is pleasant with average temperatures of 20-23°C. Estelí remains one of the most Sandinista cities in Nicaragua and the party colours of black and red can be seen all around the town. ▸▸ For listings, see pages 257-262.

Arriving in Estelí → *Population: 107,458. Altitude: 844 m. Colour map 1, C4.*

Getting there and around Estelí is a major transport hub for the north with express bus services from Managua, Matagalpa and León. Regular buses connect it with Somoto and Ocotal, both of which have regular services to the border with Honduras. The city centre lies well to the west of the highway, with the focus of its life and commerce on a north–south avenue that skirts the Parque Central's west side. Taxis are cheap in the town and walking is safe in the daytime. However, use caution at night, and don't wander around the barrios. ►► *For further details, see Transport, page 261.*

Tourist information INTUR ① *southwest corner of the Parque Central, ½ c abajo, 2nd floor of the red building, T2713-6799,* has information on local attractions including nature reserves, cigar factories and Spanish schools. A great source of English-language information is the **Treehuggers tourism office** ① *east side of the cathedral, 1 c norte, T8405-8919, www.cafeluzyluna.com.*

Places in Estelí

Estelí was founded in 1711 by Spanish colonists who abruptly left Nueva Segovia, now Ciudad Antigua (see page 268), to escape joint Miskito-British attacks on the old city. Sadly the town was razed in 1978-1979 by Somoza's National Guard, which used aerial bombing and tanks to put down repeated uprisings by the population spurred on by the FSLN. As a result, there is little of visual beauty to be found in the city. The **cathedral**, first built in 1823, with upgrades in 1889, was the last to be built in the 'Nicaraguan primitive baroque' style. However, the current neoclassical façade was added in 1929. The church is not particularly inspiring inside, but it does have a pretty image of the Virgen del Rosario after which the cathedral is named.

Estelí is known as the capital of **cigars**, with the finest tobacco in Central America

Estelí

Where to stay
Alameda 2
Casa Nicarao 7
Don Vito 1
El Mesón 3
Hospedaje Luna 4
Hospedaje San Francisco 11
Hostal Tomabú 5
Los Arcos 12
Miraflor 8
Moderno 6
Panorama 1 9
Panorama 2 10

Restaurants
Ananda 1
Café Luz 2
Cafetería El Rincón Pinareño 7
Cohifer 3
Ixcotelli 5
Koma Rico 8
La Casita 10
Las Brasas 12
Pullaso's Ole 4
Repostería Gutiérrez 13
Sopas El Carao 6
Tipiscayan 14
Vuela Vuela 9

Bars & clubs
Cigarzone 11
El Chamán 15
Rincón Legal 17
Semáforo Rancho 16

grown in the surrounding mountains. The town is full of cigar factories, some of which produce among the best *puros* or *habanos* in the world. Most of the factories were founded by exiled Cubans, who brought their seeds and expertise with them in the 1960s. Many left during the 1980s but they returned in force in the following decade. The complicated and delicate process of making a fine cigar involves 73 stages. However, what interests most people is the final stage, the rolling of the cigars, which is done in male-female pairs. The man prepares the filler and the woman rolls it with wrapper leaf and a touch of glue. Many people visit Estelí to get a glimpse of this process and, although there are no set tours offered by the cigar manufacturers, a handful of local guides and tour operators now lead groups around selected factories. You can also visit independently, though you must contact the company at least two days prior to your arrival. Most Estelí cigar manufacturers have free-trade tax status for their factories, which means that many cannot (technically) sell cigars locally. Be aware that time spent with visitors is often time lost in production, so remember that you are a privileged guest. For details of tobacco factories, see What to do, page 260.

Around Estelí → *For listings, see pages 257-261.*

Reserva Natural Meseta Tisey-Estanzuela
ⓘ *The reserve is managed by Fundación Fider, Petronic El Carmen, 1½ c abajo, Estelí, T713-3918, fiderest@ibw.com.ni. Accommodation is offered by the Cerrato brothers who have some simple wood cabins, T2713-6213, ecoposadatisey@hotmail.com.*

This highland nature reserve is home to rugged mountain scenery quite different from the landscape of Nicaragua's Pacific Basin. There are pine and oak forests, moss-covered granite boulders, rivers and cascades. The biggest attraction is the lovely **Estanzuela waterfall**, accessed by a road just south of Estelí. This is perhaps the most beautiful of Nicaragua's waterfalls that can be reached without an arduous journey. The site is marked by a small sign, just south of the entrance to Estelí and the new hospital, on the highway. A dirt road leads 5 km west to the site. Most of the year this road is not passable except in 4WD, but the walk is pleasant, passing small ranches and farms and a small oak forest. After 4-5 km, turn right onto a smaller road; there used to be a sign marking the turning, but there is now only a post here. From here you pass over two crests and then down into the river valley where the beautiful **El Salto de la Estanzuela** flows into the Río La Pintada. It is a cool place and the pool at the bottom is good for swimming.

The area above the waterfall is best accessed via a dirt road that starts south of Estelí on the Pan-American Highway at the village of **Santa Cruz** and leads to San Nicolás. The park ranger station is 12 km from the highway; from there you can walk in the reserve as well as try some goat's cheese, produced by a co-operative of nuns. Near the Cerro El Quebracho is the farm of **Humberto González** and his unusual art gallery. It is a hike from his ranch up to the mountain gallery where he has carved snakes, deer, foxes, elephants, clowns and even Augusto Sandino. Ask for directions to his farm at the park ranger station.

Reserva Natural Miraflor
ⓘ *For information on lodging and excursion possibilities inside the reserve, visit Miraflor Eco-tours and Adventure, east side of the cathedral, 1 c norte, T8405-8919, www.cafeluzyluna.com, inside the Treehuggers tourism office.*

Despite only being 206 sq km, this pristine mountain nature reserve is full of diverse wildlife and vegetation and opportunities to visit and stay in local communities (see box, page 256). The ecosystem changes with altitude from tropical savannah to tropical dry

Community tourism around Estelí

The beautiful **Miraflor Nature Reserve** is home to Nicaragua's best community tourism project, the Unión de Cooperativas Agropecuarias (UCA) Miraflor. There is so much to see and do here that you should devote at least a few days to exploring it all and soaking up the rural way of life. A popular route leads from the lowlands up to the highlands. Along the way you could sample the locally produced coffee in the tasting lab, play baseball with the locals on Sunday, ride horses through the hills, hear gripping stories of the revolution, or just relax in a hammock, enjoying the soporific pace. But most people come here to hike. Miraflor has 206 sq km of diverse ecosystems, home to abundant birdlife including the resplendent quetzal. In the humid zone, the communities of **El Cebollal**, **La Perla** and **Puertas Azules** provide access to rich cloud forests, Miraflor lagoon (see below), a revolutionary mural, an orchid centre and a modest archaeolgoical site. In the intermediary zone, the friendly community of **Sontule** provides access to a great viewpoint look and the Apaguis cave system, apparently inhabited by *duendes*

(leprechauns). **El Coyolito** and **La Pita** in the dry zone lead to bearded oak forests, waterfalls and viewpoints.

There are 46 communities in Miraflor and a wide range of mostly rustic accommodation. Private rooms in a family house cost US$15 per person including meals, private cabins are US$20 per person (cheaper for a group) and camping is from US$2. Meals cost US$3-US$4. Guides are US$15 per group of one to three people, US$5 for each additional person. Horses are US$7 per person plus the guide. Specialist tours to see birds, orchids or coffee facilities cost US$30 per group.

Before visiting, it is best to discuss your options with Miraflor Eco-tours and Adventure (east side of the cathedral, 1 cuadra norte, T8405-8919, www.cafeluzyluna.com), inside the Treehuggers tourism office. They can also help with volunteer placements inside the reserve, though Spanish speakers and a six-month commitment is preferred. All other enquires should be directed to UCA Miraflor's main office (costado noreste de la Catedral, 2 cuadras al norte y 2 cuadras al este, T2713-2971, www.ucamiraflor.com).

forest, then to pine forest and finally cloud forest at its highest elevations. The legendary quetzal lives here, along with trogons, magpie jays, the turquoise-browed mot-mot, many birds of prey, howler monkeys, mountain lions, ocelots, deer, sloths, river otters, racoons and tree frogs. The reserve also has some gallery forest, ideal for viewing wildlife, a variety of orchids and a 60-m waterfall that flows during the rainy season.

Laguna de Miraflor is a 1.5-ha body of water at an altitude of 1380 m; it has an unknown depth. The reserve is shared by the departments of Estelí and Jinotega, but access is much easier from the Estelí side of the mountains. Access is from the Pan-American Highway heading north out of Estelí; at the Texaco petrol station, a dirt road leads towards Yalí and passes the entrance to the reserve. The narrow track (often difficult conditions in rainy season) leads up into the mountains with spectacular views of the valley below. The entrance to the park is beyond the rocky fields of bearded oaks.

San Juan de Limay

North of Estelí, a very poor dirt road runs west to the rural village of San Juan de Limay. It can take up to two hours to travel the 44 km, but it's worth it for those who like off-the-beaten-path villages and local crafts. The village was founded by the Chorotega, who escaped the colonial invasions of Estelí (the area is rich in pre-Columbian remains with at least three good petroglyphs sites at **Los Quesos**, **La Bruja** and **El Chorro**) and is famous across Nicaragua for the beautiful soapstone (*marmolina*) carvings produced by more than 50 carvers who work in the area. The material is extracted from the Cerro Tipiscayán and transformed into all kinds of objects, varying in size from small tropical birds and reptiles up to 75-kg sculptures of (mostly) humans, especially large, heavy woman. The workmanship is very good and can be found in markets all over Central America. The locals are happy to receive visitors in their houses, which double as their workshops. The artisans have a **main office** ⓘ *de los Juzgados 3½ c norte, T2719-5115*, for sales.

Condega

On the east side of the highway, about 25 km north of Estelí, is the sleepy village of Condega, another vehemently Sandinista town, with a mainly indigenous population. The name Condega means 'land of potters' and the artisans make traditional, red-clay pottery that is both attractive and functional. Condega's central park is a quiet place with an 18th-century church, **Iglesia San Isidro**, that was recently rebuilt. The area around the church comes alive during the week of 15 May to celebrate its patron, the saint of the *campesinos* (peasants), in the hope that he will bring a healthy rainy season for planting.

On the southeastern side of the square is the **Casa de Cultura** ⓘ *Mon-Fri 0800-1200, 1400-1600, Sat 0800-1200*, which produces plays, holds art classes and has a good little pre-Columbian museum. The people of Condega have a love of the *guitarra*, with more than a dozen musical groups in the municipality. You may be able to visit an artisan guitar-maker's shop, located in the back of the cultural centre.

There is a curious **park** at the south end of town above the cemetery, with great views of the surrounding mountains and valleys. The park monument is an old aeroplane from Somoza's National Guard. It was downed by FSLN rebels in 1979 and now sits like the rusting carcass of a dinosaur, staring across the valley, forever grounded but tickled at night by romantic couples and their graffiti.

One kilometre north of Condega, then 3 km west from the highway, is the **Taller Cerámica Ducuale Grande** ⓘ *T2715-2418, Mon-Fri 0700-1700*. This co-operative was founded in 1990 to help improve the quality and sales of what has been a tradition in this area for thousands of years. The pottery is lovely, burnt-brick red and rustic (no colours are added). Visiting the workshop provides an opportunity to meet with the artists and buy their work, which is not available for sale at many markets in the country. The woman of the co-operative usually work in complete silence – quite a contrast from the artisans of Masaya. It's possible to walk here from Condega town centre in about one hour.

⊚ Estelí listings

For sleeping and eating price codes and other relevant information, see pages 28-30.

⊙ Where to stay

Estelí *p253, map p254*
For directions, keep in mind that the cathedral faces due west. Directions from

the central park start at the street that runs along the other side of the park, opposite the church; directions from the church start at the street that passes directly in front of the church.
$$ Alameda, Shell Esquipulas, 1 c arriba, 1½ c sur, T2713-6292. Large hotel with clean, bright rooms. Services include internet,

pool, parking and bar-restaurant. Very comfortable and decent, but far from the centre; use a taxi or car. Discounts for groups.

$$ Hotel Don Vito, Parque Infantil, 1½ c arriba, T2713-4318, www.hoteldonvitoesteli. com. A comfortable new business hotel with 26 clean, generic, well-appointed rooms. Most have hot water, a/c, a few cheaper ones have fan. Other services include restaurant, laundry, cable TV and Wi-Fi.

$$ Hotel Los Arcos, northeast corner of the cathedral, ½ c norte, T2713-3830, www. familiasunidas.org/hotelosarcos.htm. This brightly painted, professionally managed and comfortable hotel has 32 clean, spacious rooms with private bath, a/c or fan, and cable TV. There's also parking, laundry service and Wi-Fi. The attached restaurant, **Vuela Vuela**, is also reputable, and profits go to social projects. Breakfast included.

$$ Hotel Panorama 1, Km 147, Carretera Panamericana, T2713-3147, h.panorama@ yahoo.com. Inconveniently located away from the centre, but good if you need to catch an early morning bus. The newer section is brightly painted and has comfortable rooms with private bath, hot water, a/c and cable TV. The older section is cheaper and less attractive, but still quite comfortable. Wi-Fi and restaurant services.

$ Casa Hotel Nicarao, Parque Central, 1½ c sur, T2713-2490. 9 clean, comfortable rooms with fan and private bath, all set around a relaxing, sociable courtyard filled with plants, paintings and sitting space. Very friendly management and a nice atmosphere, but the walls are a bit thin. There are cheaper rooms without bath.

$ El Mesón, Av Bolívar, Parque Central, 1 c norte, T2713-2655, hotelelmeson-esteli. com. Clean, comfortable rooms at this friendly, helpful hotel, all with hot water and cable TV. There's also Wi-Fi, parking and a restaurant, as well as a good travel agency next door and an *artesanía* shop over the road. Recommended.

$ Hospedaje Luna, catedral, 1 c al norte, 1 c arriba, T8441-8466, www.cafeluzyluna.com.

This popular hostel is part of an excellent non-profit social enterprise. Facilities include 2 dorms, 2 private rooms, hammock space, an activities board, tourist information, DVDs, lockers, tours and drinking water. Volunteer work in Miraflor can be arranged here – 3 months' commitment and Spanish speakers preferred. Discounts for longer stays and groups. Highly recommended.

$ Hospedaje San Francisco, next to Parque Infantil. Just one of a handful of cheapies in this area. Rooms are basic and clean with outside bathroom. The hotel is friendly and pleasant. Shabby, but the price is right.

$ Hostal Tomabú, opposite the Parque Infantil, T8914-3963, hostaltomabu.esteli@ gmail.com. Friendly, family-run hotel whose name means 'place of the sun'. 15 good, clean rooms with hot water, fan and cable TV. Bright colours and potted flowers. Lots of connections with tour operators and professional, personal attention. Recommended.

$ Hotel Miraflor, Parque Central, ½ c norte, T2713-2003. 7 simple, economical rooms with hot water, cable TV and private bath. The attached restaurant serves *comida típica*. Popular with Nicas.

$ Hotel Panorama 2, catedral, 1 c sur, ½ c arriba, T2713-5023, h.panorama@yahoo. com. Similar features as **Hotel Panorama 1** (see above), but much quieter at night, with good access to central restaurants, secure parking, rooms upstairs nicer. Clean, simple and OK. If leaving on early bus pay in advance and ask for a receipt.

$ Moderno, catedral, 2½ c sur, T2713-2378. Clean and comfortable rooms with a/c, hot water and cable TV (cheaper with fan). There's a restaurant for guests and breakfast is included. Friendly desk staff and Wi-Fi.

Reserva Natural Miraflor *p255*
Numerous interesting and highly recommended homestay options are available in several communities; book through **Miraflor Eco-tours and Adventure**, east side of the cathedral, 1 c norte, T8405-

8919, www.cafeluzyluna.com, inside the Treehuggers tourism office. Alternatively, try:
$$ Finca Neblina del Bosque, Rampla, T8701-1400, www.visitamiraflor.com, contact in advance of visit. These rustic cabins are set in flower-filled gardens and are some of the more private and comfortable lodgings in the reserve. Some good reports from former guests. Activities include tours, horse riding and Spanish classes.

Condega *p257*
$ Hospedaje Framar, on main plaza next to Casa de Cultura, T2715-2393. 14 very clean and pleasant rooms, cold showers, nice garden, safe, friendly, owner speaks English, excellent value. Safe parking for motorbikes.
$ Pensión Baldovinos, opposite the park, T2715-2222. *Pensión* with 20 rooms, cheaper with shared bath. Fan, group discounts, good food.

● Restaurants

Estelí *p253, map p254*
$$$-$$ Cohifer, catedral, 1 c arriba, ½ c al sur. A very decent establishment that promises a fulfilling gastronomic experience. They serve a range of excellent steaks, chicken and fish dishes, as well as some lighter, more economical fare, including burgers and sandwiches. Well established.
$$ Ixcotelli, Almacén Sony, ½ c arriba, T2714-2212. Fine Nicaraguan cuisine in a pleasant, ranch-style setting.
$$ Las Brasas, just off northwest corner of central park, T2713-4985. Tue-Sun 1130-2400. Popular, lively place, with stacks of booze and bottles lining the walls. They serve Nicaraguan food and a range of beef dishes, inlcuding steak fillets, *brochetas* and *mixtas*. Try the *cerdo asado*. Recommended.
$$ Tipiscayan, northeast corner of Parque Central, 2 c norte, 2½ c arriba. A relaxing space with lots of interesting artwork and a good balcony upstairs. They serve a range of meat and chicken dishes in *jalapeño* and other sauces.

$$ Vuela Vuela, in Hotel Los Arcos (see above). A pleasant interior and a nice place for an evening meal. They serve meat, chicken and fish dishes, tempting specials like stuffed prawns, and snacks, including tacos and sandwiches. Some dishes, like the export-quality steak and paella, are tasty but pricey (**$$$**).
$$-$ Café Luz, catedral, 1 c al norte, 1 c arriba. This English-owned café is part of a non-profit enterprise that supports communities in Miraflor. They serve a range of breakfasts, including fruit salads with yogurt and granola, pancakes with honey, and – for those homesick Brits – egg and bacon buttie. They also sell *artesanías* and light lunches. Recommended.
$$-$ Cafetería El Rincón Pinareño, Enitel, ½ c sur. Cuban and Nicaraguan dishes and home-made pastries, try *vaca frita* (shredded fried beef with onions and bell peppers), *sandwich cubano*, good service and food, crowded for lunch. Recommended.
$ Koma Rico, Enitel, 1 c norte, 1½ c arriba. Some of the best street food in the city. They serve tasty grilled meats and chicken. Very popular with locals.
$ Sopas El Carao, Almacén Sony, 1 c sur, 1 c abajo, T2713-3678. Daily 0900-2000. Chicken, crab and iguana soups, grilled meats, bull balls consommé. Authentic and recommended.

Cafés, juice bars and bakeries
Ananda, Enitel, 10 vrs abajo. Chilled-out yoga centre full of happy-looking plants. They serve delicious and healthy fresh fruit *licuados* – the perfect nutrient boost. Highly recommended.
La Casita, opposite la Barranca, at south entrance to Estelí on Panamericana, T2713-4917, casita@sdnnic.org.ni. Nicaragua's best home-made yogurt in tropical fruit flavours. Very cute place with pleasant outdoor seating underneath trees on back patio. Recommended.
Repostería Gutiérrez, Parque Infantil, 1 c sur. A good, cheap bakery with bread, *rosquillas* and cakes.

Condega *p257*

$ Bar y Restaurante Linda Vista, on
Panamerican just south of Condega.
Cheap *comida corriente* and cheap-to-
moderate other dishes, very good *sopa
de frijoles* (bean soup), *gallo pinto* and
leche con banano (milk and banana).

$ La Cocina de Virfrank, Km 191, Carretera
Panamericana, T2715-2391. Daily 0630-2000.
Very cute roadside eatery set in a little
garden with excellent food, economical
prices, traditional Nicaraguan dishes and
drinks, also rooms for rent.

ⓝ Bars and clubs

Estelí *p253, map p254*
There are endless options for dancing in
Estelí, Thu-Sun. Most clubs are concentrated
on the Pan-American Highway on the south
side of town. Always use taxis and exercise
caution after dark.

Café Luz, see Restaurants, above. Most
evenings at **Café Luz** see an eclectic mix
of expats, Nicas, volunteers and travellers
gathering to drink beer, coffee or rum, or
otherwise engage in relaxed conversation.

Cigarszone, Carretera Panamericana,
southern entrance to the city. Estelí's most
modern and popular disco. Also features live
music and boisterous young things.

El Chamán, Hospital San Juan de Dios,
200 m sur. Lively place that's attracts a
young, energetic crowd.

Rincón Legal, Hospital San Juan de Dios,
200 m sur. Some say this classic Sandinista
bar has lost its appeal since moving to
its new location. If you're in the area, it's
worth popping in to see the revolutionary
memorabilia and perhaps shake hands with
the manager, an FSLN comrade. Live music
and rousing Sandinista tunes.

Semáforo Rancho Bar, Hospital San Juan
de Dios, 400 m sur. Don your dancing
shoes for Estelí's quintessential night spot.
It hosts some of the best live music in the
country, with nationally and internationally
renowned acts performing regularly.

ⓞ Shopping

Estelí *p253, map p254*
Crafts
Artesanía Sorpresa, opposite Enitel. A new
shop with locally produced handicrafts.
Casa Estelí, Monumento centenario, 20 m
al sur, T713 2584, www.asdenic.org. On the
Pan-American Highway, this information
centre displays arts and crafts by local talent
and co-operatives.
La Esquina, costado oeste de catedral, 1 c
norte. Owned by **Hotel El Méson**, opposite,
they have a decent stock of crafts.

ⓦ What to do

Estelí *p253, map p254*
Cigar making
Estelí's famous cigar factories can be toured
with independent guides or agencies. **Leo
Flores Lovo**, T8415-2428, tourdeltabaco@
gmail.com, leads popular 1-hr tours that
include a chance to roll your own. Also
recommended are **Treehuggers Tours**,
catedral, 1 c al norte, 1 c arriba, inside Hospedaje
Luna, whose tours leave after breakfast,
Mon-Fri, from Café Luz across the street.

Alternatively, you can contact the factories
directly (a comprehensive list is available
from INTUR), although not all of them offer
tours. All visits must be arranged in advance:
Nicaprosa, Star Mark, 400 m northeast,
T2713-9373, nicaprosa@alfanumerie.com.ni.
Tabacos Cubanica, SA, de Obispado, 1 c
al sur, T2713-2383, ileana_06@yahoo.com.
Makes the superb *Padrón* line, routinely
rated in the top 5 in the world.
Tabacalera Cubana García Fernández,
opposite the Monumento Centenario,
T2713-9312, tacubaventas@turbonet.com.ni.
Tabacalera Olivas, CEPAC, 2 c al norte, T2713-
7376, tacunisa@ibww.com.ni. Excellent cigars
and a very professional operation.
Tabacos Puros de Nicaragua, Km 141
Carretera Panamericana, T2713-2758, tpn@
ibww.com.ni. Mon-Fri 0700-1130, 1400-
1630. The oldest of the cigar factories.

Cultural and community tourism

La Garnacha, Reserva Tisey-Estanzuela, contact Yadira Moreno, T2713-7785. At the friendly community you can undertake several hikes and witness the production of their famous goat's cheese. Tours cost US$5 and there are now various self-guided trails and basic lodgings at the Tisey Posada several kilometres away (see page 255).

UCA Miraflor, information and bookings managed by Miraflor Eco-tours and Adventure, east side of the cathedral, 1 c norte, T8405-8919, www.cafeluzyluna.com, inside the Treehuggers tourism office. Many have reported wonderful experiences with this organization that arranges visits to the communities of Miraflor nature reserve. See box, page 256.

Condega *p257*
Cultural and community tourism

Communidad Venecia Cantagallo, Condega, Ramón or William Padilla, T2621-4573. Located 22 km east of Condega, this rural community offers lodging, rowing on the lagoon and guided tours of the surroundings.

◎ Transport

Estelí *p253, map p254*
Bus

Buses enter and leave Estelí via 2 terminals, both on the Pan-American highway. The north terminal deals with northern destinations like Somoto and Ocotal. The south terminal, a short distance away, deals with southern destinations like Managua. A handful of Managua express buses also stop at the Shell station, east of the centre on the Pan-American highway.

North station: to **Somoto**, every hr, 0530-1810, US$1.10, 2½ hrs, use this service to connect to El Espino border bus. To **Ocotal**, every hr, 0600-1730, US$1.40, 2 hrs, use this for bus to Las Manos crossing. To **Jinotega**, every hour, 0445, 0730, 0830, 1330, 1600, US$2.25, 2 hrs. To **El Sauce**, 0900, US$1.25, 3 hrs. To **San Juan de Limay**, 0530,

0700, 1000, 1215, 1400, 1500, US$2.25, 3 hrs. To **Miraflor**, take a bus heading towards **San Sebastián de Yalí** (not one that goes to Condega first), 3 daily 0600, 1200, 1600, US$2, 1½ hrs. Return bus passes at 0700, 1100 and 1620.

South station: express bus to **León**, 0645, US$2.75, 3 hrs. To **Managua**, every 30 mins, 0330-1800, US$2, 3 hrs; express buses, roughly 30 mins, 0545-1515, US$2.75, 2 hrs. To **Matagalpa**, every 30 mins, 0520-1650, US$1.40, 2 hrs; express buses, 0805, 1435, US$1.50, 1½ hrs.

International buses For fares and schedules, see individual agencies: Ticabus, Esteli Drug Store, ½ norte, T713-7350, www.ticabus.com; Transnica, Centro Comercial Estela Módulo 3, T713-6574, www.transnica.com.

Car hire

Budget Rent a Car, catedral, 1 c norte, T713-4030. **Toyota Rent a Car**, Edif Casa Pellas, Km 48, Carretera Panamericana, T713-2716.

Taxi

Taxis are common on the Carretera Panamericana in Estelí, at the bus stations and in the town proper. Fares per person, inside the city centre US$0.50, from the bus stations to centre US$1. Night fares are higher and trips to the dance clubs on the outskirts cost US$2-3. As always, agree on fare before long rides; in town just get in.

Condega *p257*

Buses north- and south-bound pass through the Parque Central in Condega every ½ hr. Bus to **Ocotal** or **Somoto**, both 1 hr, both US$0.75 and to **Estelí** US$0.50, 40 mins.

❶ Directory

Estelí *p253, map p254*

Banks Almost every bank in the city is located in 1 city block. BAC, T2713-7101, changes all brands of TCs. **Fire** T2713-2413.

Hospital San Juan de Dios, Carretera Panamericana, T2713-6300. **Internet** Cafés all over town, US$0.50-1; many are clustered along the central avenue. **Immigration** T713-2086. **Language schools** CENAC, Centro Nicaragüense de Aprendizaje y Cultura, Apdo 40, Estelí, T2713-5437, T2713-5437. 2 offices: Texaco, 5 c arriba, ½ c sur; and de los Bancos 1 c sur, T2713-2025, ½ c arriba. 20 hrs of Spanish classes, living with a family, full board, trips to countryside, meetings and seminars, opportunities to work on community projects, US$140 per week. Also teaches English to Nicaraguans and others and welcomes volunteer tutors. **Horizonte Nica**, INISER, 2 c arriba, ½ c al norte, T2713-4117, www.ibw.com.ni/~horizont. Intensive Spanish courses with a programme of activities and homestay. They offer excursions and voluntary work, and aim to educate you about local communities as well as the language. US$165 for 20 hrs and homestay. **Los Pipitos-Sacuanjoche Escuela de Español**, Costado Noreste Catedral, 1 c norte, ½ c abajo, T2713-5511, www.lospipitosesteli.org.ni. Social projects are a part of the course and all profits go to disabled children and their families. Excursions to local co-operatives and homestay available. US$120-170, flexible options. **Police** T2713-2615. **Post** Correos de Nicaragua, 75 m east of the banks, T2713-2085. **Red Cross** T2713-2330. **Telephone** Enitel, catedral, 1 c sur, T2713-3280.

Somoto

The last major village along the Pan-American Highway before Honduras is Somoto, set in a landscape of rugged mountains and pine forests. Despite being the provincial capital of Madriz, everything happens in its own time here, and its peacefulness can be overwhelming. The population is as quiet as the town, with a shy smile often breaking their sombre exterior. Somoto also takes the title of 'donkey capital' of Nicaragua: the animals are everywhere, chomping at grass in the fields, pulling twice their weight as a beast of burden, or waiting patiently for their owners outside a bar in Somoto. It is safe to say that there are more donkeys than tourists in Somoto, but this may change as tourists discover the Canyon of Somoto, just north of the village. Hope reigns supreme that the canyon will make Somoto a destination for foreign visitors and action is being taken to declare it a National Park. Aside from the canyon, there are beautiful walks and horse rides in the surrounding mountains, including a municipal forest reserve on a mountain west of the village. ▶▶ *For listings, see page 265.*

Arriving in Somoto → *Population: 14.000. Colour map 1, B3.*

Getting there and around There is a regular bus service from Managua and Estelí using the Pan-American Highway. Somoto is a short drive from the Honduran border at El Espino. Walking is good and very safe in the area. Taxis are available in Somoto for trips near the town, otherwise there are intercity buses or private transport. ▶▶ *For futher details, see Transport, page 265.*

Places in Somoto

Somoto is known as one of the safest towns in the country, renowned for its superb *rosquillas* (baked corn and cheese biscuits) – practically a religion – and for its world-famous sons, the folk musicians Carlos and Luis Enrique Mejía Godoy. Their mother, Elsa, has moved back from Managua to the profound peace of the town, and lives across from the INSS office, but the sons are still in Managua and give weekly concerts. The place makes a decent base from which to explore this area and the residents are very welcoming to visitors.

Somoto's church, **La Iglesia Santiago**, was built in 1661 and is an original adobe structure with tile roof, a simple, cool interior and a black Christ above the altar. The Christ figure, *El Señor de los Milagros*, is credited with repelling English pirates in the 17th century. Both this Christ figure and the one in Ciudad Antigua (see page 268) are said to have been brought to Nicaragua in the same year by Spanish missionaries. They left the white icon of Christ in Antigua, where the population was mostly Spanish, and brought the black Christ to Somoto, which is largely indigenous. The old church is charming and must be of very sound construction as it has survived centuries of tremors and earthquakes, including one good shaker in 1954 when General Somoza García was inside attending Mass. As elderly locals recall with bemused smiles, the powerful dictator was the first one to sprint outside. Somoto has a small but important pre-Columbian **museum** ① *Parque Central, T2722-2138, Mon-Fri 0800-1200, 1400-1700*, which displays ceramics with unusual iconography and evidence of trade with Honduras.

For those interested in gastronomic tourism, try visiting one of Somoto's 53 *rosquilla* bakeries. No-one seems sure when *rosquillas* became a tradition here, but the oldest residents recall that they were already popular in the 1920s. The most famous baker could be **Betty Espinoza** ① *Enitel, 3 c norte, T2722-2173, Mon-Sat 0500-1000*, who is happy for visitors to watch the process of butter, corn, eggs, milk, sugar and Nicaraguan feta cheese being made into *rosquillas*; her seven employees and big wood-burning ovens crank out 3000 of them per day. Betty learned from her great-grandmother and 80% of her production is shipped to Managua.

There are also good artisans in Somoto. Crafts include white-clay ceramics and rope art. The **Taller de Cerámica Arturo Machado** ① *on the exit to El Espino at Cruz Roja, 2 c norte*, is worth a look. His work can also be seen at the fabulous crafts store in the **Hotel Panamericano** on Parque Central in Somoto, which has a fine selection of northern crafts, with examples from all over Somoto, Condega, Mozonte, Jinotega and more. The owner, Danilo Morazán, knows most of the artists personally so he can tell you where to find them if you're interested in a visit. The artisans in Somoto and San Lucas often work in henequen (*pita*), which is grown in the area and woven into thread and rope to make beautiful mats and other crafts. You can visit the very friendly Ivania Moncada at the **Cooperativa de Henequeneros de Madriz** ① *Profamilia, 5 c arriba, T2722-2343*.

Grand Canyon of Somoto

① *Follow the highway about 15 km north of Somoto, where you'll find a signposted dirt track at the bridge that crosses over the Tapacalí River. The canyon is accessed by a 20-minute walk from here. Follow the track 3 km to the end where you will meet guides with a boat who will ferry you to the canyon. They may also have inner tubes for hire. Once inside the canyon, you don't need a guide to pass over the rocks, but it's recommended because they're slippery. A taxi here will cost around US$5.*

Fifteen kilometres north of Somoto is one of Nicaragua's most impressive canyons, known locally as *Namancambre*. Its jagged walls soar above crystal-clear waters at the source of the great Río Coco – Central America's longest river – which travels more than 750 km to meet the Caribbean Sea. The canyon is at the convergence of the Río Tapacalí and Río Comalí: the former fed by the mountains of Honduras, the latter by the range behind Somoto. The canyon is 3 km long with a depth of 80-100 m and is extremely narrow at some points.

Border crossings: Nicaragua–Honduras

El Espino/Somoto

There's nowhere to stay in El Espino, 20 km beyond Somoto and 5 km from the Honduran border at La Playa. There's a duty-free shop and a food bar on the Nicaraguan side and several cafés on the Honduran side.

Nicaraguan immigration The Nicaraguan side is open 24 hours. If you're arriving in Nicaragua you'll have to pay US$12 plus a US$1 Alcaldía charge; if you're leaving, US$2 plus a US$1 charge.

Crossing by private vehicle Motorists leaving Nicaragua should enquire in Somoto if an exit permit has to be obtained there or at El Espino. This applies to cyclists too.

Transport Buses run from Somoto to El Espino every hour 0615-1710, US$0.50, 40 minutes. See Somoto for routes to Managua and other destinations. On the Honduran side, taxis go between the border and the Mi Esperanza bus stops, when totally full, 9-10 people, US$1 for foreigners, less for locals. On the Nicaraguan side taxis wait to take you to Somoto, they may try to overcharge; pay no more than US$8.

Money exchange No money changers on Nicaraguan side but locals will oblige, even with lempiras.

Las Manos/Ocotal

This is recommended as the best route from Tegucigalpa to Managua.

Nicaraguan immigration Open 24 hours. All those arriving must fill in an immigration card, present their luggage to the customs authorities, obtain a receipt, and then present these to immigration authorities along with passport and entry fees. When leaving the country, fill out a card, pay the tax and get your passport stamped.

Crossing by private vehicle After completing immigration procedures, go to Tránsito to pay for the vehicle permit, obtain clearance from Revisión, and get your vehicle permit from Aduana (Customs). Travellers advise that if it is busy, go first to Customs and get your number in the queue. On leaving the country, complete the immigration requirements, then go to Tránsito to have the vehicle checked, and to Customs to have the vehicle stamp in the passport cancelled. Surrender the vehicle permit at Customs and take another form back to Tránsito; this will be stamped, signed and finally handed over at the exit gate.

Transport Buses run from Las Manos to Ocotal, every 30 minutes or when full, 0615-1730, US$0.80, 45 minutes. Taxis are also available for US$7-8; agree fare before boarding.

Money exchange Money changers operate on both sides, offering córdobas at a little better than the street market rate in Nicaragua. Rates for cash and TC exchange are usually better in Estelí.

Now protected as part of the **Reserva Tepesomoto-Pataste**, a walk in the canyon is both a contemplative and adventurous experience, requiring careful hiking over slippery shore rocks hugging the sides of the canyon walls. A rest stop reveals trees glimmering in the sun, caressed by gentle winds and the muffled babble of the stream. This is a solitary slot in the earth that a 13-million-year-old knife of water has cut through solid rock. From inside the canyon, with its green water and marvellously sculpted reddish stone, the sky is but a narrow blue glimmer. You can swim in the waters of the canyon during the dry season, but it can be very dangerous in the rainy season (June to November) even if not swimming, as water levels can change quickly and currents are very strong.

⊙ Somoto listings

For sleeping and eating price codes and other relevant information, see pages 28-30.

⊙ Where to stay

Somoto *p262*

$$ Hotel Colonial, Iglesia, ½ c sur, T2722-2040. An attractive, professionally managed hotel with decent rooms; all have private bath, cable TV and fan. Popular with businessmen and NGOs.

$ El Bambú, Policía Nacional, 2 c norte, T2722-2330. 20 simple, cheap rooms with cable TV. Some have bath, some don't. Close to the highway and bus station.

$ Hotel Panamericano, on north side of Parque Central, T2722-2355. Good-value rooms at this interesting hotel, where you'll find an orchid collection, a craft shop and a menagerie of animals. The annexed section, a few roads away, has a lovely garden an recreation area. They arrange trips to the Canyon and surrounding countryside. Highly recommended.

$ Hospedaje La Provedencia, Intel, 2½ c norte, T2722-2089. 6 simple rooms with 2 shared baths inside a house. Friendly, family-run and basic.

⊙ Restaurants

Somoto *p262*

$$-$ La Llanta, Petronic, 1 c abajo, T2722-2291. Mon-Fri 1000-2200, Sat-Sun 1000-2400. Good pork dishes, hot pepper steak, *comida corriente*.

$$-$ Restaurante Almendro, Iglesia, ½ c sur. Famous for its steaks, and serves good *comida corriente*. The big tree in the centre gives the restaurant its name and is famous for being mentioned in a Mejía Godoy song.

$$-$ Restaurante Somoteño, Parque Central, 2 c abajo, 75 vrs norte, on Carretera Panamericana, T2722-2518. Cheery outdoor seating with bamboo walls, great beef grill with friendly service and monumental portions: *corriente* (normal), *semi à la carte* (too big) and *à la carte* (way too big). Sat is karaoke night. Recommended.

$ Cafetería Bambi, Enitel, 2½ c sur, T2722-2231. Tue-Sun 0900-2200. Surprisingly no deer on the menu, just sandwiches, hamburgers, hot dogs, tacos and fruit juices.

$ Comedor Familiar, Iglesia Santiago, 1 c al sur, ½ c al este. Locals' haunt that's good for a cheap meal and discreet people-watching.

⊖ Transport

Somoto *p262*

Buses to **El Espino** and the Honduran border, every hour, 0515-1715, US$0.50, 40 mins. To **Estelí**, every hour, 0520-1700, US$1.25, 2½ hrs; express buses are Managua-bound, US$1.65, 1½ hrs, they will drop you off at the Shell station, just east of central Estelí. Express bus to **Managua**, Mon-Sat, 0345, 0500, 0615, 0730, 1400, 1515, Sun 1400, 1515, US$4, 3½ hrs. To **Ocotal**, every 45 mins, 0345-1635, US$0.75, 1½ hrs.

⊙ Directory

Somoto *p262*

Banks Banco de Finanzas (BDF), T2722-2240, in front of the Alcaldía. **Hospital** West side of Parque Central, T2722-2247. **Fire** T2722-2776. **Police** T2722-2359. **Post** Correos de Nicaragua, southeast corner of park, T2722-2437. **Red Cross** T2722-2285. **Telephone** Enitel, behind church, T2722-2374.

Nueva Segovia

Along with León and Granada, Nueva Segovia is Nicaragua's oldest Spanish province, founded in the early 16th century for mining purposes. Located in the extreme north of Nicaragua the province contains the peaceful and historic indigenous communities of Totogalpa and Mozonte, the trading centre of Ocotal, which has decent accommodation, and the ancient forgotten village of Ciudad Antigua. With just two paved roads, the area is deeply rural and a 4WD is a valuable tool because local buses are slow and dusty. This is also an alternative route to Honduras, via the highway to Ocotal and Las Manos. Travelling further from the Pan-American Highway, the Carretera a Ocotal runs north and the landscape changes into jagged hills and pine trees. The bridge just before Ocotal crosses Central America's longest river, the Río Coco, before which is the historic red-earth indigenous village of Totogalpa. ▸▸ *For listings see pages 269-270.*

Arriving in Nueva Segovia

Getting there and around There are regular buses from Managua and Estelí along the Pan-American Highway. Somoto is a short drive from the Honduran border at Las Manos. Walking is not ideal around Ocotal but Totogalpa and Ciudad Antigua offer better hiking opportunities. Taxis are available in Ocotal for trips near to the town, otherwise intercity buses and private transport are available. ▸▸ *For further details, see Transport, page 270.*

Comunidad Indígena de Totogalpa → *For listings, see pages 269-270.*

Arriving in Totogalpa, technically in the department of Madriz, feels like arriving at the very end of the earth. This seemingly forgotten town, with its romantic colonial-period churches and ageing population, has seen its youth move to cities and foreign lands in search of work. The bright red clay streets and its crumbling, yet attractive, adobe homes add to the town's rustic other-worldliness. The original settlement dates back more than 1600 years and is located in the community of San José, northeast of the current village along the banks of the Río Coco. This is now a major archaeological site yet to be excavated but check with the mayor's office if you're interested in a visit. The remains of circular stone houses and ceramics suggest that this was a large settlement from AD 400-600. Today's indigenous community plans to build a new museum to house the recovered artefacts.

Totogalpa celebrates its patron saint, Virgen de la Merced, from 8 to 23 September. The festival of María Magdalena takes place during the week of 22 July and may afford the opportunity to see an **ancient indigenous dance** that was banned by the church on numerous occasions but is still practised by some indigenous communities in the Northern Highlands – mainly at funerals where they dance with palm fronds around the deceased. During the Magdalena festival the local dance group *Nido de Aves* performs *La Danza de la Palma*.

The British naturalist Thomas Belt visited Totogalpa in 1871, during one of its festival days. He didn't mention which saint the community was celebrating but he did describe the men drinking *chicha* in *jícaro* bowls and the women decorating the interior of Totogalpa's charming parish. "We found a number of the Indian women with great baskets full of the most beautiful and sweet-smelling flowers, making garlands and bouquets to decorate the holy images and church. The beautiful flowers were twined in wreathes or stuck on prepared stands and shapes, and their fragrance filled the church. At other mestizo towns, where the churches were like dilapidated barns, we heard much of the religious fervour of the Indians of Totogalpa."

La Cueva del Duende

ⓘ *It is said that once inside La Cueva del Duende all torches immediately stop working.*

In the area surrounding Totogalpa there are opportunities for hiking, caving and rafting along the Río Coco between the Canyon of Somoto and Ocotal. One kilometre north of Totogalpa is **Cerro de las Rocas** and a trail that leads to a cave inside the mountain, La Cueva del Duende. The name, 'Leprechaun's Cave', relates to a widely held local belief in leprechauns. Danni Altamirano, at the **Hotel El Camino** in Totogalpa, is brave enough to take visitors to the cave. He, or his brother, can also organize rafting trips along the Río Coco.

Ocotal → *For listings, see pages 269-270.*

This little city with its sprawling suburbs is the financial and trading centre for the region, but has little to offer visitors. The population is more serious and less friendly than in most parts of the country. Ocotal is, however, a useful jumping-off point for visiting some of the beautiful villages in the region, such as Mozonte or Ciudad Antigua, or to rest before or after the border crossing at Las Manos. **INTUR** ⓘ *Procredit, ½ c abajo, T2732-3429, ocotal@ intur.gob.ni,* has brochures of general interest in English, ask about some very interesting farm stays available in the highlands of Dipilto. Check www.ocotalnicaragua.com for a great English-language source of information about the town.

Ocotal's main attraction is its Parque Central, which is like no other in Nicaragua. **Parque Las Madres**, as it is called, is a lush tropical garden designed by the ex-mayor of Ocotal and tropical plant expert, Don Fausto Sánchez. It contains a stunning display of plant diversity with its dense tapestry of greens, reds, oranges, yellows and pinks. Set within the relative ugliness of Ocotal, the park is a leafy refuge and a reminder of the stunning fertility of the tropics. If you are fortunate enough to find Don Fausto inside the park caring for his garden, he may take you on an impromptu tour, naming over 100 species and highlighting each plant's special charm. The church on the Parque Central is attractive and also worth a look. Founded in 1803, **El Templo Parroquial de Ocotal** was not finished until 1869. Its baroque and neoclassical façade hide a simple and attractive interior with pine (*ocotl*) columns and comfortable curved pews. There are some very pretty icons inside, which are said to have been imported from La Antigua, Guatemala.

The patron saint of Ocotal is the *Virgen de la Asunción* whose day of celebration is 15 August. The festival lasts all week and includes a parade of 22 brightly decorated ox carts, one of which holds the festival queen. On 11 August is the northern Nicaraguan version of Carnival – a sort of a mini-Woodstock held in Parque Central, with an endless flow of bands.

Ocotal, named after the ocotl species of pine tree that once enveloped the town, has the dubious distinction of being the first town in the world to be bombed by a fleet of military aeroplanes in combat circumstances. The co-ordinated bombing raid was courtesy of the US Marines in July 1927. This was a practice that would continue throughout Nicaragua's northern mountains from 1927 to 1933 as the Marines and newly formed National Guard fought in vain to destroy Sandino's rebel army. In May 1927, Sandino rejected a pact made between liberal generals and the US military. On 11 July the US Marine captain gave Sandino 48 hours to turn over his arms in Ocotal. Sandino waited until 16 July and at 0115 attacked the Marine base, today Ocotal's **Casa de Cultura** ⓘ *east side of the Parque Central, T2732-2839.* The battle lasted until five Marine biplanes arrived at 1435, dropping over

300 fragmentation bombs during a one-hour period, forcing Sandino's troops to retreat. From then on, Sandino changed his tactics, avoiding face-to-face confrontation whenever possible and moving towards modern guerrilla warfare.

Comunidad Indígena de Mozonte

Four kilometres east of Ocotal is the sleepy, ancient village of Mozonte, renowned for its ceramic artisans. Mozonte (often spelt Mosonte) has a special beauty and a proud population that has done much to preserve its indigenous form of government. The system is run by a council of elders and relies on the spirit of community co-operation. This is apparent in the way the ceramic artisans share tools like kilns and shops, while simultaneously keeping independent business ownership. There are several **co-operatives** of over 50 artisans working in ceramics, one of which is located at Km 3.5 on the highway from Ocotal (T732-2810). The most common theme is a floral vase with a country village carved out in relief and painted with bright colours. This is one of the poorest municipalities in Nicaragua, so a good way to support the community is to buy from the talented artisans who are happy to receive visitors.

There are two interesting churches in Mozonte. **Iglesia Mozonte** in the central square dates to 1703 and is one of the oldest parish churches in its original state in the country. The other temple, **Ermita de la Virgen de Guadalupe**, built in 1763, contains several relics dating back to its construction. It is an eerie-looking chapel that sits alone on the summit of the hill to the north of the village. The *Loma Santa* (holy hilltop) chapel is reached by a long flight of steps in the extreme north of the town and affords fabulous views.

Ciudad Antigua → *For listings, see pages 269-270.*

Nestled in a valley of rolling hills, the Ciudad Antigua of today is truly in the middle of nowhere, but that was not always the case. Originally called Nueva Ciudad Segovia, it was founded in 1611 by Spanish colonists who hurriedly abandoned the first Ciudad Segovia settlement (founded between 1541 and 1543 near current-day Quilalí), as a result of continued attacks by the indigenous populations. In the late 1600s, the city was attacked by pirates and most of the population fled to found Ocotal, or further south to found Estelí at the turn of the 18th century. The economy of Ciudad Antigua was based on pine pitch extraction, which had value as caulking for sailing ships, and also to seal barrels that were used to transport wine from Peru.

The church in Ciudad Antigua is one of the finest examples of *mudéjar* (Spanish Arab influenced) construction and is very similar to the churches of Totogalpa and Sutiava. From the 17th century onwards the town was attacked by English and French pirates, one of whom, Ravenau de Lussan, wrote a description of the church and town that is still accurate today. The British pirate, Charles Morgan, was another pirate who sacked the town and residents of 21st-century Ciudad Antigua claim that these pirates are to blame for their current state of poverty. During the Contra War, 1982-1990, Ciudad Antigua was the scene of heavy fighting between Contra and Sandinista troops and the countryside around the town was a free fire zone.

Places in Ciudad Antigua

The village has not changed much for the last few centuries, providing an excellent opportunity to step back in time. **Parque Central** lies to the left of the road entrance. The park is elegant, inexplicably large and infallibly empty. The lovely **church** was built in 1654 and many of its original 17th-century doors and walls are intact. The interior is whitewashed adobe, with an ornate gold-leaf altar that bears a famous image of Jesus or *El Señor de los Milagros*, donated by an Austrian queen. The image is said to have been brought to Ciudad Antigua, along with the heavy altar, via a Caribbean port in Honduras and transported here by manpower alone. According to local legend, *El Señor de los Milagros* was not willing to be stolen. During the numerous pirate raids, the icon grew so large that it was impossible to extract it through the massive front doors. He is celebrated every 20 January with processions throughout the town.

The **Museo Religioso de Ciudad Antigua** ⓘ *T2732-2227, Mon-Fri*, is a small, musty and delightful museum of ancient religious artefacts next to the church. Doña Rosivel (often found in the little crucifix store in front of the church) has the key and is the best guide in town. She can take you into the museum to see rare colonial artefacts (and bats). The talkative Roque Toledo, the official town guide, is a lot of fun, but if your Spanish is not perfect his long-winded explanations can be exhausting, bewildering or both. Roque will also take you to the southern outskirts of town to see the baseball stadium and the ruins of the **Iglesia La Merced**.

ⓦ Nueva Segovia listings

For sleeping and eating price codes and other relevant information, see pages 28-30.

ⓦ Where to stay

Totogalpa *p266*
$ Hotel El Camino, along the main entrance road to the village. Private bath, fan, parking, clean, light rooms. Cheap meals are available in the owner's house. Recommended.

Ocotal *p267*
Ocotal has a large mosquito population, even in the dry season; bring a net.
$$ Hotel Frontera, behind the Shell station on the highway to Las Manos, T2732-2668, hosfrosa@turbonett.com. This is the best hotel in town, even if it looks like a prison compound from outside. It has an inviting swimming pool, bar, restaurant and events room. The rooms are clean and comfortable, if uninspiring, and cheaper without a/c (**$**). They also offer Wi-Fi, laundry service and international call facility.
$ Casa Huésped 'Llamarada del Bosque', Parque Central, T2732-2643, llamaradadelbosque@hotmail.com. Conveniently located, this reasonably priced hotel has a wide range of rooms, but those upstairs are more spacious, modern and comfortable (**$$**). Services include Wi-Fi, cable TV, fan, hot water and conference room. They also own the popular restaurant on the corner of the plaza.
$ Hostal Canada, Instituto Nacional de Segovia, 2 c oeste, T2732-0309. Quiet, friendly hotel with 7 simple rooms, all equipped with private bath and fan. Good kitchen and a comfortable sitting room with TV. Breakfast is offered but not included.
$ Hotel Belrive, Shell station on the highway, 1 c oeste, T2732-2146. This motel-style place has rooms with bath, hot water and cable TV. There's parking and a restaurant. Pleasant and friendly. Cheaper without a/c.
$ Hotel Benmoral, at south entrance to city, opposite FINOSA, T2732-2824. 24 dark, clean rooms with a/c or fan, cable TV, Wi-Fi and hot water. Food is available, and there's parking space. Friendly and helpful.
$ Hotel Restaurant Mirador, opposite bus station, T2732-2496. 22 rooms with cable TV, private bath and hot water. Some are nicer than others. As the name suggests, there's a small restaurant attached.

🍴 Restaurants

Ocotal *p267*
Most restaurants have a mid-range menu with cheap *comida corriente* available.

$$-$ Llamarada del Bosque, south side of Parque Central, T2732-2643. Popular locals' joint that serves tasty and cheap buffet food and *comida típica*.

$$-$ Restaurante El Paraíso, at south entrance to Ocotal, T2732-3301. Pleasant open-air setting, steak, chicken and pork dishes, moderate prices.

$$-$ Restaurante La Cabaña, next to Hotel Benmoral, T2732-2415. Daily 1000-2300. Good steak dishes like *filete a la cabaña* or *jalapeño* steak, moderate prices, avoid the shrimps. Lovely garden setting with banana trees and separate gazebos for the tables.

$$-$ Restaurante La Yunta, Casa Pellas 75 vrs al sur, T732-2180. Daily 1100-2300. A range of beef, steak and fillet dishes to delight any carnivore, good sea bass and grilled pork. Recommended.

$ Comedor la Esquinita, Esso, 1 c al sur. Clean, pleasant *comedor* with tables set around a leafy courtyard. They serve cheap Nica fare for breakfast and lunch, but service is brusque.

🚌 Transport

Totogalpa *p266*
Buses pass the village on the highway, every 15 mins for **Ocotal** US$0.40 and **Estelí** US$0.80.

Ocotal *p267*
Bus
The bus station for Ocotal is on the highway, 1 km south of the town centre, 15-20 mins' walk from Parque Central. Buses to **Las Manos/Honduras border** (see page 264) every 30 mins, 0500-1645, US$0.80, 45 mins. To **Somoto**, every 45 mins, 0545-1830, US$0.75, 2½ hrs. Express bus to **Managua**, 10 daily, 0400-1530, US$4.50, 4 hrs. To **Ciudad Antigua**, 0500, 1200, US$1.25, 1½ hrs. To **Estelí**, leaves the city market every hour, 0445-1800, US$1.30, 2½ hrs; express buses are Managua-bound, 2 hrs, US$1.65, they will drop you off at the Shell station, just east of central Estelí.

Taxi
Ocotal taxis are cheap, with rides within town costing about US$0.40. A ride to **Las Manos** and the border with Honduras will cost US$7-9.

Ciudad Antigua *p268*
There is 1 bus per day to **Ocotal** at 1400, 1½ hrs, US$1.50.

ℹ️ Directory

Ocotal *p267*
Bank Bancentro, Parque Central, 1 c norte, 1 c abajo, has a Visa ATM and money-changing facility; as does Banco Procredit, Parque Central, 1 c abajo. **Fire** T2732-2390. **Hospital** T2732-2491. **Police** T2732-2657. **Post** Correos de Nicaragua, Esso, 2 c sur, T2732-3021. **Red Cross** T2732-2485. **Telephone** Enitel is on the north side of Parque Central, ½ c norte, T2732-2321.

Contents

Footprint features

Caribbean Coast & Islands

At a glance

⊖ **Getting around** There are few roads in the region and those that exist are mostly unpaved and washed out in the wet season. Single-propeller planes and rugged 4WDs are necessary to access some areas; otherwise nearly all travel is conducted by boat.

⊙ **Time required** 7-14 days.

☼ **Weather** Rainfall is significantly higher on the Caribbean side than the Pacific. Typically, May-Jul are the wettest months, but you should expect torrential storms at any time of the year.

⊗ **When not to go** If you intend to navigate the rivers, late in the dry season is a bad time to visit. Snorkelling and diving are comparatively poor in the wet season, as is hiking, when conditions are boggy and bug-infested. There's a risk of hurricanes Jun-Nov – take particular care travelling in RAAN during that time.

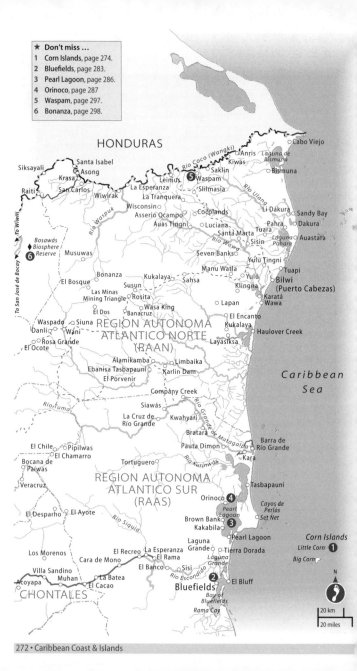

HONDURAS

Cabo Viejo

Siksayali
Santa Isabel
Krasa
Asong
Raiti
San Carlos
Wiwirak
Río Coco (Wangki)
Anris
Laguna de Bismuna
Kiwas
Leimus
Waspam
Saklin
Bismuna
La Esperanza
Slilmasia
La Tranquera

To Wiwili

Río Waspuk

Wisconsino
Asserio Ocampo
Auas Tingni
Cocolands
Li Dákura
Luciana
Santa Marta
Río Wawa
Sisin
Pahra
Sandy Bay
Dakura
Laguna Pahara
Auastara
Seven Banks
Yulu Tingni
Tuapi

Bosawás Biosphere Reserve
Musuwas
Manu Watla
Yulu
Bilwi (Puerto Cabezas)
Klingna
Karatá
Wawa

Bonanza
Kukalaya
Sahsa
El Bosque
Susun
Las Minas Mining Triangle
Rosita
Wasa King
Lapan
El Dos
Banacruz
El Encanto
Kukalaya
Waspado
Siuna
Haulover Creek
Danlí
Wani
REGION AUTONOMA ATLANTICO NORTE (RAAN)
Layasiksa
Rosa Grande
El Ocote

Alamikamba
Limbaika
Ebanisa Tasbapauni
Karlin Dam
El Porvenir

Caribbean Sea

Company Creek

Río Tuma

Siawás
La Cruz de Río Grande
Kwahyari
Río Grande de Matagalpa
Bratara
Barra de Río Grande
El Chile
Pipilwas
El Chamarro
Pauta Dimon
Kara
Bocana de Paiwas
Tortuguero
Río Kurinwás
Veracruz
REGION AUTONOMA ATLANTICO SUR (RAAS)
Tasbapauni

El Desparho
El Ayote
Río Siquia
Orinoco
Cayos de Perlas
Set Net
Brown Bank
Pearl Lagoon
Kakabila
Pearl Lagoon

Los Morenos
Laguna Grande
Tierra Dorada
Corn Islands
Cara de Mono
El Recreo
La Esperanza
El Rama
Laguna Grande
Little Corn
Villa Sandino
El Banco
Sisi
Big Corn
Acoyapa
Muhan
La Batea
El Cacao
Río Escondido
El Bluff
CHONTALES
Bluefields
Bay of Bluefields
Rama Cay

N

20 km
20 miles

Nicaragua's Caribbean Coast enjoys a thriving multicultural heritage that sets it apart from its Pacific cousin. British buccaneers, Jamaican labourers, Chinese immigrants, Afro-descendent Garífunas, indigenous Miskitos, Mayagnas and Ramas have all contributed to the region's exotic flavours. Lilting Creole English, not Spanish, is the traditional lingua franca. Take the single propeller plane over and you'll soon see why La Costa Atlántica has developed along its own unique lines – an unrelenting carpet of green treetops, meandering toffee-coloured rivers and swollen lagoons separate it from the rest of Nicaragua. Few roads – or Spanish colonists – have ever penetrated this inhospitable wilderness of rainforest and swamp.

The Corn Islands are the region's principal attraction: two dazzling offshore atolls with white-sand beaches, scintillating coral reefs and turquoise waters. Little Corn is a low-key dive centre, Big Corn is home to diverse fishing communities and a good place to sample authentic Caribbean life while it lasts. On the mainland, Bluefields is the nearest city of any size, a decaying and shambolic spectre, but ripe with all the sights, sounds and smells of any bustling tropical port. This is the place to drink rum and watch the tropical storms roll in.

The coast's isolation has allowed the Miskito peoples to thrive here, asserting their political will through the Yatama political party and controlling municipal governments since 2004. In the North Atlantic Autonomous Region (RAAN), Bilwi is the administrative capital of the Miskito world, but Waspam is its spiritual heart. Located on the banks of the formidable Río Coco, only the truly brave and adventurous will get this far. Surrounded by dense forests, a sturdy boat and a trustworthy guide will be necessary to navigate the river, its complex network of tributaries and the many remote communities that comprise the obscure and truly fascinating Miskito nation.

Corn Islands

The Corn Islands are a portrait of Caribbean indolence with their languid palm trees, colourful clapboard houses and easy, rum-soaked dilapidation. Divorced from the mainland by 70 km of turquoise sea, many islanders are incurable eccentrics. Few, if any, pay much mind to the world outside, concerning themselves only with the friendships, feuds and often entertaining gossip that is the staple diet of island life. But a burgeoning tourist trade and Colombian 'business interests' mean the islands are no longer the place to experience the authentic Caribbean life of days gone by. Outsiders are steadily infiltrating, bringing tourists, foreign-owned hotels and crime. But like everything else here, the pace of change has been slow. For now, the islands remain distinctly low-key, staunchly individualistic, and governed by a handful of families who have been here for generations. Scratch the surface and you'll discover that many things are as they have always been: rains come and go, mangoes fall, and waves lap the sugar-white beaches in perpetuity. ▶ For listings, see pages 277-282.

Arriving in the Corn Islands → *Population: 6370. Altitude: 4-90 m. Colour map 4, B3.*

Getting there The islands are 70 km off the mainland of Nicaragua. The big island is 13 sq km and the little one is 3.5 sq km. About 7 km of Caribbean Sea separates them. La Costeña flies twice daily to Big Corn and there are boat services three times a week from Bluefields. Transport to Little Corn is on a twice-daily skiff with two big outboards and good native navigators. The boat has no roofing to protect from rain and sun and it can be a wet ride if it's rough – not for the weak-hearted. ▶ *For further details, see Transport, page 282.*

Getting around The big island has one paved road that does a lap of the island with two buses and nearly 100 taxis. The small island has no roads; walking or boating are the only way of getting around.

Tourist information There is an official tourist office inside the island's Alcaldía, Brig Bay, otherwise your best bet is to chat to locals. A good online source of information is www.bigcornisland.com.

Safety Paradise has a dark side and you should use common sense at all times. Avoid walking at night on the island anywhere, always use a taxi to get between bars and your hotel. Theoretically, there is now a police force on Little Corn, but they may be hard to find. It's better not to walk alone in the bush, and don't walk there at night at all. Don't go out with locals unless recommended by your hotel; thieves, known as 'pirates', sometimes pose as informal tour guides.

Background

During his fourth and final exploratory voyage, Columbus encountered the islands and named them *Islas Limonares*. At the time, they were inhabited by the Kukra people, of which little is known today except for a reported tendency towards cannibalism. During the 18th century the islands became a haven for pirates resting in between pillages. Eventually they were settled by Afro-Caribbeans, mostly Jamaicans, who arrived from the neighbouring islands of San Andrés. The local economy was based on the production of palm oil until the devastating winds of Hurricane Joan in 1988, which reached over 200 kph and destroyed most of the palm trees on the island. Lobster fishing took over as the biggest industry, but supplies are being depleted rapidly. Tourism and 'white lobster' (cocaine) are taking over as the biggest sources of income for the islanders (see box, page 285). Thanks to their proximity to the San Andrés Islands, which come under Colombian jurisdiction (although located inside Nicaragua's ocean platform), drug traffickers have had a lot of involvement here, using Little Corn as a refuelling stop for many years. Today there's a meagre police presence, frequently rotated to keep hands (and noses) clean. But there is still a lot of drug money on both islands, and parcels of coke are still dumped at sea (albeit less and less frequently), allowing locals to fish for the lucrative 'white lobster'. Meanwhile, there has been a migration of Miskito communities from the mainland to the islands to dive for real lobster, although dwindling supplies have created unemployment in both native and

Big Corn Island

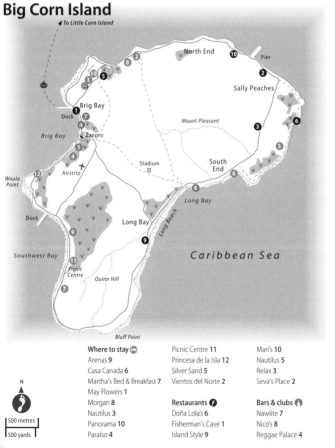

Where to stay	Picnic Centre 11	Mari's 10
Arenas 9	Princesa de la Isla 12	Nautilus 5
Casa Canada 6	Silver Sand 5	Relax 3
Martha's Bed & Breakfast 7	Vientos del Norte 2	Seva's Place 2
May Flowers 1		
Morgan 8	Restaurants	Bars & clubs
Nautilus 3	Doña Lola's 6	Nawlite 7
Panorama 10	Fisherman's Cave 1	Nico's 8
Paraíso 4	Island Style 9	Reggae Palace 4

migrant populations, with some desperate people turning to crime. Yet there is a surprising affluence to both islands that can probably only be explained by tourism or drugs. Either way, the Corn Island natives remain some of the most hospitable, polite and welcoming people in Nicaragua; a people with a profound understanding of the word 'relaxed'.

Big Corn → *For listings, see pages 277-282.*

Big Corn has a good landing strip, airport terminal and quite a few decent hotels. Around Waula Point is **Picnic Centre**, a fine beach for swimming and sunbathing. On the sparsely populated southeastern part of the island is the long and tranquil **Long Beach** in Long Bay. With Quinn Hill rising above the western part of the bay it is also very scenic – climb the hill to see an interesting pyramid art sculpture, the **Soul of the World**, www.souloftheworld. com, part of a global installation with counterparts in Botswana, Argentina, Australia and other far-off destinations. The most interesting nature is to be found beneath the water, with beautiful reefs and rich marine life. There are also several ancient canons belonging to a sunken Spanish galleon, but you'll need a boat to reach them. Snorkelling is best on the northern coast of Big Corn, just west of **Sally Peaches**. The eastern side of the island is the most rustic and quieter. Facing the Atlantic, it has good waves for most of the year and plenty of rocks. There are numerous estuaries and wetlands all around the island, containing a startling amount of fresh water. Birdlife is generally disappointing.

The beaches on the west and southern side of the island are best for swimming. Walking around the island takes about three hours. Big Corn does not offer the natural beauty of Little Corn, but it is more lively and those who bore easily or are not interested in snorkelling or diving might prefer the big island. The eastern part of the island has a lovely community called **South End**, the most idyllic example of Afro-Caribbean culture on the islands. Most of the island's social life, however, is concentrated in the built-up community around Brig Bay. To celebrate the abolition of slavery in 1841, Big Corn holds an annual festival, culminating on the anniversary of the decree on 27 August (book accommodation well in advance for this week) with the **Crab Soup Festival**. Various activities take place, including the election of a Crab Festival Queen, and copious amounts of crab soup are served.

Little Corn → *For listings, see pages 277-282.*

The small island has some of the finest coral reefs in Nicaragua and is a superb place for snorkelling and diving. *National Geographic Explorer* gave the reefs nine out of 10. Little Corn is more relaxed and less developed than its larger neighbour, although it now suffers from low-level crime and sees huge numbers of visitors in the high season. The locals on the island are keenly aware of the beauty of their home and are learning to adapt to its growing popularity.

The island has good opportunities for walking, with the north end of the island a mixture of scrub forest and grazing land leading down to the brilliant turquoise sea. The prettiest side of the island is also the windward side; visiting during a windy period can be disappointing for snorkellers but helps calm mosquitoes and the heat. The most developed areas are along the western shores of the narrow southern part of the island, separated from the windswept east coast by a large swamp. This is where the boats arrive and there are numerous options for sleeping and eating. The water is calm and good for swimming and there is a good sense of community spirit here.

There are lovely highlands at both southern and northern tips of the island. The highlands of the southeast have been cordoned off by the **Casa Iguana** (see page 279), but the northern ones are open to all and have great beaches and only a few foreign settlers. South of an attractive Southeast Asian-style lodge called **Derek's** (see page 279), there is a long spectacular beach that runs the entire length of the island, broken only by some small rocky points. Near the southern end of this beach there are good places to eat right on the sand and simple lodges. All the beaches have sugar-white sand, although it disappears at high tide. There is some very interesting and unique artisan jewellery sold south of Hotel **Los Delfines** (see page 279), near the village at the 'bottle house' of Vice Mayor 'Tall Boy' Robert Knight, which also sells shoes, sandals and T-shirts.

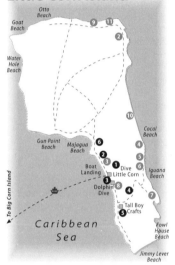

Little Corn Island

Otto Beach
Goat Beach
Water Hole Beach
Gun Point Beach
Majagua Beach
Boat Landing
Dive Little Corn
Dolphin Dive
Tall Boy Crafts
Cocal Beach
Iguana Beach
Fowl House Beach
Jimmy Lever Beach
Caribbean Sea
To Big Corn Island

N
10 km
10 miles

Where to stay
Casa Iguana 7
Derek's 2
Elsa's 6
Ensueños 9
Grace Cool Spot 5
Little Corn Beach and Bungalows 10
Lobster Inn 3
Los Delfines 8
Peace and Love Farm 11
Sunrise Paradise 4

Restaurants
Café Tranquilo 3
Doña Rosa's 4
Habana Libre 2
Mango's Pizza 5
Miss Bridgette's 1
Triángulo 6

Corn Islands listings

For sleeping and eating price codes and other relevant information, see pages 28-30.

Where to stay

Big Corn *p276, map p275*
$$$ Arenas Hotel, Picnic Centre, T2222-6574, www.arenasbeachhotel.com. This professionally managed hotel is the closest thing Big Corn has to a resort. It has modern double rooms, comfortable wooden bungalows and luxury suites overlooking the ocean, all with cable TV, hot water, a/c and hammocks. There's a restaurant and conference centre, and a range of other services too. Free use of kayaks and breakfast included.
$$$ Casa Canada, South End, T8644-0925, www.casa-canada.com. Sophisticated, luxurious rooms with ocean views. Each is splendidly equipped with a DVD player, minibar, coffee-maker, leather chairs and mahogany furniture. There's free Wi-Fi for guests and a beautiful infinity pool overlooks the waves. Friendly and hospitable management. Recommended.
$$$-$$ Hotel Paraíso, Brig Bay, T2575-5111, www.paraisoclub.com. A professional, friendly hotel, managed by 2 Dutch gentlemen, Mike and Ton, who contribute to local social projects. They have 9 doubles (**$$**) and 5 bungalows (**$$$**), all clean, comfortable and well fitted with a/c, hammocks and mosquito nets. Hotel Paraíso is right on the beach, and there's good

snorkelling at the wreck offshore. Tours, massages and fishing trips can be arranged; ask Mike about seeing the reefs or touring the island in a golf cart. Prices include breakfast at their restaurant, which has free Wi-Fi and an internet terminal. Highly recommended.

$$$-$$ Princesa de la Isla, Waula Point, T8854-2403, www.laprincesadelaisla.com. The Princess' setting on a windswept point is eternally romantic. They have 2 bungalows (**$$$**) – often reserved for honeymooners – and a handful of rooms (**$$**), all with hot water, hammocks and unusual furnishings. The friendly Italian owners also offer good coffee, wine and Italian food (**$$$**) – call 3-4 hrs in advance to get the pasta cooking. Wi-Fi available.

$$ Martha's Bed & Breakfast, Southwest Bay, just south of Picnic Centre, T8835-5930. This hotel has lovely landscaped grounds and 8 clean, unpretentious rooms with private bath, a/c and cable TV. Comfortable enough, but the value isn't great.

$$ Picnic Centre, Picnic Centre Beach, T2575-5285. **Picnic Centre** has several average rooms with private bath, cable TV and a/c. They have a very popular ranch on the beach for eating (**$$-$**) and drinking, and worth a visit if sleeping elsewhere. Good ambience and great location.

$$ Vientos del Norte, North End, T2575-5112, www.bigcornisland.com/vientosdelnorte.html. Also known as Ike's place, **Vientos del Norte** offers a range of well-equipped quarters with fridge, coffee machine, microwave and toaster. Those overlooking the ocean or with a/c cost slightly more. They also have an annex with well-furnished family-sized lodgings and some economy rooms. Friendly, recommended.

$$-$ Hotel Morgan, North Point, T2575-5052. **Hotel Morgan** has a restaurant, Wi-Fi service, trim lawn, hammocks and many bright pink structures of concrete and wood. They offer a range of accommodation, including 3 *cabañas* (**$$**) equipped with

hot water, a/c and fridge. Their cheapest rooms (**$**) have TV, fan and shared bath, whilst those with a/c and own bath cost a little more.

$$-$ Panorama, Iglesia Católica, ½ c al este, T2575-5065. This gently fading motel-style place near a small beach has simple a/c rooms with private bath, porch, mosquito net and deckchairs. The economy rooms lack a/c or porch and are quite musty. Mosquitoes are an issue; bring repellent.

$ May Flowers, Brig Bay, on the beach, T8821-8749. This guesthouse on the beach has 5 good, clean, straightforward rooms with private bath and fan. A good option for budget travellers and couples. Quiet and peaceful but just a short walk from the action on Brig Bay. Recommended.

$ Nautilus, Brig Bay, T2575-5055. This friendly hostel evokes the old-school travel spirit of the 60s and 70s. They have 12 dorm beds and extras including lockers, kitchen, fridge, cable TV, Wi-Fi and garden. A little cramped and grungy, but OK. Recommended for budget wanderers.

$ Silver Sand, Sally Peaches, south of rocky point, T8948-1436. Managed by the colourful Ira Gómez, who could well be a character from a *Pirates of the Caribbean* movie. His rustic fishermen's cabins have seen better days, but their secluded setting near the beach is tranquil and pleasant. Ira can organize fishing trips, and cook up the catch in his bar-restaurant on the beach. Look out for the feisty turkeys and pack insect repellent.

Little Corn *p276, map p277*
The north end is the greenest, wildest area, but somewhat isolated and difficult to reach at night. The cheapest lodgings are clustered on the south side of the island.

$$$ Peace and Love Farm, north end of the island, www.farmpeacelove.com. Not a hotel, **Peace and Love Farm** has 1 cottage and 1 'suite', both with fully equipped kitchens and enough space for 3 adults, or 2 adults and 2 children under 10 (sharing a bed). This is the place for people who wish to self-cater and get away from it all. Book your stay well in advance, as they are often full. They also offer Italian food (**$$$**) – order 24 hrs in advance through **Casa Iguana's** dive shop.

$$$-$$ Casa Iguana, on southeastern bluff, www.casaiguana.net. This is a famous, popular lodging, beautifully located with stunning views of the beaches. They have 4 'economy' cabañas with shared bath (**$$**), 9 casitas with private bath (**$$$**), and 2 'luxury' casitas (**$$$**). They grow their own food in lush, attractive gardens, offer great breakfasts, sociable dining and an expensive internet café (US$10 per hr). An interesting outfit, if something of a gringo summer camp. Book in advance, especially in high season.

$$$-$$ Little Corn Beach and Bungalows, on the east coast, north of **Sunrise Paradise**, T8333-0956, www.littlecornbb.com. A new place on the beach with a mixture of smart bunkhouses (**$$**), rooms (**$$**) and bungalows (**$$$**). All come with fan and sleep up to 4 (US$5 extra for each additional person). The bungalows are particularly comfortable and have good views, wooden floors and decent showers. Restaurant attached.

$$ Derek's, at northeastern tip, www.dereks placelittlecorn.com. Attractive wooden cabins on stilts, faintly reminiscent of Southeast Asia. All are equipped with renewable energy, mosquito nets, orthopaedic mattresses, hammocks, porches and sea views; showers and toilets are shared. The restaurant serves flavourful and interesting food, including fresh fruit juices, fruit salads, wine, home-made bread, and various coconut-based dishes, including curries. Derek's place is a tranquil, social spot by the beach, and Derek is a friendly host. Prices drop by US$10 in low season.

$$ Los Delfines, in village just south of boat landing, T820-2242, www.hotellos delfines.com.ni. A rather conventional hotel with motel-style rooms dotted around landscaped grounds. Clean and comfortable with cable TV, a/c and sporadic hot water. The attached restaurant has nice views, but service is slack. Value isn't great; ask about deals if studying at the adjoining dive shop.

$$-$ Ensueños, Otto Beach, www.ensuenos-littlecornisland.com. Trippy, rustic cabins with sculpted Lord of the Rings-style interiors; some have electricity, some don't. The grounds are wonderfully lush and filled with exuberant fruit trees, and naturalist owner Ramón Gil is an interesting and friendly host. There are comfortable houses too (**$$**) and good meals are available. Recommended.

$ Elsa's, north along beach from Casa Iguana (see above). The long-established **Elsa's** offers simple wooden cabins with sea views and own bath, as well as cheaper lodgings without either. The restaurant serves lobster, fish and vegetarian food for US$6-10 a plate. Snorkels, tours, hammocks and beer available. Hospitable, friendly, safe and relaxed. 'Everyone welcome'.

$ Grace Cool Spot, just north of Elsa's (see above), T8617-0239. 17 rough and ready backpackers' cabins filling the grounds like a small village. Brightly painted and daubed in Jamaican colours, each has its own hammock, and the sometimes cleanish facilities are outdoors. Kitchen, snorkels and mosquito nets available. Breakfast is included for an extra couple of dollars. Friendly management.

$ Lobster Inn, in the village, just north of boat landing, T8847-1736. You'll find 13 rooms in this 2-storey, centrally located hotel. They're small but clean, all with private bath, TV and fan. Economical comida corriente is served in the restaurant. Hints of shady connections.

$ Sunrise Paradise, on east coast just north of Grace's (see above), T8414-4074. Also known as Carlito's, and managed by the head of the island's informal security service, who is a real gentleman. They offer a range of simple cabins all with fan and electricity. Those with shared bath are cheaper, but the facilities are inadequate for the number of guests sharing. They also have food, beer and hammocks, and the grounds are pleasant.

❼ Restaurants

Seafood lovers will be in heaven, others could go hungry, but chicken and coconut bread should sustain the non-fish eaters. Both islands are populated by big, menacing-looking land crabs that aren't good for eating whole, but make a very hearty soup.

Big Corn *p276, map p275*
$$$ Doña Lola's, also known as Casa Oro del Negro, Sally Peaches, access road is signed. Loud, occasionally outrageous and thoroughly hospitable seafood restaurant overlooking the waves. Here, the irrepressible Doña Lola cooks up a tasty range of local and Ecuadorian dishes, including wholesome lobster and fish recipes. Belting atmosphere driven by country and Western tunes at top volume.
$$$-$$ The Buccaneer, Brig Bay, inside Hotel Paraíso, see Where to stay, above. Clean, friendly and presentable restaurant with a thatched palapa roof. They serve seafood and meat dishes, including lobster, shrimp, *filete mignon* and hamburgers. Open for breakfast, lunch and dinner, with plans for a regular BBQ night.
$$ Nautilus Restaurant, North Point. Open 0800-2200. Fabulously eclectic menu with Caribbean curry and classic dishes like rondon soup, containing vegetables, coconut milk and seafood. They also do pizza and will deliver. Generally tasty, but gringo prices mean it's not great value.
$$-$ Fisherman's Cave, next to dock. This great little seafood restaurant overlooks the water and fishing boats. Usually a relaxing spot, although it's sometimes loud with inebriated fishermen. Open for breakfast, lunch or dinner, and good for a coffee or beer whilst awaiting the boat to Little Corn. Check out the pools filled with live fish.

$$-$ Island Style, Long Beach. Formerly only open during Semana Santa, this restaurant-bar is earning a reputation as a cool dining and drinking spot. Open air, with loud music and authentic local vibe. Lunch and dinner only.
$$-$ Mari's, North End. Friendly, low-key place with outdoor tables and chairs. They serve pancakes, coffee, seafood, tacos and, with advance notice. Open for breakfast, lunch and dinner.
$$-$ Seva's Place, 500 m east of Anastasia's in Sally Peaches. One of the island's best and longest-established restaurants. They serve great seafood, meat and chicken from a fine location with rooftop seats and ocean views. Try the lobster *a la plancha*.

Ice cream parlours
Relax, South End. 0800-2000. Also known as Virgil's Place, they do the best ice cream on the island and some light meals too, including fried chicken.

Little Corn *p276, map p277*
Dining options on Little Corn are slowly improving. You'll find various cheap and cheerful *comedores* around the port. Most hotels have restaurants too.
$$$-$$ Habana Libre, just north of boat landing. Really tasty, flavourful dishes including succulent veal, fish and lobster served with interesting sauces. There's terraced seating, good music and amiable staff. Cuban specialities are available on request and in advance. Be sure to try a *mojito* – they're outstanding.
$$ Café Tranquilo, the port, 100 m south. A range of snacks and light dishes, including bruschetta, ceviche, cheeseburgers, chicken fillets, sandwiches, tacos, *quesadillas* and cookies. Very popular with the gringos, quite tasty but a bit pricey. Seating is outdoors on a wooden veranda with various games, like dominoes and chess. Wi-Fi available at US$6 per hr. Gift shop attached. Breakfast and lunch only.

$$ Mango's Pizza, the port, 200 m south.
This pizza restaurant, housed by Tall
Boy's bottle house, has seats on the cliffs
overlooking the water. A pleasant spot.
$$-$ Doña Rosa's, the port, 175 m south,
100 m east, on the path to Casa Iguana.
Reasonably priced for the island, you can get
a 3-course meal for US$6 or so, including
fish and shrimp dishes. The portions are on
the small side though.
$$-$ Miss Bridgette's, the dock, 20 m
south, then slightly east, off the path.
A lovely little *comedor* serving wholesome,
home-cooked fare. Service is very Caribbean,
so be prepared to wait.
$$-$ Triángulo, the port, 150 m north,
where the path forks. A nice people-
watching spot where they sell cheap
tacos and bread, as well as full meals.
OK, but don't expect too much.

🍸 Bars and clubs

Big Corn *p276, map p275*

After dark, always use taxis to get between
your hotel and the bars, even if they're close
to each other.
Bar Nawilte, Brigg Bay. 1900-0200.
Daubed in Jamaican colours and also
known as Nancy's Bar. Good for cold
beer, reggae and raucous dancing most
nights of the week, but Fri night is busiest
(Tue night 'happy night' and Thu night is
ladies' night). Lovely owner.
Nico's, South End. 1900-0200. The action
kicks off on Sun, with wall-to-wall drinking
and dancing by the waves. They serve
beef soup when you need perking up.
Thu features country and western.
Reggae Palace, Brigg Bay. 1900-0200.
Sat night is the big night here. As usual,
reggae, salsa and rum in heavy doses.

⭕ What to do

Big Corn *p276, map p275*
Bicycles, golf carts and motorbikes
Corn Island Car Rental, Southwest Bay,
next to Arenas, T8653-9881, also available
at Sunrise Hotel, South End. A range of golf
carts available, US$50 for 6 hrs; US$82 for
24 hrs (4 people). Scooters US$26 for 6 hrs;
US$46 for 24 hrs. Bicycles US$6 for 6 hrs;
US$18 for 24 hrs.

Diving
Nautilus Resort & Dive Centre, Brig Bay,
T2575-5077, www.nautilus-dive-nicaragua.
com. Diving and snorkelling tours to see
the cannons of the old Spanish galleon,
Blowing Rock and coral reefs, as well as trips
further afield. PADI open water certification
from US$280, advanced certification from
US$230, night dives and 2-tank dives US$65
per person (Little Corn and Blowing Rock,
US$95), snorkelling trips and glass-bottom
boat tours at US$20 per person.

Fishing
Ira Gómez, Silver Sand hotel, Sally Peaches,
south of rocky point, T8948-1436. One of
those irresistible local characters, Ira is an
enthusiastic fishing man and can organize
your trip.

Little Corn *p276, map p277*
Diving
Little Corn Island is one of the best and
cheapest places in the world to get diving
qualifications. The island's 2 dive shops
charge the same for their services. Excluding
manuals, an open water certificate costs
US$305; advanced open water US$225.
A 1-tank dive cost US$35; 2-tanks US$65.
Dive Little Corn, boat landing in village,
T8823-1154, www.divelittlecorn.com.
There's a strong PADI ethos at this 5-star,
gold palm centre, with training right
up to assistant instructor level. They
also offer night dives, single and 2-tank
dives, snorkelling tours, and 5- or 10-dive

packages – trips leave several times daily. There's a 10% discount if you stay with **Casa Iguana** in the high season; consult their website for more details.
Dolphin Dive, in the village, south of the dock, T8690-0225, www.dolphindive littlecorn.com. **Dolphin Dive** offers PADI instruction to dive master level, and a range of customized trips for diving, fishing or snorkelling. Underwater digital camera rental costs US$20 including a CD. Various dive packages are available, including discounts at **Hotel Delfines** next door. Groups are kept small.

⊖ Transport

Air
La Costeña flies from Big Corn to **Managua** with a stop in **Bluefields**, daily at 0810 and 1540, US$107 one-way, US$165 return, 1½ hrs. Re-confirm seats 1-2 days before travelling or you might be moved to a later flight. **La Costeña** office is at the airport on Big Corn, T2575-5131.

Boat
Inter-island boats Big Corn to Little Corn, daily 1000, 1630, US$6.50, 40 mins. Little Corn to Big Corn, daily 0700, 1330, US$6.50, 40 mins. Boats leave from main dock, first come, first served. US$0.20 charge to get into the dock area. Buy big blue plastic bags to keep luggage dry at shop across from dock entrance, best to sit near the back.

Mainland boats Schedules are always changing, check locally for the latest; 5 boats travel between Corn Islands and **Bluefields**, US$10-12 one-way, including: *Genesis*, Mon, 1800; *Río Escondido*, Thu, 0900; *Captain D*, Sat, 0000; *Island Express*, Sun, 1700; *Humberto C*, Sun, 1700. One service per month Corn Islands to Bilwi, *Captain D*, usually Fri, 1700, US$25.

Bus
2 buses circle the paved island road on Big Corn every 20 mins, US$0.50.

Taxi
Taxis charge US$1-2 for trips to and from the airport or any trip after 2000. The usual fare to most destinations is US$0.75. Hourly taxi rates are US$6 per hr, poor value, as there are many taxis and trip fares are cheap.

⊕ Directory

Banks 'Bucks' are córdobas in island speak. There is a **Banpro** with a working ATM, Brig Bay, Mon-Fri 0800-1630, Sat 0800-1200; however, it has been known to break down, so bring cash reserves in case of complications. TCs are not accepted or changed anywhere, but dollars are widely used. If stuck, you might get a credit card advance at the airport. **Hospital** Brig Bay, T2575-5236. **Internet** Big Corn has a café near Nautilus, Cyber Island Spring, Mon-Fri 0800-1200 and 1330-1800, US$1.50 per hr. Little Corn has extortionate connections at **Peace and Love Farm**, US$6 per hr, **Café Tranquilo**, US$6 per hr and **Casa Iguana**, US$12 per hr! **Police** T2575-5201. There are few, if any police on the Little Corn – ask around. **Telephone** Enitel, T2575-5061.

Bluefields

Dirty and chaotic but curiously inviting, Bluefields is the heart and soul of Nicaragua's Caribbean world and the capital of Southern Atlantic Autonomous Region, known by its acronym RAAS. It is located at the mouth of the Río Escondido, which opens into Bluefields Bay in front of the city. The majority of the population is Afro-Caribbean, though the other ethnic groups of the region are represented and the main attraction of the town is its ethnic diversity and west Caribbean demeanour. The main church of the city is Moravian, the language is Creole English and the music is calypso and reggae. Bluefields is a good jumping-off point to visit Pearl Lagoon and other less explored areas of the wide-open region. ** For listings, see pages 289-293.*

Bluefields

Where to stay
Anabis **2**
Bluefields Bay **1**
Caribbean Dreams **9**
Hospedaje Pearl Lagoon **5**
Hostal Doña Vero **3**
La Isleña **4**
Los Pipitos **7**
Marda Maus **8**
Mini Hotel Central **10**
Oasis **11**
South Atlantic II **6**

Restaurants
Bella Vista **1**
Chez Marcel **2**
Comedor Vera Blanca **7**
El Flotante **4**
Irie Food and
 Honey Sweet's **12**
La Loma **5**
Luna Ranch **6**
Pelican **13**
Pizza Martinuzi **8**
Salmar **3**

Bars & clubs
Cima Club **9**
Four Brothers **10**
La La Place **14**

Arriving in Bluefields → *Population 42,665. Altitude 20 m. Colour map 4, B3.*

Getting there and around La Costeña flies three times daily from Managua's domestic terminal, twice daily from the Corn Islands, and three times a week from Bilwi. Getting there by land is more complicated. The classic route uses a long-distance bus from Managua to connect with boats at El Rama, from where you travel downstream to the coast. A road from El Rama to Bluefields has been promised for years and that now looks as though it may soon become a reality. Most of Bluefields can be seen on foot, though taxis are recommended at night. All visits to surrounding attractions are by boat. ** For further details, see Transport, page 293.*

Tourist information INTUR① *opposite the police station, Barrio Punta Fría, T2572-0221, raas@intur.gob.ni, Mon-Fri 0800-1700,* has very limited information on local attractions and Spanish-speaking staff. Online, try the entertaining **Right Side Guide**① *www.right sideguide.com.*

Background

Bluefields is named after the Dutch pirate Henry Bluefeldt (or Blauvedlt) who hid in the bay's waters in 1610. The native Kukra were hired by Dutch and British pirates to help them with boat repairs and small time trade began with the Europeans. The first permanent European settlers arrived at the end of the 18th century and the ethnic mix of the area began to change. The 19th century saw a healthy trade in bananas and an influx of Afro-Caribbeans from Jamaica to work in the plantations and administer the Anglican and Moravian churches. During the 20th century Chinese immigrants also came to Bluefields creating what was thought to be the largest Chinese community in Central America. The fighting of the Revolution did not affect the area much, but the Contras of the 1980s used the eastern coast to harass Sandinista positions and many of the Chinese left during these years.

Bluefields was nearly wiped off the map by Hurricane Joan in October 1988. Some 25,000 residents were evacuated and most of the structures were destroyed. An army member arriving the day after the hurricane described the city as appearing trampled by a giant, with nothing left of the buildings but wooden footprints. The famous *Bluefields Express* boat that worked the 96-km journey from Rama to Bluefields was later found wrecked inside thick forest – 4 km from the riverbanks.

The town, like the entire region, is struggling against the Columbian drug runners. Bluefields is used as a landing and strategic post. Local dealers are also getting involved and, although consumption is well below US and European rates, slowly the corruption of the Bluefields/eastern Chontales corridor is being consolidated.

Places in Bluefields

Lacking any conventional tourist attractions, the appeal of Bluefields lies in getting to know its people – anyone willing to scratch the city's surface will find no shortage of strange stories and colourful characters. A good place to begin learning about Bluefields' swashbuckling past is the CIDCA-BICU **Historical Museum of the Atlantic Coast** ① *Barrio Punta Fría, Mon-Fri 0900-1700, entry by donation*, where you'll find an intriguing collection of artefacts including a photo collection showing the city before it was destroyed by Hurricane Joan. Downstairs there is a very good cultural library.

Within Nicaragua, Bluefields is best known for its dancing and it is the **reggae** capital of the country. The best time to see the locals dance is at the annual **Palo de Mayo** (maypole) celebrations (also known as ¡Mayo Ya!). The festival is celebrated throughout May and there are countless dance contests between different neighbourhoods. The only rule is to hang on to the ribbon connected to the maypole and move. There is also some interesting local music and poetry in the festival.

Although Bluefields is doing its part to pollute the bay that surrounds it, the sheer expanse of water (30 km from north to south and 6 km wide) means that it is still beautiful. If you have some time in Bluefields, a boat excursion to see some of the bay provides a different perspective on the tired city waterfront.

Around Bluefields → *For listings, see pages 289-293.*

Rama Cay

① *A boat ride to the island will cost US$15-50 depending on the number of passengers. Check at the dock next to the market to see if any boats are going; if you hitch a ride, returning could be a problem.*

This island in the Bay of Bluefields, only 20-30 minutes by *panga* from Bluefields, is home to the last tribe of Rama, led by an elderly woman chief. The Rama, calm and friendly people who are renowned for their kindness and generosity, are pretty accustomed to visitors but sadly this is the least studied group of all the indigenous peoples in Nicaragua and the most likely to lose its language. They may have been the dominant group on the

Fishing for white lobster: cocaine and complicity

Cocaine is the one of the most powerful and lucrative drugs of all time, boasting a market value of US$70 billion. Colombian cartels manage the production and distribution of cocaine, processing farm-grown coca leaves into the precious crystalline powder that Westerners like to snort for fun.

Poorly policed and effectively lawless, Nicaragua's Caribbean Coast was easily consolidated by the Colombians in the 1990s, when they established a sea route for their traffickers and a network of refuelling bases on the region's isolated islands. Today this route is one of the most frequented and dangerous smuggling lanes in the world. The coast guard, underfunded and under-resourced, is easily outmaneuvered by the sophisticated Colombian speedboats that are equipped with powerful engines, GPS, machine guns and radar. When pursuits do end in capture, the parcels of merchandise are usually dumped at sea before they can be confiscated.

These parcels, often containing many kilos of pure cocaine, wash ashore to be claimed by local fishermen, a new and highly lucrative catch known locally as 'white lobster'. Dealers will typically buy back their stash for US$4000 per kilo – several times less than the US street value, but still an inordinate amount for the region's impoverished inhabitants. Some church ministers have hailed the white lobster as a gift from God, citing the financial miracles it works for their communities (and their donation boxes).

The continued survival of the cocaine industry demands complicity at all points of the supply chain. The farmers who grow coca, the communities who harbor smugglers, the corrupt customs officials, and the high-ranking politicians who take a share of the pie; all are bought, all turn a blind eye to the violent excesses. And when complicity can't be bought, it can be traded for false promises. Increasingly, a portion of the high-grade cocaine that passes through Nicaragua is converted to crack, hooking the poor and disadvantaged.

And if complicity can't be traded at all, it is simply taken. In 2004, a gang of Colombians stormed Bluefields police station and cut the throats of four policemen, stamping their authority on the town for all time. The merciless ambitions of the cartels, the woeful ignorance of the recreational user, and the staggering economic realities of this global trade mean that cocaine isn't likely to fade away any time soon.

coast before the arrival of the Europeans but their reluctance to support the British in their pirate attacks against the Spanish led to the rise of the Miskitos, who allied with the British (and were given muskets, hence their name). With the help of firepower and economic support, the Miskitos eventually took over almost all of the Rama territory and much of the Mayagna, an area comprising the Caribbean Coast from Cape Camarón in Honduras to Río Grande in Nicaragua. The exception is the little island of Rama Cay and the Río San Juan, where the Rama are making a comeback.

The Rama are highly skilled at languages, often speaking Rama, Creole English, Spanish and some even Miskito, despite receiving little or no formal schooling. The Rama language is related to that of the northern Amazonian peoples and it is believed they migrated from that area. The Rama are proud of their culture and are glad to receive visitors. Rama schoolteacher Ervin Hodgson runs a blog with more information on the island, www.ramacay.com. He is happy to provide assistance if you require a guide or accomodation.

El Bluff

El Bluff is a peninsula that separates the sea from the Bay of Bluefields. In happier days it was a busy port, but now a fleet of rusting shrimping boats evidence the town's decline. Nonetheless, it has retained its role as a maritime processing station with many large ships passing through its port. It is also home to a large petrochemical plant and a military installation. El Bluff's beach is the nearest stretch of sand to Bluefields – long, wide and a little bit dirty, but OK for an afternoon. It is infested with sand flies so bring plenty of repellent. There is also a good walk to the lighthouse with a fine view of the bay and the sea. El Bluff has a single working hotel, **Hospedaje Sandra**, but if you are staying overnight to catch the early boat to Bluefields, take care walking to the port in the dark. Boats to El Bluff leave from the southern dock in Bluefields next to the market. The boat costs US\$3 and leaves when full, 0730-1730.

Reserva Silvestre Privada Greenfields

ⓘ *T2279-0589 (Managua), www.greenfields.com.ni. The reserve at Kukra Hill can be reached by a regular panga from Bluefields, or an infrequent bus from El Rama or Pearl Lagoon. One-day entrance is US\$15, but call ahead of your visit.*

Greenfields is a 284-ha, privately managed nature reserve of mangroves, rivers and forests. There's a botanical park and 30 km of paths snaking through the Swiss-owned wildlife sanctuary, sometimes visited by scientists and home to jaguars, tapirs, monkeys caymans and otters. There are pricey ecolodgings (US\$250 for a two-day all inclusive stay) and camping facilities.

Pearl Lagoon Basin → *For listings, see pages 289-293.*

This oval-shaped coastal lagoon, 80 km north of Bluefields, covers 518 sq km and is one of the most beautiful places on the coast. The lagoon is fed principally by the jungle-lined Río Kurinwás but also by the rivers Wawashán, Patch, Orinoco and Ñari. Pearl Lagoon's shores range from pine forests and mangroves to savannah and rainforest. The cultural diversity is equally broad with Afro-Caribbean, Miskito and Garífuna settlements at different points around the lagoon. To get the most out of a trip, hire a guide or use a tour operator.

Pearl Lagoon village

The village of **Pearl Lagoon**, in the far southwest of the estuary, is the most developed place in the region. It is friendly, welcoming and well accustomed to visitors – a good place to start when planning a trip. The local community is predominantly Afro-Caribbean but there are plenty of Miskito and mestizo inhabitants too. You'll find the best accommodation in the entire region here and there are boat services to Bluefields a few times a day.

A good 20-minute walk out of town passes through interesting wetlands (much more scenic in the wet season) to the Miskito village of **Raitipura**, complete with traditional wooden housing. Continue on the road for another five minutes and you'll come to another Miskito community, **Awas**, known for its fine views over the lagoon, its *rancho* and its swimming area. The road to Raitipura and Awas is paved and easy to find, but it's better to walk in a group. Avoid it completely after dark.

Pearl Cays

The village of Pearl Lagoon is a popular point of departure for the Pearl Cays, a dazzling white-sand archipelago around 1½ hours away by high-speed *panga*. The cays – composed of numerous small but verdant islands – are tranquil and idyllic, but tourism here is uncontrolled and an ongoing point of contention. For over a decade, many of the islands have been privately 'owned', but locals insist they were sold illegally and rightfully belong to the communities. The cays are also the site of a massive annual hawksbill turtle migration – a spectacular natural phenomena that local tour operators have so far failed to capitalize on. In the future, responsible tours to nesting sites may be available, but for now you are asked to tread carefully and consider the implications of visiting these fragile and disputed isles.

Orinoco

North of Pearl Lagoon village is the community of Orinoco, home to Nicaragua's most significant population of Garífuna people. This group has been studied by anthropologists in Honduras, but went unnoticed in Nicaragua until finally being recognized by the government in 1987 – after more than 150 years of settlement. The language and many of the dances and culinary customs of the Garífuna remain intact, in a mixture of old African and indigenous influences that has taken on a life of its own.

Drumming is a central part of Garífuna culture. A typical performance uses three deer-skin drums which symbolize the past, present and future. Interestingly, the drummers take their lead from a group of dancers, who determine the tempo with their dance steps. If you would like to experience a performance, talk to **Hostal Garífuna** (see page 291) about finding a troupe (there are many). The *hostal* can also help arrange tours to observe wildlife in Wawashán Wildlife Reserve – don't miss the phenomena of 'burn water', only in the dry season, when the river lights up with millions of bio-luminescent organisms. A pleasant 30- to 40-minute walk from Orinoco lies the terminally sleepy village of **Marshall Point** with its mixed Creole and Garífuna heritage. Orinoco has an annual cultural festival from 17-19 November.

Tasbapauni

Between Pearl Lagoon and the Caribbean Sea is the Miskito village of Tasbapauni – or Tasba, as it's known locally. One hour from the village of Pearl Lagoon, it has around 2000 inhabitants living on a strip of land less than 1 km wide between the sea and the lagoon. Though it can have debris, the beach here is pleasant and the locals have started to clean it up.

In recent years, Tasba has earned an infamous reputation as a centre for drug trafficking and it is quite common to see giant concrete mansions standing alongside weathered fishermen's huts. For this reason, take extreme care when visiting the area – stay indoors after dark and know that the north side of the village ('uptown') is much friendlier than the south side ('downtown'). Use a guide if you want to explore the coastline north or south and never go wandering alone on the beach.

Beyond the Pearl Lagoon basin

The **Río Kurinwás** area is a fascinating, largely uninhabited jungle where it is possible to see monkeys and much other wildlife. It might occasionally be possible to get a boat to the town of **Tortuguero** (also called **Nuevo Amanecer**), a mestizo town that will really give you a taste of the frontier. Tortuguero is about a six-hour speedboat ride from Bluefields up Río Kurinwás, or several days by regular boat.

Río Grande is the next river north of Río Kurinwás, connected to the Pearl Lagoon by the Top-Lock Canal. At its mouth are five interesting villages: the four Miskito communities of **Kara**, **Karawala**, **Sandy Bay Sirpi** and **Walpa**, and the Creole village of **La Barra**. Sandy Bay Sirpi is on both the river and the Caribbean, and has a good beach.

Nicaragua's British coast: La Miskitia

Although the post-Conquest history of the Pacific Coast of Nicaragua began early in the 16th century, that of the Caribbean Coast began much later. Throughout the 16th century, the Spaniards were not even close to having a presence on the Caribbean Coast, and the first Spanish governor appointed to the area, Diego de Gutiérrez, was eaten by the Miskito in 1545. By 1610 the *indígenas* had run the Spaniards out of their easternmost town, Nueva Segovia, and forced them to rebuild it 90 km west, at present-day Ciudad Antigua. After that, the Spaniards kept a healthy distance and remained inland.

The first successful European interaction with the coastal communities was when the British set up a colony on the Caribbean island of Providencia (today occupied by Colombia) to begin trading with the Miskito. After some conflicts with Spaniards on Caribbean islands, the British created the hoax of the Miskito Kingdom, complete with a 'Miskito King', to guard their own interests in the mid-1600s. Their interests, along what is now the whole of the east coast of Nicaragua, were a military alliance with the natives, safe harbours for ship repair and resupply, and a profitable trade with the natives, for turtle shells, dye woods, sarsaparilla and vanilla extract.

The headquarters of operations for the British interests was Bluefields. As a result, whenever Great Britain and Spain were at war, Bluefields was used as base for attacks on Nicaragua. The War of Spanish Succession (1700-1713), The War of Jenkins' Ear (1739-1748), The Seven Years' War (1756-1763) and the War Between Great Britain, France and Spain (1778-1783) all brought British incursions to Spanish Nicaragua from the Caribbean Coast. Finally, the Treaty of Paris of 1783 settled the matter for the time being, with Great Britain agreeing to remove all colonists from the Caribbean shore, with the exception of Belize. By 1787 this process was complete.

With the collapse of the Spanish Empire in 1821, helped along by British foreign policy, the British sought to take control of the Miskito Coast again. They simply revived the Miskito Kingdom, which demanded British protection as soon as it was resuscitated. In 1850 the United States and Great Britain agreed to divide control and influence of the Miskito Coast, with neither party having complete control of the area. With the Treaty of Managua of 1860, the British agreed to give up all interests in the Miskito Coast, but they never got around to actually pulling out. Only when Nicaraguan President José Santos Zelaya sent General Cabezas to take control of the Miskito Coast by military force in 1894, did the British control over the Caribbean Coast of Nicaragua finally come to an end.

Travelling upriver, the Río Grande is a noticeable contrast to the Río Kurinwás; it is much more settled, dotted with farms and cattle grazing. Some distance upriver (about a six-hour speedboat ride from Bluefields, several days by regular boat), you reach the mestizo town of **La Cruz de Río Grande**. It was founded around 1922 by Chinese traders to serve workers from a banana plantation (now defunct). La Cruz has a very pretty church, and there are resident expatriate (US) monks of the Capuchin order in the town. The truly adventurous can walk between La Cruz and Tortuguero; each way takes about 10 hours in the dry season, 12 hours in the rainy season.

El Rama

There is not much to see in El Rama, an important transport hub en route to the central Caribbean Coast. The village was an ancient Rama trading centre and has been settled by Europeans since at least 1747, but there is no surviving evidence of this. El Rama's greatest asset is also its worst: water. The Río Siquia, Río Mico and Río Rama converge on the little port, and the Río Escondido that drains into the Bay of Bluefields. In the last 20 years the village has been erased from the map three times by hurricanes – the worst of which left El Rama beneath 15 m of water. The level was so high that Army rescue boats tangled their propellers on power cables.

Once upon a time, El Rama was the end of the road – all travellers had to disembark here and continue by boat to Bluefields. That has now changed with a new road from El Rama to Pearl Lagoon. At present, only a single daily bus plies this modest byway at 1600, the journey time is three hours (you may find trucks that leave sooner). From Pearl Lagoon you can easily catch a *panga* south along the coast to Bluefields, but not until the next day. This route is longer, but it is far more scenic and interesting.The regular route to Bluefields (from Managua via El Rama) is now an eight- to 10-hour trip with improvements to the highway; the bus from Managua to El Rama takes six to eight hours; the boat from El Rama to Bluefields takes two hours, as long as you arrive early enough to find a seat. There are rumours that a new road from El Rama to Bluefields is scheduled to open soon, but such rumours have been in circulation for years now. See Transport, page 293, for boat and bus schedules.

⊙ Bluefields listings

For sleeping and eating price codes and other relevant information, see pages 28-30.

⊙ Where to stay

Bluefields *p283, map p283*
Many hotels in Bluefields are quite basic and grim. Check rooms before accepting.
$$$ Hotel Oasis, 150 m from Bluefields Bay, T2572-2812, www.oasishotelcasino.net. The best hotel in town with spacious modern rooms, comfortable furnishings, Wi-Fi, cable TV and professional service. There are lots of slot machines downstairs, should you fancy a low-key punt. Breakfast included.
$$ Bluefields Bay Hotel, Barrio Pointeen, T2572-2143. Owned by the region's university, this hotel has clean, simple rooms with private bath and hot water. The rooms upstairs are better and less damp; some have views. There's a restaurant on the water's edge and excursions are offered to surrounding areas. Breakfast included, but still a little overpriced. Friendly.

$$ Hotel Anabis, Barrio Central, opposite Farmacia Godoy, T2572-2640. A large red building that you can't fail to notice, this quiet and gently fading business hotel has a conference centre, bar and restaurant. Rooms are equipped with hot water, a/c and cable TV, but are on the small side. They do weddings and 'sweet 15s', should you wish to celebrate either of these in Bluefields.
$$ South Atlantic II, Barrio Central, next to petrol station Levy, T2572-2265. Upstairs are clean rooms with reasonable mattresses, private bath, cable TV and a/c. Downstairs you'll find the economy quarters (**$**), which all have a fan and private bath but are also quite damp and dingy. There's a sports bar-restaurant that's good for a beer. Friendly.
$ Caribbean Dreams, Barrio Punta Fría, Pescafrito, ½ c sur, T2572-1943. 27 rooms with private bath, a/c or fan, and cable TV. Services including restaurant with home cooking and à la carte menu, Wi-Fi (US$2 per day) and laundry. Clean and often booked, call ahead. Owners helpful.

$ Hospedaje Pearl Lagoon, Barrio Central, across from UNAG, T2572-2411. Possibly the cheapest place in town, with very basic rooms and cranky owners who would prefer 'husband and wife' couples only. A little dismal, but the nightly rate will cheer hard-core budget travellers.

$ Hostal Doña Vero, Barrio Central, opposite Mercadito Mas x Menos, T2572-2166. New, clean, well-attended budget lodgings and without doubt the best deal in town. Rooms on the top floor are large, comfortable and great value. Those downstairs are smaller. Some ultra-cheap quarters have shared bath. Very secure and pleasant, with good attention to detail. Thoughtful and friendly. Highly recommended.

$ La Isleña, Barrio Central, next to Joyería Isamar, T2572-0706. New, friendly place with reasonably priced rooms, most with fan, cable TV and private bath, a few with a/c. Some reports of loud music in the evening, so ask for a quiet room if this bothers you. There's also a garden and pleasant restaurant attached. Not bad.

$ Los Pipitos, Barrio Central, next to the Oficina Dirección General de Ingreso, T2572-1590. 4 simple rooms with TV, private bath and a/c, cheaper with fan. There's a bakery on the premises that serves good coffee and cake. Friendly.

$ Marda Maus, pier, 50 m abajo, T2572-2429. Occupying a colourful spot near the market, this long-running hotel is a little run-down, but friendly enough. Rooms are simple, smallish and cleanish, with TV, private bath and fan. Not bad for a budget choice, but view the room before accepting it.

$ Mini Hotel Central, Barrio Punta Fría, opposite Bancentro, T2572-2362. 14 simple and fairly uninspiring rooms with private bath, a/c, TV. Cheaper with fan, although the cheapest rooms are very no frills and those downstairs may be noisy. There's a mediocre restaurant attached. OK for the budget traveller, but not fantastic.

Rama Cay *p284*

A handful of families offer lodgings to visitors, including that of the Moravian pastor. Enquire locally or at the tourist office.

El Bluff *p286*

$ Hospedaje Sandra, 500 m from the port (ask for directions), T2557-0007. The only working hotel in town. Rooms come with fan and own bath. Reasonable enough, but lock your door at night and avoid those rooms near the front of the building, which are quite damp.

Pearl Lagoon *p286*

$$ Casa Ulrich, Muelle Principal, 300 vrs norte, at the end of the paved road, T8603-5173, casaulrich@hotmail.com. The only hotel in town with a waterfront location and swimming off the terrace at the back. They have 10 comfortable rooms with a/c, cable TV and private bath (a few cheaper rooms have fan, **$**). The upstairs bar has views of the lagoon, there's also a restaurant, parking, internet and boats for excursions and fishing. Nice, hospitable owners. A happy place. Recommended.

$$-$ Hotelito Casa Blanca, in May 4 sector, T2572-0508, www.casablancapearllagoon. fortunecity.com. One of the best hotels in town, with a range of clean, light, comfortable rooms; 5 have private bath (**$$**), 6 have shared bath (**$**). The owners, Sven and Miss Dell, are very hospitable and friendly, and offer fishing expeditions, trips to the cays, general information and community tours. They're happy to answer questions by email, and prefer reservations in advance. Restaurant attached and internet available. A nice family house, recommended.

$ Green Lodge, Muelle Principal, 150 vrs sur, T2572-0507. This homely and friendly hotel has 7 basic rooms with fan and shared bath, as well as 4 comfortable, newly built rooms with a/c, TV and private bath (more expensive). The owner, Wesley, is a decent fellow and very knowledgeable about the area. He has good contacts and can help arrange tours. They cook cheap grub too.

$ Hotel Slilma, Enitel tower, 50 vrs sur, 75 vrs arriba on the left-hand turn, T2572-0523, rondownleiva@hotmail.com. Also known by its Spanish name, **Las Estrellas**, **Hotel Slilma** is a friendly, helpful lodging, highly recommended for budget travellers. They have 20 rooms, most with shared bath, cable TV and fan, but a few new ones also have private bath and a/c (**$**). The restaurant serves good, inexpensive home-cooked fish, shrimp and chicken. Various hammocks and porches for chilling out.

$ Sweet Pearly, from dock, 1 c sur, T8400-1916. A real rough-around-the-edges locals' hotel, with average, slightly grubby a/c rooms (cheaper with fan) and an OK restaurant (**$$-$**). Sometimes, noisy from the church and bar downstairs. A good budget choice (cheapest rooms have no bath or TV) but don't expect much comfort or charm.

Orinoco *p287*

$ Hostal Garífuna, 50 m from the dock, T8937-0123, www.hostalgarifuna.net. Owned and managed by Kensy Sambola, a respected Garífuna anthropologist, **Hostal Garífuna** is your one-stop shop for cultural information and tours. Rooms are clean and comfortable with shared bath and there's also a pleasant garden slung with hammocks. Meals are served. Highly recommended.

Tasbapauni *p287*

There's a handful of very cheap and basic lodgings in Tasba, none of them particularly clean or inviting. Ask for **Miss Nora** – she is trustworthy and has some ultra-cheap rustic rooms in her garden outside (**$**).

❶ Restaurants

Bluefields *p283, map p283*
$$$-$$ Chez Marcel, Alcaldía, 1 c sur, ½ c abajo, T2572-2347. The fading red curtains speak of better days, but the food is still OK

and the service attentive. As you may be the only customers, the atmosphere can be a bit lifeless. Dishes include *filete mignon*, shrimp in garlic butter and grilled lobster.

$$ Bella Vista, Barrio Punta Fría, T2572-2385. Daily 1000-2300. On the water's edge, overlooking the tired old boats and bay, this seafood restaurant serves shrimp, lobster, meat and *comida económica*.

$$ El Flotante, Barrio Punta Fría, T2572-2988. Daily 1000-2200. Built over the water at the end of the main street with a great view of the fishing boats and islets. They serve good shrimp and lobster, but service is slow. Dancing at weekends.

$$ Luna Ranch, Santa Matilde opposite URACAN. On a hill with views over the bay, this long-established 'cultural restaurant' is often recommended by locals. Interesting photos and paraphernalia, but service was surly and food mediocre when we visited. You pay for views and atmosphere.

$$ Pelican, Barrio Pointeen, La Punta, at the end of the road. Evenings here are often buzzing with drinkers and diners. Great breezes from the balcony, comfortable interior, friendly service and average food, including seafood and meat. Not a bad place to spend an evening. Good for rum and beer at least.

$$ Salmar, Alcaldía, 1 c sur, ½ c abajo, T2572-2128. Daily 1600-2400. If you're bored of seafood and rice, this long-running restaurant serves reasonable (but not fantastic) Tex Mex, including burritos, as well as the usual local fare. Attentive service. The best place in town at last check.

$$-$ La Loma, Barrio San Pedro, opposite University BICU, T2572-2875. An open-air ranch on the top of a hill. They serve a wide range of pricey food including meat, chicken and fish dishes. A good spot for a beer, breezes and occasional live music. Nice atmosphere.

$$-$ Pizza Martinuzi, Alcaldía, 1 c sur, ½ c abajo. Greasy pizza, chicken and burgers. Not too bad, especially after beer.

$ Comedor Vera Blanca, Barrio Central, opposite ADEPHCA. A simple *comedor* offering high-carb food, including the obligatory chicken and fish dishes. Often packed with locals for lunch and dinner.
$ Irie Food and Honey Sweet's, Obelisco, 25 vrs sur. An intimate, unpretentious little place that serves great shrimps and fish fillet in coconut sauce. Excellent value and often frequented by locals at both lunch and dinner time. A pleasant, colourful interior and service with a smile. The best restaurant in town. Highly recommended.

Pearl Lagoon *p286*
A few new restaurants have started appearing in Pearl Lagoon. Lobster is pricey; the season runs Jul-Jan. For a cheap breakfast of coconut bread and patties, try the house on the corner opposite the dock.
$$ Queen Lobster, Muelle Principal, 200 vrs norte, T8662-3393, www.queenlobster.com. Owned by Nuria Dixon Curtis, this is possibly the best place in town. This ranch-style eatery on the water's edge serves good seafood, including lobster and crab in red or coconut sauce. Order 'Mr Snapper' and you'll get a whole pound of fish. Good views and recommended.

🍸 Bars and clubs

Bluefields *p283, map p283*
Some of the bars are quite shady, but the ones below are safe for gringos. The action starts at **La La**, later moves to **Cima** and ends during the early hours at **Four Brothers**.
Cima Club, Banpro, 1 c abajo. It's hard to miss this centrally located dance hall with 2 floors and a large sign. Popular and often recommended by locals.
Four Brothers, Cotton tree, from Alcaldía, 1 c al mar, 4½ c sur. The best reggae spot in Nicaragua, a big ranch full of great dancing. Usually open Tue-Sun, ask around to see what kind of music is playing. Admission US$1.

La La Place, Barrio Pointeen. This wooden construction on the water's edge is popular with the city's Creole population, especially on Fri, Sat and Sun night. They play reggae, country and salsa through very large speakers. There's also a restaurant serving rondon and other Caribbean food.

⏱ What to do

Bluefields *p283, map p283*
Fishing
Rumble in the Jungle, www.nicaragua fishing.net, T8853-4080. Sport fishing tours on the rivers and offshore cays. Various packages, including guides, accommodation and equipment. Fish include giant snook and tarpon, jacks, mackerel and others. English spoken.

Pearl Lagoon *p286*
Tour operators
Many hoteliers are able to arrange guides or transport to the Pearl Cays or Pearl Lagoon communities, including **Casa Blanca** (see page 290), one of the best. Otherwise try:
Pearl of the Caribbean, Muelle Principal, T8447-9522, pearlofcaribbeantour@gmail. com. A range of tours led by Augusto Taylor, including fishing, snorkelling, beach and jungle river tours. Tours to Wawashan reserve and Orinoco are also possible. If you're looking for something more relaxed, there's a covered pontoon for cruising the bay. Well equipped and ready to go.
Queen Lobster, Muelle Principal, 200 vrs norte, T8662-3393, www.queenlobster. com. The most organized and forward-thinking outfit in town. They offer cooking classes, including a fishing expedition and trip to the market; sport fishing to the rich waters of northern lagoon (own equipment necessary), where homestay on a *finca* is possible; community and rural tourism, including camping, farming, fishing and living the Miskito life; trips to Wawasha Reserve; bicycle rental; and transport to the Pearl Cays. Recommended.

❸ Transport

Bluefields *p283, map p283*

Air

The airport is 3 km south of the city centre, either walk (30 mins) or take a taxi US$0.75 per person. **La Costeña** office, inside the terminal, T2572-2500. All schedules are subject to random and seasonal changes. It's best to get your name on the list several days in advance, if possible, and especially if travelling to Bilwi.

To **Managua**, daily 0815, 1110, 1600, US$83 one-way, US$128 return, 1 hr. To **Corn Islands**, daily 0730, 1510, US$64 one-way, US$99 return, 20 mins. To **Bilwi**, Mon, Wed, Fri, 1110, US$96 one-way, US$148 return, 1 hr.

Boat

Motorboats (*pangas*) depart when full. The early ones are more reliable, and services on Sun are restricted. Note that all schedules (especially Corn Island boats) are subject to change; confirm departure times at the port well in advance of your trip. Pregnant women or those with back problems should think twice before taking long *panga* trips. Use heavy-duty plastic bags to protect your luggage. If the Corn Island ferry is grounded no replacement will be made available.

To **Pearl Lagoon**, from 0830, several daily, US$7.50, 1-1½ hrs. To **Tasbapauni**, Mon-Sat 0900, US$12, 2½ hrs. To **El Rama**, 0530-1600, several daily, US$10, 2 hrs. To **Kukra Hill**, from 0830, several daily, US$6, 1 hr. To **Orinoco**, Mon, Tue, Sun 0730, US$11, 2 hrs. To **San Juan del Norte**, usually one a week, days change, enquire at the port. To **Corn Islands**, US$10-12. *Río Escondido*, Wed, 0900-1200; *Captain D*, Wed, 1200, stopping in El Bluff until 1700; *Island Express*, Fri, leaves directly from El Bluff 0200-0400; *Humberto C'*, Fri, leaves directly from El Bluff, 0500; *Genesis*, Sun, leaves directly from El Bluff, 0550. To **El Bluff**, several daily, depart when full from the dock near the market, 0630-1730, US$1.50, 15 mins.

Taxi

Taxi rides anywhere in the city are US$0.50 per person (US$0.75 to the airport or at night).

Pearl Lagoon *p286*

To **Bluefields**, boat schedules are irregular with boats leaving when full. The first of the day, 0630, US$7.50, 1-1½ hrs, is the only one guaranteed, although there are usually a few more after that. Get to the dock at 0600 to get your name on the passenger list. Services are restricted on Sun when it may be quicker to go via Kukra Hill. Bus to **El Rama**, 0600, US$7.50, 3 hrs. To Managua, it's possible to drive all the way, but the roads are rough. A strong 4WD can get you there in 6 hrs, on a good day. Otherwise, it may take twice that long.

El Rama *p289*

To **Bluefields**, *pangas* depart when full, several daily, 0530-1600, US$10, 2 hrs. The ferry is slightly cheaper and much slower. It departs Mon and Thu in the early morning (around 0800 when the bus has arrived), US$8, 8 hrs.

Bus to **Managua**, every hr, 0300-1100, 1900, 2200, 2300, US$8, 9 hrs. Express bus to **Managua** (recommended) leaves once a day at 0800, US$9.50, 7 hrs. To **Juigalpa**, every hour, 0800-1500, US$6.50, 6 hrs. To **Pearl Lagoon**, 1600, US$7.50, 3 hrs.

❹ Directory

Bluefields *p283, map p283*

Banks At the moment none of them will change TCs. If desperate try **BanPro** in Barrio Central opposite the Moravian church, T2822-2261, which also has an ATM. Another ATM can be found next to the Alcaldía on the the plaza. **Fire** T2822-2298. **Hospital** T2822-2391. **Internet** Several places in town, try a block south of the Alcaldía, or along the main road towards the sea. **Police** T2822-2448. **Post** Correos de Nicaragua, Lotería

Nacional, 1 c abajo, T2822-1784. **Red Cross** T2822-2582. **Telephone** Enitel, Alcaldía 1 c al mar, T2822-2222.

Pearl Lagoon *p286*
Banks There are no banks or ATMs in Pearl Lagoon – bring all the cash you need. If you get really stuck there's a **Western Union** office opposite the dock. Simply log onto the internet and send yourself cash using a credit card. **Internet** Connections, like water and light, are sporadic. There is a café 1 block west and 50 m south of the Claro tower. Also try **Casa Blanca** and **Queen Lobster**.

Bilwi (Puerto Cabezas)

Bilwi, or Puerto Cabezas as it has been known for the last century, has now legally changed back to its original name. It is the capital of the RAAN, the Northern Atlantic Autonomous Region, and it has a distinctly different atmosphere from Bluefields. It is principally a large Miskito village and, although Waspam on the Río Coco is the heart and soul of the Miskito world, it is here that the Miskito political party Yatama became the first indigenous party to have control of a provincial capital in the country's modern history. The town offers an excellent introduction to the Miskito part of the country. There are also significant minorities of Hispanics (referred to as españoles*) and Afro-Caribbeans (referred to as* ingleses*) here but Spanish is mainly a second language (although most who live in Bilwi speak it well; outside the town many do not as the municipality is 80% indigenous).* ▶▶ *For listings, see pages 299-302.*

Arriving in Bilwi (Puerto Cabezas) → *Population 50,941. Altitude 10 m.*
Getting there and around **La Costeña** flies twice daily to Bilwi from Managua's domestic terminal and three times a week from Bluefields. There is a very bad road from Siuna that connects to Managua and it is best traversed during the dry season. It is a gruelling 560-km drive (20-hour bus ride) through some of the most solitary places in Central America. Downtown Bilwi is small and easy to walk round but take a taxi at night. There are seasonal roads around the city, but many surrounding attractions are only accessible by boat. ▶▶ *For futher details, see Transport, page 301.*

Tourist information **INTUR** ① *corner opposite Carnicería Río Blanco, Barrio Pedro Joaquín Chamorro, T2792-1564, raan@intur.gob.ni,* has limited information on the region. Tourism is generally underdeveloped out here, although some of the locals are working to change that. Hotel owners can be helpful with suggestions, also try **La Asociación de Mujeres Indígenas de la Costa Atlántica** (**AMICA**) ① *Barrio La Libertad, T2792-2219, asociacionamica@yahoo.es,* whose goal is to promote community tourism and protect the environment. They have extensive contacts with rural communities.

Background
The name Bilwi is of Mayagna origin. The Mayagna people have traditionally occupied the Río Grande in Matagalpa and northwards but they were forced east by the advances of Hispanic Nicaragua and this brought them into conflict with the Miskitos, who used their alliance with the British in the 17th and 18th centuries to dominate most of the Mayagna land and nearly all of the Rama territory. The Mayagna, Rama and Miskito are believed to have migrated from South America around 3000 BC. While the Rama language branched off around 2000 years ago, the Miskitos and Mayagna were heavily influenced by Afro-Caribbean migration and intermarriage. The Mayagna and Miskito

share some 50% of words and both claim to have originated from the shores of the Río Patuka near its confluence with Río Wampú. It is likely that before the migrations from central Mexico around AD 750, all of Nicaragua, including the Pacific slope, was occupied by variations of these groups.

The first European contact with the region was by Christopher Columbus, who arrived in the midst of a storm and found refuge in the bay at the mouth of the Río Coco. He named it Cabo Gracias a Dios (Cape Thank God) for the protection it afforded his boats from the raging sea. In the early 1600s, the British started trading with people on the coast and eventually made allies out of the Miskitos. Various shipwrecks, from pirates to slave ships, brought new influences to the area, but Bilwi itself is not thought to have been founded until the mid-19th century when Moravian missionaries were landed on the northern coast. More foreign interest arrived in the late 19th and early 20th century in the form of logging and banana-growing operations. After the Caribbean was formally integrated into the rest of Nicaragua in the late 19th century, the name was changed from Bilwi to Puerto Cabezas in honour of the Nicaraguan general who was given the task of integration. The 'Bay of Pigs' invasion of Cuba was launched from here in 1961 and during the Contra War the village grew from 5000 to more than 30,000 residents due to fighting in the region and enforced Sandanista relocation programmes along the Río Coco. The port was important during the Sandinista period for the unloading of Cuban and Soviet military aid. The original name of Bilwi is now legally restored, as a statement of indigenous recognition, and also a sign of frustration with the central government that is seen as selling off resources without any benefit for the local population.

On 4 September 2007, Bilwi was struck by Hurricane Felix, a massive category 5 storm with 260-kph winds. Over 130 people were killed, including 25 Miskito fishermen whose boat was swept away in the chaos. Many thousands more were stranded and displaced by the violent hurricane, which destroyed 9000 houses and caused significant flooding throughout the region.

Bilwi

To Airport
To Poza Verde
Moravian
INTUR
Alcadia
To Hospital (200m)
To Market
Catholic
Cyber Gina
Enitel
Banpro
Supermarket Monter
AMICA
Caribbean Sea
Dock
N

200 metres
200 yards

Where to stay
Casa Museo **5**
El Cortijo **1**
Hospedaje Bilwi **2**
Liwa Mairin **4**
Moncada **7**
Pérez **6**
Tangny **3**

Restaurants
Comedor Avril **6**
Crisfa **2**
El Malecón **1**
Kabu Payaska **4**
María Bonita **3**

Bars & clubs
Coco Bongo **5**
Jumbo **7**
Zaire **8**

Places in Bilwi (Puerto Cabezas)

The town itself will not win any beauty contests, but does have an end-of-the-earth feel and a 730-m pier that stretches into the Caribbean Sea. The main reasons to visit are to experience Nicaragua's only indigenous-run provincial capital and to meet its friendly population. Bilwi has two main roads which run parallel to each other and to the sea. The airport is at the northern end of the town; the port at the southern end, and a walk along the pier at sunset is highly recommended. The main market occupies the centre of town and there is a beach on the outskirts, but it is dirty. **Poza Verde**, several kilometres to the north, is a good, clean beach with white sand and calm water, although there can be sandflies. Take the road out of town for about 15 minutes and turn right onto the track marked 'SW Tuapi' (SW stands for switch); follow it for a few kilometres to the sea. You can also walk 6 km along the beach from Bilwi, or take a taxi (US$30).

Around Bilwi

The Miskito communities around Bilwi offer some of the most interesting and adventurous community tourism in Central America. Many of these fishing villages are politically autonomous and have ancient roots in Nicaragua's indigenous past. If you're lucky, you might witness traditional dances, learn about native medicine and discarnate spirits, or hear fading legends of the Miskito nation. Many of these lesser-visited communities can only be reached by riverboat, making them the preserve of only the more intrepid travellers. After you've explored the local culture, you can strike out into a wilderness of rainforests and rivers.

Located 18 km south of Bilwi pier on the shores of a large lagoon, the 2000-strong community of **Karatá** is equipped with *cabañas* and offers fishing, hiking, birdwatching and cultural tours. Nearby, the sandy beach at **Wawa Bar** overlooks the Caribbean. **Haulover** was founded by German missionaries in the 19th century and also has a sand bar, *cabañas* and large population of migratory birds. West of the village, **Laguna de Huouhnta** backs onto the nature reserves of **Laguna Kukulaya** and **Laguna Layasiska**, easily explored by boat and connected to the outside world by dirt roads. **Tuapi** is a small community of 98 families, just 8 km south of Bilwi and easily reached as a day trip. Consider this if you want a taste of village life but don't have the time, resources or inclination to venture far. **Krukira** is a gateway to **Pahara Wildlife Reserve**, a large lagoon with abundant wildlife. There's little infrastructure out there – this is for adventure tourists who want to get back to nature.

Off the mainland, several wonderfully isolated cays have powder white-sand beaches, including **Miskito**, **Wilpin** and **Mahara cays**. Take care, though, this is the haunt of drug runners, so check the security situation before heading out and always use a guide.

The **Asociación de Mujeres Indígenas de la Costa Atlántica (AMICA)** ① *Barrio La Libertad, Bilwi, T2792-2219, asociacionamica@yahoo.es*, are the people to contact when planning a trip to the communities around Bilwi. You are advised not to turn up unannounced with a backpack unless you know what you're doing. AMICA offer easy all-inclusive packages which are reasonable for groups of 10, but quite expensive for solo travellers or couples. In such cases you might be better off hitching a ride, organizing your own transport or making enquiries at the pier to see if any public boats are scheduled. AMICA can still help you find guides and lodgings and brief you on what to expect in the community, so don't leave without speaking to them.

Waspam and the Río Coco (Wangki)

This is the heart and soul of Miskito country and though some Spanish is spoken in Waspam, only Miskito is spoken in the surrounding villages. For the Miskitos, Waspam is considered the capital of the Río Coco, a trading centre for the 116 communities that line the great waterway. Most travel is by motorized canoes dug out of a single tree (*cayucos*). In the dry season they are punted using long poles. The residents of Waspam and many other communities along the river were seen as allies to the Contra rebels in the 1980s and were evacuated by force as their crops and homes were burned to the ground by government troops. They were allowed to return, but were once again hard hit by Hurricane Mitch in 1998, when the Río Coco's 780 km of water rose to more than 10 m above normal.

The source of the Río Coco is in the mountains near Somoto in northwestern Nicaragua. The river passes through Nueva Segovia before heading north to the border with Honduras and then all the way out to the coastal Laguna de Bismuna (about 80 km downriver from Waspam) and finally out to the Caribbean. The river marks the border between Nicaragua and Honduras, but for the Miskitos and Mayagna who live there the divide is hypothetical. Sadly, much of the river's banks have been deforested as a result of logging and agriculture, and by the brutal currents of Hurricanes Mitch and Felix. The riverbanks and tributaries suffer from a major erosion problem and, during the dry season, the Río Coco now has islands of sandbars, making navigation and communication between communities more difficult.

There is a good place to stay in Waspam, though water supply is reported to be unreliable. The road from Bilwi to Waspam is only open during the dry season. It is a 130-km trip that takes at least three hours by 4WD and six to eight hours by public bus (see page 301). The bus can be boarded at several points along the road leading out of town. This trip will take you through the pine forests and red plains north of Bilwi towards the Río Coco (also the border with Honduras), and you will pass through several Miskito villages including **Sisin** and **Santa Marta**. Hitching is possible; if you cannot get all the way to Waspam, make sure you are left at Sisin, Santa Marta or La Tranquera. You can accepts lifts from the military; never travel at night.

If you don't have the time or inclination to travel far out of Waspam, the traditional village of Kisalaya lies an hour's walk away. Take plenty of water as there is little shade and nowhere to buy drinks. The dirt tracks between Waspam and Bilwi are great for mountain biking; use good maps as it's easy to get lost.

Las Minas mining triangle (Siuna–Rosita–Bonanza)

These three towns are known for their gold and silver mines which are dominated by Canadian mining companies whose employees, along with Evangelist missionaries and US Peace Corps, make up the majority of the foreign population. There is great tourism potential here, but security has always been a big issue. Many locals returned after the war years to face 80% unemployment and subsequently turned to criminal activities. Drug-running, kidnapping and highway robbery were widespread until recently, with most of this lawlessness perpetrated by the Andrés Casto United Front (FUAC), whose mission was to divert funds and attention into the area. This organization of disenchanted ex-soldiers and mercenaries was effectively broken up by the government in 2001. Still, everyone in this region seems to carry a gun, and land mines may be lurking in the wilderness, despite government assertions to the contrary. Ultimately, any pleasure visits here have to be weighed against potential risks. Tourism is certainly increasing and, despite heavy logging (much of it illegal) and cattle ranching, the area still holds plenty of natural and cultural interest, including more than 50 female medicinal healers, an abundance of pristine forests, wildlife, indigenous communities and old gold mines. With increased security and environmental protection, this area could be one of the great future areas for travel in Nicaragua.

It is possible to go to the Bosawás Reserve without travelling through the mining triangle, but **Siuna** offers the easiest access to the reserve and local guides are widely available here (see page 299 for more information). It is the largest of the three towns and home to lots of interesting wooden architecture faintly reminiscent of the old west. The population is predominately mestizo but there is a Creole minority.

The town of **Bonanza**, 170 km from Bilwi, has seen huge improvements in recent years, thanks in part to the ever-rising value of gold, which is still mined in the surrounding hills. The Alcaldía can help arrange visits to old mines, processing plants and panning streams. Jewellery is widely available throughout town but those buying very large quantities of the yellow stuff may be targeted by bandits. The surrounding countryside is great for hiking and travellers often head to **Cerro Cola Blanca**; guided trips to the summit usually include an overnight stop in the village of **Kukalaya** (bring a blanket, food and water purification tablets). For commanding views over Bonanza, head to a well-known strip-mined hill known as **El Elefante** (taxi US$7 round trip including a one-hour wait).

The rural areas around Bonanza have a significant Mayagna population. Perched on the banks of the Río Waspuk, a major tributary of the Río Coco, the capital of their world is **Musuwas**. All travellers to Musuwas – or anywhere else in the Mayagna territory – must first organize permission with the Casa de Gobierno in Salkiwas, the nearest Mayagna community to Bonanza. For a fee, they will issue you with a 'Carta Aval' granting you right of passage; keep it on your person at all times. They can also advise on routes and guides – Mauricio Samuel Flores has been recommended.

If travelling to Musuwas, there is a rough road as far as Suniwas, 9 km beyond Salkiwas, and reports of a new *rancho* there with simple rustic accommodation. From Suniwas you can hike, ride horses (US$10) or hire a boat (US$250) to take you the final kilometres to the Mayagna capital. Note the road is extremely muddy, even in the dry season, and rubber boots are recommended. Once inside Musuwas, the town's *pulpería* next to the Moravian church is a good place to enquire about making trips further afield. It is worth bringing food with you to Musuwas, as there are sometimes shortages – a few jars of instant coffee will certainly raise your prestige.

The town of **Rosita** used to be entirely owned by the Rosario Mining Company, but the mines were nationalized in 1979 by the Sandinista government, who moved all the mining operations to Siuna and forcibly evacuated the local inhabitants. Today, the **Foundation for Unity and Reconstruction of the Atlantic Coast (FURCA)** ① *T2794-1045, furca@sdnnic. org.ni*, can arrange tours of the indigenous communities in the area.

From Rosita you can catch a direct bus to the Miskito town of **Alamikamba**, the main community of the twisting Prinzapolka river. If coming from Siuna, you will have to wait for connections at the highway's turn-off, where you'll find the small village of El Empalme – a good place to stock up on supplies, especially fuel, which is reportedly good quality. Most people come to Alamikamba for the superb sport fishing – the river's waters are teeming with giant, easy-to-snag snook and tarpon. To organize a fishing trip, contact 'Papatara' Erminger, T8618-2750, a former peace corp volunteer from Arkansas who now owns probably the finest lodge in RAAN (see page 300). He has several different boats and engines, lures and other fishing equipment and is generally an excellent and experienced guide.

Reserva de la Biosfera Bosawás

This is the largest forest reserve in Central America. The area is not only the most important swathe of rainforest on the isthmus, but also the most important cloud forest, with numerous isolated mountains and rivers. In addition to all the species mentioned in the Indio-Maíz Reserve (see page 186), the reserve also has altitude-specific wildlife and vegetation. There are seven mountains above 1200 m, the highest of which is **Cerro Saslaya** at 1650 m. The principal rivers that cross the reserve and feed into the Río Coco are: Río Bocay, Wina, Amaka, Lakus and Waspuk.

Visiting the reserve is still a challenge. The easiest and most organized way to visit is via Siuna. Contact the unsigned **Proyecto Bosawás** ① *2 blocks from the airstrip on the road to Rosita, T2794-2036*, for advice, queries and guides. The town's Alcaldía, T8823-7094, may be able to help too. Ecotourism projects are planned but are a long way off, due to the remoteness of the reserve and the instability of the region. However, there is at least one good project, the **Proyecto Ecoturístico Rosa Grande**, supported by Nature Conservancy and the Peace Corps.

The community of **Rosa Grande**, 25 km from Siuna, is near an area of virgin forest with a trail, waterfall on the Río Labú and lots of wildlife including monkeys and big cats. One path leads to a lookout with a view over Cerro Saslaya; a circular path to the northwest goes to the **Rancho Alegre falls**. Guides can be hired for US$7 a day plus food. Excursions for two or more days cost as little as US$13 per person for a guide, food and camping equipment. You may have to pay for a camp guard while hiking. Clarify what is included in the price and be aware of extras that may be added to the bill. Be certain you have enough supplies for your stay. For information contact Don Trinidad at the *comedor* on arrival in Santa Rosa.

There is an alternative way to experience the wilderness of Bosawás. With a great deal of time, patience and a bit of luck, you can see the great forest of Bosawás and explore a large part of the Río Coco in the process. Access is via **Jinotega** in central Nicaragua (see page 247).

⊕ Bilwi (Puerto Cabezas) listings

For sleeping and eating price codes and other relevant information, see pages 28-30.

⊕ Where to stay

Bilwi *p294, map p295*

$$ Liwa Mairin, Enitel, 2 c este, 20 vrs norte, T2792-2315, www.hotelliwamairan.com. The best in town. This new hotel has great big, airy double rooms with lots of light, balconies, sea views (US$10 extra), a/c, cable TV and tasteful, comfortable furnishings. There's also Wi-Fi, restaurant and steps down to the beach. Good value and recommended.

$$-$ Hotel Moncada, Parque Central, T2792-2061. A new, well-appointed place on the plaza. They have a variety of rooms, small (**$$**) or large (**$**), equipped with a/c, private bath and TV. Very clean and well serviced, although there's a possibility of noise from the plaza (get a room at the back). High-speed internet and restaurant service available.

$ Casa Museo, next to Centro de Computación Ansell, T2792-2225. Also known as Miss Judy's, this lovely house has lots of interesting art and artefacts in the attached museum and gallery. Rooms are spacious and comfortable and have private bath, TV and a/c (cheaper with fan). Friendly and interesting, with lots of family history. Restaurant attached, excellent value and highly recommended.

$ El Cortijo, Barrio Revolución, T2792-2340. Big Caribbean house with largish rooms, big TVs, acceptable mattresses, Wi-Fi and a/c. The rooms upstairs are more expensive and have hot water. There's also laundry, parking and breakfast on request (extra cost). Friendly and helpful. Also owns El Cortijo 2, which has very similar rooms and views of the moon rising over the beach. Visa accepted.

$ Hospedaje Bilwi, in front of pier. Tucked away from the paved road, this large, basic hotel has 19 rooms, some with fan, some with a/c and TV. Good view of the dock from the back balcony. There's a seafood restaurant downstairs. A reliable cheapie.

$ Hotel Pérez, Calle Central, T2792-2362. Friendly, family house with a range of simple rooms. Some have private bath, some have a/c, some have fan. The rooms at the back of the building are nicer, but all are a bit pokey. Breakfast, lunch and dinner available to guests, including lobster, chicken, natural juices and rondon. Prices negotiable. Pleasant garden and balconies.

$ Hotel Tangny, Entitel, 1 c arriba, 50 m norte. Clean and simple. They offer a range of cost-effective rooms with or without TV and own bath. A reasonable economical choice.

Waspam *p297*
$ La Casa de la Rose, almost next to the airport, roseck@ibw.com.ni. This comfortable wooden hotel has rooms with private bath, hammocks and screened windows. Tasty home-cooked meals are available, as well as on-site internet access. Look out for the red macaws. Recommended.

Las Minas mining triangle *p297*
$ Hotel Bonanza, Bonanza, T2794-0177. Also known as Hotelito Isa, Bonanza's best hotel has 2 types of room. The more expensive ones are tiled and come with big TVs. The more basic rooms are in a separate building across the street.

$ Hotel Papatara, Alamikamba, T8618-2750. This beautiful guesthouse has immaculately clean, comfortable, polished-wood rooms with orthopaedic beds. Built and managed by a former peace corp volunteer, Papatara Erminger, who stayed on in the region as a lumberman. An authority on sport fishing and local culture and fully equipped for expeditions. Highly recommended.

$ Hotel Siu, Siuna, T2794-2028. The best in town, with orthopaedic beds, fans, cable TV, Wi-Fi and a lush garden. Can do tours.

Reserva de la Biosfera Bosawás *p299*
$ BOSAWAS field station, on the Río Labú. Very limited hammocks, clean but simple, locally produced food for US$1.25.

🍽 Restaurants

Bilwi *p294, map p295*
In addition to those below, there are numerous *comedores* in the San Jerónimo Market.

$$ El Malecón, close to the dock, La Bocana. A popular seafood restaurant overlooking the water. It gets busy in the evenings with families and couples. One of the best in town. Recommended.

$$-$ Crisfa, Entitel, 2½ c norte, 1 c oeste. Tasty *comida típica*, meat and chicken dishes. Not bad, one of the better ones.

$$-$ Kabu Payaska, hospital, 200 vrs al mar. Often recommended by the locals, this restaurant overlooking the water serves some of the best seafood and *comida típica* in town.

$ Comedor Avril, opposite Banpro. Cheap home-cooked fare, *comida típica* and breakfasts.

$ María Bonita, Entitel, 2½ c norte. Friendly place serving *comida corrida*, à la carte food and economical home cooking, including chicken, fish and other wholesome Nica staples. Not bad.

Reserva de la Biosfera Bosawás *p299*
$ Comedor Melania, Rosa Grande. A meal costs about US$1.

🎵 Bars and clubs

Bilwi *p294, map p295*
Bilwi has a colourful and somewhat sketchy nightlife reminiscent of a Hogarth illustration. It's not safe to be out late, but if you want to explore, 3 rough-and-ready drinking holes are next to each other – **Jumbo**, **Coco Bongo** and **Zaire**; from the Entel tower, 1½ c norte. Exercise caution at all times.

🚍 Transport

Bilwi *p294, map p295*
Air
The newly renovated airport is 3 km north of town, from where taxis charge US$2 to anywhere in Bilwi. If flying to Bluefields, try to get your name on the list several days in advance. To **Bluefields**, Mon, Wed, Fri, 1210, US$96 1-way, US$148 return, 1 hr. To **Managua**, La Costeña, daily 0820, 1220, 1610, US$97 1-way, US$148 round-trip;
   Note: Bring your passport as there are immigration checks by the police in Bilwi and sometimes in the waiting lounge in Managua. All bags are x-rayed coming into the domestic terminal from any destination.

Boat
Destinations around Bilwi depart from the tiny river port of Lamlaya, 3 km out of town and best reached by taxi. Boats to destinations south of the city are said to start loading from 0630-0700 with no set departure schedule. To **Wawa**, US$3.50, 20 mins. To **Haulover**, US$4, 40 mins. To **Karatá**, US$2.50, 15 mins. To **Wounta**, US$15, 1½ hrs. Return transport leaves

at 0600, but always check locally. Boats to destinations north of Bilwi are less frequent – enquire at the main pier in town. As ever, Sun brings diminished services.
   To **Corn Islands**, once a month, night departure, US$30, 3 days. It is recommended that you do not hire a boat with fewer than 2 people. Always check for safety and crowding before boarding any long-haul vessel.
   Indepedent travel to the **Cayos Miskitos** is not recommended due to problems with drug runners from Colombia using the islands as a refuge. Contact an agency like AMICA to arrange a guided visit.
   A good boat trip is to **Laguna Bismuna** on the northern coast, reportedly one of the most beautiful in Nicaragua, though easiest access is via Waspam.

Bus
The bus station is a few kilometres out of town; take a taxi, US$0.50. To **Managua**, 1100, 1300, US$21, 18-24 hrs. To **Rosita**, 0700, US$8, 4-6 hrs. To **Siuna**, 0800, 8-9 hrs, US$17. To **Waspam**, 0600, US$6, 6 hrs. All these journeys require a strong back and stomach.

Las Minas mining triangle *p297*
From Bonanza to **Managua**, daily 1630, Mon, Tue, Fri, 1000, US$15, 18 hrs, reserve several days in advance. To **Rosita**, 6 daily, 0600-1630, US$2.50, 1½ hrs. To **Salkiwas**, 0800, 0900, 1530, US$1.50, 1 hr. To **Suniwas** (stopping in Salkiwas), 0600, 0700, 1300, U$2, 1½ hrs.
   From Siuna to **Managua**, 0330, 0500 (directo), 1200, 1500, 1700, 2000 (directo), US$8 ordinario, US$9 directo, 9-11 hrs. To **Bilwi**, 0400, US$12, 12-14 hrs. To **Rosita**, several daily, US$4, 4-5 hrs. To **Rosa Grande**, Carretera Awaslala buses, several daily, US$2.75, 1½ hrs.
   From Rosita to **Bonanza**, several daily, US$2.50, 1½ hrs. To **Siuna**, several daily, US$4, 4-5 hrs. To **Alamikamba**, 3 daily, US$4, 4½ hrs.

⊙ Directory

Bilwi *p294, map p295*
Bank Next to Enitel, BanPro has cashed TCs in the past, but do not rely on them. Bring as much cash as necessary.

Fire T2792-2255. **Hospital** Nuevo Amanecer, T2792-2259. **Police** T2792-2257. **Post and telephone** Just south of the park, Enitel handles mail during the week and telephone service daily, T2792-2237. **Red Cross** T2792-2719.

Contents

Background

History of Nicaragua

Pre-Columbian

Nicaragua was at the crossroads between northern and southern pre-Hispanic cultures for thousands of years. The migration from Asia across the Bering Strait is believed to have reached Nicaragua sometime before 18,000 BC. In Museo Las Huellas de Acahualinca in Managua, there are some well-preserved human and animal footprints of what appears to be a family of 10 people leaving the Lake Managua area after a volcanic event in the year 4000 BC. Ceramic evidence of organized settlement in Nicaragua begins around 2500 BC in San Marcos, and by 1500 BC settlements are evident in much of the Pacific area. Nicaragua continued to receive migrations from both north and south until the first arrival of the Spanish explorers in 1523. The best understood culture is that of the **Nicaraguas**, whose final migration to Nicaragua from central Mexico to the shores of Lake Nicaragua occurred just 150-200 years before the arrival of the Spanish. They spoke Náhuat (a rustic version of the Aztec Náhuatl), which became the lingua franca for the indigenous people after the conquest and may have already been widely used for trading in the region before the arrival of the first Europeans.

The Nicaraguas shared the Pacific Basin of Nicaragua with the **Chorotegas** and **Maribios**. The Chorotegas also came from Mexico, though earlier, around AD 800 and were Mangue speakers. The two tribes seemed to have found some common commercial and perhaps religious ground and dominated most of the area west of the lakes. The Maribios, Hokano speakers, and believed to be originally from California and Baja California in Mexico, populated the western slope of what is today the Maribios volcanic range, in northwestern Nicaragua. The Nicaraguas and Chorotegas were a very successful society sitting in the middle of a trade route that stretched from Mexico to Peru.

On the east side of the great lakes of Nicaragua the cultures were of South American origin. The **Chontales** and **Matagalpas** may have used the same language root (Chibcha) as the Caribbean Basin Rama, Mayagna and Miskito (a Mayagna derivative) cultures. In fact it could be that the Mayagna are descendants of the original inhabitants of the Pacific that lost ground to the invading tribes of Chorotegas in the ninth century. The Chontales appear to have been the most developed of the group, though little is known about their culture to date, despite ample and impressive archaeological evidence. Their name means 'barbarian' or 'foreigner' in Náhuatl, and has been applied to many different Mesoamerican groups.

The Conquest

Christopher Columbus sailed the Caribbean shores of Nicaragua in 1502 on his fourth and final voyage and took refuge in the far northern part of today's Nicaragua before sailing to Jamaica. The Spanish explorer Gil González Dávila sailed from Panama to the Gulf of Nicoya and then travelled overland to the western shores of Lake Nicaragua to meet the famous Nicaraguas tribe chief, Niqueragua, in April 1523. After converting the Nicaragua elite to Christianity, and taking plenty of gold away with him, González Dávila travelled further north before being chased out of the area by a surprise attack of Chorotega warriors led by legendary chieftain, Diriangén. The Spaniards fled to Panama to regroup. In 1524 a stronger army of 229 men was sent and the local populace was overcome by force. The

The Conquest of Nicaragua: a business trip

The meeting of the Spanish explorer Gil González and the philosophical Chief Niqueragua is a romantic story filled with fate, adventure and tragedy. But a brief glimpse at the cold numbers of the original expedition and the conquest that followed paints a very different picture. According to local historian Patrick Werner, Gil González received authorization for the expedition to make Europe's first business trip to the land of Nicaragua. A company was formed with four shareholders: the Spanish Crown 48%, Andrés Niño 28%, Cristóbal de Haro 15% and Gil González with 9% of the shares. The original investment totalled 8000 gold pesos. They even took an accountant with them, Andrés de Cereceda who later reported the returns on the four-month business trip. The bottom line looked a lot better than your average start-up company: 112,524 gold pesos collected on an 8000-peso investment.

Soon after, it was the turn of Pedrarias Dávila to form a new company, especially for Nicaragua. The chief negotiator for this trip, Captain Francisco Hernández de Córdoba, with an army of 229 soldiers, produced spectacular returns on the investment, recovering 158,000 gold pesos while founding the cities of León and Granada. Within one year of the Conquest, the new franchises of León and Granada had collected a further 392,000 gold pesos. It was all the gold the Indians had ever owned; in less than three years, 700-800 years of accumulated gold had been taken.

captain of the expedition, Francisco Hernández de Córdoba, founded the cities of Granada and León (Viejo) on the shores of Lake Nicaragua and Lake Managua respectively. A little is known about the actual battles of the conquest, thanks to a lost letter from Córdoba to the country's first governor describing the events. Nueva Segovia was founded as third city in 1543 to try and capitalize on mineral resources in the northern mountains. The famously cruel Pedrarias Dávila (see page 218) was given the first governor's post in Nicaragua, a position he used as a licence to run a personal empire. His rule set the stage for a tradition of *caudillos* (rulers of personality and favouritism, rather than of constitution and law) that would run and ruin Nicaragua, almost without exception, until the 21st century.

Colonial era

By the middle of the 16th century, the Spanish had realized that Nicaragua was not going to produce the same kind of mineral riches as Mexico and Peru. What Nicaragua did have was a solid population base and this was exploited to its maximum. There are no accurate figures for slave trade in early to mid-16th century Nicaragua as it was not an approved activity and was made officially illegal by the Spanish Crown in 1542. However, it is estimated that somewhere between 200,000 to 500,000 Nicaraguans were exported as slaves to work in Panama and Peru or forced to work in the gold mines near Nueva Segovia. The Consejo de Indias (Indian council) and the Casa de Contratación (legal office) in Seville managed affairs in Spain for Nicaragua. These administrative bodies controlled immigration to the Americas, acted as a court for disputes, and provided nominees for local rulers to the Spanish Crown. On a local level the province of Nicaragua belonged to the Reino de Guatemala (Kingdom of Guatemala) and was administered by a Spanish governor in León. While the *conquistadores* were busy pillaging the New World, there were serious discussions in Spain as to the legality of Spanish action in the Americas. Thanks in part to some tough lobbying by the humanist priest, Fray Bartolomé de Las Casas, laws were passed in 1542 to protect the rights of the Indians, outlawing slavery and granting them (in theory) equal rights. Sadly, enforcement of these laws was nearly impossible due to local resistance, communication obstacles and the sheer distance of the colony from Spain. The estimated indigenous population of the Pacific Basin on the arrival of the Spanish was at least 500,000. Within 40 years the total population was no more than 50,000 people, and by 1610 the indigenous residents of the Pacific slope had been reduced to around 12,000. (It wasn't until the 20th century that the population of Nicaragua returned to match pre-Conquest numbers.)

Due to the exhaustion of the indigenous population and mineral resources, many of the Spanish left Nicaragua looking for greener pastures. The ones who stayed on became involved in agriculture. Cattle were introduced and they took over cacao production, which was already very big, upon their arrival. Indigo was the other principal crop, along with some trade in wood. The beef, leather and indigo were exported to Guatemala, the cacao to El Salvador. The exports were traded for other goods, such as food and clothing, and the local population lived primarily off locally grown corn and beans. There was also a busy commercial route between Granada and the Caribbean colonial states via the Río San Juan and trade between Nicaragua and Peru. Granada became much wealthier thanks to its advantageous position along the international trade routes (although this made it a target for attacks from Dutch, French and British pirates during the 17th century), but administrative and church authority remained in León, creating a rivalry that would explode after Independence from Spain.

Independence from Spain

After 297 years as a colony of Spain, Nicaragua achieved independence. It was not a hard fought independence, but it was one that would release built-up tensions and rivalries into an open and bloody playing field. What followed was the least stable period in the history of the country: a general anarchy that only an outside invader would stop, by uniting Nicaraguans in a common cause, against a common enemy.

The greatest impulse for the demise of Spanish rule came from a new social class created during the colonial period, known locally as *criollos*, the descendants of Spaniards born in Nicaragua. At the beginning of the 19th century they still only represented 5% of the population, but they were the owners of great agricultural empires, wealthy and increasingly powerful, a class only the Spanish Crown could rival. The *criollos* did not openly oppose the colonial system, but rather chipped away at its control, in search of the power that they knew would be theirs without colonial rule.

They continued to organize and institutionalize power until 5 November 1811 when El Salvador moved to replace all the Spaniards in its local government with *criollos*. One week later, in León, the local population rebelled. The people of León took to the streets demanding the creation of a new government, new judges, and abolition of the government monopoly to produce liquor, lower prices for tobacco and an end to taxes on beef, paper and general sales. All the demands were granted. There were also demonstrations in Masaya, Rivas and Granada.

In September 1821 Mexico declared Independence from Spain. A meeting was called in Guatemala City on 15 September 1821. At the meeting were the representatives of the central government in Spain, Spanish representatives from every country in

Central America, the heads of the Catholic Church from each province, the archbishop of Guatemala and the local senators of the provinces. Independence from Spain was declared; yet in Nicaragua the wars had just begun.

León versus Granada

In October 1821 the authorities in León declared that Nicaragua would become part of the Mexican Empire, while the Guatemalan office of Central America created a local Central American government office in Granada, increasing sentiments of separatism in Granada. Regardless, Nicaragua remained more or less part of the federation of Mexico and Central America until 1823 when the United Provinces of Central America met and declared themselves free of Mexican domain and any other foreign power. The five members – Guatemala, El Salvador, Honduras, Nicaragua and Costa Rica – were a federation free to administer their own countries and in November 1824 a new constitution for the Central America Federation was decreed. Nicaraguans, however, were already fighting among themselves.

In April 1824 León and Granada had both proclaimed themselves capital of the country. Other cities chose sides with one or the other, while Managua created a third 'government', proclaiming Managua as Nicaragua's capital. The in-fighting continued until, in 1827, civil war erupted. It was not until Guatemala sent another general that peace was achieved and a new chief of state named in 1834. The civilian head of state was Dr José Núñez, but the military chiefs were not pleased and he was soon thrown out. In 1835 José Zepeda was named head of state but still more violence followed. In 1836 Zepeda was thrown in prison, put against a wall and shot. By this time, the federal government in Guatemala was increasingly helpless and impotent and, as the power vacuum of 300 years of colonial rule wreaked havoc upon the isthmus, the state of anarchy in Nicaragua was common across Central America.

On 30 April 1838 the legislative assembly of Nicaragua, in a rare moment of relevance, declared Nicaragua independent of any other power and the Central American Federation collapsed, with the other states also declaring the Federation to be history. A new constitution was written for Nicaragua, but it was one that would have little effect on the constant power struggle.

In 1853 Granada General Fruto Chamorro took over the post of Director of State, with hope of establishing something that resembled peace. Informed of an armed uprising being planned in León, he ordered the capture of the principal perpetrators, but most escaped to Honduras. In 1854 yet another new constitution was written. This one changed the post of Director of State to 'President' which meant that Conservative General Fruto Chamorro was technically no longer in power. However the assembly, going against the constitution they had just approved, named him as president anyway. The Liberal León generals in Honduras had seen enough and decided to attack. Máximo Jérez led the attack against the Conservatives and Chamorro, the León contingent hiring US mercenary Byron Cole to give them a hand against Granada. He signed a contract and returned to the US where he gave the job to the man every single Nicaraguan (but not a single North American) school child has heard of.

William Walker and the Guerra Nacional

On 13 June 1855, North American William Walker and his 55 hired guns set sail for Nicaragua. The group was armed with the latest in firepower and a very well-planned scheme to create a new slave state in Nicaragua. His idea was for a new colony to be settled by North American Anglos (to own the lands and slaves) and blacks (to do all the work). William Walker planned to conquer and colonize not only Nicaragua, but all of Central America, isolating what remained of Mexico, which had just lost one-third of its territory to the US in the Mexican-American War.

In September of the same year, Walker and his little battalion landed in San Juan del Sur, confronted Granada's Conservative Party army in La Virgen and won easily. On 13 October 1855 he travelled north, attacked and took Granada with the local generals escaping to Masaya and later signing a peace pact. As per prior agreement, Patricio Rivas of León's Liberal Party was named President of the Republic and Walker as the head of the military. Rivas, following Walker's wishes, confiscated the steamship line of Vanderbilt, which Walker then used to ship in more arms, ammunitions and mercenary soldiers from the US. Soon he had the best-equipped and most modern fighting force in Central America.

On 6 June 1856, Walker appeared in León, demanding that he be allowed to confiscate the properties of the León elite. President Patricio Rivas and his ministers refused and after numerous meetings and no agreements William Walker left León for Granada. The people with power in León had finally realised what they were up against and contacted generals in El Salvador and Guatemala for help. Soon all of Central America would be united against the army of William Walker.

From 22-24 June 1856 farcical elections were held and William Walker was named President of the Republic. On 12 July, Walker officially took office with a pompous parade through Granada, while flying his new flag for the country. A series of decrees were proclaimed during that month, including the legalization of slavery, and the immediate confiscation of all properties of all 'enemies of the state'. English was made the official language of business (to ensure that North American colonists would receive all the land confiscated).

The turning point in William Walker's troops' apparent invincibility came at the little ranch north of Tipitapa called San Jacinto. It is a museum today and a mandatory visit for all Nicaraguan primary school children. Walker had never been able to control Matagalpa and a division of the rebel Nicaraguan army was sent south from Matagalpa to try and stop the confiscation of cattle ranches in the area of San Jacinto. The two forces met. The Nicaraguan division used the little house in San Jacinto, with its thick adobe walls, as their fort and it provided great protection. A battle on 5 September was a slight victory for the Nicaraguans, but both sent for reinforcements and on 14 September (the national holiday now celebrated annually), 200 of Walker's troops lost a bloody and difficult battle to 160 Nicaraguan troops. The tide had turned and battles in Masaya, Rivas and Granada would prove victorious for the combined Central American forces. William Walker escaped to a steamship from where he watched the final grisly actions of his troops in Granada, who, completely drunk, proceeded to rape and kill the fleeing natives and then burned the city to the ground. Walker's administrators mounted a mock procession in Granada, burying a coffin in Central Park with a sign above it that said, "Here was Granada".

Walker would later return to Nicaragua, before just escaping with his life. He then tried his luck in Honduras where he was taken prisoner by Captain Salmon of the British navy and handed over to the Honduran authorities. He was tried, put against a wall and shot by the Honduran armed forces on 12 September 1860.

General José Santos Zelaya

For the next 30-plus years, the wealthy families of Granada would control the government (now based in Managua), thanks partly to a law stating that, to have the right to vote, you must have 100 pesos, and in order to be a presidential candidate, over 4000 pesos. But, in 1893, the Conservative president was overthrown by a movement led by Liberal Party General José Santos Zelaya.

General Zelaya did much to modernize Nicaragua. A new constitution was written in 1893 and put into effect the following year. The separation of church and state was instituted, with ideas of equality and liberty for all, respect for private property, civil marriage, divorce, mandatory schooling for all, the death penalty abolished and debtors' prison banned and freedom of expression guaranteed. Construction was rampant, with new roads, docks, postal offices, shipping routes and electricity installed in Managua and Chinandega. A whole raft of new laws were passed to facilitate business, proper police and military codes, and a Supreme Court was created. The Caribbean Coast was finally officially incorporated into the country in 1894. Despite all of this, however, Zelaya did not endear himself to the US. With the canal project close at hand in either Panama or Nicaragua, Zelaya insisted that no single country would be permitted to finance a canal project in Nicaragua and, what's more, only Nicaragua could have sovereignty over a canal inside its country. The project went to Panama. In 1909 as Zelaya was flirting with Japan to build a rival canal, he was pushed out of power with the help of the US Marines.

US Marines – Augusto C Sandino

In 1909 there was an uprising in Bluefields against Zelaya. Led by General Juan Estrada, with the support of the Granada Conservative Party, two American mercenaries were caught and executed during the battles. The US Marines entered in May 1910 to secure power for Estrada who took control of the east coast in what they termed a 'neutral zone'. General Estrada marched into Managua to install himself as the new president of Nicaragua. Stuck with debts from European creditors, Juan Estrada was forced to borrow from the North American banks. He then gave the US control over collection of duties, as a guarantee for those loans. The Nicaraguan National Bank and a new monetary unit called the *córdoba* were established in 1912. The Granada aristocrats were not happy with General Estrada and a new round of fighting between León Liberals and Granada Conservatives erupted.

On 4 August the US Marines entered Managua to secure order and establish their choice, Adolfo Díaz, as president of the country. Two years later, under occupation of the Marines, Nicaragua signed the Chamorro-Bryan Treaty, with Nicaragua conceding perpetual rights of any Nicaraguan canal project to the US, in exchange for US$3 million, which went to pay US banks for outstanding debts. There was no intention to build a canal in Nicaragua; the deal was rather to keep Nicaragua from building a competing one.

In 1917, with Emiliano Chamorro in control of the presidency, more problems followed. Díaz, still fighting to regain the presidency, called for more Marines to be sent from the US. Over 2000 troops arrived and Díaz was put back into the presidency, but nothing could be done to bring together the various factions.

In what were then considered to be fair elections (albeit under occupation) in 1924, moderate Conservative Carlos Solórzano was elected to the presidency with Liberal Party physician Dr Juan Sacasa his VP. In 1925 the Marines withdrew from Nicaragua. Two and a half months later a revolt broke out led by hard-line Conservative Emiliano Chamorro.

Solórzano fled with his Liberal VP Sacasa to Honduras. Chamorro purged congress and was declared president in 1926. The Liberals rebelled, but the US Marines returned to prop up the president.

In May 1927, the US State Department agreed a plan with the Nicaraguan authorities to organize a non-political army, disarm both the Liberal and Conservative armies and hold new elections. The new army would be called the Guardia Nacional. Most parties agreed to the solution, with the exception of General Augusto Sandino, who had been fighting under the command of Liberal General José María Moncada. Sandino returned to the northern mountains determined to fight against the government of Adolfo Díaz, whom he panned as a US puppet president, and the occupation of the Marines, something the nationalist Sandino found unacceptable.

In 1928, José María Moncada won the elections under supervision of the US government. Despite the fact that a Liberal was now president, Sandino refused to lay down his arms as long as Nicaragua was under occupation. Fighting side by side with the Marines, to exterminate Augusto Sandino's rebel army, was the newly created Guardia Nacional. The Marines thought they would defeat General Sandino's rebel forces quickly, in particular because of their vastly superior artillery and advantage of air power. However, the charismatic general had widespread support in the north and was not defeated. He relentlessly attacked US Marine positions with what some say was the first use of modern guerrilla warfare. Finally, with elections approaching in 1933, and with the National Guard under the command of General Anastasio Somoza García, the US announced that the Marines would pull out when the new president took power. Juan Bautista Sacasa was elected, and the day he took power, 1 January 1933, the last regiment of Marines left Nicaragua by boat from Corinto. Twenty-four years of intervention had ended.

The Somoza family

With the US Marines gone, General Augusto Sandino went to the presidential palace (today the Parque Loma de Tiscapa) and signed a peace and disarmament treaty with President Sacasa. The treaty stipulated that the rebel army would gradually turn over their weapons and receive amnesty, with ample job opportunities for ex-rebel fighters. One year later, on 21 February 1934, when Sandino returned to the presidential palace for dinner with President Sacasa, the commander of the Guardia Nacional, Anastasio Somoza García plotted the abduction and death of Sandino, which was carried out while Somoza was enjoying a concert. After Sandino left the dinner party he was stopped at a road block, sent to a rural part of Managua, shot and buried. With the death of Sandino the Liberal Party was divided into two camps, one that supported Somoza and the other President Sacasa. Somoza attacked the fort above León in May 1936 and the Guardia Nacional demanded Sacasa's resignation. A month later Sacasa resigned and new elections were won by Somoza García. Yet again, a leader of Nicaragua's military took state office. Various 'presidents' were elected from 1937 to 1979, but there was never any doubt who was running the show. Anastasio Somoza García and later his son Anastasio Somoza Debayle maintained effective power as the head of the National Guard.

Nicaragua enjoyed a period of relative stability and economic growth. The relationship between the US and Nicaragua had never been better, with close co-operation, including the use of Nicaragua as a training and launching ground for the Bay of Pigs invasion in Cuba. Somoza used the Guardia Nacional to keep the populace at bay and the technique of *pactos* (political pacts) to keep Conservative political opponents in on some of the

Somoza family's ever-increasing riches and power. During the Second World War, Nicaragua entered on the side of the US and Somoza García used the war to confiscate as much property from German nationals as possible (including what is today Montelimar Beach Resort, see page 74). This formed a basis for building a business empire that used state money to grow.

After accepting the Liberal Party nomination for the election of 1956, Somoza García was shot and killed by a young León poet named Rigoberto López Pérez. Despite his death, the family dynasty continued with Somoza García's sons, Luis and Anastasio. Together they lasted 42 years in power, one of the longest dictatorships in Latin American history.

Sandinista National Liberation Front

The first attack of the FSLN was along the Río Coco in 1963 in which Tomás Borge and ageing Sandino fighter Santos López participated; they were routed. More than 200 civilians died in January 1967 when the National Guard broke up a 60,000-person opposition rally in Managua by firing into the crowd. The FSLN rebels regrouped and carried out a number of urban bank robberies and minor rural attacks, but later that year they were attacked at Pancasán, Matagalpa, and many founding members of the party were killed. In the same year one of the bank robbers, **Daniel Ortega**, was thrown in jail and Tomás Borge escaped to Cuba, leaving the FSLN almost completely disbanded or in exile. Founder Carlos Fonseca was jailed in Costa Rica in 1969 and Somoza made one of many public blunders by broadcasting the National Guard attack of an FSLN safe house. As the house was being shelled into ruins, rebel Julio Buitrago defended it alone, against tanks, troops and helicopters, inspiring the Nicaraguan public. An aeroplane hijacking achieved the release of Carlos Fonseca and Humberto Ortega from a Costa Rican jail in 1970 and the next year rebels regrouped in the northern mountains, including flamboyant rebel Edén Pastora.

In 1972 a massive earthquake destroyed Managua, killing 5000-15,000 people and leaving some 200,000 homeless. The millions of dollars of aid and reconstruction money were funnelled through Somoza's companies or went straight into his bank accounts and the Nicaraguan elite started to lose patience with the final Somoza dictator.

Somoza was elected to yet another term as president in September 1974, but on December of the same year, an FSLN commando unit led by Germán Pomares raided a Managua party of Somoza politicians, gaining sweeping concessions from the government including six million dollars in cash, a rise in the national minimum wage, the release of 14 prisoners including Daniel Ortega, and the broadcast of a 12,000-word FSLN communiqué.

The FSLN was at a crossroads in 1975, with the three principal Sandinista ideological factions at odds on how to win the war against Somoza. FSLN General Secretary Carlos Fonseca returned from five years of exile in Cuba to try and unify the forces. The most pragmatic of the three factions, led by the Ortega brothers Daniel and Humberto, proposed a strategy of combining select assassinations and the creation of broad alliances with non-Marxist groups and a whole range of ideologies. Too conveniently for some, party founder and devout Marxist Carlos Fonseca, who was in the mountains of Matagalpa expecting a reunion of the leaders of the three bickering factions, was ambushed and killed by the National Guard on 8 November 1976, one week before the three-faction summit. Early the following year the Ortega faction came out with a highly detailed 60-page plan on how to defeat Somoza; they also quickly solidified their domination of FSLN leadership, an iron grip that Daniel Ortega has held until today.

1978-1979 Revolution

During the Somoza family reign, control of the military was critical, but so was the weakness of the Conservative Party (today almost defunct), which was continually bought out by the Somozas whenever they made too much noise. The exception was *La Prensa* newspaper publisher Pedro Joaquín Chamorro. A man who could not be purchased and who was the most vocal opposition to Somoza rule in Nicaragua, PJ Chamorro was the Conservative Party's great hope, a natural to take over leadership of the country if the Liberal dictator could be disposed of. On 10 January 1978 Pedro Joaquín Chamorro was riddled with bullets in Managua on his way to the office, a murder attributed to the National Guard. The country erupted. Over the following days rioters set fire to Somoza businesses, 30,000 people attended the funeral and the entire country went on strike. The National Guard attacked many of the public gatherings in Managua; the FSLN went into action with Edén Pastora leading an attack on Rivas barracks; and Germán Pomares led attacks in Nueva Segovia in early February. The Catholic Church published a letter in *La Prensa* approving of armed resistance and one week later the indigenous community of Monimbó was tear-gassed by the National Guard at a Mass for Pedro Joaquín Chamorro and took over their town in a spontaneous rebellion that surprised even the FSLN. Somoza, after one week of defiance by citizens armed with hunting rifles and machetes, had to use tanks and planes to retake Monimbó, killing more than 200. The indigenous community of Sutiava also rebelled, as did the largely indigenous city of Diriamba in the same month. Monimbó rioted again in March 1978, and between April and August there were many rebellions and skirmishes, but the insurrection was beginning once again to stall, until the most famous act of the Revolution brought it back to life: the attack by FSLN commandos on Nicaragua's parliament in session that lasted from 22-24 August. The rebels held the Congressmen hostage, along with more than 1000 state employees in the National Palace, until demands were met. The strike, led by Edén Pastora and female Comandante Dora María Tellez, won the release of 58 prisoners and US$500,000 in cash and a plane ride for the prisoners (including Tomás Borge) and commandos to Panama.

In September 1978, the FSLN launched their most ambitious series of attacks ever, winning National Guard posts in east Managua, Masaya, León, Chinandega and Estelí, though the National Guard with air and tank support took back each city one by one causing hundreds of deaths. The National Guard was overrun again in Monimbó one week later and fighting broke out along the border with Costa Rica, while in Diriamba more than 4000 died in uprisings. The public and the rebels, sometimes together, sometimes working apart, continued harassing the National Guard for the next eight months, as international pressure was stepped up on Somoza. He in turn accused Venezuela, Panama, Cuba and Costa Rica of supporting the FSLN (which they were). From February to May 1979, rebels attacked Nicaraguan cities at will.

In June the attacks became more prolonged, the forces of the FSLN swelling with new recruits as the general public became part of the rebellion and doing even more fighting than the FSLN. There was total insurrection around the Pacific, central and northern regions, with Edén Pastora forces occupying Somoza's elite troops in a frontal battle in southern Rivas. On 20 June American news reporter Bill Stewart from ABC was put on the ground and executed by the National Guard in front of his own cameraman who captured the scene, which was broadcasted across the USA.

By the end of June, Masaya, Diriamba, eastern Managua, Chontales and other rural areas were liberated by the FSLN and under their control. By 6 July, Jinotepe, San Marcos,

Masatepe and Sébaco had fallen, cutting off supply routes for the National Guard north and south. León was finally liberated on 9 July; four days later Somoza flew to Guatemala looking for military aid which was denied. At 0100 on 17 July Somoza finally resigned and his National Guard disintegrated, some escaping out of San Juan del Sur on commandeered shrimp boats, while others fled to Miami, Honduras and Guatemala.

At the huge cost of more than 50,000 Nicaraguan lives, Somoza Debayle and the Guardia National were finally defeated. Nicaragua was in ruins, but free. A huge party was held in front of the Old Cathedral and National Palace on 20 July. Somoza escaped to Miami and later to Paraguay, where he was blown to bits by an Argentine hit squad on 17 September 1980.

Sandinista Government and the Contra War

A national reconstruction committee assumed power of Nicaragua on 20 July 1979. It was made up of five members: FSLN leader Daniel Ortega, novelist Sergio Ramírez, physics professor Dr Moisés Hassan, widow of the slain *La Prensa* publisher Violeta Barrios de Chamorro and businessman Alfonso Robelo. It looked to be a well-balanced group, but what the public did not know at the time was that Ramírez and Hassan were both sworn secret members of the FSLN, giving them three to two control of the ruling board. Within a year both Doña Violeta and Alfonso Robelo would resign.

The committee abolished the old constitution and confiscated all property belonging to Somoza and his 'allies'. A new legislative body was organized to write a new constitution. Several key bodies were created by the Sandinistas that helped them to consolidate power quickly, like the Comités de Defensa Sandinista (CDS) that was organized in the *barrios* of Managua and the countryside to be the 'eyes and ears of the Revolution'. Much of the Nicaraguan public who fought had believed that the Revolution was about getting rid of Somoza (and not much beyond that) while many also hoped to establish a democratic system based on the Costa Rican model. However, the Sandinistas' aim was to change society as a whole, installing a semi-Marxist system and, in theory, reversing over four centuries of social injustice.

The peace in Nicaragua was short lived. Thanks to the pre-victory death of legendary non-Marxist FSLN rebel leader Germán Pomares in Jinotega in May 1979 – by what was at first said to be a National Guard sniper, then revised as a 'stray bullet' – the first anti-Sandinista rebel units formed in Nueva Segovia. Four days after the first anniversary of the victory over Somoza, a group of ex-Sandinista rebels attacked Sandinista Government troops, overrunning the local military base in Quilalí. The Contra War had begun. By August 1980, ex-National Guard members were also forming groups in Honduras and, thanks to organization by CIA, at first directed via Argentine generals, and then with direct control from ex-Guard members, the movement began to formalize rebel groups. The first planned CIA attack was carried out in March 1982 with bombs planted to destroy key bridges in the north. Although the original Contras and the majority of the Contra fighters had nothing to do with the National Guard, the Resistencia Nicaragüense (better known as the Contras – short for counter-revolutionary in Spanish) was to be commanded in Honduras by former Guard members and funded by the US government under Ronald Reagan. The war waged by the Contras was one of harassment and guerrilla warfare like Sandino had used against the US Marines. But, unlike Sandino, the Contra bands attacked freely 'soft (civilian) targets' and country infrastructure as part of their strategy. A southern front against the Sandinista administration was opened up by ex-FSLN hero Edén Pastora

The Contra War

Then US President Ronald Reagan labelled the Contras the 'Freedom Fighters', and on one occasion even sported a T-shirt that read, 'I'm a Contra too'. His administration lobbied to maintain and increase military aid to the Nicaraguan Contras fighting the Sandinista Revolution during the 1980s. The first bands of Contras were organized shortly after the Sandinistas took power in 1979. The leaders were mainly ex-officials and soldiers loyal to the overthrown general Anastasio Somoza Debayle. Thanks to the United States, the Contras grew quickly and became the largest guerrilla army in Latin America. When they demobilized in May 1990, they had 15,000 troops.

The Contras divided Nicaragua in two: war zones and zones that were not at war. They also divided United States public opinion between those who supported President Reagan's policy and those who opposed it. The US House of Representatives and the Senate were likewise divided. The Contras are also associated with one of the biggest political scandals in the US after Watergate. The so-called 'Iran-Contra Affair' broke at the end of 1986, when a C-123 supply plane with a US flight crew was shot down over Nicaraguan territory. The scandal that followed caused some US government officials to resign, including Lieutenant Colonel Oliver North. The intellectual authors of the affair remained unscathed.

The most famous Contra leader was former Guardia Nacional Colonel Enrique Bermúdez, known in the war as 'Commander 3-80'. In February 1991, Bermúdez was shot dead in the parking lot of Managua's Intercontinental Hotel. The 'strange circumstances' surrounding his death were never clarified, and the killers were never apprehended. After agreeing to disarm in 1990, the majority of the Contra troops returned to a normal civilian life. However, most of them never received the land, credit, work implements, etc they had been promised. The Contras live on today as the Partido Resistencia Nicaragüense (Nicaraguan Resistance Party), which has been ineffective due to internal disputes and divisions.

who was disillusioned with the new Sandinista government and the meaningless roles he was given to play in it. By introducing mandatory military service the Sandinista army swelled to over 120,000 to fight the combined Contra forces of an estimated 10,000-20,000 soldiers. The national monetary reserves were increasingly taxed, with more than half the national budget going on military spending, and a US economic embargo that sent inflation spinning out of control, annihilating the already beleaguered economy that was finally killed by the collapse of partner states in the Soviet bloc. Massive migration to avoid the war zones changed the face of Nicaragua, with exiles choosing departmental capitals, Managua or Costa Rica, while those who could afford it fled to Miami. Indigenous groups suffered greatly during this period with the Mayagna in the heart of the Contra War and the Miskitos being forced to live in internment camps while their village homes and crops were razed by government troops. The Miskitos formed their own rebel Contra groups who attacked from the Caribbean side and the Río Coco.

The Sandinistas are credited with numerous important socio-political achievements including the **Literacy Crusade**, a fresh sense of nationalism, giant cultural advances and improved infrastructure. Yet the Contra War, US economic embargo, a thoroughly disastrous agriculture reform program, human rights abuses and dictatorial style of running the government would spell their doom. Progress in education and culture was undeniably impressive during the Sandinista years, especially considering the circumstances, but the cost was too high for the majority of the Nicaraguan people. Personal freedoms were the same or worse (especially regarding freedom of speech and press) as they had been in the time of Somoza's rule, and fatigue from the death and poverty caused by the Contra War was extreme. Hundreds of studies have been written on what happened in the 1980s in Nicaragua and defenders of the FSLN rule point out that they never had a chance to rule in peace. Their detractors, on the other hand, highlight that democracy was never on the agenda for the party.

A peace agreement was reached in Sapoá, Rivas and elections were held in 1990. Daniel Ortega (40.8%) lost to Violeta Chamorro (55.2%). After losing the elections the Sandinistas bravely handed over power to Doña Violeta. Then they proceeded frantically to divide and distribute state-held assets (which included hundreds of confiscated properties and businesses) among leading party members in the two months between the election loss and handing over power, in what has since been known simply as *la piñata*.

Nicaragua after the Contra War

After an entire century of limited personal freedoms and military-backed governments, most Nicaraguans considered the election of Doña Violeta as the beginning of true democracy in Nicaragua. She was forced to compromise on many issues and at times the country looked set to collapse back into war, but Nicaragua's first woman president spent the next six years trying to repair the damage and unite the country. The Nicaraguan military was de-politicized, put under civilian rule and reduced from over 120,000 to fewer than 18,000. Uprisings were common with small groups taking up arms or demonstrations meant to destabilize the government. But by the time Doña Violeta handed over the presidency in 1997, Nicaragua was fully at peace and beginning to recover economically.

In 1996 Liberal Party candidate Arnoldo Alemán won 51% of the vote against the 37.7% garnered by his opponent Daniel Ortega, with the rest divided among 21 different presidential candidates. However, behind closed doors, a politically expedient pact between the Liberals and the Sandinistas compromised and politicized government institutions and created much controversy. Sandinista objectors to the pact were tossed out of the party. Meanwhile, Alemán made great strides in increasing economic growth and foreign investment and improved education and road infrastructure. He also managed to steal more than US$100 million of state funds and left office with an approval rating of less than 25%.

In 2001, the electorate once again voted for the Liberals, or more precisely against Ortega, electing Liberal Party candidate Enrique Bolaños in a record turnout of 96% of registered voters. Bolaños promised to attack the corruption of his party leader Arnoldo Alemán and he did exactly that. At great political cost to Nicaragua's executive branch, Bolaños had Alemán tried, convicted and sentenced to 20 years in prison on corruption charges. But the Liberal congressmen, all purchased by Alemán, refused to abandon their leader and insisted on amnesty for Alemán, who continued to rule the Liberal party from his luxury ranch and enjoyed full movement about the country. Despite the great victory against state thievery, Bolaños' administration has been largely ineffectual; the war against corruption left him without support in the Nicaraguan congress. Furthermore, Alemán and Ortega entered into a new pact that promised freedom for Alemán after Liberal parliamentary members voted the Sandinistas into power at all levels of non-Federal government, from Parliament to the Supreme Court.

The return of Daniel Ortega

Daniel Ortega returned to the run the Executive Branch in 2007 after winning 38% of the vote. Despite ample promises of help from new allies such as Venezuela and Iran, little changed in Nicaragua's daily reality, with the rising cost of living outpacing mandated salary adjustments. More than this, despite instituting scores of seemingly progressive social programmes, Ortega was widely criticized for employing the same neo-liberal policies of the last 17 years. The *Economist* called it "Ortega's Crab Walk"; tough revolutionary, anti-Imperialist rhetoric combined with a textbook IMF economic policy. Equally, there were real concerns about Ortega's apparent ambitions for perpetual re-election. In 2009, he effectively amended the Nicaraguan constitution to allow a President to hold office for two consecutive terms. Predictably, he ran as the Sandinista candidate in the 2011 election, winning a landslide victory against a poorly organized and divided Liberal opposition. Time will tell whether he delivers on his political promises or instead descends into the kind of corruption and authoritarianism that he so rigorously fought against in the 1980s. As ever, Nicaragua's future looks as uncertain as it does volatile.

Nicaragua culture and customs

People

Ethnicity

The origin of the Nicaraguan, as with much of the Americas' population, is typically diverse. The pre-conquest cultures of the central and western sections of the countries mixed with small waves of European immigration, beginning in the 16th century and continuing today. The eastern section of Nicaragua remained in relative isolation for the first several centuries and fairly well defined indigenous ethnic cultures are still present in the communities of Miskito, Rama and Mayagna as well as Afro-Caribbeans from Jamaica (Creole) and San Vincent (Garífuna) Islands. Ultimately, however, the Hispanic mestizo culture of the western two-thirds of the country dominate the ethnic profile of the Nicaraguan. Recent surveys suggest a country 96% mestizo, with 3% indigenous and 1% Afro-Caribbean. Among the peoples classified as mestizo are many of close to pure indigenous roots who have lost their distinguishing language, but retained many cultural traits of pre-Columbian times. There is also a very small, nearly pure European sector that has traditionally controlled the country's economic and land assets. Massive movements of population during the troubled years of the 1980s has also blurred these once well-defined lines, although you can still see some definite ethnic tendencies in each province of the country.

Religion

By 1585, the majority of the local population had been converted to Christianity. Recent surveys suggest that now only 59% of the population is Roman Catholic. Evangelical groups have made great strides in recent years in attracting worshippers, and Baptist, Methodist, Church of Christ, Assembly of God, Seventh Day Adventists, Jehovah's Witness, Mormon and other churches now account for 29% of the population, with the remainder claiming no church affiliation. Religion and spirituality in general are very important parts of Nicaraguan life. The combined forces of the Evangelist churches have their own political party in Camino Cristiano (who joined in alliance with the Liberal party for the elections in 2001) and won the third largest tally of votes in the 1996 campaign. The Catholic Church has no official political wing, but plays heavily on the political scene.

Dance

During the early years of Spanish colonization, dance as a discipline did not have a defined style. Indigenous dances were considered heretical due to the ceremonial nature of some of them (although many were danced for pure pleasure) and therefore discouraged or banned. The dances considered folkloric or traditional in Nicaragua today are a mixture of African, indigenous and European dances and cultures. In the colonial period, celebrations of religious festivities saw the performance by the upper-class Spanish of European dances that were in fashion back home. The manner of dancing and behaviour of the upper class was observed by the native, African and mestizo populations and then mixed with each culture's respective dances.

The terms *el son* or *los sones* are used to define the dances that first appeared in the 1700s, such as the **Jarabe**, **Jaranas** and **Huapangos**. These dances are the local adaptations of the Fandango and Spanish tap dance. In Nicaragua the dances or *sones Jarabe Chichón* and *Jarabe Repicado* are still performed today in the festivals of Masaya and its *pueblos*. Many traditional dances have a love message; a good example is the flirtatious **Dance of the Indian Girls** (*Baile de las Inditas*) or the entertaining physical satire on relationships known as the **Dance of the Old Man and Lady** (*El Baile del Viejo y la Vieja*).

Other well-known dances are the **Dance of the Black Girls** (*Danza de las Negritas*), another dance performed by men in drag, and a spectacular and colourful traditional dance **The Little Demons** (*Los Diablitos*). This is a native mock-up of an Iberian masquerade ball, danced in the streets and with performer's costumes consisting of every possible character from Mr Death to a tiger, or a giant parrot or the Devil. One of the most traditional dances from Masaya is **El Torovenado**, which follows the rhythm of *marimbas* and *chicheros*. The participants are all male and dress in costumes representing both male and female politicians and members of the upper class. Their handmade masks and costumes are created to satirize important events happening in the country or behaviour of the moneyed class. The Torovenado is a street performance-protest against social injustice and government corruption. Another of the many traditional Nicaraguan dances is the **Dance of the Hungarians** (*Danza de la Húngaras*), which developed from early 20th-century immigration of eastern European gypsies to Nicaragua.

Masaya is far from unique in its local dances, for Nicaraguan regional dance is rich and impressive across the board. The most famous of all, **El Güegüence** (see box, page 102) has disputed origins – it is either from the highland village of Diriamba or from Masaya. The small, but historic village of Nindirí is home to many dances like **The Black Chinese** (*Los Chinegros*), **El Ensartado** and **Las Canas**. León is the origin of the spectacular joke on the early colonisers called **El Baile de La Gigantona y el Enano Cabezón**, in which a 3-m-tall blond women spins and dances in circles around an old dwarf with a big bald head. León is also home to **Los Mantudos** and **El Baile del Toro**. Managua has **La Danza de la Vaca** and Boaco has the **Dance of the Moors and the Christians** (*Los Moros y Cristianos*). Very peculiar inside Nicaragua is the dance only performed on the Island of Ometepe in the village of Altagracia called the **Dance of the Leaf-Cutter Ants** (*El Baile de Los Zompopos*).

In the northern cities of Matagalpa and Jinotega, the coffee immigrants from Germany and other parts of northern Europe in the late 19th century had violin and guitar-driven polkas, *jamaquellos* and *mazurkas*.

The Caribbean Coast is home to some little-known Garífuna dances that are now being performed in Managua and some native Miskito dances that have also been recognized and performed by dance troupes on the Pacific side. The favourite of both coasts for its raw energy may be the **Palo de Mayo** (maypole) dances, a hybrid of English maypole traditions and Afro-Caribbean rain and fertility dances.

Aside from the tradition of dancing in festivals, the dances of Nicaragua have been brought to the stage and are performed regularly by numerous groups and professional companies in Managua and Masaya with less frequent performances all over Nicaragua. Masaya often has dance groups performing on Thursday nights at the artisans' market and the **Centro Cultural Managua** and **Teatro Rubén Darío** also have regular shows.

Literature

Early Nicaraguan poetry and narrative, influenced from the beginning by the chronicles of the West Indies, uses a straightforward descriptive style to depict the life of the indigenous people and the Spanish conquest through colourful narratives. This type of **native literature** was the most prevalent during the pre-Hispanic era. One of the original works was *Canto al sol de los Nicaraguas*, dedicated to the principal cultures to inhabit this remote region, the Nicaraguas and Chorotegas. The writing of the indigenous peoples, generally pictographs, is largely anonymous. While the native languages would later become mixed with Spanish, a series of primitive dialects were conserved, so that later it was possible to recover and compile different works, including **Sumu poetry**, **Miskito songs**, **Sutiavan poems**, **Carib music** and **native myths** from different regions of Nicaragua. These were songs related to the Spanish conquest or religion – a product of the colonization process – sayings, riddles, ballads and children's games that would later reappear in different narratives and poetic forms. The first book attributed to Nicaraguan-born Spanish descendants was *Relaciones verdaderas de la deducción de los indios infieles, de la provincia de Teguzgalpa* (True Revelations about the Pagan Indians from the Province of Teguzgalpa) by Francisco Fernández Espino, which appeared in 1674. The work was little known. In 1876, according to literary critic Ricardo Llopesa, the first literary group La Montaña, was founded in Granada. Two years later the first anthology titled *Lira Nicaragüense* was published.

Rubén Darío

The Father of Modernism Rubén Darío (1867-1916) overshadowed everyone with his proposals for innovation in the Spanish language through the Modernist movement, which he himself founded. The Modernist school advocated aestheticism, the search for sensory and even sensual values, and the artistic effects of colour, sound, voice and synthesis. His first verses were published in 1879. In 1881 he edited his first complete work, *Poesías y artículos en prosa*, which was published after his death, and *Epítolas y poemas* in 1888. That same year, *Azul*, one of the fundamental works for understanding Modernism, was published. In 1896, he published *Los Raros y Prosas Profanas*, in Buenos Aires. In 1901 a second edition of this work was published. Upon returning to Valparaíso, Chile, he published *Abrojos* (1887) and his novel *Emelina*. Other Darío narratives include *El Fardo, Invernal, El Rey Burgués* and *La Ninfa*. Darío's works had a significant impact on the Spanish language, especially his literary production, personal letters and stories. In 1916, after many years of absence, Darío returned to the city of León, where he died on 6 February. See also box, page 205.

The Vanguard

A significant group of poets were followers of Darío, but with very individual styles. These included Father **Azarias H Pallais** (1884-1959), **Alfonso Cortés** (1893-1969) and **Salomón de la Selva** (1893-1959). These world-class poets were known for their innovation and experimentation. Literature, and especially poetry, has always been attractive to Nicaraguan youth. For that reason the Vanguard movement was born. Founded by **Luis Alberto Cabrales** (1901-1974) and **José Coronel Urtecho** (1906-1994) this movement exerted an important renovating influence on Nicaraguan literature. Coronel Urtecho's work *Oda a Rubén Darío* (1927) contains the essence of the new style and marks the transition from the Darío school of Modernism to the Vanguard movement. **Pablo Antonio Cuadra** (1912-2002), the movement's principal author, wrote a declaration reaffirming the national identity, which was later incorporated into his first book *Poemas Nicaragüenses* (1934). His literary production was truly prolific and included *Libro de horas* (1964), *El Jaguar y la Luna* (1959). He wrote about the life of the mammal in *Cantos de Cifar* and *Al mar dulce* (1926); his excellent treatise against dictatorships in *Siete arboles contra el atardecer* (1982) and *Poemas para un calendario* (1988). Cuadra's work has been translated into several languages. For more than a decade he was the general director of the *La Prensa* daily newspaper. Cuadra, together with Coronel Urtecho, Luis Cabrales and **Joaquín Pasos** (1914-1947) author of the dramatic poem *Canto de Guerra de las Cosas*, summarized their programme and released the *Anti-Academia de la Lengua* declaration. Another member of the Vanguard was **Manolo Cuadra** (1907-1957) who became known for his poems, *Perfil* and *La palabra que no te dije*, published in *Tres Amores* (1955).

The 1940s

The main themes of the generation of the 1940s were love and freedom, reflected in the poetry of **Francisco Pérez Estrada** (1917-1982), **Enrique Fernández Morales** (1918-1982), and **Julio Ycaza Tigerino** (1919-2001). However, this period is especially known for the emergence of two great poets. **Ernesto Mejía Sánchez** (1923-1985) cultivated a style marked by brevity and precision in his most important works *Ensalmos y conjuros* (1947) and *La carne contigua* (1948). **Carlos Martínez Rivas** (1924-1999) used a modern rhythm, making his ideas felt through quick turns of phrase and ruptures of his own language. *El paraíso recobrado* (1948) was a revelation and the publication of *Insurrección solitaria* (1953) even more so. He published a series of poems titled *Allegro irato*, in 1989, which continued a very experimental line.

Expressionist poetry

The poetry of **Ernesto Cardenal**, born 20 January 1925, reflects spoken language and contains simple expressions. He is the founder of the expressionist poetry current, which opposed the subjectivity of lyrical poetry. Through his poetry he attacked the Somoza family dictatorship for over four decades. Also a priest, he founded the Christian community of Solentiname on a group of islands in Lake Nicaragua. His extensive work has been translated into several languages. *La ciudad deshabitada* (1946), *Hora 0* (1960), *Oración por Marylin Monroe y otras poemas* (1966), are poems reflecting religious, historical and Christian themes as well as the topic of social commitment.

The 1950s and 1960s

In the 1950s, **Guillermo Rothschuh Tablada** (1926) and **Fernando Silva** (1927) stand out. Rothschuh wrote *Poemas Chontaleños* (1960), while Silva follows the traditional-regional approach, reflecting the spoken language of the rural areas. His work *Barro de Sangre* represents a vernacular renewal in the authenticity of its theme and language. In the 1960s, the left-leaning **Grupo Ventana** (Window Group) emerged led by students at the Autonomous National University of León, including **Fernando Gordillo** (1940-1967), who left only a scattered poetic work, and **Sergio Ramírez Mercado** (1942). Other poets of this generation include **Octavio Robleto** (1935) and **Francisco Valle** (1942), a surrealist and a writer of prose. **Beltrán Morales** (1945-1986) is the most outstanding poet of this generation for his synthesis and irony, reflected in *Agua Regia* (1972). Other groups emerging in this period were the **La Generación Traicionada** (The Betrayed Generations) and **Grupo M**, both from Managua, **Grupo U** from Boaco, and **Los Bandeleros** (The Bandoliers) from Granada. **Mario Cajina-Vega**, a poet and thoughtful but comic narrator, published *Breve Tribu* in 1962. **Julio Valle-Castillo**, poet, narrator and critic, published one of his first books *Materia Jubilosa* in 1953. Along with **Jorge Eduardo Arellano** (1946), Julio Valle is one of Nicaragua's most respected researchers.

The 1970s

In the 1970s, the modern short story was born in Nicaragua with **Lisandro Chávez Alfaro**'s *Los Monos de San Telmo* (1963), known for its innovative technique and themes. Chronicles from poor Managua neighbourhoods are found in *Se Alquilan Cuartos* (1975), by Juan Aburto (1918-1988). **Sergio Ramírez Mercado** is one of the best internationally known writers to have ever come out of Nicaragua. The ex-vice president of Nicaragua under Daniel Ortega has published novels and books of short stories including *De Tropeles y Tropelias* (1972) and *Charles Atlas también muere* (1976). In 1998 he won the International Prize for Fiction of the Alfagura publishing house of Spain who also published his later works. He is considered among the finest novelists in Latin America today.

Poetic revelations

The revelation of the 1970s was **Gioconda Belli**. Her first book *Sobre La Grama* (1974) is a sensual work of poems that broke ground with its frank femininity. *De La Costilla De Eva* (1987) speaks of free love at the service of revolutionary transformation. Her novels, *La mujer habitada*, *Memorias de amor y de guerra* and *El país bajo mi piel*, among others, have been published in more than 20 languages. Along with Belli, other writers emerging in this period included **Vidaluz Meneses**, **Daisy Zamora**, **Ana Ilce Gómez**, **Rosario Murillo**, and **Christian Santos**.

Exteriorism

In the 1980s, a new literary phenomenon called Exteriorism became popular. Founded by **Ernesto Cardenal**, who at the time was the Sandinista government's Minister of Culture, this movement advocated political poetry, and promoted what he called "objective poetry: using fragments of narrative, anecdotes, and employing proper nouns with imprecise details and exact statistics." This style was taught in widespread poetry workshops where members of the army, the recently literate farming population and other sectors of the country were encouraged to write. The use of a unified style for the workshops was later criticized and with the end of the Sandinista government the poetry workshops disappeared.

Modern trends

From the 1990s onwards, a more intimate poetry emerged. The traditional literary topics are prevalent: death, existentialism and love, along with new themes including homosexuality, women's rights and the environment. New writers have emerged: poets like **Blanca Castellón**, **Erick Aguirre**, **Pedro Xavier Solís**, **Juan Sobalvarro**, **Isolda Hurtado**, **Marta Leonor González** and **Ariel Montoya**. There are also new literary groups and magazines such as *400 Elefantes*, *Decenio* and *Cultura de Paz*.

Music

Music is a very integral part of Nicaraguan life with everything from traditional festivals to political rallies using music as its driving backbone. Rock, pop, folk, regional, romantic and protest music are all a part of the national offering.

Marimba

The marimba is the most traditional among these varieties of rhythms. The instrument is known as Nicaragua's 'national piano' and although its origin has never been well defined, most believe it has its roots in Africa. In musical terms it is a complex instrument: shaped in the form of a triangle and comprising 22 wood keys. The marimba player uses two sticks with rubber heads called *bolillos*. The instrument has very clear and sonorous tonalities. In the past the marimba was used to play folk pieces and typical music of the countryside, but today it has been diversified, *marimberos* performing anything from salsa to *merengue* and *cumbia*. The country's best *marimberos* are from the indigenous barrio of Masaya, Monimbó, which has a generations-long tradition of marimba playing.

Classical music

Classical music was the music of *criollos* in Nicaragua and the original European-influenced music of the country. The classical symphony music of the Nicaraguan artists in the 19th century was played by orchestras in León. Key names like **Juan Bautista Prado**, **Manuel Ibarra**, **Alfonso Zelaya**, **Salvador Martínez**, **Santos Cermeño**, **Alfonso Solórzano** and **Lizandro Ramírez** dominated the classical music scene of Nicaragua that survives today, although original compositions have diminished greatly since the end of the 1800s. The greatest of all Nicaraguan classical composers was the León artist **José de la Cruz Mena**, who received international recognition before dying of leprosy (see León, page 201). The poet **Salomón Ibarra Mayorga** wrote the Nicaraguan national anthem. The short piece was written on 16 December 1910 and performed by the greatest musicians of the time, the masters **Abraham Delgadillo Rivas** and **Carlos Alberto Ramírez Velásquez**.

Folk music

Folk music also has its roots in Masaya, with many artists known as *orejeros* (those who learn to play by ear). Nicaraguan rhythms such as *Mamá Ramona* come from the city. The *orejeros* are famous for their deft guitar playing. One of the most important creators of the Nicaraguan song is **Víctor M Leiva** who wrote the song *El Caballo Cimarrón* (The Untamed Horse) in 1948, the first Nicaraguan song recorded in the country. During his more than 50 years of performing and composing he painted portraits of the Nicaraguan's daily life, landscape and labour. Some of his most famous compositions include *Santo Domingo de Guzmán*, *Tata Chombo*, *Coffee Season*, *El Toro Huaco* and *La Chapandonga*. He received a Gold Palm award in United States, as the second greatest folkloric composer in Latin

America. Another important folk singer songwriter is **Camilo Zapata** (1917-2009), known as 'The Master of Regionalism'. He wrote his first song *Caballito Chontaleno* (Little Horse from Chontales) at the age of 14. His songs are nourished by culture and Nicaraguan critics have crowned him as the face and heart of Nicaraguan regionalism. In 1948 Zapata came to national fame with songs like *El Nandaimeno*, *El Ganado Colorado* (The Pink Cattle), *El Solar de Monimbó* (The Backyard of Monimbó), *Flor de Mi Colina* (Flower from my Hill), *Minga Rosa Pineda*, *El Arriero* (The Muleteer) and some other romantic ones such as *Facing the sun*, *Cariño*. El Maestro Zapata continued to compose and perform into his eighties.

Chicheros

Chicheros are an integral part of any festival or traditional party. The Chichero band consists of six to eight amateur musicians who play snare drums, bass drum, cymbal, trumpet, flute, clarinet and trombone. Their music ranges from energetic dance tunes to solemn funeral marches.

La Misa Campesina

With marimbas, guitars, *atabales* (drums), violins and mazurcas and Nicaraguan rhythm, a new style in popular religious music was born with *La Misa Campesina* or the Peasant Mass. The Mass is composed of 10 songs, written by legendary folk singer Carlos Mejía Godoy and recorded in the 1980s by the Popular Sound Workshop. It was composed in Solentiname, where Ernesto Cardenal was preaching, and was later extended to all the 'peoples' churches and even to Spain. The Catholic Church in Nicaragua prohibited the work on orders from Pope John Paul II. The lack of acceptance by the church did little to diminish the worldwide acceptance of the music. *La Misa Campesina* has been translated into numerous languages and is even sung by Anglicans, Mormons and Baptists in the United States. Among the most loved are the *Welcome Song*, *The Creed*, *The Meditation song*, *Kirye*, *Saint* and *Communion*. The music has also been chosen as one of the hundred hymns of the Mennonite Church in the United States.

Protest music

Protest music had its glory days during the years leading up to the Revolution. This music of pop and folkloric rhythms brought to fame such bands as Engel Ortega, Norma Elena Gadea and Eduardo Araica, the Pancasan Band, Duo Guardabarranco formed by Katia and Salvador Cardenal, Keyla Rodríguez and Luis Enrique Mejía Godoy.

Palo de Mayo

Palo de Mayo is a collection of native music from the Caribbean Coast of Nicaragua. The music is characterized by its vibrant rhythm. The songs that are a joy hymn for the Afro-Caribbean Nicaraguans include *Tululu Pass Under*, *Oh Nancy, Oh*, *Simón Canta Simón*, *Mayaya Oh*. To perform the Caribbean rhythms, local musicians incorporate instruments such as cow and donkey jawbones, combs and pots, as well as more common instruments like drums and guitars.

Nicaragua land and environment

Geography

Nicaragua can be divided into three principal sections. The **Caribbean lowlands**, which include pine savannahs in the north and, further south, the largest remaining expanse of rainforest on the Central American isthmus, are crossed by numerous rivers that drain the central mountain range to the emerald sea. The **central and northern mountains and plains** are geologically the oldest in the country, with many long-extinct volcanoes. The mountains are low, ranging from 500 m in the far south of the zone to 2000 m as they reach the border with Honduras in the north. This is a mineral-rich area that has been prospected for centuries. The diversity of the ecosystem is immense, with rainforest giving way to tropical dry forest in the south, and cloud forest to pines in the north.

The third division is the **Pacific Basin**, which is marked by numerous crater lakes, the two great lakes of Managua and Nicaragua and the lumpy spine of volcanoes, the Cordillera Los Maribios, that run from the extreme northwest at Volcán Cosigüina to the dual volcano island of Ometepe in Lake Nicaragua. The area is a mixture of tropical dry forest and savannah with two cloud forests on Volcán Mombacho and Volcán Maderas, and a pine forest on the Volcán Casita.

Lakes and rivers

In the Pacific Basin plain are 15 crater lakes and the two largest expanses of water in Central America. The capital, Managua, lies on the shores of **Lake Managua** (also known as *Xolotlán*), which is 52 km long, 15-25 km wide, and sits 39 m above sea level. Its maximum depth is only 30 m and it has a surface area of 1025 sq km. The Peninsula of Chiltepe juts out into Lake Managua and holds two crater lakes, Xiloá and Apoyeque. Managua also houses four small crater lakes. Lake Managua drains to Lake Nicaragua via the Río Tipitapa just east of the capital. The mighty **Lake Nicaragua**, often called by one of its pre-Conquest names, *Cocibolca*, is 160 km long, 65 km at its widest, and 32 m above the level of the sea. This massive sheet of water averages 20 m in depth with a maximum depth of 60 m. Lake Nicaragua covers a total of 8264 sq km. Just 18 km separates the big lake from the Pacific Ocean on the southern part of its western shores. But Lake Nicaragua drains 190 km to the Caribbean Sea via the **Río San Juan**, the second longest river in Central America behind the 680-km Río Coco in Nicaragua's north. In total there are 96 principal rivers, most lying east of the great lakes.

Volcanoes

Nicaragua is one of the most geologically active countries in the world. It lies at the intersection of the Coco and Caribe continental plates. Subduction of the Coco plate underneath the Caribe plate is at a rate of 8-9 cm per year, the fastest rate of plate collision in the hemisphere. The newest of the countries in the Americas in geological terms (8-9 million years old), its constant subterranean movement results in over 300 low level tremors per day in the region, with the majority occurring on the Pacific shelf. Another result of the land in upheaval is a line of more than 40 beautiful volcanoes, six of which have been active within the last 100 years. The volcanoes run 300 km from north to south along a fault line that is full of magma 10 km below the topsoil.

The northernmost is **Volcán Cosigüina** (800 m), overlooking the Golfo de Fonseca, with a lake in its crater. Its final eruption was in 1835, in what is believed to have been the most violent in recorded history in the Americas, with ash being thrown as far as Mexico and the ground shaking as far south as Colombia. To the southeast continues the Maribios volcanic chain, with the now-extinct **Volcán Chonco** (1105 m) and the country's highest, the cone of **Volcán San Cristóbal** (1745 m). San Cristóbal began erupting again in 1971 after a long period of inactivity following the highly explosive years of 1684-1885. Since 1999 it has been throwing up a lot of ash; its last activity was in 2006.

Just south rises the extinct cone of **Volcán Casita**, which is notable for its pine forest, the southernmost of its kind in the American continent's northern hemisphere. One side of Casita collapsed during the torrential rains of Hurricane Mitch in 1998, burying numerous villages in the municipality of Posoltega and killing more than 2000 people. Further south, just before León, is the very active **Volcán Telica** (1061 m) with eruptions occurring often in the 1990s and the last one in 2007. It was recorded erupting in 1529, 1685 and between 1965 and 1968 with more activity in 1971. It seems to erupt in unison with San Cristóbal. Next to the bald, eroding summit of Telica are the dormant cones of little **Volcán Santa Clara** (or **Volcán San Jacinto**) and **Volcán Rota** or **Volcán Orata** (836 m), which is believed to be the oldest in the chain.

Just south of León is one of the youngest volcanoes on the planet, **Cerro Negro**; born in 1850, it has risen from just above sea level to 450 m in this short period. Major eruptions have occurred 12 times since 1867, including three times since 1990. This is the most dangerous of the volcanoes with violent eruptions and lava flows, and the eruption in August 1999 opened new craters at its southern base.

Volcán Pilas is formed of various craters, the highest of which rises 1001 m and contains one active crater known as *El Hoyo*, which last erupted from 1952 to 1955, though it is still smoking. Other extinct cones lie between Pilas and the majestic **Volcán Momotombo** (1300 m), which overlooks the shores of Lake Managua. Momotombo's eruptions in the late 1500s convinced the residents of León Viejo to leave. It erupted with force in 1764, regularly erupted from 1858 to 1866, and had its most recent significant eruption in 1905 with a large lava flow to its east side. Today a geothermal plant on the base of its west side utilizes its considerable fumarolic energy on a daily basis. The chain ends with little extinct **Volcán Momotombito**, which forms an island in Lake Managua. Managua's volcanoes are all extinct and six contain crater lakes.

The **Dirianes** volcanic chain begins just north of Masaya with the complex of **Volcán Masaya**, including the smoking, lava-filled **Santiago** crater as well as four extinct craters and a lagoon. Masaya is the only volcano on the American continent, and one of four in the world, with a constant pool of lava. During its very active recent history there have been noteworthy eruptions in 1670, 1772, 1858-1859, 1902-1905, 1924, 1946, 1965 and 1970-1972. It fell dormant for two decades before coming alive again with up to 400 tonnes per day of sulphur output from 1995 until today. It had a small, but nasty little eruption on 23 April 2001, with more expected.

South between Masaya and Granada is the extinct **Apoyo**, which died very violently 20,000 years ago, leaving the deep blue Laguna de Apoyo, 6 km in diameter. Along the shores of Lake Nicaragua and shadowing Granada is dormant and mildly fumarolic **Volcán Mombacho** (1345 m), wrapped in cloud forest. Mombacho had a major structural collapse in 1570 that wiped out a Chorotega village at its base. Fall-out and lava flows from a prehistoric eruption (around 6000 BC) of the Mombacho cone created Las Isletas in Lake Nicaragua.

The **volcanoes of Lake Nicaragua** include the extinct and heavily eroded cone that forms the **Isla de Zapatera** (600 m), a national park and a very important pre-Columbian site. The last two volcanoes in the Nicaraguan chain of fire make up the stunning Isla de Ometepe. The symmetrical and active cone of **Volcán Concepción** (1610 m) became very active in 1883-1887, 1908-1910, 1921 and 1948; the last major lava flow was in 1957 and has had ash emissions as recently as 2007. The cloud forest covering **Volcán Maderas** (1394 m), believed to be extinct, holds a lake in its misty summit.

In reality there are many, many more volcanoes; some are so heavily eroded that they merge with the landscape, but Nicaragua, in essence, is one string of volcanoes from west to east varying in age from eight million to 160 years.

Flora and fauna

Like all neotropical countries, Nicaragua is blessed with rich biodiversity and, thanks to its relatively low population, economic underdevelopment and many nature reserves, much of the country's native wildlife and vegetation have been preserved. Some species endangered in neighbouring countries are prevalent here, like the **howler monkey**, which enjoys many habitats and a population of thousands. Nonetheless, Nicaragua has not been immune to the world crisis of deforestation, most of which has occurred to clear land for farming, along with limited logging. Forest coverage has been reduced from 7,000,000 ha in 1950 to under 4,000,000 ha in the 21st century. Compounding the problem is the dominant use of wood for energy, with kindling wood (*leña*) still the main fuel for cooking. *Leña* represents 57% of the national consumption of energy, while petroleum is only at 30%. The development of responsible tourism in Nicaragua's outstanding natural areas provides hope for economic viability and nature conservation.

Principal ecosystems

The Pacific Basin is dominated by **savannah** and **tropical dry forest**. There are several significant **mangrove forests** and major areas of **wetlands** in diverse parts of the country. The biggest expanse of **cloud forest** in Central America is present on Pacific volcanoes and northern mountain ranges, especially within the Bosawás reserve. **Pine forests** run along the northern territories all the way to the Caribbean with the central-northern mountains home to extensive, but dwindling numbers. Transitional **tropical wet forests** are present on the east side of the great lakes and Lake Nicaragua's southern coast. The most extensive growth of **primary rainforest** on the isthmus dominates the Río San Juan's Indio-Maíz reserve and much of the northeastern and Caribbean lowlands. **Plant species** are, of course, diverse with 350 species of tree, part of some 12,000 species of flora that have been classified so far, with at least another 5000 yet to be documented. Those classified include more than 600 species of orchid alone. **Animal species** are equally impressive, most of all the insect life, with an estimated 250,000 species, although only about 10,000 of those have been documented to date. Mammals include some 251 species along with 234 different variations of reptile and amphibian. Bird diversity is particularly impressive with the ever-growing list of species currently totalling 714.

National parks and reserves

The Ministro de Medio Ambiente y Recursos Naturales (Ministry of Environment and Natural Resources) better known as **MARENA** ⓘ *Km 12.5, Carretera Norte, Managua, T233-*

1278, www.marena.gob.ni, is responsible for the administration of Nicaragua's 83 protected areas, which cover more than 18% of its land. The organization is gravely underfunded and understaffed, but tries hard to overcome these shortcomings to preserve Nicaragua's spectacular natural resources. The ministry is open to tourism, but has yet to utilize visitors as a means of financing preservation. The exceptions are the well-organized parks where the non-profit Cocibolca Foundation has joined forces with MARENA to offer a viable ecological experience for foreign and national visitors. If you have some grasp of Spanish you will find the *guardabosques* (park guards) to be very friendly and helpful in any natural reserve. It is important to realize that the MARENA park guards are serious about their responsibility, despite being considerably underpaid. They will ask for proof of permission for entrance into some areas and should be treated with respect and appreciation for the critical role they play in the preservation of reserves and parks. Check with MARENA before setting out to visit one of the lesser-known reserves. Parks and reserves that charge admission (see individual destinations) are prepared and welcome visitors, but many areas, like the remote reaches of the Indio-Maíz Biological Reserve, cannot be entered without prior consent from MARENA.

Volcanic parks and reserves

Along with the flagship Parque Nacional Volcán Masaya, many of Nicaragua's volcanoes have forests set aside as a reserve. Ancient volcanoes in the central and eastern regions all have forest reserves on them, critical for the local climate and water tables. In many parts of the country they are covered in rain and cloud forest and there are more than 28 such reserves set aside as protected areas, including the following Pacific Basin volcanoes: **Momotombo**, **El Hoyo**, **San Cristóbal**, **Casita**, **Telica**, **Rota**, **Concepción**, **Maderas**, **Cosigüina** and **Mombacho**. Volcanic crater lakes and their forests are also set aside as protected areas, such as **Laguna de Apoyo**, **Laguna de Asososca**, **Laguna de Nejapa**, **Laguna de Tiscapa** and the two crater lakes of Península de Chiltepe, **Laguna Apoyeque** and **Laguna Xiloá**.

Turtle nesting sites and mangroves

Some of the most rewarding of all parks to visit are the wildlife refuges set aside for the arrival of egg-laying sea turtles. Along the central Pacific Coast is **Chacocente** and its tropical dry forest reserve. More accessible is the beach at **La Flor**, south of San Juan del Sur. **Isla Juan Venado** is also a place to see turtles, not in the quantity of the other reserves, but with the added attraction of accessible mangroves and their wildlife. The Pearl Cays are a major nesting site for hawksbill turtles, but they are not set up for tourism (see box, opposite).

Cloud forest reserves

Given the the great challenges of visiting the hard-to-reach protected cloud forests of the Bosawás Reserve, the best place to enjoy the wildlife of the cloud forest is on the **Volcán Mombacho**, just outside Granada, and **Volcán Maderas** on Ometepe Island. In Matagalpa, the **Selva Negra Reserve** is also easy to access, as is the **Arenal Reserve** on the border of Jinotega and Matagalpa, and **El Jaguar** in Jinotega; another good option is the **Miraflor Reserve** in Estelí.

Rainforest reserves

With the two biggest rainforest reserves in Central America, Nicaragua is the place for the rainforest enthusiast who does not need luxury lodging. The best, for its access and

Save the turtles

Nicaragua's Caribbean Coast is home to declining populations of endangered green, loggerhead, leatherback and critically endangered hawksbill turtles. Consumption of green turtle meat is permitted by law for the coast's indigenous and Afro-descendant peoples, whose traditions include the hunting of turtles for sustenance. Unfortunately, the capture and consumption of green turtles now exceeds 11,000 per year and the commercial trade in turtle meat – although a viable and potentially sustainable local economy – may soon face collapse through over-fishing. Uncontrolled development around the Pearl Cays has also harmed the numbers of nesting hawksbills, as has the trade in turtle shell jewellery and eggs. Please consider your role as a visitor to the region and adhere to the following advice:

→ Please don't eat turtles and don't provide a market for commercial turtle fishing. Many locals may expound the delicious virtues of *carne de tortuga*, but laws permitting turtle consumption were not designed with tourists in mind.

→ Please don't buy jewellery made from turtle shell, no matter how beautiful – it belongs on the turtle's back.

→ Please avoid eating turtle eggs. Nicaraguans have long attributed aphrodisiac qualities to turtle eggs which they often eat raw or in seafood stews. However, the chances of survival for hatchling turtles are slim enough as it is.

→ Please think carefully before setting out to the Pearl Cays – they may be among the most stunning offshore islands in Central America, but uncontrolled tourism here has seriously harmed local turtle populations.

→ Please donate generously to turtle conservation projects, especially the Wildlife Conservation Society, www. wcs.org, who have a research station in Pearl Lagoon and are trying to develop ecologically aware tourism programmes for the Pearl Cays.

reliable lodging, is **Indio-Maíz**. **Bosawás** is the biggest area of forest on the isthmus, accessible from the Northern Highlands or Caribbean side of the country. Travel safety is an issue in the region (see page 299 for details), and although it is improving, this vast wilderness is generally the preserve of hardened adventure travellers. If you are planning to visit Bosawás, always check with MARENA in Managua to see which entrance to the park is most advisable. They can put you in contact with guides too, as well as supply maps.

Wetland reserves

Nothing can match the natural splendour of the wetlands in **Los Guatuzos**, which one US environmental writer called "one of the most beautiful places on earth". This wildlife refuge has only basic and rustic lodging, but it is well worth the effort to see its fauna.

National monument parks

Archipiélago Solentiname is great for culture lovers as well as birders. Solentiname's 36 islands are teeming with birdlife and are home to a very interesting community of rural artists. The fortress at **El Castillo** is an important historic landmark set on a beautiful hill above the majestic Río San Juan.

Nicaragua books and films

Books

Anthropology

Field, LW *The Grimace of Macho Ratón* (Duke University, 1999). A cultural anthropological look at Nicaragua's national play, *El Güegüence*, and how it relates to Nicaraguan identity, in particular its effect on definitions of indigenous and mestizo in Pacific Nicaragua. This curious wandering work also focuses on Nicaragua's ceramic artisans as a model for understanding Nicaraguan social-behavioural traits, and on occasion slips into being a travel diary.

Gould, JL *To Die in this Way, Nicaraguan Indians and the Myth of Mestizaje 1880-1965* (Duke University Press, 1998). A fascinating, though academic, study of the tragic trajectory of Nicaragua's Pacific and central indigenous communities and the resulting effect on the definitions of the country's ethnic make-up. A very important work for anthropology and also for the history of Nicaragua and its injustice to its most vulnerable citizens. Despite the breadth and quality of the research, readers are still left wondering about the 'myth of *mestizaje*', and how should we define 'indigenous' in today's Nicaragua?

Lange, FW *Archaeology of Pacific Nicaragua* (University of New Mexico, 1992). Dr Lange is an expert on Nicaraguan archaeology. Though not meant as an introduction for the layman, this book is very interesting in its descriptions and observations about Nicaraguan archaeology in the extraordinarily ceramic-rich Pacific region.

Fiction

Belli, G *The Inhabited Women* (translated by Kathleen March, Warner Books, 1994). One of Nicaragua's most famous writer/poets, her work is famously sensual and this story is no exception. A yuppie turns revolutionary after

being inspired by a native spirits tale. The hero joins an underground rebel group for a story based partially upon historic events. It works well, at least until its action-film ending, and is an enjoyable read, with some beautiful and magical prose.

Ramírez, S *To Bury Our Fathers* (translated by Nick Caistor, Readers International, 1993). Nicaragua's finest living author (see page 320) recounts life in the Somoza García period of Nicaragua, from the viewpoint of exiled rebels in Guatemala. Sergio Ramírez paints a detailed picture of the Nicaraguan character and humour.

Narratives and travelogues

Beals, C *Banana Gold* (JB Lippincott Company, 1932). A true jewel. Although half of the book gripes about the life of a journalist travelling through southern Mexico and Central America, the half that deals with Beals' harrowing trip on horseback from Tegucigalpa to Sébaco during the war between Sandino and the US Marines is fascinating, humorous, tragic and beautiful. Beals' poetic prose further adds to the thrill as we ride along on his unrelenting quest to meet with August C Sandino and interview him. At once both a brilliant travel and political history work.

Cabezas, O *Fire from the Mountain* (translated by Kathleen Weaver, Crown Publishers, 1985). This first-hand account of a revolutionary rebel in the making, and later in action, was dictated into a tape recorder and reads like a long, tragic and often hilarious confession. This very honest book is a must for those who wish to get the feel of this time in Nicaraguan history and the irreverent Nicaraguan humour.

Rushdie, S *The Jaguar Smile* (Penguin Books, 1988). A detailed and entertaining account of Rushdie's visit to Nicaragua during the volatile Sandinista years.

Twain, M *Travels with Mr Brown* (Alfred A Knopf, 1940). Although his observations on Nicaragua make up only a small part of this book, Twain's irrepressible humour and use of language make this memoir an enjoyable read. Twain describes in detail the Nicaraguan inter-oceanic steamship route from San Francisco to New York, using the Río San Juan and Lake Nicaragua as a crossing from ocean to sea, which was so popular with gold-rushers at that time.

Walker, W *The War in Nicaragua* (University of Arizona Press, 1985). A reproduction of the 1860 original by the walking evil empire himself, General William Walker, who tried to annex Nicaragua to the USA in 1856. Walker wrote the book in the USA while planning his final attack on Central America.

Nature

Belt, T *The Naturalist in Nicaragua* (University of Chicago, 1985). Reprint of a 1874 classic. Very enlightening in its observations of insect life and acute observations of 19th-century Nicaragua. Described by Charles Darwin as "the best of all natural history journals which have ever been published", this book by a mining engineer also sheds light on the mentality of a naturalist 130 years ago. Alongside brilliant and sensitive analytical observation, Belt freely admits beating his pet monkey and shooting dozens of birds and laments not bagging a giant jaguar he encounters in the forest.

Poetry

Darío, R *Selected Poems* (translated by Lysander Kemp, prologue by Octavio Paz, University of Texas, 1988). This attractive collection of some of Darío's best-known poems has the original Spanish and English translations on facing pages.

Gullette, DG *!Gaspar! A Spanish Poet/Priest in the Nicaraguan Revolution* (Bilingual Press, 1993). A sentimental but balanced look at the Spanish Jesuit rebel-priest, Gaspar García Laviana, who died in action during the Revolution, a great hero among the

poor of Nicaragua's southern Pacific Coast during the 1970s. This volume includes poems about the plight of the Nicaraguan *campesino* in the original Spanish with English translations, as well as a biographical sketch and some humorous accounts of early botched battles.

Political history

Brody, R *Contra Terror in Nicaragua* (South End Press, 1985). Written at the height of the Contra War to demonstrate to the US Congress what was happening to the Nicaraguan public during the conflict, this is a graphic condemnation of the methods used by the Contra rebels during the war, often horrifying and tragic. A strong message directed at Ronald Reagan's many fans who must consider the full ramifications of his statement that the Contras were "the moral equivalent of our founding fathers".

Brown, TC *The Real Contra War* (University of Oklahoma Press, 2001). Written by a former 'Senior Liaison to the Contras for the US State Department' one would expect an apology for the Contras and that is exactly what one gets. However, the book grinds its axe with great elegance and brings to light some very little-known aspects of the grass-roots origins of the Contra rebellion. Well researched and a valuable counterweight to the numerous books batting on the other side of the fence.

Dickey, C *With the Contras* (Simon and Schuster, 1985). This is a mixture of journalism and sensationalist reporting, with the theme of the Contra insurgency and the US government's role in the war. Despite being too colourful for its own prose at times, the book manages to highlight many key characters in the conflict and exposes the difficulty of defining good and bad guys in real life war dramas. When Dickey enters the battlefield his self-satisfied irreverence cools off and he starts reporting. A valuable first-hand account.

Hodges, DC *Intellectual Foundations of the Nicaraguan Revolution* (University of Texas, 1986). An in-depth study of Nicaragua's

20th-century political players and the lead up to the Revolution of 1978-1979. A very good account of the nationalist hero Augusto Sandino. Written with a rare combination of balance and eloquence, this book is a must for those who wish to understand 20th-century Nicaraguan politics.

Kinzer, S *Blood of Brothers, Life and War in Nicaragua* (Doubleday, 1991). A landmark book on the Revolution and its aftermath. Kinzer spent many years in Nicaragua working for the *Boston Globe* and *New York Times* and aside from occasional fits of arrogance has produced one of the most interesting and informative books ever written by a foreigner about Nicaragua.

Mulligan, J *The Nicaraguan Church and the Revolution* (Sheep and Ward, 1991). Mulligan's book deals with liberation theology and its direct effect on the Nicaraguan Revolution and the local Catholic Church.

Pezzullo, L and R *At the Fall of Somoza* (University of Pittsburgh Press, 1993). Written by the last US Ambassador to Somoza's Nicaragua with the help of his son, this is a riveting book that is much more balanced and sympathetic to the Revolution than most would expect. Great writing on heroism during the rebellion and the head games of the US government and Somoza.

Zimmermann, M *Sandinista, Carlos Fonseca and the Nicaraguan Revolution* (Duke University Press, 2000). A very detailed biography of the founder of the FSLN who died before the final victory. A well-researched and interesting work.

Films

Cox, Alex *Walker* (USA, 1987). This counter-culture take on filibuster William Walker was shot in Nicaragua during the Contra War, mostly in Granada. Belonging to the creative sub-genre of 'acid western', it features a sound-track by Joe Strummer and was so politically contentious at the time it earned director Alex Cox a lifetime place on the Hollywood blacklist.

Herzog, Werner *Ballad of the Little Soldier* (West Germany, 1984). In this arresting 45-min documentary, Herzog turned his attentions on Nicaragua's Miskito Coast, focusing on child soldiers who had been enlisted by the Contras to fight against the Sandinistas. The film was described by the *New York Times* as "a lament about the idiotic state of the world and a praise of the human spirit."

Loach, Ken *Carla's Song* (Scotland, 1996). With big points for originality, this film ends up playing like a Sandinista party film. The film – a love story between a Glaswegian bus driver and a Nicaraguan immigrant – shows some great elements of Nicaraguan life in the 1980s.

Meiselas, Roberts and Guzetti *Pictures from a Revolution – A Memoir of the Nicaraguan Conflict* (USA, 1991). In 1978, the 30-year-old Susan Meiselas was an inexperienced documentary photographer who had never covered a major political story. Just after joining the most prestigious photo agency in the world, **Magnum**, she read about the assassination of the *La Prensa* editor Pedro Joaquín Chamorro and soon found herself in Managua with no knowledge of Spanish and doubts about what she was even to photograph there. When she returned from shooting the Nicaraguan Revolution, she had became a world-famous, award-winning war photographer. In this film she returns 10 years later to Nicaragua, with a film crew in tow, to find out what happened to her photo subjects.

Spottiswoode, Roger *Under Fire* (USA, 1983). Hollywood does the Nicaraguan Revolution. This film starring Nick Nolte and Gene Hackman is a hearty attempt at historical drama, with a lot of factual events being massaged to keep the necessary love story plot thumping along. Some interesting details in the film like authentic Nicaraguan beer and street signs of obscure villages are made all the more impressive by the sad fact that not one scene was actually shot in Nicaragua. The murder by Somoza's army of a US journalist is factual, if twisted, and gives the movie a surprise element.

Footnotes

Contents

Basic Spanish for travellers

Learning Spanish is a useful part of the preparation for a trip to Latin America and no volumes of dictionaries, phrase books or word lists will provide the same enjoyment as being able to communicate directly with the people of the country you are visiting. It is a good idea to make an effort to grasp the basics before you go. As you travel you will pick up more of the language and the more you know, the more you will benefit from your stay.

General pronunciation

Whether you have been taught the 'Castilian' pronounciation (*z* and *c* followed by *i* or *e* are pronounced as the *th* in think) or the 'American' pronounciation (they are pronounced as *s*), you will encounter little difficulty in understanding either. Regional accents and usages vary, but the basic language is essentially the same everywhere.

Vowels

a	as in English *cat*
e	as in English *best*
i	as the *ee* in English *feet*
o	as in English *shop*
u	as the *oo* in English *food*
ai	as the *i* in English *ride*
ei	as *ey* in English *they*
oi	as *oy* in English *toy*

Consonants

Most consonants can be pronounced more or less as they are in English. The exceptions are:

g	before *e* or *i* is the same as *j*
h	is always silent (except in *ch* as in *chair*)
j	as the *ch* in Scottish *loch*
ll	as the *y* in *yellow*
ñ	as the *ni* in English *onion*
rr	trilled much more than in English
x	depending on its location, pronounced *x*, *s*, *sh* or *j*

Spanish words and phrases

Greetings, courtesies

hello	*hola*	I speak Spanish	*hablo español*
good morning	*buenos días*	I don't speak Spanish	*no hablo español*
good afternoon/ evening/night	*buenas tardes/ noches*	do you speak English?	*¿habla inglés?*
goodbye	*adiós/chao*	I don't understand	*no entiendo/ no comprendo*
pleased to meet you	*mucho gusto*		
see you later	*hasta luego*	please speak slowly	*hable despacio por favor*
how are you?	*¿cómo está? ¿cómo estás?*	I am very sorry	*lo siento mucho/ disculpe*
I'm fine, thanks	*estoy muy bien, gracias*	what do you want?	*¿qué quiere? ¿qué quieres?*
I'm called...	*me llamo...*		
what is your name?	*¿cómo se llama? ¿cómo te llamas?*	I want	*quiero*
		I don't want it	*no lo quiero*
yes/no	*sí/no*	leave me alone	*déjeme en paz/ no me moleste*
please	*por favor*		
thank you (very much)	*(muchas) gracias*	good/bad	*bueno/malo*

Questions and requests

Have you got a room for two people?
¿Tiene una habitación para dos personas?
I'd like to make a long-distance phone call
Quisiera hacer una llamada de larga distancia

How do I get to_?	*¿Cómo llego a_?*
How much does it cost?	*¿Cuánto cuesta?*
	¿cuánto es?
Is service included?	*¿Está incluido el servicio?*
Is tax included?	*¿Están incluidos los impuestos?*

When does the bus leave (arrive)?
¿A qué hora sale (llega) el autobús?
Where is the nearest petrol station?
¿Dónde está la gasolinera más cercana?

When?	*¿cuándo?*
Where is_?	*¿dónde está_?*
Where can I buy tickets?	*¿Dónde puedo comprar boletos?*
Why?	*¿por qué?*

Basics

bank	*el banco*	market	*el mercado*
bathroom/toilet	*el baño*	note/coin	*le billete/la moneda*
bill	*la factura/la cuenta*	police (policeman)	*la policía (el policía)*
cash	*el efectivo*	post office	*el correo*
cheap	*barato/a*	public telephone	*el teléfono público*
credit card	*la tarjeta de crédito*	supermarket	*el supermercado*
exchange house	*la casa de cambio*	ticket office	*la taquilla*
exchange rate	*el tipo de cambio*	traveller's cheques	*los cheques de viajero/los travelers*
expensive	*caro/a*		

Getting around

aeroplane	*el avión*	to insure yourself against	*asegurarse contra*
airport	*el aeropuerto*		
arrival/departure	*la llegada/salida*	luggage	*el equipaje*
avenue	*la avenida*	motorway, freeway	*el autopista/ la carretera*
block	*la cuadra*		
border	*la frontera*	north	*norte*
bus station	*la terminal de autobuses/camiones*	south	*sur*
		west	*oeste (occidente)*
bus	*el bus/el autobús/ el camión*	east	*este (oriente)*
		oil	*el aceite*
collective/fixed-route taxi	*el colectivo*	to park	*estacionarse*
		passport	*el pasaporte*
corner	*la esquina*	petrol/gasoline	*la gasolina*
customs	*la aduana*	puncture	*el pinchazo/ la ponchadura*
first/second class	*primera/segunda clase*		
		street	*la calle*
left/right	*izquierda/derecha*	that way	*por allí/por allá*
ticket	*el boleto*	this way	*por aquí/por acá*
empty/full	*vacío/lleno*	tourist card/visa	*la tarjeta de turista*
highway, main road	*la carretera*	tyre	*la llanta*
immigration	*la inmigración*	unleaded	*sin plomo*
insurance	*el seguro*	to walk	*caminar/andar*
insured person	*el/la asegurado/a*		

Accommodation

air conditioning	*el aire acondicionado*	power cut	*el apagón/corte*
all-inclusive	*todo incluido*	restaurant	*el restaurante*
bathroom, private	*el baño privado*	room/bedroom	*el cuarto/*
bed, double/single	*la cama matrimonial/*		*la habitación*
	sencilla	sheets	*las sábanas*
blankets	*las cobijas/mantas*	shower	*la ducha/regadera*
to clean	*limpiar*	soap	*el jabón*
dining room	*el comedor*	toilet	*el sanitario/excusado*
guesthouse	*la casa de huéspedes*	toilet paper	*el papel higiénico*
hotel	*el hotel*	towels, clean/dirty	*las toallas limpias/*
noisy	*ruidoso*		*sucias*
pillows	*las almohadas*	water, hot/cold	*el agua caliente/fría*

Health

aspirin	*la aspirina*	diarrhoea	*la diarrea*
blood	*la sangre*	doctor	*el médico*
chemist	*la farmacia*	fever/sweat	*la fiebre/el sudor*
condoms	*los preservativos,*	pain	*el dolor*
	los condones	head	*la cabeza*
contact lenses	*los lentes de contacto*	period/sanitary towels	*la regla/las toallas*
contraceptives	*los anticonceptivos*		*femeninas*
contraceptive pill	*la píldora anti-*	stomach	*el estómago*
	conceptiva	altitude sickness	*el soroche*

Family

family	*la familia*	husband/wife	*el esposo (marido)/*
brother/sister	*el hermano/*		*la esposa*
	la hermana	boyfriend/girlfriend	*el novio/la novia*
daughter/son	*la hija/el hijo*	friend	*el amigo/la amiga*
father/mother	*el padre/la madre*	married	*casado/a*
		single/unmarried	*soltero/a*

Months, days and time

January	*enero*	Monday	*lunes*
February	*febrero*	Tuesday	*martes*
March	*marzo*	Wednesday	*miércoles*
April	*abril*	Thursday	*jueves*
May	*mayo*	Friday	*viernes*
June	*junio*	Saturday	*sábado*
July	*julio*	Sunday	*domingo*
August	*agosto*		
September	*septiembre*	at one o'clock	*a la una*
October	*octubre*	at half past two	*a las dos y media*
November	*noviembre*	at a quarter to three	*a cuarto para las tres/*
December	*diciembre*		*a las tres menos*
			quince

it's one o'clock	*es la una*	in ten minutes	*en diez minutos*
it's seven o'clock	*son las siete*	five hours	*cinco horas*
it's six twenty	*son las seis y veinte*	does it take long?	*¿tarda mucho?*
it's five to nine	*son las nueve menos cinco*		

Numbers

one	*uno/una*	sixteen	*dieciséis*
two	*dos*	seventeen	*diecisiete*
three	*tres*	eighteen	*dieciocho*
four	*cuatro*	nineteen	*diecinueve*
five	*cinco*	twenty	*veinte*
six	*seis*	twenty-one	*veintiuno*
seven	*siete*	thirty	*treinta*
eight	*ocho*	forty	*cuarenta*
nine	*nueve*	fifty	*cincuenta*
ten	*diez*	sixty	*sesenta*
eleven	*once*	seventy	*setenta*
twelve	*doce*	eighty	*ochenta*
thirteen	*trece*	ninety	*noventa*
fourteen	*catorce*	hundred	*cien/ciento*
fifteen	*quince*	thousand	*mil*

Food

avocado	*el aguacate*	goat	*el chivo*
baked	*al horno*	grapefruit	*la toronja/el pomelo*
bakery	*la panadería*	grill	*la parrilla*
banana	*el plátano*	grilled/griddled	*a la plancha*
beans	*los frijoles/ las habichuelas*	guava	*la guayaba*
		ham	*el jamón*
beef	*la carne de res*	hamburger	*la hamburguesa*
beef steak or pork fillet	*el bistec*	hot, spicy	*picante*
boiled rice	*el arroz blanco*	ice cream	*el helado*
bread	*el pan*	jam	*la mermelada*
breakfast	*el desayuno*	knife	*el cuchillo*
butter	*la mantequilla*	lime	*el limón*
cake	*el pastel*	lobster	*la langosta*
chewing gum	*el chicle*	lunch	*el almuerzo/ la comida*
chicken	*el pollo*		
chilli or green pepper	*el ají/pimiento*	meal	*la comida*
clear soup, stock	*el caldo*	meat	*la carne*
cooked	*cocido*	minced meat	*el picadillo*
dining room	*el comedor*	onion	*la cebolla*
egg	*el huevo*	orange	*la naranja*
fish	*el pescado*	pepper	*el pimiento*
fork	*el tenedor*	pasty, turnover	*la empanada/ el pastelito*
fried	*frito*		
garlic	*el ajo*	pork	*el cerdo*

potato	*la papa*	spoon	*la cuchara*
prawns	*los camarones*	squash	la calabaza
raw	*crudo*	squid	*los calamares*
restaurant	*el restaurante*	supper	*la cena*
salad	*la ensalada*	sweet	*dulce*
salt	*la sal*	to eat	*comer*
sandwich	*el bocadillo*	toasted	*tostado*
sauce	*la salsa*	turkey	*el pavo*
sausage	*la longaniza/*	vegetables	*los legumbres/*
	el chorizo		*vegetales*
scrambled eggs	*los huevos revueltos*	without meat	*sin carne*
seafood	*los mariscos*	yam	*el camote*
soup	*la sopa*		

Drink

beer	*la cerveza*	juice	*el jugo*
boiled	*hervido/a*	lemonade	*la limonada*
bottled	*en botella*	milk	*la leche*
camomile tea	*la manzanilla*	mint	*la menta*
canned	*en lata*	rum	*el ron*
coffee	*el café*	soft drink	*el refresco*
coffee, white	*el café con leche*	sugar	*el azúcar*
cold	*frío*	tea	*el té*
cup	*la taza*	to drink	*beber/tomar*
drink	*la bebida*	water	*el agua*
drunk	*borracho/a*	water, carbonated	*el agua mineral*
firewater	*el aguardiente*		*con gas*
fruit milkshake	*el batido/licuado*	water, still mineral	*el agua mineral*
glass	*el vaso*		*sin gas*
hot	*caliente*	wine, red	*el vino tinto*
ice/without ice	*el hielo/sin hielo*	wine, white	el vino blanco

Key verbs

to go	**ir**	there is/are	*hay*
I go	*voy*	there isn't/aren't	*no hay*
you go (familiar)	*vas*		
he, she, it goes, you (formal) go	*va*	**to be**	**ser** estar
		I am	soy estoy
we go	*vamos*	you are	eres estás
they, you (plural) go	*van*	he, she, it is, you (formal) are	es está
		we are	somos estamos
to have (possess)	**tener**	they, you (plural) are	son están
I have	*tengo*		
you (familiar) have	*tienes*	This section has been assembled on the basis of glossaries compiled by André de Mendonça and David Gilmour of South American Experience, London, and the Latin American Travel Advisor, No 9, March 1996	
he, she, it, you (formal) have	*tiene*		
we have	*tenemos*		
they, you (plural) have	*tienen*		

Nicaraguan Spanish

You've done your Spanish course and you're ready to chat up the Nicaraguan people. But wait, what's that? ¿Cómo, perdón? Err…¿Qué dice?

It seems all that hard work in class has yet to pay off. Nicaraguans (Nicas) are famous for their creativity and humour and this carries over to their use of the Spanish language, nothing is sacred. In fact the Nicaraguans are credited with hundreds of words unique to their inventive, heavily indigenous-influenced version of Spanish. Here are some essentials for a head start, ¡dale pues! (go for it!):

Nica-speak	Meaning
boludo	lazy
chele	white person
chapín	barefoot
charula	worthless thing
chiringo	old clothes
cipote	little boy
fachento	arrogant
jaña	girlfriend
palmado	broke, penniless
pinche	stingy
tapudo	big-mouth
tuanis	cool
turcazo	hard punch

Food glossary

A

aguacate canelo native avocado

ajillo garlic butter sauce

a la plancha food cooked on a sizzling plate or flat grill

asado roasted or grilled meat or fish

B

bistec encebollado steak bathed in onions

boa en salsa boa constrictor in tomato sauce

¡buen provecho! enjoy your meal

burrito flour tortilla stuffed with meat, rice and vegetables

C

cacao raw cocoa bean, ground and mixed with milk, rice, cinnamon, vanilla, ice and sugar

café de palo home-roasted coffee

café percolado percolated coffee

cajetas traditional sweets, candied fruit

cajeta de leche milk sweet

cajeta de zapoyol cooked zapote seeds and sugar

caliente hot

camarones de río freshwater prawns

carne asada grilled beef

cerdo asado grilled pork

ceviche raw fish marinated in onions and lime juice

chicha corn-based drink, sometimes fermented to alcohol

chimichangas fried burritos

churrasco steak grilled steak in garlic and parsley sauce

comidas meals

comida corriente/comida casera set menu

comida económica cheap food/menu

cocktail de pulpo octopus

cuajada lightly salted, soft feta-type cheese

curvina sea bass

curvina a la plancha grilled sea bass

cuzuco armadillo

cuzuco en salsa armadillo in tomato sauce

D

dorado a la parilla grilled dorado fish

E

empanadas pastries filled with meat or chicken

enchilada meat or chicken wrapped in flour tortilla

F

fritanga street food

G

gallo pinto fried white rice and kidney beans, with onions and sweet pepper

garbanzos chick peas

garrobo black iguana

garrobo en caldillo black iguana soup

gaseosas fizzy drinks

guardatinaja large nocturnal rodent

guapote local, large-mouthed bass

H

huevo de toro asado grilled bull's testicles

I

indio viejo cornmeal and shredded beef porridge with garlic and spices

J

jugo pure fruit juice

L

langosta lobster

langosta blanca 'white lobster' ie cocaine

lomo relleno stuffed beef

M

mahi mahi grilled dorado fish

mar y tierra surf and turf

mariscos seafood

melocotón star fruit/peach

mojarra carp

mole chocolate, chilli sauce

N

nacatamales cornmeal, pork or chicken and rice, achote (similar to paprika), peppers, peppermint leafs, potatoes, onions and cooking oil, all wrapped in a big green banana leaf and boiled
níspero brown sugar fruit

P

paca large, nocturnal rodent
pargo al vapor steamed snapper
pargo rojo/blanco red/white snapper
para llevar to take away
parrillada Argentine-style grill
pescado fish
pescado a la suyapa fresh snapper in a tomato, sweet pepper and onion sauce
piniona thin strips of candied green papaya
Pío V corn cake topped with light cream and bathed in rum sauce
pitaya cactus fruit, blended with lime and sugar
plátano plantain
plato típico typical Nicaraguan food
pollo chicken
pollo asado grilled chicken
posol grainy indigenous drink served in an original jícaro gourd cup
pupusas tortillas filled with beans, cheese and/or pork

Q

quesadillas fried tortilla with cheese, chilli and peppers
quesillos mozzarella cheese in a hot tortilla with salt and bathed in cream
queso crema moist bland cheese, good fried
queso seco slightly bitter dry cheese

R

refresco/fresco fruit juice or grains and spices mixed with water and sugar
robalo snook
rosquillas baked corn and cheese biscuits

S

sábalo/sábalo real tarpon/giant tarpon
sopa de albóndiga soup with meatballs made of chicken, eggs, garlic and cornmeal
sopa de mondongo tripe soup
sopa de tortilla soup of corn tortilla and spices
sopa huevos de toro bull testicle soup
sopa levanta muerto literally 'return from the dead' soup
sorbete ice cream
surtido sampler or mixed dish

T

tacos fried tortilla stuffed with chicken, beef or pork
tacos chinos egg rolls
tres leches very sweet cake made with three kinds of milk (fresh and tinned)
tamales cornmeal bars boiled
tilapia African lake fish introduced to Nicaragua
tiste grainy indigenous drinks served in an original jícaro gourd cup
tipitapa tomato sauce
tostones con queso flat plantain sections fried with cheese

V

vigorón banana leaf filled with fried pork rind, cabbage salad, yucca, tomato, hot chilli and lemon juice

Credits

Footprint credits

Project editor: Felicity Laughton
Layout and production: Emma Bryers
Cover and colour section: Pepi Bluck
Maps: Kevin Feeney

Managing Director: Andy Riddle
Commercial Director: Patrick Dawson
Publisher: Alan Murphy
Publishing Managers: Felicity Laughton, Nicola Gibbs, Jo Williams
Digital Editor: Tom Mellors
Marketing and PR: Liz Harper
Marketing Executive: Liz Eyles
Sales: Diane McEntee
Advertising: Renu Sibal
Finance and administration: Elizabeth Taylor

Photography credits

Front cover: Rolf Richardson / The Travel Library (Iglesia de la Recolección, León)
Back cover: Nik Wheeler / Alamy (Playa Madera, San Juan del Sur)

Colour section
Page 1: Wendy Connett / Robert Harding World Imagery
Page 2: Jean-Pierre Degas / hemis.fr
Page 5: Nik Wheeler / Alamy
Page 6: Johnnymitch / Dreamstime.com
Page 7: Jürgen Dano / age fotostock.com
Page 8: Jane Sweeney / age fotostock.com
Page 9: Jon Arnold Images Ltd / Alamy
Page 10: Margie Politzer / Alamy (top); Robert Thompson / naturepl.com (bottom)

Printed in India by Replika Press Pvt Ltd

Publishing information

Footprint Nicaragua
4th edition
© Footprint Handbooks Ltd
March 2012

ISBN: 978 1907263 57 6
CIP DATA: A catalogue record for this book is available from the British Library

® Footprint Handbooks and the Footprint mark are a registered trademark of Footprint Handbooks Ltd

Published by Footprint
6 Riverside Court
Lower Bristol Road
Bath BA2 3DZ, UK
T +44 (0)1225 469141
F +44 (0)1225 469461
footprinttravelguides.com

Distributed in the USA by Globe Pequot Press, Guilford, Connecticut

Every effort has been made to ensure that the facts in this guidebook are accurate. However, travellers should still obtain advice from consulates, airlines, etc about travel and visa requirements before travelling. The authors and publishers cannot accept responsibility for any loss, injury or inconvenience however caused.

Map symbols

- □ Capital city
- ○ Other city, town
- International border
- Regional border
- ⊖ Customs
- Contours (approx)
- ▲ Mountain, volcano
- Mountain pass
- Escarpment
- Glacier
- Salt flat
- Rocks
- Seasonal marshland
- Beach, sandbank
- Waterfall
- Reef
- Motorway
- Main road
- Minor road
- Track
- Footpath
- Railway
- Railway with station
- ✈ Airport
- Bus station
- Ⓜ Metro station
- Cable car
- Funicular
- Ferry
- Pedestrianized street
- Tunnel
- One way-street
- Steps
- Bridge
- Fortified wall
- Park, garden, stadium
- Sleeping
- Eating
- Bars & clubs

- Building
- Sight
- Cathedral, church
- Chinese temple
- Hindu temple
- Meru
- Mosque
- Stupa
- Synagogue
- Tourist office
- Museum
- ✉ Post office
- Police
- Ⓢ Bank
- @ Internet
- ♪ Telephone
- Market
- Medical services
- Ⓟ Parking
- Petrol
- Golf
- Archaeological site
- National park, wildlife reserve
- Viewing point
- Campsite
- Refuge, lodge
- Castle, fort
- Diving
- Deciduous, coniferous, palm trees
- Mangrove
- Hide
- Vineyard, winery
- Distillery
- Shipwreck
- Historic battlefield
- Related map

Map 1

Regions/States:
- NUEVA SEGOVIA
- JINOTEGA
- MADRIZ
- MATAGALPA
- BOACO

Rivers:
- Río Bocay
- Río Coco
- Río Coco
- Río Tuma
- Río Tuma
- Río Grande
- Río Grande de Matagalpa
- Río Sébaco
- Río Matagalpa

Reserves/Parks:
- Bosawás Biosphere Reserve
- El Jaguar Cloud Forest Reserve
- Reserva Natural Areñal
- Selva Negra Cloud Forest Reserve
- Reserva Natural Miraflor
- Reserva Natural Meseta Tisey Estanzuela

Towns/Places:
- Sik
- Raiti
- Tolecacinte
- Jalapa
- Wambuca
- El Plantel
- Valle Congjas
- Murra
- Wamblán
- Santa Clara
- Fernando
- Ciudad Antigua
- Susucayan
- Plan de Grama
- Wiwilí
- San José de Bocay
- El Naranja
- El Ocote
- Rosa Gra
- Wa
- Ducalí
- dega
- dra Larga
- Puerto Viejo
- San Rafael del Norte
- Sirena
- Lago de Apanás
- El Cuá
- La Dalia
- Río Blanco
- Güilique
- El Char
- stelí
- alto de
- anzuelo
- as Lajitas
- La Trinidad
- San Isidro
- Jinotega
- Disparate de Potter
- El Tuma
- Esperanza Verde/Yucul
- Santa Elsa
- Monte Grande
- Matagalpa
- La Rosa
- La Garita
- Pancasán
- San Ramón
- San Pablo
- Cordillera Dariense
- Chagüitillo
- El Caracal
- Matiguás
- Bocana de Paiwas
- Veracruz
- ta Rosa
- Peñón
- La Cruz de la India
- Ciudad Darío
- Terrabona
- Muy Muy
- Pineda
- Santa María (1210m)
- Tierra Azul
- El Trapichito
- Valle El Orégano
- Laguna Moyuá
- El Cacao
- Puertas Viejas
- Esquipulas
- San José de las Remates
- Río de Janeiro
- Santa Fe
- San Francisco
- El Guanacaste
- El Paraíso
- El Portón

Grid reference markers: A, B, C, 2, 3, 4, 5, 6

Map 2

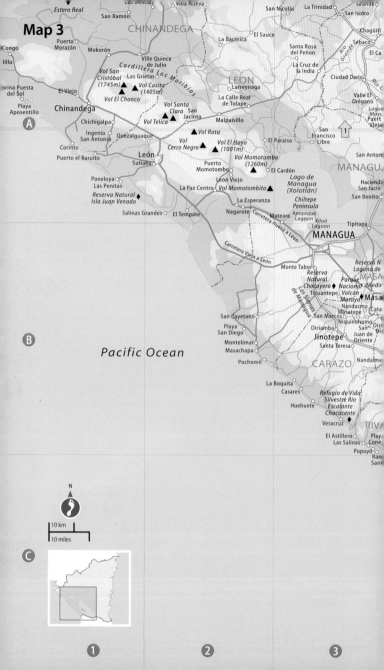

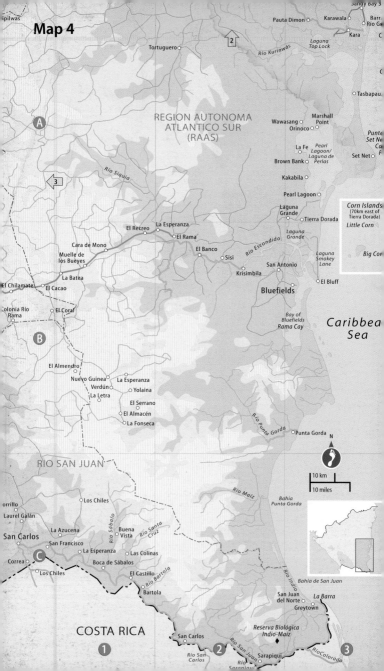

Map 4

2
3

Tortuguero

Río Kurinwás

Laguna
Top Lock

Pauta Dimon

Karawala

Sandy Bay S

Barr
Río G

Kara

Tasbapau

REGION AUTONOMA
ATLANTICO SUR
(RAAS)

Wawasang

Orinoco

Marshall
Point

Río Siquia

La Fe

Pearl
Lagoon/
Laguna de
Perlas

Punte
Set Ne
Ca

Set Net

Brown Bank

Kakabila

Pearl Lagoon

El Recreo

La Esperanza

El Rama

Laguna
Grande

Tierra Dorada

Cara de Mono

El Banco

Laguna
Grande

Muelle de
los Bueyes

Sisi

Río Escondido

Corn Islands
(70km east of
Tierra Dorada)

Little Corn

San Antonio

La Batea

Krisimbila

Laguna
Smokey
Lane

El Bluff

Big Cor

El Chilamate

El Cacao

Bluefields

Colonia Río
Rama

El Coral

Bay of
Bluefields

Rama Cay

Caribbea
Sea

El Almendro

Nuevo Guinea

La Esperanza

Verdún

Yolaina

La Letra

El Serrano

El Almacén

La Fonseca

Río Punta Gorda

Punta Gorda

N

RIO SAN JUAN

Río Maíz

10 km

10 miles

Bahía
Punta Gorda

orrillo

Los Chiles

Laurel Galán

San Carlos

La Azucena

Buena
Vista

Río Sábalo

Río Santa
Cruz

San Francisco

La Esperanza

Las Colinas

Correa

Boca de Sábalos

Río Indío

Bahía de San Juan

Los Chiles

El Castillo

Río Bartola

San Juan
del Norte

La Barra

Greytown

Bartola

COSTA RICA

San Carlos

Río San
Carlos

Río San Juan

Reserva Biológica
Indio-Maíz

Sarapiquí

RíoColorado

Río
Sarapiqu

1

2

3

Acknowledgements   First and foremost, a huge debt of gratitude is owed to Richard Leonardi, who authored this book from scratch and nurtured it through its challenging first and second editions. Thanks to his hard work, dedication and insight, you are now holding the best Nicaragua guidebook in the world.

At the Footprint offices in Bath, many thanks to Felicity Laughton for her painstaking editing, and to Alan Murphy and Pat Dawson for putting the project on the rails.

Numerous people on the road contributed useful information or made the journey interesting, entertaining or memorable in some way – many more than can be mentioned on one page. In Laguna de Apoyo, thanks to Dr Jeffrey McCrary for his hospitality and Aura for her teaching. In León, thanks to Kris Eikelenboom, Ingrid Eikelenboom, Mark Toohey, Matt Hicks and Matt Barwick for the good times. In Moyogalpa, thanks to Bob and Simone, John, Jerry and Yogi for their help, advice and hospitality. In Estelí, thanks to Janie Boyd for the handy update. On the Caribbean Coast, scores of people need to be thanked for their expertise and help, including Dolene Miller, Santiago Thomas, Silvio Hebert, Allen Clair, Edgar 'Rasta' Coulsen and Casey from Blue Energy. Particular thanks to film director David Lalé for his interest in the region, and to René Frotscher, Rasmus Sievers and Paul Rischer – look forward to seeing you all again one day soon.

Most of all, thanks to Jennifer Kennedy for her on-going love, support and companionship both on and off the road.

Back home, some friends and family deserve a quick mention. In London, thanks to Terri Wright, Al Peacock-Johns, Sym Gharial and Peter McCallan. In New York, thanks to Jo and Dan Roberts, Charlie, Thea, Frankie and Ruby.

Many thanks to the kind readers who took the time to write to us with their comments, criticisms and suggestions – these are always welcome and greatly appreciated. Finally, many thanks to the hoteliers, restaurateurs, tour operators and others who kindly informed us when their contact details changed.